KARL MARX
FREDERICK ENGELS

COLLECTED
WORKS

INTERNATIONAL PUBLISHERS
NEW YORK

KARL MARX
FREDERICK ENGELS

Volume
1

KARL MARX: 1835-43

INTERNATIONAL PUBLISHERS
NEW YORK

This volume has been prepared jointly by Lawrence & Wishart Ltd., London, International Publishers Co. Inc., New York, and Progress Publishers, Moscow, in collaboration with the Institute of Marxism-Leninism, Moscow

ISBN 0-7178-0407-0

Library of Congress Catalog Card No. LC 73-84671

First printing 1975

Printed in the Union of Soviet Socialist Republics in 1974

Contents

General Introduction XIII
Preface XXV

KARL MARX

WORKS

August 1835-March 1843

Reflections of a Young Man on the Choice of a Profession 3

Letter from Marx to His Father 10

Wild Songs 22
    The Fiddler 22
    Nocturnal Love 23

Difference Between the Democritean and Epicurean Philosophy of
    Nature 25
    Dedication 27
    Foreword 29
    Contents 32

Part One. Difference Between the Democritean and Epicurean Philosophy of
    Nature in General 34
      I. The Subject of the Treatise 34
      II. Opinions on the Relationship Between Democritean and Epicu-
      rean Physics 36
      III. Difficulties Concerning the Identity of the Democritean and
      Epicurean Philosophy of Nature 38

Part Two. On the Difference Between Democritean and Epicurean Physics
    in Detail 46

Chapter One. The Declination of the Atom from the Straight Line   46
Chapter Two. The Qualities of the Atom   53
Chapter Three. ''Ατομοι ἀρχάί and ἄτομα στοιχεῖα ····················   58
    Chapter Four. Time   63
    Chapter Five. The Meteors   66
Fragment from the Appendix: Critique of Plutarch's Polemic Against the
Theology of Epicurus   74

    II. Individual Immortality   74
        1. On Religious Feudalism. The Hell of the Populace   74

                                                                                      77
Notes   77
    Part One   89
    Part Two.. 102
    Appendix 106
    Draft of New Preface.. 109
Comments on the Latest Prussian Censorship Instruction 109

Proceedings of the Sixth Rhine Province Assembly. First Article. Debates
on Freedom of the Press and Publication of the Proceedings of the
Assembly of the Estates 132

The Question of Centralisation in Itself and with Regard to the
Supplement to No. 137 of the *Rheinische Zeitung* 182

The Leading Article in No. 179 of the *Kölnische Zeitung* 184

The Philosophical Manifesto of the Historical School of Law 203
Yet Another Word on *Bruno Bauer und die Akademische Lehrfreiheit* by
Dr. O. F. Gruppe, Berlin, 1842 211
Communism and the Augsburg *Allgemeine Zeitung* 215

Communism and the Augsburg *Allgemeine Zeitung*. Editorial Note 222

Proceedings of the Sixth Rhine Province Assembly. Third Article Debates
on the Law on Thefts of Wood 224

In Connection with the Article "Failures of the Liberal Opposition
in Hanover". Editorial Note 264

Communal Reform and the *Kölnische Zeitung* 266

The Divorce Bill. Editorial Note 274
A Correspondent of the *Kölnische Zeitung* vs. the *Rheinische Zeitung* 277
Cabinet Order on the Daily Press 280
Renard's Letter to Oberpräsident von Schaper 282
The Industrialists of Hanover and Protective Tariffs 286
The Attitude of Herwegh and Ruge to "The Free" 287
The Polemical Tactics of the Augsburg Newspaper 288
The Supplement to Nos. 335 and 336 of the Augsburg *Allgemeine
Zeitung* on the Commissions of the Estates in Prussia 292
The Divorce Bill 307

The Ban on the *Leipziger Allgemeine Zeitung* 311
Announcement by the Editors of the *Rheinische Zeitung* of Their Reply
to Oberpräsident von Schaper 331
Justification of the Correspondent from the Mosel 332
Polemical Articles Against the *Allgemeine Zeitung* 359
Marginal Notes to the Accusations of the Ministerial Rescript 361
The Local Election of Deputies to the Provincial Assembly 366
The *Rhein – und Mosel-Zeitung* as Grand Inquisitor 370
Stylistic Exercises of the *Rhein- und Mosel-Zeitung* 373
Announcement. March 17, 1843 376

LETTERS

1. To Carl Friedrich Bachmann. *April 6, 1841* 379
2. To Oscar Ludwig Bernhard Wolff. *April 7, 1841* 380
3. To Arnold Ruge. *February 10, 1842* 381
4. To Arnold Ruge. *March 5, 1842* 382
5. To Arnold Ruge. *March 20, 1842* 383
6. To Arnold Ruge. *April 27, 1842* 387
7. To Arnold Ruge. *July 9, 1842* 389
8. To Dagobert Oppenheim. *Approximately August 25, 1842* 391
9. To Arnold Ruge. *November 30, 1842* 393
10. To Arnold Ruge. *January 25, 1843* 396
11. To Arnold Ruge. *March 13, 1843* 398

FROM THE PREPARATORY MATERIALS

Notebooks on Epicurean Philosophy 403
    First Notebook 405
    Second Notebook 417
    Third Notebook 442
    Fourth Notebook 464
    Fifth Notebook 479
    Sixth Notebook 489
    Seventh Notebook 501

Plan of Hegel's Philosophy of Nature 510

EARLY LITERARY EXPERIMENTS

From the Albums of Poems Dedicated to Jenny von Westphalen 517
    Concluding Sonnets to Jenny 517
    To Jenny 521
    To Jenny. 521
    My World 523
    Feelings 525
    Transformation 528

A Book of Verse Dedicated by Marx to His Father 531
   Contents 533
   To My Father 534
      Creation 534
      Poetry 535
   The Forest Spring 535
   The Magic Harp 536
   The Abduction 537
   Yearning 538
   The Viennese Ape Theatre in Berlin 539
   Sir (G)luck's *Armide* 540
   Terms of Engagement 540
   Sentimental Souls 540
   Romanticism à la Mode 541
   To the Sun of Truth (F. Quednow) 541
   On a Certain Knight-Hero 541
   To My Neighbour Across the Street 541
   Siren Song 542
   A Philistine Wonders 545
   Mathematical Wisdom 545
   The Little Old Man of the Water 546
   To the Medical Students 547
   Medical Student Psychology 547
   Medical Student Metaphysics 547
   Medical Student Anthropology 547
   Medical Student Ethics 548
   The First Elegy of Ovid's *Tristia* 548
   Concluding Sonnet to Jenny 557
   The Madwoman 558
   Two Songs to Jenny 559
      Sought 559
      Found 559
   Flower King 560
   Sea Rock 561
   The Awakening 562
   Night Thoughts 563
   Invocation of One in Despair 563
   Three Little Lights 564
   The Man in the Moon 565
   Lucinda 565
   Dialogue with.... 571
   The Last Judgment 572
   Two Singers Accompanying Themselves on the Harp 574
   Epigrams I-VIII 575
   Concluding Epigram on the Puff-Pastry Cook 580
   Harmony 580
   Distraught 581

Man and Drum 583
Human Pride 584
Evening Stroll 587
Scenes from *Oulanem*. A Tragedy 588
Song to the Stars 608
Dream Vision 609
The Song of a Sailor at Sea 610
The Magic Ship 611
The Pale Maiden 612
Some Chapters from *Scorpion and Felix*. A Humoristic Novel 616

APPENDICES

Birth Certificate 635
Gymnasium Examination Papers Written by Marx 636
    The Union of Believers with Christ According to John 15: 1-14,
    Showing Its Basis and Essence, Its Absolute Necessity, and Its
    Effects 636
    Does the Reign of Augustus Deserve to Be Counted Among the
    Happier Periods of the Roman Empire? 639
Certificate of Maturity for Pupil of the Gymnasium in Trier Karl
Marx 643

Father's Letters (November 1835-June 1836) 645
    Heinrich Marx to Karl Marx. *November 8, 1835* 645
    Heinrich Marx to Karl Marx. *November 18-29, 1835* 645
    Heinrich Marx to Karl Marx. *Beginning of 1836* 649
    Heinrich Marx to Karl Marx. *March 19, 1836* 652
    Heinrich Marx to Karl Marx. *About May or June 1836* 653
    Father's Consent to Marx's Transfer from Bonn to Berlin Univer-
    sity 655
Certificate of Release from Bonn University 657
Father's Letters (November 1836-February 1838) 661
    Heinrich Marx to Karl Marx. *November 9, 1836* 661
    Heinrich Marx to Karl Marx. *December 28, 1836* 663
    Heinrich Marx to Karl Marx. *February 3, 1837* 667
    Heinrich Marx to Karl Marx. *March 2, 1837* 670
    Heinrich Marx to Karl Marx. *August 12, 1837* 674
    Heinrich Marx to Karl Marx. *Approximately August 20, 1837* 677
    Heinrich Marx to Karl Marx. *September 16, 1837* 679
    Heinrich Marx to Karl Marx. *November 17, 1837* 683
    Heinrich Marx to Karl Marx. *December 9, 1837* 685
    Heinrich Marx to Karl Marx. *February 10, 1838* 691
    Postscript by Heinrich Marx to Henriette Marx's Letter to Karl Marx.
    February 15-16, 1838 694

Jenny von Westphalen to Karl Marx [1839-1840] 695
Record Sheet Filled in by Marx 699

Leaving Certificate from Berlin University 703
Recommendatory Reference on the Dissertation of Karl Marx 705
Jenny von Westphalen to Karl Marx. *August 10, 1841* 707
Cologne Citizens' Petition for the Continuance of the *Rheinische
Zeitung* 710
Minutes of the General Meeting of Shareholders of the *Rheinische
Zeitung. February 12, 1843* 712
Humble Petition from the Shareholders of the *Rheinische Zeitung*
Company for the Continuance of the *Rheinische Zeitung* 725
Jenny von Westphalen to Karl Marx. *March 1843* 727

NOTES AND INDEXES

Notes 733
Name Index 761
Index of Quoted and Mentioned Literature 781
Index of Periodicals 792
Subject Index 795

ILLUSTRATIONS

Page from the gymnasium examination composition "Reflections of a Young
Man on the Choice of a Profession" 5
Letter from Karl Marx to his father, November 10-11, 1837 13
Portrait of Karl Marx in his student years 14-15
Members of the Trier Students' Association at Bonn University 14-15
Draft of the preface to *Difference Between the Democritean and Epicurean
Philosophy of Nature* 107
Page of the *Rheinische Zeitung* with Marx's article "Communism and the
Augsburg *Allgemeine Zeitung*" 217
Prometheus Bound. Allegory on the prohibition of the *Rheinische Zeitung*   374-75
Page from *Notebooks on Epicurean Philosophy* (Second Notebook) 433
Title page of Marx's *Book of Love*, with dedication to Jenny 519
Portrait of Jenny von Westphalen 526-27
Karl Marx's Birth Certificate 638-39
Trier 638-39
The house where Karl Marx was born 638-39
Gymnasium where Marx studied (front and view from courtyard) 638-39
Karl Marx's Certificate of Maturity 638-39
Certificate of Release from Bonn University 659
Leaving Certificate from Berlin University 701
Bonn University 702-03
Berlin University 702-03
Karl Marx's Doctor's Diploma 702-03
Prohibition of the *Rheinische Zeitung* 718-19
Burial of the *Rheinische Zeitung* 718-19

TRANSLATORS:

RICHARD DIXON: *Notebooks on Epicurean Philosophy*

CLEMENS DUTT: Articles, Letters and Appendices

JACK LINDSAY and the late ALICK WEST: *Oulanem*

ALEX MILLER: Poems

DIRK J. and SALLY R. STRUIK: *Doctoral Dissertation*

ALICK WEST: *Scorpion and Felix*

Karl Marx

F. Engels

General Introduction

KARL MARX and FREDERICK ENGELS were the authors of an integrated body of philosophical, economic and social-political views, the ideology of communism, which in our time has spread more widely and exercised a greater influence on the course of world history than any other.

Theirs was a unique collaboration in theoretical work and in revolutionary leadership. While the leading role in it certainly belongs to Marx, the partnership was so close, many important writings having been undertaken under their joint authorship and the greater part of the work of each from the beginning of their friendship in 1844 to Marx's death in 1883 having been discussed with the other, that their works must of necessity be collected together.

Both Marx and Engels began their adult lives as free-thinkers and revolutionary democrats in the Germany of the late 1830s and early 1840s. By the time they met and began their lifelong friendship and collaboration each had independently come to recognise in the emergent industrial working class the force that could reshape the future. As convinced materialists and Communists, they decided to collaborate in working out the fundamentals of a new revolutionary outlook. From that time their joint efforts were devoted to the aim of equipping the working-class movement with the scientific ideology and political organisation necessary for the realisation of what they saw as its historical mission, the overthrow of the power of the bourgeoisie and the creation of communism.

They were revolutionary thinkers who assailed old ideas and replaced them by new theoretical constructions, forging new means for scientifically understanding the world and human life. And they were practical revolutionaries who fought for socialism and communism against the established order of society based on capitalist property. Their revolutionary standpoint was summed up in Marx's famous aphorism: "The philosophers have only interpreted the world, in various ways; the point is to change it." This became the point of all their practical activity and theoretical labours.

Marx and Engels were never merely theoreticians, and their work can never be understood simply as productive of a theory. Indeed, the distinctive feature of Marxism, and its strength, lies above all in the combination of a theoretical approach which seeks to be governed by strictly scientific considerations with the will to revolutionary action—its unity of theory and practice. They themselves played an active part in the working-class movement, both as advisers and as active participants. In their theoretical work they drew on the movement's practical experience. And much of it is devoted to accurate and often very lively analysis of particular events and particular problems, both great and small, immediately affecting the movement at various times. From beginning to end their works show that Marxism arose and developed out of practical revolutionary activity. Both Marx and Engels were essentially fighters. And they hammered out their standpoint in the course of often bitter struggle against bourgeois ideology, petit-bourgeois and other kinds of non-proletarian socialism, anarchism, and opportunism of both the Right- and Left-wing varieties within the working-class movement.

The sum total of achievement of Marx and Engels was truly immense.

Marxism offers to the revolutionary movement of all lands a scientifically-based theory of social life and of the individual, of the laws of development of social-economic formations, of history and human activity, and of the concepts and methods man can employ for comprehending both his own existence and that of the world about him so as to frame and realise human purposes in the world.

In the light of this the character and consequences of the alienation and exploitation of labour in modern capitalist society are made clear and it becomes possible to formulate a practical aim for ending it, and in a comprehensive theory of class struggle to work out principles for deciding practical policies to realise this aim.

In their studies of the past history and present predicament of society Marx and Engels came to grips with the problems of political and state power. In their theory of the state they concluded that state power has always been the product of the development of class contradictions, and exposed the whole character of the repressive apparatus and ideology of the bourgeois state in particular.

The penetrating Marxist analysis of bourgeois society, which was the crowning achievement of Marx and Engels, set out, in Marx's words, to disclose its "law of motion", the economic laws of its development and their reflection in class and political struggle. It is from this that Marxism demonstrates the historical necessity for the revolutionary transformation of capitalism into socialism, and of the subsequent building of communist society, the realisation of human aspirations for genuine freedom and social equality. This demonstration is at once a prediction of the future course of human development and an action programme for the social forces capable of realising it.

The revolutionary programme of the dictatorship of the proletariat, the conquest of political power by the working class in alliance with the non-proletarian sections of the working people, was the culminating point of Marxism. The Marxist theory of the socialist revolution gave to the movement practical principles of the strategy and tactics of working-class struggle, demonstrated the need for well-organised independent proletarian parties and for proletarian internationalism, and forecast the basic laws of construction of the new society.

* * *

Many decades have now passed since the deaths of Marx and Engels. And from that distance in time we now have to assess the continuing validity of the teachings of Marx and Engels and the progress of the world revolutionary movement they inspired.

During their lifetime the ideas of Marx and Engels became the organising and guiding force in the struggle to overthrow capitalism. The efforts of Marx and Engels themselves made Marxism into the theoretical foundation of the programmes and activity of the first international organisations of the proletariat — the Communist League, and subsequently the First International (the International Working Men's Association) embracing socialist groups and working-class associations and trade unions of various countries. As the contradictions of the bourgeois system deepened and the working-class movement spread and grew in strength, Marxism won increasingly strong positions and more and more supporters.

The further development of Marxism on a world scale from the close of the nineteenth century is inseparably bound up with the personality, ideas and work of V. I. Lenin. Of all the political leaders and theoreticians of that time who became influential as Marxists, it was Lenin who based himself most consistently on the content and methods of the work of Marx and Engels in philosophy, political economy and the theory and practice of scientific socialism, and achieved the most creative development of their teachings. In so doing he established the organisational and political principles of a party able to lead the working class and the whole working people to the conquest of political power and the construction of socialism.

"Without revolutionary theory," Lenin said, "there can be no revolutionary movement." True to this principle, Lenin maintained that revolutionary theory must always keep pace with the march of world events and in doing so remain true to and consolidate the original theoretical positions of Marxism. To him the movement owes an analysis of imperialism, of monopoly and state-monopoly capitalism, which continued that made by Marx and Engels of capitalism in the earlier phases of its development. His immense contributions to the creative theoretical and practical development of Marxism cover the theory and practice of socialist revolution and the dictatorship of the proletariat, the agrarian, nationalities and colonial problems, the transition period from capitalism to socialism and the ways and means of building communist society, the principles of organisation and leading role of revolutionary working-class parties and, in general, the motive forces and prospects of the world revolutionary process in the epoch of imperialism and proletarian revolutions. Marxism organically absorbs the new features that were introduced by Lenin and represents in the modern epoch the integrated international doctrine of Marx, Engels and Lenin, constituting the foundation of the international communist movement.

The October Socialist Revolution of 1917 in Russia carried out, in the conditions obtaining at the time, Marx's, Engels' and Lenin's conception of the revolutionary conquest of power by the working class. It began a new epoch in world history, in which to the power of the old possessing classes are opposed not only the struggle against it of the working-class movement in capitalist countries and of the peoples dominated by imperialism, but the rule of socialism which is becoming ever more consolidated throughout a large territory of the world.

In the years that have followed, the working people of socialist countries have faced and continue to face immense problems of socialist planning and administration, of overcoming objective difficulties of development and, in a number of cases, errors, of resolving new contradictions and of organising creative labour to strengthen the socialist system and move towards the goal of communism. Marxism-Leninism has been and continues to be the basis of all the achievement of socialist countries. The same is true of the working-class movement in the capitalist countries, where a struggle is spreading for profound economic and social-political changes, for true democracy, for a transition to the road to socialism; one of the vital conditions of victory in this struggle is to eliminate the consequences of opportunism and division in the working-class movement. In the countries that have freed themselves from colonialism and are developing on new lines, leading forces of the national liberation movements are turning more and more to the guidance of this teaching in the struggle to eliminate the results of colonial slavery, neo-colonialism and racialism, and to achieve economic and cultural renaissance.

At the present time, moreover, with growing social tensions set up by the deepening of the contradictions of capitalism and the advent of the new scientific-technological revolution, Marxism attracts many people beyond the working-class movement itself. More and more do perceptive minds come to realise that in the theory of Marxism they can find the thread to lead the way out of the labyrinth of the social and political problems of modern times. The appeal of Marxism to progressive-minded people lies in its scientific approach and revolutionary spirit, its genuine humanism, its combination of a sober realistic attitude to facts with confidence in the creative abilities of working men and women the world over. The breadth and consistency of Marxism affords hope for the solution not only of economic and sociological problems but of problems of philosophy, law and ethics, including various aspects of the future of human personality, which are of particular concern to the present generation. Thus it is that despite the efforts to discredit and refute Marxism, which have been going on for well over a century and are continually stepped up, the interest in Marxism, and its influence, grow unceasingly.

* * *

The undertaking of collecting together and publishing the complete works of Marx and Engels was begun on a broad scale in the twenties of this century in the Soviet Union. In 1927, the Marx-Engels Institute in Moscow launched the publication in the original languages of Marx/Engels, *Gesamtausgabe,* initially under the general editorship of D. Ryazanov and later under the editorship of V. Adoratsky, a project that was never completed. A Russian edition was commenced and published between the years 1928 and 1947. A second Russian edition was launched in 1955, embodying an all-round study by the Institute of Marxism-Leninism of the Central Committee of the Communist Party of the Soviet Union of everything by then discovered written by Marx and Engels, of all the documents having any bearing on their work, and also of newspapers and periodicals in which their works were published in their lifetime. This edition at present consists of 39 basic and 4 supplementary volumes (47 books in all, since some of the volumes are published in two or more parts). Following this, the further labours of the Institute of Marxism-Leninism of the Central Committee of the Socialist Unity Party of Germany in Berlin led to the publication, beginning in 1956, of Marx/Engels, *Werke.* It also comprises 39 basic and 2 supplementary volumes (44 books in all).

Both in the USSR and in the German Democratic Republic new supplementary volumes continue to be prepared, containing early writings of Marx and Engels, their legacy of manuscripts, and works and letters recently discovered.

A complete edition of the works of Marx and Engels in the original languages (Marx/Engels, *Gesamtausgabe*—MEGA) has been projected jointly by the Moscow and Berlin Institutes of Marxism-Leninism. Besides containing all the works and letters of Marx and Engels, this edition will include all the extant manuscript preparatory materials for various of their published works—synopses, excerpts, marginal notes, etc.—as well as all the available letters written to them.

Many of the works of Marx and Engels, particularly their major works, are available to readers in the English-speaking countries, particularly in Great Britain and the USA, where some were translated and published while their authors were still alive (not to mention numerous articles, reports and pamphlets they themselves wrote in English and which were published in the British or

American press), and many more have been translated and published since.

A whole series of major works, particularly the economic manuscripts, remain, however, largely or even completely unknown to English readers. Many of Marx's early writings, nearly all the writings of the young Engels, the bulk of Marx and Engels' numerous contributions to the *Neue Rheinische Zeitung* (1848-49), and most of their letters, have never yet appeared in English. Many of their articles which were published in the British and American press of their day have not been republished in English and are now bibliographical rarities. From the available scattered publications in English it is difficult to gain any clear conception of the formative process of Marxist ideas, to study them in their historical development. Some of the existing translations, moreover, do not meet present-day requirements, and notes and commentaries are not always up to the standard now demanded in studies of the history of Marxism and of the international working-class movement.

In preparing this first English-language edition of the collected works of Marx and Engels these circumstances have been kept in mind. It is intended that the composition and character of this edition should reflect the present level of development of Marxist studies and be guided by both English and international experience in the publication of social-economic and political literature. The task is to take into account and use to the fullest advantage the best traditions established in this field in Great Britain, the USA, the USSR, the German Democratic Republic, and other countries, as well as the results achieved by world science in investigating the literary legacy of Marx and Engels and the history of Marxism. Thus this edition will provide for the first time to the English-speaking world a practically complete, organised and annotated collection of the works of the founders and first teachers of the international communist movement.

* * *

This English edition will include the works and letters already contained in the main volumes of the above-mentioned second Russian and German editions as well as in the supplementary volumes of these editions already published or in preparation. It will embrace all the extant works of Marx and Engels published in their lifetime and a considerable part of their legacy of manu-

scripts—manuscripts not published in their lifetime and unfinished works, outlines, rough drafts and fragments. The contents
of the main sections of the volumes will include authorised publications of speeches by Marx and Engels or reports of their speeches
which they themselves verified. Author's revisions of various works
are regarded as works in their own right and will be included
alongside the original texts. Of the available preliminary manuscript versions, however, only those that differ essentially from the
final text will be published in this edition. Nor will versions of
printed works (the texts of articles published simultaneously in
various organs of the press, and various lifetime editions of one
and the same work) be duplicated. Any important changes in these
texts made by the authors themselves will be brought to the
reader's attention, usually in footnotes.

The edition will include all the letters of Marx and Engels that
have been discovered by the time the volumes appear.

Synopses and excerpts made by Marx and Engels are considered
selectively and will appear in this edition only if they contain
considerable author's digressions and commentaries. Such works,
and also the rough versions and drafts of individual works the
final texts of which are published in the body of a given volume,
will usually be grouped together in a special section under the
heading "From the Preparatory Materials".

Several of the volumes of this edition will be supplied with
appendices containing documents and materials of a biographical
nature, such as official applications and other legal documents
written by Marx or Engels, newspaper reports and minutes,
reports of speeches and lectures never verified by the authors,
interviews which they gave to various correspondents, documents
which they helped to draw up for various organisations and letters
written on their instructions.

The whole edition will comprise fifty volumes, organised into
three main groups: (1) philosophical, historical, political, economic
and other works; (2) Marx's *Capital,* with his preliminary versions
and works directly connected with it, particularly the *Economic
Manuscripts of 1857-1858* better known under the editorial heading
Grundrisse der Kritik der Politischen Ökonomie; (3) the letters,
beginning from August 1844. According to the preliminary plan
of the edition, the first group will run from volumes 1 to 28, the
second from 29 to 37, and the third from 38 to 50.

The first three volumes will have certain specific structural
features. Before the beginning of their close friendship and
co-operation in August 1844, Marx and Engels each developed

independently as thinker, writer and revolutionary, and in these volumes their works and letters will be published separately. The first volume will contain works and letters of the young Marx up to March 1843, and the second works and letters of Engels over approximately the same period. The third volume will be divided on the same principle, giving works and letters of Marx and Engels from the spring of 1843 up to August 1844 in two separate sections. In the subsequent volumes the literary legacy of the founders of Marxism, an important feature of whose creative work from August 1844 onwards was constant collaboration, will be published together.

Within each group of volumes the material will be arranged, as a rule, chronologically according to the date when a particular work or letter was written. When the writing was spread over a long period, the date of the first publication will be used. Departures from this chronological principle will be made only when individual works or series of works of similar type are grouped in special volumes.

The distribution of material over the volumes will be determined on current principles of periodisation of the history of Marxism, so that the contents of individual volumes or several consecutive volumes correspond to specific stages in the authors' work. Provision has been made for including works referring to a particular group of subjects in one or another volume. Within any given volume, articles of a particular series will be published in chronological order. Only series of articles conceived as such by the authors and serialised during their lifetime in newspapers or periodicals will be presented as unified works.

A number of works by Marx and Engels were republished, sometimes more than once, during their lifetime, and the authors usually provided each new edition with a new introduction, preface or afterword. Sometimes these additions were separated from the works for which they were written by decades, and naturally reflect a fresh departure in Marxist thought. These prefaces and the like were essentially independent contributions containing new material and referring to a historical period that differed from that in which the main work was written. Writings of this type will be published according to the date of writing, along with other materials of the given period. Cross-references will be provided to all works that have later author's prefaces, introductions or afterwords.

All letters, irrespective of addressee, will be published in chronological order.

The editions of the works of Marx and Engels published in their lifetime and, failing these, the author's manuscripts, will provide the source of the texts used for publication. If several editions authorised by the authors themselves are available, the last of them will, as a rule, be taken as the basic one and any significant variant readings from other authorised editions will be given in footnotes. In cases where such readings are numerous they may be brought together in the form of appendices.

Any extraneous editorial additions to the texts of publications made during the authors' lifetime will be removed and information concerning them, if necessary with reproduction of the corrupted text, will be provided in the notes.

English translations that appeared during the lifetime of Marx and Engels and under their supervision and editorship are regarded as authorised by them. These texts will generally be reproduced without changes, but only after checking against the texts in the original languages and removal of any obvious mistranslations or misprints that passed unnoticed by the authors. Textual revisions introduced by a translator with the consent of the authors or on their instructions will be preserved, the translation of the text as in the original language being given in a footnote as a variant reading.

All texts will be checked for misprints, inaccuracies in the quoting of proper names, place names, numerical errors, and so on. Obvious misprints or slips of the pen in the original will be corrected without comment, while any assumed errors will be discussed in footnotes. Comments in footnotes or general notes will also be made whenever the correction of a misprint influences the reading of the subsequent text or calls for further correction (for example, in tables, arithmetical calculations, etc.).

Citations by the authors will be checked and obvious mistakes corrected. The author's deliberate condensation or revision of quoted texts will be preserved and, where this seems necessary, the exact text of the passage cited will be noted. Citations from works in languages other than English will, as a rule, appear in English translation. Deliberate uses of foreign expressions, terms, aphorisms, proverbs in the ancient language or in local dialect, etc., will be reproduced, however, as in the original, an English translation being appended in a footnote when this seems necessary.

The edition will include a detailed reference apparatus for each volume, containing information on texts, sources, bibliography and history, references to theoretical and literary sources, commentaries on obscure passages, and brief notes on persons, newspapers and periodicals referred to in the texts. Each volume will be provided with a subject index. In general, the reference apparatus, more or less uniform for all volumes, will be arranged as follows: an editorial preface for each volume, or group of volumes embracing a single work; notes; a name index; an index of quoted and mentioned literature; an index of periodicals, and a subject index.

Editorial commentary will be found in the form of footnotes and notes at the end of each volume. The footnotes will be concerned mainly with textual criticism. They will seek to explain obscurities in the texts, including oblique references to names, literary works and events. And they will cite variant readings from other authorised editions or from manuscripts and printed versions, provide cross-references, indicate possible misprints, and so on. Explanations concerning books and literary works mentioned will be given in footnotes only where the reader may have difficulty in tracing these works in the index of quoted and mentioned literature.

The notes at the end of each volume will provide more detailed information. They will deal with the history of various works and projects, including those that remained in the form of unfinished manuscripts (brief information on the first publication will also be given at the end of each work). The work of Marx and Engels on various newspapers, and their activities in various organisations, will be one of the main subjects of the notes. Historical commentary will bear mainly on the history of the working-class movement and Marx and Engels' participation in it. Notes on general historical events will be provided only when circumstances essential to an understanding of the text do not emerge clearly from the authors' own accounts.

The name index will be provided with brief annotations. A special section will list alphabetically the literary and mythological characters mentioned in the text. The index of periodicals, which includes all the newspapers, magazines, annuals, etc., referred to in the text, will also be annotated. Wherever possible the index of quoted and mentioned literature will indicate the editions used by Marx and Engels. Where this cannot be firmly established, the first edition will be indicated and, in the case of fiction, only the title and the author's name.

The volumes will include documentary illustrations, with maps and diagrams for articles dealing with military and historical subjects. Original drawings by Engels included in his letters will be reproduced.

* * *

This complete edition of the works of Marx and Engels is the product of agreement and collaboration of British, American and Soviet scholars, translators and editors. It is published by Lawrence & Wishart Ltd., London, International Publishers Co. Inc., New York, in consultation respectively with the Executive Committee of the Communist Party of Great Britain and the National Committee of the Communist Party of the United States of America, and by Progress Publishers and the Institute of Marxism-Leninism of the Central Committee of the Communist Party of the Soviet Union, Moscow.

The entire work of preparation and publication is supervised by editorial commissions appointed by the publishers in Great Britain, the United States and the Soviet Union. Together they form a team responsible for the edition as a whole.

Considerable help is being afforded, too, by the Institute of Marxism-Leninism of the Central Committee of the Socialist Unity Party of Germany, in Berlin.

All the work of arrangement, preparation and final editing of the texts and of the reference apparatus of each volume is based on agreement in the sharing of obligations between the participating publishers, the key principle being co-ordination of all major decisions and mutual cross-checking of the work. The edition is being printed in Moscow at the First Model Printers.

The general principles governing its preparation and publication were first agreed at a general conference of representatives of the three publishers in Moscow at the beginning of December 1969, and subsequently elaborated further by the agreement of the three editorial commissions. Those who took part personally in the elaboration of these principles are listed alphabetically below:

GREAT BRITAIN: Jack Cohen, Maurice Cornforth, Maurice Dobb, E. J. Hobsbawm, James Klugmann, Margaret Mynatt.

USA: James S. Allen, Philip S. Foner, the late Howard Selsam, Dirk J. Struik, William W. Weinstone.

USSR: for Progress Publishers — N. P. Karmanova, V. N. Pavlov, M. K. Shcheglova, T. Y. Solovyova; for the Institute of Marxism-Leninism — P. N. Fedoseyev, L. I. Golman, A. I. Malysh, A. G. Yegorov, V. Y. Zevin.

The publication of the first volume and preparation of subsequent volumes is being conducted under the supervision of the above-mentioned editorial commissions.

Preface

The first volume of the *Collected Works* of Karl Marx and Frederick Engels contains works and letters written by Marx between August 1835 and March 1843. The volume is divided into four sections — works, letters, preparatory material and youthful literary experiments in prose and verse, the material in each section being arranged chronologically. Relevant biographical documents are supplied in the appendices.

These writings reflect Marx's early, formative period, the path of intellectual development that led an inquiring young man, inspired while still at the gymnasium by the idea of serving the common good, to the forefront of the philosophical and political thought of his day. This was the time when Marx, as a student first at Bonn and then at Berlin University, was deeply engaged in the study of law, history and philosophy, which he combined with trying his strength in the sphere of creative writing. In these years Marx evolved his atheistic and revolutionary-democratic beliefs and began his activities as a contributor to and, later, editor of the *Rheinische Zeitung*. His work on this newspaper initiated a new stage in the formation of his ideas which was to result in his final and complete adoption of materialist and communist positions.

The first section of the volume opens with the school essay "Reflections of a Young Man on the Choice of a Profession", which Marx wrote in 1835, and which may be regarded as the starting point of his intellectual development. Unlike his other school essays (they appear in the appendices), which as a whole do not reach beyond the usual framework of ideas current among gymnasium students and in gymnasium textbooks of those days,

this composition reveals his resolve not to withdraw into the
narrow circle of personal interests but to devote his activities to the
interests of humanity. At the same time the young Marx, swayed
by the ideas of the French Enlightenment concerning the influence of the social environment on man, had begun to think also
about the objective conditions determining human activity. "Our
relations in society have to some extent already begun to be
established before we are in a position to determine them," he
wrote in this essay (see p. 4).

The "Letter from Marx to His Father", written in 1837, vividly
illustrates Marx's hard thinking as a student and shows the
versatility of his intellectual interests and the variety of problems
that stirred his imagination. The letter records an important stage
in the evolution of his ideas — his recognition of Hegelian
philosophy as a key to the understanding of reality, in contrast to
the subjective idealism of Fichte and other subjectivist philosophical systems. In his intensive search for a truly scientific conception
of the world Marx did not confine himself to becoming an
advocate of Hegel's teaching and joining the Young Hegelian
movement, whose representatives were attempting to draw atheistic and radical political conclusions from Hegel's philosophy.
Armed with Hegelian dialectics, he set about blazing his own trail
in philosophy.

An important feature of the intellectual development of the
young Marx was his study of ancient classical philosophy, which
resulted in the *Notebooks on Epicurean Philosophy* (1839) (published
in the third section) and, based on this preparatory material, the
Doctoral dissertation on the *Difference Between the Democritean and
Epicurean Philosophy of Nature* (1840-41). This work of investigation
into the major trends in classical philosophy testifies to the young
Marx's erudition and the revolutionary nature, the radicalism, of
his views. The very choice of subject, his recourse to the great
materialist philosophers of classical times, Democritus, Epicurus
and Lucretius, whom Hegel had treated with a certain degree of
scorn, indicates Marx's considerable power of independent
thought, his desire to gain his own understanding of the salient
problems of philosophy and to determine his own attitude to the
philosophical legacy of the past.

While studying the ancients, Marx kept constantly in view the
issues that stirred the minds of his contemporaries and formed the
hub of the current ideological struggle. In his comments on
excerpts from works of the classical philosophers contained in his
notebooks he is already voicing a protest against agnosticism,

against attempts to belittle the cognitive power of philosophy. He is full of faith in the power of human reason, in the power of progressive philosophy to influence life. His high estimation of Epicurus' struggle against superstition reads as a passionate defence of freedom of thought, an appeal for resolute protest against the shackling authority of religion.

In his dissertation, Marx went even further in pursuing his atheist views. He declared his profound conviction that it is necessary to know the origin and nature of religion in order to overcome it. This work also contains, in embryo, the idea of the dialectical unity of philosophy and life. "... as the world becomes philosophical, philosophy also becomes worldly" (see p. 85). Demonstrating the fertility of the dialectical method in philosophy, Marx strove to discover the elements of dialectics that were already implicit in the beliefs of the ancient philosophers. He did, in fact, reveal the dialectical nature of Epicurus' teaching on the declination of the atoms as the embodiment of the principle of self-movement.

Thus, in his Doctoral dissertation Marx faced up squarely to problems that were to play a major part in the subsequent formation of his view of the world. He became clearly aware of the need to solve the problem of the relationship between philosophy and reality. The strong atheist views that he had already adopted facilitated his subsequent transition to materialism.

Collected in this volume are all the known journalistic writings of the young Marx in the early forties. They illustrate his development as a political tribune, a revolutionary democrat and a resolute critic of the existing social and political system. It was in active journalistic work, in political struggle against the whole conservative and obsolete Establishment that the young Marx saw the way to integrating advanced philosophy with life. In the very first article "Comments on the Latest Prussian Censorship Instruction", exposing Prussian legislation on the press, Marx launched what amounted to a militant campaign against feudal monarchist reaction in Germany. Here for the first time he passed from the discussion of general philosophical problems to an analysis of specific political phenomena. By linking his criticism of existing conditions of censorship to an exposure of the Prussian political system he not only demonstrated its irrationality from the standpoint of advanced philosophy but also came near to understanding the essential hostility of the Prussian state to the people.

Marx's political convictions became even more clearly defined while he was with the *Rheinische Zeitung* (May 1842 to March 1843). Journalistic work on this paper provided him with an outlet for his enormous revolutionary energy, for publicising his revolutionary-democratic views. As its editor, Marx displayed great skill and flexibility in overcoming censorship difficulties and the opposition of the moderates on the editorial board and among the shareholders, and set about converting the paper from an organ of the liberal opposition into a tribune of revolutionary-democratic ideas. He set the tone in his own articles, which hit out against the social, political and spiritual oppression that reigned in Prussia and other German states. The revolutionary-democratic direction that Marx had given the paper led to attacks upon it from almost the whole monarchist press and also persecution by the authorities, who succeeded in having the paper closed. In the history not only of the German but also of the whole European press and social thought the *Rheinische Zeitung* occupies a distinguished place for having several years before the revolution of 1848 heralded the approaching revolutionary storm in Germany.

Marx's work on the newspaper represents an important phase in the development of his world outlook. In his articles one can trace what Lenin called "Marx's transition from idealism to materialism and from revolutionary democracy to communism" (V. I. Lenin, *Collected Works*, Vol. 21, p. 80). The forming of his political views had a considerable reciprocal effect on his philosophical position, leading him further and further beyond the bounds of Hegelian idealism. Newspaper work revealed to Marx his lack of knowledge of political economy and prompted him to undertake a serious study of economic problems, of man's material interests.

Marx's articles — some of them were never published because of the censorship and have not been preserved — ranged widely over the social problems of the Germany of his day.

In his article "Debates on Freedom of the Press and Publication of the Proceedings of the Assembly of the Estates" Marx, though he had not yet abandoned the abstract-idealist view of freedom as the "essence" of human nature, nevertheless linked his presentation of the problem with the attitudes adopted by various sections of society towards freedom of the press. His conclusion strikes a revolutionary note; only a people's press can be truly free and its main purpose is to rouse the people to defend freedom with arms in hand.

In this and a number of other articles ("The Supplement to Nos. 335 and 336 of the Augsburg *Allgemeine Zeitung* on the

Commissions of the Estates in Prussia", "The Local Election of Deputies to the Provincial Assembly", "The Divorce Bill", etc.) Marx strongly criticises the hierarchical principle on which Prussian political institutions were based and which led to the political domination of the nobility. He exposed the wretched inadequacy of the Provincial Assemblies, which were mere caricatures of representative institutions, the retrograde ideas permeating Prussian legislation, and the absolutist political system of the Prussian monarchy.

The group of articles that includes "The Philosophical Manifesto of the Historical School of Law", "The Leading Article in No. 179 of the *Kölnische Zeitung*", "Communal Reform and the *Kölnische Zeitung*", "The Polemical Tactics of the Augsburg Newspaper", and "The *Rhein- und Mosel-Zeitung* as Grand Inquisitor", was aimed against various aspects of ideological reaction in Germany. Marx spoke in defence of opposition newspapers that were being persecuted by the government and exposed the stand of the anti-democratic and reactionary press on the country's domestic affairs. He angrily exposed the preachers of religious obscurantism. He branded the representatives of the historical school of law and reactionary romanticism for attempting to justify feudal aristocratic institutions on the grounds of historical tradition. He also condemned the half-heartedness and inconsistency of the liberal opposition towards the existing regimes of the German states. Characteristic in this respect is his editorial note "In Connection with the Article 'Failures of the Liberal Opposition in Hanover'".

Marx defended the representatives of progressive philosophy of the time, particularly the Left Hegelians, from the attacks of the reactionaries in other papers as well. This can be seen from his article in the *Deutsche Jahrbücher* against Doctor Gruppe's criticism of the views of Bruno Bauer, the leader of the Young Hegelians. At the same time he took a sharply critical attitude towards anarchistic individualism, superficial and loud-mouthed criticism, addiction to the ultra-radical phrase without any clearly defined positive programme, all of which were distinctive features of the Berlin Young Hegelian circle of "The Free". In a short article on "The Attitude of Herwegh and Ruge to 'The Free'" Marx hinted that such behaviour would compromise the freedom party's cause. These disagreements with "The Free" marked the beginning of the rift that was to develop between Marx and the Young Hegelians.

Some of the material and documents published in this volume ("Renard's Letter to Oberpräsident von Schaper", "Marginal

Notes to the Accusations of the Ministerial Rescript", etc.) reflect Marx's struggle to keep up publication of the *Rheinische Zeitung*, his attempts to deflect the onslaught of the ruling circles, which in the end succeeded in having it banned.

In his articles in the *Rheinische Zeitung* Marx generally maintained idealist positions in his understanding of the state and the interrelation between material and spiritual activity, treating the Prussian state merely as a deviation from the state's essential nature. At the same time the urge to achieve a critical understanding of reality, to put the ideal of freedom into practice, the desire to comprehend and express the true interests of the people, drove Marx to probe more deeply into the life around him. He began to understand the role of social contradictions in the development of society, took the first steps towards defining the class structure of German society, and the role of the nobility as the social mainstay of the Prussian state. Outstanding in this respect are the "Debates on the Law on Thefts of Wood" and "Justification of the Correspondent from the Mosel", in which Marx came out openly in defence of the "poor, politically and socially propertyless many" (see p. 230).

Work on these articles with their analysis of the destitute condition of the working masses and its causes was of great significance in shaping Marx's beliefs. As Engels wrote, Marx told him on more than one occasion later that it was his study of the law on thefts of wood and of the condition of the Mosel peasants that prompted him to turn from pure politics to the study of economic relations and, thus, to socialism (see F. Engels to R. Fischer, April 15, 1895).

In his article "Communism and the Augsburg *Allgemeine Zeitung*" Marx touched for the first time on communism, which he regarded as a contemporary issue raised by life itself, by the struggle of a section of society "that today owns nothing" (see p. 216). Though critical in his attitude to the various utopian theories of the time and also to the practical experiments in setting up communist communities, Marx felt that his knowledge was not yet sufficient for him to express a definite opinion on these subjects. Even then, however, he saw in communism a subject worthy of profound theoretical analysis.

The second section contains letters written by Marx between 1841 and 1843, most of which are addressed to the German radical Arnold Ruge, editor of the Young Hegelian *Deutsche Jahrbücher*. The letters provide a supplement to Marx's published works of the time. Here he often expresses his views in a much sharper form, since in private correspondence he was able to write with a frankness impossible under press censorship of his critical attitude towards Prussian life and towards various trends in philosophy and literature. This part of the young Marx's literary legacy is also permeated with revolutionary-democratic ideas. The letters vividly reproduce the political atmosphere in which Marx, as a revolutionary journalist and editor of the *Rheinische Zeitung*, had to work, his struggle with the censorship and the obstacles which beset publication of the paper at every turn.

The position Marx adopted in the fierce political and philosophical arguments that had flared up in Germany can be clearly traced in his correspondence. Marx did not share the illusions of the German liberals concerning the prospects of introducing a constitutional monarchy by peaceful means and stood for revolutionary methods of struggle against absolutism. More fully than his articles in the *Rheinische Zeitung* the letters reveal Marx's conflict with the Berlin Young Hegelian circle of "The Free". Marx's letter to Ruge of November 30, 1842 (see pp. 393-95) is particularly important in this respect. Marx hailed *The Essence of Christianity* and other works of Ludwig Feuerbach as a major event in philosophical life. Indeed, this is shown not only by Marx's letters but by a number of articles in the *Rheinische Zeitung*, particularly "the Leading Article in No. 179 of the *Kölnische Zeitung*" where he ranks Feuerbach among the representatives of true philosophy, which was "the intellectual quintessence of its time" (see p. 195). Feuerbach's materialist views exercised a considerable influence on Marx. Though he had a high opinion of them, Marx nevertheless perceived some of the deficiencies in Feuerbach's contemplative materialism. He pointed out that Feuerbach "refers too much to nature and too little to politics. That, however, is the only alliance by which present-day philosophy can become truth" (see p. 400). This remark on the inseparable connection between philosophy and political struggle anticipates his thoughts in later works on the unity of revolutionary theory and practice.

The third section, "From the Preparatory Materials", includes the above-mentioned *Notebooks on Epicurean Philosophy*. These notebooks consist of lengthy excerpts from Diogenes Laertius, Sextus Empiricus, Lucretius, Cicero, Plutarch, Seneca, Clement of Alexandria and Stobaeus, accompanied by Marx's own comments on the problems of both ancient philosophical thought and the social significance of philosophy. The section also includes the *Plan of Hegel's Philosophy of Nature*, which Marx devised in his undergraduate years under the influence of Hegel's *Encyclopaedia of the Philosophical Sciences.*

The fourth section offers the reader a considerable portion of the verse and prose which Marx wrote as a young man. It does not embrace all the poems that have been preserved, but what has been included gives a clear idea of the nature of Marx's youthful contribution to *belles-lettres,* sufficient to judge the part played by these endeavours in his intellectual development.

The section includes some of the poems from the three albums that Marx wrote for his fiancée — Jenny von Westphalen. The poetical works that Marx himself selected in 1837 for a book of verse dedicated to his father are given in full. It contained ballads, romances, sonnets, epigrams, humorous verse and scenes from the unfinished tragedy *Oulanem.* A supplement to this book consisted of chapters from a humoristic novel *Scorpion and Felix,* which are also reproduced in the present volume. Marx himself evidently regarded this collection as the best of what he had written in this field and later actually decided to publish two of the poems from it. These poems, combined under the title *Wild Songs,* were published in the magazine *Athenäum* in 1841 (they appear in the first section of the present volume).

Many of these literary endeavours are, of course, somewhat imitative in character. Marx himself did not place much value on their artistic merits and later treated them with a great deal of scepticism, though he found that there was genuine warmth and sincerity of feeling in his youthful poems, particularly the ones dedicated to Jenny. But the main value of these youthful writings is that they reflect — particularly the sonnets, epigrams and jests — certain aspects of the view that the young Marx had of the world in general, his attitude to the life around him, the traits that were forming in his character. The themes of high endeavour, of dedicated effort, of contempt for philistine sluggishness, of readiness to throw oneself into battle for lofty aims stand out clearly. Regarded from this angle, the poems included here offer an important insight into the mind of the young Marx.

The appendices supply biographical documents concerning the major landmarks in Marx's life, his gymnasium essays on set subjects, papers concerned with his undergraduate years, and so on. Of great biographical interest are the letters of Heinrich Marx to his son. These letters are full of parental anxiety over a beloved child's irresistible craving for knowledge, tempestuous character and fearless free-thinking, particularly in matters of religion.

They convey a picture of the intense intellectual life Marx led as a student. The few extant letters from Jenny von Westphalen to Marx reveal the strength of the feelings that bound them together.

A special group is formed by the documents concerning the banning of the *Rheinische Zeitung* by the Prussian Government — a petition from the citizens of Cologne requesting withdrawal of the ban, and the minutes of the general meeting of the shareholders held on February 12, 1843.

* * *

Most of the items included in this volume had not previously been translated into English. Many of the articles from the *Rheinische Zeitung*, including the "Proceedings of the Sixth Rhine Province Assembly" (articles 1 and 3), "Justification of the Correspondent from the Mosel", all the letters given in the volume, the bulk of the youthful literary endeavours, and also the *Notebooks on Epicurean Philosophy* and the *Plan of Hegel's Philosophy of Nature*, appear in English for the first time. The appendices also consist entirely of material and documents not previously published in English.

The article "Luther as Arbiter Between Strauss and Feuerbach" published in previous editions of Marx's early works is not included in the present edition, for recent research has proved that it was not written by Marx.

The works that have previously appeared in English are given here in new, carefully checked translations.

The author's underlining is reproduced by italics; marks of emphasis in the margins are shown by vertical lines. Headings supplied by the editors where none existed in the original are given in square brackets. The asterisks indicate footnotes by the author; the editors' footnotes are indicated by index letters, and reference notes by superior numbers.

The compiling of the volume, the writing of the preface and notes, and the making of the subject index were the work of Tatyana Vasilyeva. The name index and the indexes of quoted literature and periodicals were prepared by Dmitry Belyaev, Tatyana Chikileva and Galina Kostryukova (CC CPSU Institute of Marxism-Leninism).

All the articles, letters, etc., in this volume have been translated from the German unless otherwise stated.

The prose translations were made by Richard Dixon, Clemens Dutt, Dirk J. and Sally R. Struik and Alick West, and edited by

Robert Browning, Maurice Cornforth, Richard Dixon, Catherine Judelson, David McLellan and Margaret Mynatt.

The poems were translated by Alex Miller in consultation with Diana Miller and Victor Schnittke except for the verse tragedy *Oulanem* translated by Jack Lindsay and Alick West and edited by Alex Miller.

The English translations of the excerpts from Cicero, Athenaeus, Diogenes Laertius, Plutarch, Seneca, Sextus Empiricus and Clement of Alexandria in Marx's *Doctoral Dissertation* and *Notebooks on Epicurean Philosophy* are based on the translations published in the Loeb Classics; those from Epicurus on *The Extant Remains*, translated by Cyril Bailey; those from Lucretius on Lucretius, *The Nature of the Universe*, translated by R. E. Latham and published by Penguin Books, London; and those from Aristotle on *The Works of Aristotle translated into English*, published by Oxford University Press. The publishers express their gratitude to Harvard University Press and the Loeb Classical Library, Penguin Books, and the Clarendon Press, Oxford, for their kind permission to use these translations.

The volume was prepared for the press by the editors Natalia Karmanova, Margarita Lopukhina, Victor Schnittke, Lyudgarda Zubrilova, and the assistant-editor Natina Perova, for Progress Publishers, and Vladimir Mosolov, scientific editor, for the Institute of Marxism-Leninism, Moscow.

KARL MARX

WORKS

August 1835-March 1843

REFLECTIONS OF A YOUNG MAN
ON THE CHOICE OF A PROFESSION[1]

Nature herself has determined the sphere of activity in which the animal should move, and it peacefully moves within that sphere, without attempting to go beyond it, without even an inkling of any other. To man, too, the Deity gave a general aim, that of ennobling mankind and himself, but he left it to man to seek the means by which this aim can be achieved; he left it to him to choose the position in society most suited to him, from which he can best uplift himself and society.

This choice is a great privilege of man over the rest of creation, but at the same time it is an act which can destroy his whole life, frustrate all his plans, and make him unhappy. Serious consideration of this choice, therefore, is certainly the first duty of a young man who is beginning his career and does not want to leave his most important affairs to chance.

Everyone has an aim in view, which to him at least seems great, and actually is so if the deepest conviction, the innermost voice of the heart declares it so, for the Deity never leaves mortal man wholly without a guide; he speaks softly but with certainty.

But this voice can easily be drowned, and what we took for inspiration can be the product of the moment, which another moment can perhaps also destroy. Our imagination, perhaps, is set on fire, our emotions excited, phantoms flit before our eyes, and we plunge headlong into what impetuous instinct suggests, which we imagine the Deity himself has pointed out to us. But what we ardently embrace soon repels us and we see our whole existence in ruins.

We must therefore seriously examine whether we have really been inspired in our choice of a profession, whether an inner voice approves it, or whether this inspiration is a delusion, and what we took to be a call from the Deity was self-deception. But how can we recognise this except by tracing the source of the inspiration itself?

What is great glitters, its glitter arouses ambition, and ambition can easily have produced the inspiration, or what we took for inspiration; but reason can no longer restrain the man who is tempted by the demon of ambition, and he plunges head-long into what impetuous instinct suggests: he no longer chooses his position in life, instead it is determined by chance and illusion.

Nor are we called upon to adopt the position which offers us the most brilliant opportunities; that is not the one which, in the long series of years in which we may perhaps hold it, will never tire us, never dampen our zeal, never let our enthusiasm grow cold, but one in which we shall soon see our wishes unfulfilled, our ideas unsatisfied, and we shall inveigh against the Deity and curse mankind.

But it is not only ambition which can arouse sudden enthusiasm for a particular profession; we may perhaps have embellished it in our imagination, and embellished it so that it appears the highest that life can offer. We have not analysed it, not considered the whole burden, the great responsibility it imposes on us; we have seen it only from a distance, and distance is deceptive.

Our own reason cannot be counsellor here; for it is supported neither by experience nor by profound observation, being deceived by emotion and blinded by fantasy. To whom then should we turn our eyes? Who should support us where our reason forsakes us?

Our parents, who have already travelled life's road and experienced the severity of fate—our heart tells us.

And if then our enthusiasm still persists, if we still continue to love a profession and believe ourselves called to it after we have examined it in cold blood, after we have perceived its burdens and become acquainted with its difficulties, then we ought to adopt it, then neither does our enthusiasm deceive us nor does overhasti-ness carry us away.

But we cannot always attain the position to which we believe we are called; our relations in society have to some extent already begun to be established before we are in a position to determine them.

Our physical constitution itself is often a threatening obstacle, and let no one scoff at its rights.

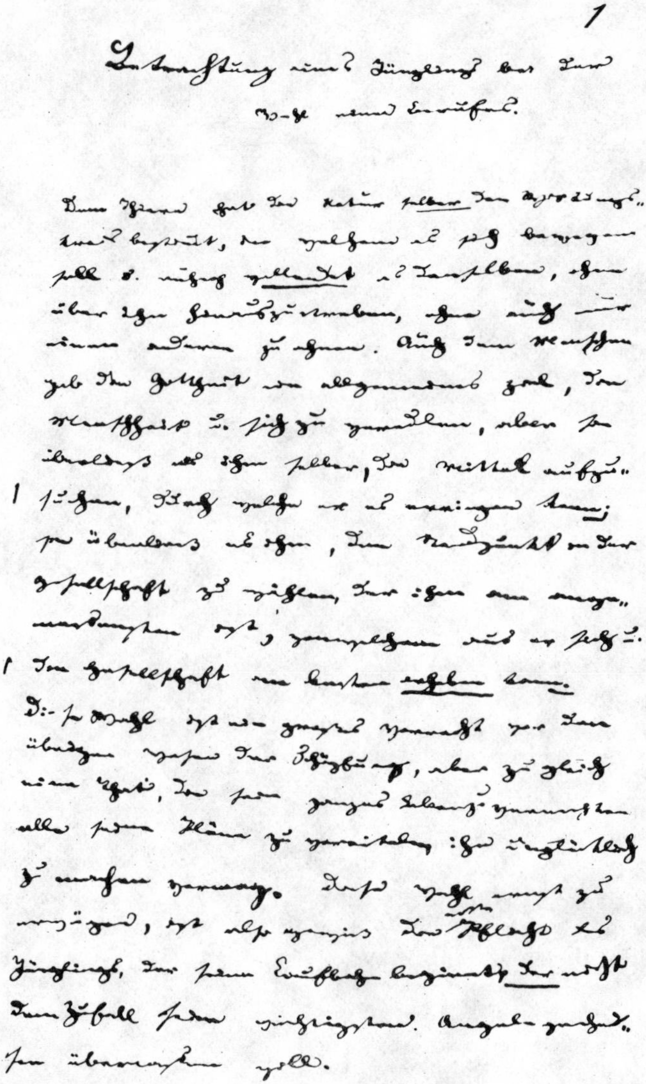

Page from the gymnasium examination composition "Reflections of a Young Man on the Choice of a Profession"

It is true that we can rise above it; but then our downfall is all the more rapid, for then we are venturing to build on crumbling ruins, then our whole life is an unhappy struggle between the mental and the bodily principle. But he who is unable to reconcile the warring elements within himself, how can he resist life's tempestuous stress, how can he act calmly? And it is from calm alone that great and fine deeds can arise; it is the only soil in which ripe fruits successfully develop.

Although we cannot work for long and seldom happily with a physical constitution which is not suited to our profession, the thought nevertheless continually arises of sacrificing our well-being to duty, of acting vigorously although we are weak. But if we have chosen a profession for which we do not possess the talent, we can never exercise it worthily, we shall soon realise with shame our own incapacity and tell ourselves that we are useless created beings, members of society who are incapable of fulfilling their vocation. Then the most natural consequence is self-contempt, and what feeling is more painful and less capable of being made up for by all that the outside world has to offer? Self-contempt is a serpent that ever gnaws at one's breast, sucking the life-blood from one's heart and mixing it with the poison of misanthropy and despair.

An illusion about our talents for a profession which we have closely examined is a fault which takes its revenge on us ourselves, and even if it does not meet with the censure of the outside world it gives rise to more terrible pain in our hearts than such censure could inflict.

If we have considered all this, and if the conditions of our life permit us to choose any profession we like, we may adopt the one that assures us the greatest worth, one which is based on ideas of whose truth we are thoroughly convinced, which offers us the widest scope to work for mankind, and for ourselves to approach closer to the general aim for which every profession is but a means — perfection.

Worth is that which most of all uplifts a man, which imparts a higher nobility to his actions and all his endeavours, which makes him invulnerable, admired by the crowd and raised above it.

But worth can be assured only by a profession in which we are not servile tools, but in which we act independently in our own sphere. It can be assured only by a profession that does not demand reprehensible acts, even if reprehensible only in outward appearance, a profession which the best can follow with noble pride. A profession which assures this in the greatest de-

gree is not always the highest, but is always the most to be preferred.

But just as a profession which gives us no assurance of worth
degrades us, we shall as surely succumb under the burdens of one
which is based on ideas that we later recognise to be false.

There we have no recourse but to self-deception, and what a
desperate salvation is that which is obtained by self-betrayal!

Those professions which are not so much involved in life itself
as concerned with abstract truths are the most dangerous for the
young man whose principles are not yet firm and whose convictions are not yet strong and unshakeable. At the same time these
professions may seem to be the most exalted if they have taken
deep root in our hearts and if we are capable of sacrificing our
lives and all endeavours for the ideas which prevail in them.

They can bestow happiness on the man who has a vocation for
them, but they destroy him who adopts them rashly, without
reflection, yielding to the impulse of the moment.

On the other hand, the high regard we have for the ideas
on which our profession is based gives us a higher standing in
society, enhances our own worth, and makes our actions un-
challengeable.

One who chooses a profession he values highly will shudder at
the idea of being unworthy of it; he will act nobly if only because
his position in society is a noble one.

But the chief guide which must direct us in the choice of a
profession is the welfare of mankind and our own perfection. It
should not be thought that these two interests could be in conflict,
that one would have to destroy the other; on the contrary, man's
nature is so constituted that he can attain his own perfection
only by working for the perfection, for the good, of his fellow
men.

If he works only for himself, he may perhaps become a famous
man of learning, a great sage, an excellent poet, but he can never
be a perfect, truly great man.

History calls those men the greatest who have ennobled themselves by working for the common good; experience acclaims as
happiest the man who has made the greatest number of people
happy; religion itself teaches us that the ideal being whom all
strive to copy sacrificed himself for the sake of mankind, and who
would dare to set at nought such judgments?

If we have chosen the position in life in which we can most of
all work for mankind, no burdens can bow us down, because they
are sacrifices for the benefit of all; then we shall experience no

petty, limited, selfish joy, but our happiness will belong to millions, our deeds will live on quietly but perpetually at work, and over our ashes will be shed the hot tears of noble people.

Written between August 10 and 16, 1835

First published in the yearly *Archiv für die Geschichte des Sozialismus und der Arbeiterbewegung*, Ed. K. Grünberg, Leipzig, 1925

Signed: *Marx*

Printed according to the manuscript

[LETTER FROM MARX TO HIS FATHER

IN TRIER][2]

Berlin, November 10[-11, 1837]

Dear Father,

There are moments in one's life which are like frontier posts marking the completion of a period but at the same time clearly indicating a new direction.

At such a moment of transition we feel compelled to view the past and the present with the eagle eye of thought in order to become conscious of our real position. Indeed, world history itself likes to look back in this way and take stock, which often gives it the appearance of retrogression or stagnation, whereas it is merely, as it were, sitting back in an armchair in order to understand itself and mentally grasp its own activity, that of the mind.

At such moments, however, a person becomes lyrical, for every metamorphosis is partly a swan song, partly the overture to a great new poem, which endeavours to achieve a stable form in brilliant colours that still merge into one another. Nevertheless, we should like to erect a memorial to what we have once lived through in order that this experience may regain in our emotions the place it has lost in our actions. And where could a more sacred dwelling place be found for it than in the heart of a parent, the most merciful judge, the most intimate sympathiser, the sun of love whose warming fire is felt at the innermost centre of our endeavours! What better amends and forgiveness could there be for much that is objectionable and blameworthy than to be seen as the manifestation of an essentially necessary state of things? How, at least, could the often ill-fated play of chance and intellectual error better escape the reproach of being due to a perverse heart?

When, therefore, now at the end of a year spent here I cast a glance back on the course of events during that time, in order, my dear father, to answer your infinitely dear letter from Ems,[a] allow me to review my affairs in the way I regard life in general, as the expression of an intellectual activity which develops in all directions, in science, art and private matters.

When I left you, a new world had come into existence for me, that of love, which in fact at the beginning was a passionately yearning and hopeless love. Even the journey to Berlin, which otherwise would have delighted me in the highest degree, would have inspired me to contemplate nature and fired my zest for life, left me cold. Indeed, it put me strikingly out of humour, for the rocks which I saw were not more rugged, more indomitable, than the emotions of my soul, the big towns not more lively than my blood, the inn meals not more extravagant, more indigestible, than the store of fantasies I carried with me, and, finally, no work of art was as beautiful as Jenny.

After my arrival in Berlin, I broke off all hitherto existing connections, made visits rarely and unwillingly, and tried to immerse myself in science and art.

In accordance with my state of mind at the time, lyrical poetry was bound to be my first subject, at least the most pleasant and immediate one. But owing to my attitude and whole previous development it was purely idealistic. My heaven, my art, became a world beyond, as remote as my love. Everything real became hazy and what is hazy has no definite outlines. All the poems of the first three volumes I sent to Jenny are marked by attacks on our times, diffuse and inchoate expressions of feeling, nothing natural, everything built out of moonshine, complete opposition between what is and what ought to be, rhetorical reflections instead of poetic thoughts, but perhaps also a certain warmth of feeling and striving for poetic fire. The whole extent of a longing that has no bounds finds expression there in many different forms and makes the poetic "composition" into "diffusion".[b]

Poetry, however, could be and had to be only an accompaniment; I had to study law and above all felt the urge to wrestle with philosophy. The two were so closely linked that, on the one hand,

---

[a] See this volume, pp. 677-78.— *Ed.*

[b] A pun on the German words *Dichten* (poetic composition or also something compact) and *Breiten* (something broad or diffuse).— *Ed.*

I read through Heineccius, Thibaut[a] and the sources quite
uncritically, in a mere schoolboy fashion; thus, for instance, I
translated the first two books of the Pandect[3] into German, and,
on the other hand, tried to elaborate a philosophy of law covering
the whole field of law. I prefaced this with some metaphysical
propositions by way of introduction and continued this unhappy
opus as far as public law, a work of almost 300 pages.[4]

Here, above all, the same opposition between what is and what
ought to be, which is characteristic of idealism, stood out as a
serious defect and was the source of the hopelessly incorrect
division of the subject-matter. First of all came what I was pleased
to call the metaphysics of law, i. e., basic principles, reflections,
definitions of concepts, divorced from all actual law and every
actual form of law, as occurs in Fichte,[b] only in my case it was
more modern and shallower. From the outset an obstacle to
grasping the truth here was the unscientific form of mathematical
dogmatism, in which the author argues hither and thither, going
round and round the subject dealt with, without the latter taking
shape as something living and developing in a many-sided way. A
triangle gives the mathematician scope for construction and proof,
it remains a mere abstract conception in space and does not
develop into anything further. It has to be put alongside something else, then it assumes other positions, and this diversity added
to it gives it different relationships and truths. On the other hand,
in the concrete expression of a living world of ideas, as exem-
plified by law, the state, nature, and philosophy as a whole, the
object itself must be studied in its development; arbitrary divisions
must not be introduced, the rational character of the object itself
must develop as something imbued with contradictions in itself
and find its unity in itself.

Next, as the second part, came the philosophy of law, that is to
say, according to my views at the time, an examination of the
development of ideas in positive Roman law, as if positive law in
its conceptual development (I do not mean in its purely finite
provisions) could ever be something different from the formation
of the concept of law, which the first part, however, should have
dealt with.

---

[a] J. G. Heineccius, *Elementa iuris civilis secundum ordinem Pandectarum, commoda
auditoribus methodo adornata*; A. F. J. Thibaut, *System des Pandekten-Rechts*,
Bd. 1-2.— *Ed.*

[b] J. G. Fichte, *Grundlage des Naturrechts nach Prinzipien der Wissenschaftslehre*,
2 Teile.— *Ed.*

Letter from Karl Marx to his father, November 10-11, 1837

Portrait of Karl Marx
in his student years

Members of the Trier Students' Association
at Bonn University

Moreover, I had further divided this part into the theory of formal law and the theory of material law, the first being the pure form of the system in its sequence and interconnections, its subdivisions and scope, whereas the second, on the other hand, was intended to describe the content, showing how the form becomes embodied in its content. This was an error I shared with Herr v. Savigny, as I discovered later in his learned work on ownership,[a] the only difference being that he applies the term formal definition of the concept to "finding the place which this or that theory occupies in the (fictitious) Roman system", the material definition being "the theory of positive content which the Romans attributed to a concept defined in this way",[5] whereas I understood by form the necessary architectonics of conceptual formulations, and by matter the necessary quality of these formulations. The mistake lay in my belief that matter and form can and must develop separately from each other, and so I obtained not a real form, but something like a desk with drawers into which I then poured sand.

The concept is indeed the mediating link between form and content. In a philosophical treatment of law, therefore, the one must arise in the other; indeed, the form should only be the continuation of the content. Thus I arrived at a division of the material such as could be devised by its author for at most an easy and shallow classification, but in which the spirit and truth of law disappeared. All law was divided into contractual and non-contractual. In order to make this clearer, I take the liberty to set out the plan up to the division of *jus publicum*,[b] which is also treated in the formal part.

<table>
<tr><td align="center">I</td><td align="center">II</td></tr>
<tr><td align="center">*jus privatum*[c]</td><td align="center">*jus publicum*</td></tr>
</table>

I. *jus privatum*

a) Conditional contractual private law.
b) Unconditional non-contractual private law.

A. *Conditional contractual private law*

a) Law of persons; b) Law of things; c) Law of persons in relation to property.

a) Law of persons

I. Commercial contracts; II. Warranties; III. Contracts of bailment.

---

[a] F. C. Savigny, *Das Recht des Besitzes.*— *Ed.*

[b] Public law.— *Ed.*

[c] Private law.— *Ed.*

I. *Commercial contracts*

2. Contracts of legal entities (*societas*). 3. *Contracts of casements (locatio conductio)*.

3. *Locatio conductio*

1. Insofar as it relates to *operae*.[a]
   a) *locatio conductio* proper (excluding Roman letting or leasing);
   b) *mandatum*.[b]
2. Insofar as it relates to *usus rei*.[c]
   a) On land: *usus fructus*[d] (also not in the purely Roman sense);
   b) On houses: *habitatio*.[e]

II. *Warranties*

1. Arbitration or conciliation contract; 2. Insurance contract.

III. *Contracts of bailment*

2. *Promissory contract*

1. *fide jussio*[f]; 2. *negotiorum gestio*.[g]

3. *Contract of gift*

1. *donatio*[h]; 2. *gratiae promissum*.[i]

b) *Law of things*

I. *Commercial contracts*

2. *permutatio stricte sic dicta*.[j]

1. *permutatio* proper; 2. *mutuum (usurae)*[k]; 3. *emptio venditio*.[l]

pignus.[m]   ### II. *Warranties*

---

[a] Services.— *Ed.*
[b] Commission.— *Ed.*
[c] Right to use of something.— *Ed.*
[d] Usufruct.— *Ed.*
[e] Right to habitation (first of all in one's own house, later in the house of another person).— *Ed.*
[f] Pledge.— *Ed.*
[g] Management without commission.— *Ed.*
[h] Gift.— *Ed.*
[i] Promise of a favour.— *Ed.*
[j] Exchange in the original sense.— *Ed.*
[k] Loan (interest).— *Ed.*
[l] Purchase and sale.— *Ed.*
[m] Pledge.— *Ed.*

III. *Contracts of bailment*

2. *commodatum*[a]; 3. *depositum*.[b]

But why should I go on filling up pages with things I myself have rejected? The whole thing is replete with tripartite divisions, it is written with tedious prolixity, and the Roman concepts are misused in the most barbaric fashion in order to force them into my system. On the other hand, in this way I did gain a general view of the material and a liking for it, at least along certain lines.

At the end of the section on material private law, I saw the falsity of the whole thing, the basic plan of which borders on that of Kant,[6] but deviates wholly from it in the execution, and again it became clear to me that there could be no headway without philosophy. So with a good conscience I was able once more to throw myself into her embrace, and I drafted a new system of metaphysical principles, but at the conclusion of it I was once more compelled to recognise that it was wrong, like all my previous efforts.

In the course of this work I adopted the habit of making extracts from all the books I read, for instance from Lessing's *Laokoon*, Solger's *Erwin*, Winckelmann's history of art, Luden's German history, and incidentally scribbled down my reflections. At the same time I translated Tacitus' *Germania*, and Ovid's *Tristia*, and began to learn English and Italian by myself, i. e., out of grammars, but I have not yet got anywhere with this. I also read Klein's criminal law and his annals, and all the most recent literature, but this last only by the way.

At the end of the term, I again sought the dances of the Muses and the music of the Satyrs. Already in the last exercise book that I sent you[c] idealism pervades forced humour (*Scorpion and Felix*) and an unsuccessful, fantastic drama (*Oulanem*), until it finally undergoes a complete transformation and becomes mere formal art, mostly without objects that inspire it and without any impassioned train of thought.

And yet these last poems are the only ones in which suddenly, as if by a magic touch—oh, the touch was at first a shattering blow—I caught sight of the glittering realm of true poetry like a distant fairy palace, and all my creations crumbled into nothing.

Busy with these various occupations, during my first term I

---

[a] Loan, loan contract.— *Ed.*

[b] Safe keeping of goods deposited.— *Ed.*

[c] See this volume, pp. 616-32.— *Ed.*

spent many a sleepless night, fought many a battle, and endured much internal and external excitement. Yet at the end I emerged not much enriched, and moreover I had neglected nature, art and the world, and shut the door on my friends. The above observations seem to have been made by my body. I was advised by a doctor to go to the country, and so it was that for the first time I traversed the whole length of the city to the gate and went to Stralow. I had no inkling that I would mature there from an anaemic weakling into a man of robust bodily strength.

A curtain had fallen, my holy of holies was rent asunder, and new gods had to be installed.

From the idealism which, by the way, I had compared and nourished with the idealism of Kant and Fichte, I arrived at the point of seeking the idea in reality itself. If previously the gods had dwelt above the earth, now they became its centre.

I had read fragments of Hegel's philosophy, the grotesque craggy melody of which did not appeal to me. Once more I wanted to dive into the sea, but with the definite intention of establishing that the nature of the mind is just as necessary, concrete and firmly based as the nature of the body. My aim was no longer to practise tricks of swordsmanship, but to bring genuine pearls into the light of day.

I wrote a dialogue of about 24 pages: "Cleanthes, or the Starting Point and Necessary Continuation of Philosophy".[7] Here art and science, which had become completely divorced from each other, were to some extent united, and like a vigorous traveller I set about the task itself, a philosophical-dialectical account of divinity, as it manifests itself as the idea-in-itself, as religion, as nature, and as history. My last proposition was the beginning of the Hegelian system. And this work, for which I had acquainted myself to some extent with natural science, Schelling, and history, which had caused me to rack my brains endlessly, and which is so [...] written (since it was actually intended to be a new logic) that now even I myself can hardly recapture my thinking about it, this work, my dearest child, reared by moonlight, like a false siren delivers me into the arms of the enemy.

For some days my vexation made me quite incapable of thinking; I ran about madly in the garden by the dirty water of the Spree, which "washes souls and dilutes the tea".[a] I even joined my landlord in a hunting excursion, rushed off to Berlin and wanted to embrace every street-corner loafer.

---

[a] H. Heine, *Die Nordsee*, 1. Zyklus, "Frieden".—*Ed.*

Shortly after that I pursued only positive studies: the study of Savigny's *Ownership*, Feuerbach's and Grolmann's criminal law, Cramer's *de verborum significatione*, Wenning-Ingenheim's Pandect system, and Mühlenbruch's *Doctrina pandectarum*, which I am still working through, and finally a few titles from Lauterbach, on civil procedure and above all canon law, the first part of which, Gratian's *Concordia discordantium canonum*, I have almost entirely read through in the *corpus* and made extracts from, as also the supplement, Lancelotti's *Institutiones*. Then I translated in part Aristotle's *Rhetoric*, read *de augmentis scientiarum* of the famous Bacon of Verulam, spent a good deal of time on Reimarus, to whose book on the artistic instincts of animals I applied my mind with delight, and also tackled German law, but chiefly only to the extent of going through the capitularies of the Franconian kings and the letters of the Popes to them.

Owing to being upset over Jenny's illness and my vain, fruitless intellectual labours, and as the result of nagging annoyance at having had to make an idol of a view that I hated, I became ill, as I have already written to you, dear Father. When I got better I burnt all the poems and outlines of stories, etc., imagining that I could give them up completely, of which so far at any rate I have not given any proofs to the contrary.

While I was ill I got to know Hegel from beginning to end, together with most of his disciples. Through a number of meetings with friends in Stralow I came across a Doctors' Club,[8] which includes some university lecturers and my most intimate Berlin friend, Dr. Rutenberg. In controversy here, many conflicting views were expressed, and I became ever more firmly bound to the modern world philosophy from which I had thought to escape, but all rich chords were silenced and I was seized with a veritable fury of irony, as could easily happen after so much had been negated. In addition, there was Jenny's silence, and I could not rest until I had acquired modernity and the outlook of contemporary science through a few bad productions such as *The Visit*,[9] etc.

If perhaps I have here neither clearly described the whole of this last term nor gone into all details, and slurred over all the nuances, excuse me, dear Father, because of my desire to speak of the present time.

Herr v. Chamisso sent me a very insignificant note in which he informed me "he regrets that the *Almanac* cannot use my contributions because it has already been printed a long time ago".[10] I swallowed this with vexation. The bookseller Wigand has sent my plan to Dr. Schmidt, publisher of Wunder's firm that trades in good cheese and bad literature. I enclose his letter; Dr. Schmidt has not yet replied. However, I am by no means abandoning this plan, especially since all the aesthetic celebrities of the Hegelian school have promised their collaboration through the help of university lecturer Bauer, who plays a big role among them, and of my colleague Dr. Rutenberg.[11]

Now, as regards the question of a career in cameralistics, my dear father, I recently made the acquaintance of an assessor, Schmidthänner, who advised me after the third law examination to transfer to it as a justiciary, which would be the more to my taste, since I really prefer jurisprudence to all administrative science. This gentleman told me that in three years he himself and many others from the Münster high provincial court in Westphalia had succeeded in reaching the position of assessor, which was not difficult, with hard work of course, since the stages there are not rigidly fixed as they are in Berlin and elsewhere. If later, as an assessor, one is awarded a doctor's degree, there are also much better prospects of obtaining a post as professor extraordinary, as happened in the case of Herr Gärtner in Bonn, who wrote a mediocre work on provincial legislation [a] and is otherwise only known as belonging to the Hegelian school of jurists. But, my dear, very good father, would it not be possible to discuss all this with you personally? Eduard's [b] condition, dear Mama's illness, your own ill health, although I hope it is not serious, all this makes me want to hurry to you, indeed it makes it almost a necessity. I would be there already if I was not definitely in doubt about your permission and consent.

Believe me, my dear, dear father, I am actuated by no selfish intention (although it would be bliss for me to see Jenny again), but there is a thought which moves me, and it is one I have no right to express. In many respects it would even be a hard step for me to take but, as my only sweet Jenny writes, these considerations are all of no account when faced with the fulfilment of duties that are sacred.

I beg you, dear Father, however you may decide, not to show this letter, at least not this page, to my angel of a mother. My sudden arrival could perhaps help this grand and wonderful woman to recover.

---

[a] G. F. Gaertner, *Ueber die Provinzial-Rechte. Sendschreiben an den Königl. Geheimen Justiz- und vortragenden Rath im hohen Justiz-Ministerium zu Berlin, Herrn A. W. Goetze.—Ed.*

[b] Karl Marx's brother.—*Ed.*

My letter to Mama was written long before the arrival of Jenny's dear letter, so perhaps I unwittingly wrote too much about matters which are not quite or even very little suitable.[12]

In the hope that gradually the clouds that have gathered about our family will pass away, that it will be granted to me to suffer and weep with you and, perhaps, when with you to give proof of my profound, heartfelt sympathy and immeasurable love, which often I can only express very badly; in the hope that you also, dear, ever beloved Father, taking into account my much agitated state of mind, will forgive me where often my heart seems to have erred, overwhelmed by my militant spirit, and that you will soon be wholly restored to health so that I can clasp you to my heart and tell you all my thoughts,

Your ever loving son,

Karl

Please, dear Father, excuse my illegible handwriting and bad style; it is almost 4 o'clock, the candle has burnt itself out, and my eyes are dim; a real unrest has taken possession of me, I shall not be able to calm the turbulent spectres until I am with you who are dear to me.

Please give greetings from me to my sweet, wonderful Jenny. I have read her letter twelve times already, and always discover new delights in it. It is in every respect, including that of style, the most beautiful letter I can imagine being written by a woman.

First published in *Die Neue Zeit* No. 1, 1897

Printed according to the original

WILD SONGS [13]

I

THE FIDDLER

The Fiddler saws the strings,
His light brown hair he tosses and flings.
    He carries a sabre at his side,
    He wears a pleated habit wide.

"Fiddler, why that frantic sound?
Why do you gaze so wildly round?
    Why leaps your blood, like the surging sea?
    What drives your bow so desperately?"

"Why do I fiddle? Or the wild waves roar?
That they might pound the rocky shore,
    That eye be blinded, that bosom swell,
    That Soul's cry carry down to Hell."

"Fiddler, with scorn you rend your heart.
A radiant God lent you your art,
    To dazzle with waves of melody,
    To soar to the star-dance in the sky."

"How so! I plunge, plunge without fail
My blood-black sabre into your soul.
    That art God neither wants nor wists,
    It leaps to the brain from Hell's black mists.

"Till heart's bewitched, till senses reel:
With Satan I have struck my deal.
    He chalks the signs, beats time for me,
    I play the death march fast and free.

"I must play dark, I must play light,
Till bowstrings break my heart outright."

The Fiddler saws the strings,
His light brown hair he tosses and flings.
  He carries a sabre at his side,
  He wears a pleated habit wide.

II

NOCTURNAL LOVE

Frantic, he holds her near,
  Darkly looks in her eye.
"Pain so burns you, Dear,
  And at my breath you sigh.

"Oh, you have drunk my soul.
  Mine is your glow, in truth.
My jewel, shine your fill.
  Glow, blood of youth."

"Sweetest, so pale your face,
  So wondrous strange your words.
See, rich in music's grace
  The lofty gliding worlds."

"Gliding, dearest, gliding,
  Glowing, stars, glowing.
Let us go heavenwards riding,
  Our souls together flowing."

His voice is muffled, low.
  Desperate, he looks about.
Glances of crackling flame
  His hollow eyes shoot out.

"You have drunk poison, Love.
  With me you must away.
The sky is dark above,
  No more I see the day."

Shuddering, he pulls her close to him.
Death in the breast doth hover.
Pain stabs her, piercing deep within,
And eyes are closed forever.

Written in 1837

First published in the *Athenäum.*
Zeitschrift für das gebildete Deutschland,
January 23, 1841

Printed according to the journal

DIFFERENCE
BETWEEN THE DEMOCRITEAN
AND EPICUREAN
PHILOSOPHY OF NATURE

With an Appendix [14]

Written between 1840 and March 1841

First published in the book:
Marx und Engels, *Aus dem literarischen Nachlass*, Stuttgart, 1902

Signed: *Karl Heinrich Marx, Ph. D.*

Printed according to the copy of the manuscript corrected by Marx

To his dear fatherly friend,
LUDWIG VON WESTPHALEN,
Geheimer Regierungsrat
at Trier,
the author dedicates these
lines as a token
of filial love

You will forgive me, *my dear fatherly friend,* if I set *your* name, so dear to me, at the head of an insignificant brochure. I am too impatient to await another opportunity of giving *you* a small proof of my love.

May everyone who doubts of the Idea be so fortunate as I, to be able to admire an old man who has the strength of youth, who greets every forward step of the times with the enthusiasm and the prudence of truth and who, with that profoundly convincing sun-bright idealism which alone knows the true word at whose call all the spirits of the world appear, never recoiled before the deep shadows of retrograde ghosts, before the often dark clouds of the times, but rather with godly energy and manly confident gaze saw through all veils the empyreum which burns at the heart of the world. *You, my fatherly friend,* were always a living *argumentum ad oculos*[a] to me, that idealism is no figment of the imagination, but a truth.

I need not pray for *your* physical well-being. The spirit is the great physician versed in magic, to whom *you* have entrusted yourself.[b]

---

[a] Visible proof.— *Ed.*

[b] This paragraph was originally: "I hope to follow soon in person this messenger of love which I send *you,* and to roam again at *your* side through our wonderfully picturesque mountains and forests. I need not pray for *your* physical well-being. The spirit and nature are the great physicians versed in magic, to whom *you* have entrusted *yourself.*"— On the left-hand margin of this page are the words, "This dedication should be printed in larger type."— *Ed.*

FOREWORD

The form of this treatise would have been on the one hand more strictly scientific, on the other hand in many of its arguments less pedantic, if its primary purpose had not been that of a doctor's dissertation. I am nevertheless constrained by external reasons to send it to the press in this form. Moreover I believe that I have solved in it a heretofore unsolved problem in the history of Greek philosophy.

The experts know that no preliminary studies that are even of the slightest use exist for the subject of this treatise. What Cicero and Plutarch have babbled has been babbled after them up to the present day. Gassendi, who freed Epicurus from the interdict which the Fathers of the Church and the whole Middle Ages, the period of realised unreason, had placed upon him, presents in his expositions[15] only one interesting element. He seeks to accommodate his Catholic conscience to his pagan knowledge and Epicurus to the Church, which certainly was wasted effort. It is as though one wanted to throw the habit of a Christian nun over the bright and flourishing body of the Greek Lais. It is rather that Gassendi learns philosophy from Epicurus than that he could teach us about Epicurus' philosophy.

This treatise is to be regarded only as the preliminary to a larger work in which I shall present in detail the cycle of Epicurean, Stoic and Sceptic philosophy in their relation to the whole of Greek speculation.[16] The shortcomings of this treatise, in form and the like, will be eliminated in that later work.

To be sure, *Hegel* has on the whole correctly defined the general aspects of the above-mentioned systems. But in the admirably great and bold plan of his history of philosophy, from which alone the history of philosophy can in general be dated, it was impossible, on the one hand, to go into detail, and on the other hand, the giant thinker was hindered by his view of what he called speculative thought *par excellence* from recognising in these systems their great importance for the history of Greek philosophy and for the Greek mind in general. These systems are the key to the true history of Greek philosophy. A more profound indication of their connection with Greek life can be found in the essay of my friend Köppen, *Friedrich der Grosse und seine Widersacher*.[17]

If a critique of Plutarch's polemic against Epicurus' theology has been added as an appendix, this is because this polemic is by no means isolated, but rather representative of an *espèce*,[a] in that it most strikingly presents in itself the relation of the theologising intellect to philosophy.

The[b] critique does not touch, among other things, on the general falsity of Plutarch's standpoint when he brings philosophy before the forum of religion. In this respect it will be enough to cite, in place of all argument, a passage from David Hume:

"... 'Tis certainly a kind of indignity to philosophy, whose *sovereign authority* ought everywhere to be acknowledged, to oblige her on every occasion to make apologies for her conclusions and justify herself to every particular art and science which may be offended at her. *This puts one in mind of a king arraign'd for high treason against his subjects.*"[18]

Philosophy, as long as a drop of blood shall pulse in its world-subduing and absolutely free heart, will never grow tired of answering its adversaries with the cry of Epicurus:

Ἀσεβὴς δὲ, οὐχ ὁ τοὺς τῶν πολλῶν θεοὺς ἀναιρῶν, ἀλλ' ὁ τὰς τῶν πολλῶν δόξας θεοῖς προσάπτων.[c][19]

Philosophy makes no secret of it. The confession of Prometheus:

ἁπλῷ λόγῳ, τοὺς πάντας ἐχθαίρω θεούς,[d]

is its own confession, its own aphorism against all heavenly and earthly gods who do not acknowledge human self-consciousness as the highest divinity. It will have none other beside.

But to those poor March hares who rejoice over the apparently

---

[a] Species, type.— *Ed.*

[b] "The" corrected by Marx from "this".— *Ed.*

[c] Not the man who denies the gods worshipped by the multitude, but he who affirms of the gods what the multitude believes about them, is truly impious.— *Ed.*

[d] In simple words, I hate the pack of gods (Aeschylus, *Prometheus Bound*).— *Ed.*

worsened civil position of philosophy, it responds again, as Prometheus replied to the servant of the gods, Hermes:

τῆς σῆς λατρείας τὴν ἐμὴν δυςπραξίαν,
σαφῶς ἐπίστασ', οὐκ ἂν ἀλλάξαιμ' ἐγώ.
κρεῖσσον γὰρ οἶμαι τῇδε λατρεύειν πέτρᾳ
ἢ πατρὶ φῦναι Ζηνὶ πιστὸν ἄγγελον. [a]

Prometheus is the most eminent saint and martyr in the philosophical calendar.

Berlin, March 1841

---

[a] Be sure of this, I would not change my state
Of evil fortune for your servitude.
Better to be the servant of this rock
Than to be faithful boy to Father Zeus.
(Ibid.)— *Ed.*

Contents

Foreword

ON THE DIFFERENCE BETWEEN THE DEMOCRITEAN
AND EPICUREAN PHILOSOPHY OF NATURE

Part One

DIFFERENCE BETWEEN THE DEMOCRITEAN
AND EPICUREAN PHILOSOPHY OF NATURE *IN GENERAL*

  I. The Subject of the Treatise
 II. Opinions on the Relationship Between Democritean and
     Epicurean Physics
III. Difficulties Concerning the Identity of the Democritean
     and Epicurean Philosophy of Nature
 IV. General Difference in Principle Between the Democritean
     and Epicurean Philosophy of Nature
  V. Result

Part Two

DIFFERENCE BETWEEN THE DEMOCRITEAN
AND EPICUREAN PHILOSOPHY OF NATURE IN DETAIL

Chapter One: The Declination of the Atom from the
             Straight Line
Chapter Two: The Qualities of the Atom
Chapter Three: Ἄτομοι ἀρχαί and ἄτομα στοιχεῖα[a]
Chapter Four: Time
Chapter Five: The Meteors

---

[a] *Atomoi archai*, indivisible principles; *atoma stoicheia*, indivisible elements.— *Ed.*

Appendix

CRITIQUE OF PLUTARCH'S POLEMIC AGAINST THE THEOLOGY
OF EPICURUS

Preliminary Note

I. The Relationship of Man to God
1. Fear and the Being Beyond
2. Cult and the Individual
3. Providence and the Degraded God

II. Individual Immortality
1. On Religious Feudalism. The Hell of the Populace
2. The Longing of the Multitude
3. The Pride of the Elected

Part One

DIFFERENCE BETWEEN THE DEMOCRITEAN AND EPICUREAN PHILOSOPHY OF NATURE IN GENERAL

I. THE SUBJECT OF THE TREATISE

Greek philosophy seems to have met with something with which a good tragedy is not supposed to meet, namely, a dull ending.[a] The objective history of philosophy in Greece seems to come to an end with[b] Aristotle, Greek philosophy's Alexander of Macedon, and even the manly-strong Stoics did not succeed[c] in what the Spartans did accomplish in their temples, the chaining of Athena[d] to Heracles so that she could not flee.

Epicureans, Stoics and Sceptics are regarded as an almost improper addition bearing no relation to its powerful premises.[e] Epicurean philosophy is taken as a syncretic combination of Democritean physics and Cyrenaic morality; Stoicism as a compound of Heraclitean speculation on nature and the Cynical-ethical view of the world, together with some Aristotelean logic; and finally Scepticism as the necessary evil confronting these dogmatisms. These philosophies are thus unconsciously linked to the Alexandrian philosophy by being made into a one-sided and tendentious eclecticism. The Alexandrian philosophy is finally regarded entirely as exaltation and derangement—a confusion in which at most the universality of the intention can be recognised.

---

[a] After "ending", Marx erased "an incoherent finale".— *Ed.*

[b] Corrected by Marx from "after".— *Ed.*

[c] The sentence "The objective history ... succeed" was originally: "With Aristotle, Greek philosophy's Alexander of Macedon, the owl of Minerva seems to lower its wings, and even the manly-strong Stoics seem not to have succeeded...." — *Ed.*

[d] Corrected by Marx from "Minerva".— *Ed.*

[e] *Prämissen* (premises) corrected by Marx from *Antezedentien* (predecessors).— *Ed.*

To be sure, it is a commonplace[a] that birth, flowering and decline constitute the iron circle in which everything human is enclosed, through which it must pass. Thus it would not have been surprising if Greek philosophy, after having reached its zenith in Aristotle, should then have withered. But the death of the hero resembles the setting of the sun, not the bursting of an inflated frog.

And then: birth, flowering and decline are very general, very vague notions under which, to be sure, everything can be arranged, but through which nothing can be understood. Decay itself is prefigured in the living; its shape should therefore be just as much grasped in its specific characteristic as the shape of life.

Finally, when we glance at history, are Epicureanism, Stoicism and Scepticism particular phenomena? Are they not the prototypes of the Roman mind, the shape in which Greece wandered to Rome? Is not their essence so full of character, so intense and eternal that the modern world itself has to admit them to full spiritual citizenship?

I lay stress on this only in order to call to mind the historical importance of these systems. Here, however, we are not at all concerned with their significance for culture in general, but with their connection with the older Greek philosophy.

Should not this relationship urge us at least to an inquiry, to see Greek philosophy ending up with two different groups of eclectic systems, one of them the cycle of Epicurean, Stoic and Sceptic philosophy, the other being classified under the collective name of Alexandrian speculation? Furthermore, is it not remarkable that after the Platonic and Aristotelean philosophies, which are universal in range, there appear new systems which do not lean on these rich intellectual forms, but look farther back and have recourse to the simplest schools — to the philosophers of nature in regard to physics, to the Socratic school in regard to ethics? Moreover, what is the reason why the systems that follow after Aristotle find their foundations as it were ready made in the past, why Democritus is linked to the Cyrenaics and Heraclitus to the Cynics? Is it an accident that with the Epicureans, Stoics and Sceptics all moments of self-consciousness are represented completely, but every moment as a particular existence? Is it an accident that these systems in their totality[b] form the complete structure of self-consciousness? And finally, the character with which Greek philosophy mythically

---

[a] Corrected by Marx from "not to be denied".— *Ed.*

[b] Marx erased after "totality" the word *gleichsam,* "so to say", or "as it were".— *Ed.*

begins in the seven wise men, and which is, so to say as its central point, embodied in Socrates as its demiurge — I mean the character of the wise man, of the *sophos* (σοφός) — is it an accident that it is asserted in those systems as the reality of true science?

It seems to me that though the earlier systems are more significant and interesting for the content, the post-Aristotelean ones, and primarily the cycle of the Epicurean, Stoic and Sceptic schools, are more significant and interesting for the subjective form, the character of Greek philosophy. But it is precisely the subjective form, the spiritual carrier of the philosophical systems, which has until now been almost entirely ignored in favour of their metaphysical characteristics.

I shall save for a more extensive discussion the presentation of the Epicurean, Stoic and Sceptic philosophies as a whole and in their total relationship to earlier and later Greek speculation.

Let it suffice here to develop this relationship as it were by an example, and only in one aspect, namely, their relationship to earlier speculation.

As such an example I select the relationship between the Epicurean and the Democritean philosophy of nature. I do not believe that it is the most convenient point of contact. Indeed, on the one hand it is an old and entrenched prejudice to identify Democritean and Epicurean physics, so that Epicurus' modifications are seen as only arbitrary vagaries. On the other hand I am forced to go into what seem to be microscopic examinations as far as details are concerned. But precisely because this prejudice is as old as the history of philosophy, because the differences are so concealed that they can be discovered as it were only with a microscope, it will be all the more important if, despite the interdependence of Democritean and Epicurean physics, an essential difference extending to the smallest details can be demonstrated. What can be demonstrated in the small can even more easily be shown where the relations are considered in larger dimensions, while conversely very general considerations leave doubt whether the result will hold when applied to details.

II. OPINIONS ON THE RELATIONSHIP BETWEEN DEMOCRITEAN AND EPICUREAN PHYSICS

The way in which my general outlook is related to earlier points of view will become quite obvious if a brief review is made of the opinions held by the ancient authors concerning the relationship between Democritean and Epicurean physics.

Posidonius the Stoic, Nicolaus and *Sotion* reproach Epicurus for having presented the Democritean doctrine of atoms and Aristippus' teaching on pleasure as his own. [1] *Cotta* the Academician asks in Cicero: "What is there in Epicurus' physics which does not belong to Democritus? True, he modifies some details, but most of it he repeats after him." [2] *Cicero* himself says similarly:

"In physics, where he is the most pretentious, Epicurus is a perfect stranger. Most of it belongs to Democritus; where he deviates from him, where he endeavours to improve, he spoils and worsens it." [3]

Although many authors reproach Epicurus for aspersions against Democritus, Leonteus, according to Plutarch, affirms on the contrary that Epicurus honoured Democritus because the latter had adhered to the true doctrine before him, because he had discovered the principles of nature earlier. [4] In the essay *De placitis philosophorum* Epicurus is called one who philosophises after the manner of Democritus. [5] Plutarch in his *Colotes* goes further. Successively comparing Epicurus with Democritus, Empedocles, Parmenides, Plato, Socrates, Stilpo, the Cyrenaics and the Academicians, he seeks to prove that "Epicurus appropriated from the whole of Greek philosophy the false and did not understand the true". [6] Likewise the treatise *De eo, quod secundum Epicurum non beate vivi possit* teems with inimical insinuations of a similar kind.

In the Fathers of the Church we find this unfavourable opinion, held by the more ancient authors, maintained. In the note I quote only one passage from Clement of Alexandria, [7] a Father of the Church who deserves to be prominently mentioned with regard to Epicurus, since he reinterprets the warning of the apostle Paul against philosophy in general into a warning against Epicurean philosophy, as one which did not even once spin fantasies concerning providence and the like. [8] But how common was the tendency to accuse Epicurus of plagiarism is shown most strikingly by *Sextus Empiricus,* who wishes to turn some quite inappropriate passages from Homer and Epicharmus into principal sources of Epicurean philosophy. [9]

It is well known that the more recent writers by and large make Epicurus, insofar as he was a philosopher of nature, a mere plagiarist of Democritus. The following statement of *Leibniz* may here represent their opinion in general:

"Nous ne savons presque de ce grand homme" (Démocrite) "que ce qu'Epicure en a emprunté, qui n'était pas capable d'en prendre toujours le meilleur." [a][10]

---

[a] "Of this great man" (Democritus) "we scarcely know anything but what Epicurus borrowed from him, and Epicurus was not capable of always taking the best."— Ed.

Thus while Cicero says that Epicurus worsened the Democritean doctrine, at the same time crediting him at least with the will to improve it and with having an eye for its defects, while Plutarch ascribes to him inconsistency [11] and a predisposition toward the inferior, hence also casts suspicion on his intentions, Leibniz denies him even the ability to make excerpts from Democritus skilfully.

But all agree that Epicurus borrowed his physics from Democritus.

III. DIFFICULTIES CONCERNING THE IDENTITY OF THE DEMOCRITEAN AND EPICUREAN PHILOSOPHY OF NATURE

Apart from historical testimony, there is much other evidence for the identity of Democritean and Epicurean physics. The principles — atoms and the void — are indisputably the same. Only in isolated cases does there seem to be arbitrary, hence unessential, difference.

However, a curious and insoluble riddle remains. Two philosophers teach exactly the same science, in exactly the same way, but — how inconsistent! — they stand diametrically opposed in all that concerns truth, certainty, application of this science, and all that refers to the relationship between thought and reality in general. I say that they stand diametrically opposed, and I shall now try to prove it.

A. The opinion of Democritus *concerning the truth and certainty of human knowledge* seems hard to ascertain. Contradictory passages are to be found, or rather it is not the passages, but Democritus' views that contradict each other. For Trendelenburg's assertion in his commentary to Aristotelean psychology, that only later authors, but not Aristotle, knew of such contradictions, is factually incorrect. Indeed, in Aristotle's *Psychology*[a] it is stated: "Democritus posits soul and mind [*Verstand*] as one and the same, since the phenomenon is the true thing." [1] But in his *Metaphysics* he writes: "Democritus asserts that nothing is true or it is concealed from us." [2] Are not these passages of Aristotle contradictory? If the phenomenon is the true thing, how can the true thing be concealed? The concealment begins only when phenomenon and truth separate.[b] But *Diogenes Laertius* reports that Democritus was

---

[a] Corrected by Marx from "Physiology".— *Ed.*
[b] This sentence and the one before were inserted by Marx.— *Ed.*

counted among the Sceptics. His saying is quoted: "In reality we know nothing, for truth lies at the deep bottom of the well." [3] Similar statements are found in *Sextus Empiricus.* [4]

This sceptical, uncertain and internally self-contradictory view held by Democritus is only further developed in *the way* in which *the relationship between the atom and the world which is apparent to the senses is determined.*

Sensuous appearance, on the one hand, does not belong to the atoms themselves. It is not *objective appearance,* but *subjective semblance [Schein].* "The *true* principles are the atoms and the void, *everything else is opinion, semblance.*" [5] "Cold exists only according to opinion, heat exists only according to opinion, but in reality there are only the atoms and the void." [6] *Unity* therefore does not truly result from the many atoms, but rather "through the combination of atoms each thing *appears* to become a unity". [7] The principles can therefore be perceived only through reason, since they are inaccessible to the sensuous eye if only because of their smallness. For this reason they are even called *ideas.* [8] The sensuous appearance is, on the other hand, the only true object, and the *aisthesis* (αἴσθησις) *is the phronesis* (φρόνησις)[a]; this true thing however is the changing, the unstable, the phenomenon. But to say that the phenomenon is the true thing is contradictory. [9] Thus now the one, now the other side is made the subjective and the objective. The contradiction therefore seems to be held apart, being divided between two worlds. Consequently, Democritus makes sensuous reality into subjective semblance; but the antinomy, banned from the world of objects, now exists in his own self-consciousness, where the concept of the atom and sensuous perception face each other as enemies.

Thus Democritus does not escape the antinomy. This is not yet the place to explain it. It is enough that we cannot deny its existence.

Now let us listen to Epicurus.

The wise man, he says, takes a *dogmatic, not* a *sceptical* position. [10] Yes, exactly this makes him superior to all the others, that he knows with conviction. [11] "All senses are heralds of the true." [12] "*Nor is there anything which can refute sensations,* neither like can refute like, because of their equal validity, nor can unlike refute unlike, because they do not pass judgment on the same thing, nor the concept, because the concept depends on the sensuous

---

[a] *Aisthesis*—sensuous perception, *phronesis*—reason, that which is rational.— *Ed.*

perceptions," [13] as it says in the *Canon*. But while *Democritus* turns the *sensuous world* into *subjective semblance*, *Epicurus* turns it into *objective appearance*. And here he differs quite consciously, since he claims that he shares *the same principles but* that he does *not* reduce the sensuous qualities to things *of mere opinion*. [14]

Since therefore sensation was in fact Epicurus' standard, since objective appearance corresponds to it: then we can only regard as a correct conclusion that at which Cicero shrugs his shoulder:

"The sun seems large to Democritus, because he is a man of science well versed in geometry; to Epicurus it seems to be about two feet large, for he pronounces it *to be* as large as it *seems*." [15]

B. *This difference* in the *theoretical judgments* of Democritus and Epicurus concerning the certainty of science and the truth of its objects *manifests* itself in the *disparate scientific energy* and *practice* of these men.

Democritus, for whom the principle does not enter into the appearance, remains without reality and existence, is faced on the other hand with the *world of sensation* as the real world, full of content. True, this world is subjective semblance, but just because of this it is torn away from the principle, left in its own independent reality. At the same time it is the unique real object and *as such* has value and significance. Democritus is therefore driven into *empirical observation*. Dissatisfied with philosophy, he throws himself into the arms of *positive knowledge*. We have already seen that Cicero calls him a *vir eruditus*.[a] He is versed in physics, ethics, mathematics, in the encyclopedic disciplines, in every art.[16] The catalogue alone of his books given by Diogenes Laertius bears witness to his erudition.[17] But since it is the characteristic trait of erudition to expand in breadth and to collect and to search on the outside, we see Democritus *wandering through half the world* in order to acquire experiences, knowledge and observations.

"I have among my contemporaries," he prides himself, "wandered through the largest part of the earth, investigating the remotest things. I have seen most climates and lands, and I have heard most learned men, and in linear composition with demonstration no one surpassed me, not even the so-called Arsipedonapts of the Egyptians." [18]

Demetrius in the *Homonymois* (ὁμωνύμοις)[b] and *Antisthenes* in the *Diadochais* (διαδοχαῖς)[c] report that he travelled to Egypt to the priests in order to learn geometry, and to the Chaldeans in Persia, and

---

[a] Man of science.— *Ed.*

[b] *Men of the Same Name.— Ed.*

[c] *Successions of Philosophers.— Ed.*

that he reached the Red Sea. Some maintain that he also met the gymnosophists [20] in India and set foot in Ethiopia. [19] On the one hand it is the *lust for knowledge* that leaves him no rest; but it is at the same time *dissatisfaction with true, i. e., philosophical, knowledge* that drives him far abroad. The knowledge which he considers true is without content, the knowledge that gives him content is without truth. It could be a fable, but a true fable, that anecdote of the ancients, since it gives a picture of the contradictory elements in his being. Democritus is supposed to have blinded himself so that the *sensuous light of the eye* would not darken the *sharpness of intellect.* [20] This is the same man who, according to Cicero, wandered through half the world.[a] But he did not find what he was looking for.

An opposite figure appears to us in Epicurus.

Epicurus is *satisfied* and *blissful in philosophy.*

"You must," he says, "serve philosophy so that true freedom will be your lot. He who has subordinated and surrendered himself to it does not need to wait, he is emancipated at once. For to serve philosophy is freedom itself." [21] Consequently he teaches: "Let no one when young delay to study philosophy, nor when he is old grow weary of his study. For no one can come too early or too late to secure the health of his soul. And the man who says that the age for philosophy has either not yet come or has gone by is like the man who says that the age for happiness is not yet come to him, or has passed away." [22]

While Democritus, dissatisfied with philosophy, throws himself into the arms of empirical knowledge, *Epicurus has nothing but contempt for the positive sciences,* since in his opinion they contribute nothing to *true perfection.* [23] He is called an *enemy of science,* a scorner of grammar. [24] He is even accused of ignorance. "But," says an Epicurean in Cicero, "it was not Epicurus who was without erudition, but those are ignorant who believe that what is shameful for a boy not to know ought still to be recited by the old man." [25]

But while *Democritus* seeks to learn from *Egyptian priests, Persian Chaldeans* and *Indian gymnosophists, Epicurus* prides himself on *not* having had a *teacher,* on being *self-taught.* [26] There are some people, he says according to Seneca, who struggle for truth without any assistance. Among these people he has himself traced out his path. And it is they, the self-taught, whom he praises most. The others, according to him, are second-rate minds. [27] While Democritus is driven into all parts of the world, Epicurus leaves his garden in Athens scarcely two or three times and travels to

---

[a] "Half the world" corrected from "the whole of infinity".— *Ed.*

Ionia, not to engage in studies, but to visit friends. [28] Finally, while Democritus, [a] despairing of acquiring knowledge, blinds himself, Epicurus, feeling the hour of death approaching, takes a warm bath, calls for pure wine and recommends to his friends that they be faithful to philosophy. [29]

C. The differences that we have just set forth should not be attributed to the accidental individuality of the two philosophers; they embody two opposite tendencies. We see as a difference of practical energy that which is expressed in the passages above as a difference of theoretical consciousness.

We consider finally the *form of reflection* which *expresses the relation of thought to being, their mutual relationship.* In the general relationship which the philosopher sees between the world and thought, he merely makes objective for himself the relation of his own particular consciousness to the real world.

Now Democritus uses *necessity* as a form of reflection of reality. [30] Aristotle says of him that he traces everything back to necessity. [31] Diogenes Laertius reports that the vortex of atoms, the origin of all, is the Democritean necessity. [32] More satisfactory explanations are given by the author of *De placitis philosophorum:*

Necessity is, according to Democritus, fate and law, providence and the creator of the world. But the substance of this necessity is the antitype and the movement and impulse of matter. [33]

A similar passage is to be found in the *Physical Selections* of *Stobaeus* [34] and in the sixth book of the *Praeparatio evangelica* of *Eusebius.* [35] In the *Ethical Selections* of Stobaeus the following aphorism of Democritus is preserved [36] — it is almost exactly repeated in the 14th book of Eusebius [37]: human beings like to create for themselves the illusion of chance — a manifestation of their own perplexity, since *chance [Zufall] is incompatible with sound thinking. Simplicius* similarly attributes to Democritus a passage in which Aristotle speaks of the ancient doctrine that does away with chance. [38]

Contrast this with Epicurus:

"*Necessity,* introduced [b] by some as the absolute ruler, *does not exist,* but some things are *accidental,* others depend on our *arbitrary will.* Necessity cannot be persuaded, but chance is unstable. It would be better to follow the myth about the gods

---

[a] Before "Democritus" Marx erased "the widely travelled".— *Ed.*

[b] "Introduced" (*eingeführt*) corrected by Marx from "played up" (*aufgeführt*).— *Ed.*

than to be a slave to the *heimarmene* (εἰμαρμενη)[a] of the physicists. For the former leaves hope for mercy if we do honour to the gods, while the latter is inexorable necessity. But it is *chance*, which must be accepted, *not God*, as the multitude believe." [39] "It is a misfortune to live in necessity, but to live in necessity is not a necessity. On all sides many short and easy paths to freedom are open. Let us therefore thank God that no man can be kept in life. It is permitted to subdue necessity itself." [40]

The Epicurean Velleius in Cicero says something similar about Stoic philosophy:

"What are we to think of a philosophy in which, as to ignorant old women, everything seems to occur through fate? ... by Epicurus we have been redeemed, set free." [41]

Thus Epicurus even *denies disjunctive judgment* so as not to have to acknowledge any concept of necessity. [42]

True, it is claimed that Democritus also used the concept of chance, but of the two passages on this matter which can be found in Simplicius [43] the one renders the other suspect, because it shows clearly that it was not Democritus who used the category of chance, but Simplicius who ascribed it to him as a consequence. For he says: Democritus assigns, generally speaking, no cause for the creation of the world, he *seems* therefore to make chance the cause. Here, however, we are concerned not with the *determination of the content*, but with the *form* used *consciously* by Democritus. The situation is similar in regard to the report by Eusebius that Democritus made chance the ruler of the universal and divine and claimed that here it is through chance that everything happens, whereas he excluded chance from human life and empirical nature and called its supporters foolish. [44]

In part, we see in these statements only a desire of the Christian bishop *Dionysius* for conclusion-forcing. In part, where the universal and divine begin, the Democritean concept of necessity ceases to differ from chance.

Hence, this much is historically certain: *Democritus* makes use of *necessity*, *Epicurus* of *chance*. And each of them rejects the opposite view with polemical irritation.

The principal consequence of this difference appears in the way individual physical phenomena are explained.

Necessity appears in finite nature as *relative necessity*, as *determinism*. Relative necessity can only be deduced from *real possibility*, i. e., it is a network of conditions, reasons, causes, etc., by means of which this necessity reveals itself. Real possibility is [b] the explica-

---

[a] What has been decreed, destiny.— *Ed.*

[b] After "is" Marx erased *gleichsam*, "as it were".— *Ed.*

tion of relative necessity. And we find it used by Democritus. We cite some passages from Simplicius.

If somebody is thirsty and drinks and feels better, Democritus will not assign chance as the cause, but thirst. For, even though he seems to use chance in regard to the creation of the world, yet he maintains that chance is not the cause of any particular event, but on the contrary leads back to other causes. Thus, for example, digging is the cause of a treasure being found, or growing the cause of the olive tree.[45]

The enthusiasm and the seriousness with which Democritus introduces this manner of explanation into the observation of nature, the importance he attaches to the striving to ascertain causes, are naively[a] expressed in his avowal:

"I would rather discover a new aetiology than acquire the Persian crown."[46]

Once again Epicurus stands directly opposed to Democritus. Chance, for him, is a reality which has only the value of possibility. *Abstract possibility,* however, is the direct *antipode of real possibility.* The latter is restricted within sharp boundaries, as is the intellect; the former is unbounded, as is the imagination. Real possibility seeks to explain the necessity and reality of its object; abstract possibility is not interested in the object which is explained, but in the subject which does the explaining. The object need only be possible, conceivable. That which is abstractly possible, which can be conceived, constitutes no obstacle to the thinking subject, no limit, no stumbling-block. Whether this possibility is also real is irrelevant, since here the interest does not extend to the object as object.

Epicurus therefore proceeds with a boundless nonchalance in the explanation of separate physical phenomena.

More light will be thrown upon this fact by the letter to Pythocles, later to be considered. Suffice it here to draw attention to Epicurus' attitude to the opinions of earlier physicists. Where the author of *De placitis philosophorum* and Stobaeus quote the different views of the philosophers concerning the substance of the stars, the size and shape of the sun and similar matters, it is always said of Epicurus: He rejects none of these opinions, *all could* be right, he adheres to the *possible.*[47] Yes, Epicurus *polemicises* even against the rationally determining, and for precisely this reason one-sided, method of explanation by real possibility.

Thus *Seneca* says in his *Quaestiones naturales*: Epicurus maintains

---

[a] After "naively" Marx erased "also".— *Ed.*

that all these causes are possible, and then attempts in addition still other explanations. He *blames* those who claim that any particular one of them occurs, because it is rash to judge apodictically about that which can only be deduced from conjectures.[48]

One can see that there is no interest in investigating the real causes of objects. All that matters is the tranquillity of the explaining subject. Since everything possible is admitted as possible, which corresponds to the character of abstract possibility, the *chance of being* is clearly transferred only into the *chance of thought.* The only rule which Epicurus prescribes, namely, that "the explanation should *not contradict* sensation", is self-evident; for to be abstractly possible consists precisely in being free from contradiction, which therefore must be avoided.[49] And Epicurus confesses finally that his method of explaining aims only at the *ataraxy*[21] *of self-consciousness, not at knowledge of nature in and for itself.*[50]

It requires no further clarification to show how in this matter, too, Epicurus differs from Democritus.

We thus see that the two men are opposed to each other at every single step. The one is a sceptic, the other a dogmatist; the one considers the sensuous world as subjective semblance, the other as objective appearance. He who considers the sensuous world as subjective semblance applies himself to empirical natural science and to positive knowledge, and represents the unrest of observation, experimenting, learning everywhere, ranging over the wide, wide world. The other, who considers the phenomenal world to be real, scorns empiricism; embodied in him are the serenity of thought satisfied in itself, the self-sufficiency that draws its knowledge *ex principio interno.*[a] But the contradiction goes still farther. The *sceptic* and *empiricist,* who holds sensuous nature to be subjective semblance, considers it from the point of view of *necessity* and endeavours to explain and to understand the real existence of things. The *philosopher* and *dogmatist,* on the other hand, who considers appearance to be real, sees everywhere only *chance,* and his method of explanation tends rather to negate all objective reality of nature. There seems to be a certain absurdity in these contradictions.

It hardly seems still possible to presume that these men, who contradict each other on all points, will adhere to one and the same doctrine. And yet they seem to be chained to each other.

The task of the next section is to comprehend their relationship in general.[22]

---

[a] From an inner principle.— *Ed.*

Part Two

ON THE DIFFERENCE BETWEEN DEMOCRITEAN AND EPICUREAN PHYSICS IN DETAIL

Chapter One

THE DECLINATION OF THE ATOM FROM THE STRAIGHT LINE

Epicurus assumes a *threefold* motion of the atoms in the void.[1] One motion is the *fall in a straight line*, the second originates in the *deviation* of the atom *from the straight line*, and the third is established through the *repulsion of the many atoms*. Both Democritus and Epicurus accept the first and the third motion. The *declination of the atom* from the straight line differentiates the one from the other.[2]

This motion of declination[a] has often been made the subject of a joke. *Cicero* more than any other is inexhaustible when he touches on this theme. Thus we read in him, among other things:

"Epicurus maintains that the atoms are thrust downwards in a straight line by their weight; this motion is said to be the natural motion of bodies. But then it occurred to him that if all atoms were thrust downwards, no atom could ever meet another one. Epicurus therefore resorted to a lie. He said that the atom makes a very tiny swerve, which is, of course, entirely impossible. From this arose complexities, combinations and adhesions of the atoms with one another, and out of this came the world, all parts of it and its contents. Besides all this being a puerile invention, he does not even achieve what he desires."[3]

We find another version in the first book of Cicero's treatise *On the Nature of the Gods*:

"Since Epicurus saw that, if the atoms travelled downwards by their own weight, nothing would be within our control, for their motion would be determined and necessary, he invented a means for escaping this necessity, a means which had escaped the notice of Democritus. He says that the atom, although thrust downwards by its weight and gravity, makes a very slight swerve. To assert this is more disgraceful than to be incapable of defending what he wants."[4]

---

[a] Corrected by Marx from "last motion".— *Ed.*

Pierre Bayle expresses a similar opinion:

"Avant lui" (c.-à-d. Epicure) "on n'avait admis dans les atomes que le mouve-ment de pesanteur, et celui de réflexion. [...] Epicure supposa que même au milieu du vide, les atomes déclinaient un peu de la ligne droite, et de là venait la liberté, disait-il... Remarquons en passant que ce ne fut [pas] le seul motif qui le porta à inventer ce mouvement de déclinaison, il le fit servir aussi à expliquer la rencontre des atomes; car il vit bien qu'en supposant qu'ils se mouvaient [tous] avec une égale vitesse par des lignes droites qui tendaient toutes de haut en bas, il ne ferait jamais comprendre qu'ils eussent pu se rencontrer, et qu'ainsi la production du monde aurait été impossible. Il fallut donc [...] qu'ils s'écartaient de la ligne droite." [a][5]

For the present I leave the validity of these reflections an open question. This much everyone will notice in passing, that the most recent critic of Epicurus, *Schaubach,* has misunderstood Cicero when he says:

"The atoms are all thrust downwards by gravity, hence parallel, owing to physical causes, but through mutual repulsion they acquire another motion, according to Cicero (*De natura deorum*, I, xxv [, 69]) an oblique motion due to accidental causes, and indeed from all eternity." [6]

In the first place, Cicero in the quoted passage does not make the repulsion the reason for the oblique direction, but rather the oblique direction the reason for the repulsion. In the second place, he does not speak of accidental causes, but rather criticises the fact that no causes at all are mentioned, as it would be in and for itself contradictory to assume repulsion and at the same time accidental causes as the reason for the oblique direction. At best one could then still speak of accidental causes of the repulsion, but not of accidental causes of the oblique direction.

For the rest, one peculiarity in Cicero's and Bayle's reflections is too obvious not to be stressed immediately. They foist upon Epicurus motives of which the one nullifies the other. Epicurus is supposed to have assumed a declination of the atoms in order to explain the repulsion on one occasion, and on another freedom. But if the atoms do *not* meet without declination, then declination as an explanation of freedom is superfluous; for the opposite of

---

[a] "Before him" (i.e., Epicurus) "only the motion of weight and that of reflection were conceded to the atom.... Epicurus supposed that even in the midst of the void the atoms declined slightly from the straight line, and from this, he said, arose freedom.... It must be noted, in passing, that this was not the only motive that led him to invent this motion of declination. He also used it to explain the meeting of atoms; for he saw clearly that supposing they [all] move with equal speed downwards along straight lines, he would never be able to explain that they could meet, and that thus the creation of the world would have been impossible. It was necessary, then, that they should deviate from the straight line." — *Ed.*

freedom begins, as we see in *Lucretius*,[7] only with the deterministic and forced meeting of atoms. But if the atoms meet *without* declination, then this is superfluous for explaining repulsion. I maintain that this contradiction arises when the causes for the declination of the atom from the straight line are understood so superficially and disconnectedly as they are by Cicero and Bayle. We shall find in Lucretius, the only one in general of all the ancients who has understood Epicurean physics, a more profound exposition.

We now shall consider the declination itself.

Just as the point is negated [*aufgehoben*] in the line, so is every falling body negated in the straight line it describes. Its specific quality does not matter here at all. A falling apple describes a perpendicular line just as a piece of iron does. Every body, insofar as we are concerned with the motion of falling, is therefore nothing but a moving point, and indeed a point without independence, which in a certain mode of being—the straight line which it describes—surrenders its individuality [*Einzelheit*]. Aristotle therefore is correct when he objects against the Pythagoreans: "You say that the motion of the line is the surface, that of the point the line; then the motions of the monads will also be lines." [8] The consequence of this for the monads as well as for the atoms would therefore be—since they are in constant motion [9]—that neither monads nor atoms exist, but rather disappear in the straight line; for the solidity of the atom does not even enter into the picture, insofar as it is only considered as something falling in a straight line. To begin with, if the void is imagined as spatial void, then the *atom* is the *immediate negation of abstract space*, hence *a spatial point*. The solidity, the intensity, which maintains itself in itself against the incohesion of space, can only be added by virtue of a principle which negates space in its entire domain, a principle such as time is in real nature. Moreover, if this itself is not admitted, the atom, insofar as its motion is a straight line, is determined only by space and is prescribed a relative being and a purely material existence. But we have seen that one moment in the concept of the atom is that of being pure form, negation of all relativity, of all relation to another mode of being. We have noted at the same time that· Epicurus objectifies for himself both moments which, although they contradict one another, are nevertheless inherent in the concept of the atom.

How then can Epicurus give reality to the pure form-determination of the atom, the concept of pure individuality, negating any mode of being determined by another being?

Since he is moving in the domain of immediate being, all determinations are immediate. Opposite determinations are therefore opposed to one another as immediate realities.

But the *relative existence* which confronts the atom, *the mode of being which it has to negate,* is *the straight line.* The immediate negation of this motion is *another motion,* which, therefore, spatially conceived, is the *declination from the straight line.*

The atoms are purely self-sufficient bodies or rather bodies conceived in absolute self-sufficiency, like the heavenly bodies. Hence, again like the heavenly bodies, they move not in straight, but in oblique lines. *The motion of falling is the motion of non-self-sufficiency.*

If Epicurus therefore represents the materiality of the atom in terms of its motion along a straight line, he has given reality to its form-determination in the declination from the straight line, and these opposed determinations are represented as directly opposed motions.

Lucretius therefore is correct when he maintains that the declination breaks the *fati foedera*,[a10)] and, since he applies this immediately to consciousness,[11)] it can be said of the atom that the declination is that something in its breast that can fight back and resist.

But when Cicero reproaches Epicurus that

"he does not even attain the goal for which he made all this up—for if all atoms declined, none of them would ever combine, or some would deviate, others would be driven straight ahead by their motion. So it would be necessary as it were to give the atoms definite assignments beforehand: which had to move straight ahead and which obliquely",[12)]

this objection has the justification that the two moments inherent in the concept of the atom are represented as directly different motions, and therefore must be allotted to different individuals: an inconsistency, but a consistent one, since the domain of the atom is immediacy.

Epicurus feels this inherent contradiction quite well. He therefore endeavours to represent the declination as being as *imperceptible* as possible *to the senses*; it takes place

Nec regione loci certa, nec tempore certo,[b13)]

it occurs in the smallest possible space.[14)]

---

[a] The bonds of fate.— *Ed.*
[b] In time, in place unfixt (Lucretius, *De rerum natura*, II, 294).— *Ed.*

Moreover *Cicero,*[15] and, according to Plutarch, several ancient authors, [16] reproach Epicurus for saying that the declination of the atom occurs *without cause.* Nothing more disgraceful, says Cicero, can happen to a physicist. [17] But, in the first place, a physical cause such as Cicero wants would throw the declination of the atom back into the domain of determinism, out of which it was precisely to be lifted. *And then, the atom is by no means complete before it has been submitted to the determination of declination.* To inquire after the cause of this determination means therefore to inquire after the cause that makes the atom a principle — a clearly meaningless inquiry to anyone for whom the atom is the cause of everything, hence without cause itself.

Finally, *Bayle,*[18] supported by the authority of *Augustine,*[19] who states that Democritus ascribed to the atom a spiritual principle — an authority, by the way, who in contrast to Aristotle and the other ancients is without any importance — reproaches Epicurus for having thought out the concept of declination instead of this spiritual principle. But, on the contrary, merely a word would have been gained with this "soul of the atom", whereas the declination represents the real soul of the atom, the concept of abstract individuality.

Before we consider the consequence of the declination of the atom from the straight line, we must draw attention to another, most important element, which up to now has been entirely overlooked.

The declination of the atom from the straight line is, namely, not a particular determination which appears accidentally in Epicurean physics. On the contrary, the law which it expresses goes through the whole Epicurean philosophy, in such a way, however, that, as goes without saying, the determination of its appearance depends on the domain in which it is applied.

As a matter of fact, abstract individuality can make its concept, its form-determination, the pure being-for-itself, the independence from immediate being, the negation of all relativity, effective only by *abstracting from the being that confronts it;* for in order truly to overcome it, abstract individuality had to idealise it, a thing only generality can accomplish.

Thus, while the atom frees itself from its relative existence, the straight line, by abstracting from it, by swerving away from it; so the entire Epicurean philosophy swerves away from the restrictive mode of being wherever the concept of abstract individuality, self-sufficiency and negation of all relation to other things must be represented in its existence.

The purpose of action is to be found therefore in abstracting, swerving away from pain and confusion, in ataraxy.[20] Hence the good is the flight from evil,[21] pleasure the swerving away from suffering.[22] Finally, where abstract individuality appears in its highest freedom and independence, in its totality, there it follows that the being which is swerved away from, is *all being; for this reason, the gods swerve away from the world,* do not bother with it and live outside it.[23]

These gods of Epicurus have often been ridiculed, these gods who, like human beings, dwell in the intermundia[a] of the real world, have no body but a quasi-body, no blood but quasi-blood,[24] and, content to abide in blissful peace, lend no ear to any supplication, are unconcerned with us and the world, are honoured because of their beauty, their majesty and their superior nature, and not for any gain.

And yet these gods are no fiction of Epicurus. They did exist. *They are the plastic gods of Greek art.*[23] *Cicero,* the *Roman,* rightly scoffs at them,[25] but *Plutarch,* the *Greek,* has forgotten the whole Greek outlook when he claims that although this doctrine of the gods does away with fear and superstition, it produces no joy or favour in the gods, but instead bestows on us that relation to them that we have to the Hyrcanian[24] fish, from which we expect neither harm nor advantage.[26] Theoretical calm is one of the chief characteristics of the Greek gods. As *Aristotle* says:

"What is best has no need of action, for it is its own end."[27]

We now consider the *consequence* that follows directly from the declination of the atom. In it is expressed the atom's negation of all motion and relation by which it is determined as a particular mode of being by another being. This is represented in such a way that the atom abstracts from the opposing being and withdraws itself from it. But what is contained herein, namely, *its negation of all relation to something else,* must be *realised, positively established.* This can only be done if *the being to which it relates itself* is *none other than itself,* hence equally *an atom,* and, since it itself is directly determined, *many atoms. The repulsion of the many atoms is therefore the necessary realisation of the lex atomi,*[b] as *Lucretius* calls the declination. But since here every determination is established as a particular being, repulsion is added as a third motion to the former ones. Lucretius is therefore correct when he says that, if

---

[a] The spaces between the worlds (literally: inter-worlds).— *Ed.*
[b] Law of the atom.— *Ed.*

the atoms were not to decline, neither their repulsion nor their meeting would have taken place, and the world would never have been created.[28] For atoms are *their own sole object and can only be related to themselves*, hence speaking in spatial terms, they can only *meet*, because every relative existence of these atoms by which they would be related to other beings is negated. And this relative existence is, as we have seen, their original motion, that of falling in a straight line. Hence they meet only by virtue of their declination from the straight line. It has nothing to do with merely material fragmentation.[29]

And in truth: the immediately existing individuality is only realised conceptually, inasmuch as it relates to something else which actually is itself — even when the other thing confronts it in the form of immediate existence. Thus man ceases to be a product of nature only when the other being to which he relates himself is not a different existence but is itself an individual human being, even if it is not yet the mind [*Geist*]. But for man as man to become his own real object, he must have crushed within himself his relative being, the power of desire and of mere nature. *Repulsion is the first form of self-consciousness*, it corresponds therefore to that self-consciousness which conceives itself as immediate-being, as abstractly individual.

The concept of the atom is therefore realised in repulsion, inasmuch as it is abstract form, but no less also the opposite, inasmuch as it is abstract matter; for that to which it relates itself consists, to be true, of atoms, but *other* atoms. *But when I relate myself to myself as to something which is directly another, then my relationship is a material one.* This is the most extreme degree of externality that can be conceived. In the repulsion of the atoms, therefore, their materiality, which was posited in the fall in a straight line, and the form-determination, which was established in the declination, are united synthetically.

Democritus, in contrast to Epicurus, transforms into an enforced motion, into an act of blind necessity, that which to Epicurus is the realisation of the concept of the atom. We have already seen above that he considers the vortex ($\delta\acute{\iota}\nu\eta$) resulting from the repulsion and collision of the atoms to be the substance of necessity. He therefore sees in the repulsion only the material side, the fragmentation, the change, and not the ideal side, according to which all relation to something else is negated and motion is established as self-determination. This can be clearly seen from the fact that he conceives one and the same body divided through empty space into many parts quite sensuously, like gold broken up into pieces.[30] Thus he scarcely conceived of the One as the concept of the atom.

Aristotle correctly argues against him:

"Hence Leucippus and Democritus, who assert that the primary bodies always moved in the void and in the infinite, should say what kind of motion this is, and what is the motion natural to them. For if each of the elements is forcibly moved by the other, then it is still necessary that each should have also a natural motion, outside which is the enforced one. And this first motion must not be enforced but natural. Otherwise the procedure goes on to infinity."[31]

The Epicurean declination of the atom thus changed the whole inner structure of the domain of the atoms, since through it the form-determination is validated and the contradiction inherent in the concept of the atom is realised. Epicurus was therefore the first to grasp the essence of the repulsion—even if only in sensuous form, whereas Democritus only knew of its material existence.

Hence we find also more concrete forms of the repulsion applied by Epicurus. In the political domain there is the *covenant*,[32] in the social domain *friendship*,[33] which is praised as the highest good.[a]

Chapter Two

THE QUALITIES OF THE ATOM

It contradicts the concept of the atom that the atom should have properties, because, as Epicurus says, every property is variable but the atoms do not change.[1] Nevertheless it is a *necessary consequence* to attribute properties to atoms. Indeed, the many atoms of repulsion separated by sensuous space must necessarily be *immediately different from one another* and *from their pure essence*, i.e., they must possess *qualities*.

In the following analysis I therefore take no account of the assertion made by *Schneider* and *Nürnberger* that "Epicurus attributed no qualities to the atoms, paragraphs 44 and 54 of the letter to Herodotus in Diogenes Laertius have been interpolated". If this were truly so, how is one to invalidate the evidence of Lucretius, Plutarch, and indeed of all other authors who speak of Epicurus? Moreover, Diogenes Laertius mentions the qualities of the atom not in two, but in ten paragraphs: Nos. 42, 43, 44, 54, 55, 56, 57, 58, 59 and 61. The grounds these critics give for their conten-

---

[a] This paragraph was added by Marx in the manuscript.— *Ed.*

tion—that "they did not know how to reconcile the qualities of the atom with its concept"—are very shallow.[25] *Spinoza* says that ignorance is no argument.[a] If one was to delete the passages in the ancients which he does not understand, how quickly would we have a *tabula rasa*[b]!

Through the qualities the atom acquires an existence which contradicts its concept; it is assumed as an *externalised being different* from *its essence*. It is this contradiction which mainly interests Epicurus. Hence, as soon as he posits a property and thus draws the consequence of the material nature of the atom, he counterposits at the same time determinations which again destroy this property in its own sphere and validate instead the concept of the atom. *He therefore determines all properties in such a way that they contradict themselves.* Democritus, on the other hand, nowhere considers the properties in relation to the atom itself, nor does he objectify the contradiction between concept and existence which is inherent in them. His whole interest lies rather in representing the qualities in relation to concrete nature, which is to be formed out of them. To him they are merely hypotheses to explain the plurality which makes its appearance. It follows that the concept of the atom has nothing to do with them.

In order to prove our assertion it is first of all necessary to elucidate the sources which here seem to contradict one another.

In the treatise *De placitis philosophorum* we read:

"*Epicurus* asserts that the atoms have three qualities: size, shape, weight. Democritus only assumed two: size and shape. Epicurus added weight as the third."[2]

The same passage is repeated word for word in the *Praeparatio evangelica* of *Eusebius*.[3]

It is confirmed by the testimony of *Simplicius*[4] and *Philoponus*,[5] according to whom Democritus attributed to the atoms only difference in size and shape. Directly contrary stands *Aristotle* who, in the book *De generatione et corruptione*, attributes to the atoms of Democritus difference in weight.[6] In another passage (in the first book of *De caelo*) *Aristotle* leaves undecided the question of whether or not Democritus ascribed weight to the atoms, for he says:

"Thus none of the bodies will be absolutely light if they all have weight; but if all have lightness, none will be heavy."[7]

---

[a] B. Spinoza, *Ethics*, Part I, Prop. 36, Appendix.— *Ed.*
[b] An empty slate.— *Ed.*

In his *Geschichte der alten Philosophie, Ritter*, basing himself on the authority of Aristotle, rejects the assertions of Plutarch, Eusebius and Stobaeus.[8] He does not consider the testimony of Simplicius and Philoponus.

Let us see whether these passages are really so contradictory. In the passage cited, Aristotle does not speak of the qualities of the atom *ex professo*.[a] On the other hand, we read in the eighth book of the *Metaphysics*:

> "Democritus assumes three differences between atoms. For the underlying body is one and the same with respect to matter, but it differs in *rhysmos* (ῥυσμός), meaning shape, in *trope* (τροπή), meaning position, or in *diathige* (διαθιγή), meaning arrangement."[9]

This much can be immediately concluded from this passage.[b] Weight is not mentioned as a property of the Democritean atoms. The fragmented pieces of matter, kept apart by the void, must have special forms, and these are quite externally perceived from the observation of space. This emerges even more clearly from the following passage of Aristotle:

> "Leucippus and his companion Democritus hold that the elements are the full and the void.... These are the basis of being as matter. Just as those who assume only one fundamental substance generate all other things by its affections, assuming rarity and density as the principles of qualities — in the same way Leucippus and Democritus also teach that the differences between the atoms are the causes of the other things, for the underlying being differs only by *rhysmos*, *diathige* and *trope*.... That is, A differs from N in shape, AN from NA in arrangement, Z from N in position."[10]

It is evident from this quotation that Democritus considers the properties of the atom only in relation to the formation of the differences in the world of appearances, and not in relation to the atom itself. It follows further that Democritus does not single out weight as an essential property of the atoms. For him weight is taken for granted, since everything corporeal has weight. In the same way, according to him, even size is not a basic quality. It is an accidental determination which is already given to the atoms together with figure. Only the diversity of the figures is of interest to Democritus, since nothing more is contained in shape, position and arrangement. Size, shape and weight, by being combined as they are by Epicurus, are differences which the atom in itself possesses. Shape, position and arrangement are differences which the atom possesses in relation to something else. Whereas we find

---

[a] Professionally, as a man who knows his field of study.— *Ed.*

[b] The following sentence was erased by Marx: "Democritus does not posit the ⟨difference⟩ contradiction between the quality of the atom and its concept."— *Ed.*

in Democritus mere hypothetical determinations to explain the world of appearances, in Epicurus the consequence of the principle itself will be presented to us. We shall therefore discuss in detail his determinations of the properties of the atom.

First of all, the atoms have *size.*[11] And then again, size is also negated. That is to say, they do not have *every* size;[12] but only *some* differences in size among them must be admitted.[13] Indeed, only the negation of the large can be ascribed to them, the small,[14]—also not the minimum, for this would be merely a spatial determination, but the infinitely small, which expresses the contradiction.[15] *Rosinius,* in his notes on the fragments of Epicurus, therefore translates one passage incorrectly and completely ignores the other, when he says:

"Hujusmodi autem tenuitatem atomorum incredibili parvitate arguebat Epicurus, utpote quas nulla magnitudine praeditas ajebat, teste Laertio, X, 44." [a][16]

Now I shall not concern myself with the fact that, according to *Eusebius,* Epicurus was the first to ascribe infinite smallness to the atoms,[17] whereas Democritus also assumed atoms of the largest size — *Stobaeus* says even as large as the world.[18]

This, on the one hand, contradicts the testimony of *Aristotle.*[19] On the other hand, Eusebius, or rather the Alexandrian bishop *Dionysius,* from whom he takes excerpts, contradicts himself; for in the same book we read that Democritus assumed as the principles of nature indivisible bodies perceptible through reason.[20] This much at least is clear: Democritus was not aware of the contradiction; he did not pay attention to it, whereas it was the chief interest of Epicurus.

The *second* property of the Epicurean atoms is *shape.*[21] But this determination also contradicts the concept of the atom, and its opposite must be assumed. Abstract individuality is abstract identity-to-itself and therefore without shape. The differences in the shape of the atoms cannot, therefore, be determined,[22] although they are not absolutely infinite.[23] It is rather by a definite and finite number of shapes that the atoms are differentiated from one another.[24] From this it is obvious that there are not as many different figures as there are atoms,[25] while Democritus assumes an infinite number of figures.[26] If every atom had a particular shape, then there would have to be atoms of infinite size[27]; for they would have an infinite difference, the difference from all the others,

---

[a] "In this way Epicurus tried to make plausible the tenuity of the atoms of incredible smallness, by saying, according to Laertius, X, 44, that they have no size."— *Ed.*

in themselves [*an sich*], like the monads of Leibniz. This leads to the inversion of Leibniz's assertion that no two things are identical, and there are infinitely many atoms of the same shape.[28] This obviously negates again the determination of the shape, because a shape which no longer differs from another is not shape.[a]

Finally,[b] it is highly important that Epicurus makes *weight* the *third* quality,[29] for in the centre of gravity matter possesses the ideal individuality which forms a principal determination of the atom. Hence, once the atoms are brought into the realm of presentation, they must also have weight.

But weight also directly contradicts the concept of the atom, because it is the individuality of matter as an ideal point which lies outside matter. But the atom is itself this individuality, as it were the centre of gravity presented as an individual existence. Weight therefore exists for Epicurus only as *different weight,* and the atoms are themselves *substantial centres of gravity* like the heavenly bodies. If this is applied to the concrete, then the obvious result is the fact which old *Brucker* finds so amazing[30] and of which *Lucretius* assures us,[31] namely, that the earth has no centre towards which everything strives, and that there are no antipodes. Furthermore since weight belongs only to that atom which is different from the other, hence externalised and endowed with properties, then it is clear that where the atoms are not thought of as many in their differentiation from one another, but only in relation to the void, the determination of weight ceases to exist. The atoms, as different as they may be in mass and shape, move therefore with equal speed in empty space.[32] Epicurus thus applies weight only in regard to repulsion and the resulting compositions. This has led to the assertion[c] that only the conglomerations of the atoms are endowed with weight, but not the atoms themselves. [33]

Gassendi already[d] praises Epicurus because, led purely by reason, he anticipated the experimentally demonstrated fact that all bodies, although very different in weight and mass, have the same velocity when they fall from above to below.[e][34]

---

[a] Marx erased the following paragraph: "Epicurus therefore has here also objectified the contradiction, while Democritus, only considering the material side, does not show in the further determination any consequence of the principle."— *Ed.*

[b] "Finally" added by Marx.— *Ed.*

[c] Marx erased the words "that they can be considered as cause of it and".— *Ed.*

[d] "Already" added by Marx.— *Ed.*

[e] Marx erased the sentence: "We have added to this praise the explanation of the principle of Epicurus."— *Ed.*

The consideration of the properties of the atoms leads us therefore to the same result as the consideration of the declination, namely, that Epicurus objectifies the contradiction in the concept of the atom between essence and existence. He thus gave us the science of atomistics. In Democritus, on the other hand, there is no realisation of the principle itself. He only maintains the material side and offers hypotheses for the benefit of empirical observation.

Chapter Three

Ἄτομοι ἀρχαί AND ἄτομα στοιχεῖα [a]

Schaubach, in his treatise on the astronomical concepts of Epicurus, to which we have already referred, makes the following assertion:

> "*Epicurus*, as well as *Aristotle*, has made a distinction between *principles* [*Anfänge*] (*atomoi archai*, Diogenes Laertius, X, 41) and *elements* (*atoma stoicheia*, Diogenes Laertius, X, 86). The former are the atoms recognisable only through reason and do not occupy space.[1] These are called *atoms* not because they are the smallest bodies, but because they are indivisible in space. According to these conceptions one might think that Epicurus did not attribute any spatial properties to the atom.[2] But in the letter to Herodotus (Diogenes Laertius, X, 44, 54) he gives the atoms not only weight but also size and shape.... I therefore consider these atoms as belonging to the second species, those that have developed out of the former but can still be regarded again as elementary particles of the bodies." [3]

Let us look more closely at the passage which *Schaubach* cites from Diogenes Laertius. It reads: Οἷον, ὅτι τὸ πᾶν, σῶμα καὶ ἀναφὴς φύσις ἐστίν· ἢ ὅτι ἄτομα στοιχεῖα, καὶ πάντα τὰ τοιαῦτα.[b]

Epicurus here teaches Pythocles, to whom he is writing, that the teaching about meteors differs from all other doctrines in physics, for example, that everything is either body or void, that there are indivisible basic elements. It is obvious that there is here no reason to assume that it is a question of a second species of atoms.[c] It may perhaps seem that the disjunction between τὸ πᾶν, σῶμα καὶ ἀναφὴς

---

[a] *Atomoi archai*—indivisible principles (or beginnings), and *atoma stoicheia*—indivisible elements.—*Ed.*

[b] For instance such propositions that the All consists of bodies and non-corporeal nature, or that there are indivisible elements and other such statements.—*Ed.*

[c] Here Marx erased the sentence: "We can equally conclude (justly or unjustly) from the passage ἀρχὴ δέ τούτων οὐκ ἔστιν, αἰτίων τῶν ἀτόμων οὐσῶν [for this there is no beginning, the atoms being the cause],[4] that Epicurus has assumed a *third* kind, the *atoma aitia* (ἄτομα αἴτια) [atoms as cause]."—*Ed.*

φύσις and ὅτι τὰ ἄτομα στοιχεῖα[a] establishes a difference between *soma* (σῶμα)[b] and *atoma stoicheia* (ἄτομα στοιχεῖα), so that we might say that *soma* stands for atoms of the first kind in contrast to the *atoma stoicheia*. But this is quite out of the question. *Soma* means the *corporeal* in contrast to the *void*, which for this reason is called *asomaton* (ἀσώματον)[c5]. The term *soma* therefore includes the atoms as well as compound bodies. For example, in the letter to Herodotus we read: Τὸ πᾶν ἐστι τὸ σῶμα.... εἰ μὴ ἦν, ὃ κενὸν καὶ χώραν καὶ ἀναφῆ φύσιν ὀνομάζομεν..... Τῶν σωμάτων τὰ μέν ἐστι συγκρίσεις, τὰ δ' ἐξ ὧν αἱ συγκρίσεις πεποίηνται. Ταῦτα δέ ἐστιν ἄτομα καὶ ἀμετάβλητα..... Ὥςτε τὰς ἀρχάς, ἀτόμους ἀναγκαῖον εἶναι σωμάτων φύσεις .[d6]

Epicurus is thus speaking in the passage cited first of the *corporeal* in general, in contrast to the *void*, and then of the corporeal in particular, the atoms.[e]

Schaubach's reference to Aristotle proves just as little. True the difference between *arche* (ἀρχή) and *stoicheion* (στοιχεῖον),[f] which the Stoics particularly insist upon,[7] can indeed also be found in Aristotle,[8] but he nonetheless assumes the identity of the two expressions.[9] He even teaches explicitly that *stoicheion* (στοιχεῖον) denotes primarily the atom.[10] Leucippus and Democritus likewise call the πλῆρες καὶ κενὸν [g]: "στοιχεῖον".[11]

In Lucretius, in Epicurus' letters as quoted by Diogenes Laertius, in the *Colotes* of Plutarch,[12] in Sextus Empiricus,[13] the properties are ascribed to the atoms themselves, and for this reason they were determined as transcending themselves [*sich selbst aufhebend*].

However, if it is thought an antinomy that bodies perceptible only to reason should be endowed with spatial qualities, then it is

---

[a] "The All consisting of bodies and non-corporeal bodies" and "that there are indivisible elements".— *Ed.*

[b] Body, matter.— *Ed.*

[c] Non-corporeal, immaterial.— *Ed.*

[d] The All is *body* ... if there were not that which we call *void*, space and non-corporeal nature.... Among bodies some are *corpound*, others the things out of which the compounds are made, and *these latter* are *indivisible* and unchangeable.... Consequently these first principles are necessarily of indivisible corporeal nature.— *Ed.*

[e] Here Marx erased the sentence: "'*Atoma stoicheia* here has no other meaning than *atomoi physeis* (ἄτομοι φύσεις) [indivisible natures], of which it is said in the last quoted passage that they are *archai* (ἀρχαί) [beginnings, first principles]."— *Ed.*

[f] "Beginning (first principle)" and "element".— *Ed.*

[g] Fullness and void.— *Ed.*

an even greater antinomy that the spatial qualities themselves can be perceived only through the intellect.[14]

Finally, *Schaubach*, in further support of his view, cites the following passage from Stobaeus: ' Ἐπίκουρος ..... τά [...]. πρῶτα (sc.σώματα) δὲ ἁπλᾶ, τὰ δὲ ἐξ ἐκείνων συγκρίματα πάντα βάρος ἔχειν.[a]

To this passage from Stobaeus could be added the following, in which *atoma stoicheia* are mentioned as a particular kind of atom: (Plutarch.) *De placit. philosoph.*, I, 246 and 249, and Stob., *Physical Selections*, I, p. 5.[15] For the rest it is by no means claimed in these passages that the original atoms are without size, shape and weight. On the contrary, weight alone is mentioned as a distinctive characteristic of the *atomoi archai* (ἄτομοι ἀρχαί) and *atoma stoicheia* (ἄτομα στοιχεῖα). But we observed already in the preceding chapter that weight is applied only in regard to repulsion and the conglomerations arising therefrom.

With the invention of the *atoma stoicheia* we also gain nothing. It is just as difficult to pass from the *atomoi archai* to the *atoma stoicheia* as it is to ascribe properties directly to them. Nevertheless I do not deny such a differentiation entirely. I only deny that there are two different and fixed kinds of atoms. They are rather different determinations of one and the same kind.

Before discussing this difference I would like to call attention to a procedure typical of Epicurus. He likes to assume the different determinations of a concept as different independent existences. Just as his principle is the atom, so is the manner of his cognition itself atomistic. Every moment of the development is at once transformed in his hands into a fixed reality which, so to say, is separated from its relations to other things by empty space; every determination assumes the form of isolated individuality.

This procedure may be made clear by the following example. The infinite, *to apeiron* (τὸ ἄπειρον), or the *infinitio*, as Cicero translates it, is occasionally used by Epicurus as a particular nature; and precisely in the same passages in which we find the *stoicheia* described as a fixed fundamental substance, we also find the *apeiron* turned into something independent.[16]

However, according to Epicurus' own definitions, the infinite is neither a particular substance nor something outside of the atoms and the void, but rather an accidental determination of the void. We find in fact three meanings of *apeiron*.

---

[a] Epicurus [states] that the primary (bodies) should be simple, those bodies compounded from them however should have weight.— *Ed.*

First, *apeiron* expresses for Epicurus a quality common to the atoms and the void. It means in this sense the infinitude of the All, which is infinite by virtue of the infinite multiplicity of the atoms, by virtue of the infinite size of the void.[17]

Secondly, *apeiria* (ἀπειρία) is the multiplicity of the atoms, so that not the atom, but the infinitely many atoms are placed in opposition to the void.[18]

Finally, if we may draw from Democritus a conclusion about Epicurus, *apeiron* also means exactly the opposite, the unlimited void, which is placed in opposition to the atom determined in itself and limited by itself.[19]

In all these meanings — and they are the only ones, even the only possible ones for atomistics — the infinite is a mere determination of the atoms and of the void. Nevertheless, it is singled out as a particular existence, even set up as a specific nature alongside the principles whose determination it expresses.[a]

Therefore, even if Epicurus himself thus fixed the determination by which the atom becomes *stoicheion* as an independent original kind of atom — which, by the way, is not the case judging by the historical superiority of one source over the other, even if Metrodorus,[26] the disciple of Epicurus — as it seems more probable to us — was the first to change the differentiated determination into a differentiated existence[20]; we must ascribe to the subjective mode of atomistic consciousness the changing of separate moments into something independently existing. The granting of the form of existence to different determinations has not resulted in understanding of their difference.

For Democritus the atom means only *stoicheion,* a material substrate. The distinction between the atom as *arche* and *stoicheion,* as principle and foundation, belongs to Epicurus. Its importance will be clear from what follows.

The contradiction between existence and essence, between matter and form, which is inherent in the concept of the atom, emerges in the individual atom itself once it is endowed with qualities. Through the quality the atom is alienated from its concept, but at the same time is perfected in its construction. It is from repulsion and the ensuing conglomerations of the qualified atoms that the world of appearance now emerges.

In this transition from the world of essence to the world of appearance, the contradiction in the concept of the atom clearly

---

[a] Marx erased the sentence: "This example is convincing." — *Ed.*

reaches its harshest realisation. For the atom is conceptually the absolute, essential form of nature. *This absolute form has now been degraded to absolute matter, to the formless substrate of the world of appearance.*

The atoms are, it is true, the substance of nature,[21] out of which everything emerges, into which everything dissolves[22]; but the continuous annihilation of the world of appearance comes to no result. New appearances are formed; but the atom itself always remains at the bottom as the foundation.[23] Thus insofar as the atom is considered as pure concept, its existence is empty space, annihilated nature. Insofar as it proceeds to reality, it sinks down to the material basis which, as the bearer of a world of manifold relations, never exists but in forms which are indifferent and external to it. This is a necessary consequence, since the atom, presupposed as abstractly individual and complete, cannot actualise itself as the idealising and pervading power of this manifold.

Abstract individuality is freedom from being, not freedom in being. It cannot shine in the light of being. This is an element in which this individuality loses its character and becomes material. For this reason the atom does not enter into the daylight of appearance,[24] or it sinks down to the material basis when it does enter it. The atom as such only exists in the void. The death of nature has thus become its immortal substance; and Lucretius correctly exclaims:

Mortalem vitam mors [...] immortalis ademit.[a]

But the fact that Epicurus grasps the contradiction at this its highest peak and objectifies it, and therefore distinguishes the atom where it becomes the basis of appearance as *stoicheion* from the atom as it exists in the void as *arche*—this constitutes his philosophical difference from Democritus, who only objectifies the one moment. This is the same distinction which in the world of essence, in the realm of the atoms and of the void, separates Epicurus from Democritus. However, since only the atom with qualities is the complete one, since the world of appearance can only emerge from the atom which is complete and alienated from its concept, Epicurus expresses this by stating that only the qualified atom becomes *stoicheion* or only the *atomon stoicheion* is endowed with qualities.

---

[a] When death immortal claims his mortal life (*De rerum natura*, III, 869).— *Ed.*

Chapter Four

TIME

Since in the atom matter, as pure relationship to itself, is exempted from all relativity and changeability, it follows immediately that time has to be excluded from the concept of the atom, the world of essence. For matter is eternal and independent only insofar as in it abstraction is made of the time moment. On this Democritus and Epicurus agree. But they differ in regard to the manner in which time, removed from the world of atoms, is now determined, whither it is transferred.

For Democritus time has neither significance nor necessity for the system. He explains time in order to negate it [*aufzuheben*]. It is determined as eternal, in order that—as *Aristotle*[1] and Simplicius[2] state—the emergence and passing away, hence the temporal, is removed from the atoms. Time itself offers proof that not everything need have an origin, a moment of beginning.

There is something more profound to be recognised in this notion. The imagining intellect that does not grasp the independence of substance inquires into its becoming in time. It fails to grasp that by making substance temporal it also makes time substantial and thus negates its concept, because time made absolute is no longer temporal.

But this solution is unsatisfactory from another point of view. Time excluded from the world of essence is transferred into the self-consciousness of the philosophising subject but does not make any contact with the world itself.

Quite otherwise with Epicurus. *Time*, excluded from the world of essence, becomes for him *the absolute form of appearance*. That is to say, time is determined as accidens of the accidens. The accidens is the change of substance in general. The accidens of the accidens is the change as reflecting in itself, the change as change. This pure form of the world of appearance is time.[3]

Composition is the merely passive form of concrete nature, time its active form. If I consider composition in terms of its being, then the atom exists beyond it, in the void, in the imagination. If I consider the atom in terms of its concept, then composition either does not exist at all or exists only in the subjective imagination. For composition is a relationship in which the atoms, independent, self-enclosed, as it were uninterested in one another, have likewise no relationship to one another. Time, in contrast, the change of the finite to the extent that change is posited as change, is just as much the real form which separates appearance from essence, and posits it as appearance, while leading it back into essence. Composition expresses merely the materiality of the atoms as well as of nature emerging from them. Time, in contrast, is in the world of appearance what the concept of the atom is in the world of essence, namely, the abstraction, destruction and reduction of all determined being into being-for-itself.

The following consequences can be drawn from these observations. *First*, Epicurus makes the contradiction between matter and form the characteristic of the nature of appearance, which thus becomes the counter-image of the nature of essence, the atom. This is done by time being opposed to space, the active form of appearance to the passive form. *Second*, Epicurus was the first to grasp appearance as appearance, that is, as alienation of the essence, activating itself in its reality as such an alienation. On the other hand, for Democritus, who considers composition as the only form of the nature of appearance, appearance does not by itself show that it is appearance, something different from essence. Thus when appearance is considered in terms of its existence, essence becomes totally blended [*konfundiert*] with it; when considered in terms of its concept, essence is totally separated from existence, so that it descends to the level of subjective semblance. The composition behaves indifferently and materially towards its essential foundations. Time, on the other hand, is the fire of essence, eternally consuming appearance, and stamping it with dependence and non-essence. *Finally*, since according to Epicurus time is change as change, the reflection of appearance in itself, the nature of appearance is justly posited as objective, sensation is justly made the real criterion of concrete nature, although the atom, its foundation, is only perceived through reason.

Indeed, time being the abstract form of sensation, according to the atomism of Epicurean consciousness the necessity arises for it to be fixed as a nature having a separate existence within nature. The changeability of the sensuous world, its change as change, this reflection of appearance in itself which constitutes the concept of time, has its separate existence in conscious sensuousness. *Human sensuousness is therefore embodied time, the existing reflection of the sensuous world in itself.*

Just as this follows immediately from the definition of the concept of time in *Epicurus*, so it can also be quite definitely demonstrated in detail. In the letter from Epicurus to Herodotus[4] time is so defined that it emerges when the accidentals of bodies, perceived by the senses, are thought of as accidentals. Sensuous perception reflected in itself is thus here the source of time and time itself. Hence time cannot be defined by analogy nor can anything else be said about it, but it is necessary to keep firmly to the *Enargie* itself; for sensuous perception reflected in itself is time itself, and there is no going beyond it.

On the other hand, in *Lucretius, Sextus Empiricus* and *Stobaeus,*[5] the accidens of the accidens, change reflected in itself, is defined as time. The reflection of the accidentals in sensuous perception and their reflection in themselves are hence posited as one and the same.

Because of this interconnection between time and sensuousness, the *eidola* (εἴδωλα),[a] equally found in Democritus, also acquire a more consistent status.

The *eidola* are the forms of natural bodies which, as surfaces, as it were detach themselves like skins and transfer these bodies into appearance.[6] These forms of the things stream constantly forth from them and penetrate into the senses and in precisely this way allow the objects to appear. Thus in hearing nature hears itself, in smelling it smells itself, in seeing it sees itself.[7] Human sensuousness is therefore the medium in which natural processes are reflected as in a focus and ignited into the light of appearance.

In *Democritus* this is an inconsistency, since appearance is only subjective; in Epicurus it is a necessary consequence, since sensuousness is the reflection of the world of appearance in itself, its embodied time.

Finally, the interconnection between sensuousness and time is revealed in such a way *that the temporal character of things and their appearance to the senses are posited as intrinsically one.* For it is precisely because bodies appear to the senses that they pass away.[8] Indeed, the *eidola,* by constantly separating themselves from the bodies and flowing into the senses, by having their sensuous existence outside themselves as another nature, by not returning into themselves, that is, out of the diremption, dissolve and pass away.

Therefore: just as the atom is nothing but the natural form of abstract, individual self-consciousness, so sensuous nature is only the objectified, empirical, individual self-consciousness, and this is the sensuous. Hence the senses are the only criteria in concrete nature, just as abstract reason is the only criterion in the world of the atoms.

---

[a] Images.— *Ed.*

4*

Chapter Five

THE METEORS

Ingenious as *Democritus'* astronomical opinions may be for his
time, they present no philosophical interest. They neither go
beyond the domain of empirical reflection, nor have they any
more definite intrinsic connection with the atomic doctrine.

By contrast, *Epicurus'* theory of the celestial bodies and the
processes connected with them, or his theory of *meteors* (in this one
term he includes it all), stands in opposition not only to Democritus, but to the opinion of Greek philosophy as a whole. Worship
of the celestial bodies is a cult practised by all Greek philosophers.
The system of the celestial bodies is the first naive and nature-
determined existence of true reason [*Vernunft*]. The same position
is taken by Greek self-consciousness in the domain of the mind
[*Geist*]. It is the solar system of the mind. The Greek philosophers
therefore worshipped their own mind in the celestial bodies.

Anaxagoras himself, who first gave a physical explanation of
heaven and in this way brought it down to earth in a sense
different from that of Socrates, answered, when asked for what
purpose he was born: εἰς θεωρίαν ἡλίου καὶ σελήνης καὶ οὐρανοῦ.[a)1]
Xenophanes, however, looked up at heaven and said: The One is
God.[2] The religious attitude of the *Pythagoreans, Plato* and *Aristotle*
to the heavenly bodies is well known.

Indeed, Epicurus opposes the outlook of the whole Greek
people.

Aristotle says it often seems that the concept provides evidence
for the phenomena and the phenomena for the concept. Thus all
men have an idea of the gods and assign the highest region to the
divine, barbarians as well as Hellenes, and in general all who
believe in the existence of the gods, evidently connecting the
immortal with the immortal, for otherwise it is impossible. Thus if
the divine exists—as it actually does—then what we say about the
substance of the celestial bodies is also correct. But this corresponds also to sensuous perception, insofar as human conviction is
concerned. For throughout the time that has passed, according to
the memories handed down from people to people, nothing seems
to have changed, either in heaven as a whole, or in any part of
it. Even the name seems to have been handed down from the
ancients to the present time, and they assumed that which we also

---

[a] For the observation of the sun, the moon and the heaven.— *Ed.*

say. For not once, not twice, but an infinite number of times have the same views come down to us. For since the primary body is something different, apart from the earth and the fire and the air and the water, they called the highest region "ether", from *thein aei* (θεῖν ἀεί),[a] giving it the by-name: eternal time.[3] But the ancients assigned heaven and the highest region to the gods, because it alone is immortal. But the present teaching testifies that it is indestructible, ungenerated and not subject to any mortal ills. In this way our concepts correspond at the same time to intimations about God.[4] But that there is *one* heaven is evident. It is a tradition handed down from our ancestors and the ancients and surviving in the form of the myths of later generations, that the heavenly bodies are gods and that the divine encompasses all nature. The rest was added in mythical form for the belief of the masses, as useful for the laws and for life. Thus the myths make the gods resemble man and some of the other living creatures, and invent similar things connected with and related to this. If we discard the additions and hold fast only to the first, namely, the belief that the primary substances are gods, then we must consider this as having been divinely revealed, and we must hold that after all sorts of art and philosophy had, in one way or another, been invented and lost again, these opinions came down to us like relics.[5]

Epicurus, on the contrary, says:

To all this we must add that the greatest confusion of the human soul arises from the fact that men hold that the heavenly bodies are blessed and indestructible and have conflicting desires and actions, and conceive suspicion according to the myths.[6] As to the meteors, we must believe that motion and position and eclipse and rising and setting and related phenomena do not originate in them owing to One ruling and ordering or having ordered, One who at the same time is supposed to possess all bliss and indestructibility. For actions do not accord with bliss, but they occur due to causes most closely related to weakness, fear and need. Nor is it to be supposed that some fire-like bodies endowed with bliss arbitrarily submit to these motions. If one does not agree with this, then this contradiction itself produces the greatest confusion in men's souls.[7]

Aristotle reproached[b] the ancients for their belief that heaven required the support of Atlas [8] who: πρὸς ἑσπέρους τόπους ἔστηκε

---

[a] To run always.— *Ed.*

[b] Corrected by Marx from "blamed".— *Ed.*

χίον' οὐρανοῦ τε καὶ χθονὸς ὤμοιν ἐρείδων,[a] Epicurus, on the other hand, blames those who believe that man needs heaven. He finds the Atlas by whom heaven is supported in human stupidity and superstition. Stupidity and superstition also are Titans.

The letter of Epicurus to Pythocles deals entirely with the theory of the heavenly bodies, with the exception of the last section, which closes the letter with ethical precepts. And appropriately,[b] ethical precepts are appended to the teaching on the meteors. For Epicurus this theory is a matter of conscience. Our study will therefore be based mainly on this letter to Pythocles. We shall supplement it from the letter to Herodotus, to which Epicurus himself refers in writing to Pythocles.[9]

First, it must not be supposed that any other goal but ataraxy and firm assurance can be attained from knowledge of the meteors, either taken as a whole or in part, just as from the other natural sciences.[10] Our life does not need speculation and empty hypotheses, but that we should live without confusion. Just as it is the business of the study of nature in general to investigate the foundations of what is most important: so happiness lies also in knowledge of the meteors. In and for itself the theory of setting and rising, of position and eclipse, contains no particular grounds for happiness; only terror possesses those who see these things without understanding their nature and their principal causes.[11] So far, only the *precedence* which the theory of the meteors is supposed to have over other sciences has been denied; and this theory has been placed on the same level as others.

But the theory of the meteors is *also specifically different* in comparison both with the method of ethics and with other physical problems, for example, the existence of indivisible elements and the like, where only one explanation corresponds to the phenomena. For this is not the case with the meteors.[12] Their origin has no simple cause, and they have more than one category of essence corresponding to the phenomena. For the study of nature cannot be pursued in accordance with empty axioms and laws.[13] It is constantly repeated that the meteors are not to be explained *haplos* (ἁπλῶς) (simply, absolutely), but *pollachos* (πολλαχῶς) (in many ways).

---

[a] In the places of the West stands, supporting with his shoulders the pillar of heaven and earth (Aeschylus, *Prometh.*, 348 ff.). The quotation was inserted by Marx in Greek in place of the Latin translation, which he struck out.— *Ed.*

[b] "Appropriately" corrected by Marx from "not accidentally".— *Ed.*

This also holds for the rising and setting of the sun and the moon,[14] the waxing and waning of the moon,[15] the semblance of a face on the moon,[16] the changes of duration of day and night,[17] and other celestial phenomena.

How then is it to be explained?

Every explanation is sufficient. Only the myth must be removed. It will be removed when we observe the phenomena and draw conclusions from them concerning the invisible.[18] We must hold fast to the appearance, the sensation. Hence analogy must be applied. In this way we can explain fear away and free ourselves from it, by showing the causes of meteors and other things that are always happening and causing the utmost alarm to other people.[19]

The great number of explanations, the multitude of possibilities, should not only tranquillise our minds and remove causes for fear, but also at the same time negate in the heavenly bodies their very unity, the absolute law that is always equal to itself. These heavenly bodies may behave sometimes in one way, sometimes in another; this possibility conforming to no law is the characteristic of their reality; everything in them is declared to be impermanent and unstable.[20] *The multitude of the explanations should at the same time remove [aufheben] the unity of the object.*

Thus while *Aristotle,* in agreement with other Greek philosophers, considers the heavenly bodies to be eternal and immortal, because they always behave in the same way; while he even ascribes to them an element of their own, higher and not subjected to the force of gravity; *Epicurus* in contrast claims the direct opposite. He reasons that the theory of the meteors is specifically distinguished from all other physical doctrine in this respect, that in the meteors everything occurs in a multiple and unregulated way, that everything in them is to be explained by a manifold of indefinitely many causes. Yes, in wrath and passionate violence he rejects the opposite opinion, and declares that those who adhere to only one method of explanation to the exclusion of all others, those who accept something Unique, hence Eternal and Divine in the meteors, fall victim to idle explanation-making and to the slavish artifices of the astrologers; they overstep the bounds of the study of nature and throw themselves into the arms of myth; they try to achieve the impossible, and exert themselves over absurdities; they do not even realise where ataraxy itself becomes endangered. Their chatter is to be despised.[21] We must avoid the prejudice that investigation into these subjects cannot be sufficiently thorough and subtle if it aims only at our own ataraxy and bliss.[22] On the contrary, it is an absolute law that nothing that can disturb ataraxy, that can cause danger, can belong to an indestructible and eternal nature. Consciousness must understand that this is an absolute law.[23]

Hence Epicurus concludes: *Since eternity of the heavenly bodies would disturb the ataraxy of self-consciousness, it is a necessary, a stringent consequence that they are not eternal.*

But how can we understand this peculiar view of Epicurus?

All authors who have written on Epicurean philosophy have presented this teaching as incompatible with all the rest of physics, with the atomic doctrine. The fight against the Stoics, against superstition, against astrology is taken as sufficient grounds.

And we have seen that Epicurus himself distinguishes the *method* applied in the theory of the meteors from the method of the rest of physics. But in which definition of his principle can the necessity of this distinction be found? How does the idea occur to him?

And he fights not only against astrology, but also against astronomy itself, against eternal law and rationality in the heavenly system. Finally, opposition to the Stoics explains nothing. Their superstition and their whole point of view had already been refuted when the heavenly bodies were declared to be accidental complexes of atoms and their processes accidental motions of the atoms. Thereby their eternal nature was destroyed, a consequence which Democritus was content to draw from these premises.[24] In fact, their very being was disposed of [*aufgehoben*].[25] The atomist therefore was in no need of a new method.

But this is not yet the full difficulty. An even more perplexing antinomy appears.

The atom is matter in the form of independence, of individuality, as it were the representative of weight. But the heavenly bodies are the supreme realisation of weight. In them all antinomies between form and matter, between concept and existence, which constituted the development of the atom, are resolved; in them all required determinations are realised. The heavenly bodies are eternal and unchangeable; they have their centre of gravity in, not outside, themselves. Their only action is motion, and, separated by empty space, they swerve from the straight line, and form a system of repulsion and attraction while at the same time preserving their own independence and also, finally, generating time out of themselves as the form of their appearance. *The heavenly bodies are therefore the atoms become real.* In them matter has received in itself individuality. Here Epicurus must therefore have glimpsed the highest existence of his principle, the peak and culminating point of his system. He asserted that he assumed the atom so that nature would be provided with immortal foundations. He alleged that he was concerned with the substantial individuality of matter. But when he comes upon the reality of his nature (and he knows no other nature but the mechanical), when he comes upon independent, indestructible matter in the heavenly bodies whose eternity and unchangeability were proved by the belief of the people, the judgment of philosophy, the evidence of the senses: then his one and only desire is to pull it down into earthly transience. He turns vehemently against those who worship an independent nature containing in itself the quality of individuality. This is his most glaring contradiction.

Hence Epicurus feels that here his previous categories break down, that the method of his theory[a] becomes different. And the *profoundest knowledge* achieved by his system, its most thorough consistency, is that he is aware of this and expresses it consciously.

Indeed, we have seen how the whole Epicurean philosophy of nature is pervaded with the contradiction between essence and existence, between form and matter. *But this contradiction is resolved in the heavenly bodies,* the conflicting moments are reconciled. In the celestial system matter has received form into itself, has taken up the individuality into itself and has thus achieved its independence. *But at this point it ceases to be affirmation of abstract self-consciousness.* In the world of the atoms, as in the world of appearance, form struggled against matter; the one determination transcended the other and precisely *in this contradiction abstract-individual self-consciousness felt its nature objectified.* The abstract form, which, in the shape of matter, fought against abstract matter, was *this self-consciousness itself.* But now, when matter has reconciled itself with the form and has been rendered self-sufficient, individual self-consciousness emerges from its pupation, proclaims itself the true principle and opposes nature, which has become independent.

All this can also be expressed from another point of view in the following way: *Matter,* having received into itself individuality, form, as is the case with the heavenly bodies, *has ceased to be abstract individuality; it has become concrete individuality, universality.* In the meteors, therefore, abstract-individual self-consciousness is met by

---

[a] "Method of his theory" was corrected by Marx from "theory of his method."— *Ed.*

its contradiction, shining in its materialised form, the universal which has become existence and nature. Hence it recognises in the meteors its deadly enemy, and it ascribes to them, as Epicurus does, all the anxiety and confusion of men. Indeed, the anxiety and dissolution of the abstract-individual is precisely the universal. Here therefore Epicurus' true principle, abstract-individual self-consciousness, can no longer be concealed. It steps out from its hiding place and, freed from material mummery, it seeks to destroy the reality of nature which has become independent by an explanation according to abstract possibility: what is possible may also be otherwise, the opposite of what is possible is also possible. Hence the polemic against those who explain the heavenly bodies *haplos* (ἁπλῶς),[a] that is, in one particular way, for the One is the Necessary and that which is Independent-in-itself.

Thus as long as nature as atom and appearance expresses individual self-consciousness and its contradiction, the subjectivity of self-consciousness appears only in the form of matter itself. Where, on the other hand, it becomes independent, it reflects itself in itself, confronts matter in its own shape as independent form.

It could have been said from the beginning that where Epicurus' principle becomes reality it will cease to have reality for him. For if individual self-consciousness were posited in reality under the determination of nature, or nature under the determination of individual consciousness, then its determination, that is, its existence, would have ceased, because only the universal in free distinction from itself can know at the same time its own affirmation.

In the theory of meteors therefore appears the soul of the Epicurean philosophy of nature. Nothing is eternal which destroys the ataraxy of individual self-consciousness. The heavenly bodies disturb its ataraxy, its equanimity with itself, because they are the existing universality, because in them nature has become independent.

Thus the principle of Epicurean philosophy is not the *gastrology* of *Archestratus* as *Chrysippus* believes,[26] but the absoluteness and freedom of self-consciousness — even if self-consciousness is only conceived in the form of individuality.

If abstract-individual self-consciousness is posited as an absolute principle, then, indeed, all true and real science is done away with [*aufgehoben*] inasmuch as individuality does not rule within the nature of things themselves. But then, too, everything collapses

---

[a] Simply, absolutely.— *Ed.*

that is transcendentally related to human consciousness and therefore belongs to the imagining mind. On the other hand, if that self-consciousness which knows itself only in the form of abstract universality is raised to an absolute principle, then the door is opened wide to superstitious and unfree mysticism. Stoic philosophy provides the historic proof of this. Abstract-universal self-consciousness has, indeed, the intrinsic urge to affirm itself in the things themselves in which it can only affirm itself by negating them.

Epicurus is therefore the greatest representative of Greek Enlightenment, and he deserves the praise of Lucretius[27]:

> Humana ante oculos foede cum vita iaceret
> In terris oppressa gravi sub religione
> Quae caput a caeli regionibus ostendebat
> Horribili super aspectu mortalibus instans,
> Primum Graius homo mortalis tollere contra.
> Est oculos ausus primusque obsistere contra,
> Quem neque fama deum nec fulmina nec minitanti
> Murmure compressit caelum............
> Quare religio pedibus subiecta vicissim
> Obteritur, nos exaequat victoria caelo.[a]

The difference between Democritean and Epicurean philosophy of nature which we established at the end of the general section has been elaborated and confirmed in all domains of nature. In *Epicurus*, therefore, *atomistics* with all its contradictions has been carried through and completed *as the natural science of self-consciousness*. This self-consciousness under the form of abstract individuality is an absolute principle. Epicurus has thus carried atomistics to its final conclusion, which is its dissolution and conscious opposition to the universal. For *Democritus*, on the other hand, the *atom* is only the *general objective expression of the empirical investigation of nature as a whole*. Hence the atom remains for him a pure and abstract category, a hypothesis, the result of experience, not its active [*energisches*] principle. This hypothesis remains therefore without realisation, just as it plays no further part in determining the real investigation of nature.

---

[a] When human life lay grovelling in all men's sight, crushed to the earth under the dead weight of religion whose grim features loured menacingly upon mortals from the four quarters of the sky, a man of Greece was first to raise mortal eyes in defiance, first to stand erect and brave the challenge. Fables of the gods did not crush him, nor the lightning flash and growling menace of the sky.... Therefore religion in its turn lies crushed beneath his feet, and we by his triumph are lifted level with the skies.— *Ed.*

[Fragment from the Appendix]

[CRITIQUE OF PLUTARCH'S POLEMIC AGAINST THE THEOLOGY OF EPICURUS] [27]

[II. INDIVIDUAL IMMORTALITY]

[1. On Religious Feudalism. The Hell of the Populace]

The study is again divided into the relation *ton adikon kai poneron* (τῶν ἀδίχων χαὶ πονήρῶν),[a] then of the *pollon kai idioton* (πολλῶν χαὶ ἰδιωτῶν),[b] and finally of the *epieikon kai noun echonton* (ἐπιειχῶν χαὶ νοῦν ἐχόντων)[c] (l. c. 1104)[28] to the doctrine of the continued existence of the soul. Already this division into fixed qualitative distinctions shows how little Plutarch understands Epicurus, who, as a philosopher, investigates the essential relationship of the human soul in general.

Then he brings fear up again as the means to reform the evil-doers and thus justifies the terrors of the underworld for the sensuous consciousness. We have already considered this objection of his. Since in fear, and specifically in an inner fear that cannot be extinguished, man is determined as an animal, we do not care at all how an animal is kept in restraint.

Now we proceed to the view of the *polloi* (πολλοί),[d] although it turns out at the end that few people are not included in this term; although, to tell the truth, all people, *deo legein pantas* (δέω λέγειν πάντας),[e] vow allegiance to this banner.

τοῖς δὲ πολλοῖς χαὶ ἄνευ φόβου περὶ τῶν ἐν ἅ δου ἡ περὶ τὸ μυθῶδες τῆς ἀϊδιότητος ἐλπὶς, χαὶ ο πόθος τοῦ εἶναι, πάντων ἐρώτων πρεσβύτατος ὢν χαὶ μέγιστος, ἡδονῆς ὑπερβάλλει χαὶ γλυχυθυμίας τὸ παιδιχὸν ἐχεῖνο δέος. P.1104, l.c. ἤ χαὶ τέχνα χαὶ γυναῖχα χαὶ φίλους ἀποβάλλοντες, εἶναί που μᾶλλον ἐθέλουσι χαὶ διαμένειν χαχοπαθοῦντες, ἤ παντάπασιν ἐξη-

---

[a] Of the evil-doers and rascals.— *Ed.*
[b] Masses and uncivilised.— *Ed.*
[c] Decent and intelligent ones.— *Ed.*
[d] Multitude.— *Ed.*
[e] I had almost said all men.— *Ed.*

ρῆσθαι καὶ διεφθάρθαι καὶ γεγονέναι τὸ μηθέν. ἡδέως δὲ τῶν ὀνομάτων τοῦ
μεθιστάσθαι τὸν θνῄσκοντα καὶ μεταλλάττειν, καὶ ὅσα δηλοῖ μεταβολὴν
ὄντα τῆς ψυχῆς, οὐ φθοράν, τὸν θάνατον ἀκροῶνται... P.1104, 1.c.
[...] καὶ πρὸς τὸ ἀπόλωλε, καὶ τὸ ἀνῄρηται, καὶ τὸ οὐκέστι, ταράσσονται...
ἢ καὶ προσεπισφάττουσιν οἱ ταυτὶ λέγουτες, ἅπαξ ἄνθρωποι γεγόναμεν, δὶς
δὲ οὐκ ἔστι γενέσθαι... [P. 1104, 1.c.] καὶ γὰρ τὸ παρὸν ὡς
μικρὸν, μᾶλλον δὲ μηδοτιοῦν πρὸς τὸ σύμπαντα ἀτιμήσαντες ἀναπόλαυστα
προϊενται, καὶ ὀλιγωροῦσιν ἀρετῆς καὶ πράξεως, οἷον ἐξαθυμοῦντες, καὶ
καταφρονοῦντες ἑαυτῶν ὡς ἐφημέρων καὶ ἀβεβαίων καὶ πρὸς οὐδὲν ἀξιόλογον
γεγονότων. τὸ γὰρ ἀναίσθητον καὶ λυθὲν καὶ μηδὲν εἶναι πρὸς ἡμᾶς τὸ ἀναι-
σθητοῦν, οὐκ ἀναιρεῖ τὸ τοῦ θανάτου δέος, ἀλλ' ὥσπερ ἀπόδειξιν αὐτοῦ
προστίθησιν. αὐτὸ γὰρ τοῦτό ἐστιν ὃ δέδοικεν ἡ φύσις... τὴν εἰς τὸ μὴ φρονοῦν
μηδὲ αἰσθανόμενον διάλυσιν τῆς ψυχῆς, ἣν Ἐπίκουρος εἰς κενὸν καὶ ἀτόμους
διασποραν ποιῶν, ἔτι μᾶλλον ἐκκόπτει τὴν ἐλπίδα τῆς ἀφθαρσίας· δι' ἣν
ὀλίγου δέω λέγειν πάντας εἶναι καὶ πάσας προθύμους τῷ Κερβέρῳ διαδάκ-
νεσθαι, καὶ φορεῖν εἰς τὸν ἄτρητον, ὅπως ἐν τῷ εἶναι [μόνον] διαμένωσι,
μηδὲ ἀναιρεθῶσι. P. [1104—]1105, l.c.[a]

There is really no qualitative difference between this and the
previous category. What in the first case appeared in the shape of
animal fear, appears here in the shape of human fear, the form of
sentiment. The content remains the same.

We are told that the desire of being is the oldest love; to be
sure, the most abstract and hence oldest love is the love of self, the

---

[a] In the masses, who have no fear of what comes after death, the myth-inspired
hope of eternal life and the desire of being, the oldest and most powerful of all
passions, produces joy and a feeling of happiness and overcomes that childish
terror. Hence, whoever has lost children, a wife, and friends would rather have
them continue to be somewhere and continue to exist, even if in hardship, than be
utterly taken away and destroyed and reduced to nothing. On the other hand, they
willingly hear such expressions as "the dying person goes somewhere else and
changes his dwelling", and whatever else intimates that death is a change of the
soul's dwelling, and not destruction ... and such expressions as "he is lost" and "he
has perished" and "he is no more" disturb them.... They hold in store for them
utter death who say: "We men are born only once; one cannot be born a second
time".... For the present is of little account to them, or rather of none at all, in
comparison with eternity, and they let it pass without enjoying it and neglect virtue
and action, spiritless and despising themselves as creatures of a day, impermanent, and beings worth nothing to speak of. For the doctrine that "being-with-
out-sensation and being-dissolved and what has no sensation is nothing to us"
does not remove the terror of death, but rather confirms it. For this is the very
thing nature dreads ... the dissolution of the soul into what has neither thought nor
sensation; Epicurus, by making this a scattering into emptiness and atoms, does still
more destroy our hope of immortality, a hope for which (I would almost say) all
men and all women are ready to be torn asunder by Cerberus and to carry
constantly [water] into the barrel [of the Danaides], so that they may [only] stay in
being and not be extinguished.— Ed.

love of one's particular being. But that was expressing this fact too bluntly, and so it is retracted and an ennobling halo is cast around it by the semblance of sentiment.

Thus he who loses wife and children would rather that they were somewhere, even under bad conditions, than that they had totally ceased to exist. If the issue were only love, then the wife and the child of the individual would be preserved in the greatest purity in his heart, a state of being far superior to that of empirical existence. But the facts are otherwise. Wife and child as such are only in empirical existence insofar as the individual to whom they belong exists empirically himself. That the individual therefore prefers to know that they are somewhere in sensuous space, even under bad conditions, rather than nowhere, only means that he wants to preserve the consciousness of his own empirical existence. The mantle of love was only a shadow. The naked empirical Ego, the love of self, the oldest love, is the core and has not rejuvenated itself into a more concrete, more ideal shape.

Plutarch believes that the word "change" has a more pleasing sound than "total cessation". But the change is not supposed to be a qualitative one, the individual Ego in its individual being is supposed to persist, the word therefore is only the sensuous image of what the word stands for and has to stand for its opposite. The thing is not supposed to be changed, only placed in a dark spot. The qualitative leap—and every qualitative distinction is a leap, without such leaping no ideality—is then obscured by the interposition of a fantastic distance.

Plutarch also thinks that this consciousness....[a]

---

[a] Here the manuscript breaks off.— *Ed.*

[Notes]

Part One

DIFFERENCE BETWEEN THE DEMOCRITEAN AND EPICUREAN PHILOSOPHY OF NATURE IN GENERAL

II. OPINIONS ON THE RELATIONSHIP BETWEEN DEMOCRITEAN AND EPICUREAN PHYSICS

[1] **Diogenes Laertius,** X, 4. They are followed by Posidonius the Stoic and his school, and Nicolaus and Sotion ... [allege that] he (Epicurus) put forward as his own the doctrines of Democritus about atoms and of Aristippus about pleasure.[a]

[2] **Cicero,** *On the Nature of the Gods,* I, xxvi [73]. What is there in Epicurus' natural philosophy that does not come from Democritus? Since even if he *introduced some alterations* ... yet most of his system is the same....

[3] **Id.,** *On the Highest Goods and Evils,* I, vi [21]. Thus where Epicurus alters the doctrines of Democritus, he alters them for the worse; while for those ideas which he adopts, the credit belongs entirely to Democritus....

Ibid. [17, 18] ... the subject of Natural Philosophy, which is Epicurus' particular boast. Here, in the first place, *he is entirely second-hand.* His doctrines are those of Democritus, with 'a very few modifications. And as for the latter, where he attempts to *improve* upon his original, in my opinion he only succeeds in making things *worse*.... Epicurus for his part, where he follows Democritus, does not generally blunder.

[4] **Plutarch,** *Reply to Colotes* (published by Xylander), 1108. Leonteus ... writes ... that Democritus was honoured by Epicurus for having reached the correct approach to knowledge before him ... because Democritus had first hit upon the first principles of natural philosophy. Comp. *ibid.,* 1111.

[5] **(Id.,)** *On the Sentiments of the Philosophers,* V, 235, published by Tauchnitz. Epicurus, the son of Neocles, from Athens, who philosophised according to Democritus....

[6] **Id.,** *Reply to Colotes,* 1111, 1112, 1114, 1115, 1117, 1119, 1120 seqq.

[7] **Clement of Alexandria,** *The Miscellanies,* VI, p. 629, Cologne edition [2]. Epicurus also has pilfered his leading dogmas from Democritus.

[8] **Ibid.,** p. 295 [I, 11]. "Beware lest any man despoil you through philosophy and vain deceit, after the tradition of men, after the elements of the world and

---

[a] The translation of Latin and Greek texts follows, when possible, that of the Loeb Classical Library. The translation differs in details from the text in the dissertation, which is the English translation of Marx's text, and therefore also of Marx's German translation of the Latin and Greek texts.— *Ed.*

not after Christ" [Col. ii, 8], branding not all philosophy, but the Epicurean, which Paul mentions in the Acts of the Apostles [Acts xvii, 18], which abolishes providence ... and whatever other philosophy honours the elements, but places not over them the efficient cause, nor apprehends the Creator.

9) **Sextus Empiricus,** *Against the Professors* (Geneva edition) [I, 273]. Epicurus has been detected as guilty of having filched the best of his dogmas from the poets. For he has been shown to have taken his definition of the intensity of pleasures,—that it is "the removal of everything painful" — from this one verse:

"When they had now put aside all longing for drinking and eating." [a]

And as to death, that "it is nothing to us", Epicharmus had already pointed this out to him when he said,

"To die or to be dead concerns me not."

So, too, he stole the notion that dead bodies have no feeling from Homer, where he writes,

"'Tis dumb clay that he beats with abuse in his violent fury." [b]

10) *Letter of* **Leibniz** *to Mr. Des Maizeaux, containing [some] clarifications....* [*Opera omnia,*] ed. L. Dutens, Vol. 2, p[p]. 66[-67].

11) **Plutarch,** *Reply to Colotes,* 1111. Democritus is therefore to be censured not for admitting the consequences that flow from his principles, but for setting up principles that lead to these consequences.... If "does not say" means "does not admit it is so", he is following his familiar practice; thus he (Epicurus) does away with providence but says he has left us with piety; he chooses friends for the pleasure he gets, but says that he assumes the greatest pains on their behalf; and he says that while he posits an infinite universe he does not eliminate "up" and "down".

III. DIFFICULTIES CONCERNING THE IDENTITY OF THE DEMOCRITEAN AND EPICUREAN PHILOSOPHY OF NATURE

1) **Aristotle,** *On the Soul,* I, p. 8 (published by Trendelenburg) [2, 404[a], 27-29]. Democritus roundly identifies soul and mind, for he identifies what appears with what is true.

2) **Id.,** *Metaphysics,* IV, 5 [1009[b], 11-18]. And this is why Democritus, at any rate, says that either there is no truth or to us at least it is not evident. And in general it is because they [i.e., these thinkers] suppose knowledge to be sensation, and this to be a physical alteration, that they say that what appears to our senses must be true; for it is for these reasons that both Empedocles and Democritus and, one may almost say, all the others have fallen victims to opinions of this sort. For Empedocles says that when men change their condition they change their knowledge.

By the way, the contradiction is expressed in this passage of the *Metaphysics* itself.[c]

---

[a] Homer, *Iliad,* I, 469.— *Ed.*

[b] Ibid., XXIV, 54.— *Ed.*

[c] Marx wrote this sentence with a corresponding reference in the left margin of the page.— *Ed.*

[3] **Diogenes Laertius,** IX, 72. Furthermore, they find Xenophanes, Zeno of Elea, and Democritus to be sceptics.... Democritus [says:] "Of a truth we know nothing, for truth is in a well."

[4] Comp. **Ritter,** *History of Ancient Philosophy* [in German], Part I, pp. 579 seqq. [2^d improved edition, 1836, pp. 619 seqq.]

[5] **Diogenes Laertius,** IX, 44. His (Democritus') opinions are these: The first principles of the universe are atoms and empty space; everything else is merely thought to exist.

[6] **Ibid.,** IX, 72. Democritus rejects qualities, saying: "Opinion says hot or cold, but the reality is atoms and empty space."

[7] **Simplicius,** *Scholia to Aristotle* (collected by Brandis), p. 488. ... yet he (Democritus) does not really allow one being to be formed out of them, for it is quite foolish, he says, that two or more become one.

P. 514. [...] and therefore they (Democritus and Leucippus) said that neither the one becomes many nor do the many become the truly inseparable one but through the combination of atoms each thing appears to become a unity.

[8] **Plutarch,** *Reply to Colotes,* 1111. The atoms, which he (Democritus) calls *"ideas".*

[9] Comp. **Aristotle,** l. c.

[10] **Diogenes Laertius,** X, 121. He [the wise man] will be a dogmatist but not a mere sceptic.

[11] **Plutarch,** *Reply to Colotes,* 1117. For it is one of Epicurus' tenets that none but the sage is unalterably convinced of anything.

[12] **Cicero,** *One the Nature of the Gods,* I, xxv [70]. He (Epicurus) therefore said that *all the senses give a true report.*

Comp. **id.,** *On the Highest Goods and Evils,* I, vii.

(Plutarch,) *On the Sentiments of the Philosophers,* IV, p. 287 [8]. Epicurus holds that every impression and every phantasy is true.

[13] **Diogenes Laertius,** X, 31. Now in *The Canon* Epicurus affirms that our sensations and preconceptions and our feelings are the standards of truth.... 32. Nor is there anything which can refute sensations or convict them of error: one sensation cannot convict another and kindred sensation, for they are equally valid; nor can one sensation refute another which is not kindred but heterogeneous, for the objects which the two senses judge are not the same; nor again can reason refute them, for reason is wholly dependent on sensation.

[14] **Plutarch,** *Reply to Colotes,* l. c. [1110-1111]. He [Colotes] says that Democritus' words "colour is by convention, sweet by convention, a compound by convention", and so the rest, "what is real are the void and the atoms", are an attack on the senses.... I cannot deny the truth of this, but I can affirm that this view is as inseparable from Epicurus' theories as shape and weight are by their own assertion inseparable from the atom. For what does Democritus say? That entities infinite in number, indivisible and indestructible, destitute moreover of quality, and incapable of modification, move scattered about in the void; that when they draw near one another or collide or become entangled the resulting aggregate appears in the one case to be water, in others fire, a plant, or a man, but that everything really is the indivisible "forms", as he calls them [or: atoms, "ideas", as he calls them], and nothing else. For there is no generation from the non-existent, and again nothing can be generated from the existent, as the atoms are too solid to be affected and changed. From this it follows that there is no colour, since it would have to come from things colourless, and no natural entity or mind, since they

would have to come from things without qualities.... Democritus is therefore to be censured, not for admitting the consequences that flow from his principles, but for setting up principles that lead to these consequences.... *Epicurus claims to lay down the same first principles, but nevertheless does not say that "colour is by convention", and so with the qualities [sweet, bitter] and the rest.*

15) **Cicero,** *On the Highest Goods and Evils,* I, vi. Democritus, being an educated man and well versed in geometry, thinks the sun is of vast size; Epicurus considers it perhaps two feet in diameter, for he pronounces it *to be* exactly as large as it *appears.* Comp. **(Plutarch,)** *On the Sentiments of the Philosophers,* II, p. 265.

16) **Diogenes Laertius,** IX, 37. [And truly Democritus] had trained himself both in physics and in ethics, nay more, in mathematics and the routine subjects of education, and was quite an expert in the arts.

17) Comp. **Diogenes Laertius,** [IX,] 46[-49].

18) **Eusebius,** *Preparation for the Gospel,* X, p. 472. And somewhere he (Democritus) says proudly about himself: "I have wandered through a larger part of the earth than any of my contemporaries, investigating the remotest things, and I have seen most climates and lands, and I have heard the most learned men, and in linear composition with demonstration no one surpassed me, not even the so-called Arsipedonapts of the Egyptians, whose guest I was when already turning eighty." For he went as far as Babylon and Persia and Egypt, where he also studied with the Egyptian priests.

19) **Diogenes Laertius,** IX, 35. According to Demetrius in his book on *Men of the Same Name* and Antisthenes in his *Successions of Philosophers* he (Democritus) travelled into Egypt to learn geometry from the priests, and he also went into Persia to visit the Chaldaeans as well as to the Red Sea. Some say that he associated with the gymnosophists in India and went to Aethiopia.

20) **Cicero,** *Tusculan Disputations,* V, 39. When Democritus lost his sight.... And this man believed that the sight of the eyes was an obstacle to the piercing vision of the soul, and whilst others often failed to see what lay at their feet, he ranged freely into the infinite without finding any boundary that brought him to a halt.

Id., *On the Highest Goods and Evils,* V, xxix [87]. It is related of Democritus that he deprived himself of eyesight; and it is certain that [he did so] *in order that his mind should be distracted as little as possible from reflection.*

21) **Luc. Ann. Seneca,** *Works,* II, p. 24, Amsterdam, 1672, Epistle VIII. I am still conning Epicurus.... "If you would enjoy real freedom, you must be the slave of Philosophy." The man who submits and surrenders himself to her is not kept waiting; he is emancipated on the spot. For the very service of Philosophy is freedom.

22) **Diogenes Laertius,** X, 122. Let no one be slow to seek wisdom when he is young nor weary in the search thereof when he is grown old. For no age is too early or too late for the health of the soul. And to say that the season for studying philosophy has not yet come, or that it is past and gone, is like saying that the season for happiness is not yet or that it is now no more. Therefore, both old and young ought to seek wisdom, the former in order that, as age comes over him, he may be young in good things because of the grace of what has been, and the latter in order that, while he is young, he may at the same time be old, because he has no fear of the things which are to come. Comp. **Clement of Alexandria,** IV, 501.

23) **Sextus Empiricus,** *Against the Professors,* I, 1. The case against the mathematici [or: Professors of Arts and Sciences] has been set forth in a general way, it would seem, both by Epicurus and by the School of Pyrrho, although the

standpoints they adopt are different. Epicurus took the ground that the subjects taught are of no help in perfecting wisdom....

24) **Ibid.**, p. 11 [I, 49]. And amongst them we must place Epicurus, although he seems to be bitterly hostile to the Professors of Arts and Sciences.

Ibid., p. 54 [I, 272]. ... those accusers of grammar, Pyrrho, and Epicurus.... Comp. **Plutarch,** *That Epicurus Actually Makes a Pleasant Life Impossible*, 1094.

25) **Cicero,** *On the Highest Goods and Evils*, I, xxi [72]. No! Epicurus was not uneducated: the real ignoramuses are those who ask us to go on studying till old age the subjects that we ought to be ashamed not to have learnt in boyhood.

26) **Diogenes Laertius,** X, 13. Apollodorus in his *Chronology* tells us that our philosopher (i.e., Epicurus) was a pupil of Nausiphanes and Praxiphanes; but in his letter to Eurydicus, Epicurus himself denies it and says that he was self-taught.

Cicero, *On the Nature of the Gods*, I, xxvi [72]. For he (Epicurus) boasted that he had never had a teacher. This I for my part could well believe, even if he did not proclaim it....

27) **Seneca,** *Epistle LII*, p. 177. Epicurus remarks that certain men have worked their way to the truth without any one's assistance, carving out their own passage. And he gives special praise to these, for their impulse has come from within, and they have forged to the front by themselves. Again, he says, there are others who need outside help, who will not proceed unless someone leads the way, but who will follow faithfully. Of these, he says, Metrodorus was one; this type of man is also excellent, but belongs to the second grade.

28) **Diogenes Laertius,** X, 10. He spent all his life in Greece, notwithstanding the calamities which had befallen her in that age; when he did once or twice take a trip to Ionia, it was to visit his friends there. Friends indeed came to him from all parts and lived with him in his garden. This is stated by Apollodorus, who also says that he purchased the garden for eighty minae.

29) **Ibid.**, X, 15, 16. Hermippus relates that he entered a bronze bath of lukewarm water and asked for unmixed wine, which he swallowed, and then, having bidden his friends remember his doctrines, breathed his last.

30) **Cicero,** *On Fate*, x [22, 23]. Epicurus [thinks] that the necessity of fate can be avoided.... Democritus preferred to accept the view that all events are caused by necessity.

Id., *On the Nature of the Gods*, I, xxv [69]. He [Epicurus] therefore invented a device to escape from determinism (the point had apparently escaped the notice of Democritus)....

Eusebius, *Preparation for the Gospel*, I, pp. 23 seqq. Democritus of Abdera [assumed] ... that all, the past as well as the present and the future, has been determined always, since time immemorial, by necessity.

31) **Aristotle,** *On the Generation of Animals*, V, 8 [789^b, 2-3]. Democritus ... reduces to *necessity* all the operations of Nature.

32) **Diogenes Laertius,** IX, 45. All things happen by virtue of necessity, the vortex being the cause of the creation of all things, and this he (Democritus) calls *necessity*.

33) **(Plutarch,)** *On the Sentiments of the Philosophers*, p. 252 [I, 25]. Parmenides and Democritus [say] that there is nothing in the world but what is *necessary*, and that this same necessity is otherwise called *fate, right, providence* and the *creator of the world.*

34) **Stobaeus,** *Physical Selections*, I, 8. Parmenides and Democritus [say] that everything occurs by *necessity*, this being *fate, justice, providence* [and the architect of the world]. Leucippus [says] that everything [occurs] by *necessity*, this being *fate*. For he says ... nothing originates without cause, but everything because of a cause and of *necessity*.

35) **Eusebius,** *Preparation for the Gospel*, VI, p. 257. ... *fate*, that ... for the others (i.e., Democritus) depends on these small bodies, which are carried downward and then ascend again, that conglomerate and again dissipate, that run away from each other and then come together again by *necessity*.

36) **Stobaeus,** *Ethical Selections*, II [4]. Men like to create for themselves the illusion of chance—an excuse for their own perplexity; since chance is incompatible with sound thinking.

37) **Eusebius,** *Preparation for the Gospel*, XIV, p. 782. ... and he (i.e., Democritus) has made chance the master and ruler of the universal and divine, and has claimed that everything happens through chance. At the same time he keeps it away from human life and has decried as stupid those who proclaim it. Indeed, at the beginning of his teachings he says: "Men like to create for themselves the illusion of chance—an excuse for their own folly; since it is natural that sound thinking is incompatible with chance; and they have said that this worst enemy of thinking rules; or rather, they accept chance instead of thinking by totally removing and abolishing sound thinking. For they do not appreciate thinking as blissful, but chance as the most reasonable."

38) **Simplicius,** l. c., p. 351. The expression "like the ancient doctrine that removes chance" seems to refer to Democritus....

39) **Diogenes Laertius,** X, 133, 134. ... Destiny,[a] which some introduce as sovereign over all things, he laughs to scorn, affirming rather that some things happen of necessity, others by chance, others through our own agency. For he sees that necessity destroys responsibility and that chance or fortune is inconstant; whereas our own actions are free, and it is to them that praise and blame naturally attach. It were better, indeed, to accept the legends of the gods than to bow beneath the yoke of destiny which the natural philosophers have imposed. The one holds out some faint hope that we may escape if we honour the gods, while the necessity of the naturalists is deaf to all entreaties. But he holds to chance, not to a god, as the world in general [*hoi polloi*] does....

40) **Seneca,** *Epistle XII*, p. 42. "It is wrong to live under necessity; but no man is constrained to live under necessity.... On all sides lie many short and simple paths to freedom; and let us thank God that no man can be kept in life. We may spurn the very constraints that hold us." Epicurus ... uttered these words....

41) **Cicero,** *On the Nature of the Gods*, I, xx [55-56]. But what value can be assigned to a philosophy (i. e., the Stoic) which thinks that everything happens by fate? It is a belief for old women, and ignorant old women at that.... But Epicurus has set us free [from superstitious terrors] and delivered us out of captivity....

42) **Ibid.,** I, xxv [70]. He (i. e., Epicurus) does the same in his battle with the logicians. Their accepted doctrine is that in every disjunctive proposition of the form "*so-and-so either is or not*" one of the two alternatives must be true. Epicurus took alarm; if such a proposition as "*Epicurus either will or will not be alive tomorrow*"

---

[a] Translated by "necessity" in the text of the dissertation.— *Ed.*

were granted, one or the other alternative would be necessary. Accordingly he denied the necessity of a disjunctive proposition altogether.

[43] **Simplicius**, l. c., p. 351. But also Democritus states, where he brings it up, that the different kinds must separate themselves from the totality, but not how and because of what reason, and seems to let them originate automatically and by chance.

Ibid., p. 351. ... and since this man (i. e., Democritus) has apparently applied chance in the creation of the world....

[44] Comp. **Eusebius**, l. c., XIV, [p]p. [781-]782. ... and this [said] one (i. e., Democritus), who had sought vainly and without reason for a cause, since he started from an empty principle and a faulty hypothesis, and has taken as the greatest wisdom the understanding of unreasonable [and foolish] happenings, without seeing the root and general necessity of things....

[45] **Simplicius**, l. c., p. 351. ... indeed, when somebody is thirsty, he drinks cold water and feels fine again; but Democritus will probably not accept chance as the cause, but the thirst.

Ibid., p. 351. ... for, even though he (Democritus) seems to use chance in regard to the creation of the world, yet he maintains that in individual cases chance is not the cause of anything, but refers us back to other causes. For instance: the cause of treasure trove is the digging or the planting of the olive tree....

Comp. **ibid**, p. 351. ... but in individual cases, he (Democritus) says, [chance] is not the cause.

[46] **Eusebius**, l. c., XIV, 781. Indeed, Democritus himself is supposed to have said that he would rather discover a new causal explanation than acquire the Persian crown.

[47] **(Plutarch,)** *On the Sentiments of the Philosophers*, II, p. 261 [13]. Epicurus rejects none of these opinions,[a] [for he keeps to] what is possible.

Ibid., II, p. 265 [21]. Epicurus says again that all the foregoing is possible.

Ibid. [II, 22] Epicurus believes that all the foregoing is possible.

Stobaeus, *Physical Selections*, I, p. 54. Epicurus rejects none of these opinions, for he keeps to what is possible.

[48] **Seneca**, *Questions of Nature*, [VI,] XX, [5,] p. 802. Epicurus asserts that all the foregoing may be causes, but he tries to introduce some additional ones. He criticises other authors for affirming too positively that some particular one of the causes is responsible, as it is difficult to pronounce anything as certain in matters in which conjecture must be resorted to.

[49] Comp. Part II, Chapter 5.

Diogenes Laertius, X, 88. However, we must observe each fact as presented, and further separate from it all the facts presented along with it, the occurrence of which from various causes is not contradicted by facts within our experience.... All these alternatives are possible; they are contradicted by none of the facts....

[50] **Diogenes Laertius**, X, 80. We must not suppose that our treatment of these matters fails of accuracy, so far as it is needful to ensure our tranquillity [ataraxy] and happiness.

---

[a] Marx added here: "(i.e., opinions of the philosophers on the substance of the stars)".— *Ed.*

IV. GENERAL DIFFERENCE IN PRINCIPLE BETWEEN THE DEMOCRITEAN AND EPICUREAN PHILOSOPHY OF NATURE

[1] Plutarch, in his biography of Marius, provides us with an appalling historical example of the way in which this type of morality destroys all theoretical and practical unselfishness. After describing the terrible downfall of the Cimbri, he relates that the number of corpses was so great that the Massilians [30] were able to manure their orchards with them. Then it rained and that year was the best for wine and fruit. Now, what kind of reflections occur to our noble historian in connection with the tragical ruin of those people? Plutarch considers it a moral act of God, that he allowed a whole, great, noble people to perish and rot away in order to provide the philistines of Massilia with a bumper fruit harvest. Thus even the transformation of a people into a heap of manure offers a desirable occasion for a happy revelling in morality!

[2] Also in relation to Hegel it is mere ignorance on the part of his pupils, when they explain one or the other determination of his system by his desire for accommodation and the like, hence, in one word, explain it in terms of *morality*. They forget that only a short time ago they were enthusiastic about all his idiosyncrasies [*Einseitigkeiten*], as can be clearly demonstrated from their writings.

If they were really so affected by the ready-made science they acquired that they gave themselves up to it in naive uncritical trust, then how unscrupulous is their attempt to reproach the Master for a hidden intention behind his insight! The Master, to whom the science was not something received, but something in the process of becoming, to whose uttermost periphery his own intellectual heart's blood was pulsating! On the contrary, they rendered themselves suspect of not having been serious before. And now they oppose their own former condition, and ascribe it to Hegel, forgetting however that his relation to his system was immediate, substantial, while theirs is only a reflected one.

It is quite thinkable for a philosopher to fall into one or another apparent inconsistency through some sort of accommodation; he himself may be conscious of it. But what he is not conscious of, is the possibility that this apparent accommodation has its deepest roots in an inadequacy or in an inadequate formulation of his principle itself. Suppose therefore that a philosopher has really accommodated himself, then his pupils must explain *from his inner essential consciousness* that which *for him himself* had the form of *an exoteric consciousness*. In this way, that which appears as progress of conscience is at the same time progress of knowledge. No suspicion is cast upon the particular conscience of the philosopher, but his essential form of consciousness is construed, raised to a definite shape and meaning and in this way also transcended.

By the way, I consider this unphilosophical trend in a large section of Hegel's school as a phenomenon which will always accompany the transition from discipline to freedom.

It is a psychological law that the theoretical mind, once liberated in itself, turns into practical energy, and, leaving the shadowy empire of Amenthes as *will*, turns itself against the reality of the world existing without it. (From a philosophical point of view, however, it is important to specify these aspects better, since from the specific manner of this turn we can reason back towards the immanent determination and the universal historic character of a philosophy. We see here, as it were, its *curriculum vitae*[a] narrowed down to its subjective point.) But the *practice* of philosophy is itself *theoretical*. It is the *critique* that measures the individual existence by the essence, the particular reality by the Idea. But this *immediate realisation* of philosophy is in its deepest essence afflicted with contradictions, and this its essence takes form in the appearance and imprints its seal upon it.

When philosophy turns itself as will against the world of appearance, then the system is lowered to an abstract totality, that is, it has become one aspect of the world which opposes another one. Its relationship to the world is that of reflection. Inspired by the urge to realise itself, it enters into tension against the other. The inner self-contentment and completeness has been broken. What was inner light has become consuming flame turning outwards. The result is that as the world becomes philosophical, philosophy also becomes worldly, that its realisation is also its loss, that what it struggles against on the outside is its own inner deficiency, that in the very struggle it falls precisely into those defects which it fights as defects in the opposite camp, and that it can only overcome these defects by falling into them. That which opposes it and that which it fights is always the same as itself, only with factors inverted.

This is the one side, when we consider this matter *purely objectively* as immediate realisation of philosophy. However, it has also a *subjective* aspect, which is merely another form of it. This is *the relationship of the philosophical system* which is realised *to its intellectual carriers*, to the individual self-consciousnesses in which its progress appears. This relationship results in what confronts

---

[a] Course of life.— *Ed.*

the world in the realisation of philosophy itself, namely, in the fact that these individual self-consciousnesses always carry *a double-edged demand*, one edge turned against the world, the other against philosophy itself. Indeed, what in the thing itself appears as a relationship inverted in itself, appears in these self-consciousnesses as a double one, a demand and an action contradicting each other. Their liberation of the world from un-philosophy is at the same time their own liberation from the philosophy that held them in fetters as a particular system. Since they are themselves engaged merely in the act and immediate energy of development— and hence have not yet theoretically emerged from that system— they perceive only the contradiction with the plastic equality-with-self [*Sich-selbst-Gleichheit*] of the system and do not know that by turning against it they only realise its individual moments.

This duality of philosophical self-consciousness appears finally as a double trend, each side utterly opposed to the other. One side, the *liberal* party, as we may call it in general, maintains as its main determination the concept and the principle of philosophy; the other side, its *non-concept*, the moment of reality. This second side is *positive philosophy*.[31] The act of the first side is critique, hence precisely that turning-towards-the-outside of philosophy; the act of the second is the attempt to philosophise, hence the turning-in-towards-itself of philosophy. This second side knows that the inadequacy is immanent in philosophy, while the first understands it as inadequacy of the world which has to be made philosophical. Each of these parties does exactly what the other one wants to do and what it itself does not want to do. The first, however, is, despite its inner contradiction, conscious of both its principle in general and its goal. In the second party the inversion [*Verkehrtheit*], we may well say the madness [*Verrücktheit*], appears as such. As to the content: only the liberal party achieves real progress, because it is the party of the concept, while positive philosophy is only able to produce demands and tendencies whose form contradicts their meaning.

That which in the first place appears as an inverted [*verkehrtes*] relationship and inimical trend of philosophy with respect to the world, becomes in the second place a diremption of individual self-consciousness in itself and appears finally as an external separation and duality of philosophy, as two opposed philosophical trends.

It is obvious that apart from this there also emerge a number of subordinate, querulous formations without individuality. Some of them place themselves behind a philosophical giant of the past—but the ass is soon detected under the lion's skin; the whimpering voice of a manikin of today or yesterday blubbers in comical contrast to the majestic voice resounding through the ages—say of Aristotle, whose unwelcome organ it has appointed itself. It is as if a mute would help himself to a voice by means of a speaking-trumpet of enormous size. Or as if some Lilliputian armed with double spectacles stands on a tiny spot of the posterior of the giant and announces full of amazement to the world the astonishingly novel vista his *punctum visus*[a] offers and makes himself ridiculous explaining that not in a flowing heart, but in the solid substantial ground on which he stands, has been found the point of Archimedes, *pou sto* (ποῦ στῶ), on which the world hinges. Thus we obtain hair-, nail-, toe-, excrement-philosophers and others, who have to represent an even worse function in the mystical world man [*Weltmensch*] of Swedenborg. However, all these slugs belong essentially to the two above-mentioned sides as to their element. As to these sides themselves: in another place I shall completely explain their relation, in part to each other, in part to Hegel's philosophy, as well as the particular historical moments in which this development reveals itself.

[3)] **Diogenes Laertius,** IX, 44. Nothing can come into being from that which is not, nor pass away into that which is not (Democritus).

Ibid., X, 38. To begin with, nothing comes into being out of what is non-existent. For in that case anything would have arisen out of anything.... 39. And if that which disappears had been destroyed and become non-existent, everything would have perished, that into which the things were dissolved being non-existent. Moreover, the sum total of things was always as it is now, and such it will ever remain. For there is nothing into which it can change (Epicurus).

[4)] **Aristotle,** *Physics,* I, 4 [187[a], 32-35]. ...for since everything that comes into being must arise either from what is or from what is not, and it is impossible for it to arise from what is not (on this point all the physicists agree)....

[5)] **Themistius,** *Scholia to Aristotle* (collected by Brandis), folio 42, p. 383. Just as there is no distinction in the nothing, so there is none in the void, for the void is *something non-existent* and *privation,* says [Democritus], etc.

[6)] **Aristotle,** *Metaphysics,* I, 4 [985[b], 4-9]. Leucippus and his associate Democritus say that the full and the empty are the elements, calling the one being and the other non-being—the full and solid being being, the empty non-being (whence they say being no more is than non-being, because the solid no more is than the empty).

[7)] **Simplicius,** l.c., p. 326. Democritus also [says that there are] the Full and the Void, of which he says that the first is "what is" and the second "what is not" [...].

---

[a] Point of view.— *Ed.*

Themistius, l.c., p. 383. For the void is something non-existent and privation, says Democritus.

[8] **Simplicius,** l.c., p. 488. Democritus believes that the nature of the Eternal consists of small beings, infinite in number; he assigns to them a dwelling-place of infinite magnitude; this place he calls by the terms the Void, the Nothing, the Infinite, and each being by: that there, the solid, the being.

[9] Comp. **Simplicius,** l.c., p. 514. The One and the Many.

[10] **Diogenes Laertius,** l.c., 40. ... and if there were no space (which we call also *Void* and place and intangible nature)....

Stobaeus, *Physical Selections,* I, p. 39. Epicurus uses all names: void, place, space, one beside the other.

[11] **Stobaeus,** *Physical Selections,* I, p. 27. It is called atom, not because it is the smallest....

[12] **Simplicius,** l.c., p. 405. ... it was said by those who denied infinite divisibility—since it would be impossible for us to divide infinitely and thus convince ourselves that such division is unattainable—that bodies consist of indivisibles and can be divided as far as the indivisibles. Apart from the fact that Leucippus and Democritus consider not only impassibility[a] as cause of the indivisibility of the primary bodies, but also their smallness and the lack of parts, Epicurus later did not suppose them to be without parts but says that they are indivisible because of impassibility. Aristotle has repeatedly examined critically the opinion of Democritus and Leucippus, and it probably was because of these criticisms, unfavourable to being-without-parts, that Epicurus (who lived later), who sympathised with the opinion of Democritus and Leucippus concerning the primary bodies, maintained that they were impassible.

[13] **Aristotle,** *On Becoming and Decaying,* I, 2 [316[a], 5-14]. Lack of experience diminishes our power of taking a comprehensive view of the admitted facts. Hence those who dwell in intimate association with nature and its phenomena grow more and more able to formulate, as the foundations of their theories, principles such as to admit of a wide and coherent development: while those whom devotion to abstract discussions has rendered unobservant of the facts are too ready to dogmatise on the basis of a few observations. The rival treatments of the subject now before us will serve to illustrate how great is the difference between a "scientific" and a "dialectical" method of inquiry. For, whereas the Platonists argue that there must be atomic magnitudes "because otherwise 'The Triangle' will be more than one", Democritus would appear to have been convinced by arguments appropriate to the subject, i.e., drawn from the science of nature.

[14] **Diogenes Laertius,** IX, [40,] 7,8. Aristoxenus in his *Historical Notes* affirms that Plato wished to burn all the writings of Democritus that he could collect, but that Amyclas and Clinias the Pythagoreans prevented him, saying that there was no advantage in doing so, for already the books were widely circulated. And there is clear evidence for this in the fact that Plato, who mentions almost all the early philosophers, never once alludes to Democritus, not even where it would be necessary to controvert him, obviously because he knew that he would have to match himself against the prince of philosophers....

---

[a] Ἀπάθειαν—i.e., the atom is not affected by anything outside itself.— *Ed.*

Part Two

ON THE DIFFERENCE BETWEEN DEMOCRITEAN
AND EPICUREAN PHYSICS IN DETAIL

Chapter One

THE DECLINATION OF THE ATOM
FROM THE STRAIGHT LINE

[1] **Stobaeus,** *Physical Selections,* I, p. 33. Epicurus says ... that the atoms move sometimes vertically downwards, at other times by deviating from a straight line, but the motion upward is due to collision and recoil.

Comp. **Cicero,** *On the Highest Goods and Evils,* I, vi. **(Plutarch,)** *On the Sentiments of the Philosophers,* p. 249 [I, 12]. **Stobaeus,** l.c., p. 40.

[2] **Cicero,** *On the Nature of the Gods,* I, xxvi [73]. What is there in Epicurus' natural philosophy that does not come from Democritus? Since even if he *introduced some alterations,* for instance the *swerve of the atoms* of which I spoke just now....

[3] **Cicero,** *On the Highest Goods and Evils,* I, vi [18-19]. He (Epicurus) believes that these same indivisible solid bodies are borne by their own weight perpendicularly downward, which he holds is the natural motion of all bodies; but thereupon this *clever fellow,* encountering the difficulty that if they all travelled downwards in a straight line, and, as I said, perpendicularly, no one atom would ever be able to overtake any other atom, accordingly introduced an idea of his own invention: he said that the atom makes a very tiny swerve,—the smallest divergence possible; and so are produced entanglements and combinations and cohesions of atoms with atoms, which result in the creation of the world and all its parts, and of all that is in them.

[4] **Cicero,** *On the Nature of the Gods,* I, xxv [69-70]. Epicurus saw that if the atoms travelled downwards by their own weight, we should have no freedom of the will, since the motion of the atoms would be determined by necessity. He therefore invented a device to escape from determinism (the point had apparently escaped the notice of Democritus): he said that the atom while travelling vertically downward by the force of gravity makes a very slight swerve to one side. This defence discredits him more than if he had had to abandon his original position. Comp. **Cicero,** *On Fate,* x [22-23].

[5] **Bayle,** *Dictionnaire historique et critique* (Historical and Critical Dictionary), art. Epicurus.

[6] **Schaubach,** *On Epicurus' Astronomical Concepts* [in German], in *Archiv für Philologie und Pädagogik,* V, 4, [1839,] p. 549.

[7] **Lucretius,** *On the Nature of Things,* II, 251 ff. Again, if all movement is always interconnected, the new rising from the old in a determinate order ... what is the source of the free will?

[8] **Aristotle,** *On the Soul,* I, 4 [409 [a], 1-5]. How are we to imagine a unit [monad] being moved? By what agency? What sort of movement can be attributed to what is without parts or internal differences? If the unit is both originative of movement and itself capable of being moved, it must contain differences. *Further, since they say a moving line generates a surface and a moving point a line, the movements of the psychic units must be lines.*

[9] **Diogenes Laertius,** X, 43. The atoms are in *continual* motion.

    Simplicius, l.c., p. 424. ... the followers of Epicurus ... [taught] *eternal* motion.

[10] **Lucretius,** *On the Nature of Things,* II, 251, 253-255. ... if the atoms never swerve so as to originate some new movement that will snap the bonds of fate, the everlasting sequence of cause and effect....

[11] **Ibid.,** II, 279-280. ... there is within the human breast something that can fight against this force and resist it.

[12] **Cicero,** *On the Highest Goods and Evils,* I, vi [19-20]. ... yet he does not attain the object for the sake of which this fiction was devised. For, if all the atoms swerve, none will ever come to cohere together; or if some swerve while others travel in a straight line, by their own natural tendency, in the first place this will be tantamount to assigning to the atoms their different spheres of action, some to travel straight and some sideways....

[13] **Lucretius,** l.c., 293.

[14] **Cicero,** *On Fate,* x [22]. ... when the atom swerves sideways a minimal space, termed [by Epicurus] *elachiston* [the smallest].

[15] **Ibid.** Also he is compelled to profess in reality, if not quite explicitly, that this swerve takes place without cause....

[16] **Plutarch,** *On the Creation of the Soul,* VI (VI, p. 8, stereotyped edition). For they do not agree with Epicurus that the atom swerves somewhat, since he introduces a motion without cause out of the non-being.

[17] **Cicero,** *On the Highest Goods and Evils,* I, vi [19]. The swerving is itself an arbitrary fiction (for Epicurus says *the atoms swerve without a cause, yet this is a capital offence in a natural philosopher, to speak of something taking place uncaused*). Then also he gratuitously deprives the atoms of what he himself declared to be the natural motion of all heavy bodies, namely, movement in a straight line downwards....

[18] **Bayle,** l.c.

[19] **Augustine,** Letter 56.

[20] **Diogenes Laertius,** X, 128. For the end of all our actions is to be free from pain and fear.

[21] **Plutarch,** *That Epicurus Actually Makes a Pleasant Life Impossible,* 1091. Epicurus too makes a similar statement to the effect that the Good is a thing that arises out of your very escape from evil....

[22] **Clement of Alexandria,** *The Miscellanies,* II, p. 415 [21]. ...Epicurus also says that the removal of pain is pleasure....

[23] **Seneca,** *On Benefits,* IV [,4, 1], p. 699. Yes, and therefore God does not give benefits, but, free from all care and unconcerned about us, he turns his back on the world... and benefits no more concern him than injuries....

[24] **Cicero,** *On the Nature of the Gods,* I, xxiv [68]. ... you gave us the formula just now—God has not body but a semblance of body, not blood but a kind of blood.

[25] **Ibid.,** xl [112, 115-116]. Well then, what meat and drink, what harmonies of music and flowers of various colours, what delights of touch and smell will you assign to the gods, so as to keep them steeped in pleasure?... Why, what reason have you for maintaining that men owe worship to the gods, if the gods not only pay no regard to men, but care for nothing and do nothing at all? "But deity possesses an excellence and pre-eminence which must of its own nature attract the worship of the wise." Now how can there be any excellence in a being so engrossed in the delights of his own pleasure that he always has been, is, and will continue to be entirely idle and inactive?

[26] **Plutarch,** *That Epicurus Actually Makes a Pleasant Life Impossible,* [1100-]1101. ...their theory ... does remove a certain superstitious fear; but it allows no joy and delight to come to us from the gods. Instead, it puts us in the same state of mind with regard to the gods, of neither being alarmed nor rejoicing, that we have regarding the Hyrcanian fish. We expect nothing from them either good or evil.

[27] **Aristotle,** *On the Heavens,* II, 12 [292^b, 4-6]. ...while the perfectly conditioned has no need of action, since it is itself the end....

[28] **Lucretius,** *On the Nature of Things,* II, 221, 223-224. If it were not for this swerve, everything would fall downwards like rain-drops through the abyss of space. No collision would take place and no impact of atom on atom would be created. Thus nature would never have created anything.

[29] **Ibid.,** II, 284-292. So also in the atoms ... besides weight and impact there must be a third cause of movement, the source of this inborn power of ours....
But the fact that the mind itself has no internal necessity to determine its every act and compel it to suffer in helpless passivity—this is due to the slight swerve of the atoms....

[30] **Aristotle,** *On the Heavens,* I, 7 [275^b, 30-276^a, 1]. If the whole is not continuous, but exists, as Democritus and Leucippus think, in the form of parts separated by void, there must necessarily be one movement of all the multitude. ... but their nature is one, like many pieces of gold separated from one another.

[31] **Ibid.,** III, 2 [300^b, 9-17]. Hence Leucippus and Democritus, who say that the primary bodies are in perpetual movement in the void or infinite, may be asked to explain the manner of their motion and the kind of movement which is natural to them. For if the various elements are constrained by one another to move as they do, each must still have a natural movement which the constrained contravenes, and the prime mover must cause motion not by constraint but naturally. If there is no ultimate natural cause of movement and each preceding term in the series is always moved by constraint, we shall have an infinite process.

[32] **Diogenes Laertius,** X, 150. Those animals which are incapable of making *covenants* with one another, to the end that they may neither inflict nor suffer harm, *are without either justice or injustice.* And those tribes which either could not or would not form mutual covenants to the same end are in like case. There never was an absolute justice, but only an agreement made in reciprocal intercourse, in whatever localities, now and again, from time to time, providing against the infliction or suffering of harm.

33)^a

---

^{a} Notes 32) and 33) were later added to the text by Marx. The text of Note 33) was not inserted.—*Ed.*

Chapter Two

THE QUALITIES OF THE ATOM

[1] **Diogenes Laertius,** X, 54. For every quality changes, but the atoms do not change.

Lucretius, *On the Nature of Things,* II, 861-863. They must be kept far apart from the atoms, if we wish to provide the universe with imperishable foundations on which it may rest secure....

[2] **(Plutarch,)** *On the Sentiments of the Philosophers* [I, 3]. Epicurus ... affirms that ... bodies are subject to these three accidents, shape, size and weight. Democritus [acknowledged] but two: size and shape. Epicurus added the third, to wit, weight, for he pronounced that it is necessary ... that bodies receive their motion from that impulsion which springs from weight.... Comp. **Sextus Empiricus,** *Against the Professors,* p. 421 [X, 240].

[3] **Eusebius,** *Preparation for the Gospel,* XIV, p. 749 [14].

[4] **Simplicius,** l.c., p. 362. ...giving (i.e., Democritus) them (i.e., the atoms) the difference with regard to size and shape....

[5] **Philoponus,** ibid. He (Democritus) assigns a unique common nature of the body to all shapes; its parts are the atoms, which differ from each other in size and shape; for they have not only different shape but some of them are bigger, the others smaller.

[6] **Aristotle,** *On Becoming and Decaying,* I, 8 [326^a, 10]. ...and yet he [Democritus] says "the more any indivisible exceeds, the heavier it is".

[7] **Aristotle,** *On the Heavens,* I, 7 [276^a, 1-2, 4-7]. But each piece must, as we assert, have the same motion.... So that if it be weight that all possess, no body is, strictly speaking, light; and if lightness be universal, none is heavy. Moreover, whatever possesses weight or lightness will have its place either at one of the extremes or in the middle region.

[8] **Ritter,** *History of Ancient Philosophy* [in German], I, p. 568, Note 2 [2^d improved edition, 1836, p. 602, Note 2].

[9] **Aristotle,** *Metaphysics,* VIII, 2 [1042^b, 11-14]. Democritus seems to think there are three kinds of difference between things [atoms]; the underlying body, the matter, is one and the same, but they differ either in rhythm, i. e. shape, or in turning, i. e. position, or in inter-contact, i. e. order.

[10] **Ibid.,** I, 4 [985^b, 4-19]. Leucippus and his associate Democritus say that the full and the empty are the elements, calling the one being and the other non-being—the full and solid being being, the empty non-being (whence they say being no more is than non-being, because the solid no more is than the empty); and they make these the material causes of things. And as those who make the underlying substance one generate all other things by its modifications, supposing the rare and the dense to be the sources of modifications, in the same way these philosophers say the differences in the elements are the causes of all other qualities. These differences, they say, are three—shape and order and position. For they say the real is differentiated only by "rhythm" and "inter-contact" and "turning"; and of these rhythm is shape, inter-contact is order, and turning is position; for A differs from N in shape, AN from NA in order, and Z from N in position.

[11] **Diogenes Laertius,** X, 44. ...atoms have no quality at all except shape, *size* and weight. ... further, that they are not of any and every *size*; at any rate no atom has ever been seen by our senses.

[12] **Ibid.,** X, 56. But to attribute *any* and every size to the atoms does not help to explain the differences of quality in things; moreover, in that case atoms would exist large enough to be perceived by us, which is never observed to occur; nor can we conceive how such an occurrence should be possible, i. e., that an atom should become visible.

[13] **Ibid.,** X, 55. Again, you should not suppose that the atoms have any and every size ... but *some* differences of size must be admitted.

[14] **Ibid.,** X, 59. On the analogy of things within our experience we have declared that the atom has size; and this, small as it is, we have merely reproduced on a larger scale.

[15] Comp. **ibid.,** X, 58. **Stobaeus,** *Physical Selections*, I, p. 27.

[16] **Epicurus,** *Fragments* (On Nature, II and XI), collected by Rosinius, ed. by Orelli, p. 26.

[17] **Eusebius,** *Preparation for the Gospel*, XIV, p. 773 (Paris ed.). But they differed in that one of them (i.e., Epicurus) assumed that all atoms were infinitely small and could therefore not be perceived, while Democritus assumed that some large atoms existed too.

[18] **Stobaeus,** *Physical Selections*, I, 17. Democritus even says ... that an atom is possible as large as the world. Comp. **(Plutarch,)** *On the Sentiments of the Philosophers*, I, p. 235 [I, 3].

[19] **Aristotle,** *On Becoming and Decaying*, I, 8 [324^b, 30]. ... invisible ... owing to their minuteness....

[20] **Eusebius,** *Preparation for the Gospel*, XIV, p. 749. Democritus ... [assumed] as the principles of the things indivisible ... bodies perceptible through reason.... Comp. **(Plutarch,)** *On the Sentiments of the Philosophers*, I, p. 235 [3].

[21] **Diogenes Laertius,** X, 54. Moreover, we must hold that the atoms in fact possess none of the qualities belonging to the world which come under our observation, except *shape*, weight, and size, and the properties necessarily conjoined with *shape*. Comp. § 44.

[22] **Ibid.,** X, 42. Furthermore, the atoms ... vary indefinitely in their shapes.

[23] **Ibid.,** X, 42. ... but the variety of shapes, though indefinitely larger, is not absolutely infinite.

[24] **Lucretius,** *On the Nature of Things*, II, 513-514. ... you must acknowledge a corresponding limit to the different forms of matter.
   Eusebius, *Preparation for the Gospel*, XIV, p. 749. Epicurus ... [says] ... that the shapes of the atoms themselves are limited, and not infinite.... Comp. **(Plutarch,)** *On the Sentiments of the Philosophers*, l.c.

[25] **Diogenes Laertius,** X, 42. The like atoms of each shape are absolutely infinite.
   Lucretius, *On the Nature of Things*, II, 525-528. Since the varieties of form are limited, the number of uniform atoms must be unlimited. Otherwise the totality of matter would be finite, which I have proved in my verses is not so.

[26] **Aristotle,** *On the Heavens*, III, 4 [303^a, 3-5, 10-15]. There is, further, another view — that of Leucippus and Democritus of Abdera — the implications of which

are also unacceptable.... and further, they say that since the atomic bodies differ in shape, and there is an infinity of shapes, there is an infinity of simple bodies. But they have never explained in detail the shapes of the various elements, except so, far as to allot the sphere to fire. Air, water and the rest....

Philoponus, l.c. They have ... not only entirely different shapes....

[27)] **Lucretius,** *On the Nature of Things,* II, 474-484, 491-492, 495-497. ... the number of different forms of atoms is finite. If it were not so, some of the atoms would have to be of infinite magnitude. Within the narrow limits of any single particle, there can be only a limited range of forms....
... if you wish to vary its form still further ... the arrangement will demand still other parts.... Variation in shape goes with increase in size. You cannot believe, therefore, that the atoms are distinguished by an infinity of forms....

[28)] Comp. Note 25).

[29)] **Diogenes Laertius,** X, 44 and 54.

[30)] **Brucker,** *Institutions of the History of Philosophy* [Latin, 1747], p. 224.

[31)] **Lucretius,** *On the Nature of Things,* I, 1051-1052. 0, Memmius, here you must give up fully the belief that all things strive — as they say — to the middle of the world.

[32)] **Diogenes Laertius,** X, 43. The atoms move with equal speed, since the void makes way for the lightest and heaviest alike through all eternity.... 61. When they are travelling through the void and meet with no resistance, the atoms must move with equal speed. Neither will heavy atoms travel more quickly than small and light ones, so long as nothing meets them, nor will small atoms travel more quickly than large ones, provided they always find a passage suitable to their size; and provided that they meet with no obstruction.

Lucretius, *On the Nature of Things,* II, 235-239. But empty space can offer no resistance to any object in any quarter at any time, so as not to yield free passage as its own nature demands. Therefore, through undisturbed vacuum all bodies must travel at equal speed though impelled by unequal weights.

[33)] Comp. Ch. 3.

[34)] **Feuerbach,** *History of the Newer Philosophy.* [1833, quotations from] **Gassendi,** l. c., XXXIII, No. 7. Although Epicurus had perhaps never thought about this experiment, he [still] reached, led by reason, the same opinion about atoms that experiment has recently taught us. This opinion is that all bodies..., although very different in weight and bulk, have the same velocity when they fall from above to below. Thus he was of opinion that all atoms, however much they may differ in size and weight, move with an equal velocity.

Chapter Three
''Ατομοι ἀρχαί AND ἄτομα στοιχεῖα

[1)] *Ametocha kenou* (ἀμέτοχα κενοῦ) [**Stobaeus,** *Physical Selections,* I, p. 306] does not at all mean "*do not fill space*", but "*have no part of the void*", it is the same as what at another place *Diogenes Laertius* says: "though they are without distinction of parts". In the same way we must explain this expression in **(Plutarch,)** *On the Sentiments of the Philosophers,* I, p. 236, and **Simplicius,** p. 405.

2) This also is a wrong consequence. That which cannot be divided in space is not therefore outside of space or without spatial relation.

3) **Schaubach,** l.c., [p]p. [549-]550.

4) **Diogenes Laertius,** X, 44.

5) **Ibid.,** X, 67. But it is impossible to conceive anything that is *incorporeal* as self-existent, except *empty space.*

6) **Ibid.,** X, 39, 40 and 41.

7) **Ibid.,** VII, [Ch.] 1 [134]. There is a difference, according to them (i. e., the Stoics), between principles and elements; the former being without generation or destruction, whereas the elements are destroyed when all things are resolved into fire.

8) **Aristotle,** *Metaphysics,* IV, 1 and 3.

9) Comp. l. c.

10) **Ibid.,** V, 3[1014^a, 31-34; 1014^b, 5-6]. Similarly those who speak of the elements of bodies mean the things into which bodies are ultimately divided, while they are no longer divided into other things differing in kind; ... for which reason what is small and simple and indivisible is called an element.

11) **Ibid.,** I, 4.

12) **Diogenes Laertius,** X, 54.
Plutarch, *Reply to Colotes,* 1110. ... that this view is as inseparable from Epicurus' theories as shape and weight are by their (i.e., the Epicureans) own assertion inseparable from the atom.

13) **Sextus Empiricus,** *Against the Professors,* p. 420.

14) **Eusebius,** *Preparation for the Gospel,* XIV, p. 773. ... Epicurus ... [assumed that] they [i.e., the atoms] cannot be perceived.... P. 749. ... but they [i.e., the atoms] have their own shape perceivable by reason.

15) **(Plutarch,)** *On the Sentiments of the Philosophers,* I, p. 246 [7]. The same (Epicurus) asserts that there are four other natural beings which are immortal—of this sort are atoms, the vacuum, the infinite and the similar parts; and these last are [called] homoeomerias and likewise elements. 12. Epicurus [thinks that] bodies are not to be limited, but the first bodies are simple bodies, and all those composed of them possess weight....
Stobaeus, *Physical Selections,* I, p. 52. Metrodorus, the teacher of Epicurus, [says] ... that the causes, however, are the atoms and elements. P. 5. Epicurus [assumes] ... four substances essentially indestructible: the atoms, the void, the infinite and the similar parts, and these are called homoeomerias and elements.

16) Comp. l.c.

17) **Cicero,** *On the Highest Goods and Evils,* I, vi. ... that which he follows ... the atoms, the void ... infinity itself, that they [i.e., the Epicureans] call *apeiria....*
Diogenes Laertius, X, 41. Again, the sum of things is infinite.... Moreover, the sum of things is unlimited both by reason of the multitude of the atoms and the extent of the void.

18) **Plutarch,** *Reply to Colotes,* 1114. Now look at the sort of first principles [you people adopt] to account for generation: infinity and the void—the void incapable of action, incapable of being acted upon, bodiless; the infinite disordered, irrational, incapable of formulation, disrupting and confounding itself because of a multiplicity that defies control or limitation.

19) **Simplicius,** l.c., p. 488.

20) **(Plutarch,)** *On the Sentiments of the Philosophers*, p. 239 [I, 5]. But Metrodorus says ... that the number of worlds is infinite, and this can be seen from the fact that the number of causes is infinite.... But the causes are the atoms or the elements.

　　Stobaeus, *Physical Selections*, I, p. 52. Metrodorus, the teacher of Epicurus, [says] ... that the causes, however, are the atoms and elements.

21) **Lucretius,** *On the Nature of Things*, I, 820-821. For the same elements compose sky, sea and lands, rivers and sun, crops, trees and animals....

　　Diogenes Laertius, X, 39. Moreover, the sum total of things was always such as it is now, and such it will ever remain. For there is nothing into which it can change. For outside the sum of things there is nothing which could enter into it and bring about the change.... The whole of being consists of bodies.... 41. These elements are indivisible and unchangeable, and necessarily so, if things are not all to be destroyed and pass into non-existence, but are to be strong enough to endure when the composite bodies are broken up, because they possess a solid nature and are incapable of being anywhere or anyhow dissolved.

22) **Diogenes Laertius,** X, 73. ... and all things are again dissolved, some faster, some slower, some through the action of one set of causes, others through the action of others. 74. It is clear, then, that he [Epicurus] also makes the worlds perishable, as their parts are subject to change.

　　Lucretius, V, 109-110. May reason rather than the event itself convince you that the whole world can collapse with one ear-splitting crack!

　　Ibid., V, 373-375. It follows, then, that the doorway of death is not barred to sky and sun and earth and the sea's unfathomed floods. It lies tremendously open and confronts them with a yawning chasm.

23) **Simplicius,** l.c., p. 425.

24) **Lucretius,** II, 796. ...and the atoms do not emerge into the light....

Chapter Four

TIME

1) **Aristotle,** *Physics*, VIII, 1 [251^b, 15-17]. ...in fact, it is just this that enables Democritus to show that all things cannot have had a becoming; for time, he says, is uncreated.

2) **Simplicius,** l.c., p. 426. Democritus was so strongly convinced that time is eternal, that, in order to show that not all things have an origin, he considered it evident that time has no origin.

3) **Lucretius,** I, 459, 462-463. Similarly, time by itself does not exist.... It must not be claimed that anyone can sense time by itself apart from the movement of things or their restful immobility.

　　Ibid., I, 479-482. So you may see that events cannot be said to be by themselves like matter or in the same sense as space. Rather, you should describe them as accidents of matter, or of the place in which things happen.

　　Sextus Empiricus, *Against the Professors*, p. 420. Here Epicurus calls time accident of accidents (*symptoma symptomaton*).

Stobaeus, *Physical Selections,* I, 8. Epicurus [calls time] an accident, i.e., something that accompanies motions.

[4] **Diogenes Laertius,** X, 72. There is another thing which we must consider carefully. We must not investigate time as we do the other accidents which we investigate in a subject, namely, by referring them to the preconceptions envisaged in our minds; but we must take into account the plain fact itself, in virtue of which we speak of time as long or short, linking to it in intimate connection this attribute of duration. We need not adopt any fresh terms as preferable, but should employ the usual expression about it. Nor need we predicate anything else of time, as if this something else contained the same essence as is contained in the proper meaning of the word "time" (for this also is done by some). We must chiefly reflect upon that to which we attach this peculiar character of time, and by which we measure it. 73. No further proof is required: we have only to reflect that we attach the attribute of time to days and nights and their parts, and likewise to feelings of pleasure and pain and to neutral states, to states of movement and states of rest, conceiving a peculiar accident of these to be this very characteristic which we express by the word "time". He [i.e., Epicurus] says this both in the second book *On Nature* and in the *Larger Epitome.*

[5] **Lucretius,** *On the Nature of Things,* l.c.

Sextus Empiricus, *Against the Professors,* p. 420 [X, 238, 240, 241, 244]. ... accident of accidents.... For this reason Epicurus compels us to think that an existing body consists of non-existing bodies, since he says that we have to think of the body as a composition of size and shape, resistance and weight.... Hence there must be accidents for time to exist, but for accidents to be present themselves there must be an underlying circumstance. However, if no underlying circumstance exists, then there can be no time.... When this therefore is time, and Epicurus says that accidents are the nature [of time], then time, according to Epicurus, must be its own accident. Comp. **Stobaeus,** l.c.

[6] **Diogenes Laertius,** X, 46. Again, there are outlines or films, which are of the same shape as solid bodies, but of a thinness far exceeding that of any object that we see.... To these films we give the name of "images" or "idols".... 48. ... the production of the images is as quick as thought ... though no diminution of the bodies is observed, because other particles take their place. And those given off retain the position and arrangement which their atoms had when they formed part of the solid bodies....

Lucretius, IV, 30-32. ..."images" of things, a sort of outer skin perpetually peeled off the surface of objects and flying about this way and that through the air.

Ibid., IV, 51-52. ... because each particular floating image wears the aspect and form of the object from whose body it has emanated.

[7] **Diogenes Laertius,** X, 49. We must also consider that it is by the entrance of something coming from external objects that we see their shapes and think of them. For external things would not stamp on us their own nature ... so well as by *the entrance into our eyes* or minds, to whichever their size is suitable, of certain films coming from the things themselves, these films or outlines being of the same colour and shape as the external things themselves.... 50. [...] and this again explains why they present the appearance of a single continuous object and retain the mutual interconnection which they had with the object.... 52. Again, *hearing* takes place when a current passes from the object, whether person or thing, which emits voice or sound or noise, or produces the sensation of hearing in any way whatever. This

current is broken up into homogeneous particles, which at the same time preserve a certain mutual connection.... 53. ... Again, we must believe that *smelling*, like hearing, would produce no sensation, were there not particles conveyed from the object which are of the proper sort for exciting the organ of smelling.

   [8] **Lucretius,** *On the Nature of Things,* II, 1145-1146. It is natural, therefore, that everything should perish when it is thinned out....

Chapter Five
THE METEORS

[1] **Diogenes Laertius,** II, 3, 10.

[2] **Aristotle,** *Metaphysics,* I, 5 [986^b, 25]. The One is God.

[3] **Aristotle,** *On the Heavens,* I, 3 [270^b, 4-24]. Our theory seems to confirm experience and to be confirmed by it. For all men have some conception of the nature of gods, and all who believe in the existence of gods at all, whether barbarian or Greek, agree in allotting the highest place to the deity, surely because they suppose that immortal is linked with immortal and regard any other supposition as inconceivable. If then there is, as there certainly is, anything divine, what we have just said about the primary bodily substance was well said. The mere evidence of the senses is enough to convince us of this at least with human certainty. For in the whole range of time past, so far as our inherited records reach, no change appears to have taken place either in the whole scheme of the outermost heaven or in any of its proper parts. The common name, too, which has been handed down from our distant ancestors even to our own day, seems to show that they conceived of it in the fashion which we have been expressing. The same ideas, one must believe, recur to men's minds not once or twice but again and again. And so, implying that the primary body is something else beyond earth, fire, air and water, they gave to the highest place a name of its own, *aither,* derived from the fact that it "runs always" (*thein aei,* ϑεῖν ἀει) for an eternity of time.

[4] **Ibid.,** II, 1 [284^a, 11-15, 284^b, 2-5]. The ancients gave the Gods the heaven or upper place, as being alone immortal; and our present argument testifies that it is indestructible and ungenerated. Further, it is unaffected by any mortal discomfort ... it is not only more appropriate so to conceive of its eternity, but also on this hypothesis alone are we able to advance a theory consistent with popular divinations of the divine nature.

[5] **Aristotle,** *Metaphysics,* XI (XII), 8 [1074^a, 31, 38-1074^b, 3]. Evidently there is but one heaven.... Our forefathers in the most remote ages have handed down to their posterity a tradition, in the form of a myth, that these bodies are gods and that the divine encloses the whole of nature. The rest of the tradition has been added later in a mythical form with a view to the persuasion of the multitude and to its legal and utilitarian expediency; they say these gods are in the form of men or like some of the other animals, and they say other things consequent on and similar to those which we have mentioned. But if one were to separate the first point from these additions and take it alone that they thought the first substances to be gods, one must regard this as an inspired utterance; and reflect that, while probably each art and each science has often been developed as far as possible and has again perished, these opinions, with others, have been preserved until the present like relics of the ancient treasure.

6) **Diogenes Laertius**, X, 81. There is yet one more point to seize, namely, that the greatest anxiety of the human mind arises through the belief that the heavenly bodies are blessed and indestructible, and that at the same time they have volitions and actions ... inconsistent with this belief ... apprehending some evil because of the myths....

7) **Ibid.**, X, 76. Nay more, we are bound to believe that in the sky revolution, solstices, eclipses, risings and settings, and the like, take place without the ministration or command, either now or in the future, of any being who at the same time enjoys perfect bliss along with immortality. 77. For troubles and anxieties ... do not accord with bliss, but always imply weakness and fear and dependence upon one's neighbours. Nor, again, must we hold that things which are no more than globular masses of fire, being at the same time endowed with bliss, assume these motions at will.... Otherwise such inconsistency will of itself suffice to produce the worst disturbance in our minds.

8) **Aristotle**, *On the Heavens*, II, 1 [284^a, 18-20]. Hence we must not believe the old tale which says that the world needs some Atlas to keep it safe.

9) **Diogenes Laertius**, X, 85. So you (i.e., Pythocles) will do well to take and learn them and get them up quickly along with the short epitome in my letter to Herodotus.

10) **Ibid.**, X, 85. In the first place, remember that, like everything else, knowledge of celestial phenomena, whether taken along with other things or in isolation, as well as of the other sciences, has no other end in view than peace of mind and firm conviction.

Ibid., X, 82. But mental tranquillity means being released from all these troubles and cherishing a continual remembrance of the highest and most important truths.

11) **Ibid.**, X, 87. For our life has no need now of ideologies and false opinions; our one need is untroubled existence.

Ibid., X, 78. Further, we must hold that to arrive at accurate knowledge of the cause of things of most moment is the business of natural science, and that happiness depends on this (viz. on the knowledge of celestial phenomena).

Ibid., X, 79. There is nothing in the knowledge of risings and settings and solstices and eclipses and all kindred subjects that contributes to our happiness; but those who are well informed about such matters and yet are ignorant what the heavenly bodies really are, and what are the most important causes of phenomena, feel quite as much fear as those who have no such special information — nay, perhaps even greater fear.

12) **Ibid.**, X, 86. We do not seek to wrest by force what is impossible, nor to understand all matters equally well, nor make our treatment always as clear as when we discuss human life or explain the principles of ethics in general ... for instance, that the whole of being consists of bodies and intangible nature, or that the ultimate elements of things are indivisible, or any other proposition which admits only one explanation of the phenomena to be possible. But this is not the case with celestial phenomena.

13) **Ibid.**, X, 86. These at any rate admit of manifold causes for their occurrence and manifold accounts, none of them contradictory of sensation, of their nature.

For in the study of nature [physiology] we must not conform to empty assumptions and arbitrary laws, but follow the promptings of the facts.

14) **Ibid.**, X, 92.

15) **Ibid.**, X, 94.

16) **Ibid.**, X, 95 and 96.

17) **Ibid.**, X, 98.

18) **Ibid.**, X, 104. And [says Epicurus] there are several other ways in which thunderbolts may possibly be produced. Exclusion of myth is the sole condition necessary; and it will be excluded, if one properly attends to the facts and hence draws inferences to interpret what is obscure.

19) **Ibid.**, X, 80. When, therefore, we investigate the causes of celestial phenomena, as of all that is unknown, we must take into account the variety of ways in which analogous occurrences happen within our experience.

Ibid., X, 82. But mental tranquillity means being released from all these troubles.... Hence we must attend to present feelings and sense perceptions, whether those of mankind in general or those peculiar to the individual, and also attend to all the clear evidence available, as given by each of the standards of truth. For by studying them we shall rightly trace to its cause and banish the source of disturbance and dread, accounting for celestial phenomena and for all other things which from time to time befall us and cause the utmost alarm to the rest of mankind.

Ibid., X, 87. Some phenomena within our experience afford evidence by which we may interpret what goes on in the heavens. We see how the former really take place, but not how the celestial phenomena take place, for their occurrence may possibly be due to a variety of causes. [88.] However, we must observe each fact as presented, and further separate from it all the facts presented along with it, the occurrence of which from various causes is not contradicted by facts within our experience.

20) **Ibid.**, X, 78. Further, we must recognise on such points as this plurality of causes or contingency....

Ibid., X, 86. These [celestial phenomena] at any rate admit of manifold causes for their occurrence....

Ibid., X, 87. All things go on uninterruptedly, if all be explained by the method of plurality of causes ... so soon as we duly understand what may be plausibly alleged respecting them....

21) **Ibid.**, X, 98. Whereas those who adopt only one explanation are in conflict with the facts and are utterly mistaken as to the way in which man can attain knowledge.

Ibid., X, 113. To assign a single cause for these effects when the facts suggest several causes is madness and a strange inconsistency; yet it is done by adherents of rash astrology, who assign meaningless causes for the stars whenever they persist in saddling the divinity with burdensome tasks.

Ibid., X, 97. And further, let the regularity of their orbits be explained in the same way as certain ordinary incidents within our own experience; the divine nature must not on any account be adduced to explain this, but must be kept free from the task and in perfect bliss. Unless this be done, the whole study of celestial phenomena will be in vain, as indeed it has proved to be with some who did not lay hold of a possible method, but fell into the folly of supposing that these events happen in one single way only and of rejecting all the others which are possible, suffering themselves to be carried into the realm of the unintelligible, and being unable to take a comprehensive view of the facts which must be taken as clues to the rest.

Ibid., X, 93. ...unmoved by the servile artifices of the astrologers.

Ibid., X, 87. ...we clearly fall away from the study of nature altogether and tumble into myth.

Ibid., X, 80. Therefore we must ... investigate the causes of celestial phenomena, as of all that is unknown, [...] while as for those who do not recognise the difference between what is or comes about from a single cause and that which may be the effect of any one of several causes, overlooking the fact that the objects are only seen at a distance, and are moreover ignorant of the conditions that render, or do not render, peace of mind impossible — all such persons we must treat with contempt.

[22] **Ibid.,** X, 80. We must not suppose that our treatment of these matters fails of accuracy, so far as it is needful to ensure our tranquillity and happiness.

[23] **Ibid.,** X, 78. ... but we must hold that nothing suggestive of conflict or disquiet is compatible with an immortal and blessed nature. And the mind can grasp the absolute truth of this.

[24] Comp. **Aristotle,** *On the Heavens,* I, 10.

[25] **Ibid.,** I, 10 [279^b, 25-26]. Suppose that the world was formed out of elements which were formerly otherwise conditioned than as they are now. Then ... if their condition was always so and could not have been otherwise, the world could never have come into being.

[26] **Athenaeus,** *Banquet of the Learned,* III, 104. ... One ... must with good reason approve the noble Chrysippus for his shrewd comprehension of Epicurus' "Nature", and his remark that the very centre of the Epicurean philosophy is the *Gastrology* of Archestratus....

[27] **Lucretius,** *On the Nature of Things,* I, 63-70, 79-80.

Appendix

CRITIQUE OF PLUTARCH'S POLEMIC
AGAINST THE THEOLOGY OF EPICURUS

I. THE RELATIONSHIP OF MAN TO GOD

1. Fear and the Being Beyond

[1] **Plutarch,** *That Epicurus Actually Makes a Pleasant Life Impossible* (published by Xylander), II, 1100. ...one point, that of pleasure they derive from these views, has, I should say, been dealt with (i.e., from Epicurus): ... their theory ... does remove a certain superstitious fear; but it allows no joy and delight to come to us from the gods.

[2] **[Holbach,]** *System of Nature* (London, 1770), II, p. 9.[32] The idea of such powerful agencies has always been associated with that of terror; their name always reminded man of his own calamities or those of his fathers; we tremble today because our ancestors have trembled for thousands of years. The idea of Divinity always awakens in us distressing ideas ... our present fears and lugubrious thoughts ... rise every time before our mind when we hear his name. Comp. p. 79. When man bases morality on the not too moral character of a God who changes his behaviour, then he can never know what he owes to God nor what he owes to himself or to others. Nothing therefore could be more dangerous than to persuade man that a being superior to nature exists, a being before whom reason must be silent and to whom man must sacrifice all to receive happiness.

[3] **Plutarch,** l.c., 1101. For since they fear him [God] as a ruler mild to the good and hating the wicked, by this one fear, which keeps them from doing wrong, they are freed from the many that attend on crime, and since they keep their viciousness within themselves, where it gradually as it were dies down, they are less tormented than those who make free with it and venture on overt acts, only to be filled at once with terror and regret.

2. Cult and the Individual

[4] **Plutarch,** l.c., 1101. No, wherever it [i.e., the soul] believes and conceives most firmly that the god is present, there more than anywhere else it puts away all feelings of pain, of fear and of worry, and gives itself up so far to pleasure that it indulges in a playful and merry inebriation, in amatory matters....

[5] **Ibid.,** l.c.

[6] **Ibid.,** l.c., 1102. For it is not the abundance of wine or the roast meats that cheer the heart at festivals, but good hope and the belief in the benign presence of the god and his gracious acceptance of what is done.

3. Providence and the Degraded God

[7] **Plutarch,** l.c., 1102. ... how great their pleasures are, since their beliefs about God are purified from error: that he is our guide to all blessings, the father of everything honourable, and that he may no more do than suffer anything base. For he is good, and in none that is good arises envy about aught or fear or anger or hatred; for it is as much the function of heat to chill instead of warm as it is of good to harm. By its nature anger is farthest removed from favour, wrath from goodwill, and from love of man and kindliness, hostility and the spreading of terror; for the one set belong to virtue and power, the other to weakness and vice. Consequently it is not true that Heaven is prey to feelings of anger and favour; rather, because it is God's nature to bestow favour and lend aid, it is not his nature to be angry and do harm....

[8] **Ibid.** Do you think that deniers of providence require any other punishment, and are not adequately punished when they extirpate from themselves so great a pleasure and delight?

[9]a "But he is not a *weak* intellect who does not know an objective God, but he who *wants* to know one." *Schelling,* "Philosophical Letters on Dogmatism and Criticism" [in German] in *Philosophische Schriften,* Vol. I, Landshut, 1809, p. 127, Letter II.

Herr Schelling should at any rate be advised to give again some thought to his first writings. For example, we read in his essay "on the Ego as principle of philosophy":

For example, let us assume *God,* insofar as he is determined as object, "as the *real foundation* of our cognition, then he belongs *himself,* insofar as he is object, in the *sphere of our cognition,* and therefore cannot be for us the ultimate point on which this entire sphere is suspended" (l.c., p. 5).

Finally, we remind Herr Schelling of the last words of the letter from which we have just quoted:

"*The time has come* to proclaim to the *better part* of humanity the *freedom of minds,* and *not to tolerate any longer that they deplore the loss of their fetters*". P. 129, l.c.

When the time already had come in 1795, how about the year 1841?[33]

We might bring up for this occasion a theme that has well-nigh become notorious, namely, the *proofs of the existence of God.* Hegel has turned all these theological demonstrations upside-down, that is, he has rejected them in order to justify them. What kind of clients are those whom the defending lawyer can only save from conviction by killing them himself? For instance, Hegel interpreted the conclusion from the world to God as meaning: "Since the accidental does *not* exist, God or Absolute exists."[34] However, the theological demonstration is the opposite: "Since the accidental

---

a This Note 9) was subsequently inserted by Marx; italics in quotations from Schelling are mostly by Marx.— *Ed.*

has true being, God exists." God is the guarantee for the world of the accidental. It is obvious that with this the opposite also has been stated.

The proofs of the existence of God are either mere *hollow tautologies*. Take for instance the ontological proof. This only means:

"that which I conceive for myself in a real way (*realiter*), is a real concept for me",

something that works on me. In this sense *all gods*, the pagan as well as the Christian ones, have possessed a real existence.[a] Did not the ancient Moloch reign[b]? Was not the Delphic Apollo a real power in the life of the Greeks? Kant's critique[35] means nothing in this respect. If somebody imagines that he has a hundred talers, if this concept is not for him an arbitrary, subjective one, if he believes in it, then these hundred imagined talers have for him the same value as a hundred real ones. For instance, he will incur debts on the strength of his imagination, his imagination will *work, in the same way as all humanity has incurred debts on its gods.* The contrary is true. Kant's example might have enforced the ontological proof. Real talers have the same existence that the imagined gods have. Has a real taler any existence except in the imagination, if only in the general or rather common imagination of man?[36] Bring paper money into a country where this use of paper is unknown, and everyone will laugh at your subjective imagination. Come with your gods into a country where other gods are worshipped, and you will be shown to suffer from fantasies and abstractions. And justly so. He who would have brought a Wendic[37] god to the ancient Greeks would have found the proof of this god's non-existence. Indeed, for the Greeks he did not exist. *That which a particular country is for particular alien gods, the country of reason is for God in general, a region in which he ceases to exist.*[c]

As to the second alternative, that such proofs are *proofs of the existence of essential human self-consciousness, logical explanations of it,* take for example the ontological proof. Which being is immediate when made the subject of thought? Self-consciousness.

Taken in this sense all proofs of the existence of God are proofs

---

[a] "Existence" corrected from "power".— *Ed.*

[b] After "reign" the words "to whom human sacrifices were offered" were crossed out.— *Ed.*

[c] "He ceases to exist" corrected from "his non-existence is demonstrated".— *Ed.*

of his *non-existence*. They are *refutations* of all concepts of a God. The true proofs should have the opposite character: "Since nature has been badly constructed, God exists", "Because the world is without reason, therefore God exists", "Because there is no thought, there is God". But what does that say, except that, *for whom the world appears without reason, hence who is without reason himself, for him God exists? Or lack of reason is the existence of God.*

"... when you presuppose the *idea* of an *objective God*, how can you talk of *laws* that *reason* produces *out of itself*, since *autonomy* can only belong to an *absolutely free being.*" Schelling, l.c., p. 198 [Letter X].

"It is a crime against humanity to hide principles that can be generally communicated." Ibid., p. 199.

DRAFT OF NEW PREFACE[38]

The treatise that I herewith submit to the public is an old piece of work and was originally intended as part of a comprehensive exposition of Epicurean, Stoic, and Sceptic philosophy.[a] At present, however, political and philosophical arrangements of an entirely different kind prevent me from bringing such a task to completion.[b]

Only now the time has come in which the systems of the Epicureans, Stoics and Sceptics can be understood. They are the *philosophers of self-consciousness*. These lines will at any rate show how little has so far been achieved towards solving this problem.

Written in late 1841 and early 1842

Published in: Marx/Engels, *Gesamtausgabe*, Abt. 1, Bd. 1, Hb. 2, 1929

Printed according to the manuscript

Published in English for the first time

---

[a] The following passage is crossed out in the manuscript: "Since in the meantime political as well as philosophical work of more immediate interest prevents for the time being my finishing a complete exposition of these philosophies—since I do not know when I shall again have the opportunity to return to this subject—I am content to...." — *Ed.*

[b] The following passage is crossed out in the manuscript: "The Epicurean, Stoic, Sceptic philosophy, the *philosophies of self-consciousness* were just as much underestimated up to now by the philosophers as unspeculative and by the learned schoolmasters who *also* write history of philosophy as...." — *Ed.*

Draft of the preface to *Difference Between the Democritean and Epicurean Philosophy of Nature*

COMMENTS ON THE LATEST PRUSSIAN
CENSORSHIP INSTRUCTION [39]

We are not one of those malcontents who, even before the appearance of the new Prussian censorship decree, exclaim: *Timeo Danaos et dona ferentes.*[a] On the contrary, since an examination of already promulgated laws is approved in the new instruction, even if it should prove not to agree with the government's views, we are making a start with this at once. *Censorship* is *official criticism*; its standards are critical standards, hence they least of all can be exempted from criticism, being on the same plane as the latter.

Certainly everyone can only approve of the *general trend* expressed in the introduction to the instruction:

"In order *already now* to free the press from improper restrictions, which are against the intentions of the All-Highest, His Majesty the King, by a supreme order issued to the royal state ministry on the 10th of this month, has been pleased to disapprove expressly of any undue constraint on the activity of writers and, recognising the value and need of frank and decent publicity, has empowered us to direct the censors anew to due observance of Article II of the censorship decree of October 18, 1819."

Certainly! If censorship is a necessity, frank liberal censorship is still more necessary.

What might immediately arouse some surprise is the *date* of the law cited; it is dated October 18, 1819. What? Is it perhaps a law which conditions of time made it necessary to repeal? Apparently not; for the censors are only directed "*anew*" to ensure observance of it. Hence the law has existed until 1842, but it has not been observed, for it has been called to mind "in order *already now*" to

---

[a] I fear the Greeks, even when bringing gifts (Virgil, *Aeneid*, II, 49).— *Ed.*

free the press from improper restrictions, which are against the intentions of the All-Highest.

The press, *in spite of the law*, has until now been subjected to improper restrictions—that is the immediate conclusion to be drawn from this introduction.

Is this then an argument *against the law* or *against the censors*?

We *can* hardly assert the latter. For twenty-two years illegal actions have been committed by an authority which has in its charge the highest interest of the citizens, *their minds*, by an authority which regulates, even more than the Roman censors did, not only the behaviour of individual citizens, but even the behaviour of the public mind. Can such unscrupulous behaviour of the highest servants of the state, such a thoroughgoing lack of loyalty, be possible in the well-organised Prussian state, which is proud of its administration? Or has the state, in continual delusion, selected the most incapable persons for the most difficult posts? Or, finally, has the subject of the Prussian state no possibility of complaining against illegal actions? Are all Prussian writers so ignorant and foolish as to be unacquainted with the laws which concern their existence, or are they too cowardly to demand their observance?

If we put the blame on the *censors*, not only their own honour, but the honour of the Prussian state, and of the Prussian writers, is compromised.

Moreover, the more than twenty years of illegal behaviour of the censors in defiance of the law would provide *argumentum ad hominem*[a] that the press needs other guarantees than such general instructions for such irresponsible persons; it would provide the proof that there is a basic defect in the nature of the censorship which no law can remedy.

If, however, the censors were capable, and *the law was no good*, why appeal to it afresh for removal of the evil it has caused?

Or should, perhaps, the *objective defects* of an institution be ascribed to *individuals*, in order fraudulently to give the impression of an improvement without making any essential improvement? It is the habit of *pseudo-liberalism*, when compelled to make concessions, to sacrifice persons, the instruments, and to preserve the thing itself, the institution. In this way the attention of a superficial public is diverted.

Resentment against the thing itself becomes resentment against persons. It is believed that by a change of persons the thing itself

---

[a] Convincing proof (literally: an argument to the man).— *Ed.*

has been changed. Attention is deflected from the censorship to individual censors, and those petty writers of progress by command allow themselves petty audacities against those who have fallen out of favour and perform just as many acts of homage towards the government.

Yet another difficulty confronts us.

Some newspaper correspondents take the censorship instruction for the new censorship decree itself. They are mistaken, but their mistake is pardonable. The censorship decree of October 18, 1819, was to continue only provisionally until 1824, and it would have remained a provisional law to the present day if we had not learnt from the instruction now before us that it has never been implemented.

The 1819 decree was also an *interim* measure, with the difference that in its case a definite period of expectation of five years was indicated, whereas in the new instruction it is of unlimited duration, and that *at that time laws on the freedom of the press* were the object of expectation whereas *now* it is *laws on censorship*.

Other newspaper correspondents regard the censorship instruction as a refurbishing of the old censorship decree. Their error will be refuted by the instruction itself.

We regard the censorship instruction as the *anticipated spirit* of the presumable censorship law. In so doing we adhere strictly to the spirit of the 1819 censorship decree, according to which *laws* and *ordinances* are of equal significance for the press. (See the above-mentioned decree, Article XVI, No. 2.)

Let us return to the instruction.

"According to this law," namely, Article II, "the censorship should not prevent serious and modest investigation of truth, nor impose undue constraint on writers, or hinder the book trade from operating freely."

The investigation of truth which should not be prevented by the censorship is more particularly defined as one which is *serious* and *modest*. Both these definitions concern not the content of the investigation, but rather something which lies outside its content. From the outset they draw the investigation away from truth and make it pay attention to an unknown third thing. An investigation which continually has its eyes fixed on this third element, to which the law gives a legitimate capriciousness, will it not lose sight of the truth? Is it not the first duty of the seeker after truth to aim directly at the truth, without looking to the right or left? Will I not forget the essence of the matter, if I am obliged not to forget to state it in the prescribed form?

Truth is as little modest as light, and towards whom should it be so? Towards itself? *Verum index sui et falsi.*[a] Therefore, *towards falsehood?*

If modesty is the characteristic feature of the investigation, then it is a sign that truth is feared rather than falsehood. It is a means of discouragement at every step forward I take. *It is the imposition on the investigation of a fear of reaching a result,* a means of guarding against the truth.

Further, truth is general, it does not belong to me alone, it belongs to all, it owns me, I do not own it. My property is the *form,* which is my spiritual individuality. *Le style c'est l'homme.*[b] Yes, indeed! The law permits me to write, only I must write in a style that is not *mine!* I may show my spiritual countenance, but I must first set it in the *prescribed folds!* What man of honour will not blush at this presumption and not prefer to hide his head under the toga? Under the toga at least one has an inkling of a Jupiter's head. The prescribed folds mean nothing but *bonne mine à mauvais jeu.*[c]

You admire the delightful variety, the inexhaustible riches of nature. You do not demand that the rose should smell like the violet, but must the greatest riches of all, the spirit, exist in only *one* variety? I am humorous, but the law bids me write seriously. I am audacious, but the law commands that my style be modest. *Grey, all grey,* is the sole, the rightful colour of freedom. Every drop of dew on which the sun shines glistens with an inexhaustible play of colours, but the spiritual sun, however many the persons and whatever the objects in which it is refracted, must produce only the *official colour!* The most essential form of the spirit is *cheerfulness, light,* but you make *shadow* the sole manifestation of the spirit; it must be clothed only in black, yet among flowers there are no black ones. The essence of the spirit is *always truth itself* but what do you make its essence? *Modesty.* Only the mean wretch is modest, says Goethe,[d] and you want to turn the spirit into such a mean wretch? Or if modesty is to be the modesty of genius of which Schiller[e] speaks, then first of all turn all your citizens and above all your censors into geniuses. But then the modesty of genius does not consist in what educated speech

---

[a] Truth is the touchstone of itself and of falsehood (Spinoza, *Ethics,* Part II, Prop. 43).— *Ed.*

[b] Style is the man.— *Ed.*

[c] To put a good face on a bad job.— *Ed.*

[d] J. Goethe, *Rechenschaft.— Ed.*

[e] F. Schiller, *Über naive und sentimentalische Dichtung.— Ed.*

consists in, the absence of accent and dialect, but rather in speaking with the accent of the matter and in the dialect of its essence. It consists in forgetting modesty and immodesty and getting to the heart of the matter. The universal modesty of the mind is reason, that universal liberality of thought which reacts to *each thing* according to *the latter's essential nature.*

Further, if seriousness is not to come under Tristram Shandy's [a] definition according to which it is a hypocritical behaviour of the body in order to conceal defects of the soul, but signifies seriousness *in substance*, then the entire prescription falls to the ground. For I treat the ludicrous seriously when I treat it ludicrously, and the most serious immodesty of the mind is to be modest in the face of immodesty.

Serious and modest! What fluctuating, relative concepts! Where does seriousness cease and jocularity begin? Where does modesty cease and immodesty begin? We are dependent on the *temperament* of the censor. It would be as wrong to prescribe temperament for the censor as to prescribe style for the writer. If you want to be consistent in your aesthetic criticism, then forbid also a *too serious* and *too modest* investigation of the truth, for too great seriousness is the most ludicrous thing of all, and too great modesty is the bitterest irony.

Finally, the starting point is a completely perverted and abstract view of *truth* itself. All objects of the writer's activity are comprehended in the one general concept "*truth*". Even if we leave the *subjective* side out of account, viz., that one and the same object is refracted differently as seen by different persons and its different aspects converted into as many different spiritual characters, ought the *character of the object* to have no influence, not even the slightest, on the investigation? Truth includes not only the result but also the path to it. The investigation of truth must itself be true; true investigation is developed truth, the dispersed elements of which are brought together in the result. And should not the manner of investigation alter according to the object? If the object is a matter for laughter, the manner has to seem serious, if the object is disagreeable, it has to be modest. Thus you violate the right of the object as you do that of the subject. You conceive truth abstractly and turn the spirit into an *examining magistrate*, who draws up a dry *protocol* of it.

Or is there no need of this metaphysical twisting? Is *truth* to be understood as being simply *what the government decrees*, so that *investigation* is added as a superfluous, intrusive element, but

---

L. Sterne, *The Life and Opinions of Tristram Shandy, Gentleman*, Vol. I, Ch. XI.— *Ed.*

which for *etiquette's sake* is not to be entirely rejected? It almost seems so. For investigation is understood in advance as in *contradiction* to truth and therefore appears with the suspicious official accompaniment of seriousness and modesty, which of course is fitting for the layman in relation to the priest. The government's understanding is the only state reason. True, in certain circumstances of time, concessions have to be made to a different understanding and its chatter, but this understanding comes on the scene conscious of the concession and of its own lack of right, modest and submissive, serious and tedious. If Voltaire says: "*Tous les genres sont bons, excepté le genre ennuyeux*",[a] in the present case the genre *ennuyant*[b] becomes the exclusive one, as is already sufficiently proved by the reference to the "proceedings of the Rhine Province Assembly". Why not rather the good old German curialistic style? You may write freely, but at the same time every word must be a curtsey to the liberal censorship, which allows you to express your equally serious and modest opinions. Indeed, do not lose your feeling of reverence!

The *legal emphasis* is not on truth but on modesty and seriousness. Hence everything here arouses suspicion: seriousness, modesty and, above all, truth, the indefinite scope of which seems to conceal a very definite but very doubtful kind of truth.

"The censorship," the instruction states further, "should therefore by no means be implemented in a narrow-minded interpretation going beyond this law."

By *this law* is meant in the first place Article II of the 1819 decree, but later the instruction refers to the "*spirit*" of the censorship decree as a whole. The two provisions are easily combined. Article II is the *concentrated spirit* of the censorship decree, the further subdivision and more detailed specification of this spirit being found in the other articles. We believe the above-mentioned spirit cannot be better characterised than by the *following expressions of it:*

Article VII. "*The freedom from censorship hitherto accorded the Academy of Sciences and the universities is hereby suspended for five years.*"

§10. "*The present temporary decision* shall remain in force for five years from today. Before the expiry of this term there shall be a thorough investigation in the Bundestag of how the kind of provisions regarding *freedom of the press proposed* in Article 18 of the Bundesakte *could* be put into effect, and thereby a definite decision reached on the legitimate *limits of freedom of the press* in Germany."

A law which suspends *freedom of the press* where it has hitherto

---

[a] "All kinds are good except the kind that bores you." F. Voltaire, *L'enfant prodigue.*— *Ed.*

[b] The annoying kind.— *Ed.*

existed, and makes it superfluous through *censorship* where it was to be brought into existence, can hardly be called one favourable to the press. Moreover, §10 directly admits that provisionally a *censorship law* will be introduced instead of the *freedom of the press*[40] proposed in Article 18 of the Bundesakte and perhaps intended to be put into effect at some time. This *quid pro quo*[a] at least reveals that the circumstances of the time called for restrictions on the press, and that the decree owes its origin to distrust of the press. This annoyance is even excused by being termed provisional, valid for only five years — unfortunately it has lasted for 22 years.

The very next line of the instruction shows how it becomes involved in a contradiction. On the one hand, it will not have the censorship implemented in any interpretation that goes beyond the decree, and at the same time it prescribes such excess:

"The censor can very well permit a frank discussion also of internal affairs."

The censor *can*, but he does not have to, there is no necessity. Even this cautious liberalism very definitely goes not only beyond the spirit but beyond the definite demands of the censorship decree. The old censorship decree, to be exact, Article II cited in the instruction, not only does not permit any *frank discussion* of Prussian affairs, but not even of *Chinese* affairs.

"Here," namely, among violations of the security of the Prussian state and the German Federated States, the instruction comments, "are included all attempts to present in a *favourable light* parties existing *in any country* which work for the overthrow of the state system."

Is this the way a *frank* discussion of Chinese or Turkish national affairs is permitted? And if even such remote relations endanger the precarious security of the German Federation, how can any word of disapproval about *internal* affairs fail to do so?

Thus, on the one hand, the instruction goes beyond the spirit of Article II of the censorship decree in the direction of liberalism — an *excess* whose *content* will become clear later, but which is already *formally* suspicious inasmuch as it claims to be the consequence of Article II, of which wisely only the *first half* is quoted, the censor however being referred at the same time to the *article itself*. On the other hand, the instruction just as much goes beyond *the censorship decree* in an *illiberal direction* and adds *new press restrictions* to the old ones.

In the above-quoted Article II of the censorship decree it is stated:

---

[a] The confusion of one thing with another.— *Ed.*

"Its aim" (that of the censorship) "is to check all that is contrary to the *general principles* of religion, *irrespective* of the opinions and doctrines of *individual* religious parties and sects permitted in the state."

In 1819, rationalism still prevailed, which understood by religion in general the so-called religion of reason. This *rationalist point of view* is also that of the censorship decree, which at any rate is so inconsistent as to adopt the irreligious point of view while its aim is to protect religion. For it is already contrary to the general principles of religion to separate them from the positive content and particular features of religion, since each religion believes itself distinguished from the various other *would-be* religions by its *special nature,* and that precisely its *particular features* make it the *true religion.* In quoting Article II, the new censorship instruction omits the *restrictive additional clause* by which individual religious parties and sects are excluded from inviolability, but it does not stop at this and makes the following comment:

"Anything aimed in a *frivolous, hostile* way against the *Christian* religion in general, or against a *particular article of faith,* must not be tolerated."

The old censorship decree does not mention the *Christian* religion at all; on the contrary, it distinguishes between religion and *all* individual religious parties and sects. The new censorship instruction does not only convert religion in general into the *Christian* religion, but adds *further* a *particular article of faith.* A delightful product of our Christianised science! Who will still deny that it has forged new fetters for the press? Religion, it is said, must not be attacked, *whether in general or in particular.* Or do you perhaps believe that the words frivolous and hostile have made the new fetters into chains of roses? How adroitly it is written: *frivolous, hostile!* The adjective frivolous appeals to the citizen's sense of decorum, it is the exoteric word for the world at large, but the adjective hostile is whispered into the censor's ear, it is the legal interpretation of frivolity. We shall find in this instruction more examples of this subtle tact, which offers the public a subjective word that makes it blush and offers the censor an objective word that makes the author grow pale. In this way even *lettres de cachet*[41] could be set to music.

And in what a remarkable contradiction the censorship instruction has entangled itself! It is only a half-hearted attack that is frivolous, one which keeps to individual aspects of a phenomenon, without being sufficiently profound and serious to touch the essence of the matter; it is precisely an attack on a *merely particular feature as such* that is frivolous. If, therefore, an attack on the

Christian religion in general is forbidden, it follows that only a frivolous attack on it is permitted. On the other hand, an attack on the general principles of religion, on its essence, on a particular feature *insofar as it is a manifestation* of the essence, is a hostile attack. Religion can only be attacked in *a hostile or a frivolous* way, there is no third way. This inconsistency in which the instruction entangles itself is, of course, only a *seeming* one, for it depends on the semblance that in general *some kind* of attack on religion is still permitted. But an unbiassed glance suffices to realise that this semblance is only a semblance. Religion must not be attacked, whether in a hostile or a frivolous way, whether in general or in particular, *therefore not at all.*

But if the instruction, in open contradiction to the 1819 censorship decree, imposes new fetters on the *philosophical press*, it should at least be sufficiently consistent as to free the *religious press* from the old fetters imposed on it by the former rationalist decree. For it declares that the aim of the censorship is also

"to oppose fanatical transference of religious articles of faith into politics and the *confusion of ideas* resulting therefrom".

The new instruction, it is true, is clever enough not to mention this provision in its *commentary*, nevertheless it accepts it in *citing Article II*. What does fanatical transference of religious articles of faith into politics mean? It means making religious articles of faith, by their specific nature, a determining factor of the state; it means making the *particular nature of a religion the measuring-rod of the state*. The old censorship decree could rightly oppose this confusion of ideas, for it left a particular religion, its definite content, open to criticism. The old decree, however, was based on the shallow, superficial *rationalism* which you yourselves despised. But you, who base the state even in details on *faith* and *Christianity*, who want to have a *Christian state*, how can you still recommend the censorship to prevent this confusion of ideas?

The confusion of the political with the Christian-religious principle has indeed become *official doctrine*. We want to make this confusion clear in a few words. Speaking only of Christianity as the recognised religion, you have in your state Catholics and Protestants. Both make equal claims on the state, just as they have equal duties to it. They both leave their religious differences out of account and demand equally that the state should be the realisation of political and juridical reason. But you want a *Christian state*. If your state is only *Lutheran-Christian*, then for the *Catholic* it becomes a church to which he does not belong, which he must reject as heretical, and whose innermost essence is contrary to him. It is just the same the other way round. If, however, you make the *general spirit of Christianity* the *particular* spirit of your state, you nevertheless decide on the basis of your Protestant views *what* the general spirit of Christianity is. You define *what* a *Christian state* is, although the recent period has taught you that some government officials are unable to draw the line between the religious and the secular, between state and church. In regard to this *confusion of ideas*, it was not *censors* but *diplomats* who had, not to *decide*, but to *negotiate*.[42] Finally, you are adopting a *heretical* point of view when you reject definite dogma as non-essential. If you call your state a *general Christian* state, you are admitting with a diplomatic turn of phrase that it is *un-Chris-tian*. Hence either forbid religion to be introduced at all into poli-tics — but you don't want that, for you want to base the state not on free reason, but on faith, religion being for you the *general sanction for what exists* — or allow also the *fanatical* introduction of religion into politics. Let religion concern itself with politics in *its own way*, but you don't want that either. Religion has to support the secular authority, without the latter subordinating itself to religion. Once you introduce religion into politics, it is intolerable, indeed *irreli-gious*, arrogance to want to determine *secularly how* religion has to act in political matters. He who wants to ally himself with religion owing to religious feelings must concede it the decisive voice in all questions, or do you perhaps understand by religion the *cult of your own unlimited authority and governmental wisdom*?

There is yet another way in which the *orthodox spirit* of the new censorship instruction comes into conflict with the *rationalism* of the old censorship decree. The latter includes under the aim of the censorship also suppression of "what offends against *morality* and good manners". The instruction reproduces this passage as a *quotation* from Article II. *Its commentary*, however, while making additions as regards religion, contains omissions as regards morali-ty. Offending against *morality* and *good manners* becomes violation of "propriety and manners and external decorum". One sees: *morality as such*, as the *principle of a world* that obeys its own laws, *disappears*, and in place of the essence external manifestations make their appearance, *police respectability, conventional decorum*. Honour to whom honour is due, we recognise true consistency here. The specifically Christian legislator *cannot recognise morality* as an independent sphere that is sacrosanct in itself, for he claims that its inner general essence belongs to religion. Independent morality offends against the general principles of religion, but the particular concepts of religion conflict with morality. Morality recognises only its own universal and rational religion, and religion recognises only its particular positive morality. Hence, according to this instruction, the censorship must reject the intellectual heroes of morality, such as Kant, Fichte and Spinoza, as irreligious, as violating propriety, manners, and external decorum. All these moralists start out from a contradiction in principle between morality and religion, for *morality* is based on the *autonomy* of the human mind, *religion* on its *heteronomy*. Let us turn from these undesirable innovations of the censorship—on the one hand, the weakening of its moral conscience, on the other hand, the rigorous heightening of its religious conscience—to what is more welcome, the *concessions*.

It "follows in particular that writings in which the state administration is assessed as a whole or in its individual branches, laws that have been or are still to be promulgated are examined for their inner value, mistakes and misconceptions revealed, improvements indicated or suggested, are not to be rejected because they are written in a spirit that does not agree with the government's views, as long as their formulation is decent and their *tendency well-meaning*".

Modesty and seriousness of investigation—both the new instruction and the censorship decree make this demand, but for the former *decorous* formulation is as little sufficient as truth of content. For it the *tendency* is the main criterion, indeed it is its all-pervading thought, whereas in the decree itself not even the *word* tendency is to be found. Nor does the new instruction say what constitutes tendency, but how important it is for it may be seen from the following extract:

"In this connection it is an *indispensable* premise that the *tendency* of remonstrances expressed against measures of the government should not be spiteful or malevolent, but well-intentioned, and goodwill and insight are required of the censor so that he knows how to distinguish between the one case and the other. Considering this, the censors must also pay special attention to the form and tone of writings for the press and insofar as, owing to passion, vehemence and arrogance, *their tendency* is found to be pernicious, must not allow them to be printed."

The writer, therefore, has fallen victim to the *most frightful terrorism*, and is subjected to the *jurisdiction of suspicion*. Laws against *tendency*, laws giving no objective standards, are laws of terrorism, such as were invented owing to the emergency needs of the state under Robespierre and the corruption of the state under the Roman emperors. Laws which make their main criterion not *actions as such*, but the *frame of mind* of the doer, are nothing but *positive sanctions for lawlessness.* Better like that Russian Tsar[a] to have everyone's beard cut off by Cossacks in his service than to make the state of mind due to which I wear a beard the criterion for the cutting.

Only insofar as I *manifest* myself externally, enter the sphere of the actual, do I enter the sphere of the legislator. Apart from *my actions*, I have no existence for the law, am no object for it. My actions are the sole thing by which the law has a hold on me; for they are the sole thing for which I demand a right of existence, a *right of actuality*, owing to which therefore I come within the sphere of *actual law.* The law which punishes tendency, however, punishes me not only for what I do, but for what I think, *apart* from my actions. It is therefore an insult to the honour of the citizen, a vexatious law which threatens my existence.

I can turn and twist as I will, it is not a question of the facts. My existence is under suspicion, my innermost being, my individuality, is considered *bad*, and it is *for this opinion* of me that I am *punished.* The law punishes me not for any wrong I commit, but for the wrong I do not commit. I am really being punished because my action is *not against the law*, for only because of that do I compel the lenient, well-meaning judge to seize on my *bad frame of mind*, which is clever enough not to come out in the open.

The law against a frame of mind is *not a law of the state* promulgated for its *citizens*, but the *law of one party against another party.* The law which punishes tendency abolishes the equality of the citizens before the law. It is a law which divides, not one which unites, and all laws which divide are reactionary. It is not a law, but a *privilege.* One may do what another may not do, not because the latter lacks some objective quality, like a minor in regard to concluding contracts; no, because his good intentions and his frame of mind are under suspicion. The *moral state* assumes its members to have the *frame of mind of the state*, even if they act in *opposition to an organ of the state*, against the *government.* But in a society in which *one* organ imagines itself the sole, exclusive possessor of state reason and state morality, in a government which opposes the people in principle and hence regards *its anti-state frame of mind* as the general, normal frame of mind, the bad conscience of a faction invents laws against tendency, *laws of revenge*, laws against a frame of mind which has its seat only in the government members themselves. Laws against frame of mind are based on an unprincipled frame of mind, on an immoral, material view of the state.

---

[a] Peter the Great.—*Ed.*

They are the involuntary cry of a bad conscience. And how is a law of this kind to be implemented? By a means more revolting than the law itself: by *spies*, or by previous agreement to regard entire literary trends as suspicious, in which case, of course, the trend to which an individual belongs must also be inquired into. Just as in the law against tendency the *legal form contradicts* the *content*, just as the *government* which issues it lashes out against what it is itself, against the anti-state frame of mind, so also in each particular case it forms as it were the *reverse world* to its laws, for it applies a double measuring-rod. What for one side is right, for the other side is wrong. *The very laws issued by the government are the opposite of what they make into law.*

The *new censorship instruction*, too, becomes entangled in this dialectic. It contains the contradiction of itself doing, and making it the censor's duty to do, everything that it condemns as anti-state in the case of the press.

Thus the instruction forbids writers to cast suspicion on the frame of mind of individuals or whole classes, and in the same breath it bids the censor divide all citizens into suspicious and un-suspicious, into well-intentioned and evil-intentioned. The press is deprived of the right to criticise, but criticism becomes the daily duty of the governmental critic. This reversal, however, does not end the matter. Within the press what was anti-state as regards content appeared as something particular, but from the aspect of its form it was something universal, that is to say, subject to universal appraisal.

However, now the thing is turned upside-down: the particular now appears justified *in regard to its content*, what is anti-state appears as the view of the state, as state law; in regard to its form, however, what is anti-state appears as something particular, that cannot be brought to the general light of day, that is relegated from the open air of publicity to the office files of the governmen-tal critic. Thus the instruction wants to protect religion, but it violates the most general principle of all religions, the sanctity and inviolability of the subjective frame of mind. It makes the censor instead of God the judge of the heart. Thus it prohibits offensive utterances and defamatory judgments on individuals, but it ex-poses you every day to the defamatory and offensive judgment of the censor. Thus the instruction wants the gossip of evil-mind-ed or ill-informed persons suppressed, but it compels the cen-sor to rely on such gossip, on spying by ill-informed and evil-minded persons, degrading judgment from the sphere of ob-jective content to that of subjective opinion or arbitrary action.

Thus suspicion must not be cast on the intention of the state, but the instruction starts out from suspicion in respect of the state. Thus no bad frame of mind must be concealed under a good appearance, but the instruction itself is based on a false appearance. Thus the instruction wants to enhance national feeling, but it is based on a view that humiliates the nation. Lawful behaviour and respect for the law are demanded of us, but at the same time we have to honour institutions which put us outside the law and introduce arbitrariness in place of law. We are required to recognise the principle of personality to such an extent that we trust the censor despite the defects of the institution of censorship, and you violate the principle of personality to such an extent that you cause personality to be judged not according to its actions but according to an opinion of the opinion of its actions. You demand modesty and your starting point is the monstrous immodesty of appointing individual servants of the state to spy on people's hearts, to be omniscient, philosophers, theologians, politicians, Delphic Apollos. On the one hand, you make it our duty to respect immodesty and, on the other hand, you forbid us to be immodest. The real immodesty consists in ascribing perfection of the genus to particular individuals. The censor is a particular individual, but the press becomes the embodiment of the whole genus. You order us to have trust, and you give distrust the force of law. You repose so much trust in your state institutions that you think they will convert a weak mortal, an official, into a saint, and make the impossible possible for him. But you distrust your state organism so much that you are afraid of the isolated opinion of a private person; for you treat the press as a private person. You assume that the officials will act quite impersonally, without animosity, passion, narrow-mindedness or human weakness. But what is impersonal, *ideas*, you suspect of being full of personal intrigue and subjective vileness. The instruction demands unlimited trust in the estate of officials, and it proceeds from unlimited distrust in the estate of non-officials. Why should we not pay tit for tat? Why should we not look with suspicion on precisely this estate of officials? Equally as regards character. From the outset one who is impartial should have more respect for the character of the critic who acts publicly than for the character of the critic who acts in secret.

What is at all bad remains bad, whoever personifies this badness, whether a private critic or one appointed by the government, but in the latter case the badness is authorised and regarded from above as a necessity to realise goodness from below.

The *censorship of tendency* and the *tendency of censorship* are a *gift of the new liberal instruction.* No one will blame us if we turn to the further provisions of the instruction with a certain misgiving.

"Offensive utterances and defamatory judgments on individuals are not suitable for publication."

Not suitable for publication! Instead of this mildness we could wish that an objective definition of offensive and defamatory judgments had been given.

"The same holds good for suspicion of the frame of mind of individuals *or*" (a significant or) "whole classes, for the use of *party names* and other such personal attacks."

Inadmissible, therefore, also are classification by categories, attacks on whole classes, use of party names — and man, like Adam, has to give everything a name for it to exist for him; party names are essential categories for the political press,

> "Because, as Dr. Sassafras supposes,
> Every illness for its cure
> Must first receive a name."[a]

All this is included in *personal attacks.* How then is one to make a start? One must not attack an individual, and just as little the class, the general, the juridical person. The state will — and here it is right — tolerate no insults, no personal attacks; but by a simple "or" the general is also included in the personal. By "or" the general comes into it, and by means of a little "and" we learn finally that the whole question has been only of personal attacks. But as a perfectly simple consequence it follows that the press is forbidden all control over officials as over such institutions that exist as a class of individuals.

"If censorship is exercised in accordance with these directives in the spirit of the censorship decree of October 18, 1819, adequate scope will be afforded for decorous and candid publicity, and it is to be expected that thereby greater sympathy for the interests of the Fatherland will be aroused and thus national feeling enhanced."

We are ready to admit that in accordance with these directives for *decorous* publicity, decorous in the sense understood by the censorship, a more than adequate field of play[b] is afforded — the term field of play is happily chosen, for the field is calculated for a sportive press that is satisfied with leaps in the air. Whether it is adequate for a *candid* publicity, and where its *candidness* lies,

---

[a] C. M. Wieland, *Der Neue Amadis*, No. 36.— *Ed.*

[b] A pun on the German word *Spielraum*, which means "scope" and "field of play".— *Ed.*

we leave to the readers' perspicacity. As for *expectations* held out by the instruction, *national feeling* may, of course, be enhanced just as the sending of a bow-string enhances the feeling of Turkish nationality: but whether the press, as modest as it is serious, will arouse sympathy for the interests of the Fatherland we shall leave it to decide for itself; a meagre press cannot be fattened with quinine. Perhaps, however, we have taken too serious a view of the passage quoted. We shall, perhaps, get at the meaning better if we regard it as merely a thorn in the wreath of roses. Perhaps this liberal thorn holds a pearl of very ambiguous value. Let us see. It all depends on the context. The enhancement of national feeling and the arousing of sympathy for the interests of the Fatherland, which in the above-cited passage are spoken of as an *expectation,* secretly turn into an *order,* which imposes a *new constraint* on our poor, consumptive *daily press.*

> "In this way it may be hoped that both political literature and the daily press will realise their function better, that with the acquirement of richer material they will also adopt a more dignified tone, and in future will scorn to speculate on the curiosity of their readers through communication of baseless reports taken from foreign newspapers and originating from evil-minded or badly informed correspondents, by gossip and personal attacks—a trend against which it is the undoubted duty of the censorship to take measures."

In the way indicated it is *hoped* that political literature and the daily press will realise their function better, etc. However, *better realisation* cannot be ordered, moreover it is a fruit still to be awaited, and hope remains hope. But the instruction is much too practical to be satisfied with hopes and pious wishes. While the press is granted the hope of its future improvement *as a new consolation,* the kindly instruction at the same time deprives it of a right it has at present. In the hope of its improvement it loses what it still has. It fares like poor Sancho Panza, from whom all the food was snatched away under his eyes by the court doctor in order that his stomach should not be upset and make him incapable of performing the duties imposed on him by the duke.[a]

At the same time we ought not to miss the opportunity of inviting the Prussian writer to adopt this kind of decorous style. In the first part of the sentence it is stated: "In this way it may be hoped *that*". This *that* governs a whole series of provisions, namely, that political literature and the daily press will realise their function better, that they will adopt a more dignified tone, etc.,

---

[a] Cervantes, *Don Quixote,* Part IV, Ch. 47.— *Ed.*

etc., that they will scorn communication of baseless reports, etc., taken from foreign newspapers. All these provisions are still matters for hope; but the conclusion, which is joined to the foregoing by a *dash*: "a trend against which it is the undoubted duty of the censorship to take measures", absolves the censor from the boring task of awaiting the hoped-for improvement of the daily press, and instead empowers him to delete what he finds undesirable without more ado. *Internal treatment* has been replaced by *amputation.*

"To approach this aim more closely, however, requires that great care be taken in agreeing to new publications and new editors, so that the daily press will be entrusted only to completely irreproachable persons, whose scientific ability, position and character guarantee the seriousness of their efforts and the loyalty of their mode of thought."

Before we go into details, let us make one general observation. The approval of new editors, hence of future editors in general, is entrusted wholly to the *"great care"*, naturally of the *state officials*, of the censorship, whereas at least the old censorship decree left the choice of editors, with certain guarantees, to the *discretion of the publisher:*

"Article IX. The supreme censorship authority is entitled to inform the publisher of a newspaper that a proposed editor is not such as to inspire the requisite trust, in which case the publisher is bound either to take another editor *or,* if he *wants to retain* the one designated, to furnish for him a *security to be determined* by our above-mentioned state ministries on the proposal of the above-mentioned supreme censorship authority."

The new censorship instruction expresses a quite different profundity, one could call it a *romanticism* of the spirit. Whereas the old censorship decree demands an external, prosaic, hence legally definable, security, on the guarantee of which even the objectionable editor is to be allowed, the instruction on the other hand takes away *all independent will* from the publisher of a newspaper. Moreover, it draws the attention of the preventive wisdom of the government, the great care and intellectual profundity of the authorities, to internal, subjective, externally indefinable, qualities. If, however, the indefiniteness, delicate sensitivity, and subjective extravagance of *romanticism* become *purely external,* merely in the sense that external chance no longer appears in its prosaic definiteness and limitation, but in a fantastic glory, in an imaginary profundity and splendour — then the instruction, too, can hardly avoid this *romantic fate.*

The editors of the daily press, a category which includes all journalistic activity, must be completely irreproachable men. "*Scien-*

tific qualification" is put forward in the first place as a guarantee of this complete irreproachability. Not the slightest doubt arises as to whether the censor can have the scientific qualification to pass judgment on scientific qualification of every kind. If such a crowd of universal geniuses known to the government are to be found in Prussia—every town has at least one censor—why do not these encyclopaedic minds come forward as writers? If these officials, overwhelming in their numbers and mighty owing to their scientific knowledge and genius, were all at once to rise up and smother by their weight those miserable writers, each of whom can write in only one genre, and even in that without officially attested ability, an end could be put to the irregularities of the press much better than through the censorship. Why do these experts who, like the Roman geese, could save the Capitol by their cackling remain silent? Their modesty is too great. The scientific public does not know them, but the government does.

And if these men are indeed such as no state has succeeded in discovering, for never has a state known whole classes composed solely of universal geniuses and encyclopaedic minds—how much greater must be the genius of the selectors of these men! What secret science must be theirs for them to be able to issue a certificate of universal scientific qualification to officials unknown in the republic of science! The higher we rise in this *bureaucracy of intelligence,* the more remarkable are the minds we encounter. For a state which possesses such pillars of a perfect press, is it worth the trouble, is it expedient to make these men the *guardians* of a defective press, to degrade the perfect into a means for dealing with the imperfect?

The more of these censors you appoint, the more you deprive the realm of the press of chances of improvement. You take away the healthy from your army in order to make them physicians of the unhealthy.

Merely stamp on the ground like Pompey and a Pallas Athena in complete armour will spring from every government building. Confronted by the *official press,* the shallow daily press will disintegrate into nothing. The existence of light suffices to expel darkness. Let your light shine, and hide it not under a bushel. Instead of a defective censorship whose full effectiveness you yourselves regard as problematic, give us a perfect press to whom you have only to give an order and a model of which has been in existence for centuries in the *Chinese* state.

But to make *scientific qualification* the sole, necessary condition for writers of the daily press, is that not a provision concerning the mind, no favouring of privilege, no conventional demand? Is it not a stipulation as regards the matter, not a stipulation as regards the person?

Unfortunately the censorship instruction interrupts our panegyric. Alongside the guarantee of scientific qualification is the demand for that of *position and character*. Position and character!

Character, which follows so immediately after position, seems almost to be a mere outcome of the latter. Let us, therefore, take a look at *position* in the first place. It is so squeezed in between scientific qualification and character that one is almost tempted to doubt the good conscience that called for it.

The *general* demand for scientific qualification, how *liberal!* The *special* demand for position, how *illiberal!* Scientific qualification and position together, how *pseudo-liberal!* Since scientific qualification and character are very indefinite things, whereas position, on the other hand, is very definite, why should we not conclude that by a necessary law of logic the indefinite will be supported by the definite and obtain stability and content from it? Would it then be a great mistake on the part of the censor if he interpreted the instruction as meaning that *position* is the *external form* in which scientific qualification and character manifest themselves socially, the more so since his own position as censor is a guarantee for him that this view is the state's view? Without this interpretation it remains at least quite incomprehensible why scientific qualification and character are not adequate guarantees for a writer, why position is a necessary third. Now if the censor were to find himself in a quandary, if these guarantees were seldom or never present together, where should his choice fall? A choice has to be made, for someone has to edit newspapers and periodicals. Scientific qualification and character without position could present a problem for the censor on account of their indefiniteness, just as in general it must rightly be a surprise to him that such qualities could exist separately from position. On the other hand, ought the censor to have any doubts about character and science where position is present? In that case he would have less confidence in the judgment of the state than in his own, whereas in the opposite case he would have more confidence in the writer than in the state. Ought a censor to be so tactless, so ill-disposed? It is not to be expected and will certainly not be expected. *Position,* because it is the decisive criterion *in case of doubt,* is in general the *absolutely decisive criterion.*

Hence, just as earlier the instruction was in conflict with the *censorship decree* owing to its *orthodoxy,* now it is so owing to its *romanticism,* which at the same time is always the poetry of *tendency.* The *cash security,* which is a prosaic, real guarantee, becomes an imaginary one, and this imaginary guarantee turns into the wholly *real* and *individual* position, which acquires a magical fictitious significance. In the same way the significance of the guarantee becomes transformed. The publisher no longer *chooses* an editor, for whom *he* gives a guarantee to the authorities, instead the authorities choose an editor *for him,* one for whom they give a guarantee to themselves. The old decree looked for the work of the editor, for which the publisher's cash security served as guarantee. The instruction, however, is not concerned with the *work* of the editor, but with his *person.* It demands a definite personal individuality, which the *publisher's money* should provide. The new instruction is just as superficial as the old decree. But whereas the latter by its nature expressed and delimited prosaically defined provisions, the instruction gives an imaginary significance to the purest chance and expresses what is merely individual with the fervour of generality.

Whereas, however, as regards the editor the romantic instruction expresses the extremely superficial definiteness in a tone of the most ,easy-going indefiniteness, as regards the censor it expresses the vaguest indefiniteness in a tone of legal definiteness.

"The same caution must be exercised in the appointment of censors, so that the post of censor shall be entrusted only to men of tested frame of mind and *ability,* who fully correspond to the honourable trust which that office presupposes; to men who are both right-thinking and keen-sighted, who are able to separate the form from the essence of the matter and with sure *tact* know how to set aside doubt where the meaning and *tendency* of a writing do not in themselves justify this doubt."

Instead of position and character as required of the writer, we have here the tested frame of mind, since position is already there. More significant is that whereas *scientific qualification* is demanded of the writer, what is demanded of the censor is *ability* without further definition. The old decree, which is drawn up in a rational spirit except in respect of politics, calls in Article III for "*scientifically-trained*" and even "*enlightened*" censors. In the instruction both attributes have been dropped, and instead of the *qualification* of the writer, which signifies a definite, well-developed ability that has become a reality, there appears in the case of the censor the *aptitude for qualification,* ability in general. Hence the *aptitude for ability* has to *act as censor* of *actual qualification,* however much in the nature of things the relationship should obviously be the reverse. Finally, merely in passing, we note that the ability of the censor is not more closely defined as regards its *objective* content, and this, of course, makes its character *ambiguous*.

Further, the post of censor is to be entrusted to men "who *fully correspond* to the honourable trust which that office presupposes". This pleonastic pseudo-definition, to select for an office men in whom one has trust that they (*will?*) *fully correspond* to the honourable trust, certainly a very full trust, reposed in them, is not worth further discussion.

Finally, the censors must be men

"who are both right-thinking and keen-sighted, who are able to *separate* the *form* from the *essence* of the matter and with *sure tact* know how to *set aside doubt* where the *meaning* and *tendency* of a writing do not *in themselves* justify this doubt".

Earlier, on the other hand, the instruction prescribes:

"Considering this" (namely, the investigation of tendency), "the censors must also pay special attention to the *form* and *tone* of writings for the press and insofar as, owing to passion, vehemence and arrogance, their tendency is found to be pernicious, must not allow them to be printed."

On one occasion, therefore, the censor has to judge of the *tendency from the form*, on another occasion, of the *form from the tendency*. If previously *content* had already disappeared as a criterion for censorship, now *form* also disappears. As long as the tendency is good, *faults of form* do not matter. Even if the work cannot be regarded exactly as very serious and modest, even if it may appear to be vehement, passionate, arrogant, who would let himself be frightened by the *rough exterior*? One has to know how to distinguish between *form* and *essence*. All semblance of definitions had to be abandoned, the instruction had to end in a *complete contradiction with itself*; for everything by which tendency is supposed to be recognised is, on the contrary, determined by the tendency and must be recognised from the tendency. The vehemence of the patriot is holy zeal, his passionateness is the sensitiveness of the lover, his arrogance a devoted sympathy which is too immeasurable to be moderate.

All objective standards are abandoned, everything is finally reduced to the *personal* relation, and the censor's *tact has* to be called a guarantee. What then can the censor violate? Tact. But tactlessness is no crime. What is threatened as far as the writer is concerned? His existence. What state has ever made the existence of whole classes depend on the tact of individual officials?

I repeat, *all objective standards are abandoned*. As regards the writer, tendency is the ultimate content that is demanded from him and prescribed to him. Tendency as formless opinion appears

6*

as object. Tendency as subject, as opinion of opinion, is the censor's tact and his sole criterion.

But whereas the arbitrariness of the censor—and to sanction the authority of mere opinion is to sanction arbitrariness—is a logical consequence which was concealed under a semblance of objective definitions, the instruction on the other hand quite consciously expresses the arbitrariness of the *Oberpräsidium*; trust is reposed in the latter without reserve, and *this trust reposed in the Oberpräsident* is the ultimate *guarantee of the press*. Thus the essence of the censorship in general is based on the arrogant imaginary idea that the police state has of its officials. There is no confidence in the intelligence and goodwill of the general public even in the simplest matter; but even the impossible is considered possible for the officials.

This fundamental defect is inherent in all our institutions. Thus, for example, in criminal proceedings judge, accuser and defender are combined in *a single person*. This combination contradicts all the laws of psychology. But the official is raised above the laws of psychology, while the general public remains under them. Nevertheless, one could excuse a defective principle of state; it becomes unpardonable, however, if it is not honest enough to be consistent. The *responsibility* of the officials ought to be as immeasurably above that of the general public as the officials are above the latter, and it is precisely here, where consistency alone could justify the principle and make it legitimate within its sphere, it is precisely here that it is abandoned and the opposite principle applied.

The censor, too, is accuser, defender and judge in a single person; *control of the mind* is entrusted to the censor; he is *irresponsible*.

The censorship could have only a *provisionally* loyal character if it was subordinated to the *regular courts*, which of course is impossible so long as there are no objective laws governing censorship. But the worst method of all is to subject the censorship to censorship again, as by an Oberpräsident or supreme college of censors.

Everything that holds good of the relation of the press to the censorship holds good also of the relation of the censorship to the supreme censorship and that of the writer to the supreme censor, although an *intermediate link* is interposed. It is the same relation placed on a higher plane, the remarkable error of leaving matters alone and wanting to give them another nature through other persons. If the *coercive state* wanted to be loyal, it would abolish itself. Every point would require the same coercion and the same counter-pressure. The supreme censorship would have to be subjected to censorship in its turn. In order to escape from this vicious circle, it is decided to be disloyal; lawlessness now begins in the third or ninety-ninth stage. Because the bureaucratic state is vaguely conscious of this, it tries at least to place the sphere of lawlessness so high that it escapes the eye, and then believes that lawlessness has disappeared.

The real, *radical cure for the censorship* would be its *abolition*; for the institution itself is a bad one, and institutions are more powerful than people. Our view may be right or not, but in any case the Prussian writers stand to *gain through the new instruction*, either in *real freedom*, or in freedom of *ideas*, in *consciousness*.

Rara temporum felicitas, ubi quae velis sentire et quae sentias dicere licet.[a]

Written between January 15 and February 10, 1842

First published in the symposium
Anekdota zur neuesten deutschen Philosophie und Publicistik, Bd. I, 1843

Signed: *By a Rhinelander*

Printed according to the symposium

---

[a] O rare happiness of the times, where it is permitted to think what you will and to say what you think (Tacitus, *Historiae*, 1, 1).— *Ed.*

Abonnements-Preis:
viertel-) In Köln 1 Thlr. 13½ Sgr.
jährlich) Auswärts 1 Thlr. 22½ Sgr.

Rheinische Zeitung

für

Politik, Handel und Gewerbe.

Insertions-Gebühren:
Die eugedruckte Petitzeile 1 Sgr.
Briefe werden frankiert erbeten.

Nº 125. Köln, Donnerstag den 5. Mai **1842**

PROCEEDINGS OF THE SIXTH RHINE PROVINCE ASSEMBLY [43]

First Article [44]

DEBATES ON FREEDOM OF THE PRESS AND PUBLICATION OF THE PROCEEDINGS OF THE ASSEMBLY OF THE ESTATES [45]

[Rheinische Zeitung No. 125, May 5, 1842, Supplement]

To the amazement of all writing and reading Germany the *Preussische Staats-Zeitung* one fine Berlin spring morning published its *self-confession*.[46] Of course, it chose an elegant, diplomatic, not exactly amusing, form for its confession. It gave itself the appearance of wanting to hold up the mirror for its sisters to recognise themselves; it spoke mysteriously only about other Prussian newspapers, while it was really speaking about the Prussian newspaper *par excellence*, itself.

This fact allows of many different explanations. *Caesar* spoke about himself in the third person. Why should the *Preussische Staats-Zeitung*, in speaking about third persons, not mean itself? *Children*, when speaking about themselves, are in the habit of saying not "I", but "George", etc. Why should not the *Preussische Staats-Zeitung* be allowed to use for its "I" the *Vossische*,[47] *Spenersche*,[48] or some other saint's name?

The new censorship instruction had appeared. Our newspapers believed they had to adopt the outward appearance and conventional forms of freedom. The *Preussische Staats-Zeitung*, too, was compelled to awake and have some kind of liberal — or at least independent — ideas.

The first essential condition for freedom, however, is self-knowledge, and self-knowledge is an impossibility without self-confession.

Hence one should firmly keep in mind that the *Preussische Staats-Zeitung* has written *self-confessions*; one should never forget that we see here the first awakening to self-consciousness of a semi-official press-child, and then all riddles will be solved. One will be convinced that the *Preussische Staats-Zeitung* "utters with composure many a great word", and will only remain undecided whether one should admire more the composure of its greatness or the greatness of its composure.

Hardly had the censorship instruction appeared, hardly had the *Staats-Zeitung* recovered from this blow, before it came out with the question: "What use has the greater freedom from censorship been to you Prussian newspapers?"

Obviously, what it means to say by this is: What use have the many years of strict observance of the censorship been to me? What have I become, in spite of the most scrupulous and thoroughgoing supervision and tutelage? And what should now become of me? I have not learnt to walk and a sensation-loving public is expecting *entrechats* from one who has a dislocated hipjoint! So will it be for you, too, my sisters! Let us confess our weaknesses to the Prussian people, but let us be diplomatic in our confession. We shall not tell them outright that we are uninteresting. We shall tell them that if the Prussian newspapers are uninteresting for the Prussian people, the Prussian state is uninteresting for the newspapers.

The bold question of the *Staats-Zeitung* and the still bolder answer are mere preludes to its awakening, dream-like allusions in the text to the role that it will perform. It is awakening to consciousness, it is speaking its mind. Listen to Epimenides!

It is well known that the first theoretical activity of the mind that still wavers between sensuous perception and thinking is *counting*. Counting is the first free theoretical mental act of the child. *Let us count,* the *Preussische Staats-Zeitung* calls to its sisters. *Statistics* is the premier political science! I know a man's head when I know how many hairs grow on it.

Do as you would be done by. And how could one better appreciate us and especially me, the *Preussische Staats-Zeitung*, than statistically! Statistics will not merely prove that I appear as often as any French or English newspaper, but also that I am less read than any newspaper in the civilised world. Discount the officials who half-heartedly have to be interested in me, subtract the public places which must have a semi-official organ, and who reads me, I ask, who? Calculate what I cost; calculate the income I receive, and you will admit that it is not a profitable business to utter great words with composure. See how cogent statistics are, how counting makes more far-reaching mental operations superfluous! Therefore count! Numerical tables instruct the public without exciting their emotions.

And the *Staats-Zeitung* with the importance it attaches to statistics not only puts itself on a par with the Chinese and with the universal statistician Pythagoras [49]! It shows that it has been influenced by the great natural philosopher of recent times [a], who wanted to represent the differences between animals, etc., by a series of numbers.

Thus the *Preussische Staats-Zeitung* is not without modern philosophical foundations, in spite of its apparent positivism.[50]

The *Staats-Zeitung* is many-sided. It does not stop at *number, temporal magnitude*. It carries the recognition of the quantitative principle further and proclaims the justification of *spatial magnitude*. Space is the first thing whose magnitude impresses the *child*. It is the first magnitude which the child encounters in the world. Hence the child holds a big man to be a great man, and in the same childish way the *Staats-Zeitung* informs us that *thick* books are incomparably better than *thin ones,* and much more so than single leaflets or *newspapers,* which produce only one printed sheet daily.

You Germans can only express yourselves at great length! Write really voluminous books on the organisation of the state, books of solid learning, which no one reads except the Herr Author and the Herr Reviewer, but bear in mind that your newspapers are not books. Think how many printed sheets go to make a solid work of three volumes! Therefore do not seek the spirit of our day or time in newspapers, which offer you statistical tables, but seek it in books, whose size guarantees their solidity.

Bear in mind, you good children, that it is a matter here of "learned" things. Study in the school of thick books and you will quickly get to love us newspapers on account of our flimsy format, our gentlemanly lightness, which is truly refreshing after the thick books.

Of course! Of course! Our time has no longer that real taste for size that we admire in the Middle Ages. Look at our paltry little pietistic tracts, look at our philosophical systems in small octavo, and then cast your eyes on the twenty gigantic folios of Duns Scotus. You do not need to read the books; their exciting aspect suffices to touch your heart and strike your senses, something like a Gothic cathedral. These primitive gigantic works materially affect the mind; it feels oppressed under their mass, and the feeling of oppression is the beginning of awe. You do not master the books, they master you. You are an unimportant appendage to

---

[a] Lorenz Oken.— *Ed.*

them, and in the same way, in the view of the *Preussische Staats-Zeitung*, the people should be an unimportant appendage of their political literature.

Thus the *Staats-Zeitung*, although its language is quite modern, is not without historical foundations belonging to the sterling period of the Middle Ages.

If, however, the theoretical thinking of the *child* is quantitative, its judgment, like its practical thought, is primarily practical and sensuous. The sensuous quality of the child is the first link that connects it with the world. The *practical organs of senses*, primarily the nose and mouth, are the first organs by means of which it *judges* the world. Hence the childish *Preussische Staats-Zeitung* judges the value of newspapers, and therefore its own value, by means of its *nose*. If a Greek thinker[a] held that dry souls were the best,[51] the *Staats-Zeitung* holds that "*pleasant-smelling*" newspapers are "*good*" newspapers. It cannot praise too highly the "*literary fragrance*" of the Augsburg *Allgemeine* and the *Journal des Débats*. Rare, praiseworthy naivety! Great Pompey, greatest of all!

After allowing us, therefore, a deep insight into the state of its soul by means of a number of separate praiseworthy utterances, the *Staats-Zeitung* sums up its view of the state in a profound reflection, the crux of which is the great discovery:

"that in Prussia the state administration and the whole organisation of the state are remote from the political spirit, and therefore cannot be of *political* interest either to the people or to the newspapers".

In the *opinion* of the *Preussische Staats-Zeitung*, therefore, in Prussia the state administration has no political spirit, or the political spirit has no state administration. How crude of the *Staats-Zeitung* to assert what the bitterest opponent could not express more brutally, namely, that the real life of the state is without any political spirit, and that the political spirit does not live in the real state!

But we ought not to forget the *childish-sensuous standpoint* of the *Preussische Staats-Zeitung*. It tells us that in regard to railways one should think only of rails and ways, in regard to trade contracts only of sugar and coffee, and in regard to leather factories only of leather. The child, of course, does not go beyond *sensuous perception*, it sees a thing only in isolation, and the invisible nerve threads which link the particular with the universal, which in the state as everywhere make the material parts into soul-possessing members of the spiritual whole, are for the child non-existent.

---

[a] Heraclitus.— *Ed.*

The child believes that the sun revolves around the earth; that the universal revolves around the particular. Hence the child does not believe in the *spirit*, but it believes in *spectres*.

Thus the *Preussische Staats-Zeitung* regards the political spirit as a French spectre; and it thinks it exorcises the spectre if it throws leather, sugar, bayonets and numbers at it.

However, our reader will interrupt us, we wanted to discuss the "Rhine Province Assembly proceedings" and instead we are being presented with the *"innocent angel"*, that senile child of the press, the *Preussische Staats-Zeitung*, and a repetition of the old-time lullabies with which it again and again tries to lull itself and its sisters into wholesome hibernation.

But does not Schiller say:

> "But what the sage's reason fails to see
> A *childish* nature grasps in all *simplicity*." [a]

The *Preussische Staats-Zeitung* *"in all simplicity"* has reminded us that we in Prussia, no less than in England, have *assemblies of the estates*, whose proceedings the daily press would indeed be *allowed* to discuss, if it *could*; for the *Staats-Zeitung* in its great, classical self-consciousness takes the view that what the Prussian newspapers lack is not *permission* but *ability*. We concede it the latter as its special privilege, while at the same time, without further explanation of its ability, we take the liberty of actually implementing the idea it had in all simplicity.

The *publication* of the Assembly proceedings will only become a reality when they are treated as *"public facts"*, i.e., as subject-matter for the press. The last *Rhine* Province Assembly is the one with which we are most immediately concerned.

We begin with its *"Debates on Freedom of the Press"* and must remark as a preliminary that, while we sometimes give our own positive view of this question as a participant, in later articles we shall follow and present the course of the proceedings more as a historical spectator.

The nature of the proceedings themselves determines this difference in the method of presentation. For in all the other debates we find that the various opinions of the Assembly representatives are on about the same level. In the question of the press, on the other hand, the opponents of a free press have a considerable advantage. Apart from the catchwords and commonplaces which fill the air, we find among these opponents of press freedom

---

[a] F. Schiller, *Die Worte des Glaubens.—Ed.*

a *pathological emotion,* a passionate partisanship, which gives them a *real,* not an imaginary, attitude to the press, whereas the *defenders* of the press in this Assembly have on the whole *no real relation* to what they are defending. They have never come to know freedom of the press as a *vital need.* For them it is a matter of the head, in which the heart plays no part. For them it is an "exotic" plant, to which they are attached by mere "sentiment". Hence it happens that all too general, vague arguments are put forward to counter the especially "weighty" grounds of the opponents, and the most narrow-minded idea is held to be important as long as it is not demolished.

Goethe once said that the painter succeeds only with a type of feminine beauty which he has loved in at least one living being.[a] Freedom of the press, too, has its beauty—if not exactly a feminine one—which one must have loved to be able to defend it. If I truly love something, I feel that its existence is essential, that it is something which I need, without which my nature can have no full, satisfied, complete existence. The above-mentioned defenders of freedom of the press seem to enjoy a complete existence even in the absence of any freedom of the press.

[*Rheinische Zeitung* No. 128, May 8, 1842, Supplement]

The *liberal opposition* shows us the level of a political assembly, just as the opposition in general shows the level of development that a society has reached. A time in which it is philosophical audacity to doubt the existence of ghosts, in which it is regarded as a paradox to oppose witch trials, is the time in which ghosts and witch trials are *legitimate.* A country which, like ancient Athens, regards lickspittles, parasites and flatterers as exceptions to the good sense of the people, as *fools among the people,* is a country of independence and self-reliance. But a people which, like all peoples of the good old times, claims the right to think and utter the truth only for *court-jesters,* can only be a people without independence or personality. An assembly of the estates in which the opposition assures us that freedom of the will is inherent in human nature, is at least not an assembly in which freedom of the will prevails. The exception proves the rule. The liberal opposition shows us what the liberal position has become, to what extent freedom is embodied in man.

Therefore, if we have remarked that the defenders of freedom of the press in the Assembly of the Estates are by no means equal

---

[a] J. Goethe, *Verschiedenes über Kunst.* Kapitel 2.— *Ed.*

to their task, this applies still more to the Provincial Assembly as a whole.

Nevertheless, we begin our account of the Assembly proceedings at this point, not merely out of a special interest in freedom of the press, but equally out of a general interest in the Assembly. For we find the *specific estate* spirit nowhere more clearly, decisively and fully expressed than in the debates on the press. This holds good especially of the *opposition to freedom of the press,* just as in general it is in opposition to a *general freedom* that the spirit of a definite sphere in society, the individual interest of a particular estate and its natural one-sidedness of character are expressed most bluntly and recklessly and, as it were, show their teeth.

The debates provide us with a polemic of the princely social estate against freedom of the press, a polemic of the knightly estate, and a polemic of the urban estate, so that it is not the *individual,* but the *social estate* that conducts the polemic. What mirror, therefore, could reflect the inner nature of the Assembly better than the debates on the press?

We begin with the *opponents of a free press,* and, as is only fair, with a *speaker from the princely estate.*

We shall not deal with the content of the first part of his speech, to the effect "that freedom of the press and censorship are both evils, etc.", for this theme is more thoroughly expounded by another speaker. But we must not pass over his *characteristic method of argument.*

"Censorship," he said, "is a lesser evil than excesses on the part of the press." "*This conviction* has gradually so taken root in *our* Germany" (the question is: which part of Germany that is) "that the *Federation,* too, issued *laws* on the subject, which Prussia joined in approving and observing." [52]

The Assembly discusses liberation of the press from its bonds. These bonds themselves, proclaims the speaker, the fetters with which the press is shackled, prove that it is not destined for free activity. Its fettered existence testifies against its essential nature. The laws against freedom of the press are a refutation of freedom of the press.

This is a *diplomatic* argument against all reform, one which most decisively expresses the *classical theory* of a certain party.[53] Every restriction of freedom is a factual, irrefutable proof that at one time those who held power were convinced that freedom must be restricted, and this conviction then serves as a guiding principle for later views.

People were once ordered to believe that the earth did not go round the sun. Was Galileo refuted by this?

Similarly, in *our Germany* legal sanction was given to the conviction of the empire, which the individual princes shared, that serfdom was a quality inherent in certain human beings, that truth could be made most evident by surgical operation, we mean torture, and that the flames of hell could already be demonstrated to heretics by means of flames on earth.

Was not legal serfdom a factual proof against the rationalist fantasy that the human body was no object for handling and possession? Did not the primitive method of torture refute the false theory that truth could not be extracted by opening veins, that stretching limbs on the rack did not break down the victim's silence, that convulsions were not confessions?

Thus, in the speaker's opinion, the fact of censorship refutes freedom of the press, a statement which has its factual correctness, being a truth of such a factual character that its magnitude can be measured topographically, since beyond certain frontier barriers it ceases to be factual and true.

"Neither in speech nor in writing," we are further instructed, "neither in our Rhine Province nor in Germany as a whole, are any shackles to be seen on our true and nobler spiritual development."

The noble lustre of truth in our press is supposed to be a gift of the censorship.

We shall first of all turn the speaker's previous argument against himself; instead of a rational proof we shall give him an ordinance. In the recent Prussian censorship instruction it is officially made known that the press has hitherto been subjected to excessive restrictions, that it has still to achieve true national content. The speaker can see that convictions in *our Germany* are liable to change.

But what an illogical paradox to regard the censorship as a basis for improving our press!

The greatest orator of the French revolution, whose *voix toujours tonnante*[a] still echoes in our day; the lion whose roar one must have heard oneself in order to join with the people in calling out to him: "Well roared, lion!"[b] — *Mirabeau* — developed his talent in prison. Are prisons on that account schools of eloquence?

If, despite all spiritual toll systems, the German spirit has become capable of large-scale enterprise, it is a truly princely prejudice to think that it is the customs barriers and cordons that have made it

---

[a] Ever thundering voice.— *Ed.*

[b] W. Shakespeare, *A Midsummer Night's Dream*, Act V, Scene 1.— *Ed.*

so. The spiritual development of Germany has gone forward not *owing to,* but *in spite of,* the censorship. If the press under the censorship becomes stunted and wretched, this is put forward as an argument against a free press although it only testifies against an unfree press. If the press, in spite of censorship, retains its characteristic essence, this is put forward in support of censorship although it only testifies in favour of the spirit and not the fetters.

By the way, *"true and nobler development"* is another question.

In the period of strict observance of censorship from 1819 to 1830 (later, in a large part of Germany although not in "our Germany", the censorship itself came under censorship owing to the circumstances of the time and the unusual convictions which had been formed) our literature experienced its *"Abendblatt period",* which can be called "true and noble and spiritual and rich in development" with as much right as the editor of the *Abendzeitung,* named *"Winkler",* had in humorously adopting the pseudonym *"Bright",* although we cannot even credit him with the brightness of a bog at midnight. This "backwoodsman"[a] with the trade name "Bright" is the prototype of the literature of the time, and that Lenten period will convince posterity that if few saints could endure forty days without food, the whole of Germany, which was not even saint-like, managed to live over twenty years without producing or consuming spiritual nourishment. The press had become *vile,* and one could only hesitate to say whether the lack of understanding exceeded the lack of character, and whether the absence of form exceeded the absence of content, or the reverse. For Germany, criticism would reach its zenith if it could prove that that period never existed. The sole literary field in which at that time the pulse of a living spirit could still be felt, the *philosophical* field, ceased to speak German, for German had ceased to be the language of thought. The spirit spoke in incomprehensible mysterious words because comprehensible words were no longer allowed to be comprehended.

As far then as the example of *Rhenish literature* is concerned—and, of course, this example rather closely concerns the Rhine Province Assembly—one could wander through all five administrative districts with Diogenes' lantern and nowhere would one meet "this man". We do not regard this as a defect of the Rhine Province, but rather as a proof of its practical and political good sense. The Rhine Province can produce a *"free press",* but for an *"unfree"* one it lacks adroitness and illusions.

---

[a] In German "Krähwinkler", a pun on the man's name.— *Ed.*

The literary period that has just ended, which we could call the "literary period of strict censorship", is therefore clear historical proof that the censorship has undoubtedly influenced the development of the German spirit in a disastrous, irresponsible way, and that therefore it is by no means destined, as the speaker imagined, to be *magister bonarum artium*.[a] Or should one understand by a "nobler and true press" one which bears its chains with decency?

If the speaker "took the liberty" of recalling "a well-known saying about the little finger and the whole hand", we take the liberty in return of asking whether it does not most befit the dignity of a government to give the spirit of the people not merely *one* whole hand but both hands whole?

As we have seen, our speaker disposes of the relation between censorship and spiritual development in a carelessly aristocratic, diplomatically sober way. He represents the negative aspect of his social estate still more resolutely in his attack on the *historical shaping of freedom of the press*.

As regards freedom of the press among other nations, he says:

"*England* cannot serve as a measuring-rod, because, it is claimed, centuries ago conditions were *historically* created there which could not be brought about in any other country by the application of theories, but which had their justification in *England's specific conditions*." "In *Holland*, freedom of the press was unable to save the country from an *oppressive national debt* and to a very large extent it helped to *bring about a revolution* which resulted in the loss of half the country."

We shall pass over France, to come back to it later.

"Finally, should it not be possible to find in *Switzerland* an Eldorado blessed by freedom of the press? Does one not think with *disgust* of the savage party quarrels carried on in the newspapers there, in which the parties, with a correct sense of their small degree of human dignity, are named *after parts of an animal's body*, being divided into *horn-men* and *claw-men*, and have made themselves despised by all their neighbours on account of their boorish, abusive speeches!"

The *English* press, he says, is not an argument in favour of freedom of the press in general, *because* of its *historical foundations*. The press in England has merit *only* because it developed historically, not as a press in general, for then, he alleges, it would have had to develop *without* historical foundations. History therefore has the merit here, and not the press. As if the press, too, were not part of history, as if the English press under Henry VIII, the Catholic Mary, Elizabeth and James did not have to wage a hard and often savage struggle in order to win for the English nation its historical foundations!

---

[a] Teacher of the fine arts.— *Ed.*

And would it not, on the contrary, testify in favour of freedom of the press if the English press, having the greatest freedom from restraint, did not destructively affect the historical foundations? However, the speaker is not consistent.

The English press is no proof *in favour of* the press in general, *because* it is English. The Dutch press testifies *against* the press in general, *although* it is only Dutch. In the one case all the merits of the press are ascribed to the historical foundations, in the other case all the defects of the historical foundations are ascribed to the press. In the one case the press is not supposed to have had its share also in historical progress, in the other case history is not supposed to have had its share also in the defects of the press. Just as the press in England is bound up with the latter's history and specific conditions, so also in Holland and Switzerland.

Is the press supposed to reflect, abolish or develop the historical foundations? The speaker makes each into a matter of reproach for the press.

He blames the *Dutch* press, *because of* its *historical* development. It ought to have *prevented* the course of *history*, it ought to have saved Holland from an *oppressive national debt*! What an unhistorical demand! The Dutch press could not prevent the period of Louis XIV; the Dutch press could not prevent the English navy under Cromwell from rising to the first place in Europe; it could not cast a spell on the ocean which would have saved Holland from the painful role of being the arena of the warring continental powers; it was as little able as all the censors in Germany put together to annul Napoleon's despotic decrees.

But has a *free* press ever increased national debts? When, under the regency of the Duke of Orleans, the whole of France plunged into Law's financial lunacies, who opposed this fantastic storm and stress period of money speculations except for a few satirists, who of course received not banknotes but notes sending them to the Bastille.

The demand that the press should be the saviour from the *national debt*, which can be extended to say that it should also pay the debts of individuals, reminds one of that writer who always grumbled at the doctor because, although the latter cured his bodily ailments, he did not at the same time correct the misprints in his writings. Freedom of the press is as little able to promise to make a human being or a nation perfect as the physician. It is itself no perfection.[a] What a trivial way of behaving it is to abuse

---

[a] According to the errata to the *Rheinische Zeitung* No. 130, May 10, 1842, this should read: "It is itself perfection."— *Ed.*

what is good for being some specific good and not all good at
once, for being *this* particular good and *not some other*. Of course,
if freedom of the press were all in all it would make all other
functions of a nation, and the nation itself, superfluous.

The speaker blames the Dutch press for the *Belgian revolution*
No one with any historical education will deny that the separation of Belgium from Holland was an incomparably *greater
historical event* than their union.[54]

The press in Holland is said to have brought about the Belgian
revolution. Which press? The progressive or the reactionary? It is
a question which we can also raise in France; if the speaker blames
the clerical Belgian press, which at the same time was democratic, he should also blame the clerical press in France, which at the
same time was absolutist. Both helped to overthrow their governments. In France it was not freedom of the press but censorship
that made for revolution.

But leaving this out of account, the Belgian revolution *appeared*
at first as a spiritual revolution, as a revolution of the press. The
assertion that the press caused the Belgian revolution has no sense
beyond that. But is that a matter for blame? Must the revolution at
once assume a *material form*? Strike instead of speaking? The
government can materialise a spiritual revolution; a material revolution must first spiritualise the government.

The Belgian revolution is a product of the Belgian spirit. So the
press, too, the freest manifestation of the spirit in our day, has its
share in the Belgian revolution. The Belgian press would not have
been the Belgian press if it had stood aloof from the revolution,
but equally the Belgian revolution would not have been Belgian if
it had not been at the same time a revolution of the press. The
Revolution of a people is *total*; that is, each sphere carries it out
in its own way; why not also the press as the press?

In blaming the Belgian press, therefore, the speaker is *blaming
Belgium*, not the press. It is here that we find the starting point of
his historical view of freedom of the press. The *popular* character
of the free press — and it is well known that even the artist does
not paint great historical pictures with water-colours — the historical individuality of the free press, which makes it the specific
expression of its specific popular spirit, are repugnant to the speaker from the princely estate. He demands instead that the press
of the various nations should always be a press holding *his* views,
a press of *haute volée*,[a] and should revolve around certain individ-

---

[a] High society.— *Ed.*

uals instead of around the spiritual heavenly bodies, the nations. This demand stands out undisguised in his verdict on the
Swiss press.

We permit ourselves a preliminary question. Why did the
speaker not recall that the Swiss press through Albrecht von
Haller opposed the Voltairean enlightenment? Why does he not
bear in mind that even if Switzerland is not exactly an Eldorado,
nevertheless it has produced the prophet of the future princely
Eldorado, once again a certain Herr von Haller, who in his
Restauration der Staatswissenschaften laid the foundation for the
"nobler and true" press, for the *Berliner politisches Wochenblatt?* By
their fruits ye shall know them. And what other country in the
world could oppose to Switzerland a fruit of this luscious legitimacy?

The speaker finds fault with the *Swiss press* for adopting the
"animal party names" of "horn-men and claw-men", in short
because it speaks in the *Swiss language* and to *Swiss people,* who live
in a certain patriarchal harmony with oxen and cows. *The press of
this country is the press of precisely this country.* There is nothing
more to be said about it. At the same time, however, a free press
transcends the limitations of a country's particularism, as once
again the Swiss press proves.

As regards *animal party names* in particular, let us remark that
religion itself reveres the *animal* as a symbol of the spiritual. Our
speaker, of course, will condemn the *Indian* press, which has
revered with religious fervour Sabala the cow and Hanuman the
monkey. He will reproach the Indian press for the Indian religion,
just as he does the Swiss press for the Swiss character. But there is
a press which he will hardly want to subject to censorship; we
refer to the *holy press,* the *Bible.* Does this not divide all mankind
into the two great parties of *sheep* and *goats?* Does not God Himself
describe his attitude to the houses of Judah and Israel in the
following terms: I shall be to the house of Judah as a *moth* and to
the house of Israel as a *maggot.*[a] Or, what is more familiar to us
laymen, is there not a *princely literature* which turns all *anthropology*
into *zoology?* We mean the literature of *heraldry.* That contains
things still more curious than horn-men and claw-men.

What, therefore, was the accusation the speaker levelled against
freedom of the press? *That the defects of a nation are at the same time
the defects of its press,* that the press is the ruthless language and
manifest image of the historical spirit of the people. Did he prove

---

[a] Hosea 5:12, paraphrased.— *Ed.*

that the *spirit of the German people* is an exception to this great natural privilege? He showed that every nation expresses *its* spirit through *its* press. Ought not the philosophically educated spirit of the Germans to be entitled to what, according to the speaker's own assertion, is to be found among the animal-fettered Swiss?

Finally, does the speaker think that the *national* defects of a free press are not just as much *national defects of the censors?* Are the censors excluded from the historical whole? Are they unaffected by the spirit of a time? Unfortunately, it may be so, but what man of sound mind would not rather pardon sins of the nation and the time in the press than sins against the nation and the time in the censorship?

We remarked in the introduction that the various speakers voice the polemic of their *particular estate* against freedom of the press. The speaker from the princely estate put forward in the first place *diplomatic* grounds. He proved that freedom of the press was wrong on the basis of the *princely convictions* clearly enough expressed in the censorship laws. He considered that the nobler and true development of the German spirit has been *created* by the restrictions from above. Finally, he waged a polemic *against the peoples* and with noble dread repudiated freedom of the press as the tactless, indiscreet speech of the people addressed to itself.

[*Rheinische Zeitung* No. 130, May 10, 1842, Supplement]

The speaker from the knightly estate, to whom we now come, wages his polemic not against the peoples, but against persons. He questions *human freedom* in *freedom of the press,* and *law* in the *law on the press.* Before dealing with the actual question of freedom of the press, he takes up the question of *unabridged and daily publication of the Assembly debates.* We shall follow him step by step.

"The first of the proposals for *publication of our proceedings* suffices." "Let it be in the *hands of the Provincial Assembly* to make a *wise use* of the permission granted."

That is precisely the *punctum quaestionis.*[a] The province believes that the Provincial Assembly will be under its control only when the publication of the debates is no longer left to the arbitrary decision of the Assembly in its wisdom, but has become a legal necessity. We should have to call the new concession a new step backwards if it had to be interpreted in such a way that publication depends on an arbitrary decision by the Assembly of the Estates. *Privileges of the estates are in no way rights of the province.* On the

---

[a] The crux of the question.— *Ed.*

contrary, the rights of the province cease when they become privileges of the estates. Thus the estates of the Middle Ages appropriated for themselves all the country's constitutional rights and turned them into privileges against the country.

The citizen does not want to have anything to do with right as a privilege. Can he regard it as a right if new privileged persons are added to the old ones?

In this way, the rights of the Provincial Assembly are no longer *rights of the province*, but *rights against the province*, and the Assembly itself would be the *greatest wrong against the province* but with the mystical significance of being supposed to embody its greatest right.

How greatly the *speaker from the knightly estate* is imbued with this *medieval* conception of the Assembly, how unreservedly he upholds the privilege of the estate against the rights of the province, will be seen from the continuation of his speech.

"The extension of this permission" (for publication of the debates) "could only result from *inner* conviction, but not from *external* influences."

A surprising turn of phrase! The influence of the province on *its* Assembly is characterised as something *external* to which the conviction of the Assembly of the Estates is contrasted as a *delicate inner feeling* whose highly sensitive nature calls out to the province: *Noli me tangere!*[a] This plaintive rhetoric about *"inner conviction"* in contrast to the rude, external, unauthorised north wind of "public conviction" is the more noteworthy since the purpose of the proposal was precisely to make the inner conviction of the Assembly of the Estates external. Here too, of course, there is an inconsistency. Where it seems to the speaker more convenient, in *church* controversies, he appeals to the province.

"We," continues the speaker, "would *let* it" (publication) "*take place* where *we* consider this expedient, and would *restrict* it where an extension would appear to *us* purposeless or *even* harmful."

We will do what *we* like. *Sic volo, sic jubeo, stat pro ratione voluntas.*[b] It is truly the language of a ruler, which naturally has a pathetic flavour when coming from a modern baron.

Who are *we*? The *estates.* The publication of the debates is intended for the province and not for the estates, but the speaker teaches us to know better. Publication of the debates also is a *privilege* of the Assembly of the Estates, which has the right, if it

---

[a] Touch me not! — *Ed.*

[b] Thus I wish it, thus I order it; the will takes the place of reason (Juvenal, *Satires*, vi, 223).— *Ed.*

thinks fit, to have its wisdom echoed by the many voices of the press.

The speaker knows only the province of the estates, not the estates of the province. The Assembly of the Estates has a province to which the privilege of its activity extends, but the province has no estates through which it could itself be active. Of course, the province has the right, under prescribed conditions, to create these gods for itself, but as soon as they are created, it must, like a fetish worshipper, forget that these gods are its own handiwork.

In this connection there is no telling, *inter alia,* why a *monarchy without a Provincial Assembly* is not of more value than a *monarchy with a Provincial Assembly,* for if the Assembly does not represent the will of the province, we have more confidence in the public intelligence of the government than in the private intelligence of landed property.

We are confronted here with the peculiar spectacle, due perhaps to the nature of the Provincial Assembly, of the province having to fight not so much through its representatives as against them. According to the speaker, the Assembly does not regard the general rights of the province as the Assembly's only privileges, for in that case the daily unabridged publication of the Assembly proceedings would be a new right of the Assembly, because it would be a new right of the province; on the contrary, according to the speaker, the province must regard the privileges of the Assembly of the Estates as the province's only rights; and why not also the privileges of some class of officials and of the nobility or the clergy!

Indeed, our speaker declares quite openly that the privileges of the Assembly of the Estates decrease in proportion as the rights of the province increase.

"Just as it seems to *him* desirable that *here in the Assembly* there should be *freedom of discussion* and that an over-anxious weighing of words should be avoided, it seems to him equally necessary, *in order to maintain this freedom of expression* and *this frankness* of speech, that *our words* at the time should be judged only by *those for whom they are intended.*"

Precisely because freedom of discussion, the speaker concludes, is desirable in our Assembly — and what freedoms would we not find desirable where we are concerned? — precisely for that reason freedom of discussion is not desirable in the province. Because it is desirable that we speak *frankly,* it is still more desirable to keep the province *in thrall* to secrecy. *Our* words are not *intended* for the province.

One must acknowledge the tact with which the speaker has perceived that by unabridged publication of its debates the Assembly would become a right of the province instead of a privilege of the Assembly of the Estates, that the Assembly, having become an immediate object of the public spirit, would have to decide to be a personification of the latter, and that, having been put in the light of the general consciousness, it would have to renounce its particular nature in favour of the general one.

But whereas the knightly speaker mistakenly regards personal privileges and individual freedoms *vis-à-vis* the nation and the government as general rights, and thereby unquestionably and pertinently expresses the exclusive spirit of his *estate*, on the other hand he interprets the spirit of the province in an absolutely wrong way by likewise transforming its general demands into personal desires.

Thus the speaker seems to impute to the province a personally passionate curiosity as regards *our words* (i.e., those of prominent persons in the Assembly of 'the Estates).

We assure him that the province is by no means curious about "the words" of the representatives of the estates as individuals, and only "such" words can they rightly call "their" words. On the contrary, the province demands that the words of the representatives of the estates should be converted into the publicly audible voice of the country.

The question is whether the province should be *conscious of being represented* or not! Should a new mystery of representation be added to the mystery of government? In the government, too, the people is represented. Hence a new representation of the people through the estates is quite meaningless unless its specific character is precisely that in this case matters are not dealt with on behalf of the province but, on the contrary, the province itself deals with them; that the province is not represented in it but rather represents itself. A representation which is divorced from the consciousness of those whom it represents is no representation. What I do not know, I do not worry about. It is a senseless contradiction that the functioning of the state, which primarily expresses the *self-activity* of the individual provinces, takes place without their *formal* co-operation, without their joint *knowledge*; it is a senseless contradiction that my self-activity should consist of acts unknown to me and done by another.

A publication of the Assembly proceedings that depends on the arbitrary ruling of the Assembly of the Estates, however, is worse than none at all, for if the Assembly tells me not what it is in reality, but what it wants to seem to be in my eyes, I shall take it for what it gives itself out to be, for mere semblance, and things are bad when semblance has a legal existence.

Indeed, can even daily, unabridged publication *by printing* be rightly called *unabridged* and *public*? Is there no abridgement in substituting the written for the spoken word, graphic systems for persons, action on paper for real action? Or does publicity consist only in a *real* matter being reported to the public, and not rather in its being reported to the *real public*, i.e., not to an imaginary reading public, but to the living and actually present public?

Nothing is more contradictory than that the *highest public* activity of the province is secret, that in private lawsuits the doors of the court are open to the province, but that in its own lawsuit the province has to remain outside.

In its true consistent meaning, therefore, unabridged publication of the Assembly proceedings can only be *full publicity for the activity of the Assembly*.

Our speaker, however, proceeds to regard the Assembly as a kind of club.

"From *many years' acquaintance, a good personal understanding* has developed among most of us in spite of the most diverse views on various matters, a relationship which is *inherited by newcomers*.

"Precisely for that reason we are most of all able to appreciate the *value of our words*, and do so the more frankly as we allow ourselves to be less subject to *external* influences, which could only be useful if they came to us in the form of *well-meaning* counsel, but not in the form of a *dogmatic judgment*, of praise or blame, seeking to influence *our personality* through *public opinion*."

The Herr Speaker appeals to our feelings.

We are so intimate together, we discuss things so openly, we weigh the *value of our words* so exactly; are we to allow our attitude, which is so patriarchal, so distinguished, so convenient, to be changed by the judgment of the province, which perhaps attaches less value to our words?

God help us! The Assembly cannot bear the light of day. We feel more at ease in the darkness of private life. If the whole province has sufficient confidence to entrust its rights to single individuals, it is obvious that these individuals are condescending enough to accept the confidence of the province, but it would be really extravagant to demand that they should repay like for like and trustingly surrender themselves, their achievements, their personalities, to the judgment of the province, which has already pronounced a significant judgment on them. In any case, it is more important that the personality of the representatives of

the estates should not be endangered by the province than that
the interests of the province should not be endangered by the
representatives of the estates.

We want to be both fair and very gracious. It is true that
we — and we are a sort of government — permit no dogmatic
judgment, no praise or blame, no influence of public opinion on
our *persona sacrosancta,* but we do allow *well-meaning counsel,* not in
the abstract sense that it means well for the country, but in the
fuller-sounding sense that it expresses a passionate tenderness for
the members of the estates, a specially high opinion of their
excellence.

True, one might think that if publicity is harmful to good
understanding among us, then the latter must be harmful to
publicity. However this sophistry forgets that the Provincial Assembly is the Assembly of the Estates and not the Assembly of the
Province. And who could resist the most convincing of all
arguments? If, in accordance with the constitution, the province
appoints estates *to represent* its *general intelligence,* it thereby totally
renounces *all its own judgment* and understanding, which are now
solely incorporated in the chosen representatives. Just as the
legend has it that great inventors were put to death or, what is no
legend, that they were buried alive in fortresses as soon as they
had imparted their secret to the ruler, so the political reason of
the province always falls on its own sword as soon as it has made
its great invention of the Assembly, but of course to rise again like
the phoenix for the next elections.

After these obtrusively emotional descriptions of the dangers
threatening the personalities of the estates from outside, i.e., from
the province, through publication of the proceedings, the speaker
closes this diatribe with the *guiding* thought that we have traced
through his speech up to now.

"Parliamentary freedom," a very fine-sounding expression, "is in its first period of
development. It must gain by *protection* and *care* that *internal* force and *independence*
which are absolutely necessary before it can be exposed without detriment to
external storms."

Once again the old fatal antithesis of the Assembly as something
internal and the province as something *external.*

In any case, we have long been of the opinion that *parliamentary
freedom* is at the beginning of its beginning, and the above speech
has convinced us afresh that the *primitiae studiorum in politicis*[a]
have still not been completed. But by that we by no means im-

---

[a] Primary studies in politics.— *Ed.*

ply—and the above speech once again confirms our opinion—
that the Assembly should be given a still longer time in which to
continue its independent ossification in *opposition* to the province.
Perhaps by *parliamentary freedom* the speaker understands the freedom of the *old French* parliaments. According to his own admission, a *many years'* acquaintance prevails among the Assembly of the
Estates, its spirit is even transmitted as a *hereditary disease* to the
homines novi, yet the time has still not come for publicity? The
Twelfth Assembly may give the same reply as the Sixth, only with
the more emphatic expression that it is *too* independent to allow
itself to be deprived of the *aristocratic privilege of secret proceedings.*

Of course, the development of *parliamentary* freedom in the old
French sense, independence from public opinion, and the stagnation of the caste spirit, advance most thoroughly through isolation,
but to warn against precisely this development cannot be prema-
ture. A truly political assembly flourishes only under the great
protection of the *public spirit,* just as living things flourish only
in the *open air.* Only "exotic" plants, which have been transferred to a climate that is foreign to them, require the protection
and care of a *greenhouse.* Does the speaker regard the Assembly
as an "exotic" plant in the free, serene climate of the Rhine
Province?

In view of the fact that our speaker from the knightly estate
expounded with almost comic seriousness, with almost melancholy
dignity and almost religious pathos, the thesis of the *lofty wisdom* of
the Assembly of the Estates, as also of its medieval *freedom* and
independence, the uninitiated will be surprised to see him sink in
the question of the *freedom of the press* from the lofty wisdom of the
Provincial Assembly to the general *lack of wisdom of the human race,*
from the independence and freedom of the privileged social
estates he had extolled only just before to the *fundamental lack of
freedom and independence of human nature.* We are not surprised to
encounter here one of the present-day numerous champions of
the Christian-knightly, modern feudal principle, in short the
romantic principle.

These gentlemen, because they want to regard freedom not as
the natural gift of the universal sunlight of reason, but as the
supernatural gift of a specially favourable constellation of the
stars, because they regard freedom as merely an *individual property*
of certain persons and social estates, are in consequence compelled
to include universal reason and universal freedom among the *bad
ideas* and phantoms of "*logically constructed systems*". In order to
save the special freedoms of privilege, they proscribe the universal

freedom of human nature. Since, however, the bad brood of the nineteenth century, and the very consciousness of the modern knights that has been infected by this century, cannot comprehend what is in itself incomprehensible, because devoid of idea, namely, how internal, essential, universal determinations prove to be linked with certain human individuals by external, fortuitous, particular features, without being connected with the human essence, with reason in general, and therefore common to all individuals — because of this they necessarily have recourse to the *miraculous* and the *mystical*. Further, because the *real* position of these gentlemen in the modern state does not at all correspond to the notion they have of that position, because they live in a world *beyond the real one*, and because therefore *imagination* is their head and heart, being dissatisfied with their practical activity, they necessarily have recourse to theory, but to the *theory of the other world*, to *religion*, which in their hands, however, is given a polemical bitterness impregnated with political tendencies and becomes more or less consciously only a holy cloak for very secular, but at the same time fantastic desires.

Thus we shall find that to practical demands our speaker counterposes a mystical religious theory of the imagination, to real theories — a pettily clever, pragmatically cunning wisdom of experience drawn from the most superficial practice, to the human understanding — superhuman holiness, and to the real holiness of ideas — the arbitrariness and disbelief characterising a base point of view. The more aristocratic, more nonchalant, and therefore more sober, language of the speaker from the princely estate is superseded here by emotional affectation and fantastically extravagant unction, which previously withdrew much more into the background before the feeling of privilege.

"The less it is possible to deny that the press nowadays is a political power, the more erroneous seems to him the equally widespread view that truth and light will emerge *from the struggle between the good and the bad press* and can be expected to become more widely and effectively disseminated. *Man, individually and in the mass, is always one and the same. He is by his nature imperfect* and *immature* and needs *education* as long as his *development* continues, and it ceases only with his *death*. The art of education, however, does not consist in punishing prohibited actions, but in furthering good influences and keeping away evil ones. It is, however, inseparable from this *human imperfection* that the *siren song of evil* has a powerful effect on the masses and opposes the simple and sober voice of truth as an obstacle which, even if not absolute, is in any case difficult to overcome. The *bad* press appeals only to men's passions; no means are too bad for it when it is a question of attaining *its aim* by arousing passions — that aim being the *greatest possible dissemination of bad principles* and the *greatest possible furtherance of bad frames of mind*; it has at its disposal all the advantages of that most dangerous of all *offensives*, for which there are objectively no restrictions of right and subjectively no laws of morality or even of external decency. On the other hand, the *good press* is *always confined* to the *defensive*. For the most part its effect can only be that of *defending, restraining* and *consolidating*, without being able to boast of any significant progress in enemy territory. It is good fortune enough if external obstacles do not render this still more difficult".

We have given this passage in full in order not to weaken its possible emotional impression on the reader.

The speaker has put himself *à la hauteur des principes*.[a] In order to combat *freedom of the press*, the thesis of the *permanent immaturity* of the human race has to be defended. It is sheer tautology to assert that if absence of freedom is men's essence, freedom is contrary to his essence. Malicious sceptics could be daring enough not to take the speaker at his word.

If the immaturity of the human race is the mystical ground for opposing freedom of the press, then the censorship at any rate is a highly reasonable means against the maturity of the human race.

What undergoes development is imperfect. Development ends only with death. Hence it would be truly consistent to kill man in order to free him from this state of imperfection. That at least is what the speaker concludes in order to kill freedom of the press. In his view, true education consists in keeping a person wrapped up in a cradle throughout his life, for as soon as he learns to walk, he learns also to fall, and only by falling does he learn to walk. But if we all remain in swaddling-clothes, who is to wrap us in them? If we all remain in the cradle, who is to rock us? If we are all prisoners, who is to be prison warder?

Man, individually and in the mass, is imperfect by nature. *De principiis non est disputandum*.[b] Granted! What follows from that? The arguments of our speaker are imperfect, governments are imperfect, assemblies are imperfect, freedom of the press is imperfect, every sphere of human existence is imperfect. Hence if one of these spheres ought not to exist because of this imperfection, none of them has the right to exist, man in general has no right to exist.

Given man's fundamental imperfection—let us assume it is true—then we know in advance that all human institutions are imperfect. There is no need to touch on that further, it does not speak for them or against them, it is not their *specific character*, it is not their distinctive mark.

---

[a] On the level of his principles.—*Ed.*

[b] There can be no dispute about principles.—*Ed.*

Amid all these imperfections, why should precisely the free press be perfect? Why does an imperfect provincial estate demand a perfect press?

The imperfect requires education. Is not education also human and therefore imperfect? Does not education itself also require education?

If then, by *its very existence*, everything human is imperfect, ought we therefore to lump everything together, have the same respect for everything, good and evil, truth and falsehood? The true conclusion must be that as in looking at a picture I have to leave the spot from which I see only blots of colour but not colours, irregularly intersecting lines but not a drawing, similarly I must abandon the point of view which shows me the world and human relations only in their most external appearance, and recognise that this point of view is unsuitable for judging the value of things; for how could I judge, distinguish things, from a point of view which admits only the one flat idea about the whole universe that everything in it is imperfect? This point of view itself is the most imperfect of all the imperfections it sees around it. We must therefore take the essence of the inner idea as the measure to evaluate the existence of things. Then we shall less allow ourselves to be led astray by a one-sided and trivial experience, since in such cases the result is indeed that all experience ceases, all judgment is abolished, all cows are black.

[*Rheinische Zeitung* No. 132, May 12, 1842, Supplement]

From the standpoint of the idea, it is self-evident that freedom of the press has a justification quite different from that of censorship because it is itself an embodiment of the idea, an embodiment of freedom, a positive good, whereas censorship is an embodiment of unfreedom, the polemic of a world outlook of semblance against the world outlook of essence; it has a merely negative nature.

No! No! No! our speaker breaks in. I do not find fault with the semblance, but with the essence. Freedom is the wicked feature of freedom of the press. Freedom creates the possibility of evil. Therefore freedom is evil.

Evil freedom!

"He has stabbed her in the dark forest
And sunk the body in the depths of the Rhine!" [a]

_____
[a] L. Uhland, *Die Rache* (paraphrased).— *Ed.*

But:

> "This time I must talk to you,
> Lord and master, hear me calmly!" [a]

But does not freedom of the press exist in the land of censorship? The press in general is a realisation of human freedom. Consequently, where is a press there is freedom of the press.

True, in the land of censorship the state has no freedom of the press, but one organ of the state has it, viz., the *government.* Apart from the fact that official government documents enjoy perfect freedom of the press, does not the censor exercise daily an unconditional freedom of the press, if not directly, then indirectly?

Writers are, as it were, his secretaries. When the secretary does not express the opinion of his chief, the latter strikes out the botch. Hence the censorship makes the press.

The censor's deletions are for the press what the straight lines — kus [55] — of the Chinese are for their thought. The censor's kus are the categories of literature, and it is well known that the categories are the typical souls of the whole content.

Freedom is so much the essence of man that even its opponents implement it while combating its reality; they want to appropriate for themselves as a most precious ornament what they have rejected as an ornament of human nature.

No man combats freedom; at most he combats the freedom of others. Hence every kind of freedom has always existed, only at one time as a special privilege, at another as a universal right.

The question has now for the first time been given a *consistent meaning.* It is not a question whether freedom of the press ought to exist, for it always exists. The question is whether freedom of the press is a privilege of particular individuals or whether it is a privilege of the human mind. The question is whether a right of one side ought to be a wrong for the other side. The question is whether *"freedom of the mind"* has more right than *"freedom against the mind".*

If, however, the *"free press"* and *"freedom of the press"* as the realisation of *"universal freedom"* are to be rejected, then this applies still more to *censorship* and the *censored press* as the realisation of a *special freedom,* for how can the *species* be good if the *genus* is bad? If the speaker were consistent he would have to reject not the free press, but the press as a whole. According to him, the press would only be good if it were not a product of freedom, i.e., not a *human* product. Hence in general only *animals* or *gods* would have the right to a press.

---

[a] J. Goethe, *Der Zauberlehrling.*—Ed.

Or ought we perhaps—the speaker dare not say it out-right—to suppose *divine inspiration* of the government and of the speaker himself?

If a private person boasts of divine inspiration, there is only one speaker in our society who can refute him officially, viz., the *psychiatrist*.

English history, however, has sufficiently well demonstrated how the assertion of divine inspiration from above gives rise to the counter-assertion of divine inspiration from below; Charles I went to the scaffold as the result of divine inspiration from below.

True, our speaker from the knightly estate proceeds, as we shall hear later, to describe censorship and freedom of the press, the censored press and the free press, as *two evils*, but he does not go so far as to admit that the press in general is *an evil*.

On the contrary! He divides the entire press into "*good*" and "*bad*".

About the *bad* press, we are told something incredible: that its aim is badness and the greatest possible dissemination of badness. We pass over the fact that the speaker has too much confidence in our credulity when he demands that we should take his word for it and believe in *badness as a profession*. We merely remind him of the axiom that everything human is imperfect. Will not, therefore, the bad press also be imperfectly bad, and therefore good, and the good press imperfectly good, and therefore bad?

The speaker, however, shows us the reverse side. He asserts that the bad press is better than the good press, for it is always on the *offensive*, whereas the good press is on the *defensive*. But he has himself told us that man's *development* ends only with his death. Of course, he has not told us much by that, he has said nothing but that life ends with death. But if human life is development and the good press is always on the defensive, acting only by "defending, restraining and consolidating" itself, does it not thereby continually oppose development, and therefore life? Hence either this good defensive press is bad, or development is the bad thing. In view of this, the speaker's previous assertion, too, that the aim of the "bad press is the greatest possible dissemination of bad principles and the greatest possible furtherance of bad frames of mind" loses its mystical incredibility in a rational interpretation: the bad feature of the bad press lies in the greatest possible dissemination of principles and the greatest possible furtherance of a frame of mind.

The relation of the good press to the bad press becomes still stranger when the speaker assures us that the good press is *impotent* and the bad press *omnipotent,* for the former is without effect on the people, whereas the latter has an irresistible effect. For the speaker, the good press and the impotent press are identical. Does he want to say, therefore, that what is good is impotent or that what is impotent is good?

He contrasts the sober voice of the good press to the siren song of the bad press. But surely a sober voice allows of the best and most effective singing. The speaker seems to be acquainted only with the sensuous heat of passion, but not with the hot passion of truth, not with the victory-assured enthusiasm of reason, not the irresistible ardour of moral powers.

Under the frames of mind of the bad press he includes "pride, which recognises no authority in church and state", "envy", which preaches abolition of the aristocracy, and other things, which we shall deal with later. For the time being, let us be satisfied with the question: Whence does the speaker know that this isolated element is the good? If the universal powers of life are bad and we have heard that the bad is omnipotent, that it is what influences the masses, *what* or *who* has still any right to claim to be good? The arrogant assertion is this: my individuality is the good, those few individuals who are in accord with my individuality are the good, and the wicked, bad press refuses to recognise it. The bad press!

If at the beginning the speaker turned his attack on freedom of the press into an attack on freedom in general, here he turns it into an attack on the good. His fear of the bad is seen to be a fear of the good. Hence he founds censorship on a recognition of the bad and a refusal to recognise the good. Do I not despise a man to whom I say in advance: your opponent is bound to be victorious in the struggle, because, although you yourself are a very sober fellow and a very good neighbour, you are a very poor hero; because, although you bear consecrated arms, you do not know how to use them; because, although you and I, both of us, are perfectly convinced of your perfection, the world will never share this conviction; because, although things are all right as regards your intention, they are in a bad way as regards your energy?

Although the speaker's distinction between the good press and the bad press makes any further refutation superfluous, since this distinction becomes entangled in its own contradictions, nevertheless we must not lose sight of the main thing, namely, that the speaker has formulated the question quite incorrectly and has based himself on what he had to prove.

If one wants to speak of two kinds of press, the distinction between them must be drawn from the nature of the press itself, not from considerations lying outside it. The censored press or the free press, one of these two must be the good or the bad press. The debate turns precisely on whether the censored press or the free press is good or bad, i.e., whether it is in the nature of the press to have a free or unfree existence. To make the bad press a refutation of the free press is to maintain that the free press is bad and the censored press good, which is precisely what had to be proved.

Base frames of mind, personal intrigues, infamies, occur alike in the censored and the free press. Therefore the generic difference between them is not that they produce individual products of this or that kind; flowers grow also in swamps. We are concerned here with the essence, the inner character, which distinguishes the censored from the free press.

A free press that is bad does not correspond to its essence. The censored press with its hypocrisy, its lack of character, its eunuch's language, its dog-like tail-wagging, merely realises the inner conditions of its essential nature.

The censored press remains bad even when it turns out good products, for these products are good only insofar as they represent the free press within the censored press, and insofar as it is not in their character to be products of the censored press. The free press remains good even when it produces bad products, for the latter are deviations from the essential nature of the free press. A eunuch remains a bad human being even when he has a good voice. Nature remains good even when she produces monstrosities.

The essence of the free press is the characterful, rational, moral essence of freedom. The character of the censored press is the characterless monster of unfreedom; it is a civilised monster, a perfumed abortion.

Or does it still need to be proved that freedom of the press is in accord with the essence of the press, whereas censorship contradicts it? Is it not self-evident that external barriers to a spiritual life are not part of the inner nature of this life, that they deny this life and do not affirm it?

In order really to justify censorship, the speaker would have had to prove that censorship is part of the essence of freedom of the press; instead he proves that freedom is not part of man's essence. He rejects the whole genus in order to obtain one good species, for is not freedom after all the generic essence of all spiritual existence, and therefore of the press as well? In order to abolish the possibility of evil, he abolishes the possibility of good and realises evil, for only that which is a realisation of freedom can be humanly good.

We shall therefore continue to regard the censored press as a bad press so long as it has not been proved to us that censorship arises from the very essence of freedom of the press.

But even supposing that censorship and the nature of the press come into being together, although no animal, let alone an intelligent being, comes into the world in chains, what follows from that? That freedom of the press, as it exists from the official viewpoint, that is, the censorship, also needs censorship. And who is to censor the governmental press, if not the popular press?

True, another speaker thinks that the evil of censorship would be removed by being tripled, by the local censorship being put under provincial censorship, and the latter in its turn under Berlin censorship, freedom of the press being made one-sided, and the censorship many-sided. So many roundabout ways merely to live! Who is to censor the Berlin censorship? Let us therefore return to *our* speaker.

At the very beginning, he informed us that no light would emerge from the *struggle* between the good and the bad press. But, we may now ask, does he not want to make this *useless* struggle *permanent*? According to his own statement, is not the struggle itself between the censorship and the press a struggle between the good and the bad press?

Censorship does not abolish the struggle, it makes it one-sided, it converts an open struggle into a hidden one, it converts a struggle over principles into a struggle of principle without power against power without principle. The true censorship, based on the very essence of freedom of the press, is *criticism*. This is the tribunal which freedom of the press gives rise to of itself. Censorship is criticism as a monopoly of the government. But does not criticism lose its rational character if it is not open but secret, if it is not theoretical but practical, if it is not above parties but itself a party, if it operates not with the sharp knife of reason but with the blunt scissors of arbitrariness, if it only exersises criticism but will not submit to it, if it disavows itself during its realisation, and, finally, if it is so uncritical as to mistake an individual person for universal wisdom, peremptory orders for rational statements, ink spots for patches of sunlight, the crooked deletions of the censor for mathematical constructions, and crude force for decisive arguments?

During our exposal, we have shown how the fantastic, unctuous, soft-hearted mysticism of the speaker turns into the hard-heartedness of pettifogging mental pragmatism and into the narrow-mindedness of an unprincipled empirical calculation. In his arguments *on the relation between the censorship law* and *the press law, between preventive* and *repressive measures,* he spares us this trouble by proceeding himself to make a *conscious application* of his mysticism.

"*Preventive* or *repressive measures,* censorship or press law, this *alone* is the question at issue, in which connection it would not be inexpedient to examine somewhat more closely the *dangers* which have to be removed on one side or the other. Whereas censorship seeks to *prevent* what is evil, the press law seeks by punishment to guard against its *repetition.* Like *all* human institutions, both are *imperfect,* but the question here is which is the *less* so. Since it is a matter of purely spiritual things, *one* problem — indeed the most important for both of them — can never be solved. That is the problem of finding a form which expresses the intention of the legislator so clearly and definitely that right and wrong seem to be sharply separated and *all arbitrariness* removed. But what is *arbitrariness* except acting according to *individual discretion?* And how are the effects of individual discretion to be removed where purely spiritual things are concerned? To find the guiding line, so sharply drawn that inherent in it is the necessity of *having to be applied* in every *single* case in the meaning intended by the legislator, that is the philosopher's stone, which has not been discovered so far and is hardly likely to be. Hence *arbitrariness,* if by that one understands acting according to individual discretion, is inseparable both from censorship and from the *press law.* Therefore we have to consider both in their necessary imperfection and its consequences. If the censorship suppresses much that is good, the press law will not be capable of preventing much that is bad. Truth, however, cannot be suppressed for long. The more obstacles are put in its way, the more keenly it pursues its goal, and the more resoundingly it achieves it. But the bad word, like *Greek fire,* cannot be stopped after it has left the ballista, and is incalculable in its effects, because for it nothing is holy, and it is inextinguishable because it finds nourishment and means of propagation in human hearts."

The speaker is not fortunate in his comparisons. He is overcome with a poetic exultation as soon as he begins to describe the omnipotence of the bad. We have already heard how the voice of the good has an impotent, because sober, sound when pitted against the *siren song of evil.* Now evil even becomes *Greek fire,* whereas the speaker has nothing at all with which to compare truth, and if we were to put his "sober" words into a comparison, truth would be at best a *flint,* which scatters sparks the more brightly the more it is struck. A fine argument for slave traders — to bring out the Negro's human nature by flogging, an excellent maxim for the legislator — to issue repressive laws against truth so that it will the more keenly pursue its goal. The speaker seems to have respect for truth only when it becomes *primitive and spontaneous* and is manifested *tangibly.* The more barriers you put in the way of truth, the more vigorous is the truth you obtain! Up with the barriers!

But let us allow the sirens to sing!

The speaker's mystical *"theory of imperfection"* has at last borne its earthly fruits; it has thrown its moonstones at us; let us examine the moonstones!

Everything is imperfect. The censorship is imperfect, the press law is imperfect. That determines their essence. There is nothing more to say about the *correctness of their idea*, nothing remains for us to do except, from the standpoint of the very lowest empiricism, to find out by calculating probabilities on which side the most dangers lie. It is purely a difference of time whether measures are taken to prevent the evil itself by means of censorship or repetition of the evil by means of the press law.

One sees how the speaker, by the empty phrase about "human imperfection", manages to evade the essential, internal, characteristic difference between censorship and press law and transforms the controversy from a question of principle into a fairground dispute as to whether more bruised noses result from the censorship or from the press law.

If, however, a contrast is drawn between the press law and the censorship law, it is, in the first place, not a question of their consequences, but of their basis, not of their individual application, but of their legitimacy in general. Montesquieu has already taught us that despotism is more convenient to apply than legality and Machiavelli asserts that for princes the bad has better consequences than the good. Therefore, if we do not want to confirm the old *Jesuitical* maxim that a good end — and we doubt even the goodness of the end — justifies bad means, we have above all to investigate whether censorship by its essence is a *good* means.

The speaker is right in calling the censorship law a preventive measure, it is a precautionary measure of the police against freedom, but he is wrong in calling the press law a repressive measure. It is the rule of freedom itself which makes itself the yardstick of its own exceptions. The censorship measure is not a law. The press law is not a measure.

In the press law, freedom punishes. In the censorship law, freedom is punished. The censorship law is a law of suspicion against freedom. The press law is a vote of confidence which freedom gives itself. The press law punishes the abuse of freedom. The censorship law punishes freedom as an abuse. It treats freedom as a criminal, or is it not regarded in every sphere as a degrading punishment to be under police supervision? The censorship law has only the *form* of a law. The press law is a *real* law.

The press law is a *real law* because it is the positive existence of freedom. It regards freedom as the *normal* state of the press, the press as the mode of existence of freedom, and hence only comes into conflict with a press offence as an exception that contravenes its own rules and therefore annuls itself. Freedom of the press asserts itself as a press law, against attacks on freedom of the press itself, i.e., against press offences. The press law declares freedom to be inherent in the nature of the criminal. Hence what he has done against freedom he has done against himself and this self-injury appears to him as a *punishment* in which he sees a recognition of his freedom.

The press law, therefore, is far from being a repressive measure against freedom of the press, a mere means of preventing the repetition of a crime through fear of punishment. On the contrary, the *absence of press legislation* must be regarded as an exclusion of freedom of the press from the sphere of legal freedom, for legally recognised freedom exists in the state as *law.* Laws are in no way repressive measures against freedom, any more than the law of gravity is a repressive measure against motion, because while, as the law of gravitation, it governs the eternal motions of the celestial bodies, as the law of falling it kills me if I violate it and want to dance in the air. Laws are rather the positive, clear, universal norms in which freedom has acquired an impersonal, theoretical existence independent of the arbitrariness of the individual. A statute-book is a people's bible of freedom.

Therefore the *press law* is the *legal recognition of freedom of the press.* It constitutes *right,* because it is the positive existence of freedom. It must therefore exist, even if it is never put into application, as in North America, whereas censorship, like slavery, can never become lawful, even if it exists a thousand times over as a law.

There are no actual preventive laws. Law prevents only as a *command.* It only becomes *effective* law when it is infringed, for it is *true* law only when in it the unconscious natural law of freedom has become conscious state law. Where the law is real law, i.e., a form of existence of freedom, it is the real existence of freedom for man. Laws therefore, cannot prevent a man's actions, for they are indeed the inner laws of life of his action itself, the conscious reflections of his life. Hence law withdraws into the background in the face of man's life as a life of freedom, and only when his actual behaviour has shown that he has ceased to obey the natural law of freedom does law in the form of state law compel him to be free, just as the laws of physics confront me as something alien only when my life has ceased to be the life of these laws, when it has been *struck by illness*. Hence a *preventive law* is a *meaningless contradiction*.

A preventive law, therefore, has within it no *measure*, no *rational rule*, for a rational rule can only result from the nature of a thing, in this instance of freedom. It is *without measure*, for if prevention of freedom is to be effective, it must be as all-embracing as its object, i.e., unlimited. A preventive law is therefore the contradiction of an *unlimited limitation*, and the boundary where it ceases is fixed not by necessity, but by the fortuitousness of arbitrariness, as the censorship daily demonstrates *ad oculos*.[a]

The human body is mortal by nature. Hence illnesses are inevitable. Why does a man only go to the doctor when he is ill, and not when he is well? Because not only the illness, but even the doctor is an evil. Under constant medical tutelage, life would be regarded as an evil and the human body as an object for treatment by medical institutions. Is not death more desirable than life that is a mere preventive measure against death? Does not life involve also free movement? What is any illness except life that is hampered in its freedom? A perpetual physician would be an illness in which one would not even have the prospect of dying, but only of living. Let life die; death must not live. Has not the spirit more right than the body? Of course, this right has often been interpreted to mean that for minds capable of free motion physical freedom of movement is even harmful and therefore they are to be deprived of it. The starting point of the censorship is that illness is the normal state, or that the normal state, freedom, is to be regarded as an illness. The censorship continually assures the press that it, the press, is ill; and even if the latter furnishes the best proofs of its bodily health, it has to allow itself to be treated. But the censorship is not even a learned physician who applies different internal remedies according to the illness. It is a country surgeon who knows only a single mechanical panacea for everything, the scissors. It is not even a surgeon who aims at restoring my health, it is a surgical aesthete who considers superfluous everything about my body that displeases him, and removes whatever he finds repugnant; it is a quack who drives back a rash so that it is not seen, without caring in the least whether it then affects more sensitive internal parts.

You think it wrong to put birds in cages. Is not the cage a preventive measure against birds of prey, bullets and storms? You think it barbaric to blind nightingales, but it does not seem to you

---

[a] Before one's eyes.— *Ed.*

at all barbaric to put out the eyes of the press with the sharp pens of the censorship. You regard it as despotic to cut a free person's hair against his will, but the censorship daily cuts into the flesh of thinking people and allows only bodies without hearts, submissive bodies which show no reaction, to pass as healthy!

[*Rheinische Zeitung* No. 135, May 15, 1842, Supplement]

We have shown how the press law expresses a right and the censorship law a wrong. The censorship itself, however, admits that it is not an end in itself, that it is not something good in and for itself, that its basis therefore is the principle: "The end justifies the means." But an end which requires unjustified means is no justifiable end, and could not the press also adopt the principle and boast: "The end justifies the means"?

The censorship law, therefore, is not a law, it is a police measure; but it is a *bad police measure*, for it does not achieve what it intends, and it does not intend what it achieves.

If the censorship law wants to *prevent freedom* as something objectionable, the result is precisely the opposite. In a country of censorship, every forbidden piece of printed matter, i.e., printed without being censored, is an event. It is considered a martyr, and there is no martyr without a halo and without believers. It is regarded as an exception, and if freedom can never cease to be of value to mankind, so much the more valuable is an exception to the general lack of freedom. Every mystery has its attraction. Where public opinion is a mystery to itself, it is won over from the outset by every piece of writing that formally breaks through the mystical barriers. The censorship makes every forbidden work, whether good or bad, into an extraordinary document, whereas freedom of the press deprives every written work of an externally imposing effect.

If the censorship is *honest* in its intention, it would like to prevent arbitrariness, but it makes arbitrariness into a law. No danger that it can avert is greater than itself. The mortal danger for every being lies in losing itself. Hence lack of freedom is the real mortal danger for mankind. For the time being, leaving aside the moral consequences, bear in mind that you cannot enjoy the advantages of a free press without putting up with its inconveniences. You cannot pluck the rose without its thorns! And what do you lose with a free press?

The free press is the ubiquitous vigilant eye of a people's soul, the embodiment of a people's faith in itself, the eloquent link that connects the individual with the state and the world, the embodied culture that transforms material struggles into intellectual struggles and idealises their crude material form. It is a people's frank confession to itself, and the redeeming power of confession is well known. It is the spiritual mirror in which a people can see itself, and self-examination is the first condition of wisdom. It is the spirit of the state, which can be delivered into every cottage, cheaper than coal gas. It is all-sided, ubiquitous, omniscient. It is the ideal world which always wells up out of the real world and flows back into it with ever greater spiritual riches and renews its soul.

In the course of our exposal we have shown that censorship and press law are as different as arbitrariness and freedom, as formal law and actual law. But what holds good of the essence, holds good also of the appearance. What rightly holds good of both, holds good also of *their application*. Just as a press law is different from a censorship law, so the *judge's* attitude to the press *differs* from the *attitude of the censor*.

Of course, our speaker, whose eyes are fixed on the heavens, sees the earth far below him as a contemptible heap of dust, so that he has nothing to say about any flowers except that they are dusty. Here too, therefore, he sees only two measures which are *equally arbitrary* in their application, for arbitrariness is acting according to individual discretion, and the latter, he says, is inseparable from spiritual things, etc., etc. If the understanding of spiritual things is *individual,* how can one spiritual view be more right than another, the opinion of the censor more right than the opinion of the author? But we understand the speaker. It is notable that he goes out of his way to describe both censorship and press law as being without right in their application, in order to prove the right of the censorship, for since he knows everything in the world is imperfect, the only question for him is whether arbitrariness should be on the side of the people or on the side of the government.

His *mysticism* turns into the *licence* of putting *law* and *arbitrariness* on the same level and seeing only a formal difference where moral and legal opposites are concerned, for his polemic is directed not against the *press law,* but against *law in general.* Or is there any law which is necessarily such that in *every single case* it *must* be applied as the legislator intended and all *arbitrariness absolutely* excluded? Incredible audacity is needed to call such a meaningless task the *philosopher's stone,* since it could only be put forward by the most extreme ignorance. The law is universal. The case which has to be settled in accordance with the law is a particular case. To include the particular in the universal involves a judgment. The judgment is problematic. The law requires also a *judge*. If laws applied themselves, courts would be superfluous.

But everything human is imperfect! Therefore, *edite, bibite!* [a] Why do you want judges, since judges are human? Why do you want laws, since laws can only be executed by human beings, and all human operations are imperfect? Submit yourselves then to the goodwill of your superiors! Rhenish justice, like that of Turkey, is imperfect! Therefore, *edite, bibite!*

What a difference there is between a judge and a censor!

The censor has no law but his superiors. The judge has no superiors but the law. The judge, however, has the duty of interpreting the law, as *he understands* it after conscientious examination, in order to apply it in a particular case. The censor's duty is to understand the law as *officially interpreted* for him in a particular case. The independent judge belongs neither to me nor to the government. The dependent censor is himself a government organ. In the case of the judge, there is involved at most the unreliability of an individual intellect, in the case of the censor the unreliability of an individual character. The judge has a *definite* press offence put before him; confronting the censor is the spirit of the press. The judge judges my act according to a definite law; the censor not only punishes the crime, he *makes* it. If I am brought before the court, I am accused of disobeying an existing law, and for a law to be violated it must indeed exist. Where there is no press law there is no law which can be violated by the press. The censorship does not accuse me of violating an existing law. It condemns my opinion because it is not the opinion of the censor and his superiors. My openly performed act, which is willing to submit itself to the world and its judgment, to the state and its law, has sentence passed on it by a hidden, purely negative power, which cannot give itself the form of law, which shuns the light of day, and which is not bound by any general principles.

A *censorship law is an impossibility* because it seeks to punish not offences but opinions, because it cannot be anything but a *formula for the censor,* because no state has the courage to put in general legal terms what it can carry out in practice through the agency of the censor. For that reason, too, the operation of the censorship is entrusted not to the courts but to the police.

Even if censorship were in fact the same thing as justice, in the first place this would remain a fact without being a necessity. But, further, freedom includes not only *what* my life is, but equally *how*

---

[a] Eat, drink! (Words from a German student song.) — *Ed.*

I live, not only that I do what is free, but also that I do it freely. Otherwise what difference would there be between an architect and a beaver except that the beaver would be an architect with fur and the architect a beaver without fur?

Our speaker returns superfluously once again to the effects of freedom of the press in the countries where it actually exists. Since we have already dwelt on this subject at length, we shall here only touch further on the *French* press. Apart from the fact that the defects of the French press are the defects of the French nation, we find that the evil is not where the speaker looks for it. The French press is not too free; it is not free enough. It is true that it is not subject to a spiritual censorship, but it is subject to a material censorship, in the shape of high money sureties. It operates materially precisely because it is taken out of its proper sphere and drawn into the sphere of large trade speculations. Moreover, large trade speculations are a matter for large towns. Hence the French press is concentrated at few points, and if a material force has a demoniac effect when concentrated at few points, why should this not apply to a spiritual force also?

If, however, you are bent on judging freedom of the press not by its idea, but by its historical existence, why do you not look for it where it historically exists? Naturalists seek by experiment to reproduce a natural phenomenon in its purest conditions. You do not need to make any experiments. You find the natural phenomenon of freedom of the press in *North America* in its purest, most natural form. But if there are great historical foundations for freedom of the press in North America, those foundations are still greater in Germany. The literature of a people, and the intellectual culture bound up with it, are indeed not only the direct historical foundations of the press, but are the latter's history itself. And what people in the world can boast of these most immediate historical foundations for freedom of the press more than the German people can?

But, our speaker again breaks in, woe to Germany's morals if its press were to become free, for freedom of the press produces "an inner *demoralisation,* which seeks to undermine faith in man's higher purpose and thereby the basis of true civilisation".

It is the *censored press* that has a *demoralising* effect. Inseparable from it is the most powerful vice, hypocrisy, and from this, its basic vice, come all its other defects, which lack even the rudiments of virtue, and its vice of passivity, loathsome even from the aesthetic point of view. The government hears only *its own voice,* it knows that it hears only its own voice, yet it harbours the illusion that it hears the voice of the people, and it demands that the people, too, should itself harbour this illusion. For its part, therefore, the people sinks partly into political superstition, partly into political disbelief, or, completely turning away from political life, becomes a *rabble of private individuals*.

Since the press daily praises the government-inspired creations in the way that God spoke of His Creations only on the Sixth day: "And, behold, it was *very* good", and since, however, one day necessarily contradicts the other, the press lies continually and has to deny even any consciousness of lying, and must cast off all shame.

Since the nation is forced to regard free writings as unlawful, it becomes accustomed to regard what is unlawful as free, freedom as unlawful and what is lawful as unfree. In this way censorship kills the state spirit.

But our speaker is afraid of freedom of the press owing to his concern for "*private persons*". He overlooks that censorship is a permanent attack on the rights of private persons, and still more on ideas. He grows passionate about the danger to individual persons, and ought we not to grow passionate about the danger threatening society as a whole?

We cannot draw a sharper distinction between his view and ours than by contrasting his definitions of "bad frames of mind" to ours.

A bad frame of mind, he says, is "pride, which recognises no authority in church and state". And ought we not to regard as a bad frame of mind the refusal to recognise the authority of reason and law?

"It is envy which preaches abolition of everything that the rabble calls aristocracy."

But we say, it is envy which wants to abolish the eternal aristocracy of human nature, freedom, an aristocracy about which even the rabble can have no doubt.

"It is the malicious gloating which delights in personalities, whether lies or truth, and imperiously demands publicity so that no scandal of private life will remain hidden."

It is the malicious gloating which extracts tittle-tattle and personalities from the great life of the peoples, ignores historical reason and serves up to the public only the scandals of history; being quite incapable of judging the essence of a matter, it fastens on single aspects of a phenomenon and on individuals, and imperiously demands mystery so that every blot on public life will remain hidden.

"It is the impurity of the heart and imagination which is titillated by obscene pictures."

It is the impurity of the heart and imagination which is titillated by obscene pictures of the omnipotence of evil and the impotence of good, it is the imagination which takes pride in sin, it is the impure heart which conceals its secular arrogance in mystical images.

"It is despair of one's own salvation which seeks to stifle the voice of conscience by denial of God."

It is despair of one's own salvation which makes personal weaknesses into weaknesses of mankind, in order to rid one's own conscience of them; it is despair of the salvation of mankind which prevents mankind from obeying its innate natural laws and preaches the necessity of immaturity; it is hypocrisy which shelters behind God without believing in His reality and in the omnipotence of the good; it is self-seeking which puts personal salvation above the salvation of all.

These people doubt mankind in general but canonise individuals. They draw a horrifying picture of human nature and at the same time demand that we should bow down before the holy image of certain privileged individuals. We know that man singly is weak, but we know also that the whole is strong.

Finally, the speaker recalled the words proclaimed from the branches of the tree of knowledge for whose fruits *we* negotiate today as *then*:

"Ye shall not surely die, in the day that ye eat thereof, then your eyes shall be opened, and ye shall be as gods, knowing good and evil."

Although we doubt that the speaker has eaten of the tree of knowledge, and that *we* (the Rhine Province Assembly of the Estates) *then* negotiated with the devil, about which at least Genesis tells us nothing, nevertheless we concur with the view of the speaker and merely remind him that the devil *did not lie to us then,* for God himself says: "Behold, the man is become as one of us, to know good and evil."

We can reasonably let the speaker's own words be the epilogue to this speech:

"*Writing and speaking are mechanical accomplishments.*"

However much our readers may be tired of these "mechanical accomplishments", we must, for the sake of completeness, let the *urban estate,* after the princely and knightly estates, also give vent to its feelings *against* freedom of the press. We are faced here with the opposition of the *bourgeois,* not of the *citoyen.*

The speaker from the urban estate believes that he joins Sieyès in making the philistine remark:

"Freedom of the press is a *fine thing*, so long as *bad persons* do not meddle in it." "Against that no proven remedy has yet been found", etc., etc.

The point of view which calls freedom of the press *a thing* deserves praise at least on account of its naivety. This speaker can be reproached with anything at all, but not with lack of sobriety or excess of imagination.

So freedom of the press is a fine thing, and something which embellishes the sweet customary mode of life, a pleasant, worthy thing. But there are also bad persons, who misuse speech to tell lies, the brain to plot, the hands to steal, the feet to desert. Speech and thought, hands and feet would be fine things—good speech, pleasant thought, skilful hands, most excellent feet—if only there were no bad persons to misuse them! No remedy against that has yet been found.

"Sympathy for the constitution and freedom of the press must necessarily be weakened when it is seen that they are bound up with eternally changeable conditions in that country" (France) "and with an alarming uncertainty about the future."

When for the first time the discovery in the science of the universe was made that the earth is a *mobile perpetuum*, many a phlegmatic German must have taken a tight hold of his nightcap and sighed over the eternally changeable conditions of his Fatherland, and an alarming uncertainty about the future must have made him dislike a house that turned upside down at every moment.

[*Rheinische Zeitung* No. 139, May 19, 1842, Supplement]

Freedom of the press is as little *responsible* for the "changeable conditions" as the astronomer's telescope is for the unceasing motion of the universe. Evil astronomy! What a fine time that was when the earth, like a respectable townsman, still sat in the centre of the universe, calmly smoked its clay pipe, and did not even have to put on the light for itself, since the sun, moon and stars like so many obedient night lamps and "fine things" revolved around it.

"He who never destroys what he has built, ever stands
On this terrestrial world, which itself never stands still,"

says Hariri, who is no Frenchman by birth, but an Arab. [56]

The *estate* of the speaker finds expression very definitely in the thought:

"The true, honest patriot is unable to suppress his feeling that constitution and freedom of the press exist not for the welfare of the people, but to satisfy the ambition of individuals and for the domination of parties."

It is well known that a certain kind of psychology explains big things by means of small causes and, correctly sensing that everything for which man struggles is a matter of his interest, arrives at the incorrect opinion that there are only "petty" interests, only the interests of a stereotyped self-seeking. Further, it is well known that this kind of psychology and knowledge of mankind is to be found particularly in *towns*, where moreover it is considered the sign of a clever mind to see through the world and perceive that behind the passing clouds of ideas and facts there are quite small, envious, intriguing manikins, who pull the strings setting everything in motion. However, it is equally well known that if one looks too closely into a glass, one bumps *one's own head*, and hence these clever people's knowledge of mankind and the universe is primarily a mystified bump of their own heads.

Half-heartedness and indecision are also characteristic of the speaker's estate.

"His feeling of independence inclines him to favour freedom of the press" (in the sense of the mover of the motion), "but he must listen to the voice of reason and experience."

If the speaker had said in conclusion that while his reason disposed him in favour of freedom of the press his feeling of dependence set him against it, his speech would have been a perfect genre picture of urban reaction.

"He who has a tongue and does not speak,
Who has a sword and does not fight,
What is he indeed but a wretched wight?"

We come now to the *defenders of press freedom* and begin with the *main motion.* We pass over the more general material, which is aptly and well expressed in the introductory words of the motion, in order at once to stress the peculiar and characteristic standpoint of this speech.

The mover of the motion desires that *freedom of the press* should not be excluded from the *general freedom to carry on a trade,* a state of things that still prevails, and by which the inner contradiction appears as a classical example of inconsistency.

"The work of arms and legs is free, but that of the brain is under tutelage. Of cleverer brains no doubt? God forbid, that does not come into question as far as the censors are concerned. To him whom God gives an official post, He gives also understanding!"

The first thing that strikes one is to see *freedom of the press* included under *freedom of trade.* However, we cannot simply reject the speaker's view. *Rembrandt* painted the Madonna as a Dutch peasant woman; why should our speaker not depict freedom in a form which is dear and familiar to him?

No more can we deny that the speaker's point of view has a certain *relative* truth. If the press *itself* is regarded *merely* as a trade, then, as a trade carried on by means of the brain, it deserves greater freedom than a trade carried on by means of arms and legs. The emancipation of arms and legs only becomes humanly significant through the emancipation of the brain, for it is well known that arms and legs become human arms and legs only because of the head which they serve.

Therefore, however peculiar the speaker's point of view may appear at first glance, we must absolutely prefer it to the empty, nebulous and blurry arguments of those German liberals who think freedom is honoured by being placed in the starry firmament of the imagination instead of on the solid ground of reality. It is in part to these exponents of the imagination, these sentimental enthusiasts, who shy away from any contact of their ideal with ordinary reality as a profanation, that we Germans owe the fact that freedom has remained until now a fantasy and sentimentality.

Germans are in general inclined to sentiment and high-flown extravagance, they have a weakness for music of the blue sky. It is therefore gratifying when the great problem of the idea is demonstrated to them from a tough, real standpoint derived from the immediate environment. Germans are by nature most devoted, servile and respectful. Out of sheer respect for ideas they fail to realise them. They make the worship of them into a cult, but they do not cultivate them. Hence the way adopted by the speaker seems suitable for *familiarising* Germans with his ideas, for showing them that it is not a question here of something inaccessible to them, but of their immediate interests, suitable for translating the language of the gods into that of man.

We know that the Greeks believed that in the Egyptian, Lydian and even Scythian gods they could recognise their Apollo, their Athena, their Zeus, and they disregarded the specific features of the foreign cults as subsidiary. It is no crime, therefore, if the German takes the goddess of freedom of the press, a goddess unknown to him, for one of his familiar goddesses, and accordingly calls it freedom of trade or freedom of property.

Precisely because we are able to acknowledge and appreciate the speaker's point of view, we *criticise* it the more severely.

"One could very well imagine the continued existence of crafts side by side with freedom of the press, because trade based on brain work could require a *higher degree of skill,* putting it on the same level as the seven free arts of old; but the continued unfreedom of the press alongside freedom of trade is a sin against the Holy Ghost."

Of course! The lower form of freedom is obviously considered to be without rights if the higher form has no rights. The right of the individual citizen is a folly if the right of the state is not recognised. If freedom in general is rightful, it goes without saying that a particular form of freedom is the more rightful as freedom has achieved in it a finer and better-developed existence. If the *polyp* has a right to existence because the life of nature is at least dimly evident in it, how much more so the *lion,* in which life rages and roars?

However correct the conclusion that the existence of a higher form of right can be considered proved by the existence of a lower form, the *application* is wrong when it makes the lower sphere a *measure* of the higher and turns its laws, reasonable within their own limits, into caricatures by claiming that they are not laws of their own sphere, but of a higher one. It is as if I wanted to compel a giant to live in the house of a pigmy.

Freedom of trade, freedom of property, of conscience, of the press, of the courts, are all *species* of one and the same genus, of *freedom without any specific name.* But it is quite incorrect to forget the difference because of the unity and to go so far as to make a *particular species* the measure, the standard, the sphere of other species. This is an *intolerance* on the part of one species of freedom, which is only prepared to tolerate the existence of others if they renounce themselves and declare themselves to be its vassals.

Freedom of trade is precisely freedom of trade and no other freedom because within it the nature of the trade develops unhindered according to the inner rules of its life. Freedom of the courts is freedom of the courts if they follow their own inherent laws of right and not those of some other sphere, such as religion. Every particular sphere of freedom is the freedom of a particular sphere, just as every particular mode of life is the mode of life of a particular nature. How wrong it would be to demand that the lion should adapt himself to the laws of life of the polyp! How false would be my understanding of the interconnection and unity of the bodily organism if I were to conclude: since arms and legs function in their specific way, the eye and ear — organs which take man away from his individuality and make him the mirror and echo of the universe — must have a still greater right to activity, and consequently must be *intensified* arm-and-leg activity.

As in the universe each planet, while turning on its own axis, moves only around the sun, so in the system of freedom each of its worlds, while turning on its own axis, revolves only around the central sun of freedom. To make freedom of the press a variety of freedom of trade is a defence that kills it before defending it, for do I not abolish the freedom of a particular character if I demand that it should be free in the manner of a different character? Your freedom is not my freedom, says the press to a trade. As you obey the laws of your sphere, so will I obey the laws of my sphere. To be free in your way is for me identical with being unfree, just as a cabinet-maker would hardly feel pleased if he demanded freedom for his craft and was given as equivalent the freedom of the philosopher.

Let us lay bare the thought of the speaker. What is freedom? He replies: *Freedom of trade,* which is as if a student, when asked what is freedom, were to reply: *It is freedom to be out at night.*

With as much right as freedom of the press, one could include every kind of freedom in freedom of trade. The judge practises the trade of law, the preacher that of religion, the father of a family that of bringing up children. But does that express the essence of legal, religious and moral freedom?

One could also put it the other way round and call freedom of trade merely *a variety of freedom of the press.* Do craftsmen work only with hands and legs and not with the brain as well? Is the language of words the only language of thought? Is not the language of the mechanic through the steam-engine easily perceptible to my ear, is not the language of the bed manufacturer very obvious to my back, that of the cook comprehensible to my stomach? Is it not a contradiction that all these varieties of freedom of the press are permitted, the sole exception being the one that speaks to my intellect through the medium of printer's ink?

In order to defend, and even to understand, the freedom of a particular sphere, I must proceed from its essential character and not its external relations. But is the press true to its character, does it act in accordance with the nobility of its nature, *is the press free* which degrades itself to the level of a *trade*? The writer, of course, must earn in order to be able to live and write, but he must by no means live and write to earn.

When *Béranger* sings:

> Je ne vis que pour faire des chansons,
> Si vous m'ôtez ma place Monseigneur,
> Je ferai des chansons pour vivre, [a]

___

[a] I live only to compose songs.
If you dismiss me, Monseigneur,
I shall compose songs in order to live.— *Ed.*

this threat contains the ironic admission that the poet deserts his proper sphere when for him poetry becomes a means.

The writer does not at all look on his work as a *means*. It is an *end in itself*; it is so little a means for him himself and for others that, if need be, he sacrifices *his* existence to *its* existence. He is, in another way, like the preacher of religion who adopts the principle: "Obey God rather than man", including under man himself with his human needs and desires. On the other hand, what if a tailor from whom I had ordered a Parisian frock-coat were to come and bring me a Roman toga on the ground that it was more in keeping with the eternal law of beauty!

The primary freedom of the press lies in not being a trade. The writer who degrades the press into being a material means deserves as punishment for this internal unfreedom the external unfreedom of censorship, or rather his very existence is his punishment.

Of course, the press exists also as a trade, but then it is not the affair of writers, but of printers and booksellers. However, we are concerned here not with the freedom of trade of printers and booksellers, but with freedom of the press.

Indeed, our speaker does not stop at regarding the right to freedom of the press proved because of freedom of trade; he demands that freedom of the press, instead of being subject to its own laws, should be subject to the laws of freedom of trade. He even joins issue with the spokesman of the commission, who defends a higher view of freedom of the press, and he puts forward demands which can only produce a comic effect, for it becomes comic when the laws of a lower sphere are applied to a higher one, just as, conversely, it has a comic effect when children become passionate.

"He speaks of *authorised* and *unauthorised* authors. He understands by this that even in the sphere of freedom of trade the exercise of a right that has been granted is always bound up with some condition which is more or less difficult to fulfil, depending on the occupation in question. Obviously, masons, carpenters and master builders have to fulfil conditions from which most other trades are exempt." "His motion concerns a right *in particular*, not *in general*."

First of all, *who* is to grant *authority?* Kant would not have admitted Fichte's authority as a philosopher, Ptolemy would not have admitted that Copernicus had authority as an astronomer, nor Bernard of Clairvaux Luther's authority as a theologian. Every man of learning regards his critics as "*unauthorised authors*". Or should the unlearned decide who should have the authority of a man of learning? Obviously the judgment would have to be left to the unauthorised authors, for the authorised cannot be judges in their own case. Or should authority be linked with *estate*? The cobbler Jakob Böhme was a great philosopher.[a] Many a philosopher of repute is merely a great cobbler.

By the way, when speaking of authorised or unauthorised authors, to be consistent one must not rest content with distinguishing between individual *persons*, one must divide the press as a trade into *various trades* and draw up different trade certificates for the different spheres of literary activity. Or ought the authorised writer to be able to write about everything? From the outset, the cobbler has more authority than the lawyer to write about leather. The day-labourer has just as much authority as the theologian to write about whether one should work or not on holidays. If, therefore, authority is linked with special objective conditions, every citizen will be at one and the same time an authorised and an unauthorised writer, authorised in matters concerning his profession, and unauthorised in all others.

Apart from the fact that in this way the world of the press, instead of being a bond uniting the nation, would be a sure means of dividing it, that the difference between the estates would thus be fixed intellectually, and the history of literature would sink to the level of the natural history of the particular intelligent breeds of animals; apart from the disputes over the dividing lines between them and conflicts which could neither be settled nor avoided; apart from the fact that lack of talent and narrow-mindedness would become a law for the press, for the particular can be seen intellectually and freely only in connection with the whole and therefore not in separation from it—apart from all this, since *reading* is as important as writing, there would have to be *authorised* and *unauthorised readers*, a consequence which was drawn in Egypt, where the priests, the authorised authors, were at the same time the sole authorised readers. And it is highly expedient that only the authorised authors should be given authority to buy and read their own works.

What inconsistency! If privilege prevails, the government has every right to maintain that it is the *sole authorised author* as regards what it does or does not do. For if you consider yourself authorised as a citizen to write not only about your particular estate, but about what is most general, viz., the state, should not other mortals, whom you wish to exclude, be authorised as human beings to pass judgment on a very particular matter, viz., *your authority* and your writings?

---

[a] Cf. H. Heine, *Die romantische Schule*, II, 3.— *Ed.*

The result would be the comical contradiction that the authorised author might write without censorship about the state, but the unauthorised author might write about the authorised author only by permission of the censorship.

Freedom of the press will certainly not be achieved by a crowd of official writers being recruited by you from your ranks. The authorised authors would be the *official* authors, *the struggle between censorship and freedom of the press would be converted into a struggle between authorised and unauthorised writers.*

Hence a member of the fourth estate correctly replies to this:

"If some restriction on the press must still exist, let it be equal for all parties, that is, that in this respect no one class of citizens is allowed more rights than another".

The censorship holds us all in subjection, just as under a despotic regime all are equal, if not in value, then in absence of value; that kind of freedom of the press seeks to introduce oligarchy in the sphere of intellectual life. The censorship declares that an author is at most inconvenient, unsuitable within the bounds of its realm. That kind of freedom of the press claims to anticipate world history, to know in advance the voice of the people, which hitherto has been the sole judge as to which writer has "authority" and which is "without authority". Whereas Solon did not venture to judge a man until *after* his life was over, *after his death,* this view presumes to judge a writer even *before his birth.*

The press is the most general way by which individuals can communicate their intellectual being. It knows no respect for persons, but only respect for intelligence. Do you want ability for intellectual communication to be determined officially by special external signs? What I cannot be for others, I am not and cannot be for myself. If I am not allowed to be a spiritual force for others, then I have no right to be a spiritual force for myself; and do you want to give certain individuals the privilege of being spiritual forces? Just as everyone learns to read and write, so everyone must *have the right* to read and write.

For whom, then, is the division of writers into "authorised" and "unauthorised" intended? Obviously not for the truly authorised, for they can make their influence felt without that. Is it therefore for the "unauthorised" who want to protect themselves and impress others by means of an external privilege?

Moreover, this palliative does not even make a *press law* unnecessary, for, as a speaker from the peasant estate remarks:

"Cannot a privileged person, too, exceed his authority and be liable to punishment? Therefore, in any case, a press law would be necessary, with the result that one would encounter the same difficulties as with a *general law on the press.*"

If the German looks back on his history, he will find *one* of the
main reasons for his slow political development, as also for the
wretched state of literature prior to *Lessing,* in the existence of
"authorised writers". The learned men by profession, guild or
privilege, the doctors and others, the colourless university writers
of the seventeenth and eighteenth centuries, with their stiff
pigtails and their distinguished pedantry and their petty hair-splitting dissertations, interposed themselves between the people and
the mind, between life and science, between freedom and mankind. It was the *unauthorised* writers who created our literature.
Gottsched and *Lessing*—there you have the choice between an
"authorised" and "unauthorised" writer!

In general, we have no liking for "freedom" that *only* holds
good in the plural. England is a proof on a big historical scale how
dangerous for *"freedom"* is the restricted horizon of *"freedoms".*

"Ce mot des *libertés,*" says Voltaire, "des *privilèges,* suppose l'assujettissement.
Des libertés sont des *exemptions* de la *servitude générale."* [a]

Further, if our speaker wants to exclude *anonymous* and
pseudonymous writers from freedom of the press and subject them
to censorship, we would point out that in the press it is not the
name that matters, but that, where a press law is in force, the
publisher, and through him the anonymous and pseudonymous
writer as well, is liable to prosecution in the courts. Moreover,
when Adam gave names to all the animals in paradise, he forgot
to give names to the German newspaper correspondents, and they
will remain *nameless in saecula saeculorum.* [b]

Whereas the mover of the motion sought to impose restrictions
on *persons,* the subjects of the press, other estates want to restrict
the *objective material* of the press, the *scope of its operation and
existence.* The result is a soulless bargaining and haggling as to *how
much freedom freedom of the press ought to have.*

One estate wants to limit the press to discussing the material,
intellectual and religious state of affairs in the Rhine Province;
another wants the publication of "local newspapers", whose title
indicates their restricted content; a third even wants free expression of opinion to be allowed *in one newspaper only* in each
province!!!

All these attempts remind one of the gymnastics teacher who

---

[a] "This word of the *liberties,* of the *privileges,* supposes subjection. Liberties are
exemptions from the *general servitude."— Ed.*

[b] For ever and ever.— *Ed.*

suggested that the best way to teach how to jump was to take the pupil to a big ditch and show him by means of a cotton thread how far he ought to jump *across* the ditch. Of course, the pupil had first to practise jumping and would not be allowed to clear the whole ditch on the first day, but from time to time the thread would be moved farther away. Unfortunately, during his first lesson the pupil fell into the ditch, and he has been lying there ever since. The teacher was a German and the pupil's name was "freedom".

According to the average *normal type*, therefore, the *defenders of freedom of the press* in the Sixth Rhine Province Assembly differ from their *opponents* not as regards content, but in their trend. The narrow-mindedness of a *particular estate* opposes the press in one case, and defends it in another; some want the government alone to have privileges, others want them to be shared among more persons; some want a full censorship, others a half censorship; some want three-eighths freedom of the press, others none at all. God save me from my friends!

Completely at variance with the *general spirit* of the Assembly, however, are the speeches of the commission's *spokesman* and those of some members of the *peasant estate*.

Among other things, the spokesman declared:

"In the life of peoples, as in that of individuals, it happens that the fetters of a too long tutelage become intolerable, that there is an urge for independence, and that everyone wants to be responsible himself for his actions. Thereupon the censorship has outlived its time; where it still exists it will be regarded as a *hateful* constraint which prohibits what is openly said from being written."

Write as you speak, and speak as you write, our primary schoolteachers taught us. Later what we are told is: say what has been prescribed for you, and write what you repeat after others.

"Whenever the inevitable progress of time causes a new, important interest to develop and gives rise to a new need, for which no adequate provision is contained in the existing legislation, new laws are necessary to regulate this new state of society. Precisely such a case confronts us here."

That is the *truly historical* view in contrast to the illusory one which kills the reason of history in order subsequently to honour its bones as historical relics.

"Of course, the problem" (of a press code) "may not be quite easy to solve; the first attempt that is made will perhaps remain very incomplete! But all states will owe a debt of gratitude to the legislator who is the first to take up this matter, and under a king like ours, it is perhaps the Prussian government that is destined to have the *honour* to precede other countries along this path, which alone can lead to the goal."

Our whole exposal has shown how *isolated* this courageous, dignified and resolute view was in the Assembly. This was also abundantly pointed out to the spokesman of the commission by the chairman himself. Finally, it was expressed also by a member of the peasant estate in an ill-humoured but excellent speech:

"The speakers have gone round and round the question before us like a cat round hot porridge." "The human spirit must develop freely *in accordance with its inherent laws* and be allowed to communicate its achievements, otherwise a clear, vitalising stream will become a pestiferous swamp. If any nation is suitable for freedom of the press it is surely the calm, good-natured German nation, which stands more in need of being roused from its torpor than of the strait jacket of censorship. For it not to be allowed freely to communicate its thoughts and feelings to its fellow men very much resembles the North American system of solitary confinement for criminals, which when rigidly enforced often leads to madness. From one who is not permitted to find fault, praise also is valueless; in absence of expression it is like a Chinese picture in which shade is lacking. Let us not find ourselves put in the same company as this enervated nation!"

If we now look back on the press debates as a whole, we cannot overcome the dreary and uneasy impression produced by an assembly of representatives of the *Rhine Province* who wavered only between the deliberate obduracy of privilege and the natural impotence of a half-hearted liberalism. Above all, we cannot help noting with displeasure the almost entire absence of general and broad points of view, as also the negligent superficiality with which the question of a free press was debated and disposed of. Once more, therefore, we ask ourselves whether the press was a matter too remote from the Assembly of the Estates, and with which they had too little real contact, for them to be able to defend freedom of the press with the thorough and serious interest that was required?

Freedom of the press presented its petition to the estates with the *most subtle captatio benevolentiae.*[a]

At the very beginning of the Assembly session, a debate arose in which the *chairman* pointed out that the *printing of the Assembly proceedings,* like all other writings, was subject to *censorship,* but that in this case *he* took the place of the censor.

On this *one* point, did not the question of *freedom of the press* coincide with that of *freedom of the Assembly?* The conflict here is the more interesting because the Assembly in its own person was given proof how the absence of freedom of the press makes all other freedoms illusory. One form of freedom governs another just as one limb of the body does another. Whenever a particular freedom is put in question, freedom in general is put in question.

---

[a] Attempt to arouse goodwill.— *Ed.*

Whenever one form of freedom is rejected, freedom in general is rejected and henceforth can have only a semblance of existence, since the sphere in which absence of freedom is dominant becomes a matter of pure chance. Absence of freedom is the rule and freedom an exception, a fortuitous and arbitrary occurrence. There can, therefore, be nothing wronger than to think that when it is a question of a *particular* form of existence of freedom, it is a *particular question*. It is the general question within a particular sphere. Freedom remains freedom whether it finds expression in printer's ink, in property, in the conscience, or in a political assembly. But the loyal friend of freedom whose sense of honour would be offended by the mere fact that he had to vote on the question whether *freedom* was *to be or not to be*—this friend becomes perplexed when confronted with the peculiar material form in which freedom appears. He fails to recognise the genus in the species; because of the press, he forgets about freedom, he believes he is judging something whose essence is alien to him, and he condemns his own essence. Thus the Sixth Rhine Province Assembly condemned itself by passing sentence on freedom of the press.

The highly sage, practical bureaucrats who secretly and unjustifiably think of themselves in the way that *Pericles* openly and rightly boasted of himself: "I am a man who is the equal of anyone both in knowing the needs of the state and in the art of expounding them" [a]—these hereditary leaseholders of political intelligence will shrug their shoulders and remark with oracular good breeding that the defenders of freedom of the press are wasting their efforts, for a *mild* censorship is better than a *harsh* freedom of the press. We reply to them with the words of the Spartans *Sperthias* and *Bulis* to the *Persian satrap* Hydarnes:

"Hydarnes, you have not equally weighed each side in your advice to us. For you have tried the one which you advise, the other has remained untried by you. You know what it means to be a slave, but you have never yet tried freedom, to know whether it is sweet or not. For if you had tried it, you would have advised us to fight for it, not merely with spears, but also with axes." [b]

Written in April 1842

First published in the Supplement to the *Rheinische Zeitung* Nos. 125, 128, 130, 132, 135 and 139, May 5, 8, 10, 12, 15 and 19, 1842

Printed according to the newspaper

Published in English for the first time

Signed: *By a Rhinelander*

---

[a] Thucydides, *The History of the Peloponnesian War*, Vol. I, Book 2, 60.— *Ed.*
[b] Herodot, *Historiae*, Vol. II, Book 7, 135.— *Ed.*

THE QUESTION OF CENTRALISATION
IN ITSELF AND WITH REGARD
TO THE SUPPLEMENT TO No. 137
OF THE *RHEINISCHE ZEITUNG,*
TUESDAY, MAY 17, 1842 [57]

"Germany and France with regard to the question of centralisation" with the sign $\overset{.}{\underset{.}{-}} \overset{.}{\underset{.}{-}}$.

"Whether *state power* should *issue* from a single point or whether each province, each locality, should administer itself, and the central government, only acting as the power of the whole, should rule also the individual parts of the state when the state has to be represented externally—this is a question on which views are still very much divided."

The fate which a question of the time has in common with every question justified by its content, and therefore rational, is that the *question* and not the *answer* constitutes the main difficulty. True criticism, therefore, analyses the questions and not the answers. Just as the solution of an algebraic equation is given once the problem has been put in its simplest and sharpest form, so every question is answered as soon as it has become a *real* question. World history itself has no other method than that of answering and disposing of old questions by putting new ones. The riddles of each period are therefore easy to discover. They are questions of the time, and although the intention and insight of a single individual may play an important role in the answers, and a practised eye is needed to separate what belongs to the individual from what belongs to the time, the *questions,* on the other hand, are the frank, uncompromising voices of the time embracing all individuals; they are its mottoes, they are the supremely *practical* utterances proclaiming the state of its soul. In each period, therefore, reactionaries are as sure indicators of its spiritual condition as dogs are of the weather. To the public, it looks as if the reactionaries *make* the questions. Hence the public believes that if some obscurantist or other does not combat a modern trend, if he does not subject something to question, then the question does not *exist*. The public itself, therefore, regards the reactionaries as the true men of progress.

"Whether state power should issue from a single point", i.e., whether a *single point* should rule, or whether each province, etc., should administer itself and the central government act only externally as the power of the whole "in relation to the exterior"—the question of centralisation cannot be formulated in this way. The author[a] assures us that

"this question, considered from a higher standpoint, falls away of itself as being futile", for "if man is really what he should be by his essence, individual freedom is not separate from general freedom". "If, therefore, one assumes a nation to be made up of *righteous* people, the question under consideration cannot arise at all." "The central power would live in all members, etc., etc." "But just as in general every external law, every positive institution, etc., would be superfluous, so would any central state power, etc. Such a society would be not a *state*, but the *ideal* of mankind." "One can make it astonishingly easy to solve the most difficult state problems if one looks at our social life from a high philosophical standpoint. And *theoretically*, such a solution of the problems is quite correct, indeed the only correct one. But it is a question here not of a theoretical, etc., but of a practical, naturally merely empirical and relative, answer to the question of centralisation, etc."

The author of the article begins with a *self-criticism* of his question. Seen from a higher standpoint, it does not exist, but at the same time we are told that, seen from this high standpoint, all laws, positive institutions, the central state power and finally the state itself, disappear. The author rightly praises the "astonishing ease" with which this standpoint is able to orient itself, but he is not right in calling such a solution of the problems "quite correct, indeed the only correct one", he is not right in calling this standpoint a "philosophical" one. Philosophy must seriously protest at being confused with imagination. The fiction of a nation of "righteous" people is as alien to philosophy as the fiction of "praying hyenas" is to nature. The author substitutes "his abstractions" for philosophy.[b]

Written after May 17, 1842
First published in: Marx/Engels, *Gesamtausgabe*, Abt. 1, Bd. 1, Hb. 1, 1927

Printed according to the manuscript

---

[a] Moses Hess.—*Ed.*
[b] The manuscript breaks off here.—*Ed.*

THE LEADING ARTICLE IN No. 179
OF THE *KÖLNISCHE ZEITUNG*[58]

[*Rheinische Zeitung* No. 191, July 10, 1842, Supplement]

Up to now we have respected the *Kölnische Zeitung,* if not as the *"organ of the Rhenish intelligentsia"* at any rate as the Rhenish *"information sheet".*[a] We regarded above all its, "leading political articles" as a means, both wise and select, for making politics repugnant to the reader, so that he will the more eagerly turn to the vitally refreshing realm of the advertisements which reflects the pulsating life of industry and is often wittily piquant, so that here too the motto would be: *per aspera ad astra,* through politics to the oysters.[b] However, the finely even balance which the *Kölnische Zeitung* had hitherto succeeded in maintaining between politics and advertisements has recently been upset by a kind of advertisements which can be called "advertisements of political industry". In the initial uncertainty as to where this new genus should be placed, it happened that an advertisement was transformed into a leading article, and the leading article into an advertisement, and indeed into one which in the language of the political world is called a "denunciation",[c] but if paid for is called simply an "advertisement".

It is a custom in the North that before the meagre meals, the guests are given a drink of exquisitely fine spirits. In following this custom, we are the more pleased to offer some spirits to our

---

[a] A pun on the German word *Intelligenz,* which can mean both "intelligentsia" and "information".— *Ed.*

[b] By rough paths to the stars. A pun based on the similarity of the Latin *astra*—stars, to the German *Auster*—oyster.— *Ed.*

[c] A pun on the German word *Anzeige,* which can mean both "advertisement" and "denunciation".— *Ed.*

Northern guest because in the meal itself, in the very "ailing" [a] article in No. 179 of the *Kölnische Zeitung*, we find no trace of spirit. Therefore we present first of all a scene from Lucian's *Dialogues of the Gods*, which we give here in a "generally comprehensible" translation,[59] because among our readers there is bound to be at least *one* who is no Hellene.

Lucian's *Dialogues of the Gods*

XXIV. HERMES' COMPLAINTS

Hermes. Maia

Hermes. Is there, dear Mother, in all heaven a god who is more tormented than I am?

Maia. Don't say such things, my son!

Hermes. Why shouldn't I? I, who have such a lot of things to attend to, who have to do everything myself, and have to submit to so many servile duties? In the morning I have to be among the very first to get up, sweep out the dining-room, and put the cushions straight in the council chamber. When everything is in order I have to wait on Jupiter and spend the whole day as his messenger, going to and fro on his errands. Hardly have I returned, and while still covered with dust, I have to serve ambrosia. Worst of all, I am the only one who is allowed no rest even at night, for I have to lead the souls of the dead to Pluto and perform the duties of attendant while the dead are being judged. For it is not enough that in my daytime labours I have to be present at *gymnastic exercises*, act as *herald* at meetings of the people, and help the people's orators to memorise their speeches. Nay, torn between so many duties, I must also look after *all matters concerning the dead*.

Since his expulsion from Olympus, Hermes, by force of habit, still performs "servile duties" and looks after all matters concerning the dead.

Whether Hermes himself, or his son, the goat-god Pan, wrote the ailing article of No. 179, let the reader decide, bearing in mind that the Greek Hermes was the god of eloquence and logic.

"To spread philosophical and religious views by means of the newspapers, or to combat them in the newspapers, we consider equally impermissible."

While the old man chattered on in this way, I became well aware that he intended to deliver a tedious litany of oracular pronouncements. However, I curbed my impatience, for ought I not to believe this discerning man who is so ingenuous as to express his opinion with the utmost candour in his own house, and I went on reading. But—lo and behold!—this article, which, it is true,

---

[a] A pun on the German words *leitender*, which means "leading", and *leidender*, meaning "ailing".— *Ed.*

cannot be reproached for any philosophical views, at least has the tendency to combat philosophical views and spread religious views.

What are we to make of an article which disputes the right to its own existence, which prefaces itself with a declaration of its own incompetence? The loquacious author will reply to us. He explains how his pretentious articles are to be read. He confines himself to giving some fragments, the "arrangement and connection" of which he leaves to the "perspicacity of the reader" — the most convenient method for the kind of advertisements which he makes it his business to deal with. We should like to "arrange and connect" these fragments, and it is not our fault if the rosary does not become a string of pearls.

The author declares:

"A party which employs these means" (i. e., spreads philosophical and religious views in newspapers and combats such views) "shows thereby, in *our* opinion, that its intentions are *not honest,* and that it is less concerned with instructing and enlightening the people than with achieving *other external aims."*

This being *his* opinion, the article can have no other intention than the achievement of external aims. These "external aims" will not fail to show themselves.

The state, he says, has not only the right but the duty to "put a stop to the activities of *unbidden* chatterers". The writer is obviously referring to *opponents* of his view, for he has long ago convinced himself that he is a *bidden* chatterer.

It is a question, therefore, of a new intensification of the censorship in religious matters, of new police measures against the press, which has hardly been able to draw breath as yet.

"In our opinion, the state is to be reproached, not for excessive severity, but for indulgence carried too far."

The leader writer, however, has second thoughts. It is dangerous to reproach the state. Therefore he addresses himself to the authorities, his accusation against freedom of the press turns into an accusation against the censors. He accuses them of exercising "too little censorship".

"Reprehensible indulgence has hitherto been shown also, *not by the state, it is true,* but by *'individual authorities',* in that the new philosophical school has been allowed to make most disgraceful attacks on Christianity in public papers and other publications intended for a readership that is not purely scientific."

Once again, however, the author comes to a halt; again he has second thoughts. Less than eight days ago he found that the freedom of the censorship allowed too little freedom of the press;

now he finds that the compulsion of the censors results in too little compulsion of the censorship.

That again has to be remedied.

"As long as the censorship exists it is its most urgent duty to excise such abhorrent offshoots of a childish presumption as have repeatedly offended our eyes in recent days."

Weak eyes! Weak eyes! And

"the weakest eye will be offended by an expression which can be intended only for the level of understanding of the broad masses".

If the relaxed censorship already allows abhorrent offshoots to appear, what would happen with freedom of the press? If our eyes are too weak to bear the "presumption" of the censored press, how would they be strong enough to bear the "audacity" [a] of a free press?

"As long as the censorship exists it is its most urgent duty." And when it ceases to exist? The phrase must be interpreted as meaning: it is the most urgent duty of the censorship to remain in existence as long as possible.

But again the author has second thoughts.

"It is not our function to act as *public* prosecutor, and therefore we refrain from any more detailed designation."

What heavenly goodness there is in this man! He refrains from any more detailed "designation", and yet it is only by quite detailed, quite definite signs that he could prove and show what *his* view aims at. He lets fall only vague, half audible words intended to arouse suspicions; it is not his function to be a *public* prosecutor, his function is to be a *hidden prosecutor.*

For the last time the unfortunate man has second thoughts, remembering that his function is to write liberal leading articles, and that he has to present himself as a "loyal friend of freedom of the press". Hence he quickly takes up his final position:

"We could not fail to protest against a course which, if it is not the consequence of accidental negligence, can have no other purpose than to discredit the freer movement of the press in the eyes of the public, to play into the hands of opponents who are afraid of failing to achieve their aim in an open way."

The censorship—we are told by this defender of freedom of the press, who is as bold as he is sharp-witted—if it is not the

---

[a] A pun on the German words *Übermut*—presumption, and *Mut*—audacity.— *Ed.*

English leopard with the inscription: "I sleep, wake me not!" [a], has adopted this "disastrous" course in order to discredit the freer movement of the press in the eyes of the public.

Is there any further need to discredit a movement of the press which calls the attention of the censorship to "*accidental negligences*", and which expects to obtain its renown in public opinion through the "*penknife of the censor*"?

This movement can be called "free" insofar as the licence of shamelessness is also sometimes called "free", and is it not the shamelessness of stupidity and hypocrisy to claim to be a defender of the freer movement of the press while at the same time teaching that the press will at once fall into the gutter unless it is supported under the arms by two policemen?

And what need is there of censorship, what need is there of this leading article, if the philosophical press discredits itself in the eyes of the public? Of course, the author does not want to restrict in any way "*the freedom of scientific research*".

"In our day, *scientific research* is rightly allowed the widest, most unrestricted scope."

But how our author conceives scientific research can be seen from the following utterance:

. "In this connection a sharp distinction must be drawn between the requirements of freedom of scientific research, through which Christianity can only gain, and what lies outside the limits of scientific research."

Who is to decide on the limits of scientific research if not scientific research itself? According to the leading article, limits should be prescribed to science. The leading article, therefore, knows of an "*official reason*" which does not learn from scientific research, but teaches it, which is a learned providence that establishes the length every hair should have to convert a scientist's beard into a beard of world importance. The leading article believes in the scientific inspiration of the censorship.

Before going further into these "silly" explanations of the leading article on the subject of "scientific research", let us sample for a moment the "*philosophy of religion*" of Herr H.,[b] his "own science"!

"Religion is the basis of the state and the most necessary condition for every social association which does not aim merely at achieving some external aim."

---

[a] Marx wrote these words in English.— *Ed.*
[b] Hermes.— *Ed.*

The proof: "In its crudest form as *childish fetishism* it nevertheless to some extent raises man above his sensuous desires which, if he allowed himself to be ruled exclusively by them, could *degrade him to the level of an animal* and make him incapable of fulfilling any higher aim."

The author of the leading article calls fetishism the *"crudest form"* of religion. He concedes, therefore, what all "men of science" regard as established even without his agreement, that *"animal worship"* is a *higher* form of religion than fetishism. But does not animal worship degrade man below the animal, does it not make the animal man's god?

And now, indeed, "fetishism"! Truly, the erudition of a penny magazine! Fetishism is so far from raising man *above* his sensuous desires that, on the contrary, it is "the *religion of sensuous desire*". Fantasy arising from desire deceives the fetish-worshipper into believing that an "inanimate object" will give up its natural character in order to comply with his desires. Hence the crude desire of the fetish-worshipper *smashes* the fetish when it ceases to be its most obedient servant.

"In those nations which attained higher historical significance, the flowering of their national life coincides with the highest development of their religious consciousness, and the decline of their greatness and their power coincides with the decline of their religious culture."

To arrive at the truth, the author's assertion must be directly reversed; he has stood history on its head. Among the peoples of the ancient world, Greece and Rome are certainly countries of the highest "historical culture". Greece flourished at its best internally in the time of Pericles, externally in the time of Alexander. In the age of Pericles the Sophists, and Socrates, who could be called the embodiment of philosophy, art and rhetoric supplanted religion. The age of Alexander was the age of Aristotle, who rejected the eternity of the "individual" spirit and the God of positive religions. And as for Rome! Read Cicero! The Epicurean, Stoic or Sceptic philosophies were the religions of cultured Romans when Rome had reached the zenith of its development. That with the downfall of the ancient states their religions also disappeared requires no further explanation, for the "true religion" of the ancients was the cult of "their nationality", of their "state". It was not the downfall of the old religions that caused the downfall of the ancient states, but the downfall of the ancient states that caused the downfall of the old religions. And such ignorance as is found in this leading article proclaims itself the "legislator of scientific research" and writes "decrees" for philosophy.

"The entire ancient world had to collapse because the progress achieved by the peoples in their scientific development was necessarily bound up with a revelation of the errors on which their religious views were based."

According to the leading article, therefore, the entire ancient world collapsed because scientific research revealed the errors of the old religions. Would the ancient world not have perished if scientific research had kept silent about the errors of religion, if the Roman authorities had been recommended by the author of the leading article to excise the writings of Lucretius and Lucian?

For the rest, we shall permit ourselves to enlarge Herr H.'s erudition in another communication.

[*Rheinische Zeitung* No. 193, July 12, 1842, Supplement]

At the very time when the downfall of the ancient world was approaching, there arose the *Alexandrine school*, which strove to prove by force the "eternal truth" of Greek mythology and its complete agreement "with the results of scientific research". The Emperor Julian, too, belonged to this trend, which believed that it could make the newly developing spirit of the times disappear by keeping its eyes closed so as not to see it. However, let us continue with the conclusion arrived at by H.! In the old religions, "the feeble notion of the divine was shrouded in the blackest night of error", and therefore could not stand up to scientific research. Under Christianity, the opposite is the case, as any thinking machine will conclude. At all events, H. says:

"The greatest results of scientific research have so far only served to confirm the truths of the Christian religion."

We leave aside the fact that all the philosophies of the past without exception have been accused by the theologians of abandoning the Christian religion, even those of the pious Malebranche and the divinely inspired Jakob Böhme, and that Leibniz was accused of being a "Löwenix" (a believer in nothing) by the Brunswick peasants, and of being an atheist by the Englishman Clarke and other supporters of Newton. We leave aside, too, the fact that, as the most capable and consistent section of Protestant theologians has maintained, Christianity cannot be reconciled with reason because "secular" and "spiritual" reason contradict each other, which Tertullian classically expressed by saying: "*verum est, quia absurdum est.*" [a] Leaving aside all this, we ask: how is the agreement of scientific research with religion to be

---

[a] "It is true because it is absurd" (*Carne Christi*, II, 5).— *Ed.*

proved, except by allowing it to take its own course and so compelling it to resolve itself into religion? Any other compulsion is at least no proof.

Of course, if from the outset you recognise as the result of scientific research only that which agrees with your own view, it is easy to pose as a prophet. But in that case how are your assertions superior to those of the Indian Brahmin who proves the holiness of the Vedas [60] by reserving to himself alone the right to read them?

Yes, says H., it is a question of "scientific research". But every research that contradicts Christianity "stops halfway" or "takes a wrong road". Could there be a more convenient way of arguing?

Scientific research, once it has *"'made clear'* to itself the content of its results, will never conflict with the truths of Christianity". At the same time, however, the state must ensure that this *"clarification"* is impossible, for research must never adapt itself to the level of understanding of the broad mass, i. e., it must never become popular and clear *to itself*. Even when it is attacked by unscientific investigators in all newspapers of the monarchy, it must be modest and remain silent.

Christianity precludes the possibility of "any new decline", but the police must be on their guard to see that philosophising newspaper writers do not bring about such a decline; they must guard against this with the utmost strictness. In the struggle with truth, error will of itself be recognised as such, without the need of any suppression by external force; but the state must facilitate this struggle of the truth, not, indeed, by depriving the champions of "error" of inner freedom, which it cannot take away from them, but by depriving them of the possibility of this freedom, the possibility of existence.

Christianity is sure of its victory, but according to H. it is not so sure of it as to spurn the aid of the police.

If from the outset everything that contradicts your faith is error, and has to be treated as error, what distinguishes your claims from those of the Mohammedan or of any other religion? Should philosophy, in order not to contradict the basic tenets of dogma, adopt different principles in each country, in accordance with the saying "every country has its own customs"? Should it believe in one country that $3 \times 1 = 1$, in another that women have no souls, and in a third that beer is drunk in heaven? Is there no *universal human* nature, as there is a universal nature of plants and stars? Philosophy asks what is true, not what is held to be true. It asks what is true for all mankind, not what is true for some people. Its metaphysical truths do not recognise the boundaries of political geography; its political truths know too well where the "bounds" begin for it to confuse the illusory horizon of a particular world or national outlook with the true horizon of the human mind. Of all the defenders of Christianity, H. is the weakest.

The *long existence* of Christianity is his sole proof in its favour. But has not philosophy also existed from Thales down to the present day, and indeed does not H. himself assert that it now puts forward greater claims and has a higher opinion of its importance than ever before?

Finally, how does H. prove that the state is a "Christian" state, that its aim is not a free association of moral human beings, but an association of believers, not the realisation of freedom, but the realisation of dogma?

"All our European states have Christianity as their basis."

The *French* state too? The Charter, Article 3, does not say: "every Christian" or "only a Christian", but:

"*tous les Français* sont également admissibles aux emplois civiles et militaires".[a][61]

Prussian Law, too, Part II, Section XIII, says:

"The *primary* duty of the head of state is to maintain tranquillity and security, both internally and externally, and to protect everyone from violence and interference in regard to what belongs to him."[62]

According to § 1, the head of state combines in his person all the "duties and rights of the state". It does not say that the primary duty of the state is to suppress heretical errors and to ensure citizens the bliss of the other world.

But if some European states are in fact based on Christianity, do these states correspond to their concept and is the "pure existence" of a condition the right of that condition to exist?

According to the view of our H., of course, this is the case, for he reminds adherents of Young Hegelianism

"that, according to the laws which are in force in the greater part of the state, a *marriage without consecration by the church* is regarded as *concubinage* and as such is punishable under *police* regulations".

Therefore, if "marriage without consecration by the church" is regarded on the Rhine as "marriage" according to the Napoleonic Code,[63] but on the Spree as "concubinage" according to Prussian Law, then punishment "under police regulations" ought to be an

---

[a] "*All Frenchmen* are equally eligible for civil and military posts."—*Ed.*

argument for philosophers that what is right in one place is wrong in another, that it is not the Napoleonic Code, but Prussian Law which has the scientific, moral and rational conception of marriage. This "philosophy of punishment under police regulations" may be convincing in some places, but it is not convincing in *Prussia*. Furthermore, how little the standpoint of "holy" marriage coincides with that of Prussian Law can be seen from § 12, Part II, Section I, which states:

. "Nevertheless, a marriage which is permitted by the laws of the land loses none of its *civil* validity because the dispensation of the spiritual authorities has not been sought or has been refused."

Hence in Prussia, too, marriage is partially emancipated from the "spiritual authorities" and its "civil" validity is distinguished from its "ecclesiastical" validity.

That our great Christian philosopher of the state has no "high" opinion of the state goes without saying.

"Since our states are not merely *legal associations*, but at the same time true *educational institutions*, with the only difference that they extend their care to a *wider* circle than the institutions devoted to the education of youth", etc., "the whole of public education" rests "on the basis of Christianity".

The education of our school youth is based just as much on the ancient classics and the sciences in general as on the catechism.

According to H., the state differs from an institution for young children not in content, but in magnitude, its "care" is wider.

The true "public" education carried out by the state lies in the rational and public existence of the state; the state itself educates its members by making them its members, by converting the aims of the individual into general aims, crude instinct into moral inclination, natural independence into spiritual freedom, by the individual finding his good in the life of the whole, and the whole in the frame of mind of the individual.

The leading article, on the other hand, makes the state not an association of free human beings who educate one another, but a crowd of adults who are destined to be educated from above and to pass from a "narrow" schoolroom into a "wider" one.

This theory of education and tutelage is put forward here by a friend of freedom of the press, who, out of love for this beauty, points out the "negligences of the censorship", who knows how to describe in the appropriate place the "level of understanding of the broad masses" (perhaps the "level of understanding of the broad masses" has *recently* begun to appear so doubtful to the *Kölnische Zeitung* because this mass has ceased to appreciate the superiority of the "unphilosophical newspaper"?) and who advises the learned to keep one view for the stage and another for the backstage!

In the same way that the leading article gives documentary evidence of its *"inferior"* opinion of the state, so it does now of its *low opinion of "Christianity."*

"All the newspaper articles in the world will never be able to convince a people which on the whole feels well and happy that it is in an unfortunate condition."

We should think so! The *Material* feeling of well-being and happiness is a more reliable bulwark against newspaper articles then the blissful and all-conquering trust in faith! H. does not sing: "A reliable fortress is our God." [a] According to him, the truly believing disposition of the "broad masses" is more exposed to the rust of doubt than the refined worldly culture of the "few"!

"Even incitements to revolt" are less feared by H. "in a *well-ordered* state" than in a "well-ordered church", which, moreover, is guided in all truth by the "spirit of God". A fine believer he is! And now for the reason for it! Namely, the masses can understand political articles but they find philosophical articles incomprehensible!

Finally, if the hint in the leading article that "the *half* measures adopted recently against Young Hegelianism have had the usual consequences of half measures" is put alongside the *ingenuous* wish that the latest efforts of the Hegelings may pass "without *altogether harmful* consequences", one can understand the words of Cornwall in *King Lear*:

> He cannot flatter, he,—
> An honest mind and plain,—he must speak truth:
> And they will take it, so; if not, he's plain.
> These kind of knaves I know, which in this plainness
> Harbour more craft, and more corrupter ends,
> Than twenty silly ducking observants,
> That stretch their duties nicely. [b]

We believe we would be insulting the readers of the *Rheinische Zeitung* if we imagined that they would be satisfied with the spectacle, more comic than serious, of a *ci-devant* liberal, a "young man of days gone by",[64] cut down to his proper size. We should like to say a few words on *"the heart of the matter"*. As long as we were occupied with the polemic against the ailing article, it would have been wrong to interrupt him in his work of self-destruction.

---

[a] First lines of Martin Luther's choral, Ein Feste Burg.— *Ed.*

[b] W. Shakespeare, *King Lear*, Act II, Scene 2.— *Ed.*

[*Rheinische Zeitung* No. 195, July 14, 1842, Supplement]

First of all, the question is raised: "Ought philosophy to discuss religious matters also in newspaper articles?"

This question can be answered only by criticising it.

Philosophy, especially German philosophy, has an urge for isolation, for systematic seclusion, for dispassionate self-examination which from the start places it in estranged contrast to the quick-witted and alive-to-events newspapers, whose only delight is in information. Philosophy, taken in its systematic development, is unpopular; its secret life within itself seems to the layman a pursuit as extravagant as it is unpractical, it is regarded as a professor of magic arts, whose incantations sound awe-inspiring because no one understands them;

True to its nature, philosophy has never taken the first step towards exchanging the ascetic frock of the priest for the light, conventional garb of the newspapers. However, philosophers do not spring up like mushrooms out of the ground; they are products of their time, of their nation, whose most subtle, valuable and invisible juices flow in the ideas of philosophy. The same spirit that constructs railways with the hands of workers, constructs philosophical systems in the brains of philosophers. Philosophy does not exist outside the world, any more than the brain exists outside man because it is not situated in the stomach. But philosophy, of course, exists in the world through the brain before it stands with its feet on the ground, whereas many other spheres of human activity have long had their feet rooted in the ground and pluck with their hands the fruits of the world before they have any inkling that the "head" also belongs to this world, or that this world is the world of the head.

Since every true philosophy is the intellectual quintessence of its time, the time must come when philosophy not only internally by its content, but also externally through its form, comes into contact and interaction with the real world of its day. Philosophy then ceases to be a particular system in relation to other particular systems, it becomes philosophy in general in relation to the world, it becomes the philosophy of the contemporary world. The external forms which confirm that philosophy has attained this significance, that it is the living soul of culture, that philosophy has become worldly and the world has become philosophical, have been the same in all ages. One can consult any history book and find repeated with stereotyped fidelity the simplest rituals which unmistakably mark the penetration of philosophy into salons, priests' studies, editorial offices of newspapers and court antechambers, into the love and the hate of contemporaries. Philosophy comes into the world amid the loud cries of its enemies, who betray their inner infection by wild shouts for help against the fiery ardour of ideas. This cry of its enemies has the same significance for philosophy as the first cry of the new-born babe has for the anxiously listening ear of the mother: it is the cry testifying to the life of its ideas, which have burst the orderly hieroglyphic husk of the system and become citizens of the world. The Corybantes and Cabiri,[65] whose loud fanfares announce to the world the birth of the infant Zeus, attack first of all the religious section of the philosophers, partly because the inquisitorial instinct is more certain to have an appeal for the sentimental side of the public, partly because the public, which includes also the opponents of philosophy, can feel the sphere of philosophical ideas only by means of its ideal antennae, and the only circle of ideas in the value of which the public believes almost as much as in the system of material needs is the circle of religious ideas; and finally because religion polemises not against a particular system of philosophy, but against the philosophy of all particular systems.

The true philosophy of the present day does not differ from the true philosophies of the past by this destiny. On the contrary, this destiny is a proof which history owed to its truth.

For six years German newspapers have been drumming against, calumniating, distorting and bowdlerising the religious trend in philosophy.[66] The Augsburg *Allgemeine* sang bravura arias, almost every overture played the leitmotif, to the effect that philosophy did not deserve to be discussed by this wise lady, that it was a rodomontade of youth, a fashion of blasé coteries. But, in spite of all this, it was impossible to get away from philosophy, and the drumming was continually renewed, for the Augsburg paper plays only one instrument in its anti-philosophical cat's concert, the monotonous kettle-drum. All German newspapers, from the *Berliner politisches Wochenblatt* and the *Hamburger Correspondent* down to the obscure local newspapers, down to the *Kölnische Zeitung*, reverberated with the names of Hegel and Schelling, Feuerbach and Bauer, the *Deutsche Jahrbücher*,[67] etc. Finally, the public became eager to see the Leviathan itself, the more so because semi-official articles threatened to have a legal syllabus officially prescribed for philosophy, and it was precisely then that philosophy made its appearance in the newspapers. For a long time philosophy had remained silent in the face of the self-satisfied superficiality which boasted that by means of a few hackneyed newspaper phrases it would blow away like soap-bubbles the long years of study by genius, the hard-won fruits of self-sacrificing solitude, the results of the unseen but slowly exhausting struggles of contemplative thought. Philosophy had even *protested against the newspapers* as an unsuitable arena, but finally it had to break its silence; it became a newspaper correspondent, and then — unheard-of diversion! — it suddenly occurred to the loquacious purveyors of newspapers that philosophy was not a fitting pabulum for their readers. They could not fail to bring to the notice of the governments that it was dishonest to introduce philosophical and₁ religious questions into the sphere of the newspapers not for the enlightenment of the public but to achieve external aims.

What could philosophy say about religion or about itself that would be worse than your newspaper hullabaloo had already long ago attributed to it in a worse and more frivolous form? It only has to repeat what you unphilosophical Capuchins preach about it in thousands and thousands of controversial speeches — and the worst will have been said.

But philosophy speaks about religious and philosophical matters in a different way than you have spoken about them. You speak without having studied them, philosophy speaks after studying them; you appeal to the emotions, it appeals to reason; you anathematise, it teaches; you promise heaven and earth, it promises nothing but the truth; you demand belief in your beliefs, it demands not belief in its results but the testing of doubts; you frighten, it calms. And, in truth, philosophy has enough knowledge of the world to realise that its results do not flatter the pleasure-seeking and egoism of either the heavenly or the earthly world. But the public, which loves truth and knowledge for their own sakes, will be well able to measure its judgment and morality against the judgment and morality of ignorant, servile, inconsistent and venal scribblers.

Of course, there may be some persons who misinterpret philosophy owing to the wretchedness of their understanding and attitude. But do not you Protestants believe that Catholics misinterpret Christianity, do you not reproach the Christian religion on account of the shameful times of the eighth and ninth centuries, or St. Bartholomew's night, or the Inquisition? There is clear proof that Protestant theology's hatred of philosophers arises largely from the tolerance shown by philosophy towards each particular creed as such. Feuerbach and Strauss have been more reproached for regarding Catholic dogmas as Christian than for declaring that the dogmas of Christianity are not dogmas of reason.

But if some individuals cannot digest modern philosophy and die of philosophical indigestion, that is no more evidence against philosophy than the occasional bursting of an engine boiler, with consequent injury to passengers, is evidence against the science of mechanics.

The question whether philosophical and religious matters ought to be discussed in the newspapers dissolves in its own lack of ideas.

When such questions begin to interest the public as *questions for newspapers,* they have become *questions of the time.* Then the problem is not whether they should be discussed, but where and how they should be discussed, whether in inner circles of the families and the salons, in schools and churches, but not by the press; by opponents of philosophy, but not by philosophers; in the obscure language of private opinion, but not in the clarifying language of public reason. Then the question is whether the sphere of the press should include what exists as a reality; it is no longer a matter of a particular content of the press, but of the general question whether the press ought to be a genuine press, i.e., a free press.

The second question we separate entirely from the first: "Should the newspapers treat politics philosophically in a so-called Christian state?"

When religion becomes a political factor, a subject-matter of politics, it hardly needs to be said that the newspapers not only may, but must discuss political questions. It seems obvious that philosophy, the wisdom of the world, has a greater right to concern itself with the realm of this world, with the state, than has the wisdom of the other world, religion. The question here is not whether there should be any philosophising about the state, but whether this should be done well or badly, philosophically or unphilosophically, with or without prejudice, with or without consciousness, consistently or inconsistently, quite rationally or semi-rationally. If you make religion into a theory of constitutional law, then you are making religion itself into a kind of philosophy.

Was it not Christianity above all that separated church and state?

Read St. Augustine's *De civitate Dei,* study the Fathers of the Church and the spirit of Christianity, and then come back and tell us whether the state or the church is the "Christian state"! Or does not every moment of your practical life brand your theory as a lie? Do you consider it wrong to appeal to the courts if you have been cheated? But the apostle writes that it is wrong. If you have been struck on one cheek, do you turn the other also, or do you not rather start an action for assault? But the gospel forbids it. Do you not demand rational right in this world, do you not grumble at the slightest raising of taxes, are you not beside yourself at the least infringement of your personal liberty? But you have been told that suffering in this life is not to be compared with the bliss of the future, that passive sufferance and blissful hope are the cardinal virtues.

Are not most of your court cases and most of your civil laws concerned with property? But you have been told that your treasure is not of this world. Or if you plead that you render unto Caesar the things that are Caesar's and to God the things that are God's, then you should regard not only golden Mammon, but at least as much free reason, as the ruler of this world, and the "action of free reason" is what we call philosophising.

When it was proposed to form a quasi-religious union of states in the shape of the Holy Alliance and to make religion the state emblem of Europe, the *Pope*, with profound intelligence and perfect consistency, refused to join it, on the grounds that the universal Christian link between peoples is the church and not diplomacy, not a secular union of states.

The truly religious state is the theocratic state; the head of such states must be either the God of religion, Jehovah himself, as in the Jewish state, or God's representative, the Dalai Lama, as in Tibet, or finally, as Görres rightly demands in his recent book, all the Christian states must subordinate themselves to a church which is an "infallible church". For where, as under Protestantism, there is no supreme head of the church, the rule of religion is nothing but the religion of rule, the cult of the government's will.

Once a state includes several creeds having equal rights, it can no longer be a religious state without being a violation of the rights of the particular creeds, a church which condemns all adherents of a different creed as heretics, which makes every morsel of bread depend on one's faith, and which makes dogma the link between individuals and their existence as citizens of the state. Ask the Catholic inhabitants of "poor green Erin",[a] ask the Huguenots before the French revolution; they did not appeal to religion, for their religion was not the state religion; they appealed to the "Rights of Humanity", and philosophy interprets the rights of humanity and demands that the state should be a state of human nature.

---

[a] Ireland.— *Ed.*

But, according to the assertions of half-hearted, narrow-minded rationalism, which is in equal measure unbelieving and theological, the general spirit of Christianity, irrespective of differences of creed, should be the spirit of the state! It is the greatest irreligion, it is the arrogance of secular reason, to divorce the general spirit of religion from actually existing religion. This separation of religion from its dogmas and institutions is tantamount to asserting that the general spirit of the law ought to prevail in the state irrespective of particular laws and positive legal institutions.

If you presume yourself raised so high above religion that you are entitled to separate its general spirit from its positive provisions, how can you reproach the philosophers if they carry out this separation completely and not halfway, if they call the general spirit of religion the human spirit, and not the Christian spirit?

Christians live in states with different political constitutions, some in a republic, others in an absolute monarchy, and others again in a constitutional monarchy. Christianity does not decide whether the constitutions are *good*, for it knows no distinction between them. It teaches, as religion is bound to teach: submit to authority, for *all authority* is from God. Therefore, you must judge the rightfulness of state constitutions not on the basis of Christianity, but on the basis of the state's own nature and essence, not on the basis of the nature of Christian society, but on the basis of the nature of human society.

The Byzantine state was the real religious state, for in it dogmas were questions of state, but the Byzantine state was the worst of states. The states of the *ancien régime* were the most Christian states of all; nevertheless, they were states dependent on the "will of the court".

There exists a dilemma in the face of which "common" sense is powerless.

Either the Christian state corresponds to the concept of the state as the realisation of rational freedom, and then the state only needs to be a rational state in order to be a Christian state and it suffices to derive the state from the rational character of human relations, a task which philosophy accomplishes; or the state of rational freedom cannot be derived from Christianity, and then you yourself will admit that this derivation is not intended by Christianity, since it does not want a bad state, and a state that is not the realisation of rational freedom is a bad state.

You may solve this dilemma in whatever way you like, you will have to admit that the state must be built on the basis of free reason, and not of religion. Only the crassest ignorance could assert that this theory, the conversion of the concept of the state into an independent concept, is a passing whim of recent philosophers.

In the political sphere, philosophy has done nothing that physics, mathematics, medicine, and every science, have not done in their respective spheres. Bacon of Verulam said that theological physics was a virgin dedicated to God and barren,[a] he emancipated physics from theology and it became fertile. Just as you do not ask the physician whether he is a believer, you have no reason to ask the politician either. Immediately before and after the time of Copernicus' great discovery of the true solar system, the law of gravitation of the state was discovered, its own gravity was found in the state itself. The various European governments tried, in the superficial way of first practical attempts, to apply this result in order to establish a system of equilibrium of states. Earlier, however, Machiavelli and Campanella, and later Hobbes, Spinoza, Hugo Grotius, right down to Rousseau, Fichte and Hegel, began to regard the state through human eyes and to deduce its natural laws from reason and experience, and not from theology. In so doing, they were as little deterred as Copernicus was by the fact that Joshua bade the sun stand still over Gideon and the moon in the valley of Ajalon. Recent philosophy has only continued the work begun by Heraclitus and Aristotle. You wage a polemic, therefore, not against the rational character of recent philosophy, but against the ever new philosophy of reason. Of course, the ignorance which perhaps only yesterday or the day before yesterday discovered for the first time age-old ideas about the state in the *Rheinische* or the *Königsberger Zeitung,* regards these ideas of history as having suddenly occurred to certain individuals overnight, because they are new to it and reached it only overnight; it forgets that it itself is assuming the old role of the doctor of the Sorbonne who considered it his duty to accuse Montesquieu publicly of being so frivolous as to declare that the supreme merit of the state was political, not ecclesiastical, virtue. It forgets that it is assuming the role of Joachim Lange, who denounced Wolff on the ground that his doctrine of predestination would lead to desertion by the soldiers and thus the weakening of military discipline, and in the long run the collapse of the state. Finally, it forgets that Prussian Law was derived from the philosophical school of precisely "this Wolff", and that the French Napoleonic

---

[a] F. Baconi Baronis de Verulamio, *De dignitate et augmentis scientiarum,* Liber I, 3.— *Ed.*

Code was derived not from the Old Testament, but from the school of ideas of Voltaire, Rousseau, Condorcet, Mirabeau, and Montesquieu, and from the French revolution. Ignorance is a demon, we fear that it will yet be the cause of many a tragedy; the greatest Greek poets rightly depicted it as tragic fate in the soul-shattering dramas of the royal houses of Mycenae and Thebes.

Whereas the earlier philosophers of constitutional law proceeded in their account of the formation of the state from the instincts, either of ambition or gregariousness, or even from reason, though not social reason, but the reason of the individual, the more ideal and profound view of recent philosophy proceeds from the idea of the whole. It looks on the state as the great organism, in which legal, moral, and political freedom must be realised, and in which the individual citizen in obeying the laws of the state only obeys the natural laws of his own reason, of human reason. *Sapienti sat.*[a]

In conclusion, we turn once more to the *Kölnische Zeitung* with a few philosophical words of farewell. It was very sensible of it to take a liberal "of a former day" into its service. One can very conveniently be both liberal and reactionary if only one is always adroit enough to address oneself to the liberals of the recent past who know no other dilemma than that of Vidocq: either "prisoner or gaoler". It was still more sensible for the liberals of the recent past to join issue with the liberals of the present time. Without parties there is no development, without demarcation there is no progress. We hope that the leading article in No. 179 has opened a new era for the *Kölnische Zeitung,* the era of character.

Written between June 29 and July 4, 1842
First published in the Supplement to the *Rheinische Zeitung* Nos. 191, 193 and 195, July 10, 12 and 14, 1842

Printed according to the newspaper

---

[a] It is enough for the wise.— *Ed.*

THE PHILOSOPHICAL MANIFESTO
OF THE HISTORICAL SCHOOL OF LAW[68]

It is commonly held that the *historical school* is a *reaction* against the *frivolous spirit* of the *eighteenth* century. The currency of this view is in inverse ratio to its truth. In fact, the eighteenth century had only *one* product, the *essential character* of which is frivolity, and this *sole frivolous* product is the *historical school*.

The historical school has taken the study of sources as its watchword, it has carried its love for sources to such an extreme that it calls on the boatman to ignore the river and row only on its source-head. Hence it will only find it right that we go back to *its sources*, to *Hugo's natural law. Its philosophy* is *ahead* of its development; therefore in its development one will search in vain for philosophy.

According to a fiction current in the eighteenth century, the natural state was considered the true state of human nature. People wanted to see the idea of man through the eyes of the body and created *men of nature, Papagenos,* the naivety of which idea extended even to covering the skin with feathers.[69] During the last decades of the eighteenth century, it was supposed that *peoples in a state of nature* possessed primeval wisdom and everywhere one could hear bird-catchers imitating the twittering method of singing of the Iroquois, the Indians, etc., in the belief that by these arts the birds themselves could be enticed into a trap. All these eccentricities were based on the correct idea that the *primitive* state was a naive Dutch picture of the *true* state.

The *man of nature of the historical school,* still without any of the trappings of romantic culture, is *Hugo.* His textbook of *natural law* is the *Old Testament* of the historical school. *Herder's* view that natural men are *poets,* and that the *sacred* books of natural peoples are *poetic* works, presents no obstacle to us, although Hugo talks the most trivial and sober prose, for just as every century has its own peculiar nature, so too it gives birth to its own peculiar natural men. Hence, although Hugo does not *write poerty,* he does *write fiction,* and *fiction* is the *poerty of prose* corresponding to the prosaic nature of the eighteenth century.

By describing Herr Hugo as the forefather and creator of the historical school, however, we are acting in accord with the latter's *own view,* as is proved by the *gala programme* of the most famous historical jurist[a] in honour of Hugo's jubilee.[70] By regarding Herr Hugo as a child of the eighteenth century, we are acting even in the *spirit* of Herr Hugo himself, as he testifies by his claim that he is a *pupil* of Kant and that his natural law is an offshoot of *Kantian philosophy.* We shall begin with this item of his *manifesto.*

Hugo *misinterprets* his teacher *Kant* by supposing that because we cannot know what is *true,* we consequently allow the *untrue,* if it *exists* at all, to pass as *fully valid.* He is a *sceptic* as regards the *necessary essence* of things, so as to be a *courtier* as regards their *accidental appearance.* Therefore, he by no means tries to prove that the *positive* is *rational;* he tries to prove that the *positive* is *irrational.* With self-satisfied zeal he adduces arguments from everywhere to provide additional evidence that no rational necessity is inherent in the positive institutions, e.g., property, the state constitution, marriage, etc., that they are even *contrary* to reason, and at most allow of idle *chatter* for and against. One must not in any way blame this *method* on his accidental individuality; it is rather the *method of his principle,* it is the *frank, naive, reckless* method of the historical school. If the *positive* is supposed to be *valid because* it is *positive,* then I have to *prove* that the *positive* is *not* valid *because* it is *rational,* and how could I make this more evident than by proving that the unreasonable is positive and the positive unreasonable, that the positive exists not *owing to* reason, but *in spite of* reason? If *reason* were the *measure of the positive,* the *positive* would not be the *measure of reason.* "Though this be madness, yet there is method in't!"[b] Hugo, therefore, *profanes* all that the just, moral, political man regards as holy, but he smashes these holy things only to be able to honour them as *historical relics;* he desecrates them in the *eyes of reason* in order afterwards to make them honourable in the *eyes of history,* and at the same time to make the *eyes of the historical school* honourable.

---

[a] F. C. Savigny.— *Ed.*

[b] W. Shakespeare, *Hamlet, Prince of Denmark,* Act II, Scene 2.— *Ed.*

Hugo's *reasoning*, like his *principle*, is *positive*, i.e., *uncritical*. He knows *no distinctions*. *Everything existing* serves him as an *authority*, every authority serves him as an *argument*. Thus, in a single paragraph he quotes *Moses* and *Voltaire*, *Richardson* and *Homer*, *Montaigne* and *Ammon*, *Rousseau's Contrat social* and *Augustine's De civitate Dei.* The same levelling procedure is applied to *peoples.* According to Hugo, the *Siamese*, who considers it an eternal law of nature that his king should have the mouths of chatterers sewn up and the mouth of a clumsy orator slit to the ears, is just as *positive* as the *Englishman*, who would consider it a political anomaly if his king were autocratically to impose even a penny tax. The shameless *Conci*, who runs about naked and at most covers himself with mud, is as positive as the *Frenchman*, who not only dresses, but dresses elegantly. The *German*, who brings up his daughter as the jewel of the family, is not more positive than the *Rajput*, who kills his daughter to save himself the trouble of feeding her. In short, *a rash is just as positive as the skin itself.*

In one place, one thing is positive, in another something else; the one is as irrational as the other. Submit yourself to what is positive in your own home.

Hugo, therefore, is the *complete sceptic*. With him, the *eighteenth-century scepticism* in regard to the *rationality of what exists* appears as *scepticism* in regard to the *existence of rationality*. He accepts the *Enlightenment, he no longer sees anything rational in the positive, but only in order no longer to see anything positive in the rational.* He thinks the appearance of reason has been expelled from the positive in order to recognise the positive *without* the appearance of reason. He thinks the *false flowers* have been plucked from the chains in order to wear *real chains* without any flowers.

Hugo's relation to the *other Enlighteners* of the eighteenth century is about the same as that between the *dissolution of the French state* at the debauched *court of the Regent*[a] and the dissolution of the French state during the *National Assembly*. In both cases there is dissolution! In the former case it appears as *debauched frivolity*, which realises and ridicules the hollow lack of ideas of the existing state of things, but only in order, having got rid of all rational and moral ties, to *make sport* of the decaying ruins, and then itself to be made sport of by them and dissolved. It is the *corruption of the then existing world, which takes pleasure in itself.* In the *National Assembly*, on the other hand, the *dissolution* appears as the *liberation of the new spirit from old forms*, which were no longer of any *value*

---

[a] Philippe II of Orleans.— *Ed.*

or *capable* of containing it. It is the *new life's feeling of its own power,* which *shatters* what has been *shattered* and *rejects* what has been *rejected.* If, therefore, *Kant's philosophy* must be rightly regarded as the *German theory* of the French revolution, *Hugo's natural law* is the *German theory* of the French *ancien régime.* We find in it once more the whole *frivolity* of those *roues,*[a] the *base scepticism,* which, insolent towards ideas but most subservient towards what is palpably evident, begins to feel clever only where it has killed the *spirit* of the positive, in order to possess the purely positive as a residue and to feel comfortable in this *animal* state. Even when Hugo weighs up the force of the arguments, he finds with an unerring sure instinct that what is rational and moral in institutions is *doubtful* for reason. Only *what is animal* seems to *his reason* to be *indubitable.* But let us listen to our enlightener from the standpoint of the *ancien régime!* Hugo's views must be heard from Hugo himself. To all his combinations should be added: αὐτὸς ἔφα.[b]

Introduction

"The sole juristic distinguishing feature of man is his animal nature."

The Chapter on Freedom

"A limitation of freedom" (of a *rational* being) *"lies even in the fact that it cannot of its own accord cease to be a rational being,* i.e., a being which can and should act rationally."

"Absence of freedom in no way alters the animal and rational nature of the *unfree man* or of *other men. All the obligations of conscience* remain. *Slavery* is not only *physically* possible, but also possible *from a rational standpoint,* and any research which teaches us the contrary must be based on some kind of error. Of course, slavery is not *absolutely lawful,* i.e., it does not follow from man's animal nature, or from his rational nature, or from his nature as a citizen. But that it can be *provisionally lawful, just as much* as *anything* acknowledged by its opponents, is shown by comparison with *private law* and *public law."* The proof is: "From the point of view of *animal* nature, he that is *owned* by a rich man, who suffers a loss without him and is heedful of his needs, is obviously more secure against want than the poor man whom his fellow men make use of so long as he has anything for them to use, etc." "The right to *maltreat* and *cripple servi*[c] is not essential, and *even when it occurs* it is *not much worse* than what the poor have to endure, and, as regards the *body,* it is not so bad as *war,* from participation in which slaves as such should everywhere be exempt. Even *beauty* is more likely to be found in a *Circassian slave girl* than in a *beggar girl."* (Listen to the old man!)

---

[a] Rogues.—*Ed.*
[b] He himself said.—*Ed.*
[c] Slaves.—*Ed.*

"As regards its *rational* nature, slavery has the advantage over poverty that the slave-owner, even from *well-understood economic considerations,* is much more likely to expend something on the education of a slave who shows ability than in the case of a beggar child. Under a *constitution,* the slave is spared very many kinds of oppression. Is the slave more unfortunate than the prisoner of war, whose guards' only concern is that they are temporarily responsible for him, or more unfortunate than the convict labourer over whom the government has placed an overseer?"

"Whether slavery as such is advantageous or disadvantageous for *reproduction* is a question still in dispute."

The Chapter on Marriage

"Regarded from the *philosophical* standpoint of positive law, *marriage* is already often considered *much more essential* and *much more rational* than would appear from a quite free examination."

It is precisely the *satisfaction of the sexual instinct* in marriage that suits Herr Hugo. He even draws a *wholesome moral* from this fact:

"From this, as from countless other circumstances, it *should have been clear* that to *treat the human body as a means to an end* is not always *immoral,* as people, including presumably *Kant himself,* have incorrectly understood this expression."

But the sanctification of the sexual instinct by *exclusiveness,* the bridling of this instinct through laws, the *moral beauty* which idealises the bidding of nature and makes it an element of spiritual union, the *spiritual essence* of marriage, that is precisely what Herr Hugo finds *dubious* in marriage. But before we go further into his *frivolous shamelessness,* let us listen for a moment to the French *philosopher* in contrast to the *historical* German.

"C'est en renonçant pour un seul homme à cette réserve mystérieuse, dont la règle divine est imprimée dans son cœur, que la femme se voue à cet homme, pour lequel elle suspend, dans un abandon momentané, cette pudeur, qui ne la quitte jamais; pour lequel seul elle écarte des voiles qui sont d'ailleurs son asile et sa parure. De là cette confiance intime dans son époux, résultat d'une relation exclusive, qui ne peut exister qu'entre elle et lui, sans qu'aussitôt elle se sente flétrie; de là dans cet époux la reconnaissance pour un sacrifice et ce mélange de désir et de respect pour un être qui, même en partageant ses plaisirs, ne semble encore que lui céder; de là tout ce qu'il y a de *régulier* dans notre *ordre social.*" [a]

So says the liberal philosophical *Frenchman Benjamin Constant!* [71] And now let us listen to the servile, historical German:

---

[a] "By renouncing for one man alone that mysterious reserve which divine law has implanted in her heart, the woman pledges herself to this man for whose sake she momentarily suspends the modesty which she never loses, for whom alone she lifts the veils which otherwise are her refuge and her adornment. Hence this intimate confidence in her husband, the result of an exclusive relation which can only exist between her and him, and without which she feels herself dishonoured. Hence her husband's thankfulness for the sacrifice and that mixture of desire and respect for a being who, even while sharing his pleasures, seems only to be submitting to him. Hence the source of all that is *orderly* in our *social system.*"— *Ed.*

"Much *more dubious* is the second circumstance, that *outside marriage the satisfaction of this instinct* is *not* permitted! *Animal nature is against this restriction. Rational* nature is still more so, because"... (guess!)... "because a man must be *almost omniscient* in order to foresee what result it will have, because it is therefore *tempting God* to pledge oneself to satisfy one of the most powerful natural instincts only when this can take place with one particular person!" "*The sense of the beautiful,* which is *free* by its very nature, has to be fettered and what depends on it has to be wholly divorced from it."

See *what kind* of schooling our *Young Germans* have received! [72]

"This institution conflicts with the nature of *civil society* insofar as ... finally the *police* undertake an *almost insoluble task!*"

Clumsy philosophy, which has no such consideration for the *police*!

"Everything that follows as a consequence from a more precise definition of the marriage law, shows us that marriage, whatever principles are adopted in relation to it, is still a *very imperfect institution.*"

"This restriction of the sexual instinct to marriage has *nevertheless also important* advantages, namely, by its means *infectious diseases* are usually *avoided. Marriage* saves the government a lot of *trouble.* Finally, there is also the *consideration,* which is everywhere so important, that in regard to marriage *civil law* is the *customary one.*" "*Fichte says:* An unmarried man is only *half* a man. I" (i.e., Hugo) "am extremely sorry, however, to have to declare that such a beautiful utterance, putting me above Christ, Fénelon, Kant and Hume, is a *monstrous exaggeration.*"

"As regards monogamy and polygamy, this is *obviously* a matter of man's *animal* nature"!!

The Chapter on Education

We learn at once that: "The art of education gives rise to no less objection against the juridical relation connected with it" (education in the family) "than the *art of loving* does against *marriage.*"

"The difficulty that education may only be carried out within such a relation, however, gives rise to far fewer doubts than is the case with the satisfaction of the sexual instinct if for no other reason than that it is permissible to entrust education by contract to a third person, so that he who feels a very strong urge in this respect can easily satisfy it, only not, of course, necessarily in regard to the *particular person* whom he would like to engage. It is, however, also irrational that, by virtue of *such a relationship,* someone to whom no one would entrust a child, may carry on education and exclude others from education." "Finally, here also there is *compulsion,* partly because the educator is often not permitted by positive law to *give up this relationship,* and partly because the one to be educated is compelled to let himself be educated by this particular teacher." "The reality of this relationship depends mostly on the *mere accident* of birth, which is connected with the *father* through *marriage.* This *way of originating* the relationship is obviously not very rational, if only because it usually opens the way to *preference,* which itself is already an obstacle to a good education. That it is not even absolutely necessary is evident from the fact that education is given also to children whose parents are already dead."

The Chapter on Civil Law

§ 107 tells us that the *"necessity of civil law in general is imaginary"*

The Chapter on Constitutional Law

"It is a *holy duty of conscience to obey the authorities in whose hands power lies.*" "As regards the *division of governmental powers,* it is true that *no* particular constitution is absolutely lawful, but *every* constitution is *provisionally lawful, whatever the division of governmental powers.*"

Has not Hugo proved that man can cast off even the *last fetter of freedom,* namely, that of being a *rational being?*

These few extracts from the *philosophical manifesto of the historical school* suffice, we think, for pronouncing a historical verdict on this school, instead of unhistorical fantasies, vague figments of the brain, and deliberate fictions; they suffice for deciding whether *Hugo's successors* are *fit* to be the *legislators of our time.*[73]

At all events, in the course of time and civilisation, this *crude genealogical tree* of the historical school has been shrouded in mist by the *smokescreen of mysticism,* fantastically wrought by *romanticism,* and inoculated with *speculation;* the many fruits of *erudition* have been shaken off the tree, dried and deposited with much boasting in the great storehouse of German erudition. Truly, however, little *criticism* is needed to recognise behind all these fragrant modern phrases the dirty old idea of our enlightener of the *ancien régime,* and his dissolute frivolity behind all the extravagant unctuosity.

If Hugo says: "*Animal* nature is the distinctive *juristic* feature of *man*", from which it follows: law is *animal* law, the educated *moderns* say, instead of the crude, frank "*animal*" law, something like "*organic*" law, for who on hearing the word "*organism*" thinks at once of the *animal organism?* If Hugo says that *marriage* and other *moral-legal* institutions are *irrational,* the *moderns* say that these institutions are indeed *not creations of human reason,* but are *representations* of a higher "*positive*" reason, and so on in regard to all the other articles. Only *one* conclusion is voiced by *all* with equal crudity: *the right of arbitrary power.*

The juridical and historical theories of *Haller, Stahl, Leo,* and their fellow thinkers should be regarded only as *codices rescripti*[a] of *Hugo's natural law,* which after some operations of *critical analysis* allow the old *original text* to be made legible again, as we shall show in more detail at a suitable time.

---

[a] Palimpsest.— *Ed.*

All the *tricks of embellishment* are the more in vain as we still have the *old manifesto,* which, if not *intelligent,* is nevertheless *very easy to understand.*

Written between April and early
August 1842

First published (without "The Chapter
on Marriage") in the Supplement to the
Rheiniche Zeitung No. 221, August 9, 1842;
"The Chapter on Marriage" was first
published in: Marx/Engels, *Gesamtausgabe,*
Abt. 1, Bd. 1, Hb. 1, 1927

Printed according to the newspaper text checked with the copy
of the manuscript; "The Chapter
on Marriage" is printed according
to the copy of the manuscript

YET ANOTHER WORD ON *BRUNO BAUER UND DIE AKADEMISCHE LEHRFREIHEIT* BY Dr. O. F. GRUPPE, BERLIN, 1842 [74]

If someone in Germany wanted to write a *comedy of dilettantism,* Herr *Dr. O. F. Gruppe* would be an indispensable character in it. Fate has equipped him with that iron tenacity which great men cannot do without, least of all the great men of dilettantism. Even if most of his adventures, like those of Sancho Panza, meet with ambiguous signs of acknowledgment, the monotony of this success is relieved and varied by the comic ingenuousness and touching naivety with which Herr Gruppe accepts his laurels. One cannot fail to perceive even a certain magnanimity in the consistency which has taught Herr Gruppe to conclude: Because I have been thrown out of the schoolroom of philology, it will be my mission to be thrown out also from the ball-room of aesthetics and the halls of philosophy. That is a lot, but it is not all. I shall not have played out my role until I have been thrown out of the temple of theology: and Herr Gruppe is conscientious enough to play out his role.

In his latest performance, however, Herr Gruppe has to some extent departed from the height of his standpoint. We do not doubt for a moment that his latest work *Bruno Bauer and Academic Freedom of Teaching* has been by no means written "in the service of a party or under an influence". Herr Gruppe felt the need to be thrown out of theology, but *worldly wisdom* here came to the aid of his comic instinct. As is fitting for comic characters, Herr Gruppe up to now has worked with most delightful seriousness and most unusual pomposity. Incompleteness, superficiality, and misunderstandings were his *fate,* but they were not his *tendency.* The great man acted according to his nature, but he acted for himself and not for others. He was a *buffoon by profession:* we have no doubt that in his latest performance he is a *buffoon by order and for remuneration.* The evil intention, the unscrupulous distortion, the base perfidy, will leave the reader, too, in no doubt about it.

It would be contrary to our view of comic characters to waste an extensive critical apparatus on Herr Gruppe. Who wants a critical account of Eulenspiegel? *Anecdotes* are wanted, and we give an anecdote about Herr Gruppe which is *the anecdote of his pamphlet.* It concerns Bauer's exposition of St. Matthew 12: 38-42. The kind reader will have to put up with theological matters for an instant, but he will not forget that it is our purpose to deal with Herr Gruppe and not with theology. He will find it only fair that the characteristic features of Bauer's opponents should be brought to the notice of the newspaper public, since Bauer's character and teaching has been made a newspaper myth.

We shall quote the passage in question from St. Matthew in its entirety.

"Then certain of the scribes and of the Pharisees answered, saying, Master, we would see a sign from thee.

"But he answered and said unto them. An evil and adulterous generation seeketh after a sign; and there shall *no sign* be given to it, but the sign of the prophet *Jonas:* For as Jonas was three days and three nights in the whale's belly; so shall the Son of man be three days and three nights in the heart of the earth. The men of Nineveh shall rise in the judgment with this generation, and shall condemn it: because they *repented* at the *preaching of Jonas; and, behold, a greater than Jonas is here.* The queen of the south shall rise up in the judgment with this generation, and shall condemn it: for she came from the uttermost parts of the earth to hear the *wisdom of Solomon; and, behold, a greater than Solomon is here."*

The Protestant theologians were struck by the contradiction that Jesus here rejects miracles, whereas otherwise he performs miracles. They were struck by the even greater contradiction that at the very time when the Lord refuses the demand for a miracle, he promises a miracle, and indeed a great miracle, his three days' stay in the underworld.

Since the Protestant theologians are too ungodly to admit a contradiction of the scripture *with their* understanding, since they are too sanctimonious to admit a contradiction of their understanding *with the scripture,* they falsify, distort and twist the clear words and the simple meaning of the scripture. They maintain that Jesus here does not *counterpose* his *teaching* and his *spiritual personality* to the demand for a sign; they maintain that

"he is speaking of the whole of his manifestation, which is more than the manifestation of Solomon and of Jonas, and of which 'in particular' *his miracles* also were a part".[75]

By the most thoroughgoing exegesis, Bauer proves to them the absurdity of this explanation. He quotes for them St. Luke [11 : 29-30], in which the troublesome passage about the whale and the three days' stay under the earth is missing. It says:

"This is an evil generation: they seek a sign; and there shall no sign be given it, but the sign of Jonas the prophet. For as Jonas was a sign unto the Ninevites, so shall also the Son of man be to this generation",

upon which St. Luke makes the Lord relate how the men of Nineveh repented at the *preaching* of Jonas and the queen of the south came from the uttermost parts of the earth to hear the *wisdom* of Solomon. Bauer shows that the crux is given still more simply in St. Mark [8: 12-13].

"Why," says Jesus, "doth this generation seek after a sign? verily I say unto you, There shall no sign be given unto this generation. And he left them."

Bauer comes out against the theologians' false interpretation and arbitrary distortion of the texts, and he refers them to what is *actually written* by once more summing up the *meaning of Jesus' speech* in the following words:

"*Keep away from me, theologian!* For, *it is written: a greater than Jonas is here, a greater than Solomon,* that is to say, the men of Nineveh repented at the *preaching* of Jonas, the queen of the south came from the uttermost parts of the earth to hear the *wisdom* of Solomon. But you have given no credence to my words, to my speech, yet these words are the expression of *a personality, whose spiritual compass is infinite, whereas the personalities of Jonas and Solomon were still limited.* But so it shall be, only the sign of Jonas shall be given to you, you shall not see any other sign than this *my person* and its expression, even if infinite, in the word."

After presenting *Jesus' speech* in this way, Bauer adds:

"Where *then* in particular are the miracles?"[76]

And Herr Gruppe? Herr Gruppe says:

"The most unusual thing in this connection is that Bauer in his own baroque *manner presents himself as a prophet.* On p. 296 we read the emphatic passage: *keep away from me, theologian!*" etc. (p. 20).

Herr Gruppe is so shameless as to want to make the reader believe that Bauer is speaking *about himself,* that he is making himself out to be the *infinite personality,* whereas Bauer is *explaining Jesus' speech.* Much as we might like to, we cannot excuse this *qui pro quo,* this Eulenspiegel trick, as due to Herr Gruppe's notorious weakness of intellect and dilettantist ignorance. The *deception* is obvious. It is not merely that Herr Gruppe does not tell the reader what it is all about. We might still think that the dilettante had accidentally opened Bauer's work at p. 296 and in the happy-go-lucky haste of compiling his book did not have time to read the preceding and following statements. But Herr Gruppe *suppresses* the conclusion of the "emphatic passage", the conclusion, which is beyond all possible misunderstanding: "But so it shall be, *only* the sign of Jonas shall be given to you, you shall not see any other sign than *this my person* and its expression, even if infinite, in the word. Where *then* 'in particular' are the miracles?"

Herr Gruppe was aware that even the biassed reader, the reader who was so foolish as to look for Bauer not in Bauer's writings, but in the writings of Herr Gruppe, could not fail to be convinced that Bauer was not speaking on his own account, but that he was saying *what is written*. Disregarding all other absurdities, what else could have been implied by the words "Where then in particular are the miracles?"

We doubt whether German literature has a similar specimen of shamelessness to offer.

Herr Gruppe says in his foreword:

"During my work it has become increasingly evident to me that we are living in an age of rhetoricians and sophists" (p. iv).

If this is meant to be a *confession*, we must seriously protest against it. Herr Gruppe is neither a rhetorician nor a sophist. Until the period of his pamphlet on Bauer, he was a *comical character*, he was a rogue in the naive sense; since then he has lost nothing but his naivety, and hence he is now — but let his conscience tell him that. For the rest, Bauer can regard it an acknowledgment of his intellectual superiority that he could be opposed only by men so low in intelligence and so remote from any superiority that he could hit them only by allowing himself to *fall* to their level.

Written in early September 1842
First published in the journal *Deutsche Jahrbücher für Wissenschaft und Kunst*, 5. Jg., No. 273, November 16, 1842

Signed: *K. M.*

Printed according to the journal

Published in English for the first time

COMMUNISM AND THE AUGSBURG
ALLGEMEINE ZEITUNG[77]

Cologne, October 15. No. 284 of the *Augsburg newspaper* has been so clumsy as to claim it has discovered that the *Rheinische Zeitung* is a Prussian *woman Communist*, true not a real Communist, but nevertheless one who in her imagination coquettes with communism and ogles it in a platonic fashion.

Whether this naughty flight of fancy on the part of the lady of Augsburg is unselfish, or whether this idle illusion of her over-heated imagination is bound up with speculation and diplomatic dealings, we leave the reader to judge — after we have presented the alleged *corpus delicti*.

The *Rheinische Zeitung*, we are told, published a communist article on the Berlin family houses,[78] and accompanied it with the following comment: This information *"should not be without interest for the history of this important question of the time"*. It follows, therefore, according to the Augsburg newspaper's logic, that the *Rheinische Zeitung*

"served up this kind of unwashed stuff with a recommendation".

So if I say, for instance, "the following information of the *Mefisto-feles* on the domestic affairs of the Augsburg newspaper should be *not without interest* for the history of this pompous lady",[79] am I then recommending the *dirty "stuff"* from which the lady of Augsburg tailors her gay wardrobe? Or should communism not be consid-ered an important question of the time simply because it is not one suitable for drawing-rooms and because it wears dirty linen and does not smell of rose-water?

However, the lady of Augsburg quite rightly resents our lack of understanding. The importance of communism is not that it is a highly serious question of the time for France and England. Communism has the *European importance* of having been used as a phrase by the Augsburg newspaper. One of its Paris correspondents, a convert who treats history as a pastry-cook does botany, recently had a sudden idea: the monarchy ought to try to appropriate socialist and communist ideas in its own way. You understand now the annoyance of the lady of Augsburg, who will never forgive us for presenting communism to the public in all its *unwashed* nakedness; you understand the sullen *irony* which exclaims: that is how you *recommend* communism, which once had the fortunate elegance of serving as a phrase for the Augsburg newspaper!

The second reproach levelled against the *Rheinische Zeitung* is the conclusion of a report from Strasbourg on the communist speeches delivered at the Congress[80] there; the two stepsisters had divided the material between them in such a way that the *Rhineland* one took over the *proceedings* and the *Bavarian* one the *dinners* of the Strasbourg savants. The passage incriminated was literally as follows:

"The position of the middle estate today resembles that of the nobility in 1789; at that time, the middle estate claimed for itself the privileges of the nobility and obtained them; *today the estate that owns nothing demands to share in the wealth of the middle classes, which are now at the helm.* Today the middle estate is better protected against a sudden onslaught than were the nobility in 1789, and it is to be expected that the problem will be solved in a peaceful way."

That the prophecy of Sieyès came true[81] and that the *tiers état* has become all, and wants to be all, is admitted with the most rueful indignation by Bülow-Cummerow, by the former *Berliner politisches Wochenblatt*,[a] by Dr. Kosegarten, and all the feudal-minded writers. That the estate that today owns nothing *demands* to share in the wealth of the middle classes is a fact which, without the talk at Strasbourg, and in spite of Augsburg's silence, is obvious to everyone in Manchester, Paris and Lyons.[82] Does the lady of Augsburg believe that her displeasure and her silence have refuted the facts of the time? She is *impertinent even when fleeing.* She shies away from insidious phenomena of the day and believes that the dust she raises behind her in doing so, as also the abuse which she nervously mutters between her teeth as she flees, will have blinded and confused both the uncomforting phenomena of the day and the comfortable reader.

---

[a] Hint at Frederick William IV.— *Ed.*

Rheinische Zeitung

für

Politik, Handel und Gewerbe.

N⁰ 289   Köln, Sonntag den 16. Oktober   1842

Uebersicht des Inhalts.

Amtliche Nachrichten.

Deutschland. Köln, 15. Okt.

Amtliche Nachrichten.

Chronik des Tages.

Berlin, 12. Okt.

Deutschland.

Köln, 15. Oktober.

Alter und Jugend.

Von

R. E. Prutz.

Page of the Rheinische Zeitung *with Marx's article "Communism and the Augsburg* Allgemeine Zeitung

Or does the lady of Augsburg resent our correspondent's expectation that the undeniable collision will be settled "in a *peaceful* way"? Or does she reproach us for not having at once prescribed a proven remedy and supplied the astonished reader with a report as clear as the sun at noon on the solution of the problem which cannot be regarded as a standard one? We have not mastered the art of disposing by a *single* phrase of problems which *two* nations are working to solve.

But, dearest, most worthy lady of Augsburg, in connection with communism you have given us to understand that Germany at present is poor in people enjoying independence, that nine-tenths of the better-educated youth have to beg bread from the state to assure their future, that our rivers' are neglected, that our shipping is at a standstill, that our once flourishing trading towns lack their former prosperity, that free institutions are achieved very slowly in Prussia, that our surplus population roams helplessly about, ceasing to exist as Germans among foreign nationalities; and for all these problems you offer not a single remedy, make no attempt to become *"clearer about the means for accomplishing"* the great deed that should absolve us from all these sins! Or do you expect no peaceful solution? There seems to be almost an indication of this in another article in the same issue, datelined from Karlsruhe,[83] which even in regard to the Customs Union addresses the following insidious question to Prussia:

"Can one believe that such a crisis will pass away like a row about smoking tobacco in the Zoological Gardens?"

The reason you advance for your lack of belief is a *communist* one.

"Well, then, let a crisis break out in industry, let capital amounting to millions be lost, and thousands of workers find themselves without bread."

How inopportune you must have found our *"peaceful expectation"* once you had decided to *allow* a bloody crisis to *break out,* which is no doubt why in your article, in accordance with your own logic, you *recommend* Great Britain to take note of the demagogic physician, Dr. M'Douall, who emigrated to America because *"there was nothing to be done with this royal breed".*[84]

Before we take leave of you, we should like in passing to call your attention to your own wisdom, since by your method of phrase-making you can hardly avoid now and again, in a harmless way, *expressing* an idea, although it is not *your* idea. You find that the polemic of Herr Hennequin from Paris against the parcellation of landed property puts him in surprising harmony with the autonomists[85]! Surprise, says Aristotle, is the beginning of philosophising.[a] You have come to an end at the beginning. Would otherwise the surprising fact have escaped you that communist principles are being disseminated in Germany not by liberals, but by your *reactionary* friends?

Who is it that talks of *artisans' corporations?* The reactionaries. The artisans' estate, they say, ought to form a state within the state. Do you find it remarkable that such ideas, expressed in modern language, therefore take the form: "The state ought to be turned into an estate of the artisans"? If for the artisan his estate ought to be the state, and if the modern artisan, like every modern person, understands, and can understand, by the state only the sphere common to all his fellow citizens, how can you combine these two ideas except in the idea of an *artisans' state?*

Who carries on a polemic against *parcellation of landed property?* The reactionaries. In a quite recent work (Kosegarten on parcellation[86]) written in a feudalistic spirit, the author goes so far as to call *private property* a *privilege.* That is *Fourier's* basic principle. Once there is unity on basic principles, cannot there be any dispute over consequences and application?

The *Rheinische Zeitung,* which does not admit that communist ideas in their present form possess even *theoretical reality,* and therefore can still less desire their *practical realisation,* or even consider it possible, will subject these ideas to thoroughgoing criticism. But if the lady of Augsburg demanded more, and was capable of more, than smooth-sounding phrases, it would be obvious to her that such writings as those of Leroux, Considérant, and above all the sharp-witted work by Proudhon,[b] cannot be criticised on the basis of superficial flashes of thought, but only after long and profound study. We must take such *theoretical* works the more seriously because we do not agree with the Augsburg newspaper, which finds the *"reality"* of communist *ideas* not in *Plato,* but in its *obscure acquaintance,* who was not without merit in some fields of scientific research, but who gave up all he possessed at the time and washed plates and cleaned boots for his comrades in accordance with the wishes of Father Enfantin. We are firmly convinced that the real *danger* lies not in *practical attempts,* but in the *theoretical elaboration* of communist ideas, for practical attempts, even *mass attempts,* can be answered by *cannon* as soon as they become dangerous, whereas *ideas,* which have

---

[a] Aristotle, *Metaphysics,* Book I, Ch. 2 (982[b]).— *Ed.*

[b] P. J. Proudhon, *Qu'est-ce que la propriété?* — *Ed.*

conquered our intellect and taken possession of our minds, ideas to which reason has fettered our conscience, are chains from which one cannot free oneself without a broken heart; they are demons which human beings can vanquish only by submitting to them. But the Augsburg newspaper has never known the *pangs of conscience* called forth by the rebellion of man's subjective wishes against the objective views of his mind, *since it has neither a mind of its own, nor views of its own, nor even a conscience of its own.*

Written on October 15, 1842

First published in the *Rheinische Zeitung* No. 289, October 16, 1842

Printed according to the newspaper

COMMUNISM AND THE AUGSBURG
ALLGEMEINE ZEITUNG

Editorial Note

Cologne, October 22. Following the reprint by the *Rheinische Zeitung* No. 292[a] of an article from the *Mannheimer Abendzeitung* "from Pfalz, October 12", which begins with the words:

"I was really surprised when I found yesterday that the Augsburg *Allgemeine Zeitung* had printed an article (on communism), taken from Aachen news-sheets, which truly did not deserve to be accepted by a newspaper which otherwise has such good material",

the *Aachener Zeitung* No. 293[b] has published a reply, extracts from which we certainly do not want to withhold from our readers, in view of a special wish expressed by the editorial board of this newspaper, and all the more since it affords us the opportunity we desire for a subsequent correction. The *Aachener Zeitung* rightly believes that the *Rheinische*

"could have known that the Augsburg *Allgemeine Zeitung* had torn out only a few passages from its article on the Communists (in No. 277[c] of the *Aachener Zeitung*) and added comments of its own, which of course gave a different complexion to the article".

As stated, the *Rheinische Zeitung* was not only aware of this, but knew also that the *Aachener Zeitung* was quite innocent in regard to those fragments, insipidly and cunningly put together by the Augsburg newspaper No. 284, which were aimed solely at the *Rheinische Zeitung.* Therefore, in settling accounts with the Augsburg newspaper in No. 289, the *Rheinische Zeitung* very properly did not draw the *Aachener Zeitung* into the debate. But if someone

---

[a] October 19, 1842.— *Ed.*
[b] October 22, 1842.— *Ed.*
[c] October 6, 1842.— *Ed.*

from Pfalz could be misled into a false assumption by the heading in spaced type of that Augsburg newspaper's article[87]: "*We Read Aachen News-sheets*", that is at any rate an indication that the *Aachener Zeitung* could have anticipated earlier such a misunderstanding in respect of the Augsburg *Allgemeine Zeitung*. Having once undertaken to deal wholly on its own account with the Augsburg article, the *Rheinische Zeitung* could very well allow the incidental reprint of the note in the *Mannheimer Abendzeitung* to pass without any guide-mark since, of course, its readers already knew where that came from. The following passage from today's article in the *Aachener Zeitung* requires no further comment:

"It knows that we are not against any free research, that we shall not weaken the efforts of those who are concerned for the welfare of any class of people. We are liberal towards *all*, which is more than the majority of liberals of many varieties can so far say about themselves. What we said, however, is that communism cannot find any soil among us, but that, on the other hand, it is a natural phenomenon in France and England. We added, lastly, that we were not ourselves opposed to communist efforts in Germany, but were very definitely against any club-like brotherhoods of the kind that are said to have sprung up in Silesia. Liberal ideas are not yet so firmly rooted among us, and have not yet made such progress among us, that every endeavour does not need to be carefully fostered. As a rule, however, we see in our country far too little harmony between newspapers of the same colour. They do not bear in mind that an isolated undertaking cannot cover the whole field, and that a total effect can be produced only by each in turn becoming the bearer and disseminator of the ideas of the other."

The editorial board of the *Rheinische Zeitung*

Written on October 22, 1842

First published in the *Rheinische Zeitung* No. 296, October 23, 1842

Printed according to the newspaper

Published in English for the first time

PROCEEDINGS OF THE SIXTH RHINE PROVINCE ASSEMBLY

Third Article*

DEBATES ON THE LAW ON THEFTS OF WOOD [88]

[*Rheinische Zeitung* No. 298, October 25, 1842, Supplement]

So far we have described two most important state acts of the Provincial Assembly, namely, its confusion over freedom of the press and its unfreedom in regard to the confusion.[89] We have now come down to ground level. Before we proceed to the really earthly question in all its life-size, the question of the parcellation of landed property, we shall give our readers some genre pictures which reflect in manifold ways the spirit and, we might say, even the actual physical nature of the Assembly.

It is true that the law on thefts of wood, like the law on offences in regard to hunting, forests and fields, deserves to be discussed not only in relation to the Assembly but equally on its own account. However, we do not have the draft of the law before us. Our material is limited to some vaguely indicated additions made by the Assembly and its commission to laws that figure only as paragraph numbers. The Assembly proceedings themselves are reported so extremely meagerly, incoherently and apocryphally that the report looks like an attempt at mystification. To judge from the truncated torso available to us, the Assembly wanted by this passive quietude to pay an act of respect to our province.

One is immediately struck by a fact which is characteristic of these debates. The Assembly acts as a *supplementary legislator* alongside the state legislator. It will prove most interesting to examine the legislative qualities of the Assembly by means of an example. In view of this, the reader will forgive us for demanding from him patience and endurance, two virtues which had to be

---

* We regret that we have not been able to publish the *second* article for our readers. Editorial board of the *Rheinische Zeitung*.

constantly exercised in analysing our barren subject-matter. In our account of the Assembly debates on the law on thefts we are directly describing the *Assembly's debates on its legislative function.*

At the very beginning of the debate, one of the urban deputies objected to the *title* of the law, which extends the category of "*theft*" to include simple offences against forest regulations.

A deputy of the knightly estate replied:

"It is precisely because the pilfering of wood is not regarded as theft that it occurs so often."

By analogy with this, the legislator would have to draw the conclusion: It is because a box on the ear is not regarded as murder that it has become so frequent. It should be decreed therefore that a box on the ear is murder. –

Another deputy of the knightly estate finds it

"still more risky not to pronounce the word 'theft', because people who become acquainted with the discussion over this word could easily be led to believe that the Assembly does not regard the pilfering of wood also as theft".

The Assembly has to decide whether it considers pilfering of wood as theft; but if the Assembly does not declare it to be theft, people could believe that the Assembly really does not regard the pilfering of wood as theft. Hence it is best to leave this ticklish controversial question alone. It is a matter of a euphemism and euphemisms should be avoided. The forest owner prevents the legislator from speaking, for walls have ears.

The same deputy goes even further. He regards this whole examination of the expression "theft" as

"a dangerous preoccupation with *correcting formulations* on the part of the plenary assembly".

After these illuminating demonstrations, the Assembly voted the title of the law.

From the point of view recommended above, which mistakes the conversion of a citizen into a thief for a mere negligence in formulation and rejects all opposition to it as grammatical purism, it is obvious that even the *pilfering of fallen wood* or the gathering of dry wood is included under the heading of theft and punished as severely as the stealing of live growing timber.

It is true that the above-mentioned urban deputy remarks:

"Since the punishment could run to a long term of imprisonment, such severity would lead people who otherwise followed an honest path on to the path of crime. That would happen also because in prison they would be in the company of inveterate thieves; therefore he considered that the gathering or pilfering of dry fallen wood should be punished by a simple police penalty."

Another urban deputy, however, refuted him with the profound argument

"that in the forest areas of his region, at first only gashes were made in young trees, and later, when they were dead, they were treated as fallen wood".

It would be impossible to find a more elegant and at the same time more simple method of making the right of human beings give way to that of young trees. On the one hand, after the adoption of the paragraph, it is inevitable that many people not of a criminal disposition are cut off from the green tree of morality and cast like fallen wood into the hell of crime, infamy and misery. On the other hand, after rejection of the paragraph, there is the possibility that some young trees may be damaged, and it needs hardly be said that the wooden idols triumph and human beings are sacrificed!

The supreme penal code [90] includes under theft of wood only the pilfering of hewn wood and the cutting of wood for the purpose of theft. Indeed—our Provincial Assembly will not believe it—it states:

"If, however, in daytime someone takes fruit for eating and by its removal does no great damage, then, taking into account his personal position and the circumstances, he is to be punished by civil" (therefore, not criminal!) "proceedings."

The supreme penal code of the sixteenth century requests us to defend it against the charge of excessive humanity made by a Rhine Province Assembly of the nineteenth century, and we comply with this request.

The gathering of fallen wood and the most composite wood theft! They both have a common definition. The appropriation of wood from someone else. Therefore both are theft. That is the sum and substance of the far-sighted logic which has just issued laws.

First of all, therefore, we call attention to the *difference* between them, and if it must be admitted that the two actions are essentially different, it can hardly be maintained that they are identical from the legal standpoint.

In order to appropriate growing timber, it has to be forcibly separated from its organic association. Since this is an obvious outrage against the tree, it is therefore an obvious outrage against the owner of the tree.

Further, if felled wood is stolen from a third person, this felled wood is material that has been produced by the owner. Felled wood is wood that has been worked on. The natural connection with property has been replaced by an artificial one. Therefore, anyone who takes away felled wood takes away property.

In the case of fallen wood, on the contrary, nothing has been separated from property. It is only what has already been separated from property that is being separated from it. The wood thief pronounces on his own authority a sentence on property. The gatherer of fallen wood only carries out a sentence already pronounced by the very nature of the property, for the owner possesses only the tree, but the tree no longer possesses the branches that have fallen from it.

The gathering of fallen wood and the theft of wood are therefore essentially different things. The objects concerned are different, the actions in regard to them are no less different; hence the frame of mind must also be different, for what objective standard can be applied to the frame of mind other than the content of the action and its form? But, in spite of this essential difference, you call both of them theft and punish both of them as theft. Indeed, you punish the gathering of fallen wood more severely than the theft of wood, for you punish it already by declaring it to be theft, a punishment which you obviously do not pronounce on the actual theft of wood. You should have called it murder of wood and punished it as murder. The law is not exempt from the general obligation to tell the truth. It is doubly obliged to do so, for it is the universal and authentic exponent of the legal nature of things. Hence the legal nature of things cannot be regulated according to the law; on the contrary, the law must be regulated according to the legal nature of things. But if the law applies the term theft to an action that is scarcely even a violation of forest regulations, then the law *lies*, and the poor are sacrificed to a legal lie.

"Il y a deux genres de corruption," says Montesquieu, "l'un lorsque le peuple n'observe point les lois; l'autre lorsqu'il est corrompu par les lois: mal incurable parce qu'il est dans le remède même." [a]

You will never succeed in making us believe that there is a crime where there is no crime, you will only succeed in converting crime itself into a legal act. You have wiped out the boundary between them, but you err if you believe that you have done so only to your advantage. The people sees the punishment, but it does not

---

[a] "There are two kinds of corruption," says Montesquieu, "one when the people do not observe the laws, the other when they are corrupted by the laws: an incurable evil because it is in the very remedy itself." Ch. Montesquieu, *De l'esprit des lois*, Tome premier, livre sixième, chapitre XII.— *Ed.*

see the crime, and because it sees punishment where there is no crime, it will see no crime where there is punishment. By applying the category of theft where it ought not to be applied, you have also exonerated it where this category ought to be applied.

And does not this crude view, which lays down a common definition for different kinds of action and leaves the difference out of account, itself bring about its own destruction? If every violation of property without distinction, without a more exact definition, is termed theft, will not all private property be theft? By my private ownership do I not exclude every other person from this ownership? Do I not thereby violate his right of ownership? If you deny the difference between essentially different kinds of the same crime, you are denying that crime itself is *different from right*, you are abolishing right itself, for every crime has an aspect in common with right. Hence it is a fact, attested equally by history and reason, that undifferentiated severity makes punishment wholly unsuccessful, for it does away with punishment as a success for right.

But what are we arguing about? The Assembly, it is true, repudiates the difference between gathering fallen wood, infringement of forest regulations, and theft of wood. It repudiates the difference between these actions, refusing to regard it as determining the character of the action, when it is a question of the *interests of the infringers of forest regulations*, but it recognises this difference when it is a question of the *interests of the forest owners*.

Thus the commission proposes the following *addition*:

"to regard it as an aggravating circumstance if growing timber is hewn or cut off with edged tools and if a saw is used instead of an axe".

The Assembly approves this distinction. The same keen-sightedness which so conscientiously distinguishes between an axe and a saw when it is a matter of its own interests, is so lacking in conscience as to refuse to distinguish between fallen wood and growing wood when it is a question of other people's interests. The difference was found to be important as an aggravating circumstance but without any significance as a mitigating circumstance, although the former cannot exist if the latter is impossible.

The same logic occurred repeatedly during the debate.

In regard to §65, an urban deputy desired

"that the *value* of the stolen wood also should be used as a measure for fixing the punishment", "which was opposed by the commission's spokesman as *unpractical*".

The same urban deputy remarked in connection with §66:

"in general there is missing from the whole law any statement of value, in accordance with which the punishment would be increased or diminished".

The importance of value in determining punishment for violations of property is self-evident.

If the concept of crime involves that of punishment, the actual crime calls for a measure of punishment. An actual crime has its limit. The punishment will therefore have to be limited in order to be actual, it must be limited in accordance with a principle of law in order to be just. The problem is to make the punishment the actual consequence of the crime. It must be seen by the criminal as the necessary result of his act, and therefore as *his own act*. Hence the limit of his punishment must be the limit of his act. The definite *content* of a violation of the law is the limit of a definite crime. The *measure* of this content is therefore the measure of the crime. In the case of property this measure is its *value*. Whereas personality, whatever its limits, is always a whole, property always exists only within a definite limit that is not only determinable but determined, not only measurable but measured. Value is the civil mode of existence of property, the logical expression through which it first becomes socially comprehensible and communicable. It is clear that this objective defining element provided by the nature of the object itself must likewise be the objective and essential defining element for the punishment. Even if legislation here, where it is a matter of figures, can only be guided by external features so as not to be lost in an infinitude of definitions, it must at least regulate. It is not a question of an exhaustive definition of differences, but of establishing differences. But the Assembly was not at all disposed to devote its distinguished attention to such trifles.

But do you consider then that you can conclude that the Assembly completely excluded value in determining punishment? That would be an ill-considered, unpractical conclusion! The forest owner — we shall deal with this later in more detail — does not merely demand to be compensated by the thief for the simple general value. He even gives this value an individual character and bases his demand for special compensation on this poetic individuality. We can now understand what the commission's spokesman understands by *practical*. The practical forest owner argues as follows: This legal definition is good insofar as it is useful to me, for what is useful to me is good. But this legal definition is superfluous, it is harmful, it is unpractical, insofar as it is intended to be applied to the accused on the basis of a purely theoretical legal whim. Since the accused is harmful to me, it stands to reason that everything is harmful to me that lessens the harm coming to him. That is practical wisdom.

We unpractical people, however, demand for the poor, politically and socially propertyless many what the learned and would-be learned servility of so-called historians has discovered to be the true philosopher's stone for turning every sordid claim into the pure gold of right. We demand for the poor a *customary right*, and indeed one which is not of a local character but is a customary right of the poor in all countries. We go still further and maintain that a customary right by its very nature can *only* be a right of this lowest, propertyless and elemental mass.

The so-called customs of the privileged classes are understood to mean *customs contrary to the law*. Their origin dates to the period in which human history was part of *natural history*, and in which, according to Egyptian legend, all gods concealed themselves in the shape of animals. Mankind appeared to fall into definite species of animals which were connected not by equality, but by inequality, an inequality fixed by laws. The world condition of unfreedom required laws expressing this unfreedom, for whereas human law is the mode of existence of freedom, this animal law is the mode of existence of unfreedom. *Feudalism* in the broadest sense is the *spiritual animal kingdom*, the world of divided mankind, in contrast to the human world that creates its own distinctions and whose inequality is nothing but a refracted form of equality. In the countries of naive feudalism, in the countries of the caste system, where in the literal sense of the word people are put in separate boxes,[a] and the noble, freely interchanging members of the great sacred body, the holy Humanus, are sawn and cleft asunder, forcibly torn apart, we find therefore also the *worship of animals*, animal religion in its primitive form, for man always regards as his highest being that which is his true being. The sole equality to be found in the actual life of animals is the equality between one animal and other animals of the same species; it is the equality of the given species with itself, but not the equality of the genus. The animal genus itself is seen only in the hostile behaviour of the different animal species, which assert their particular *distinctive* characteristics one against another. In the *stomach of the beast of prey*, nature has provided the battlefield of union, the crucible of closest fusion, the organ connecting the various animal species.

---

[a] A pun on the German word *Kasten*, meaning both "castes" and "boxes".— *Ed.*

Similarly, under feudalism one species feeds at the expense of another, right down to the species which, like the polyp, grows on the ground and has only numerous arms with which to pluck the fruits of the earth for higher races while it itself eats dust; for whereas in the natural animal kingdom the worker bees kill the drones, in the spiritual animal kingdom the drones kill the worker bees, and precisely by labour. When the privileged classes appeal from *legal right* to their *customary rights*, they are demanding, instead of the human content of right, its animal form, which has now lost its reality and become a mere animal mask.

[*Rheinische Zeitung* No. 300, October 27, 1842, Supplement]

The customary rights of the aristocracy conflict by their *content* with the form of universal law. They cannot be given the form of law because they are formations of lawlessness. The fact that their content is contrary to the form of law — universality and necessity — proves that they are *customary wrongs* and cannot be asserted in opposition to the law, but as such opposition they must be abolished and even punished if the occasion arises, for no one's action ceases to be wrongful because it is his custom, just as the bandit son of a robber is not exonerated because banditry is a family idiosyncrasy. If someone intentionally acts contrary to law, he is punished for his intention; if he acts by custom, this custom of his is punished as being a bad custom. At a time when universal laws prevail, rational customary right is nothing but the *custom of legal right*, for right has not ceased to be custom because it has been embodied in law, although it has ceased to be *merely* custom. For one who acts in accordance with right, right becomes his own custom, but it is enforced against one who violates it, although it is not his custom. Right no longer depends on chance, on whether custom is rational or not, but custom becomes rational because right is legal, because custom has become the custom of the state.

Customary right as a *separate domain* alongside legal right is therefore rational only where it exists *alongside* and *in addition to* law, where custom is the *anticipation* of a legal right. Hence one cannot speak of the customary rights of the privileged estates. The law recognises not only their rational right but often even their irrational pretensions. The privileged estates have no right of anticipation in regard to law, for law has anticipated all possible consequences of their right. Hence, too, the customary rights are demanded only as a domain for *menus plaisirs*,[a] in order that the

---

[a] Little extras.— *Ed.*

same content which is dealt with in the law inside its rational limits should find in custom scope for whims and pretensions outside these rational limits.

But whereas these customary rights of the aristocracy are customs which are contrary to the conception of rational right, the customary rights of the poor are rights which are contrary to the customs of positive law. Their content does not conflict with legal form, but rather with its own lack of form. The form of law is not in contradiction to this content, on the contrary, the latter has not yet reached this form. Little thought is needed to perceive how *one-sidedly* enlightened legislation has treated and been compelled to treat the *customary rights of the poor*, of which the various *Germanic* rights [91] can be considered the most prolific source.

In regard to *civil law*, the most liberal legislations have been confined to formulating and raising to a universal level those rights which they found already in existence. Where they did not find any such rights, neither did they create any. They abolished particular customs, but in so doing forgot that whereas the wrong of the estates took the form of arbitrary pretensions, the right of those without social estate appeared in the form of accidental concessions. This course of action was correct in regard to those who, besides right, enjoyed custom, but it was incorrect in regard to those who had only customs without rights. Just as these legislations converted arbitrary pretensions into legal claims, insofar as some rational content of right was to be found in those pretensions, they ought also to have converted accidental concessions into necessary ones. We can make this clear by taking the monasteries as an example. The monasteries were abolished, their property was secularised, and it was right to do so. But the accidental support which the poor found in the monasteries was not replaced by any other positive source of income. When the property of the monasteries was converted into private property and the monasteries received some compensation, the poor who lived by the monasteries were not compensated. On the contrary, a new restriction was imposed on them, while they were deprived of an ancient right. This occurred in all transformations of privileges into rights. A positive aspect of these abuses — which was also an abuse because it turned a right of one side into something accidental — was abolished not by the accidental being converted into a necessity, but by its being left out of consideration.

These legislations were necessarily one-sided, for all customary rights of the poor were based on the fact that certain forms of property were indeterminate in character, for they were not definitely private property, but neither were they definitely common property, being a mixture of private and public right, such as we find in all the institutions of the Middle Ages. For the purpose of legislation, such ambiguous forms could be grasped only by understanding, and understanding is not only one-sided, but has the essential function of making the world one-sided, a great and remarkable work, for only one-sidedness can extract the particular from the unorganised mass of the whole and give it shape. The character of a thing is a product of understanding. Each thing must isolate itself and become isolated in order to be something. By confining each of the contents of the world in a stable definiteness and as it were solidifying the fluid essence of this content, understanding brings out the manifold diversity of the world, for the world would not be many-sided without the many one-sidednesses.

Understanding therefore abolished the hybrid, indeterminate forms of property by applying to them the existing categories of abstract civil law, the model for which was available in Roman law. The legislative mind considered it was the more justified in abolishing the obligations of this indeterminate property towards the class of the very poor, because it also abolished the state privileges of property. It forgot, however, that even from the standpoint of civil law a twofold private right was present here: a private right of the owner and a private right of the non-owner; and this apart from the fact that no legislation abolishes the privileges of property under constitutional law, but merely divests them of their strange character and gives them a civil character. If, however, every medieval form of right, and therefore of property also, was in every respect hybrid, dualistic, split into two, and understanding rightly asserted its principle of unity in respect of this contradictory determination, it nevertheless overlooked the fact that there exist objects of property which, by their very nature, can never acquire the character of predetermined private property, objects which, by their elemental nature and their accidental mode of existence, belong to the sphere of occupation rights, and therefore of the occupation right of that class which, precisely because of these occupation rights, is excluded from all other property and which has the same position in civil society as these objects have in nature.

It will be found that the customs which are customs of the entire poor class are based with a sure instinct on the *indeterminate* aspect of property; it will be found not only that this class feels an urge to satisfy a natural need, but equally that it feels the need to satisfy a rightful urge. Fallen wood provides an example of this. Such wood has as little organic connection with the growing tree as the cast-off skin has with the snake. Nature itself presents as it were a model of the antithesis between poverty and wealth in the shape of the dry, snapped twigs and branches separated from organic life in contrast to the trees and stems which are firmly rooted and full of sap, organically assimilating air, light, water and soil to develop their own proper form and individual life. It is a physical representation of poverty and wealth. Human poverty senses this kinship and deduces its right to property from this feeling of kinship. If, therefore, it claims physical organic wealth for the predetermined property owners, it claims physical poverty for need and its fortuity. In this play of elemental forces, poverty senses a beneficent power more humane than human power. The fortuitous arbitrary action of privileged individuals is replaced by the fortuitous operation of elemental forces, which take away from private property what the latter no longer voluntarily foregoes. Just as it is not fitting for the rich to lay claim to alms distributed in the street, so also in regard to these *alms of nature*. But it is by its *activity*, too, that poverty acquires its right. By its act of *gathering*, the elemental class of human society appoints itself to introduce order among the products of the elemental power of nature. The position is similar in regard to those products which, because of their wild growth, are a wholly accidental appendage of property and, if only because of their unimportance, are not an object for the activity of the actual owner. The same thing holds good also in regard to gleaning after the harvest and similar customary rights.

In these customs of the poor class, therefore, there is an instinctive sense of right; their roots are positive and legitimate, and the form of *customary right* here conforms all the more to nature because up to now the *existence of the poor class itself* has been a *mere custom* of civil society, a custom which has not found an appropriate place in the conscious organisation of the state.

The debate in question affords an example of the way in which these customary rights are treated, an example which exhaustively illustrates the method and spirit of the whole procedure.

An urban deputy opposed the provision by which the gathering of bilberries and cranberries is also treated as theft. He spoke primarily on behalf of the children of the poor, who pick these fruits to earn a trifling sum for their parents; an activity which has been permitted by the owners *since time immemorial* and has given rise to a *customary right* of the children. This fact was countered by another deputy, who remarked that "in his area these berries have already become articles of commerce and are dispatched to Holland by the barrel".

In *one locality*, therefore, things have actually gone so far that a customary right of the poor has been turned into a *monopoly* of the rich. That is exhaustive proof that common property can be monopolised, from which it naturally follows that it must be monopolised. The nature of the object calls for monopoly because private property interests here have invented this monopoly. The modern idea conceived by some money-grabbing petty traders becomes irrefutable when it provides profit for the age-old Teutonic landed interest.

The wise legislator will prevent crime in order not to have to punish it, but he will do so not by obstructing the sphere of right, but by doing away with the negative aspect of every instinct of right, giving the latter a positive sphere of action. He will not confine himself to removing the *impossibility* for members of one class to belong to a higher sphere of right, but will raise their class itself to the *real possibility* of enjoying its rights. But if the state is not humane, rich and high-minded enough for this, it is at least the legislator's absolute duty not to convert into a *crime* what circumstances alone have caused to be an *offence*. He must exercise the utmost leniency in correcting as a social *irregularity* what it would be the height of injustice for him to punish as an anti-social crime. Otherwise he will be combating the social instinct while supposing that he is combating its anti-social form. In short, if popular customary rights are suppressed, the attempt to exercise them can only be treated as the simple *contravention of a police regulation,* but never punished as a crime. Punishment by police penalties is an expedient to be used against an act which circumstances characterise as a superficial irregularity not constituting any violation of the eternal rule of law. The punishment must not inspire more repugnance than the offence, the ignominy of crime must not be turned into the ignominy of law; the basis of the state is undermined if misfortune becomes a crime or crime becomes a misfortune. Far from upholding this point of view, the Provincial Assembly does not observe even the elementary rules of legislation.

The petty, wooden, mean and selfish soul of interest sees only one point, the point in which it is wounded, like a coarse person who regards a passer-by as the most infamous, vilest creature under the sun because this unfortunate creature has trodden on his corns. He makes his corns the basis for his views and judgment, he makes the one point where the passer-by comes into contact with him into the only point where the very nature of this man comes into contact with the world. But a man may very well happen to tread on my corns without on that account ceasing to be an honest, indeed an excellent, man. Just as you must not judge people by your corns, you must not see them through the eyes of your private interest.[a] Private interest makes the one sphere in which a person comes into conflict with this interest into this person's whole sphere of life. It makes the law a *rat-catcher,* who wants only to destroy vermin, for he is not a naturalist and therefore regards rats only as vermin. But the state must regard the infringer of forest regulations as something more than a wood-pilferer, more than an *enemy to wood.* Is not the state linked with each of its citizens by a thousand vital nerves, and has it the right to sever all these nerves because this citizen has himself arbitrarily severed *one* of them? Therefore the state will regard even an infringer of forest regulations as a human being, a living member of the state, one in whom its heart's blood flows, a soldier who has to defend his Fatherland, a witness whose voice must be heard by the court, a member of the community with public duties to perform, the father of a family, whose existence is sacred, and, above all, a citizen of the state. The state will not light-heartedly exclude one of its members from all these functions, for the state amputates itself whenever it turns a citizen into a criminal. Above all, the *moral* legislator will consider it a most serious, most painful, and most dangerous matter if an action which previously was not regarded as blameworthy is classed among criminal acts.

Interest, however, is practical, and nothing in the world is more practical than to strike down one's enemy. "Hates any man the thing he would not kill?" we are already told by Shylock.[b] The true legislator should fear nothing but wrong, but the legislative interest knows only fear of the consequences of rights, fear of the evil-doers against whom the laws are made. Cruelty is a characteristic feature of laws dictated by cowardice, for cowardice can be energetic only by being cruel. Private interest, however, is always cowardly, for its heart, its soul, is an external object which can always be wrenched away and injured, and who has not trembled at the danger of losing heart and soul? How could the selfish legislator be human when something inhuman, an alien material essence, is his supreme essence? *"Quand il a peur, il est terrible,"* [c]

---

[a] A pun on the German words *Hühneraugen*—corns, and *Augen*—eyes.— *Ed.*

[b] W. Shakespeare, *The Merchant of Venice,* Act IV, Scene 1.— *Ed.*

[c] "When he is afraid, he is terrible."— *Ed.*

says the *National* about Guizot. These words could be inscribed as a motto over all *legislation inspired by self-interest,* and therefore by *cowardice.*

When the Samoyeds kill an animal, before skinning it they assure it in the most serious tones that only Russians have done it this injury, that it is being dismembered with a Russian knife, and therefore it should revenge itself only on Russians. Even without any claim to be a Samoyed, it is possible to turn the law into *Russian knife.* Let us see how this is done.

In connection with § 4, the commission proposed:

"At distances greater than two miles, the *warden who makes the charge* determines the *value* according to the existing local price."

An urban deputy protested against this as follows:

"The proposal to allow the valuation of the stolen wood to be made by the forester who brings the charge evokes serious doubt. Of course, this official has our full confidence, but only as regards the fact, by no means as regards the value. The latter should be determined according to a valuation made by the local authorities and confirmed by the district president. It is true that it has been proposed that § 14, according to which the penalty imposed should accrue to the forest owner, should not be adopted", etc. "If § 14 were to be retained, the proposed provision would be doubly dangerous. For, in the nature of things, the forester who is employed by the forest owner and paid by him would certainly have to put the value of the stolen wood as high as possible."

The Provincial Assembly approved the proposal of the commission.

We see here the enactment of patrimonial jurisdiction. The patrimonial warden is at the same time in part a judge. The valuation is part of the sentence. Hence the sentence is already partly anticipated in the record of the charge. The warden who made the charge sits in the collegium of judges; he is the expert whose decision is binding for the court, he performs a function from which the other judges are excluded by him. It is foolish to oppose inquisitorial methods when there exist even patrimonial gendarmes and denouncers who at the same time act as judges.

Apart from this fundamental violation of our institutions, it is obvious from an examination of the qualifications of the warden who makes the charge how little he is objectively able to be at the same time the valuer of the stolen wood.

As warden, he personifies the protecting genius of the forest. Protection, especially personal, physical protection, calls for an effective, energetic and loving attitude to the object of his care, an attitude in which he as it were coalesces with the growing forest. The forest must be everything to him, its value for him must be absolute. The valuer's attitude to the stolen wood, on the other hand, is one of sceptical distrust. He measures it with a keen prosaic eye by an ordinary standard and reckons how much it is worth in hellers and pfennigs. A warden and a valuer are as different as a mineralogist and a trader in minerals. The forest warden cannot estimate the value of the stolen wood, for in any record for the court giving his estimate of the value of the stolen material he is estimating *his own value*, because it is the value of his own activity, and do you believe that he would not protect the *value* of the object under his care as much as the *substance* of it?

The functions entrusted to one man, for whom severity is an official duty, are contradictory not only in relation to the object under protection, but also in relation to the *persons* concerned.

As guardian of the wood, the warden has to protect the interests of the private owner, but as valuer he has just as much to protect the interests of the infringer of forest regulations against the extravagant demands of the private owner. While he has, perhaps, to use his fists on behalf of the forest, he has immediately thereafter to use his brains on behalf of the forest's enemy. While embodying the interests of the forest owner, he has at the same time to be a guarantee against these same interests.

The warden, furthermore, is the denouncer. The charge he draws up is a denunciation. The value of the object, therefore, becomes the subject-matter of the denunciation. The warden loses his dignity as a judge, and the function of judge is most profoundly debased, because at that moment it is indistinguishable from the function of denouncer.

Finally, this denouncing warden, who cannot rank as an expert, whether in his capacity of denouncer or in that of warden, is in the pay and service of the forest owner. One might just as well leave the valuation, under oath, to the forest owner himself, since in the person of his warden he has actually only assumed the shape of a third person.

Instead, however, of finding this position of the denouncing warden even somewhat dubious, the Provincial Assembly, on the contrary, regarded as dubious the sole provision which constitutes the last semblance of the state's power in the realm of forest glory, namely, *life appointment* of the denouncing wardens. This proposal evoked the most vehement protest, and the storm seems hardly to have been allayed by the explanation of the spokesman "that already previous Provincial Assemblies had called for life appointment of wardens to be abandoned, but that the government had not agreed to this and regarded life appointment as a protection for the state's subjects."

At an earlier date, therefore, the Provincial Assembly had already tried to bargain with the government so as to make it abandon protection for its subjects, but the Assembly did not go beyond bargaining. Let us examine the arguments, as generous as they are irrefutable, advanced *against* life appointment.

A deputy from the rural communities

"finds that life appointment of wardens as a condition for confidence in them is greatly to the detriment of the small forest owners; and another deputy insists that protection must be equally effective for small and big forest owners."

A member of the princely estate remarked

"that life appointment with private persons is very inadvisable, and in France it has not been found at all necessary for ensuring confidence in the records drawn up by the wardens, but that something must of necessity be done to prevent infringements from increasing".

An *urban deputy* said:

"Credence must be given to all testimony of properly appointed and sworn forest officials. Life appointment is, so to speak, an impossibility for many communities, and especially for owners of small estates. A decision that only forest officials who have been appointed for life should be trusted, would deprive these owners of all forest protection. In a large part of the province, communities and private owners would necessarily have to entrust the protection of their wooded areas to field wardens, because their forest area is not large enough to enable them to appoint special foresters for it. It would indeed be strange if these field wardens, who have also taken an oath to protect the forests, were not to enjoy complete confidence when they reported a theft of wood, but were trusted when they testified to the infringement of forest regulations."

[*Rheinische Zeitung* No. 303, October 30, 1842, *Supplement*]

Thus *town* and *countryside* and the *princely estate* have had their say. Instead of smoothing out the difference between the rights of the infringer of forest regulations and the claims of the forest owner, they found that this difference was not great enough. There was no attempt to afford equal protection to the forest owner and the infringer of forest regulations, it was only sought to make the protection of the small forest owner equal to that of the big forest owner. In this latter case, equality down to the minutest detail is imperative, whereas in the former case inequality is an axiom. Why does the small forest owner demand the same protection as the big forest owner? Because both are forest owners. But are not both the forest owners and the infringers of forest regulations citizens of the state? If small and big forest owners have the same right to protection by the state, does this not apply even more to small and big citizens of the state?

When the member of the princely estate refers to France—for interest knows no political antipathies—he only forgets to add that in France the warden's charge concerns the fact but not the value. Similarly, the worthy urban spokesman forgets that it is inadmissible to rely on a field warden here because it is a matter not only of registering a theft of wood but also of establishing the value of the wood.

What is the gist of all the arguments we have just heard? It is that the small forest owner does not have the *means* for appointing a warden for life. What follows from this? It follows that the small forest owner is not entitled to undertake this task. But what conclusion is drawn by the small forest owner? That he is entitled to appoint a warden as a valuer who can be given notice of dismissal. His lack of means entitles him to a privilege.

Moreover, the small forest owner does not have the means to support an independent *collegium of judges.* Therefore let the state and the accused manage without an independent collegium of judges, let a manservant of the small forest owner have a seat on the tribunal, or if he has no manservant, let it be his maidservant; and if he has no maidservant, let him sit there himself. Has not the accused the same right in regard to the executive power, which is an organ of the state, as he has in regard to the judicial power? Why then should not the tribunal also be organised in accordance with the means of the small forest owner?

Can the relation between the state and the accused be altered because of the meagre resources of a private person, the forest owner? The state has a right in relation to the accused because it confronts him as the state. An immediate consequence of this is its duty to act towards the law-breaker as the state and in the manner of the state. The state has not only the means to act in a way which is as appropriate to its reason, its universality, and its dignity as it is to the right, the life and the property of the incriminated citizen; it is its absolute duty to possess and apply these means. No one will make this demand of the forest owner, whose forest is not the state and whose soul is not the soul of the state.— But what conclusion was drawn from that? It was concluded that since private property does not have means to raise itself to the standpoint of the state, the latter is obliged to lower itself to the irrational and illegal means of private property.

This claim on the part of private interest, the paltry soul of which was never illuminated and thrilled by thought of the state, is a serious and sound lesson for the latter. If the state, even in a single respect, stoops so low as to act in the manner of private property instead of in its own way, the immediate consequence is that it has to adapt itself in the form of its means to the narrow limits of private property. Private interest is sufficiently crafty to intensify this consequence to the point where private interest in its most restricted and paltry form makes itself the limit and rule for the action of the state. As a result of this, apart from the complete degradation of the state, we have the reverse effect that the most irrational and illegal means are put into operation against the accused; for supreme concern for the interests of limited private property necessarily turns into unlimited lack of concern for the interests of the accused. But if it becomes clearly evident here that private interest seeks to degrade, and is bound to degrade, the state into a means operating for the benefit of private interest, how can it fail to follow that a *body representing private interests*, the estates, will seek to degrade, and is bound to degrade, the state to the thoughts of private interest? Every modern state, however little it corresponds to its concept, will be compelled to exclaim at the first practical attempt at such legislative power: Your ways are not my ways, your thoughts are not my thoughts!

How completely unsound the temporary hiring of a denouncing warden is, cannot be more glaringly shown than by an argument advanced *against* life appointment, which cannot be attributed to a slip of the tongue, for it was read out. The following remark, namely, was read out by an urban deputy:

"Community forest wardens appointed for life are not, and cannot be, under such strict control as royal officials. Every *spur* to loyal fulfilment of duty is *paralysed* by life appointment. If the forest warden only half performs his duty and takes care that he cannot be charged with any real offence, he will always find sufficient advocacy in his favour to make a proposal for his dismissal under § 56 useless. In such circumstances the interested parties will not even dare to put forward such a proposal."

We recall that it was decreed that the warden making the charge should be given full confidence when it was a question of entrusting him with the task of valuation. We recall that § 4 was a *vote of confidence* in the warden.

We now learn for the first time that the denouncing warden needs to be controlled, and strictly controlled. For the first time he appears not merely as a man, but as a horse, since spurs and fodder are the only stimuli of his conscience, and the muscles for performing his duty are not merely slackened but completely paralysed by life appointment. We see that selfishness has a double set of weights and measures for weighing and measuring people, and two world outlooks, two pairs of spectacles, one showing everything black and the other in rosy tints. When it is a matter of making other people the victim of its tools and giving a favourable appearance to dubious means, selfishness puts on its rose-coloured spectacles, which impart an imaginary glory to these tools and means, and deludes itself and others with the unpractical, delightful dreaming of a tender and trusting soul. Every wrinkle of its countenance expresses smiling bonhomie. It presses its' opponent's hand until it hurts, but it does so as a sign of its trust in him. But suddenly it is a question of personal advantage, of carefully testing the usefulness of tools and means behind the scenes where stage illusions are absent. Being a strict judge of people, it cautiously and distrustfully puts on its world-wise dark spectacles of practice. Like an experienced horse-dealer it subjects people to a lengthy ocular inspection, overlooking no detail, and they seem to it to be as petty, as pitiful, and as dirty, as selfishness itself.

We do not intend to argue with the world outlook of selfishness, but we want to compel it to be consistent. We do not want it to reserve all worldly wisdom for itself and leave only fantasies for others. We want to make the sophistical spirit of private interest abide for a moment by its own conclusions.

If the warden making the charge is a man such as you describe, a man whom life appointment, far from giving him a feeling of independence, security and dignity in the performance of his duty, has, on the contrary, deprived of any incentive to do his duty, how can we expect this man to behave impartially towards the accused when he is the unconditional slave of your arbitrary power? If only spurs force this man to do his duty, and if you are the wearer of the spurs, what fate must we prophesy for the accused, who wears no spurs? If even you yourself cannot exercise sufficiently strict control over this warden, how can the state or the accused side in the case control him? Does not what you say of life appointment apply instead to an appointment that can be terminated: "if the forest warden only half performs his duty, he will always find sufficient advocacy in his favour to make a proposal for his dismissal under § 56 useless"? Would not all of you be advocates for him as long as he performed half his duty, namely, the protection of your interests?

The conversion of naive, excessive confidence in the forest warden into abusive, censorious distrust reveals the gist of the matter. It is not in the forest warden but in *yourselves* that you place this tremendous confidence which you want the state and the infringer of forest regulations to accept as a dogma.

It is not the warden's official position, nor his oath, nor his conscience that should be the guarantee of the accused against you; on the contrary, your sense of justice, your humanity, your disinterestedness, your moderation should be the guarantee of the accused against the forest warden. Your control is his ultimate and only guarantee. Imbued with a vague notion of your personal excellence, wrapt in poetic self-delight, you offer the parties in the case your individual qualities as a means of protection against your laws. I confess that I do not share this romantic conception of the forest owners. I do not at all believe that persons can be a guarantee against laws; on the contrary, I believe that laws must be a guarantee against persons. And can even the most daring fantasy imagine that men who in the noble work of legislation cannot for a moment rise above the narrow, practically base standpoint of self-seeking to the theoretical height of a universal and objective point of view, men who tremble even at the thought of future disadvantages and seize on anything to defend their interests, can these men become philosophers in the face of real danger? But no one, not even the most excellent legislator, can be allowed to put himself above the law he has made. No one has the right to decree a vote of confidence in himself when it entails consequences for third persons.

But whether it is permissible for you even to demand that people should place special confidence in you, may be judged from the following facts.

"He must oppose § 87," stated an urban deputy, "since its provisions would give rise to extensive and fruitless investigations, as a result of which personal freedom and freedom of intercourse would be violated. It is not permissible beforehand to regard everyone as a criminal and to assume a crime before having proof that it has been committed."

Another urban deputy said that the paragraph ought to be deleted. The vexatious provision that "everyone has to prove where he obtained his wood", with the result that everyone could be under suspicion of stealing and concealing wood, was a gross and injurious intrusion into the life of the citizen. The paragraph was adopted.

In truth, you presume too much on people's inconsistency if you expect them to proclaim as a maxim that distrust is to

their detriment and confidence is to your advantage, and if you
expect their confidence and distrust to see through the eyes
of your private interest and feel through the heart of your private
interest.

Yet another argument is advanced against life appointment, an
argument of which it is impossible to say whether it is more
calculated to evoke contempt or ridicule.

"It is also impermissible that the *free will of private persons* should be so greatly
restricted in this way, for which reason *only* appointments that can be terminated
should be allowed."

The news that man possesses free will which must not be
restricted in all kinds of ways, is certainly as comforting as it is
unexpected. The oracles which we have so far heard have resembled the ancient oracle at Dodona.[92] They are dispensed from
wood. Free will, however, does not have the quality of an estate.
How are we to understand this sudden rebellious emergence of
ideology, for as far as ideas are concerned we have before us only
followers of Napoleon?

The will of the forest owner requires freedom to deal with the
infringer of forest regulations as it sees fit and in the way it finds
most convenient and least costly. This will wants the state to hand
over the evil-doer to it to deal with at its discretion. It demands
plein pouvoir.[a] It does not oppose the restriction of free will,
it opposes the *manner* of this restriction, which is so restrictive
that it affects not only the infringer of forest regulations but
also the owner of the wood. Does not this free will want to have
numerous freedoms? Is it not a very free, an excellent, free
will? And is it not scandalous in the nineteenth century to dare
to restrict "so greatly in this way" the free will of those private persons who promulgate public laws? It is, indeed, scandalous.

Even that obstinate reformer, free will, must join the adherents
of the good arguments headed by the sophistry of private interest.
But this free will must have good manners, it must be a cautious,
loyal free will, one which is able to arrange itself in such a way
that its sphere coincides with the sphere of the arbitrary power of
those same privileged private persons. Only once has there been
mention of free will, and on this one occasion it appears in the
shape of a squat private person who hurls blocks of wood at the

---

[a] Full powers.— *Ed.*

spirit of rational will. Indeed, what need is there for this spirit where the will is chained to the most petty and selfish interests like a galley-slave to his rowing bench?

The climax of this whole argument is summarised in the following remark, which turns the relationship in question upside-down:

"While the royal forest wardens and gamekeepers may be appointed for life, in the case of rural communities and private persons this evokes the most serious misgivings."

As if the sole source of misgivings were not in that private servants act here in the place of state officials! As if life appointment was not aimed precisely against private persons, who are the ones that *evoke misgivings! Rien n'est plus terrible que la logique dans l'absurdité,*[a] that is to say, nothing is more terrible than the logic of selfishness.

This logic, which turns the servant of the forest owner into a state authority, *turns the authority of the state into a servant of the forest owner.* The state structure, the purpose of the individual administrative authorities, everything must get out of hand so that everything is degraded into an instrument of the forest owner and his interest operates as the soul governing the entire mechanism. All the organs of the state become ears, eyes, arms, legs, by means of which the interest of the forest owner hears, observes, appraises, protects, reaches out, and runs.

The commission proposed the addition to §62 of a conclusion demanding that inability to pay be certified by the tax-collector, the burgomaster and two local officials of the community in which the infringer of forest regulations lives. A deputy from the rural communities considered that to make use of the *tax-collector* was contrary to existing legislation. Of course, no attention was paid to this contradiction.

In connection with §20, the commission proposed:

"In the Rhine Province the competent forest owner should be authorised to hand over convicted persons to the local authority to perform penal labour in such a way that their working days will be put to the account of the manual services on communal roads which the forest owner is obliged to render in the rural community, and accordingly subtracted from this obligation."

Against this, the objection was raised

"that burgomasters cannot be used as executors for individual members of the rural community and that the labour of convicts cannot be accepted as compensation for the work which has to be performed by paid day-labourers or servants".

[a] Nothing is more terrible than logic carried to absurdity.— *Ed.*

The spokesman commented:

"Even if it is a burdensome task for the burgomasters to see that unwilling and insubordinate prisoners convicted of infringing forest regulations are made to work, nevertheless it is one of the functions of these officials to induce disobedient and evil-minded persons in their charge to return to the path of duty, and is it not a *noble deed* to lead the convict away from the wrong road back to the right path? Who in the countryside has more means of doing this than the *burgomasters?*"

> Reineke put on an anxious and sorrowful mien,
> Which excited the pity of many a good-natured man,
> Lampe, the hare, especially was sore distressed.[a]

The Provincial Assembly adopted the proposal.

[*Rheinische Zeitung* No. 305, November 1, 1842, Supplement]

The good burgomaster must undertake a burdensome task and perform a noble deed in order that the forest owner can fulfil his duty to the community without expense to himself. The forest owner could with equal right make use of the burgomaster as a chief cook or head waiter. Is it not a noble deed for the burgomaster to look after the kitchen or cellar of those in his charge? The convicted criminal is not in the charge of the burgomaster, but in the charge of the prison superintendent. Does not the burgomaster lose the strength and dignity of his position if, instead of representing the community, he is made an executor for individual members, if he is turned from a burgomaster into a taskmaster? Will not the other, free members of the community be insulted if their honest work for the general good is degraded to the level of penal labour for the benefit of particular individuals?

But it is superfluous to expose these sophistries. Let the spokesman be so good as to tell us himself how worldly-wise people judge humane phrases. He makes the *forest owner* address the following reply to the *farm owner* who displays humanity:

"If some ears of corn are pilfered from a landowner, the thief would say: 'I have no bread, so I take a few ears of corn from the large amount you possess', just as the wood thief says: 'I have no firewood, so I steal some wood.' The landowner is protected by Article 444 of the Criminal Code, which punishes the taking of ears of corn with 2-5 years' imprisonment. The forest owner has no such powerful protection."

This last envious exclamation of the forest owner contains a whole confession of faith. You farm owner, why are you so magnanimous where *my* interests are concerned? Because *your* interests are already looked after. So let there be no illusions! Magnanimity either costs nothing or brings something in. There-

---

[a] J. Goethe, *Reineke Fuchs*, Sechster Gesang.— *Ed.*

fore, farm owner, you cannot deceive the forest owner! Therefore, forest owner, do not deceive the burgomaster!

This intermezzo alone would suffice to prove what little meaning "noble deeds" can have in our debate, if the whole debate did not prove that moral and humane reasons occur here merely as phrases. But interest is miserly even with phrases. It invents them only in case of need, when the results are of considerable advantage. Then it becomes eloquent, its blood circulates faster, it is not sparing even with noble deeds that yield it profit at the expense of others, with flattering words and sugary endearments. And all that, all of it, is exploited only in order to convert the infringement of forest regulations into current coin for the forest owner, to make the infringer of forest regulations into a lucrative source of income, to be able to invest the capital more conveniently — for the wood thief has become a capital for the forest owner. It is not a question of misusing the burgomaster for the benefit of the infringer of forest regulations, but of misusing the burgomaster for the benefit of the forest owner. What a remarkable trick of fate it is, what a remarkable fact, that on the rare occasions when a problematic benefit for the infringer of forest regulations is given a passing mention, the forest owner is guaranteed an unquestionable benefit!

The following is yet another example of these humane sentiments!

Spokesman: "French law does not acknowledge the commutation of imprisonment into forest labour; he considers this commutation a wise and beneficial measure, for imprisonment does not always lead to reform but very often to corruption."

Previously, when innocent persons were turned into criminals, when in connection with the gathering of fallen wood a deputy remarked that in prison they were brought into contact with inveterate thieves, prisons were said to be *good.* Suddenly reformatories have been metamorphosed into institutions for corruption, for at this moment it is of advantage to the interests of the forest owner that prisons corrupt. By reform of the criminal is understood *improvement of the percentage of profit* which it is the criminal's noble function to provide for the forest owner.

Interest has no memory, for it thinks only of itself. And the *one* thing about which it is concerned, itself, it never forgets. But it is not concerned about contradictions, for it never comes into contradiction with itself. It is a constant improviser, for it has no system, only *expedients.*

Whereas humane and rightful motives have no part to play except

> Ce qu'au bal nous autres sots humains,
> Nous appelons faire tapisserie,[a]

expedients are the most active agents in the argumentative mechanism of private interest. Among these expedients, we note two that constantly recur in this debate and constitute the main categories, namely, "*good motives*" and "*harmful results*". We see sometimes the spokesman for the commission, sometimes another member of the Assembly, defending every ambiguous provision against hostile shafts of objections by means of the shield of shrewd, wise and good motives. We see every conclusion drawn from the standpoint of right rejected by referring to its harmful or dangerous results. Let us examine for a moment these extensive expedients, these expedients *par excellence*, these expedients covering everything and a little more.

Interest knows how to denigrate right by presenting a prospect of harmful results due to its effects in the external world; it knows how to whitewash what is wrong by ascribing good motives to it, that is, by retreating into the internal world of its thoughts. Law produces bad results in the external world among bad people, wrong springs from good motives in the breast of the honest man who decrees it; but both, the good motives and the harmful results, have in common the peculiar feature that they do not look at a thing in relation to itself, that they do not treat the law as an independent object, but direct attention away from the law either to the external world or to their own mind, that therefore they manoeuvre *behind the back of the law*.

What are harmful results? Our whole account has shown that they are not to be understood as harmful results for the state, the law, or the accused. Moreover, we should like to make quite clear in a few lines that they do not include harmful results for the *safety of citizens*.

We have already heard from members of the Assembly themselves that the provision by which "everyone has to prove where he obtained his wood" is a gross and injurious intrusion into the life of the citizen and makes every citizen the victim of vexatious bullying. Another provision declares that everyone in whose *keeping* stolen wood is found is to be regarded as a thief, although a deputy stated:

---

[a] What, at a ball, we simple folk call being wallflowers.— *Ed.*

"This could be dangerous for many an honest man. Wood stolen by someone nearby might be thrown into his courtyard and the innocent man punished."

Under §66 any citizen who buys a broom that is not issued under monopoly is punishable by hard labour from four weeks to two years. On this, an urban deputy commented as follows:

"This paragraph threatens with hard labour each and every citizen of the Elberfeld, Lennep and Solingen districts."

Finally, supervision and management of the game and forest police have been made not only a right but a duty of the *military*, although Article 9 of the Criminal Code speaks only of officials who are under the supervision of state prosecutors and can therefore be the object of immediate proceedings on the part of the latter, which is not the case with the military. This is a threat both to the independence of the courts and to the freedom and security of citizens.

Hence, far from there being any talk of possible harmful results for the safety of citizens, their safety itself is treated as a *circumstance having harmful results.*

What then are harmful results? Harmful is that which is harmful to the interests of the forest owner. If, therefore, the law does not result in the furtherance of his interests, its results are harmful. And in this respect interest is keen-sighted. Whereas previously it did not see what was obvious to the naked eye, it now sees even what is only visible through a microscope. The whole world is a thorn in the side of private interest, a world full of dangers, precisely because it is the world not of a single interest but of many interests. Private interest considers itself the ultimate purpose of the world. Hence if the law does not realise this ultimate purpose, it becomes inexpedient law. *Law which is harmful to private interests* is therefore *law with harmful results.*

Are *good motives* considered to be better than harmful results?

Interest does not think, it calculates. Motives are its figures. Motive is an incentive for abolishing the basis of law, and who can doubt that private interest will have many incentives for doing so? The goodness of a motive lies in the casual flexibility with which it can set aside the objective facts of the case and lull itself and others into the illusion that it is not necessary to keep one's mind on what is good, but that it suffices to have good thoughts while doing a bad thing.

Resuming the thread of our argument, we mention first of all a side line to the noble deeds recommended to the Herr Burgomaster.

"The commission proposed an amended version of §34 along the following lines: if the accused demands that the warden who drew up the charge be summoned, then he must also deposit with the forestry court *in advance* all the costs thereby incurred."

The state and the court must not do anything gratis in the interests of the accused. They must demand payment in advance which obviously in advance makes difficult any confrontation of the warden making the charge and the accused.

A noble deed! Just one single noble deed! A kingdom for a noble deed!ᵃ But the only noble deed proposed is that which the Herr Burgomaster has to perform for the benefit of the Herr Forest Owner. The burgomaster is the representative of noble deeds, their humanised expression, and the series of noble deeds is exhausted and ended for ever with the burden which was imposed with melancholy sacrifice on the burgomaster.

If, for the good of the state and the moral benefit of the criminal, the Herr Burgomaster must do more than his duty, should not the forest owners, for the sake of the same good, demand *less* than their *private interest* requires?

One might think that the reply to this question had been given in the part of the debate already dealt with, but that is a mistake. We come to the *penal provisions*.

"A deputy from the knightly estate considered that the forest owner would still be inadequately compensated even if he received (over and above the simple replacement of the value) the amount of the fine imposed, which would often not be obtainable."

An urban deputy remarked:

"The provisions of this paragraph (§ 15) could have the most serious consequences. The forest owner would receive in this way *threefold* compensation, namely: the value, then the four-, six-, or eightfold fine, and in addition a special sum as compensation for loss, which will often be assessed quite arbitrarily and will be the result of a fiction rather than of reality. In any case, it seemed necessary to him to direct that the special compensation in question should be claimed at once at the forestry court and awarded in the court's sentence. It was obvious from the nature of the case that proof of loss sustained should be supplied separately and could not be based merely on the warden's report."

Opposing this, the spokesman and another member explained how the *additional value* mentioned here could arise in various cases indicated by them. The paragraph was adopted.

ᵃ These words are reminiscent of "A horse, a horse! My kingdom for a horse!" W. Shakespeare, *King Richard III*, Act V, Scene 4.— *Ed.*

Crime becomes a lottery in which the forest owner, if he is lucky, can even win a prize. There can be additional value, but the forest owner, who already receives the simple value, can also make a profitable business out of the four-, six-, or eightfold fine. But if, besides the simple value, he receives special compensation for loss, the four-, six-, or eightfold fine is also sheer profit. If a member of the knightly estate thinks the money accruing as a fine is an inadequate guarantee because it would often not be obtainable, it would certainly not become more obtainable by the value and the compensation for loss having to be recovered as well. We shall see presently how this difficulty of receiving money from the accused is overcome.

Could the forest owner have any better insurance for his wood than that instituted here, whereby crime has been turned into a source of income? Like a clever general he converts the attack against him into an infallible opportunity for a profitable victory, since even the additional value of the wood, an economic fantasy, is turned into a substance by theft. The forest owner has to be guaranteed not only his wood, but also his wood business, while the convenient homage he pays to his business manager, the state, consists in not paying for its services. It is a remarkable idea to turn the punishment of crime from a victory of the law over attacks on it into a victory of selfishness over attacks on selfishness.

In particular, however, we draw the attention of our readers to the provision of §14, which compels us to abandon the customary idea that *leges barbarorum* are laws of barbaric peoples. *Punishment* as such, the restoration of the law, which must certainly be distinguished from restitution of the value and compensation for loss, the restoration of private property, is transformed from a *public punishment* into a *private compensation*, the fines going not to the state treasury, but to the private coffers of the forest owner.

True, an urban deputy stated: "This is contrary to the dignity of the state and the principles of correct criminal jurisprudence", but a deputy from the knightly estate appealed to the Assembly's sense of right and fairness to protect the rights of the forest owner, that is to say, he appealed to a *special* sense of right and fairness.

Barbaric peoples order the payment of a definite monetary compensation (atonement money) to the injured person for a definite crime. The notion of public punishment arose only in opposition to this view, which regards a crime merely as an injury to the individual, but the people and the theory have yet to be discovered which are so complacent as to allow an individual to claim for himself both the private punishment and that imposed by the state.

The Assembly of the Estates must have been led astray by a complete *qui pro quo*. The law-giving forest owner confused for a moment his two roles, that of legislator and that of forest owner. In one case as a forest owner he made the thief pay him for the wood, and in the other as a legislator he made the thief pay him for the thief's *criminal frame of mind*, and it quite accidentally happened that in both cases it was the forest owner who was paid. So we are no longer faced by the simple *droit du seigneur*.[a] We have passed through the era of public law to the era of double patrimonial right, patrimonial right raised to the second power. The patrimonial property owners have taken advantage of the progress of time, which is the refutation of their demands, to usurp not only the private punishment typical of the barbaric world outlook, but also the public punishment typical of the modern world outlook.

Owing to the refunding of the value and in addition a special compensation for loss, the relation between the wood thief and the forest owner has ceased to exist, for the infringement of forest regulations has been completely abolished. Both thief and property owner have returned to their former state in its entirety. The forest owner has suffered by the theft of wood only insofar as the wood has suffered, but not insofar as the law has been violated. Only the sensuously perceptible aspect of the crime affects him, but the criminal nature of the act does not consist in the attack on the wood as a material object, but in the attack on the wood as part of the state system, an attack on the right to property as such, the realisation of a wrongful frame of mind. Has the forest owner any private claims to a law-abiding frame of mind on the part of the thief? And what is the multiplication of the punishment for a repetition of the offence except a punishment for a criminal frame of mind? Can the forest owner present private demands where he has no private claims? Was the forest owner the state, prior to the theft of wood? He was not, but he becomes it after the theft. The wood possesses the remarkable property that as soon as it is stolen it bestows on its owner state qualities which previously he did not possess. But the forest owner can only get back what has been taken from him. If the state is given back to him—and it is actually given him when he is given not only a private right, but

---

[a] Right of the (feudal) lord.— *Ed.*

the state's right over the law-breaker—then he must have been robbed of the state, the state must have been his private property. Therefore the wood thief, like a second St. Christopher, bore the state itself on his back in the form of the stolen wood.

Public punishment is satisfaction for the crime to the reason of the state; it is therefore a right of the state, but it is a right which the state can no more transfer to private persons than one person can hand over his conscience to another. Every right of the state in relation to the criminal is at the same time a right of the criminal in relation to the state. No interposing of intermediate links can convert the relation of a criminal to the state into a relation between him and private persons. Even if it were desired to allow the state to give up its rights, i.e., to commit suicide, such an abandonment of its obligations on the part of the state would be not merely negligence, but a crime.

It is therefore as impossible for the forest owner to obtain from the state a private right to public punishment as it is for him to have any conceivable right, in and for himself, to impose public punishment. If, in the absence of a rightful claim to do so, I make the criminal act of a third person an independent source of income for myself, do I not thus become his accomplice? Or am I any the less his accomplice because to him falls the punishment and to me the fruit of the crime? The guilt is not attenuated by a private person abusing his status as a legislator to arrogate to himself rights belonging to the state because of a crime committed by a third person. The embezzling of public, state funds is a crime against the state, and is not the money from fines public money belonging to the state?

The wood thief has robbed the forest owner of wood, but the forest owner has made use of the wood thief to purloin the *state itself*. How literally true this is can be seen from § 19, the provisions of which do not stop at imposing a fine but also lay claim to the *body and life* of the accused. According to § 19, the infringer of forest regulations is handed over completely to the forest owner, for whom he has to perform *forest labour*. According to an urban deputy, this "could lead to great inconvenience. He wished merely to call attention to the danger of this procedure in the case of persons of the other sex".

A deputy from the knightly estate gave the following eternally memorable reply:

"It is, indeed, as necessary as it is expedient when discussing a draft law to examine and firmly establish its principles in advance, but once this has been done, there can be no going back to them in discussing each separate paragraph."

After this, the paragraph was adopted *without opposition*.

Be clever enough to start out from bad principles, and you cannot fail to be rightfully entitled to the bad consequences. You might think, of course, that the worthlessness of the principle would be revealed in the abnormity of its consequences, but if you knew the world you would realise that the clever man takes full advantage of every consequence of what he has once succeeded in carrying through. We are only surprised that the forest owner is not allowed to heat his stove with the wood thieves. Since it is a question not of right, but of the principles which the Provincial Assembly has chosen to take as its starting point, there is not the slightest obstacle in the way of this consequence.

In direct contradiction to the dogma enunciated above, a brief retrospective glance shows us how necessary it would have been to discuss the principles afresh in respect of each paragraph; how, through the voting on paragraphs which were apparently unconnected and far remote from one another, one provision after another was surreptitiously *slipped through,* and once the first has been put through in this way, then in regard to the subsequent ones even the *semblance* of the condition under which alone the first could be accepted was discarded.

[*Rheinische Zeitung* No. 307, November 3, 1842, Supplement]

When in connection with §4 the question arose of entrusting valuation to the warden making the charge, an urban deputy remarked:

"If the proposal that fines should be paid into the state treasury is not approved, the provision under discussion will be doubly dangerous."

It is clear that the forest warden will not have the same motive for overestimating if his valuation is made for the state and not for his employer. Discussion of this point was skilfully avoided, the impression being given that §14, which awards the money from the fine to the forest owner, could be rejected. §4 was put through. After voting ten paragraphs, the Assembly arrived at §14, by which §4 was given an altered and dangerous meaning. But this connection was totally ignored; §14 was adopted, providing for fines to be paid into the private coffers of the forest owners. The main, indeed the only, reason adduced for this is that it is in the interests of the forest owner, who is not adequately compensated by the replacement of the simple value. But in §15 it has been forgotten that it was voted that the fine should be paid to the forest owner and it is decreed that he should receive, besides the simple value, a special compensation for loss, because it was thought proper that he should have an additional value, as if he had not already received such an addition thanks to the fines flowing into his coffers. It was also pointed out that the fines were not always obtainable from the accused. Thus the *impression was given* that only in regard to the money was it intended to take the place of the state, but in §19 the mask is discarded and a claim advanced not only for the money, but for the criminal himself, not only for the man's purse, but for himself.

At this point the method of the deception stands out in sharp and undisguised relief, indeed in self-confessed clarity, for there is no longer any hesitation to proclaim it as a principle.

The right to replacement of the simple value and compensation for loss obviously gave the forest owner only a *private claim* against the wood thief, for the implementation of which the civil courts were available. If the wood thief is unable to pay, the forest owner is in the position of any private person faced with an impecunious debtor, and, of course, that does not give him any right to compulsory labour, corvée services, or in short, *temporary serfdom* of the debtor. What then is the basis of this claim of the forest owner? The *fine*. As we have seen, by appropriating the fine for himself, the forest owner claims not only his private right, but also the *state's right* to the wood thief, and so puts himself in the place of the state. In adjudging the fine to himself, however, the forest owner has cleverly concealed that he has adjudged himself the right of *punishment itself*. Whereas previously he spoke of the *fine* simply as a sum of *money*, he now refers to it as a *punishment* and triumphantly admits that by means of the fine he has converted a public right into his private property. Instead of recoiling ·in horror before this consequence, which is as criminal as it is revolting, people accept it precisely because it is a consequence. Common sense may maintain that it is contrary to our concept of right, to every kind of right, to hand over one citizen to another as a temporary serf, but shrugging their shoulders, people declare that the principle has been discussed, although there has been neither any principle nor any discussion. In this way, by means of the fine, the forest owner surreptitiously obtains control over the *person of the wood thief*. Only §19 reveals the double meaning of §14.

Thus we see that §4 should have been impossible because of §14, §14 because of §15, §15 because of §19, and §19 itself is simply impossible and should have made impossible the entire prin-

ciple of the punishment, precisely because in it all the viciousness
of this principle is revealed.

The principle of *divide et impera*[a] could not be more adroitly
exploited. In considering one paragraph, no attention is paid to
the next one, and when the turn of that one comes, the previous
one is forgotten. One paragraph has already been discussed, the
other has not yet been discussed, so for opposite reasons both of
them are raised to a position above all discussion. But the
acknowledged principle is "the sense of right and fairness in
protecting the interests of the forest owner", which is directly
opposed to the sense of right and fairness in protecting the
interests of those whose property consists of life, freedom, humanity, and citizenship of the state, who own nothing except themselves.

We have, however, reached a point where the forest owner, in
exchange for his piece of wood, receives what was once a human
being.

> *Shylock.*   Most learned judge!—A sentence! come, prepare!
> *Portia.*   Tarry a little; there is something else.
>   This bond doth give thee here no jot of blood;
>   The words expressly are "a pound of flesh":
>   Take then thy bond, take thou thy pound of flesh;
>   But, in the cutting it, if thou dost shed
>   One drop of Christian blood, thy lands and goods
>   Are, by the laws of Venice, confiscate
>   Unto the state of Venice.
> *Gratiano.* O upright judge! Mark, Jew. O learned judge!
> *Shylock.* Is that the law?
> *Portia.*   Thyself shaft see the act.[b]

You, too, should see the act!

What is the basis of your claim to make the wood thief into a
serf? The fine. We have shown that you have no right to the
fine money. Leaving this out of account, what is your basic principle?
It is that the interests of the forest owner shall be safeguarded
even if this results in destroying the world of law and freedom.
You are unshakeably determined that *in some way or other* the wood
thief must *compensate* you for the *loss* of your *wood*. This firm
wooden foundation of your argument is so rotten that a single
breath of sound common sense is sufficient to shatter it into a
thousand fragments.

The state can and must say: I guarantee right against all

---

[a] Divide and rule.— *Ed.*

[b] W. Shakespeare, *The Merchant of Venice*, Act IV, Scene 1.— *Ed.*

contingencies. Right alone is immortal in me, and therefore I prove to you the mortality of crime by doing away with it. But the state cannot and must not say: a private interest, a particular existence of property, a wooded plot of land, a tree, a chip of wood (and compared to the state the greatest tree is hardly more than a chip of wood) is guaranteed against all contingencies, is immortal. The state cannot go against the nature of things, it cannot make the finite proof against the conditions of the finite, against accident. Just as your property cannot be guaranteed by the state against all contingencies *before* a crime, so also a crime cannot convert this uncertain nature of your property into its opposite. Of course, the state will safeguard your private interests insofar as these can be safeguarded by rational laws and rational measures of prevention, but the state cannot concede to your private demand in respect of the criminal any other right than the right of private demands, the protection given by civil jurisdiction. If you cannot obtain any compensation from the criminal in this way owing to his lack of means, the only consequence is that *all legal means* to secure this compensation have come to an end. The world will not be unhinged on that account, nor will the state forsake the sunlit path of justice, but you will have learned that everything earthly is transitory, which will hardly be a piquant novelty for you in view of your pure religiosity, or appear more astonishing than storms, conflagrations or fevers. If, however, the state wanted to make the criminal your temporary serf, it would be sacrificing the immortality of the law to your finite private interests. It would prove thereby to the criminal the mortality of the law, whereas by punishment it ought to prove to him its immortality.

When, during the reign of King Philip, Antwerp could easily have kept the Spaniards at bay by flooding its region, the butchers' guild would not agree to this because they had fat oxen in the pastures.[93] You demand that the state should abandon its spiritual region in order to avenge your pieces of wood.

Some subsidiary provisions of § 16 should also be mentioned. An urban deputy remarked:

"According to existing legislation, eight days' imprisonment is reckoned as equivalent to a fine of 5 talers. There is no sufficient reason for departing from this." (Namely, for making it fourteen days instead of eight.)

The commission proposed the following addition to the same paragraph:

"that in no case a prison sentence should be less than 24 hours".

When someone suggested that this minimum was too great, a
deputy from the knightly estate retorted:

"The French forestry law does not have any punishment of less than three
days."

In the same breath as it opposed the provision of the French
law by making fourteen days' imprisonment instead of eight the
equivalent of a fine of 5 talers, the Assembly, out of devotion to
the French law, opposed the three days being altered to 24 hours.

The above-mentioned urban deputy remarked further:

"It would be very severe at least to impose fourteen days' imprisonment as an
equivalent for a fine of 5 talers for pilfering wood, which after all cannot be
regarded as a crime deserving heavy punishment. The result would be that one
who has the means to buy his freedom would suffer simple punishment, whereas
the punishment of a poor person would be doubled."

A deputy from the knightly estate mentioned that in the
neighbourhood of Cleve many wood thefts took place merely in
order to secure arrest and prison fare. Does not this deputy from
the knightly estate prove precisely what he wants to refute,
namely, that people are driven to steal wood by the sheer necessity
of saving themselves from starvation and homelessness? Is this
terrible need an aggravating circumstance?

The previously mentioned *urban deputy* said also:

"The cut in prison fare, which has already been condemned, must be regarded
as too severe and, especially in the case of *penal labour*, quite impracticable."

A number of deputies denounced the reduction of food to *bread*
and *water* as being too severe. But a deputy from a rural
community remarked that in the Trier district the food cut had
already been introduced and had proved to be very *effective*.

Why did the worthy speaker find that the beneficial effect in
Trier was due precisely to bread and water and not, perhaps, to
the *intensification of religious sentiment*, about which the Assembly
was able to speak so much and so movingly? Who could have
dreamed at that time that bread and water were the true means
for salvation? During certain debates one could believe that the
English Holy Parliament[94] had been revived. And now? Instead of
prayer and trust and song, we have bread and water, prison and
labour in the forest! How prodigal the Assembly is with words in
order to procure the Rhinelanders a seat in heaven! How prodigal

it is too, with words, in order that a whole class of Rhinelanders should be fed on bread and water and driven with whips to labour in the forest — an idea which a Dutch planter would hardly dare to entertain in regard to his Negroes. What does all this prove? That it is easy to be holy if one is not willing to be human. That is the way in which the following passage can be understood:

"A member of the Assembly considered the provision in §23 *inhuman;* nevertheless it was adopted."

Apart from its *inhumanity,* no information was given about this paragraph.

Our whole account has shown how the Assembly degrades the executive power, the administrative authorities, the life of the accused, the idea of the state, crime itself, and punishment as well, to *material means of private interest.* It will be found consistent, therefore, that the *sentence of the court* also is treated as a mere means, and the *legal validity* of the sentence as a superfluous prolixity.

"In §6 the commission proposed to delete the words '*legally valid*', since, in cases of judgment by default, their adoption would give the wood thief a ready means of avoiding an increased punishment for a repetition of the offence. Many deputies, however, protested against this, declaring that it was necessary to oppose the commission's proposed deletion of the expression '*legally valid sentence*' in §6 of the draft. This characterisation applied to sentences in this passage, as also in the paragraph, was certainly not made without juridical consideration. If every first sentence pronounced by the judge sufficed as grounds for imposing a severer punishment, then, of course, the intention of punishing repeated offenders more severely would be more easily and frequently achieved. It had to be considered, however, whether one was willing to sacrifice in this way an *essential legal principle* to the *interests of forest protection* stressed by the spokesman. One could not agree that the violation of an indisputable basic principle of judicial procedure could give such a result to a sentence which was still without legal validity. Another urban deputy also called for the rejection of the commission's amendment. He said the amendment violated the provisions of the criminal law by which there could be no increase of punishment until the first punishment had been established by a legally valid sentence. The spokesman for the commission retorted: 'The *whole forms an exceptional law,* and therefore also an *exceptional provision,* such as has been proposed, is permissible in it.' The commission's proposal to delete the words 'legally valid' was *approved.*"

The sentence exists merely to identify recidivism. The judicial forms seem to the greedy restlessness of private interest to be irksome and superfluous obstacles of a pedantic legal etiquette. The trial is merely a reliable escort for the adversary on his way to prison, a mere preliminary to execution, and if the trial seeks to be more than that it has to be silenced. The anxiety of self-interest spies out, calculates and conjectures most carefully how the adversary could exploit the legal terrain on which, as a necessary evil, he has to be encountered, and the most circumspect counter-manoeuvres are undertaken to forestall him. In the unbridled pursuit of private interest you come up against the law itself as an obstacle and you treat it as such. You haggle and bargain with it to secure the abrogation of a basic principle here and there, you try to silence it by the most suppliant references to the right of private interest, you slap it on the shoulder and whisper in its ear: these are exceptions and there are no rules without an exception. You try, by permitting the law as it were terrorism and meticulousness in relation to the enemy, to compensate it for the slippery ease of conscience with which you treat it as a guarantee of the accused and as an independent object. The interest of the law is allowed to speak insofar as it is the law of private interest, but it has to be silent as soon as it comes into conflict with this holy of holies.

The forest owner, who himself *punishes*, is so consistent that he himself also *judges*, for he obviously acts as a judge by declaring a sentence legally binding although it has no legal validity. How altogether foolish and impractical an illusion is an impartial judge when the legislator is not impartial! What is the use of a disinterested sentence when the law favours self-interest! The judge can only puritanically formulate the self-interest of the law, only implement it without reservation. Impartiality is then only in the form, not in the content of the sentence. The content has been anticipated by the law. If the trial is nothing but an empty form, then such a trifling formality has no independent value. According to this view, Chinese law would become French law if it was forced into the French procedure, but *material law* has its own *necessary, native form of trial*. Just as the rod necessarily figures in Chinese law, and just as torture has a place in the medieval criminal code as a form of trial, so the public, free trial, in accordance with its own nature, necessarily has a public content dictated by freedom and not by private interest. Court trial and the law are no more indifferent to each other than, for instance, the forms of plants are indifferent to the plants themselves, and the forms of animals to their flesh and blood. There must be a *single* spirit animating the trial and the law, for the trial is only the *form of life of the law*, the manifestation of its inner life.

The pirates of Tidong[95] break the arms and legs of their prisoners to ensure control over them. To ensure control over wood thieves, the Provincial Assembly has not only broken the arms and legs but has even pierced the heart of the law. We consider its merit in regard to re-establishing some categories of our trial procedure as absolutely nil; on the contrary, we must acknowledge the frankness and consistency with which it gives an unfree form to the unfree content. If private interest, which cannot bear the light of publicity, is introduced materially into our law, let it be given its appropriate form, that of secret procedure so that at least no dangerous, complacent illusions will be evoked and entertained. We consider that at the present moment it is the duty of all Rhinelanders, and especially of Rhenish jurists, to devote their main attention to the *content of the law*, so that we should not be left in the end with only an empty mask. The form is of no value if it is not the form of the content.

The commission's proposal which we have just examined and the Assembly's vote approving it are the climax to the whole debate, for here the Assembly itself becomes conscious of the *conflict between the interest of forest protection and the principles of law*, principles endorsed by our own laws. The Assembly therefore put it to the vote whether the principles of law should be sacrificed to the interest of forest protection or whether this interest should be sacrificed to the principles of law, and *interest outvoted law*. It was even realised that the whole law was an *exception to the law*, and therefore the conclusion was drawn that *every* exceptional provision it contained was permissible. The Assembly confined itself to drawing consequences that the legislator had neglected. Wherever the legislator had forgotten that it was a question of an exception to the law, and not of a law, wherever he put forward the legal point of view, our Assembly by its activity intervened with confident tactfulness to correct and supplement him, and to make private interest lay down laws to the law where the law had laid down laws to private interest.

The Provincial Assembly, therefore, *completely fulfilled its mission*. In accordance with its *function*, it represented a definite *particular interest* and treated it as the final goal. That in doing so it trampled the law under foot is a *simple consequence of its task*, for interest by its very nature is blind, immoderate, one-sided; in short, it is lawless natural instinct, and can lawlessness lay down laws? Private interest is no more made capable of legislating by being installed on the throne of the legislator than a mute is made capable of speech by being given an enormously long speaking-trumpet.

It is with reluctance that we have followed the course of this tedious and uninspired debate, but we considered it our duty to show by means of an example what is to be expected from an *Assembly of the Estates of particular interests* if it were ever seriously called upon to make laws.

We repeat once again: our estates have fulfilled their function as such, but far be it from us to desire to justify them on that account. In them, the Rhinelander ought to have been victorious over the estate, the human being ought to have been victorious over the forest owner. They themselves are legally entrusted not only with the representation of particular interests but also with the representation of the interests of the province, and however contradictory these two tasks may be, in case of conflict there should not be a moment's delay in sacrificing representation of particular interest to representation of the interests of the province. The sense of right and legality is the *most important provincial characteristic* of the Rhinelander. But it goes without saying that a particular interest, caring no more for the province than it does for the Fatherland, has also no concern for local spirit, any more than for the general spirit. In direct contradiction to those writers of fantasy who profess to find in the representation of private interests ideal romanticism, immeasurable depths of feeling, and the most fruitful source of individual and specific forms of morality, such representation on the contrary abolishes all natural and spiritual distinctions by enthroning in their stead the immoral, irrational and soulless abstraction of a particular material object and a particular consciousness which is slavishly subordinated to this object.

Wood remains wood in Siberia as in France; forest owners remain forest owners in Kamchatka as in the Rhine Province. Hence, if wood and its owners as such make laws, these laws will differ from one another only by the place of origin and the language in which they are written. This *abject materialism,* this sin against the holy spirit of the people and humanity, is an immediate consequence of the doctrine which the *Preussische Staats-Zeitung* preaches to the legislator, namely, that in connection with the law concerning wood he should think only of wood and forest and should solve each material problem *in a non-political way,* i.e., without any connection with the whole of the reason and morality of the state.

The *savages of Cuba* regarded gold as a *fetish of the Spaniards.* They celebrated a feast in its honour, sang in a circle around it and then threw it into the sea. If the Cuban savages had been present at the sitting of the Rhine Province Assembly, would they not have regarded *wood* as the *Rhinelanders' fetish?* But a subsequent sitting would have taught them that the worship of animals is connected with this fetishism, and they would have thrown the *hares* into the sea in order to save the *human beings.*[96]

Written in October 1842

First published in the Supplement to the *Rheinische Zeitung* Nos. 298, 300, 303, 305 and 307, October 25, 27 and 30, November 1 and 3, 1842

Signed: *By a Rhinelander*

Printed according to the newspaper

Published in English for the first time

IN CONNECTION WITH THE ARTICLE
"FAILURES OF THE LIBERAL OPPOSITION IN HANOVER"

Editorial Note[97]

Since the expression "*liberal* opposition" in the title originated not with the author of the article in question, but with the editorial board, the latter takes this occasion to add something to explain this designation.

Two reasons are put forward against this expression. As regards its *form*, it is said that the opposition is not liberal, *because* it is conservative, because it aims at the continuance of an existing legal situation. According to this dialectic, the July revolution was a conservative and *therefore* illiberal revolution, for it aimed first of all at preserving the *Charte*.[98] Nevertheless, liberalism claimed the July revolution as its own. Liberalism, of course, is conservative, it conserves freedom and, in the face of the assaults of crude, material force, even the stunted *status quo* forms of freedom. It should be added that, if such an abstraction wishes to be consistent, from its own point of view the opposition of a legal situation dating from the year 1833 must be regarded as progressive and liberal compared with a reaction which is forcing the year 33 back to the year 19.[99]

As regards the *content*, it is further contended that the content of the opposition, the fundamental state law of 1833, is not a content of freedom. Granted! However little the fundamental state law of 1833 is an embodiment of freedom when measured by the idea of freedom, it is very much an embodiment of freedom when measured by the existence of the fundamental state law of 1819. Altogether, it is not a question primarily of the *particular* content of this law; it is a question of opposing *illegal* usurpation in favour of *legal* content.

The editorial board was the more entitled to call the Hanover opposition liberal since almost all German assemblies acclaimed it as a liberal opposition, as an opposition of legal freedom. Whether it deserves this predicate when looked at from the judgment seat of *criticism*, whether it has progressed beyond the mere opinion and pretension of being liberal to *real* liberalism, to examine this was precisely the task of the article in question.

Incidentally, we point out that in our view true liberalism in Hanover in the future has neither to champion the fundamental state law of 1833 nor to hark back to the law of 1819, but must strive for a completely new form of state corresponding to a more profound, more thoroughly educated and *freer* popular consciousness.

The editorial board of the Rheinische Zeitung

Written about November 8, 1842

First published in the Supplement to the *Rheinische Zeitung* No. 312, November 8, 1842

Printed according to the newspaper

Published in English for the first time

COMMUNAL REFORM
AND THE *KÖLNISCHE ZEITUNG*[100]

[*Rheinische Zeitung* No. 312, November 8, 1842]

Cologne, November 7. We have not considered it appropriate when discussing the question of the Communal Reform to take into account what has appeared on the subject in the provincial papers, and in particular in the *Kölnische Zeitung*. We shall easily justify ourselves if we show by an example the approximate strength of the argument which has been advanced in defence of the separation of the urban and rural communities.

The Supplement to No. 309 of the *Kölnische Zeitung* adduces under the heading "Summing Up" the authorities for the affirmative and negative answers to the question of separation. Among other curiosities we find as grounds against the separation "some newspaper articles", and in favour of the separation "likewise newspaper articles", just as newspaper articles have "likewise" appeared in favour of censorship. In any case we must mention with the greatest praise a devotion which considers an article a ground for the mere reason that it is a newspaper article as indeed a very uncritical, but despite its comical tone, rare recognition of the periodical press. Credit for an equally praiseworthy ingenuousness by no means attaches to the juxtaposition of two other authorities for and against the separation of the urban and rural communities. Said to have been against this separation is the Provincial Assembly of 1833, which moreover was prevailed upon by a single energetic personality, and accordingly therefore only this personality was against the separation; in favour of the separation was the whole Provincial Assembly of 1827 with the exception of one vote; but, honourable Summing Up, if the 1833 Provincial Assembly is only worth as much as the single personality which it followed, then what rules out the possibility that the 1827

Provincial Assembly is worth less than the single vote which it opposed; and yet the Provincial Assembly, which is so hesitating, so unable to depend on itself, still remains an authority! If further the petitions from Cologne, Aachen and Koblenz are adduced as petitions for the separation of the urban and rural communities because these petitions are limited to Cologne, Aachen and Koblenz, in the best of cases this can prove only the limitation of these petitions, but by no means their reasonableness; besides, having in their initial haste grasped so little the generality of the question and considered the interest of the whole province, these cities have just as little conceived their particular reform in any kind of opposition to the general reform. They made a petition only for themselves, but by no means against the province. We admired immediately at the beginning the comical ingenuousness of the "Summing Up", and although it does not preserve this quality throughout but, as we have just heard, could not but occasionally lapse into small intentional subtleties, this comicality and ingenuousness nevertheless victoriously reasserts itself in the end. Said to be in favour of the separation of the city and the countryside are also

"the remaining cities of the Rhine Province, whose petitions are unknown as far as their content is concerned, but which in making their requests could presumably only speak for themselves, since no single locality can be the organ of a whole province".

So not only a newspaper article in the abstract is an authority, but even the decided mediocrity of a "presumably only" can puzzle out the unknown content of the remaining cities' petitions. That this prophet who is called "presumably only" is a false prophet is proved by the petition of the city of Trier. At the end of the "Summing Up" emerges the inner ground which is the real ground for a separation of the city and the countryside. What is wanted is not only to separate the city from the countryside, but to separate the individual cities from one another and from the province, to separate the province from its own intelligence. A single locality could not be the organ of a whole province? Correct. The single locality must not be the whole organ, but it must be a part of this organ, and hence must be for its part the organ of the whole and general interest. And does not such a view remove all possibility of even a single city communal system? If a single locality cannot be the organ of the whole province, can a single citizen be the organ of a whole city? This citizen, as follows from the argument advanced above, can only request something for himself, and not for the whole city, and since the whole city consists only of single citizens, nothing at all can be requested for the city as a whole. The "Summing Up" ends with what the separation of the city and the countryside must in general end with if it is to be consistent, with making not only the city, not only the province, but even the state itself impossible. Once the particular is to be asserted in hostile opposition to the general, in the end all political and social institutions must be made to disappear before the ultimate indivisible particular, the single individual in his physical appetites and aims. The troops that the "Summing Up" puts into the field on its side resemble, with few exceptions, Falstaff's recruits: all they are good for is to fill the breach with the corpses of thoughts.[a] Enough of the grave-digger business!

Finally, a well-intended recollection of the *Kölnische Zeitung*. For the first time a sense of modesty and mistrust of its own strength has crept into the leading article, although it is otherwise accustomed to behave as if it were the criterion *de omnibus rebus et de quibusdam aliis*.[b] Not for the first time, but indeed for all time can the *Kölnische Zeitung* become convinced on this occasion of the untenability of its editorial principle. Since all unpaid contributors are welcome, a few fingers with an itch to write and set in motion by a mediocre brain suffice to falsify the expression of public opinion. When one casts a glance at the columns of the *Kölnische Zeitung*, one would think the view favouring the separation of the city and the countryside is predominant in the Rhine Province. But if one casts a glance at the Rhine Province, one would think the Rhine Province is not predominant in the *Kölnische Zeitung*.

[*Rheinische Zeitung* No. 316, November 12, 1842]

Cologne, November 11. Our appeal to the Rhineland "provincial papers" regarding the communal reform question did not fail to produce results. The *Kölnische Zeitung* found itself moved to dip its issue of Nov. 11 into a false bright instead of the usual twilight colour and to recognise, though with unmistakable ill humour, hesitant reservations, suspicious side-glances, and deliberate ambiguity, the equal rights of town and countryside. Today once again we seize the opportunity to make the *Kölnische Zeitung* conscious of its state of mind and will not abandon the pleasant,

---

[a] Paraphrase of Falstaff's words from Shakespeare's *King Henry IV*, Part One, Act IV, Scene 2.— *Ed.*

[b] Of all things and certain others.— *Ed.*

though fantastic hope that it will renounce its point of view as soon as it has gained consciousness of its point of view.

"Incidentally," the *Kölnische Zeitung* concludes its article today, "as regards the communal system question, which has such a high claim to the general interest, the editorial board of the *Kölnische Zeitung* considers it appropriate to state that in this respect also it pays allegiance to the principle of equality of rights but considers it its duty to give as free scope as possible to discussion of the *forms* in which an improvement of the present situation, which is thoroughly unfree and acknowledged by all parties to be no longer tolerable, is to be effected."

The *Kölnische Zeitung* has so far not carried a single article about the *forms* in which the communal reform is to be effected while maintaining the principle of equality of rights. It was therefore impossible for us to fight a non-existent opponent. Or does the *Kölnische Zeitung* consider that the "separation of town and countryside", a separation which a number of its articles suggested should be simulated legally by means of a separate communal system, is likewise one of the *forms* in which the principle of equality of rights is crystallised? Does it hold that the established inequality of rights is a form of equality of rights? The struggle in the *Kölnische Zeitung* centred not on the different forms of one and the same principle, but rather on the difference of the principle itself, and, indeed, in this struggle, if we consider the articles of the *Kölnische Zeitung,* according to that paper's own suggestion, as mere articles, i.e., according to their numerical mass, most of the troops belonged to the opponents of equality. We said to the *Kölnische Zeitung*: Be honest, do not falsify the expression of public opinion, fulfil the calling of a Rhineland paper, which is to represent the spirit of the Rhineland, disregard personal considerations, in a vital question for the province close your columns to all individual opinions which have the defect of wishing to assert a separate attitude in opposition to the will of the people. And how does the *Kölnische Zeitung* reply!

It finds it "appropriate" to pay allegiance to the principle of equality of rights in relation to the communal reform, a "finding appropriate" that will be considered very clever in respect of the Rhine Province, and not precisely as a proof of the inventiveness of the *Kölnische Zeitung.* Alongside this moderate allegiance to the spirit of the province, however, the *Kölnische Zeitung* considers it its "duty" to give as free scope as possible to discussion of the "forms" of the communal reform, among which forms it also includes the forms of "inequality". This "devotion to duty" will be found appropriate from the standpoint of its private interests and private considerations, however inappropriate this standpoint itself is. To cut off all hiding places for the *Kölnische Zeitung*, which creeps into concealment behind the difference between form and content, we pose the categorical question whether it declares an inequality of town and countryside legally established by means of a separate communal system to be a "form" of equality of rights and believes it can continue to keep its columns open to pretences of such equality as a mere question of form. Tomorrow we shall return to the article of the *Kölnische Zeitung* in question.

[*Rheinische Zeitung* No. 317, November 13, 1842]

Cologne, November 12. The article in No. 314 of the *Rheinische Zeitung* on the question of the communal system, which has such a high claim to the general interest,[a] is nothing but an *avant-propos* to the detailed discussion of *communal equality for town and country* which is being carried on in our supplement.[b] The *Kölnische Zeitung* introduces its reference to this, that is, to the matter itself, with "*Incidentally*", just as the worker at the craftsmen's banquet begins his speech with "In general", but this must not at all diminish the merits of the *Kölnische Zeitung* in respect of originality, since we recognise it rather as a habit of the paper, a habit which is just as original as praiseworthy, that in dealing with a question of general interest it "*incidentally*" touches also on the "matter itself". This method of treatment, which is somewhat intentional, possesses a wonderful elasticity which makes the most curious misunderstandings possible and for a third party even probable as the proper understanding of the matter.

So the *Kölnische Zeitung* begins its article in question of November 4[c] with the anecdote that a "neighbouring paper", namely, the *Rheinische Zeitung*, has called on "all Rhine Province papers to join forces against the threat, allegedly coming from Berlin, to the equality before the law of urban and rural communities" and issued the common slogan: "Equality for all, for townspeople and for peasants." The *Kölnische Zeitung* declares itself prepared to take up this slogan

"insofar as by equality is understood not the *foolish dream of the Communists*, but, as we *presume*, the only possible equality, equality of rights".

---

[a] Here Marx has an untranslatable pun on the German articles *der, die, das*, ridiculing the stilted style of the *Kölnische Zeitung*.— *Ed.*

[b] [H. Claessen,] "Die Reform der rheinischen Gemeinde-Ordnung." Zweiter Artikel. Ueber Unterschiedenheit der Gemeinde-Ordnung für Stadt und Land. *Rheinische Zeitung*, Beiblatt, Nr. 312, 314, 317, November 8, 10, 13, 1842.— *Ed.*

[c] Obviously a misprint. It should be: "November 11".— *Ed.*

This cunning side-glance at the communist dreams would have been just as impossible as the magnanimous presumption of our non-communist tendency would have been unnecessary had the *Kölnische Zeitung* begun its report with the *matter itself*, with the fact that the *Rheinische Zeitung* wants an *equal communal system* for town and countryside and even designates this equality expressly in the article quoted as "*equality of rights* of urban and rural communities". But if the *Kölnische Zeitung* were to see this equality itself as communist foolishness, then it would simply have to be referred to its own credo introduced by the Catonic "Caeterum". [a]

The ridiculous communist side-cut is not enough. The *Kölnische Zeitung* considers it necessary to associate another confession of faith with that of equality of rights.

"But," it says, "we must admit that we cannot at all *share the concern that the wise government of Frederick William IV is contemplating an infringement of equality of rights in the Rhineland.* Before we believe this we must be presented with facts and not with assertions, which, we hope, are without any foundation."

With this clumsy and perfidious insinuation imputing to us fears of and the spreading of rumours about an *intentional* infringement of equality of rights in the Rhineland by the wise government of Frederick William IV, the *Kölnische Zeitung* flees from the field of argument to the field of suspicion and denunciation and convinces us anew that the impotence of understanding seeks as a last resort to assert itself through impotence of character, through the vain recklessness of demoralisation. What is the insinuation of the *Kölnische Zeitung* based on? Basing ourselves on information from Berlin, we reported that the Rhineland deputies to the Central Commissions [b] had before them a draft of a communal system which did *not* recognise the equality of town and countryside; we recommended that in this case the Rhine press should adopt the attitude and energy of truth. [c]

If the government submits to the opinion of the *Rhineland deputies* a communal system which separates town and countryside, it follows from this simple fact that the government, far from having any concealed intention, rather entertains the complete *conviction* that by such a separation it will *not* infringe equality of rights in the Rhine Province. If the Rhine press, the organ of the Rhine Province, is convinced that the province is of

---

[a] The opening word of Cato's famous dictum: "Ceterum censeo Carthaginem esse delendam."— *Ed.*

[b] Joint Estates Commissions of the Provincial Assemblies.— *Ed.*

[c] Reference to the article headlined "Köln, 9. Nov." in the *Rheinische Zeitung* No. 314, November 10, 1842.— *Ed.*

the opposite view, it follows just as simply that it must prove that a common communal system for town and countryside is a necessary consequence of equality of rights in the Rhine Province; or is it not even a *duty of the press to the government* not only to express the popular conviction without consideration for the exceptional opinion of single individuals, but also to prove the reasonable content of this conviction?

Finally, it is more than indecent on the part of the *Kölnische Zeitung* to bring the All-high person of His Majesty into controversies of this kind. It needs really a minimum of intelligence and a maximum of irresponsibility to make any political discussion impossible in a purely monarchical state by the simple and easy manoeuvre of disregarding the true content of the discussion, bringing in a personal relationship to the monarch and thereby turning every *objective debate* into a *debate on a question of confidence*. We expressed the hope that all Rhine Province papers would represent the view of the Rhine Province, because and insofar as we entertain the unshakeable conviction that His Majesty would not refuse to recognise the great significance of the general view of the Rhine Province, even if our Berlin information is grounded—which we have no occasion to doubt—even if the Rhine deputies approve a separation of town and countryside, which can appear to be all the less beyond all doubt[a] since just recently the articles of the *Kölnische Zeitung* proved that not all Rhinelanders are capable of understanding and sharing the conviction of the vastly overwhelming majority.

The *Rheinische Zeitung* advanced the slogan of equality of rights for town and countryside, and the *Kölnische Zeitung* accepted this slogan with the cautious condition that by "equality of rights" we understand equality of rights and no communist dream. The *Rheinische Zeitung* accompanied the Berlin information with an appeal to the feelings of the Rhine Province papers, and the *Kölnische Zeitung* denounces it for suspicions concerning His Majesty's intentions. The *Rheinische Zeitung* called on the various editorial boards of our provincial papers to sacrifice individual considerations and preconceived opinions to the Fatherland, and the *Kölnische Zeitung* comes out with a flat, entirely unexplained recognition of equality of rights for town and countryside, a recognition whose formal merit it itself nullifies, by declaring the "separation" of town and countryside to be a "form" of equality

---

[a] Marx obviously meant: of which there can be all the less doubt.— *Ed.*

of rights. Is it possible to write in a more illogical, unprincipled and wretched manner? Is it possible to proclaim more clearly freedom with the lips and unfreedom with the heart? But the *Kölnische Zeitung* knows the Shakespeare saying:

"... to be honest, as this world goes, is to be one man picked out of ten thousand",[a]

and the *Kölnische Zeitung* did not succumb to the temptation to be one out of ten thousand.

Finally, a word about the "separation of town and countryside". Even apart from general grounds, the *law* can only be the ideal, self-conscious image of reality, the *theoretical* expression, made independent, of the practical vital forces. In the *Rhine Province* town and countryside are not separated in reality. Therefore the law cannot decree this separation without decreeing its own nullity.

Written on November 7-12, 1842
Published in the *Rheinische Zeitung*
Nos. 312, 316 and 317, November 8, 12
and 13, 1842

Printed according to the newspaper
Published in English for the first time

---

[a] W. Shakespeare, *Hamlet*, Act II, Scene 2.— *Ed.*

THE DIVORCE BILL[101]

Editorial Note

CRITICISM OF A CRITICISM

The criticism of the Divorce Bill given here has been outlined from the standpoint of *Rhenish* jurisprudence just as the criticism published earlier (see the Supplement to No. 310 of the *Rhein. Ztg.*[a]) was based on the standpoint and practice of old Prussian jurisprudence. A third criticism remains to be made, a criticism from a pre-eminently general point of view, that of the *philosophy of law*. It will no longer suffice to examine the individual reasons for divorce, *pro et contra*. It will be necessary to set forth the concept of marriage and the consequences of this concept. The two articles we have so far published agree in condemning the interference of religion in matters of law, without, however, expounding to what extent the essence of marriage in and for itself is or is not religious, and without, therefore, being able to explain how the consistent legislator must necessarily proceed if he is guided by the essence of things and cannot be at all satisfied with a mere abstraction of the definition of this essence. If the legislator considers that the essence of marriage is not human morality, but spiritual sanctity, and therefore puts determination from above in the place of self-determination, a supernatural sanction in the place of inner natural consecration, and in the place of loyal subordination to the nature of the relationship puts passive obedience to commandments that stand above the nature of this relationship, can then this religious legislator be blamed if he also subordinates marriage to the church, which has the mission of implementing the demands and claims of religion, and if he places secular marriage under the supervision of the ecclesiastical au-

---

[a] Of November 6, 1842.— *Ed.*

thorities? Is that not a simple and necessary consequence? It is self-deception to believe that the religious legislator can be refuted by proving that one or other of his rulings is contrary to the secular nature of marriage. The religious legislator does not engage in a polemic against the dissolution of secular marriage; his polemic is rather against the secular essence of marriage, and he seeks partly to purge it of this secularity and partly, where this is impossible, to bring home at all times to this secularity, as a merely tolerated party, its limits and to counteract the sinful defiance of its consequences. Wholly inadequate, however, is the point of view of *Rhenish* jurisprudence, which is shrewdly expounded in the criticism published above. It is inadequate to divide the nature of marriage into two parts, a spiritual essence and a secular one, in such a way that one is assigned to the church and the individual conscience, the other to the state and the citizens' sense of law. The contradiction is not abolished by being divided between two different spheres; on the contrary, the result is a contradiction and an unresolved conflict between these two spheres of life themselves. And can the legislator be obliged to adopt a dualism, a double world outlook? Is not the conscientious legislator who adheres to the religious point of view bound to elevate to the sole authority in the real world and in secular forms that which he recognises as truth itself in the spiritual world and in religious forms, and which he worships as the sole authority? This reveals the basic defect of Rhenish jurisprudence, its dual world outlook, which, by a superficial separation of conscience and the sense of law, does not solve but cuts in two the most difficult conflicts, which severs the world of law from the world of the spirit, therefore law from the spirit, and hence jurisprudence from philosophy. On the other hand, the opposition to the present Bill reveals even more glaringly the utter lack of foundation of the old Prussian jurisprudence. If it is true that no legislation can decree morality, it is still truer that no legislation can recognise it as binding in law. Prussian law [102] is based on an intellectual abstraction which, being in itself devoid of content, conceived the natural, legal, moral content as external matter which in itself knows no laws and then tried to model, organise and arrange this spiritless and lawless matter in accordance with an external aim. It treats the objective world not in accordance with the latter's inherent laws, but in accordance with arbitrary, subjective ideas and an intention that is extraneous to the matter itself. The old Prussian jurists have shown but little insight into this character of Prussian law. They have criticised not its essence, but only individual external features of its existence. Hence, too, they have attacked not the nature and style of the new Divorce Bill, but its reforming tendency. They thought they could find in bad morals proof that the laws were bad. We demand from criticism above all that it should have a critical attitude to itself and not overlook the difficulty of its subject-matter.

The editorial board of the *Rhein. Ztg.*

Written in mid-November 1842
First published in the *Rheinische Zeitung*
No. 319, November 15, 1842

Printed according to the newspaper

A CORRESPONDENT
OF THE *KÖLNISCHE ZEITUNG*
VS. THE *RHEINISCHE ZEITUNG*

Cologne, November 16. The stoutest champion of the "separation of town and countryside" in the *Kölnische Zeitung* today again raises his rumbling voice, and today it is not the province but the *Rheinische Zeitung* which he selects for the honour of being the victim of his private intelligence and his private illusions. We believe the good man when he says that the reading of the articles on communal constitution in the *Rheinische Zeitung*[a] at breakfast numbed his head and hurled him back into "exceedingly confused dreams". We believe that it is very inconvenient for one who knows *Cologne* and *Bickendorf* well to be bustled through the Orient, through Greece, Rome, the German Empire, Gaul and France and even through *thoughts* which necessarily appear as "sophistries" and "dialectical tricks" to the *routine* of practical *intercourse* and narrowly limited outlook. We do not want to judge this cheerful self-complacency amiss for the by no means moderate courtesies which it is capable of bestowing on its own achievements, for it belongs to the character of narrow-mindedness to consider its own limitations as the limitations and the pillars of the world. And as our good and humorous friend adduces no new grounds but supports the view that a ground which has been rejected and refuted at its first presentation can, like an importunate petitioner, achieve its aim in the end if only it has the obstinacy to return again and again; as therefore our friend, true to the principles established in respect of newspaper articles, expects the effect of his well-worded and correctly ordered

---

[a] [H. Claessen,] "Die Reform der rheinischen Gemeinde-Ordnung". *Rheinische Zeitung*, Beiblatt, Nr. 307, 310, 312, 314, 317, November 3, 6, 8, 10, 13, 1842.— *Ed.*

grounds not from themselves, but from their repetition, nothing else remains for us but finally to banish from the real world a few phantasmagoria that may have come to him in "sleep" and in "confused dreams" and so to contribute as much as is in our power to eliminating the reappearing belief in ghosts, which is known to confuse its dreams of things with the things themselves. Our somnambulist saw in a dream how the peasants were alerted by the *Rheinische Zeitung* to march with spades and hoes on the towns because the latter harboured tyrannical intentions.

In his intervals of clear consciousness our somnambulist will have to agree with himself that the "towns" do not lie in the *Kölnische Zeitung*, that we have even rejected its arbitrary interpretation of the towns' intentions, and that finally a work[a] which even goes beyond the range of vision of "*one who knows Cologne and Bickendorf well*" is still less able to provoke the peasant to a demonstration with "spades and hoes"—which probably play their role as a sample of "unprejudiced views" drawn "from practical life and intercourse". On awakening, our somnambulist will further find it beyond all doubt that to *put right* an alleged "*correspondent*" of the *Kölnische Zeitung* is no "distortion of the truth", that provoking "dissatisfaction" with the *Kölnische Zeitung* and *taking sides* against its contemplative correspondent is *no* "arousing of dissatisfaction and frenzy of parties" against the state; or can it be that not only the "towns" lie in the *Kölnische Zeitung*, but the *state* itself is embodied in it and its contributors! Our friend will then also grasp that one may have the "*boundless arrogance*" to irritate the literary productions of the sign——[b] without "challenging by indecent sallies" "the highest state authorities", whom he makes responsible not only for his *opinions* but even for his *arguments* and who would like to disavow this self-styled ally.

With the present level of German science it will be more than an upheaval if the hollow theories which strain to conceive themselves as the result of *world history*, and the general range of vision of today's doctrine were to experience the bitter fate of finding their critical yardstick in the "unprejudiced" views, drawn from civil intercourse and practical life, of "*one who knows Cologne and Bickendorf well*". This gentleman will find it understandable that pending the epoch of this Reformation and of the conjectural

---

[a] See previous footnote.—*Ed.*

[b] The sign occurring under a series of anonymous articles in the *Kölnische Zeitung*.—*Ed.*

literary magnitude of the sign—.—, we consider his present isolated endeavours too fragmentary, and, with his permission, too insignificant in every respect to nourish and cultivate the dream of their importance by any further assessment of them.

Written on November 16, 1842

Published in the *Rheinische Zeitung*
No. 321, November 17, 1842

Printed according to the newspaper

Published in English for the first time

[CABINET ORDER ON THE DAILY PRESS [103]]

Cologne, November 15. Today's *Kölnische Zeitung* carries the following royal Cabinet Order, which was sent to all provincial ministries in the course of last month:

"I have already frequently pointed out that the tendency of the bad part of the daily press to mislead public opinion on matters of general concern by disseminating untruths or distorted facts should be countered by contrasting every such false report at once with the truth through a correction of the facts published in the same newspapers that were guilty of the falsifications. It does not suffice to leave counteraction against the evil tendencies of a daily newspaper, which have a pernicious effect on the public mind, to other papers that are imbued with a better spirit and to expect it only from them. The poison of corruption must be rendered harmless in the very place where it has been dispensed; that is not only the duty of the authorities to the circle of readers to whom the poison has been proffered, it is at the same time the most effective means for destroying tendencies to deception and lying as they manifest themselves, by compelling the editors themselves to publish the judgment passed on them. I have therefore noted with displeasure that little or no use has been made so far of this means, which is as legitimate as it is essential, for curbing manifestations of degeneration on the part of the press. Inasmuch as the present laws may not have sufficiently established the obligation of our domestic newspapers to publish without demur, and, moreover, without any comments or introductory remarks, all factual corrections officially sent them, I expect from the state ministry immediate proposals for the necessary supplementary legislation. If, however, they are already adequate for the purpose, it is My will that they should be vigorously implemented by My magistrates for the protection of law and truth, and I recommend this, not only to the ministries themselves, but in particular to the immediate attention of the Oberpräsidents, to whom the state ministry shall give directives to this end.

"The more deeply I have it at heart that the noble, loyal and commendably frank frame of mind, wherever it may be displayed, shall not find its freedom of speech curtailed, and that truth shall be as little as possible restricted in the sphere of public discussion, the more ruthlessly must the spirit that employs the weapons of lying and misleading be held under restraint so that freedom of speech cannot be cheated of its fruits and its blessings by being misused.

"Sanssouci, October 14, 1842

(signed) *Frederick William* "

We hasten the more urgently to communicate the above royal Cabinet Order to our readers, because we see in it *a guarantee* for the Prussian press. Every loyal newspaper can only regard it as significant support on the part of the government if *untruths* or *distorted facts,* the publication of which cannot always be avoided even with the greatest circumspection on the part of the editorial board, are corrected from an authoritative source. By these *official explanations* the government not only guarantees a certain *historical correctness* of the factual content of the daily press, but also, what is still more important, recognises the great significance of the press by positive participation, which will restrict within ever narrower bounds negative participation by *prohibition, suppression* and *censorship.* At the same time, the royal Cabinet Order presupposes a certain *independence* of the daily press, for if without such independence tendencies to deception, lying and pernicious tendencies are not likely to spring up and establish themselves in the daily press, still less is a noble, loyal and commendably frank frame of mind. This royal presupposition of a certain independence of the daily press should be welcomed by Prussian newspapers as the *most excellent guarantee of this independence* and as an *unambiguous expression of the royal will.*

Written in mid-November 1842

First published in the *Rheinische Zeitung* No. 320, November 16, 1842

Printed according to the newspaper
Published in English for the first time

[RENARD'S LETTER TO OBERPRÄSIDENT VON SCHAPER [104]]

Highly respected Herr Oberpräsident!

Your Excellency!

Through Regierungspräsident Herr von Gerlach in Cologne, on the 12th of this month, Your Excellency has put before me a rescript of the censorship ministry and, in addition, two decrees, and called for my observations on them to be minuted. Considering the importance of the explanations demanded of me, rather than making a statement to be minuted, I have preferred to address myself today to Your Excellency in writing.

1. As regards the rescript of the censorship ministry and in particular the demand that the *Rheinische Zeitung* should alter its tendency and adopt one agreeable to the government, I am able to interpret this demand only in relation to the *form*, a moderation of which, insofar as the content allows, can be conceded. Judging by the recently issued censorship instruction, and also by His Majesty's views frequently expressed elsewhere, it seems to us that the tendency of a newspaper which, like the *Rheinische*, is not a mere unprincipled amalgam of dry reports and fulsome praise, but throws light on state conditions and institutions through conscious[a] criticism inspired by a noble purpose, can only be a tendency acceptable to the government. Moreover, until now the responsible editor has never been informed of any disapproval of this tendency. Furthermore, since the *Rh. Ztg.* is subjected to the strictest censorship, how could its suppression be justified as a *first warning?*

---

[a] The words "even if sharply expressed" have been deleted here.— *Ed.*

I can assure Your Excellency that in the future, too, the *Rh. Ztg.* will continue to the best of its ability to help in paving the path of progress, along which Prussia leads the rest of Germany. For that very reason, however, I must reject the reproach levelled at me in the rescript that the *Rh. Ztg.* has sought to spread French sympathies and ideas in the Rhineland. The *Rh. Ztg.* has, on the contrary,[a] made its main task to direct towards Germany the glances which so many people still fastened on France, and to evoke a German instead of a French liberalism, which can surely not be disagreeable to the government of Frederick William IV. In this connection, the *Rh. Ztg.* has always pointed to Prussia, on whose development that of the rest of Germany depends. Proof of this tendency is provided by the articles on "Prussian hegemony",[105] aimed polemically against the anti-Prussian[b] strivings of the Augsburg newspaper. Proof is provided by all the articles on the Prussian Customs Union aimed against the articles of the Hamburg *Correspondent* and other newspapers, in which the *Rh. Ztg.* depicted in the greatest detail the accession of Hanover, Mecklenburg and the Hanseatic towns as the only beneficial course. Proof is provided above all by the continual reference to North-German science in contrast to the superficiality not only of French, but also of South-German theories. The *Rh. Zeitung* was the first Rhenish, and in general the first South-German, newspaper to introduce the North-German spirit[c] in the Rhine Province and in South Germany, and how could the divided races be more inseparably linked than by spiritual unity, which is the soul of political unity and its only guarantee against all external storms?

As to the alleged *irreligious* tendency of the *Rh. Ztg.*, it cannot be unknown to the supreme authorities that in regard to the content of a certain positive creed — and it is a question only of this and not of religion, which we have never attacked and never will attack — the whole of Germany, and especially Prussia, is divided into two camps, both of which include among their champions men occupying high positions in science and the state. In an unresolved controversy, should a newspaper take neither side or only one that has been officially prescribed to

---

[a] After "contrary", the words "contributed not a little" have been deleted.— *Ed.*

[b] After "anti-Prussian", the word "tendencies" has been deleted.— *Ed.*

[c] After "North-German spirit", the words "the Protestant spirit" have been deleted in pencil.— *Ed.*

it?[a] Moreover, we have never gone outside the terrain proper to a newspaper, but have touched on dogmas such as church doctrines and conditions in general only insofar as[b] other newspapers make religion into constitutional law and transfer it from its own sphere into that of politics. It will even be easy to cover each of our utterances with the similar and stronger utterances of a Prussian king, Frederick the Great, and we consider this authority to be one which Prussian publicists may very well invoke.

The *Rheinische Zeitung* is therefore entitled to believe that it has pre-eminently carried out the wish for an independent free-minded press which His Majesty formulated in the censorship instruction, and that it has thereby contributed not a little towards the benedictions which at the present time the whole of Germany conveys to His Majesty our King in his ascendant career.

The *Rh. Ztg.*, Your Excellency, was not founded as a commercial speculation or in expectation of any profit. A large number of the most esteemed men of Cologne and the Rhine Province, justly displeased with the pitiful state of the German press, believed that they could not better honour the will of His Majesty the King than by founding the *Rh. Ztg.* as a monument of the nation, a newspaper which voices the speech of free men in a principled and fearless way and, what is at all events a rare phenomenon, enables the King to hear the true voice of the people. The unprecedentedly rapid growth of this newspaper's circulation proves how well it has understood the wishes of the people. This was the aim for which those men contributed their capital, and for which they shrank from no sacrifice. Let Your Excellency now decide for yourself whether it is possible or permissible for me, as the spokesman of these men, to declare that the *Rheinische Zeitung* will alter its tendency, and whether its suppression would be not so much an act of violence against a private individual, but rather an act of violence against the Rhine Province and the German spirit in general.

In order, however, to prove to the government how very ready I am to comply with its wishes, insofar as they are compatible with

---

[a] The following has been deleted in pencil: "If Luther is not blamed for having attacked, in defiance of emperor and realm, the sole mode of existence of Christianity at that time, the Catholic Church, in a form that was even unbridled and exceeded all bounds, should it be forbidden in a Protestant state to advocate a view opposed to current dogma, not by isolated frivolous invectives, but by the consistent exposition of serious and primarily German science?" — *Ed.*

[b] The words "they have been utilised for political theories, maxims and prescriptions" have been deleted.— *Ed.*

the function of an independent newspaper, I am willing, as has been the case for some time past, as far as possible to set aside all ecclesiastical or religious subjects, so long as other newspapers or political conditions themselves do not necessitate reference to them.[a]

2. Secondly, as regards Your Excellency's demand for the immediate dismissal of Dr. Rutenberg, I already told Regierungspräsident von Gerlach on February 14 that Dr. Rutenberg was in no way an editor of the *Rheinische Zeitung*, but only did the work of a translator. In response to the threat, conveyed to me through Regierungspräsident von Gerlach, of the immediate suppression of the newspaper if Rutenberg were not at once dismissed, I have yielded to force and have for the time being removed him from any participation in the newspaper. Since, however, I am not aware of any legal provision which would justify this point of the rescript, I request Your Excellency to specify any such provision, and, if necessary, to give a speedy ruling whether the decision reached is to remain in force or not, so that I can claim my legal rights through the appropriate channels.

3. As regards the third point, the submission of an editor for approval, according to the censorship law of October 18, 1819, § [IX], only the supreme censorship authorities are entitled to demand the submission of an editor for approval. I know of no provision which transfers this entitlement to the Oberpräsidents. Therefore I request specification of any such provision or, if necessary, of a censorship ministry decree which orders this. Very willingly, but only in that case, will I submit an editor for approval.

Written on November 17, 1842

First published in the book *Rheinische Briefe und Akten zur Geschichte der politischen Bewegung 1830-1850*, 1. Bd., Herausgegeben von Hansen, Essen, 1919

Printed according to the manuscript

Published in English for the first time

---

[a] This paragraph was inserted subsequently. Its place was marked by ** and it is to be found at the end of the manuscript.— *Ed.*

THE INDUSTRIALISTS OF HANOVER AND PROTECTIVE TARIFFS

Editorial Note[106]

We can acknowledge the historical basis of the author's reasoning, and we can further concede, as the facts testify, that during the last 400-500 years England, especially, has done a great deal to protect its industry and crafts, although we need not necessarily agree with the system of *protective tariffs*. England's example is its own refutation because it is precisely in England that the pernicious results come into prominence of a system which is no longer the system of our time, however much it might have corresponded to medieval conditions, based on division and not on unity, which, in the absense of general protection, a rational state and a rational system of individual states, had to provide *special* protection for each *particular* sphere. Trade and industry ought to be *protected*, but the debatable point is precisely whether *protective tariffs* do in reality protect *trade* and *industry*. We regard such a system much more as the *organisation of a state of war* in time of peace, a state of war which, aimed in the first place against foreign countries, necessarily turns in its implementation against the country which organises it. But in any case an *individual* country, however much it may recognise the principle of free trade, is dependent on the state of the world in general, and therefore the question can be decided only by a congress of nations, and not by an individual government.

The editorial board of the *Rheinische Zeitung*

Written in November 1842
First published in the Supplement to the *Rheinische Zeitung* No. 326, November 22, 1842

Printed according to the newspaper
Published in English for the first time

THE ATTITUDE OF HERWEGH AND RUGE
TO "THE FREE" [107]

Berlin, November 25. The *Elberfelder Zeitung* and, from it, the *Didaskalia* contain the news that *Herwegh* has visited the society of "The *Free*", but found it beneath all criticism. Herwegh has *not* visited this society, and therefore could have found it neither beneath nor above criticism. *Herwegh* and *Ruge* found that "The Free" are compromising the cause and the party of freedom by their political romanticism, their mania for genius and boasting, and this moreover was frankly stated by them and perhaps may have given offence. Consequently, if Herwegh did not visit the society of "The Free", who as individuals are excellent people for the most part, it was not because he upholds some other cause, but solely because, as one who wants to be *free* from French authorities, he hates and finds ludicrous the frivolity, the typically Berlin style of behaviour, and the insipid aping of the French clubs. Rowdiness, blackguardism, must be loudly and resolutely[a] repudiated in a period which demands serious, manly and sober-minded persons for the achievement of its lofty aims.

Written in November 1842

First published in the *Rheinische Zeitung* No. 333, November 29, 1842

Printed according to the newspaper

Published in English for the first time

---

[a] As the result of a misprint the *Rheinische Zeitung* had "irresolutely".— *Ed.*

THE POLEMICAL TACTICS
OF THE AUGSBURG NEWSPAPER

"It is merely a lust of the blood
and a permission of the will." [a]

Cologne, November 29. In its occasional polemic against the
Rheinische Zeitung, the Augsburg *Allgemeine Zeitung* employs tactics
which are as characteristic as they are laudable and which, if
consistently pursued, cannot fail to impress the superficial section
of the public. To every rebuff merited by its attacks on the
principles and trend of the *Rheinische Zeitung,* to every essential
subject of dispute, to every principled attack on the part of the
Rheinische Zeitung, the response of the Augsburg newspaper has
been to wrap itself in the ambiguous cloak of silence, so that it
always remains impossible to decide whether this silence owes its
inconspicuous existence to a consciousness of weakness which
makes it *unable* to reply, or to a consciousness of superiority which
makes it *unwilling* to reply. We have no special reproaches to make
to the Augsburg newspaper on this account, since it merely treats
us as it treats *Germany,* for which it believes it can most beneficially
show its sympathy by a thoughtful silence, only rarely interrupted
by travel notes, health bulletins and paraphrased nuptial poems.
It may well be that the Augsburg newspaper is right to regard
its silence as a contribution to the public welfare.

Besides tactics of silence, however, the lady of Augsburg employs another method of controversy, which by its verbose, complacent and arrogant loquacity is, as it were, the active complement to the previous passive and melancholy quietude. The
lady of Augsburg is silent when it is a question of a fight over
principles, over the essence of a matter, but she lies in wait,
observes from afar, and seizes the opportunity when her opponent

---

[a] W. Shakespeare, *Othello,* Act I, Scene 3.— *Ed.*

neglects her dress, makes a *faux pas*[a] in the dance, or drops her handkerchief—and then she "minces virtue and does shake the head".[b] She blares into the air her long-suppressed, well-meant anger with imperturbable aplomb, with all the indignation of prudery in dress, and calls out to Germany: "There you see, that is the character, that is the frame of mind, that is the consistency of the *Rheinische Zeitung!*"

"There's hell, there's darkness, there is the sulphurous pit, burning, scalding stench, consumption; fie, fie, fie! pah; pah! Give me an ounce of civet; good apothecary!"[c]

By means of such noisy impromptus, the lady of Augsburg is able not only to remind the forgetful public of her vanished virtue, her honourable character and mature age, not only to adorn her sunken temples with outdated and faded recollections, but even to gain surreptitiously some other practical successes besides these petty, harmless successes of coquetry. She confronts the *Rheinische Zeitung* as a sturdy fighter, *quasi re bene gesta,*[d] blustering, upbraiding, provoking, and her petulant provocations make the world forget her senile silence and quite recent retreat. In addition, the appearance is created and diligently cultivated, that the fight between the Augsburg *A. Z.* and the *Rheinische Zeitung* turns on this kind of paltriness, scandalmongering and sartorial solecisms. The host of unintelligent and irresponsible people who fail to understand the essential fight in which we speak and the lady of Augsburg is silent, but who, on the other hand, recognise their own beautiful soul in the captious faultfinding and petty criticisms of the Augsburg *A. Z.*, applaud and pay homage to the honourable lady who castigates her unruly opponent with such skill and moderation, more to educate than to hurt her. In No. 329 of the Augsburg *A. Z.* there is another sample of this over-subtle, repellent, small-town polemic.

A correspondent reports from the Main that the Augsburg *Allg. Ztg.* praised Julius Mosen's political novel *The Congress of Verona* because it was put out by Cotta's publishing house. We confess that, owing to its worthlessness, we only occasionally glance at the literary criticism section of the Augsburg *A. Z.*, and are not acquainted with its criticism of Mosen. In this matter we put our trust *à discrétion* in the conscience of the correspondent. Assuming

---

[a] A false step.—*Ed.*

[b] W. Shakespeare, *King Lear*, Act IV, Scene 6.—*Ed.*

[c] Ibid.—*Ed.*

[d] As if everything had been done well.—*Ed.*

the fact to be correct, the report is not in itself improbable for,
according to recent explanations which have been met with a
refutation based on trickery and not solid reasons, the independence of the critical conscience of the Augsburg *A. Z.* in respect
of the place of printing in Stuttgart is at least open to doubt.
Hence all that remains is that we did not know where the political
novel was printed, and *enfin,* not to know that is not a mortal
political sin.

Later, apprised of the misstatement about the place of printing,
the editorial board stated in a note:

"We have just learnt that *The Congress of Verona,* by the poet Julius Mosen, was
not published by Cotta and we therefore request our readers to make this
correction to the report from the Main in No. 317 of this year." [108]

Since the chief reproach levelled by the Main correspondent
against the Augsburg *Allgemeine Zeitung* was based solely on the
premise that *The Congress of Verona* had been published by Cotta,
since we have explained that this was not the case, and since every
argument is invalidated if its premise is abolished, we were entitled
at any rate to make the extravagant demand on our readers'
intelligence that they should correct the report from the Main in
the light of this statement, and we could believe that we had
atoned for our injustice to the Augsburg *A. Z.* But look at the
Augsburg's logic! The Augsburg's logic interprets out correction as
follows:

"If Mosen's *Congress of Verona* had been published by Cotta, it would have to be
regarded by all friends of right and freedom as a nasty and unsaleable book; since,
however, we have subsequently learnt that it was published in Berlin, we request
our respected readers to welcome it, in the poet's own words, as one of the spirits
of eternal youth, which stride on along their radiant path and mercilessly trample
on the old gang." [109]

"That fellow handles his bow like a crow-keeper: draw me a
clothier's yard. — I' the clout, i' the clout, hewgh!" [a]

"That," exclaims the lady of Augsburg triumphantly, "that is what the
Rheinische Zeitung calls its frame of mind, its consistency!"

Has the *Rheinische Zeitung* ever declared the consistencies of the
Augsburg's logic to be its consistency or the frame of mind on
which this logic is based to be *its* frame of mind? The lady of
Augsburg was entitled only to conclude: "That is the way in which
consistency and frame of mind are misunderstood in Augsburg!"
Or does the Augsburg *Allgemeine Zeitung* seriously believe that by
means of Mosen's toast we would have liked to provide a

---

[a] W. Shakespeare, *King Lear,* Act IV, Scene 6.— *Ed.*

corrective commentary to assess *The Congress of Verona?* We discussed the Schiller festival at rather great length in a feature article. We pointed to Schiller "as the prophet of the new movement of minds" (No. 326,[a] correspondence from Leipzig) and noted the resulting significance of the Schiller festival. Why had we to repudiate Mosen's toast, which emphasised this significance? Could it be because it contains a sally against the Augsburg *Allgemeine Zeitung*, which the latter had already deserved because of its condemnation of Herwegh? All that, however, had nothing to do with the report from the Main, for then we should have had to write, as the *lady of Augsburg imputes to us*, "The reader must judge the report from the Main in No. 317 in the light of Mosen's poem in No. 320." The Augsburg's logic deliberately invents this nonsense in order to be able to throw it at us. The verdict of the *Rheinische Zeitung* in the feature article of No. 317 on Mosen's "Bernhard von Weimar" proves, although it needs no proof, that in regard to Mosen it has not departed by a hair's breadth from its customary factual criticism.

For the rest, we admit to the lady of Augsburg that even the *Rheinische Zeitung* is scarcely able to ward off the literary *condottieri*, that importunate and disgusting rabble which has sprung up all over Germany in the newspaper era of which the Augsburg *A. Z.* is the embodiment.

Finally, the Augsburg newspaper reminds us of the ballista which

"throws out big words and phrases that leave reality untouched".

The Augsburg *A. Z.*, of course, touches on every possible reality, Mexican reality, Brazilian reality, but not German reality, not even Bavarian reality, and if for once it does touch on something of the kind, it invariably takes appearance for reality and the reality for appearance. When it is a matter of spiritual and true reality, the *Rheinische Zeitung* could exclaim to the lady of Augsburg in the words of Lear: "Do thy worst, blind Cupid.... Read thou this challenge", and the lady of Augsburg would reply with Gloucester: "Were all thy letters suns, I could not see."[b]

Written on November 29, 1842

First published in the *Rheinische Zeitung* No. 334, November 30, 1842

Printed according to the newspaper

Published in English for the first time

---

[a] Of November 22, 1842.— *Ed.*

[b] W. Shakespeare, *King Lear*, Act IV, Scene 6.— *Ed.*

THE SUPPLEMENT TO Nos. 335 AND 336
OF THE AUGSBURG *ALLGEMEINE ZEITUNG*
ON THE COMMISSIONS
OF THE ESTATES IN PRUSSIA[110]

[*Rheinische Zeitung* No. 345, December 11, 1842]

Cologne, December 10. In the Supplement to No. 335 of the Augsburg *Allgemeine Zeitung* there is a not uninteresting essay on the commissions of the estates in Prussia. Since we wish to criticise it, we must preface our remarks by stressing a simple principle which, however, is often overlooked in a passionate party controversy. The presentation of a state institution is not the state institution itself. Hence a polemic against this presentation is not a polemic against the state institution. The conservative press, which continually reminds us that the view held by the critical press should be rejected as being merely an individual opinion and a distortion of reality, continually forgets that it itself is not the object in question, but only an opinion on that object, and that therefore to combat it is not always to combat that object. Every object that is made a matter for praise or blame in the press becomes a literary object, hence an object for literary discussion.

What makes the press the most powerful lever for promoting culture and the intellectual education of the people is precisely the fact that it transforms the material struggle into an ideological struggle, the struggle of flesh and blood into a struggle of minds, the struggle of need, desire, empiricism into a struggle of theory, of reason, of form.

The essay in question reduces the arguments against the institution of the commissions of the estates to two main heads, to arguments against their composition and arguments against their purpose.

At the outset we must condemn as a basic logical defect that the composition has been the first object of discussion, the examination of the purpose being reserved for a subsequent article. The composition cannot be anything but the external mechanism, the guiding and regulating soul of which lies in its purpose. But who would think of judging the expediency of a machine's composition before examining and ascertaining its purpose? It could be that the composition of the commissions is open to criticism because it corresponds to their purpose, inasmuch as this purpose itself cannot be recognised as a true purpose. It could also be that the composition of the commissions is worthy of recognition because it does not correspond to their purpose, going beyond the latter. Hence this order of the presentation is an initial mistake, but one which vitiates the whole presentation.

On almost all sides, the essay states, the complaint has been made with remarkable unanimity that

"predominantly only landed property has been taken into account in connection with the right of representation in the estates".

In opposition to this, attention has been drawn, on the one hand, to the progress of industry and, on the other hand, "with still greater emphasis" to intelligence and "its right to participate in the representation of the estates".

By the basic law on the provincial assemblies of the estates, landed property is made the condition for estate membership, a provision which was logically continued in regard to the commissions of the estates formed of members of the provincial assemblies. Thus, although landed property is the general condition for participating in the right of estate representation, it is by no means the sole criterion. Confusion of those two essentially different principles, however, underlay

"to a great extent the lively objections which have been raised against the composition of the commissions of the estates".

Landownership represents all estates. This fact the author admits. He adds, however, that it is not simply landownership as such, not abstract landownership, but landownership under certain secondary circumstances, landownership of a particular kind. Landownership is the general condition for estate representation, but it is not the sole condition.

We fully agree with the author when he asserts that the additional conditions essentially alter the general principle of representation through landownership. At the same time, however, we must declare that opponents who consider that the general principle is already too restricted cannot by any means be refuted by proof that this principle, which is restricted in itself, has been regarded as still not restricted enough, but as necessarily requiring that further restrictions alien to its nature should be added to it. Apart from the very general requirements of an unblemished reputation and a minimum age of thirty years — the former being, on the one hand, self-evident and, on the other hand, open to indefinite interpretation — there are the following special conditions:

"1. Ten years' uninterrupted landownership; 2. membership of a Christian church; 3. possession of land formerly held directly under the emperor for the first estate; 4. possession of property entailing imperial knighthood for the second estate; 5. a magistracy or civil profession for the urban estate; 6. self-management of landed property as the main occupation for the fourth estate."[111]

These are not conditions which arise from the essence of landownership, but which, from considerations foreign to the latter, add limits that are foreign to it, *restrict* its essence instead of making it more general.

According to the general principle of representation through landownership, there would be no distinction between Jewish and Christian landownership, between landownership by a lawyer and by a merchant, between landownership that is ten years old and one that is one year old. According to this general principle, all these distinctions do not exist. Hence if we ask what the author has shown, we can only reply: the restriction of the general condition of landownership by special conditions which are not part of its nature, by considerations based on the *difference between the estates*.

And the author admits:

"Closely connected is the complaint heard from many sides that, in regard to these commissions of the estates too, the difference between estates which belongs only to the past has been brought in again and applied as a principle of estate organisation, in alleged contradiction with the present state of our social conditions, and with the demands of the spirit of the time."

The author does not examine whether the general condition of landownership is in contradiction with representation of the estates or even makes it impossible! Otherwise it could hardly have escaped him that, if the estate principle were consistently applied, a condition which forms an essential feature only of the peasant estate could not possibly be made a general condition for the representation of the other estates, whose existence in no way depends on landownership. For the representation of the estates can only be determined by the essential difference between them, and hence not by anything which lies outside this essence. If, therefore, the principle of representation of landownership is annulled because of special estate considerations, then this principle of representation of the estates is annulled because of the general condition of landownership, and neither principle comes into its own. Furthermore, even if a difference between the estates is accepted, the author does not examine whether this difference which is presumed to exist in the institution in question characterises the estates of the past or those of the present. Instead he discusses the difference between the estates in general. It will be as little possible to eradicate it, he says,

"as to destroy the difference existing in nature between the elements and to go back to a chaotic unity".

One could reply to the author: just as no one would think of destroying the difference between the natural elements and going back to a chaotic unity, no one would want to *eradicate* the difference between the estates. At the same time, however, one would have to demand of the author that he should make a more thorough study of nature and rise from the first sensuous perception of the various elements to a rational perception of the organic life of nature. Instead of the spectre of a chaotic unity, he would become aware of the spirit of a living unity. Even the elements do not persist in inert separation. They are continually being transformed into one another and this transforming alone forms the first stage of the physical life of the earth, the meteorological process. In the living organism, all trace of the different elements as such has disappeared. The difference no longer consists in the separate existence of the various elements, but in the living movement of distinct functions, which are all inspired by one and the same life, so that the very difference between them does not exist ready-made prior to this life but, on the contrary, continually arises out of this life itself and as continually vanishes within it and becomes paralysed. Just as nature does not confine itself to the elements already present, but even at the lowest stage of its life proves that this diversity is a mere sensuous phenomenon that has no spiritual truth, so also the state, this natural realm of the spirit, must not and cannot seek and find its true essence in a fact apparent to the senses. The author, therefore, has provided only a superficial basis for the "divine order of the world" by confining himself to the difference between the estates as its final and definitive result.

But, in the author's opinion,

"care must be taken that the people is not set in motion as a *crude, inorganic mass*".

Therefore, there can be

"no question as to whether in general *estates* ought to *exist*, but only the question of establishing to what extent and in what proportion the *existing estates* are called upon to take part in political activity".

The question that arises here, of course, is not to what extent the estates exist, but to what extent they ought to continue their existence right up to the highest sphere of state life. If it would be unfitting to set the people in motion as a crude, inorganic mass, it would be just as much impossible to achieve an organised movement of the people if it were resolved mechanically into rigid and abstract constituents, and an independent movement, which could only be a convulsive one, were demanded of these inorganic, forcibly established parts. The author starts out from the view that in the actual *state* the people exists as a crude, inorganic mass, apart from some arbitrarily seized on differences of estate. Hence he knows no organism of the state's life itself, but only a juxta-position of heterogeneous parts which are encompassed super-ficially and mechanically by the state. But let us be frank. We do not demand that in the representation of the people actually existing differences should be left out of account. On the contrary, we demand that one should proceed from the actual differences created and conditioned by the internal structure of the state, and not fall back from the actual life of the state into imaginary spheres which that life has already robbed of their significance. And now take a look at the reality of the Prussian state as it is known and obvious to everyone. The true spheres, in accordance with which the state is ruled, judged, administered, taxed, trained and schooled, the spheres in which its entire movement takes place, are the districts, rural communities, governments, provincial administrations, and military departments, but not the four cate-gories of the estates, which are intermingled in a diverse array among these higher units and owe the distinctions between them not to life itself, but only to dossiers and registers. And those distinctions, which owing to their very essence are dissolved at every moment in the unity of the whole, are free creations of the spirit of the Prussian state, but are by no means raw materials imposed on the present time by blind natural necessity and the dissolution process of a past period! They are members but not parts, they are movements but not states, [a] they are differences of unity but not units of difference. Just as our author will not wish to assert that, for instance, the great movement by which the Prussian state changes daily into a standing army and a militia is the motion of a crude, inorganic mass, so must he not assert this of a representation of the people which is based on similar principles. We repeat once more: we demand only that the Prussian state should not break off its real state life at a sphere which should be the conscious flowering of this state life; we demand only the consistent and comprehensive implementation of the fundamental institutions of Prussia, we demand that the real organic life of the state should not be suddenly abandoned in order to sink back into unreal, mechanical, subordinated, non-state spheres of life. We demand that the state should not dissolve itself in carrying out the act that should be the supreme act of its internal unification. We shall give further criticism of the essay in question in a subsequent article.

[*Rheinische Zeitung* No. 354, December 20, 1842]

Cologne, December 19. The author wants to establish according to his point of view

"to what extent the existing estates are called upon to take part in political activity".

As already pointed out, our author does not examine to what extent the estates presupposed by the electoral law are the *existing estates*, to what extent estates exist at all; on the contrary, he takes as the basis of his examination something which it should have been the main task of his investigation to prove. Hence, he goes on to argue:

"The purpose of the commissions is so clearly laid down, both in the ordinances of June 21 of this year on their formation and in the royal Cabinet Order of August 19 on their convocation to form a central commission, that there can be absolutely no doubt on the subject. According to the wording of the above-mentioned Cabinet Order, the *estate advisory council* in the individual provinces should be supplemented by an element of *unity*. In accordance with this, therefore, first of all the general purpose of the commissions of the estates is the same as that of the provincial estates, insofar as it is likewise a matter of advisory co-operation in public affairs, and especially in the work of legislation. And, on the other hand, the characteristic feature of the activity assigned to them is its centralisation. Hence, concerning the doubts which have been raised as to the composition of the commissions of the estates, what would have to be done is to prove to what extent

---

[a] A pun on the German word *Stand*, which means "state" as well as "estate."— *Ed.*

their union in a central commission contains grounds why the *elements* from which they are formed cannot correspond to the purpose of their central activity. Instead of such a proof being attempted, it has merely been asserted that the composition of the commissions of the estates (which is based on the same principle as the composition of the provincial estates) may well suffice for advising on subordinate provincial interests, but not for an activity embracing the whole state. In contradiction to this were advanced the above-mentioned complaints, which, if they were well founded, would be applicable also to the provincial estates."

From the very beginning we have drawn attention to the illogicality of wanting to examine the expediency of the *composition* of the commissions of the estates before criticising their purpose. It was bound to happen that in an unguarded moment our author would presuppose the expediency of their "purpose" in order to be able to deduce the expediency of their "composition". He tells us that the purpose of the commissions is clear!

Granting this clarity, this formal correctness of the "purpose", does that even so much as touch on the content and the truth of this content? The *commissions*, according to our author, differ from the "provincial estates" only by their "centralisation". Hence it has to be proved, he says, "to what extent *their union* in a central commission contains grounds why the elements from which they are formed cannot correspond to the purpose of their central activity".

We must reject this demand as *illogical.* The question that arises is not to what extent the union of the provincial estates in a central commission contains grounds why the component elements cannot correspond to their central activity. On the contrary, the question is to what extent the component elements of the provincial estates contain grounds which paralyse a true union in a real central commission, and hence also real central activity. The union cannot make the component elements impossible, but the component elements can make the union impossible. If, however, a *real* union, a true centralisation is presupposed, then the question of the possibility of a central activity loses all meaning, for the central activity is *merely* the expression, the result, the vitality of a true centralisation. A central commission in itself involves a central activity. How then does the author prove that the component elements of the provincial estates are suitable for central commissions? How, therefore, does he prove the real and not illusory *existence* of a central commission?

He says:

"If they" (the complaints advanced against the composition of the commissions) "were well founded, they would be applicable also to the provincial estates."

Of course, for what is asserted is precisely that these elements are not suitable for a central whole. But can the author believe that he has refuted his opponents merely by himself becoming aware of and formulating their objections?

Instead of confining himself to the statement that complaints against the composition of the commissions of the estates are complaints against the composition of the provincial estates, he ought to show to what extent objections against the provincial estates cease to be objections against the commissions of the estates. The author should not ask himself why the commissions of the estates are *not* in accord with a central activity, he should ask himself *by what means* they should be made capable of a central activity. It has been shown at some length and with concrete examples in these pages how little the provincial estates are called upon to participate in legislation (whether this participation is in the shape of *advice* or *joint action,* which can make a difference in the *power* but by no means in the *capability* of the provincial estates). Moreover, the commissions do not even arise from the provincial assemblies as moral persons; on the contrary, they arise from the provincial assemblies resolved into their mechanical component parts. It is not the Provincial Assembly which elects the commissions, but the diverse isolated parts of the Assembly, which each separately elect their deputies to the commission. This election is therefore based on a mechanical dissolution of the body of the Assembly into its individual component parts, on an *itio in partes.*[a] Hence it is possible that not the majority, but the minority of the Assembly is represented in the commissions, for a deputy from the knightly estate, for instance can have a majority in his estate although he has no majority in the Assembly, since such a majority may in fact arise by the minority representing the knightly estate combining with representatives of the urban or the peasant estate. Consequently, the objections raised against the composition of the Assembly are not just simply, but *doubly* applicable to the commissions, since in the latter the individual estate is withdrawn from the influence of the Assembly as a whole and kept within its own special limits. But let us leave even this out of account.

We take as our starting point a fact which the author will concede without argument. We assume that the composition of the provincial estates fully corresponds to their purpose, that is to say, the purpose of representing their *particular provincial interests* from the standpoint of their *particular estate interests.* This character of the provincial assemblies will be the character of all their activities.

---

[a] Division into parts.— *Ed.*

It will therefore also be the *character of their elections* to the commissions and the character of the *commission deputies themselves,* for an assembly which corresponds to its purpose will certainly remain true to its purpose in regard to its most important activity, in regard to the representatives whom it *itself elects.* What *new* element then suddenly turns the representatives of provincial interests into representatives of state interests and gives their *particular* activity the nature of a *general* activity? Obviously, it cannot be any other element than the fact of a *common place* of assembly. But can mere abstract space give a man of character a new character and chemically decompose his spiritual essence? It would be paying homage to the most materialistic mechanism to ascribe such an organising soul to mere space, particularly in view of the fact that at the meeting of the commission the existing separateness is also *spatially* recognised and represented.

After what has been said above, we can only regard the further grounds by which our author seeks to justify the composition of the commissions as attempts to justify the *composition of the provincial estates.*

[*Rheinische Zeitung* No. 365, December 31, 1842]

Cologne, December 30. As we have shown in a previous article, what the eulogist of the commissions of the estates defends in the Augsburg *Allgemeine Zeitung* is not their composition, but the *composition of the provincial assemblies.*

It seems to him .

"*surprising* to find intelligence put forward as a *particular* element *requiring* representation as an *estate alongside* industry and landed property".

We are glad to agree for once with the author and to be able to restrict ourselves to explaining his statement instead of refuting it. What does this surprise at those claims of intelligence amount to? Does he consider that intelligence is *not at all* an element of estate representation, or are we to believe perhaps that the article in question merely asserts that it is not a *particular* element? Estate representation, however, recognises *only* particular elements, which exist side by side. Hence something that is not a *particular* element, is *not at all* an element for estate representation. The article in question quite rightly calls the way in which intelligence enters into the representation of estates "the *general property* of intelligent beings", hence not a *particular property* of estate representatives, for a property which I have in common with everyone else and to the same extent as everyone else, cannot constitute my character, my superiority, my special nature. In an assembly of naturalists it is not sufficient to share in the "general property" of an intelligent being, but in an estate assembly it is sufficient to possess intelligence as a general property, to belong to the natural-historical genus[a] of "intelligent beings".

Intelligence should have a place in the provincial estate as a general human property, but intelligence should not belong to man as a particular property of a provincial estate; that is to say, intelligence does not make man a member of a provincial estate, it merely makes the member of a provincial estate a man. Our author will concede that, consequently, no special position is allotted to intelligence in the Assembly. Every newspaper advertisement is a fact of intelligence.[b] But who on that account would seek representatives of literature in advertisements? A field cannot speak, only the owner of the field can. Hence the field must appear in an intelligent *form* in order to make its voice heard. Wishes, interests, do not speak; only man speaks. But do field, interest, wish, lose their limitation because they assert themselves as something human, something intelligent? It is not a question of mere *form*, it is a question of the *content* of intelligence. If, as we readily concede to the author, intelligence not only does not need any representation as an estate, but even needs a non-estate representation, conversely, estate representation needs intelligence, but only a very limited intelligence, just as every man needs sufficient reason to realise his aims and interests, which still does not in any way make his aims and interests the aims and interests of "reason".

The *utilitarian* intelligence which fights for its hearth and home differs, of course, from the *free* intelligence which fights for what is right despite its hearth and home. There is a kind of intelligence which serves a particular purpose, a particular matter, and there is another kind of intelligence which masters every matter and serves only itself.

The author, therefore, desires only to say: intelligence is not a property of any estate; he does not ask whether estate is an intelligent property! He comforts himself with the idea that intelligence is a general property of the estate, but he refuses us the comfort of a proof that estate is a particular property of intelligence!

---

[a] In the newspaper: "genius".— *Ed.*

[b] A pun on the German word *Intelligenzblatt*, which means "an advertising sheet", literally "an intelligence sheet".— *Ed.*

It is quite *consistent*, not only with our author's principles, but with those of *estate representation*, for him to convert the question of the right of representation of "intelligence" in the provincial assemblies into the question of the right of representation of the *learned estates*, of the estates which have made a *monopoly* of intelligence, of intelligence which has become an estate. Our author is right to the extent that, given estate representation, it can also only be a question of intelligence that has become an estate. But he is wrong in not acknowledging the right of the learned estates, for where the estate principle prevails all estates must be represented. Just as he errs in excluding clerics, teachers and private men of learning, and does not even mention lawyers, physicians, etc., as possible candidates, he completely misconceives the nature of estate representation when he puts "state servants" belonging to the government on the same footing as the above-mentioned estates of learned men. In a state based on estates, government officials are the representatives of state interests as such, and therefore are hostile towards the representatives of the private interests of the estates. Although government officials are not a contradiction under people's representation, they are very much so under estate representation.

The article in question seeks further to prove that in the French and English constitutions the representation of landed property is as great as, if not greater than, in the Prussian constitution based on estates. Even if this were really the case, would it cease to be a defect in Prussia because it occurs also in England and France? We do not need to explain that this comparison is quite inadmissible if only because the French and English deputies are elected not as *representatives of landownership* but as *representatives of the people*, and, as far as particular interests are concerned, a Fould, for instance, remains a representative of industry *although* he pays a comparatively insignificant land tax in some corner of France. We will not repeat what we pointed out in our first article, namely, that the principle of estate representation annuls the principle of land-ownership representation, and vice versa, and that hence there is neither real landownership representation nor real estate representation, but only an inconsistent amalgamation of the two principles. We do not intend to examine further the basic error of a comparison which seizes on the different *figures* for England, France and Prussia, without taking into account their necessary connection with the different *conditions* in these countries. We stress only one aspect, namely, that in France and England account is taken of the benefit the state derives from landed property and of the burdens the owner has to bear, whereas in Prussia, on the contrary, what is taken into account, for instance, in connection with the majority of manorial estates and mediatised lands [112] is how *free* they are from state burdens and how independent their private use is. Not what someone possesses, but what he possesses of advantage to the state, not ownership, but, so to speak, the state activity of ownership, gives the right to representation in France and England, whose systems, by the way, we by no means agree with.

The author seeks further to prove that big landed property is not disproportionately represented compared with small landed property. On this point, as on that discussed above, we refer the reader to the work *Ueber ständische Verfassung in Preussen* (Cotta's publishing house, Stuttgart and Tübingen) and to Ludwig Buhl's book on the Prussian provincial estates. How incorrect the existing distribution is, quite apart from the difference between big and small landed property, can be shown from the following examples. The land value of the city of Berlin is 100 million talers, whereas that of the manorial estates in the Mark of Brandenburg is only 90 million talers. Yet the former sends only three deputies to the Assembly, whereas the owners of the latter elect 20 deputies from among themselves. Even among the towns, distribution according to the accepted scale of landownership is not consistently adhered to. Potsdam sends one deputy to the Assembly, although the value of its landed property is hardly one-tenth of that of Berlin. Potsdam has one deputy per 30,000 inhabitants, whereas Berlin has one per 100,000 inhabitants. The contrast is still more glaring if the smaller towns, which for historical reasons have been granted an individual vote [*Virilstimme*],[113] are compared with the capital.

For the rest, in order to establish the true relations between representation of intelligence and representation of landed property as an estate, let us return once more to the author's classical thesis, his above-mentioned justified surprise at finding "intelligence put forward as a *particular* element *requiring* representation as an estate *alongside* industry and landed property".

The author rightly does not seek the origin of the provincial assemblies in *state necessity,* and he regards them not as a *state need,* but as a *need of particular interests* against the state. It is not the basic rational mind of the state, but the pressing need of private interests that is the architect of the political system based on *estates,* and at all events intellect is no needy, egoistic interest, but the general interest. Hence representation of intelligence in an assembly of the estates is a contradiction, a nonsensical demand. Moreover, we call the author's attention to the consequences which so inevitably follow if *need* is made the principle of people's representation that our author himself for a moment recoils from them in horror and rejects not merely particular demands coming from the representation of particular interests, but the demand for this representation itself.

Either the need is *real,* and then the state is unreal because it fosters particular elements which do not find their legitimate satisfaction in the state, and therefore become organised as special bodies alongside the state and have to enter into a contractual relation with the state. Or the need really receives satisfaction in the state, and hence its representation against the state is illusory or dangerous. For a moment the author comes down on the side of illusion. He remarks as regards *industry* that even if it were not adequately represented in the provincial assemblies, it would still have ways enough for giving effect to its interests in the state and in relation to the government. Hence he maintains that *estate representation,* representation based on the principle of *need,* is an *illusion,* because the need itself is illusory. For what holds good of industry as an estate holds good for all estates, but for the *estate of landed property* even to a higher degree than for industry, since the former is already represented through the district president [*Landrat*], the district estates, etc., that is to say, through fully constituted state bodies.

From what has been said, it is obvious that not only can we not agree with the complaints about the *restricted scope of the standing orders* of the commissions, but, on the contrary, we must seriously protest against any extension of them as being against state interests. The liberalism which wants representation of *intelligence* in the Provincial Assembly is equally wrong. Not only is intelligence not a *particular* element of representation, it is not an *element* at all; it is a *principle* which cannot take part in any *compound* of elements, but can only produce a *division into parts* based on itself. There can be no question of intelligence as an integrating part, but only as the organising soul. We are concerned here not with a *complement* but with an *antithesis.* The question is: "representation of intelligence" or "representation of estates". The question is whether a particular interest should represent political intelligence or whether the latter should represent particular interests. Political intelligence will, for example, regulate landed property according to state principles, but it will not regulate state principles according to landed property. Political intelligence will assert landed property not in accordance with its private egoism, but in accordance with the state nature of landed property. It will not determine the essence of the whole in accordance with this particular essence, but will determine the latter in accordance with the essence of the whole. On the contrary, landed property with the right of representation does not adapt itself to intelligence but adapts intelligence to itself, like a watch-maker who does not want to set his watch by the sun, but wants to make the sun follow his watch. The question can be summed up in a few words: Should landed property criticise and be master over political intelligence or should it be the other way round?

For intelligence nothing is external, because it is the inner determining soul of everything, whereas, conversely, for a definite element like landed property everything is external that is not landed property itself. Hence not only the composition of the Provincial Assembly, but its activities also are *mechanical,* for it must treat all general interests and even particular interests different from itself as things extraneous and alien. All that is particular, such as landed property, is in itself limited. It must therefore be dealt with as something limited, that is to say, it must be dealt with by a general power superior to it, but it cannot deal with the general power according to its own needs.

The provincial assemblies, owing to their specific composition, are nothing but an association of particular interests which are privileged to assert their *particular limits* against the state. They are therefore a legitimised self-constituted body of non-state elements in the state. Hence by their very *essence* they are *hostile* towards the state, for the particular in its isolated activity is always the enemy of the whole, since precisely this whole makes it feel its *insignificance* by making it feel its limitations.

If this granting of political independence to particular interests were a necessity for the state, it would be merely the external sign of an internal sickness of the state, just as an unhealthy body must break out in boils according to natural laws. One would have to decide between two views: either that the particular interests, assuming the upper hand and becoming alien to the political spirit of the state, seek to impose limits on the state, or that the state becomes concentrated solely in *government* and as compensation concedes to the restricted spirit of the people merely a field for airing its particular interests. Finally, the two views could be combined. If, therefore, the demand for representation of intellect is to have any meaning, we must expound it as the demand for conscious representation of the intelligence of the people, a representation which does not seek to assert individual needs against the state, but one whose supreme need is to assert the state itself, and indeed as its own achievement, as its own state. In general, to be represented is something passive; only what is material, spiritless, unable to rely on itself, imperilled, requires to be represented; but no element of the state should be material, spiritless, unable to rely on itself, imperilled. Representation must not be conceived as the representation of something that is not the people itself. It must be conceived only as the people's *self-representation*, as a state action which, not being its sole, exceptional state action, is distinguished from other expressions of its state life merely by the universality of its content. Representation must not be regarded as a concession to defenceless weakness, to impotence, but rather as the self-reliant vitality of the supreme force. In a true state there is no landed property, no industry, no material thing, which as a crude element of this kind could make a bargain with the state; in it there are only *spiritual forces,* and only in their state form of resurrection, in their political rebirth, are these natural forces entitled to a voice in the state. The state pervades the whole of nature with spiritual nerves, and at every point it must be apparent that what is dominant is not matter, but form, not nature without the state, but the nature of the state, not the *unfree object,* but the *free human being.*

Written on December 10, 19 and 30, 1842

First published in the *Rheinische Zeitung* Nos. 345, 354 and 365, December 11, 20 and 31, 1842

Printed according to the newspaper

Published in English for the first time

THE DIVORCE BILL[114]

Cologne, December 18. In regard to the *Divorce Bill* the *Rheinische Zeitung* has adopted *quite a special* position, and so far no proof has been given anywhere that this position is untenable. The *Rheinische Zeitung* agrees with the Bill inasmuch as it considers the hitherto existing Prussian legislation on marriage immoral, the hitherto innumerable and frivolous grounds for divorce impermissible, and the existing procedure not in accord with the dignity of the matter concerned, which, incidentally, can be said of the old Prussian court procedure as a whole. On the other hand, the *Rheinische Zeitung* has put forward the following main objections to the new Bill: 1) Instead of *reform* there has been a mere *revision,* hence Prussian law was retained as the basic law, which has resulted in considerable half-heartedness and uncertainty; 2) the legislation treats marriage not as a *moral,* but as a *religious* and *church* institution, hence the *secular* essence of marriage is ignored; 3) the procedure is very defective and consists of a superficial combination of contradictory elements; 4) it cannot be ignored that there are, on the one hand, severities of a police nature which are contrary to the concept of marriage and, on the other, too great leniency in regard to what are called considerations of fairness; 5) the whole formulation of the Bill leaves much to be desired as regards logical consistency, precision, clarity and comprehensive points of view.

Insofar as opponents of the Bill condemn one or other of these defects, we agree with them; on the other hand, we can by no means approve of their unconditional apologia for the former system. We repeat once more the statement we made previously:

"If legislation cannot decree morality, it can still less pronounce immorality to be legally valid."[a] When we ask *these* opponents (who are not opponents of the church conception and of the other shortcomings we have indicated) on what they base their arguments, they always speak to us about the unfortunate position of the husband and wife tied together against their will. They adopt a eudemonic standpoint, they think only of the two individuals and forget about the *family*. They forget that almost every divorce is the break-up of a family and that even from the purely juridical standpoint the children and their property cannot be made to depend on arbitrary will and its whims. If marriage were not the basis of the family, it would no more be the subject of legislation than, for example, friendship is. Thus, the above-mentioned opponents take into account *only* the individual will or, more correctly, the *arbitrary desire* of the married couple, but pay no attention to the *will of marriage,* the moral substance of this relationship. The legislator, however, should regard himself as a naturalist. He does not *make* the laws, he does not invent them, he only formulates them, expressing in conscious, positive laws the inner laws of spiritual relations. Just as one would have to reproach the legislator for the most unbridled arbitrary behaviour if he replaced the essence of the matter by his own notions, so also the legislator is certainly no less entitled to regard it as the most unbridled arbitrariness if private persons seek to enforce their caprices in opposition to the essence of the matter. No one is forced to contract marriage, but everyone who has done so must be compelled to obey the laws of marriage. A person who contracts marriage does not *create* marriage, does not *invent* it, any more than a swimmer creates or invents the nature and laws of water and gravity. Hence marriage cannot be subordinated to his arbitrary wishes; on the contrary, his arbitrary wishes must be subordinated to marriage. Anyone who arbitrarily breaks a marriage thereby asserts that arbitrariness, *lawlessness, is the law of marriage,* for no rational person will have the presumption to consider his actions as privileged, as concerning *him alone*; on the contrary, he will maintain that his actions are legitimate, that they *concern everybody.* But what do you oppose? You oppose the legislation of arbitrariness, but surely you do not want to raise arbitrariness to the level of a law at the very moment when you are accusing the legislator of arbitrariness.

---

[a] See this volume, p. 275.— *Ed.*

Hegel says: *In itself*, according to the concept, marriage is indissoluble, but *only* in itself, i.e., only according to the concept.[a] This says nothing *specific* about marriage. All moral relations are indissoluble according to *the concept*, as is easily realised if their *truth* is presupposed. A *true* state, a *true* marriage, a *true* friendship are indissoluble, but no state, no marriage, no friendship corresponds fully to its concept, and like real friendship, even in the family, like the real state in world history, so, too, real marriage in the state is *dissoluble*. No moral *existence* corresponds to its *essence* or, at least, it does not *have* to correspond to it. Just as in nature decay and death appear of themselves where an existence has totally ceased to correspond to its function, just as world history decides whether a state has so greatly departed from the idea of the state that it no longer deserves to exist, so, too, the state decides in what circumstances an *existing* marriage has ceased to be a marriage. Divorce is nothing but the statement of the fact that the marriage in question is a *dead* marriage, the existence of which is mere semblance and deception. It is obvious that neither the arbitrary decision of the legislator, nor the arbitrary desire of private persons, but only the *essence of the matter* can decide whether a marriage is dead or not, for it is well known that the *statement* that *death has occurred* depends on the facts, and not on the *desires* of the parties involved. But if, in the case of *physical* death, precise, irrefutable proof is required, is it not clear that the legislator should be allowed to register the fact of a *moral* death only on the basis of the most indubitable symptoms, since preserving the life of moral relationships is not only his right, but also his *duty*, the duty of his self-preservation!

Certainty that the *conditions* under which the *existence* of a moral relationship no longer corresponds to its *essence* are correctly registered, without preconceived opinions, in accordance with the level attained by science and with the generally accepted views—this certainty, of course, can only exist if the law is the conscious expression of the popular will, and therefore originates with it and is created by it. We will add a few words about making divorce easier or more difficult: Can you consider a natural object to be healthy, strong, truly organised, if every external impact, every injury, is capable of destroying it? Would you not feel insulted if someone put forward as an axiom that your friendship could not withstand the slightest accident and *must* be dissolved by

---

[a] G. W. F. Hegel, *Grundlinien der Philosophie des Rechts*. Addendum to § 163.— *Ed.*

any caprice? In regard to marriage, the legislator can only establish when it is *permissible* to dissolve it, that is to say, when in its essence it is *already dissolved.* Juridical dissolution of marriage can only be the registering of its internal dissolution. The standpoint of the legislator is the standpoint of necessity. The legislator, consequently, *gives due honour* to marriage, acknowledges its profound moral essence, if he considers it strong enough to withstand a multitude of collisions without harm to itself. Indulgence of the wishes of individuals would turn into harshness towards the essence of the individuals, towards their moral reason, which is embodied in moral relationships.

Finally, we can only term it undue haste when from many quarters the accusation of *hypocrisy* is levelled against countries with *strict laws on divorce,* among which the Rhine Province is *proud* to be included. Only people whose field of vision does not go beyond the moral corruption around them can dare to make such accusations. In the Rhine Province, for example, these accusations are considered ridiculous and are regarded at most as proof that even the *idea* of moral relationships can be lost, and every moral fact regarded as a *fairy-tale* or a falsehood. This is the direct result of laws that are not dictated by respect for human beings; it is a mistake which is not done away with by contempt for the material nature of man becoming contempt for his ideal nature and blind obedience to a super-moral and supernatural authority being demanded instead of conscious subordination to moral and natural forces.

Written on December 18, 1842

First published in the *Rheinische Zeitung* No. 353, December 19, 1842

Printed according to the newspaper

[THE BAN ON THE *LEIPZIGER ALLGEMEINE ZEITUNG*[115]]

THE BAN ON THE *LEIPZIGER ALLGEMEINE ZEITUNG* WITHIN THE PRUSSIAN STATE

[*Rheinische Zeitung* No. 1, January 1, 1843]

Cologne, December 31. The German press begins the New Year with *apparently* gloomy prospects. The ban that has just been imposed on the *Leipziger Allgemeine Zeitung* in the states of Prussia is surely a sufficiently convincing refutation of all the complacent dreams of gullible people about big *concessions* in the future. Since the *Leipziger Allgemeine Zeitung,* which is published under *Saxon censorship,* is being banned for its discussion of Prussian affairs, this at the same time puts an end to the hope of an *uncensored* discussion of our own internal affairs. This is a factual consequence which no one will deny.

The main accusations levelled against the *Leipziger Allgemeine Zeitung* were approximately the following:

"It continually reports rumours, at least half of which subsequently prove to be false. Moreover, it does not keep to the facts, but pries for hidden motives. And no matter how false its conclusions in this respect often are, it invariably voices them with all the ardour of infallibility and often with the most malicious passion. Its whole activity is unsteady, 'indiscreet' and 'immature'; in a word, it is bad activity."

Supposing all these accusations were well founded, are they accusations against the *arbitrary character* of the *Leipziger Allgemeine Zeitung,* or are they not rather accusations against the *necessary character* of the young *popular press* that is only just coming into being? Is it a question only of the existence of a *certain kind* of press or is it a question of the non-existence of a *real* press, i.e., a *popular press?*

The French, English and every kind of press began in the same way as the German press, and the same reproaches have been deserved by and made against each of them. The press is, and should be, nothing but the *public,* admittedly often "passionate, exaggerated and mistaken, expression of the daily thoughts and feelings of a people that really thinks as a people". Like life itself, therefore, it is always in a state of becoming, and never of maturity. It is rooted in the people and honestly sympathises with all the latter's hopes and fears, love and hatred, joys and sorrows. What it has learned by listening in hope and fear, it proclaims loudly, and it delivers its own judgment on it, vigorously, passionately, one-sidedly, as prompted by its feelings and thoughts at the given moment. What is erroneous in the facts or judgments it puts forward today, it will itself refute tomorrow. It represents the real "naturally arising" policy, which its opponents love so much in other cases.

The reproaches which in recent days have been continuously levelled against the young "press" cancel each other out. See, it is said, what a firm, steady, definite policy the *English* and *French* newspapers pursue. They are based on real life, their views are the views of an *existing, quite mature* force. They impose no doctrines on the people, but are themselves the real doctrines of the people and its parties. You, however, do not voice the thoughts and interests of the people, you only *manufacture* them or, rather, you foist them on the people. You create the party spirit, you are not created by it. Thus, on one occasion, the press is blamed because there are *no* political parties, on another occasion it is accused of wanting to *remedy* this defect and create political parties. But it is self-evident that where the press is *young*, the popular spirit also is *young*, and the *daily* public political thinking of an only just awakening popular spirit will be less mature, more shapeless and hasty than that of the popular spirit which has become great, strong and self-confident in the course of political struggles. Above all, a people which is only just awakening to political consciousness is less concerned about the *factual* correctness of an occurrence than about its *moral* soul, through which it has its effect. Whether fact or fiction, it remains an embodiment of the thoughts, fears and hopes of the people, a *truthful* fairy-tale. The people see this, their own nature, reflected in the nature of their press, and if they did not see this, they would regard the press as something *unessential* and not worthy of sympathy, for the people do not allow themselves to be deceived. Hence, although the young press may daily compromise itself, may allow evil passions to penetrate it, the people see in it their own condition and they know that, despite all the poison which malice or lack of understanding introduces, its essence always remains true and pure, and in its ever flowing, ever swelling stream, the poison becomes truth and a healing medicine. The people know that their press has shouldered their sins, that it is prepared to suffer humiliation for the sake of the people and that for their glory, renouncing distinction, self-satisfaction and irrefutability, it represents the rose of the moral spirit amid the thorns of the present.

We must, therefore, regard all the reproaches levelled against the *Leipziger Allgemeine Zeitung* as reproaches against the young popular press, hence against the real press, for it stands to reason that the press cannot become real without passing through the necessary stages of its development which arise from its inherent nature. We must, however, declare that to condemn the popular press is to condemn the political spirit of the people. Nevertheless, at the beginning of this article we described the prospects for the German press as *apparently* gloomy. And that is so, for the struggle against something that exists is *the first form* of its recognition, its reality and its power. And only struggle can convince both the government and the people, as well as the press itself, that the press has a real and necessary right to existence. Only struggle can show whether this right to existence is a concession or a necessity, an illusion or a truth.

THE *KÖLNISCHE ZEITUNG* AND THE BAN ON THE *LEIPZIGER ALLGEMEINE ZEITUNG*

[*Rheinische Zeitung* No. 4, January 4, 1843]

Cologne, January 3. In its issue of December 31, the *Kölnische Zeitung* printed an article dated "Leipzig, 27th" by its correspondent, which reported the ban on the *Leipziger Allgemeine Zeitung* almost exultantly. Yet the Cabinet Order on the ban, contained in the issue of the *Staats-Zeitung* received here yesterday, is dated December 28. The riddle is solved by simply noting the fact that the news of the ban on the *Leipziger Allgemeine Zeitung* was received with the post here on December 31 and the *Kölnische Zeitung* considered it proper to *fabricate* not only the correspondence, but also the correspondent, and present its *own voice* as coming from the good city of Leipzig. The "mercantile" fantasy of the *Kölnische Zeitung* was so "adroit" as to confuse concepts. It transferred the residence of the *Kölnische Zeitung* to Leipzig, because it had become impossible for the residence of the *Leipziger Zeitung* to be in Cologne. If the editors of the *Kölnische Zeitung*, even after cooler reflection, had wanted to defend the exercise of their fantasy as sober, factual truth, we should be compelled to report, in connection with the mysterious correspondence from Leipzig, yet another *fact,* which

"goes beyond all bounds of decency and even in our country" would seem "to every moderate and reasonable person to be an incomprehensible indiscretion".

As for the ban on the *Leipziger Allgemeine Zeitung* itself, we have already expressed our view. We have not disputed, as if they were sheer inventions, the shortcomings for which the *Leipziger Allgemeine Zeitung* has been condemned. But we have maintained that they are shortcomings which arise from the very *nature* of the *popular press* itself and therefore must be tolerated as arising in the course of its development, if people are at all willing to tolerate its course of development.

The *Leipziger Allgemeine Zeitung* is not the *entire* German popular press, but it is a necessary component part of it. In the natural development of the popular press, each of the different elements which determine the nature of this press must first of all discover for itself its *specific* form of development. Hence the whole body of the popular press will be divided into different newspapers with different complementary characteristics, and if, for example, the predominant interest of one is in political science, that of another will be in political practice, or if the predominant interest of one is in *new* ideas, that of another will be in *new* facts. Only if the elements of the popular press are given the opportunity of unhampered, independent and *one-sided* development and of achieving independent existence in separate organs, can a "good" popular press be formed, i.e., one which harmoniously combines all the *true* elements of the *popular spirit,* so that the true moral spirit will be entirely present in each newspaper, just as the fragrance and soul of the rose is present in each of its petals. But for the press to achieve its purpose it is above all necessary that it should not have any kind of purpose prescribed for it from outside, and that it should be accorded the recognition that is given even to a plant, namely, that it has its own *inherent laws,* which it cannot and should not arbitrarily evade.

THE GOOD AND THE BAD PRESS

[*Rheinische Zeitung* No. 6, January 6, 1843]

Cologne, January 5. We have already had to hear *in abstracto* a great deal about the difference between the "*good*" and the "*bad*" press. Let us illustrate this difference now with an example.

The *Elberfelder Zeitung* of January 5, in an article dated from Elberfeld, describes itself as a "good press". The *Elberfelder Zeitung* of January 5 carries the following report:

> "*Berlin*, December 30. The ban on the *Leipziger Allgemeine Zeitung* has on the whole made only a *slight* impression here."

On the other hand, the *Düsseldorfer Zeitung*, agreeing with the *Rheinische Zeitung*, reports:

> "*Berlin*, January 1. The unconditional ban on the *Leipziger Allgemeine Zeitung* is causing a *very great* sensation here, since it was very eagerly read by the Berliners", etc.

Which press then, the "good" or the "bad", is the *"true"* press? Which expresses actual reality, and which expresses it as it *would like* it to be? Which expresses public opinion, and which distorts it? Which, therefore, deserves the *confidence of the state?*

The explanation given by the *Kölnische Zeitung*[116] does little to satisfy us. In its reply to our remark about its reporting "almost exultantly" the ban on the *Leipziger Allgemeine Zeitung*, it confines itself not only to the part concerning *dates*, but to a misprint. The *Kölnische Zeitung* itself must know very well that the sentence: "The riddle is solved by simply noting the fact that the news of the ban on the *Leipziger Allgemeine Zeitung* was received with the post here on December 31", should have read "on December 30" and did not read so only because of a misprint. On December 30 at noon, as we can prove if necessary, the *Rheinische Zeitung*, and therefore probably also the *Kölnische Zeitung*, received this news through the local post-office.

REPLY TO THE ATTACK OF A "MODERATE" NEWSPAPER[a]

[*Rheinische Zeitung* No. 8, January 8, 1843]

Cologne, January 7. A *moderate* Rhenish newspaper, as the Augsburg *Allgemeine Zeitung* in its diplomatic language calls it, i.e., a newspaper of moderate forces, of very moderate character and of the most moderate understanding, has distorted our assertion that "the *Leipziger Allgemeine Zeitung* is a necessary component part of the German popular press", into the assertion that *lying* is a necessary part of the press.[117] We will not take undue offence at

---

[a] The *Rhein- und Mosel-Zeitung.—Ed.*

this moderate newspaper extracting a single sentence from our argument and not considering that the ideas put forward in the article in question as well as in an earlier one are worthy of its lofty and honourable attention. Just as we cannot demand of someone that he should jump out of his own skin, so we must not demand that an individual or party should jump out of its spiritual skin, and venture on a *salto mortale* beyond the limits of its mental horizon; least of all can we demand this of a party which takes its narrow-mindedness for holiness. Therefore, we will not discuss what that inhabitant of the intellectual *realm of mediocrity* should have done in order to refute us, but will only discuss its actual deeds.

First of all, the old sins of the *Leipziger Allgemeine Zeitung* are enumerated: its attitude to the Hanover events,[118] its party polemic against Catholicism (*hinc illae lacrimae!*[a] Would our lady friend regard the same behaviour, only in the opposite direction, as one of the mortal sins of the *Münchener politische Blätter?*), its bits of gossip, etc., etc. We recall, in this connection, some lines from Alphonse Karr's magazine *Les Guêpes*. M. Guizot, the story goes, calls M. Thiers a traitor, and M. Thiers calls M. Guizot a traitor, and, unfortunately, both are right. If all German newspapers of the old style wanted to reproach one another for their past, the examination of the case would be reduced to the formal question whether they sinned through what they did or through what they did *not* do. We are prepared to grant our lady friend the innocent advantage over the *Leipziger Allgemeine Zeitung* that she has not only not led a bad life, but that she has shown no signs of life at all.

Meanwhile, the article of ours which is incriminated spoke not of the past, but of the *present* character of the *Leipziger Allgemeine Zeitung*, although it stands to reason that we would have no less serious objections against a ban on the *Elberfelder Zeitung*, the *Hamburger Correspondent*, or the *Rhein- und Mosel-Zeitung* published in Koblenz, since the *legal position* is not altered by the moral character or even the political and religious opinions of individuals. On the contrary, the *lack of rights* of the press is beyond all doubt once its *existence* is made dependent on its *frame of mind*. Up to now, indeed, there has been no legal code or court of law for a frame of mind.

The "moderate" newspaper accuses the *last phase* of the *Leipziger Allgemeine Zeitung* of false information, distortions and lies,

---

[a] Hence those tears! (Terence, *Andria*, Act I, Scene 1.) — *Ed.*

and accuses us with righteous indignation of regarding *lying* as a necessary element of the *popular* press. Suppose we actually admitted this frightful conclusion, suppose we actually maintained that *lying* is a necessary element of the popular press, in particular of the *German* popular press? We do not mean a *lying frame of mind,* lying in the spiritual sense, but *lying in regard to facts,* lying in the material sense. Stone him! Stone him! our Christian-minded newspaper would cry. Stone him! Stone him! the whole chorus would join in. But let us not be too hasty, let us take the world as it is, let us not be ideologists—and we can certify that our lady friend is no ideologist. Let our "moderate" newspaper cast a critical eye over its own columns. Does it not, like the *Preussische Staats-Zeitung,* like all the German newspapers and all the world's newspapers, daily report false information from *Paris,* gossip about imminent ministerial changes in France, fables that some Paris newspaper has concocted, which the following day, or even an hour later, will be refuted? Or perhaps the *Rhein- und Mosel-Zeitung* presumes that *lying in regard to facts* is a necessary element of columns headed England, France, Spain or Turkey, but a damnable crime, meriting the death penalty, in columns headed Germany or Prussia? Whence this double set of weights and measures? Whence this dual view of truth? Why should one and the same newspaper be allowed the frivolous light-heartedness of a gossip-monger in one column, and have to display the sober irrefutability of an official organ in another column? It is obviously because for German newspapers there should exist only a French, English, Turkish, Spanish time, but no German time, only a *German timelessness.* But should not rather those newspapers be praised, and praised *from the state point of view,* which wrest from *foreign countries* and win for the *Fatherland* the attention, the feverish interest and the dramatic tension which accompany every *coming into being,* and above all the *coming into being of contemporary history!* Suppose even that these newspapers have aroused dissatisfaction, ill humour! It is, after all, *German* dissatisfaction, *German* ill humour that they arouse; after all, they have given back to the state minds that had turned away from it, even though at first these minds are excited and ill-humoured! And they have aroused not only dissatisfaction and ill humour, they have also aroused fears and hopes, joy and sorrow, they have aroused, above all, real *sympathy* for the state, they have made the state *close to the heart,* a *domestic affair* of its members. Instead of St. Petersburg, London or Paris, they have made Berlin, Dresden, Hanover, etc., the capital cities on the map of the German political mind, a feat more

glorious than the transfer of the world capital from Rome to Byzantium.

And if the German and Prussian newspapers which have set
themselves the task of making Germany and Prussia the main
interest of the Germans and Prussians, the task of transforming
the mysterious, priestly nature of the state into a clear-cut, secular
nature accessible to all and belonging to all, and of making the state
part of the flesh and blood of its citizens; if these newspapers are inferior to the French and English newspapers as regards
factual truth, if their behaviour is often unskilful and fanciful,
bear in mind that the German knows his state only from *hearsay*,
that *closed doors* are not at all *transparent to the eye*, that a *secret*
state organisation is not at all a *public* state organisation, and do
not ascribe to the newspapers what is the defect of the state
alone, a defect which precisely these newspapers are seeking to
remedy.

Therefore, we repeat once more: *"The 'Leipziger Allgemeine
Zeitung' is a necessary component part of the German popular press."* It
has primarily satisfied immediate interest in *political fact*, we have
primarily satisfied interest in *political thought*. In this connection, it
stands to reason that fact does not preclude thought any more
than thought precludes fact; but it is a matter here of the
predominant character, the *distinguishing feature*.

REPLY TO THE *DENUNCIATION*
BY A "NEIGHBOUR" NEWSPAPER

[*Rheinische Zeitung* No. 10, January 10, 1843]

Cologne, January 9. It would be quite contrary to the nature of
things if the *"good"* press everywhere did not try now to win its
knightly spurs by attacking us, headed by the Augsburg
prophetess *Hulda*,[119] whom, in response to her repeated challenge,
we shall presently take to task. Today we shall deal with our
invalid neighbour, the most worthy *Kölnische Zeitung! Toujours
perdrix!*[a]

First of all "something preliminary" or a "preliminary something", a reminder with which we wish to preface today's *denunciation* by this newspaper to make it intelligible, a most delightful
little story of the way in which the *Kölnische Zeitung* tries to gain
the *"respect"* of the government, how it asserts "true freedom" in
contrast to "arbitrariness" and knows how to set itself "bounds"

---

[a] Always the same! — *Ed.*

from within. The kind reader will recall that No. 4 of the *Rheinische Zeitung* directly accused the *Kölnische Zeitung* of having *fabricated* its correspondence from Leipzig, which announced almost exultantly the much discussed ban. The reader will recall that at the same time the *Kölnische Zeitung* was given the friendly advice to refrain from any serious attempt to defend the genuineness of that document, with the definite warning that otherwise we should be compelled "in connection with the mysterious correspondence from Leipzig" to make public yet another unpleasant *fact*. The kind reader will also recall the timid, evasive reply of the *Kölnische Zeitung* of January 5, our corrective rejoinder in No. 6, and the "patient silence" which the *Kölnische Zeitung* thought best to observe in regard to this. The fact referred to is the following: the *Kölnische Zeitung* found that the ban on the *Leipziger Allgemeine Zeitung* was justified because that newspaper published a report which

"goes beyond all bounds of decency and even in our country must seem to every moderate and reasonable person to be an incomprehensible *indiscretion*".

It is obvious that what was meant was the publication of Herwegh's letter.[120] It might perhaps have been possible to agree with this opinion of the *Kölnische Zeitung* if only the *Kölnische Zeitung* a few days earlier had not itself *wanted* to publish Herwegh's letter, and only failed to do so because it came up against "bounds" imposed from "*outside*", which thwarted its good intention.

In saying this we by no means want to accuse the *Kölnische Zeitung* of a disloyal yearning, but we must leave it to the public to judge whether it is a *comprehensible discretion*, or whether it is not, on the contrary, a violation of all the bounds of *decency* and *public morals*, when one accuses one's neighbour, as if it were a crime deserving the death penalty, of the very action that one was oneself about to perform, and which only failed to be one's *own* action because of an *external* obstacle. After this explanation, it will be understandable why the bad conscience of the *Kölnische Zeitung* has led it to reply to us today with a *denunciation*.[121] It says:

"It is asserted there" (in the *Rheinische Zeitung*) "that the exceptionally sharp, almost insulting, at any rate unpleasant, tone which the press adopts towards Prussia has *no other* basis than the desire to draw to oneself the attention of the government and to awaken it. For, according to the *Rheinische Zeitung*, the people has already far outgrown the existing state forms, which suffer from a peculiar hollowness; the people, like the press, has *no* faith in these institutions and still less in the possibility of their development from within."

The *Kölnische Zeitung* accompanies these words with the following exclamation:

"Is it not astounding that side by side with such statements complaints are still heard about inadequate freedom of the press? Can one demand more than the freedom to tell the government to its face that 'all state institutions are old rubbish, unsuitable even as a transition to something better'."

First of all we should come to an agreement about how to quote. The author of the article[122] in the *Rheinische Zeitung* raises the question: what is the explanation for this sharp tone of the press precisely in relation to Prussia? He replies: "*I think* that the reason is to be found chiefly in the following." He does not assert, as the *Kölnische Zeitung falsely attributes* to him, that there is *no other* reason; on the contrary, he gives his view merely as *his* own belief, as his *personal* opinion. The author further admits, about which the *Kölnische Zeitung* says nothing, that

"the upsurge in 1840 partially penetrated state forms, endeavouring to imbue them with a full content and life".

Nevertheless, it is felt

"that the popular spirit passes them by, hardly grazing them, and that it is almost *unable as yet to recognise* them or *take* them *into account* even as a transition to further development".

The author continues:

"We leave open the question whether these forms have a right to exist or not; it is enough that the people, like the press, has no *complete* faith in the state institutions, still less in the possibility of their *development from within and from below.*"

The *Kölnische Zeitung* changes the words "has no *complete* faith" into "has *no* faith", and in the last part of the sentence quoted above it leaves out the words "and from below", thus substantially altering the meaning.

The press, our author continues, *therefore* constantly addressed itself to the *government,* because

"it seemed to be still a matter of the forms themselves, within which the government could be told freely, openly and weightily of the justified moral will of the people, its ardent desires, and its needs".

Summing up these quotations, does the article in question assert, as the *Kölnische Zeitung* alleges it tells "the government to its face", "*that all state institutions are old rubbish, unsuitable even as a transition to something better*"?

Is it a question here of *all* state institutions? It is a question only of the state forms in which "the will of the people" could be "freely, openly and weightily" expressed. And what until recently were these *state forms?* Obviously, only the *provincial estates.* Has the people had special faith in these provincial estates? Has the people expected a great popular development out of them? Did loyal Bülow-Cummerow consider them a *true* expression of the people's will? But not only the people and the press, the *government* as well has admitted that we still *lack* state forms themselves, or would it, without such an admission, have had any reason for setting up a *new* state form in the shape of the "commissions"[123]? That, however, the commissions, too, have not been satisfactory in their present form, is a thing that we have not been alone in asserting; the same opinion has been expressed in the *Kölnische Zeitung* by a *member of a commission.*

The further assertion that the *state forms,* precisely as *forms,* are still in contrast to their content, and that the spirit of the people does not feel "at home" in them as in *its own* forms, does not recognise them as the forms of its own life, this assertion only repeats what has been said by many Prussian and foreign newspapers, but chiefly by *conservative* writers, namely, that the *bureaucracy* is still too powerful, that not the whole state, but only part of it, the "government", leads a state life in the proper sense of the term. As to how far present state forms are suitable, partly for themselves becoming imbued with living content, partly for incorporating the supplementary state forms, the *Kölnische Zeitung* should have sought the answer to this question in the articles in which we examine the provincial estates and the provincial commissions in relation to the whole system of our state organisation. There it would have found information which even its wisdom could grasp.

"We do not demand that in the representation of the people actually existing differences should be left out of account. On the contrary, we demand that one should proceed from the actual differences created and conditioned by the internal structure of the state." "We demand only the *consistent and comprehensive development of the fundamental institutions of Prussia,* we demand that the real organic life of the state should not be suddenly abandoned in order to sink back into unreal, mechanical, subordinated, non-state spheres of life" (*Rheinische Zeitung,* 1842, No. 345)[a].

But what does the worthy *Kölnische Zeitung* put into our mouths? — "that all *state institutions* are *old rubbish,* unsuitable even as a transition to something better"! It almost seems as if the *Kölnische Zeitung* thinks it can make up for the deficiency of its *own courage* by ascribing to others the impudent creations of its cowardly but malicious fantasy.

---

[a] See this volume, pp. 296 and 297.— *Ed.*

THE DENUNCIATION OF THE *KÖLNISCHE ZEITUNG* AND THE POLEMIC OF THE *RHEIN- UND MOSEL-ZEITUNG*

[*Rheinische Zeitung* No. 13, January 13, 1843]

Cologne, January 11

"Votre front à mes yeux montre peu d'allégresse!
Serait-ce ma présence, Eraste, qui vous blesse?
Qu'est-ce donc? qu'avez-vous? et sur quels déplaisirs,
Lorsque vous me voyez, poussez-vous des soupirs?" [a]

These words apply in the first place to our "lady neighbour of *Cologne*"! The *Kölnische Zeitung* prefers not to expand on the theme of its "*alleged denunciation*"; it drops this *main point* and complains only that on this occasion the "editorial board" has been involved in the polemic not in the most pleasant manner. But, dear lady neighbour, if the *Kölnische Zeitung* correspondent identifies one of our Berlin reports with the *Rheinische Zeitung*, why should not the *Rheinische Zeitung* be allowed to identify with the *Kölnische Zeitung* the Rhine report published in reply by the *Kölnische Zeitung*? Now, *ad vocem* the *fact*:

"It" (the *Rheinische Zeitung*) "accuses *us* not of any *fact*, but of an *intention!*" [124]

We accuse the *Kölnische Zeitung* not merely of an intention, but of a *fact of that intention*. Owing to *accidental external circumstances*, a fact, the acceptance of Herwegh's letter for publication, was transformed for the *Kölnische Zeitung* into an intention, although its intention had already been transformed into a fact. Every fact which has been thwarted is reduced to a mere intention, but does this make it any less a fact in the eyes of the court? At any rate it would be a very peculiar virtue that found justification for its actions in accidental circumstances which prevented their realisation and made them *not* a deed, but the mere intention of a deed. But our loyal lady neighbour puts a question not, it is true, to the *Rheinische Zeitung*, which, it has an awkward suspicion, will not be so easily "at a loss" for a reply because of its "decency and conscientiousness", but to

---

[a] "Uneasy your countenance seems to my eyes!
Because of my presence, Eraste, are you hurt?
What then is the matter? and what the distaste
That when you behold me you utter such sighs?"
(J. B. Molière, *Les Fâcheux*, Act I, Scene 5.) — *Ed.*

"that small section of the public which perhaps is not yet quite clear how far the *suspicions*" (it ought to say: defence against suspicions) "of this newspaper deserve to be believed".

The question the *Kölnische Zeitung* puts is: how does the *Rheinische Zeitung* know

"that we did not combine with this intention" (i.e., the intention to publish Herwegh's letter) "the other intention as well" (*signo haud probato*[a]), "namely, to add the rebuke which the childish petulance of the author deserved?"

But how does the *Kölnische Zeitung* know what was the *intention* of the *Leipziger Allgemeine Zeitung* in publishing Herwegh's letter? Why, for example, could it not have had the harmless intention of being the first to publish an item of news? Or why not, perhaps, the loyal intention of simply submitting the letter to the judgment of public opinion? We should like to relate an anecdote to our lady neighbour. In Rome, the publication of the Koran is prohibited. But a cunning Italian found a way out of the situation. He published a *refutation* of the Koran, i.e., a book, the title page of which bore the heading "Refutation of the Koran", but after the title page it contained a simple reprint of the Koran. Have not all heretics employed such a ruse? Was not Vanini burned at the stake in spite of the fact that in his *Theatrum mundi*,[b] while propagating atheism, he carefully and ostentatiously brought out all the arguments against it? Did not even Voltaire in his book *La Bible enfin expliquée* preach unbelief in the text and belief in the notes, and did anyone believe in the purifying power of these notes? But, our worthy lady neighbour concludes,

"if we had this intention, could our acceptance for publication of an already well-known document be put on a par with the original publication?"

But, dearest lady neighbour, the *Leipziger Allgemeine Zeitung*, too, only published a letter that had already been circulated in many copies. "In faith, my lord, you are too wilful-blame."[c]

The papal encyclical *ex cathedra*[d] of August 15, 1832, the day of the Assumption of the Virgin Mary, states:

"It is madness (*deliramentum*) to assert that every man is entitled to *freedom of conscience; freedom of the press* cannot be sufficiently abhorred."

This pronouncement transfers us from Cologne to Koblenz, to the "moderate" newspaper, the *Rhein- und Mosel-Zeitung*. After the

---

[a] In no way proved.— *Ed.*

[b] L. Vanini, *Amphitheatrum aeternae.*— *Ed.*

[c] W. Shakespeare, *King Henry IV*, Part One, Act III, Scene 1.— *Ed.*

[d] Encyclical issued from the throne of St. Peter, binding on the whole church as incontestable truth.— *Ed.*

quotation given above, that newspaper's woeful outcry against our defence of press freedom becomes understandable and justified, however strange it is after that to hear also that she would like to be included "among the very zealous friends of the press". From the paper's "moderate" columns today have sprung forth not, it is true, two lions but a lion's skin and a lion's cowl,[125] to which we shall pay due attention from the point of view of natural history. No. 1 expresses its feelings, *inter alia,* as follows:

"On its part" (i.e., of the *Rheinische Zeitung*) "the struggle is conducted in such a loyal way that from the outset it assures us that, for the sake of the *'legal position'* which is so dear to its heart, it would protest even against a ban on the *Rhein- und Mosel-Zeitung.* This assurance would be in an equal degree flattering and soothing for us but for the fact that in the same breath there happened to escape from the mouth of the knight who champions *every* freedom of the press that has been violated a *vilification* of the *Münchener historisch-politische Blätter,* which is well known to have been *long ago actually banned here.*"

It is strange that at the very moment when the *Rhein- und Mosel-Zeitung* pronounces sentence on newspapers for lying in regard to *facts,* it itself lies in regard to facts. The passage referred to reads literally as follows:

"First of all, the old sins of the *Leipziger Allgemeine Zeitung* are enumerated: its attitude to the Hanover events, its party polemic against Catholicism (*hinc illae lacrimae!*). Would our lady friend regard the same behaviour, only in the opposite direction, as one of the mortal sins of the *Münchener politische Blätter?*"[a]

In these lines the *Münchener politische Blätter* declares a "party polemic" against Protestantism. Did we thereby justify the ban? Could we have wanted to justify it by finding again in the *Münchener politische Blätter*—"only in the opposite direction"— "*the same* behaviour" that in the case of the *Leipziger Allgemeine Zeitung* we said gave *no* grounds for a ban? On the contrary! We appealed to the conscience of the *Rhein- und Mosel-Zeitung,* asking whether one and the same behaviour justified a ban when coming from one side, but did not justify a ban when coming from the other side! We asked it, therefore, whether it pronounced its sentence on the behaviour itself or rather only on the trend of the behaviour. And the *Rhein- und Mosel-Zeitung* has replied to our question, saying in effect that it does not, as *we* do, condemn religious party polemics, but *only the kind* of party polemic which has the temerity to be *Protestant.* If, at the very time when we were defending the *Leipziger Allgemeine Zeitung* against the ban "that had just been imposed" on it, we, *together* with the *Rhein- und Mosel-Zeitung,* mentioned the party polemic of the *Leipziger All-*

---

[a] See this volume, p. 316.— *Ed.*

gemeine Zeitung against Catholicism, had we not the right *without* the *Rhein- und Mosel-Zeitung* to mention the party polemic of the *Münchener politische Blätter*, which had been "banned long ago"? To the "small degree of publicness or the state", the "immaturity" of a "daily", public and inexperienced "political thinking", the nature of "contemporary history that is coming into being", all grounds on which we excused the newspapers lying in respect of *facts*, No. 1 kindly added a *new* one, namely, the factual *intellectual weakness* of a large part of the German press. The *Rhein- und Mosel-Zeitung* has proved by its own example that *incorrect* thinking inevitably and unintentionally produces *incorrect* facts, and therefore distortions and lies.

We come now to No. 2, to the lion's *cowl*, for the additional grounds of No. 1 undergo here a more extensive process of confusion. The lion's cowl first of all informs the public about the state of its feelings, which is of no great interest. It says that it had expected "an outburst of fury", but that we gave only "a *genteel rejoinder,* apparently lightly tossed off". Its thanks for this "unexpected leniency" are, however, alloyed with a vexatious doubt

"whether this unexpected leniency is in fact a sign of generosity or, on the contrary, the result of spiritual discomfort and exhaustion".

We do not intend to explain to our pious gentleman how *clerical comfort* could, indeed, be a reason for *spiritual discomfort*; we will pass on at once to the "content of the rejoinder in question". The pious gentleman admits he "unfortunately cannot conceal" that, according to his "extremely moderate understanding", the *Rheinische Zeitung* "merely seeks to conceal its embarrassment behind empty wrangling over words". And so as not, for a moment, to allow any semblance of "*hypocritical* meekness or modesty", the pious gentleman demonstrates his "extremely moderate" understanding with the most convincing, most irrefutable proofs. He begins as follows:

"'The old sins of the *Leipziger Allgemeine Zeitung*: its attitude to the Hanover events, its party polemic against Catholicism, its bits of gossip', etc., cannot, of course, be denied; but—our excellent pupil of the great philosopher Hegel supposes—*these offences are fully excused* by the fact that *other* newspapers *also* are guilty of similar transgressions (which is tantamount to saying that a scoundrel brought *before the court* could not justify himself better than by referring to the base tricks of his numerous comrades still at liberty)."

Where have we asserted that "the old sins of the *Leipziger Allgemeine Zeitung* are fully *excused* by the fact that *other* newspapers *also* are guilty of similar transgressions"? Where have we even merely *tried* to "excuse" these old sins? Our actual argument, which is easily distinguished from its reflection in the mirror of the "extremely moderate understanding", was as follows: First of all the *Rhein- und Mosel-Zeitung* enumerates the "old sins" of the *Leipziger Allgemeine Zeitung*. We specify these sins, and then we continue:

> "If *all* German newspapers of the old style wanted to reproach one another for their past, the examination of the case would be reduced to the formal question whether they sinned through what they did or through what they did *not* do. We are prepared to grant our lady friend, the *Rhein- und Mosel-Zeitung*, the innocent advantage over the *Leipziger Allgemeine Zeitung* that she has not only not led a bad life, but that she has shown no signs of life at all." [a]

Thus, we do not say "*other newspapers also*", we say "*all* German newspapers of the older style", among which we expressly include the *Rhein- und Mosel-Zeitung*, cannot excuse themselves *entirely* by references to one another but that they can *rightly* address the same reproaches to themselves. The *Rhein- und Mosel-Zeitung* could lay claim only to the doubtful advantage of having sinned by what it did *not* do, thus contrasting its sins of *omission* to the sins of *commission* of the *Leipziger Allgemeine Zeitung*. We can explain to the *Rhein- und Mosel-Zeitung* its passive badness by a fresh example. It now vents its fanatic spleen on the defunct *Leipziger Allgemeine Zeitung*, whereas during the lifetime of the latter it published extracts from it instead of refuting it. The comparison by which the "extremely moderate understanding" tries to clarify our argument requires a small, but essential correction. It should have spoken not about *one* scoundrel who excuses himself *before the court* by referring to the other scoundrels still at liberty, but about *two* scoundrels, of whom the one who has not reformed and has not been imprisoned, triumphs over the other, who has been put in prison, *although* he has reformed.

> "In addition," the "extremely moderate understanding" continues, "in addition, 'the legal position is not altered by the moral character or even the political and religious opinions of individuals'; *consequently,* even a totally bad newspaper, precisely *because it is merely bad,* has a *right* to that *bad* existence (just as everything else which is bad in the world, precisely because of its bad existence, cannot be disputed its *right* to exist)."

It seems that the pious gentleman wants to convince us not only that he never studied any of the "great" philosophers, but that he did not even study any of the "lesser" ones.

The passage, which in the fantastic exposition of our friend acquired such wonderfully distorted and confused features,

---

[a] See this volume, p. 316.— *Ed.*

read—before it was refracted through the prism of the "extremely moderate understanding"—as follows:

> "Meanwhile, the article of ours which is incriminated spoke not of the past, but
> of the *present* character of the *Leipziger Allgemeine Zeitung*, although it stands to
> reason that we would have no less serious objections against a ban, etc., etc., on the
> *Rhein- und Mosel-Zeitung* published in Koblenz, since the *legal position* is not altered
> by the moral character or even the political and religious opinions of individuals.
> On the contrary, the *lack of rights* of the press is beyond all doubt once its *existence*
> is made dependent on its *frame of mind*. *Up to now, indeed, there has been no legal code
> or court of law for a frame of mind.*"[a]

We merely assert, therefore, that a person cannot be imprisoned, or deprived of his property or any other *legal* right because
of his moral character or because of his political or *religious*
opinions. The latter assertion seems particularly to excite our
religious-minded friend. We demand that the *legal position* of a
bad being should be unassailable, not because it is bad, but insofar
as its badness remains within a *frame of mind*, for which there is *no
court of law* and *no legal code*. Thus we contrast a *bad frame of mind*, for
which no *court of law* exists, to *bad deeds*, which, if they are
illegal, come within the scope of the *court* and the *laws* punishing
such deeds. We assert, therefore, that a bad being, despite its
badness, has the right to exist, as long as it is not *illegal*. We do not
assert, as our pseudo-echo reports, that a bad being, precisely
"because it is merely bad", "cannot be disputed its right to exist".
On the contrary, our worthy well-wisher must have realised that
we dispute that he and the *Rhein- und Mosel-Zeitung* have the right
to be *bad*, and therefore we are trying as far as possible to make
them *good*, without considering we are entitled on that account to
attack the "*legal position*" of the *Rhein- und Mosel-Zeitung* and its
shield-bearer. Here is yet another example of the "measure of
understanding" of our pious zealot:

> "If, however, the organ 'of political thought' goes so far as to assert that
> newspapers such as the *Leipziger Allgemeine Zeitung* (and especially, it stands to
> reason, such as itself, the *Rheinische Zeitung*) 'should rather be praised, and
> praised *from the state point of view*', since even supposing they have aroused
> *dissatisfaction* and ill humour, it is, after all, German *dissatisfaction* and *German ill
> humour* that they have aroused, then we cannot fail to express our doubts about this
> strange 'service to the German Fatherland'."

In the original, the passage quoted reads:

> "But should not rather those newspapers be praised, and praised *from the state
> point of view*, which wrest from *foreign countries* and win for the *Fatherland* the
> attention, the feverish interest and the dramatic tension which accompany every

---

[a] See this volume, p. 316.— *Ed.*

coming into being, and above all the *coming into being of contemporary history!* *Suppose even* that these newspapers have aroused dissatisfaction, ill humour! It is, after all, *German* dissatisfaction, *German* ill humour that they arouse; after all, they have given back to the state minds that had turned away from it, even though at first these minds are excited and ill-humoured! And they have aroused not only dissatisfaction and ill humour, etc., they have aroused, above all, real *sympathy* for the state, they have made the state *close to the heart*, a *domestic affair*, etc." [a]

Our worthy man, therefore, omits the connecting *intermediate links*. It is as if we said to him, "My dear fellow, be grateful to us: we are enlightening your understanding, and even if you are a little annoyed, nevertheless it is *your* understanding that gains by it", and as if our friend replied, "What! I have to be grateful to you *because* you annoy me!" After these samples of "extremely moderate understanding", no particularly deep psychological investigations are required to understand the *immoderate* fantasy of our author, which makes it appear to him that we are already "marching with fire and sword through the German regions" *in cohorts*. Finally our friend throws off the mask. "*Ulrich von Hutten* and his companions*", who, as is well known, include *Luther*, will forgive the *lion's cowl* of the *Rhein- und Mosel-Zeitung* its impotent anger. We can only blush at an exaggeration which ranks us with such *great* men and, since one good turn deserves another, we wish to rank our friend with *chief pastor Goeze*. Therefore, with Lessing, we cry out to him:

"And here is my brief knightly *challenge*. Write, Herr Pastor, and inspire others to write as much as they possibly can. I, too, shall write. If I allow that you are right in regard to the slightest matter in which you are wrong, then I can never touch a pen again." [b]

THE *RHEIN- UND MOSEL-ZEITUNG*

[*Rheinische Zeitung* No. 16, January 16, 1843]

Cologne, January 15. No. 1 of the *Rhein- und Mosel-Zeitung*, dated January 11, which we touched upon a few days ago as an outrider of the lion's article, today tries to prove,[126] by an example, how little

"the one which overbalances in its dialectics" (the *Rheinische Zeitung*) is capable "of clearly grasping a simple, clearly formulated proposition".

No. 1 claims that in fact it did not at all say that the *Rheinische Zeitung* had tried to justify the ban on the *Münchener politische Blätter*,

---

[a] See this volume, p. 317.— *Ed.*

[b] G. E. Lessing, *Eine Parabel. Nebst einer kleinen Bitte und einem eventualen Absageschreiben.— Ed.*

"but that, at the very moment when it puts itself forward as the champion of unconditional freedom of the press, it does not hesitate to vilify a newspaper which was actually banned, and therefore the chivalry with which it gave assurance of readiness to enter the lists against a ban on the *Rhein- und Mosel-Zeitung* is not worth much".

Outrider No. 1 overlooks that there could be two reasons for his disquiet about our chivalrous behaviour in the event of a ban on the *Rhein- und Mosel-Zeitung* and that both of them have already been answered. The worthy outrider, we must suppose, does not trust our assurance because in the alleged *vilification* of the *Münchener politische Blätter* he sees a hidden justification for banning it. We had the more right to presuppose such a train of thought in our worthy outrider because that mean man has the peculiar cunning to wish to detect the true opinion behind statements that seem to him to have unconsciously "slipped out". In that case we can calm the worthy outrider by proving to him how impossible it is for there to be any connection between our statement about the *Münchener politische Blätter* and a justification for banning it.

The second possibility is that No. 1 finds it altogether regrettable and unchivalrous of us to accuse a *newspaper which has actually been banned*, such as the *Münchener politische Blätter*, of a party polemic against Protestantism. He regards this as a vilification. In that case we asked the worthy outrider:

"If, at the very time when we were defending the *Leipziger Allgemeine Zeitung* against the ban 'that had just been imposed' on it, we, *together* with the *Rhein- und Mosel-Zeitung*, mentioned the party polemic of the *Leipziger Allgemeine Zeitung* against Catholicism, had we not the right *without* the *Rhein- und Mosel-Zeitung* to mention the party polemic of the *Münchener politische Blätter*, which had been banned long ago'?" [a]

That is to say: we do not *vilify* the *Leipziger Allgemeine Zeitung* by mentioning with the *consent* of the *Rhein- und Mosel-Zeitung* its party polemic against Catholicism. Will our assertion about the pro-Catholic party polemic of the *Münchener politische Blätter* become *vilification* because it is so unfortunate as not to have the consent of the *Rhein- und Mosel-Zeitung*?

No. 1 has done nothing beyond calling our assertion a vilification, and since when have we been obliged to take No. 1's word for anything? We said: The *Münchener politische Blätter* is a Catholic party newspaper, and in this respect it is a *Leipziger Allgemeine Zeitung* in reverse. The outrider in the *Rhein- und Mosel-Zeitung* says: The *Münchener politische Blätter* is not a party

---

[a] See this volume, pp. 324-25.— *Ed.*

newspaper and is not a *Leipziger Allgemeine Zeitung* in reverse. It is not, the outrider says,

"such a repository of untruths, stupid bits of gossip and mocking at non-Catholic creeds".

We are not theological polemicists for one side or the other, but it is enough to read the *Münchener politische Blätter's* psychological description of *Luther* based on vulgar tittle-tattle, it is enough to read what the *Rhein- und Mosel-Zeitung* says about "*Hutten* and his companions", to decide whether the "moderate" newspaper adopts a standpoint from which it could objectively judge what is *religious* party polemic and what is not.

Finally, the worthy outrider promises us a "more detailed characterisation of the *Rheinische Zeitung*". *Nous verrons.* The small party between Munich and Koblenz has already once given its opinion that the "*political*" sense of the Rhinelanders should either be exploited for certain non-state pursuits or suppressed as an "annoyance". Can this party fail to be annoyed when it sees the proof of its own complete unimportance in the rapid spread of the *Rheinische Zeitung* throughout the Rhine Province? Perhaps the present moment is unfavourable for showing annoyance? We think that all this is not badly conceived and only regret that this party, not having a more important organ, has to be satisfied with the worthy outrider and his insignificant "moderate" newspaper. One can judge the strength of the *party* from this *organ*.

Written on December 31, 1842, and January 3, 5, 7, 9, 11 and 15, 1843

First published in the *Rheinische Zeitung* Nos. 1, 4, 6, 8, 10, 13 and 16, January 1, 4, 6, 8, 10, 13 and 16, 1843

Printed according to the newspaper

Published in English for the first time

[ANNOUNCEMENT BY THE EDITORS OF THE *RHEINISCHE ZEITUNG* OF THEIR REPLY TO OBERPRÄSIDENT VON SCHAPER [127]]

Cologne, January 2. Since the "corrections" made by Herr Oberpräsident von Schaper and the explanations requested of the *Rheinische Zeitung* have been widely aired in the press, we take this occasion to state that our reply, which has been delayed only because a number of investigations have become necessary, will follow in the coming week.

Written on January 2, 1843

First published in the *Rheinische Zeitung* No. 3, January 3, 1843

Printed according to the newspaper

Published in English for the first time

JUSTIFICATION OF THE CORRESPONDENT FROM THE MOSEL[128]

[*Rheinische Zeitung* No. 15, January 15, 1843]

From the Mosel, January. Nos. 346 and 348 of the *Rheinische Zeitung* contain two articles of mine, one of which deals with the distress due to lack of firewood in the Mosel region, and the other the *special* sympathy of the Mosel population for the royal Cabinet Order of December 24, 1841, and for the resulting greater freedom of the press.[129] The latter article is written in *coarse*, and, if you like, even *rude* tones. Anyone who often has to hear directly the *ruthless* voice of want among the surrounding population easily loses the aesthetic tact by which his thoughts can be expressed in the most elegant and modest images. He may perhaps even consider it his *political* duty for a time to speak in public in the popular language of distress which in his native land he had no chance of forgetting. If, however, it is a question of proving that he speaks the truth, this can hardly mean proving *literally every word*, for in that case every summary would be untrue and, in general, it would be impossible to reproduce the meaning of a speech without repeating it word for word. Thus, for example, if it was said: "the cry of distress of the vine-growers was regarded as an *insolent shrieking*", then to be fair one could demand only that this expressed an approximately correct *equation*. That is to say, it should be proved that there is an object which to a certain extent measures up to the summary description "insolent shrieking", and makes this a not inappropriate description. If such a proof is given, the question is no longer one of *truth* but only of *precision of language*, and it would be hard to give more than a problematic judgment on extremely subtle nuances of linguistic expression.

The occasion for the above remarks of mine was provided by two rescripts of Oberpräsident *von Schaper* in No. 352 of the

Rheinische Zeitung, dated "Koblenz, December 15", in which a number of questions are put to me concerning my two articles mentioned above. The *delay* in the publication of my reply is due primarily to the content of the questions themselves, since a newspaper correspondent, in transmitting *with the utmost conscientiousness* the voice of the people as he has heard it, is not at all obliged to be prepared to give an exhaustive and motivated account of the occasions and sources of his report. Apart from the fact that such work would require much time and resources, the newspaper correspondent can only consider himself as a small part of a complicated body, in which he freely chooses his particular function. While one is perhaps more concerned to depict his impression of the distressed state of the people obtained directly from their statements, another, who is a historian, will discuss the history of the situation which has arisen; the man of feeling will describe the distress itself; the economist will examine the means required for its abolition, this itself being *one* problem which can be treated from different aspects: sometimes more on a local scale, sometimes more in relation to the state as a whole, etc.

Thus, with a lively press movement, the *whole truth* will be revealed, for if the whole appears at first only as the emergence of a number of different, individual points of view which — sometimes intentionally, sometimes accidentally — develop side by side, in the end, however, this work of the press will have prepared for one of its participants the material out of which he will create a *single* whole. Thus, gradually, by means of a division of labour, the press arrives at the whole truth, not by one person doing everything, but by many doing a little.

Another reason for the delay in my reply is that the editorial board of the *Rheinische Zeitung* required further particulars after my first report. Similarly, after the second and third reports, it asked for additional data, and also the present concluding report. Finally, the editorial board, on the one hand, demanded that I myself indicate my sources, and, on the other hand, held up the publication of my reports until it had itself, by some other means, received confirmation of my data.*

Further, my reply appears *anonymously*. In this respect I am guided by the conviction that *anonymity* is an essential feature of the newspaper press, since it *transforms* the newspaper from an assemblage of many individual opinions into the organ of *one*

---

* While confirming the above statements, we point out at the same time that the various mutually explanatory letters made it necessary for us to present a combined account.—Editorial Board of the *Rheinische Zeitung.*

mind. The *name* of the author would separate one article from another as definitely as the body separates one person from another, and would thus completely suppress the function of being only a complementary part. Finally, anonymity ensures greater impartiality and freedom, not only of the author, but also of the public, since the latter sees not *who* is speaking, but *what* he is saying. Free from an empirical view of the author as a person, the public judges him solely by his intellectual personality.

Since I do not mention my own name, in all my detailed reports I shall give the names of officials and communities only when quoting printed documents that are available in bookshops, or when mentioning names will harm no one. The press is obliged to reveal and denounce *circumstances*, but I am convinced that it should not denounce *individuals*, unless there is no other way of preventing a public evil or unless publicity already prevails throughout political life so that the German concept of denunciation no longer exists.

In concluding these introductory remarks I think I am entitled to express the hope that the Herr Oberpräsident, after acquainting himself with my *whole* exposition, will be convinced of the purity of my intentions and will attribute even possible mistakes to an incorrect view of things, and not to an evil disposition. My exposition itself should show whether I have deserved the serious accusation of *slander* and of *intent* to excite *dissatisfaction and discontent*, even in the present case of continued anonymity, accusations which are the more painful coming from a man who is regarded with particularly great respect and affection in the Rhine Province.

To facilitate a survey of my reply, I have set it out under the following headings:

A. *The question of wood distribution.*
B. *The attitude of the Mosel region to the Cabinet Order of December 24, 1841, and to the resulting greater freedom of the press.*
C. *The cankers of the Mosel region.*
D. *The vampires of the Mosel region.*
E. *Proposals for a remedy.*

A

THE QUESTION OF WOOD DISTRIBUTION

In my article "From the Mosel, December 12" in No. 348 of the *Rheinische Zeitung*, I referred to the following circumstances:

"The community of several thousand souls to which I belong is the owner of most beautiful wooded areas, but I cannot *recollect* an occasion when members of the community derived direct advantage from their property by sharing in the distribution of wood."

On this, the Herr Oberpräsident comments:

"Such *procedure, which does not accord with legal provisions,* can only be motivated by quite exceptional circumstances",

and at the same time he demands, in order to verify the facts of the case, that I *name* the community.

I frankly admit: On the one hand, I believe that a procedure which does *not* accord with the law, and *therefore* contradicts it, can hardly be motivated by circumstances, but must always remain illegal; on the other hand, I can*not* find that the procedure described by me is illegal.

The instruction (dated: "Koblenz, August 31, 1839") on the management of wooded areas belonging to communities and institutions in the Koblenz and Trier administrative districts, issued on the basis of the law of December 24, 1816, and the royal Cabinet Order of August 18, 1835, and published in the Supplement to No. 62 of the official organ of the royal administration in Koblenz—this instruction states literally the following in § 37:

"In regard to the utilisation of material in the wooded areas, as a rule as much *must* be sold as is required to cover forest costs (taxes and administrative expenses).

"For the rest, it depends on the decision of the communities themselves whether the material is *sold by auction* to cover other needs of the community, *or whether* it is *distributed* among the members of the community, wholly or in part, gratis or for a definite fee. However, as a rule, firewood and material for making household articles are distributed *in natura,* but building timber, if it is not used for communal buildings or to assist individual members of the community in cases of damage by fire, etc., is sold by auction."

This instruction, issued by one of the predecessors of the Herr Oberpräsident of the Rhine Province, seems to me to prove that the distribution of firewood among the members of the community is neither made obligatory by law nor prohibited by it, but is only a question of expediency. Hence in the article in question also, I discussed *only* the expediency of the procedure. Accordingly, the basis for the Herr Oberpräsident's demand to know the *name* of the community disappears, since it is no longer a question of investigating the administration of a particular community, but only of a modification to an instruction. However, I do not object to the editorial board of the *Rheinische Zeitung,* in the event of a special demand from the Herr Oberpräsident, being empowered to name the community in which, *to the best of my recollection,* there has been no wood distribution. Such information would not be a denunciation of the local authorities but could only promote the welfare of the community.

[*Rheinische Zeitung* No. 17, January 17, 1843]

B

THE ATTITUDE OF THE MOSEL REGION TO THE CABINET ORDER OF DECEMBER 24, 1841, AND TO THE RESULTING GREATER FREEDOM OF THE PRESS

In regard to my article from Bernkastel dated December 10, in No. 346 of the *Rheinische Zeitung*, where I asserted that the Mosel population, in view of its particularly difficult situation, welcomed with exceptional enthusiasm the greater freedom of the press afforded by the royal Cabinet Order of December 24 last year, the Herr Oberpräsident makes the following comment:

"If this article has any meaning, it can only be that hitherto the Mosel population had been forbidden to discuss publicly and frankly its state of distress, the causes of it and the means to remedy it. I doubt that this is so, for in view of the efforts of the authorities to find a remedy for the admittedly distressed state of the vine-growers, nothing could be more desired by the authorities than a discussion, as public and frank as possible, of the conditions prevailing there." "I should, therefore, be greatly obliged if the author of the above article would be so good as to point out specially the cases where, even before the appearance of the royal Cabinet Order of December 24 last year, the authorities prevented a frank, public discussion of the distressed state of the inhabitants of the Mosel region."

The Herr Oberpräsident further remarks:

"In addition, I think that I can in advance certainly describe as untrue the assertion in the above-mentioned article that the cry of distress of the vine-growers was for a long time regarded in higher quarters as an *insolent shrieking*."

My reply to these questions will take the following course. I shall try to prove:

1) that, first of all, quite *apart* from the powers of the press prior to the royal Cabinet Order of December 24, 1841, the need for a free press *necessarily* arises from the specific character of the state of distress in the Mosel region;

2) that even if there were *no special* obstacles to a "frank and public discussion" before the appearance of the above-mentioned Cabinet Order, my assertion would be no less true, and the particular sympathy of the Mosel population for the royal Cabinet Order and the resulting greater freedom of the press would remain equally understandable;

3) *that in actual fact special* circumstances prevented a "frank and public" discussion.

From the whole context it will then be seen how far my assertion: "For a long time the *desperate* state of the vine-growers was doubted in higher quarters, and their cry of distress was regarded as an insolent shrieking", is true or untrue.

As regards 1. In investigating a situation *concerning the state* one is all too easily tempted to overlook the *objective nature of the circumstances* and to explain everything by the *will* of the persons concerned. However, there are *circumstances* which determine the actions of private persons and individual authorities, and which are as independent of them as the method of breathing. If from the outset we adopt this objective standpoint, we shall not assume good or evil will, exclusively on one side or on the other, but we shall see the effect of circumstances where at first glance only individuals seem to be acting. Once it is proved that a phenomenon is made *necessary* by circumstances, it will no longer be difficult to ascertain the *external* circumstances in which it must *actually* be produced and those in which it could not be produced, although the need for it already existed. This can be established with approximately the same certainty with which the chemist determines the *external* conditions under which substances having affinity are bound to form a compound. Hence we believe that by our proof "that the *necessity* for a free press follows from the *specific character* of the state of distress in the Mosel region" we give our exposition a basis that goes far beyond anything personal.

The *state of distress* in the Mosel region cannot be regarded as a *simple* state of affairs. At least *two* aspects of it have to be distinguished: the private aspect and the state aspect, for the state of distress in the Mosel region cannot be considered to lie outside the state administration any more than the Mosel region can be considered to lie outside the state. Only the *mutual relation* between these two aspects provides the *actual* state of the Mosel region. In order to show the nature of this mutual relation, we shall report an authentic exchange of opinion, certified by documents, between the respective *organs* of the two sides.

In the fourth issue of *Mitteilungen des Vereins zur Förderung der Weinkultur an der Mosel und Saar zu Trier* there is a report of negotiations between the Finance Ministry, the government at Trier and the board of the above-mentioned Society. A document presented by the Society to the Finance Ministry contains, among other things, a calculation of the income from the vineyards. The government at Trier, which also received a copy of this document, asked for an expert opinion on it from the chief of the Trier Cadastre Bureau, tax inspector *von Zuccalmaglio*, who, as the government itself says in one of its reports, seemed to be specially suitable because he

"took an active part at the time when the registers of incomes from vineyards in the Mosel region were compiled".

We shall now simply put side by side the most striking passages from the *official* opinion of Herr von Zuccalmaglio and the *reply* of the board of the Society for the Promotion of Viticulture.

The official reporter:

In the official report covering the past decade, 1829-38, the calculation of the gross income per morgen[a] of vineyards in communities belonging to the third class as regards payment of *wine tax* is based on:

1) the yield per morgen;
2) the price at which a fuder[b] of wine is sold *in the autumn*.

The calculation, however, is not based on any precisely verified data, for

"without *official* intervention and control it is impossible for either an individual or a society to collect privately trustworthy information on the quantity of wine obtained by all the individual property owners over a specified period in a large number of communities, *because many owners may be directly interested in concealing the truth as far as possible*".

The reply of the board of the Society:

"We are not surprised that the Cadastre Bureau does its utmost to defend the procedure practised by it; nevertheless, it is difficult to understand the argument which follows", etc.

"The chief of the Cadastre Bureau tries to prove by figures that the registered yields are everywhere correct; he says also that the ten-year period assumed by us cannot prove anything here", etc., etc. "We shall not argue about figures, for, as he very wisely says in the introduction to his remarks, we lack the requisite official information. Moreover, we do not regard it as necessary, since his entire calculation and argument based on *official* data can prove nothing against the facts we have presented." "Even if we admit that the registered yields were quite correct at the time of their compilation, or even that they were too low, it is impossible successfully to contest our statement that they can no longer serve as a *basis* under the present *lamentably* changed circumstances."

The official reporter:

"Hence not a fact appears anywhere justifying the assumption that the registered yields from vineyards, based on assessments in the recent period, are too high; but it would be quite easy to prove that the earlier assessments of vineyards of the rural and urban districts of Trier and of the Saarburg district are *too low*, both in themselves and compared with other crops."

The reply of the board of the Society:

"A man crying out for help finds it painful when in reply to his well-founded complaint he is told that during compilation the registered yields could have been put higher rather than lower."

"Moreover," the reply points out, "the Herr Reporter, despite all his efforts to reject our data, could hardly refute or correct anything in our figures of *income*; therefore he has tried only to quote different results as regards *expenditure*."

---

[a] *Morgen*—German measure of land equalling approximately $^1/_4$ hectare.— *Ed.*
[b] *Fuder*—large measure for wine, approximately 1,000 litres.— *Ed.*

We want now to indicate some of the most striking differences of opinion between the Herr Reporter and the board of the Society on the question of *calculating expenditure.*

The official reporter:

"In regard to point 8, it should be particularly noted that the *removal* of the usual lateral shoots, or what is called *Geitzen*, is an operation recently introduced by only a few owners of vineyards, but nowhere, neither in the Mosel nor the Saar region, can it be regarded as part of the customary method of cultivation."

The reply of the board of the Society:

"The *removal of lateral shoots* and the *loosening of soil*, according to the chief of the Cadastre Bureau, was only recently introduced by a few owners of vineyards", etc. That, however, is not the case. "The vine-grower has understood that, to save himself from going under completely, he must not fail to try anything that could in some degree improve the quality of the wine. For the prosperity of the region, this attitude should be carefully encouraged, instead of being repressed."

"And who would think of putting the cost of potato cultivation at a lower figure because there are some cultivators who leave the potatoes to their fate and God's goodness?"

The official reporter:

"The cost of the *barrel* indicated in point 14 cannot at all enter into the valuation here, since, as has already been pointed out, the cost of the barrel is *not* included in the quoted prices of wine. If then the barrel is sold together with the wine, as is usually the case, the cost of the barrel is added to the price of the wine and thus the value of the barrels is reimbursed."

The reply of the board of the Society:

"When wine is sold, the barrel is included, and there is not and even could not be the slightest question of its reimbursement. The rare cases when the innkeepers of our town buy wine without the barrel cannot be taken into account when viewing the situation as a whole." "It is not the same with wine as with other goods, which lie in a warehouse until they are sold and the packing and dispatch of which then take place at the expense of the purchaser. Since, therefore, the purchase of wine tacitly includes that of the barrel, it is clear that the price of the latter must be included in the production costs."

The official reporter:

"If the figures of yields given in the supplement are corrected to correspond to the official data on them, but the calculation of costs is accepted as correct even in all parts, and *only* the land and *wine* taxes and the cost of the *barrels* (or expenditures given in points 13, 14 and 17) are omitted from these costs, the result is as follows:

Gross income ....53 talers	21 silver groschen	6 pfennigs
Costs — not including 13, 14 and 17.....................39 "	5 " "	0 "
Net income........................14 talers	16 silver groschen	6 pfennigs

The reply of the board of the Society:

"The calculation as such is correct, but the result is incorrect. We based our calculation not on supposed figures, but on figures which express the actual amounts involved, and we found that if from 53 talers of actual expenditure 48 talers representing the actual and only income are subtracted, there remains a loss of 5 talers."

The official reporter:

"If, nevertheless, it cannot be denied that the state of distress in the Mosel region has considerably worsened compared with the period before the inauguration of the Customs Union, and that in part even a *real impoverishment* is to be *feared*, the reason for it should be sought exclusively in the former too high yields."

"Owing to the previously existing quasi-monopoly of the wine trade in the Mosel region and the rapid succession of good wine years in 1819, 1822, 1825, 1826, 1827 and 1828, an *unprecedented luxury* developed there. The large sums of money in the hands of the vine-grower induced him to buy vineyards at enormous prices and to plant new vineyards at excessive cost in places that were no longer suitable for viticulture. Everyone wanted to become an owner, and debts were incurred which previously could easily be covered by the income from a good year, but which now, with the present unfavourable economic situation, are bound to ruin completely the vine-grower who has fallen into the hands of usurers."

"One consequence of this will be that viticulture will be confined to the better holdings and will again, as formerly, come more into the hands of the rich landowners, a purpose to which it is most suited owing to the large initial expenditure involved. The rich landowners, too, can more easily withstand unfavourable years and even at such times have adequate means to improve cultivation and to obtain a product which can stand up to competition with that from the now opened countries of the Customs Union. *Of course,* during the first years *this* cannot take place *without great hardships for the poorer class of vine-growers,* most of whom, however, had become owners of vineyards in the previous favourable period. However, it should always be borne in mind that the earlier state of affairs was an *unnatural* one *for which the imprudent are now paying. The state ... will be able to confine itself to making* the transition as *easy* as possible for the present population by appropriate measures."

The reply of the board of the Society:

"Truly, one who only fears possible poverty in the Mosel region has not yet *seen* that poverty which, in its most *ghastly* form, is already deep-rooted and daily spreading among the morally healthy, tirelessly industrious population of this region. Let no one say, as the chief of the Cadastre Bureau does, that it is the impoverished vine-growers' own fault. No, all of them have been struck down to a greater or lesser degree: the prudent and the imprudent, the industrious and the negligent, the well-to-do and the indigent; and if things have now gone so far that even the well-to-do, the industrious and the thrifty vine-growers are compelled to say that they can no longer provide themselves with food, then the cause is evidently not to be sought in them.

"It is true that in the favourable years the vine-growers bought new plots at prices higher than usual and that they incurred debts, calculating that their incomes, as they saw them, would suffice gradually to pay them off. But it is incomprehensible how this, which is proof of the enterprising and industrious spirit of these people, can be called *luxury,* and how it can be said that the present position of the vine-growers has arisen because the earlier state of affairs was an unnatural one, for which the imprudent are now paying.

"The chief of the Cadastre Bureau asserts that people who, according to him, were previously not even property owners (!!), tempted by the unusually good years, increased excessively the total of vineyards, and that the *only* remedy now lies in reducing the number of vineyards.

"But how insignificant is the number of vineyards which can be adapted for growing fruit or vegetables, compared with the majority which, apart from grapes, can produce only hedges and bushes! And can it be that this highly respectable population, which is crowded into such a relatively small area because of viticulture, and is so courageously struggling against misfortune, *does not even deserve an attempt* to alleviate its distress so that it can hold out until more favourable circumstances enable it to rise again and become for the state what it was before, namely, a source of income the equal of which is not to be found on any area of equal size apart from the towns."

The official reporter:

"It is, of course, quite understandable that the richer landowners, too, *take advantage* of this distress of the poorer vine-growers in order to obtain for themselves all possible alleviations and advantages by a *vivid* description of the former happy state of affairs in contrast to the present less favourable, but nevertheless still *profitable,* position."

[*Rheinische Zeitung* No. 18, January 18, 1843]

The reply of the board of the Society:

"We owe it to our honour and our inner conviction to protest against the *accusation* that we take advantage of the distress of the poorer vine-growers in order to obtain for ourselves all possible advantages and alleviations by means of *vivid descriptions.*

"No, we assert — and that, we hope, will suffice for our justification — that we were far from having any selfish intention, and that all our efforts were directed towards making the state aware, by a *frank and truthful description* of the conditions of the poor vine-growers, of a situation the further development of which is bound to be dangerous for the state itself! Anyone who knows the transformation which the present pitiful position of the vine-growers has already increasingly brought about in their domestic life and industrial activity, and even as regards morality, cannot but shudder at the future when he thinks of a continuance or even increase of such distress."

It has to be admitted, first of all, that the government could not come to a decision but must have vacillated between the view of its reporter and the opposing view of the vine-growers. Bearing in mind, further, that the report of Herr von Zuccalmaglio is dated December 12, 1839, and the answer of the Society is dated July 15, 1840, it follows that up to this time the view of the reporter must have been, if not the *sole,* at any rate the *prevailing* view of the government collegium. In 1839, at least, it was still counterposed to the Society's memorandum as the government's judgment and therefore, as it were, a résumé of the governmental view, for if a government is consistent its latest opinion can surely be regarded as the sum total of its earlier views and experience. In the report, however, not only is the state of distress not recognised as *general,* but there is no intention of *remedying* even the *admitted* state of distress, for it is stated: "The state will be able to confine itself *solely* to *making* the *transition* as *easy* as possible for the present population by appropriate measures." Under these circumstances, transition must be taken to mean gradual *ruin*.[a] The ruin of the poorer vine-growers is regarded as a kind of natural phenomenon, to which one must be resigned in advance, seeking only to mitigate the inevitable. "Of course," it is stated, "this cannot take place without great hardships." The Society, therefore, also raises the question whether the vine-growers of the Mosel do not even deserve "*an attempt*" to save them. If the government had held a decisively opposed view, it would have modified the report at the outset, since the report makes a definite statement on such an important question as the *task and decision* of the state in this matter. Hence it is evident that the *distressed state* of the vine-growers could be *admitted* without there being any effort to *remedy* it.

We cite now yet another example of the kind of information given to the authorities about conditions in the Mosel region. In 1838, a highly placed administrative official travelled through the Mosel region. At a conference in Piesport with two district presidents, he asked one of them what the vine-growers' situation was like as regards property and received the reply:

"The vine-growers live too luxuriously and if only for that reason things cannot be going badly with them."

Yet luxury had already become a story of former days. We only incidentally point out here that this view, which coincides with the official report, has by no means been generally abandoned. We recall the statement from Koblenz published in Supplement I of the *Frankfurter Journal* No. 349 (1842), which speaks of the *alleged* state of distress of the Mosel vine-growers.

The above-quoted official view is reflected, too, in the attitude of higher quarters, which throws doubt on the "desperate" state of the vine-growers and on the *general* nature of the distress, hence also on its *general causes*. The reports of the Society quoted above contain, *inter alia*, the following replies of the *Finance Ministry* to various petitions:

"Although, as the market prices for wine show, the owners of Mosel and Saar vineyards included in the first and second classes as regards taxation have *no* cause for *dissatisfaction*, nevertheless it is not denied that vine-growers whose products are of inferior quality are not in an *equally favourable* position."

In a reply to a petition for remission of taxation for 1838, it is stated:

"In reply to your representation sent here on October 10 of last year, we have to inform you that the petition for a general remission of the entire wine tax for

---

[a] A pun on the German words *Übergang*, which means "transition," and *Untergang*, which means "ruin."— *Ed.*

1838 cannot be entertained, since you do not belong to the class which is most in need of consideration and whose *state of distress*, etc., is *explicable* by *quite other* causes than *taxation*."

Since we wish to construct our exposition solely on *factual material*, endeavouring, as far as we can, to present only facts in a general form, we shall first of all make clear the general ideas underlying the dialogue between the Trier Society for the Promotion of Viticulture and the government's reporter.

The government has to appoint an official to give an expert opinion on the memorandum presented to it. It naturally appoints an official who has the greatest possible knowledge of the subject, preferably therefore an official who himself took part in regulating the situation in the Mosel region. This official is not averse to finding in the complaints contained in the document in question *attacks* on his official understanding and his previous official activity. He is aware of his conscientious performance of his duty and of the detailed official information at his disposal; he is suddenly faced with an opposing view, and what could be more natural than that he should *take sides* against the petitioner, and that the *intentions* of the latter, which could of course always be bound up with *private interests*, should seem to him suspicious, and that therefore he should suspect them. Instead of using the data in the memorandum, he tries to refute them. In addition, the obviously poor vine-grower has neither the time nor the education to describe his condition; hence the poor vine-grower is unable to speak, whereas the vine cultivator who is able to speak is not obviously poor, and therefore his complaints seem unfounded. But if even the educated vine-grower is rebuked for not having the official understanding, how could the uneducated vine-grower hold his own against this official understanding!

For their part, private persons who have observed the real poverty of others in the full extent of its development, who see it gradually coming closer even to themselves, and who, moreover, are aware that the private interest they defend is equally a state interest, and is defended by them as a state interest, these private persons are not only bound to feel that their own honour has been impugned, but consider also that *reality* itself has been distorted under the influence of a one-sided and arbitrarily established point of view. Hence they oppose the overweening presumption of officialdom; they point out the contradiction between the real nature of the world and that ascribed to it in government offices, contrasting the practical proofs to the official proofs. And, finally, they cannot avoid suspecting that behind total misconception of their account of the actual state of affairs, which is based on well-founded convictions and clear facts, there is a selfish intention, namely, the intention to assert official judgment in opposition to the intelligence of the citizens. Consequently, they conclude also that the expert official who comes into contact with their conditions of life will not give an unprejudiced description of them, precisely because these conditions are partly the result of his activities, whereas the unprejudiced official, who could give a sufficiently impartial judgment, is not an expert. When, however, the official accuses private persons of elevating their private affairs to the level of a state interest, private persons accuse the official of degrading the state interest to the level of a private affair of his own, from which all others are excluded as being mere laymen. In this way even the most patent reality appears illusory compared with the reality depicted in the dossiers, which is official and therefore of a state character, and compared with the intelligence based on this official reality. Hence to the official only the sphere of activity of the authorities is the state, whereas the world outside this sphere of activity is merely an object of state activity, completely lacking the state *frame of mind* and state *understanding*. Finally, in the event of a notoriously bad situation, the official puts the main blame on private persons who, he alleges, are *themselves* responsible for their plight, while he refuses to allow any attack on the excellence of administrative principles or institutions, which are themselves official creations and no part of which he is willing to relinquish. The private person, on the other hand, conscious of his industriousness, his thrift, his hard struggle against nature and social conditions, demands that the official who is supposed to be the sole creative force of the state should put an end to his distress, and, since that official claims he can put everything right, that he should prove his ability to remedy the bad situation by his activity, or at least recognise that institutions which were suitable at a certain time have become unsuitable under completely changed circumstances.

The same standpoint of *superior* official knowledge and the same antithesis between the administration and the object administered are repeated within the world of officialdom itself. We see that the Cadastre Bureau, in its judgment on the Mosel region, is mainly concerned with asserting the infallibility of the Cadastre, and just as the Finance Ministry maintains that the evil is due to "quite other" causes than "taxation", so the administration will find that the basis of the distress lies not at all *in itself*, but *outside itself*. *Not intentionally*, but *necessarily*, the individual official who is in closest contact with the vine-grower sees the state of things as better or other than it actually is. He thinks that the question whether things are all right in his region amounts to the question whether *he* administers the region correctly. Whether the administrative principles and institutions are good or not is a question that lies outside his sphere, for that can only be judged in *higher* quarters where a wider and deeper *knowledge* of the *official* nature of things, i.e., of their connection with the state as a whole, prevails. He may be most honestly convinced that *he himself* administers well. Hence either he will find the situation not so entirely desperate or, if he does find it to be so, he will look for the reason *outside* the administration, partly in nature, which is independent of man, partly in private life, which is independent of the administration, and partly in accidental circumstances, which depend on no one.

The higher administrative bodies are bound to have more confidence in *their* officials than in the persons administered, who cannot be presumed to possess the same official understanding. An administrative body, moreover, has its traditions. Thus, as regards the Mosel region too, it has its once and for all established principles, it has its official picture of the region in the Cadastre, it has official data on revenue and expenditure, it has everywhere, alongside the actual reality, a *bureaucratic* reality, which retains its authority however much the times may change. In addition, the two circumstances, namely, the law of the official hierarchy and the principle that there are two categories of citizens—the active, knowledgeable citizens in the administration, and the passive, uninformed citizens who are the object of administration—these two circumstances are mutually complementary. In accordance with the principle that the state possesses conscious and active existence in the administration, every government will regard the condition of a region—insofar as the state aspect of the matter is concerned—as the result of the work of its predecessor. According to the law of hierarchy, this predecessor will in most cases already occupy a higher position, often the one immediately above. Finally, every government is actuated, on the one hand, by the consciousness that the state has laws which it must enforce in the face of all private interests, and, on the other hand, as an individual administrative authority, its duty is not to make institutions or laws, but to apply them. Hence it can try to reform not the administration itself, but only the object administered. It cannot adapt its laws to the Mosel region, it can only try to promote the welfare of the Mosel region *within the limits* of its firmly established rules of administration. *The more zealously* and *sincerely,* therefore, a government endeavours — within the limits of the already established administrative principles and institutions by which it is itself governed — to remove a *glaring state of distress* that embraces perhaps a whole *region,* and the *more stubbornly* the evil resists the measures taken against it and increases despite the *good* administration, *so much the more profound, sincere and decisive will be the conviction* that this is an incurable state of distress, which the administration, i.e., the state, can do nothing to alter, and which requires rather a change on the part of those administered.

Whereas, however, the lower administrative authorities trust the official understanding of those above them that the administrative principles are good, and are themselves ready to answer for their dutiful implementation in each separate case, the higher administrative authorities are fully convinced of the correctness of the general principles and trust the bodies subordinate to them to make the correct official judgment in each case, of which, moreover, they have official proofs.

In this way it is possible for a government *with the best intentions* to arrive at the principle expressed by the government's reporter in Trier in regard to the Mosel region: "*The state will be able to confine itself solely to making the transition as easy as possible for the present population by appropriate measures.*"

If we look now at some of the methods which have transpired and which the government has used to alleviate the distress in the Mosel region, we shall find our argument confirmed at least by the history of the administration which is accessible to all; on the secret history, of course, we cannot pass judgment. We include among these measures: *remission of taxes in bad wine years, the advice to go over to some other cultivation, such as sericulture,* and, finally, the proposal to limit *parcellation of landed property.* The *first* of these measures, obviously, can only alleviate, not remedy. It is a *temporary* measure, by which the state makes an *exception* to its rule, and an exception which does not cost it much. Moreover, it is not the *constant* state of distress which is alleviated, it is likewise an exceptional manifestation of it, not the chronic sickness to which people have become accustomed, but an acute form of it which comes as a surprise.

In regard to the other two measures, the administration goes outside the scope of its own activities. The positive activity which it undertakes here consists partly in instructing the Mosel inhabitants how they *themselves* can come to their own aid, and partly in proposing a *limitation* or even denial of a right they previously possessed. Here, therefore, we find confirmed the train of thought we described above. The administration, which considers that the distressed state of the Mosel region is incurable and due to circumstances lying outside the scope of its principles and its activity, advises the Mosel inhabitants so to arrange their life that it is adapted to the present administrative institutions and that they are able to exist in a tolerable fashion within them. The vinegrower himself is deeply pained by such proposals, even if they only reach him by rumour. He would be thankful if the government carried out experiments at its own expense, but he feels that the advice that he should undertake experiments on himself means that the government is refusing to help him by its own activity. He wants help, not advice. However much he trusts the knowledge possessed by the *administration* in its own sphere, and however confidently he turns to it in such matters, he credits himself just as much with the necessary understanding in his own sphere. But limitation of the parcellation of landed property contradicts his inherited sense of right; he regards it as a proposal to add legal poverty to his physical poverty, for he regards every violation of equality before the law as the distress of right. He feels, sometimes consciously, sometimes unconsciously, that the administration exists for the sake of the country and not the country for the sake of the administration, but that this relationship becomes reversed when the country has to transform its customs, its rights, its kind of work and its property ownership to suit the administration. The Mosel inhabitant, therefore, demands that, if he carries out the work which nature and custom have ordained for him, the state should create conditions for him in which he can grow, prosper, and live. Hence such negative devices come to nought when they encounter the reality not only of the existing conditions, but also of civic consciousness.

[*Rheinische Zeitung* No. 19, January 19, 1843]

What then is the relation of the administration to the distress in the Mosel region? The *distressed state of the Mosel region* is at the same time a *distressed state of the administration.* The *constant* state of distress of part of the country (and a state of distress, which, beginning almost unnoticed more than a decade ago, at first gradually and then irresistibly develops to a climax and assumes ever more threatening dimensions, can well be called *constant*) signifies a *contradiction between reality and administrative principles,* just as, on the other hand, not only the nation, but also the government regards the *well-being* of a region as a factual confirmation of good administration. The administration, however, owing to its *bureaucratic* nature, is *capable* of perceiving the reasons for the distress not in the sphere *administered*, but only in the sphere of *nature* and the *private citizen*, which lies outside the sphere administered. The administrative authorities, even *with the best intentions*, the most zealous humanity and the most powerful intellect, *can* find no solution for a conflict that is more than momentary or transient, the constant conflict between reality and the principles of administration, for it is not their official task, nor would it be possible, despite the best intentions, to make a breach in an *essential relation* or, if you like, *fate*.[a] This *essential relation* is the *bureaucratic* one, both within the administrative body itself and in its *relations with the administered body*.

On the other hand, the private vine-grower can no more deny that *his* judgment may be affected, intentionally or unintentionally, by *private interest*, and therefore the correctness of his judgment cannot be assumed absolutely. Moreover, he will realise that there are in the state a multitude of private interests which suffer, and the general principles of administration cannot be abandoned or modified for their sake. Furthermore, if it is asserted that there is distress of a *general* character and that the general well-being is endangered in such a manner and to such an extent that private misfortune becomes a misfortune for the state and its removal a duty which the state owes to *itself*, the rulers regard this assertion of the ruled in relation to them as inappropriate; for the rulers consider they are in the best position to judge how far the welfare of the state is endangered and that they must be presumed to have a deeper insight into the relation between the whole and the parts than the parts themselves have. Furthermore, individuals, even a large number of them, cannot claim that their voice is the voice of the people; on the contrary, their description of the situation always retains the character of a *private* complaint. Finally, even if the conviction held by the complaining private persons were the conviction of the entire Mosel region, the latter, as an individual administrative unit, as an individual part of the country, would be, in relation to its own province as also in relation to the state, in the position of a private person whose convictions and desires should be judged only by their relation to the general conviction and the general desire.

In order to solve this difficulty, therefore, the rulers and the

---

[a] A pun on the German words *Verhältnis*, which means "relation", and *Verhängnis*, which means "fate".— *Ed.*

ruled alike are in need of a *third* element, which would be *political* without being official, hence not based on bureaucratic premises, an element which would be of a *civil* nature without being bound up with private interests and their pressing need. This supplementary element with the *head of a citizen of the state* and the *heart of a citizen* is the *free press*. In the realm of the press, rulers and ruled alike have an opportunity of criticising their principles and demands, and no longer in a relation of subordination, but on terms of equality as *citizens of the state*; no longer as *individuals*, but as *intellectual forces*, as exponents of reason. The "free press", being the product of public opinion, is also the creator of public opinion. It alone can make a particular interest a general one, it alone can make the *distressed state* of the Mosel region an object of general attention and general sympathy on the part of the Fatherland, it alone can mitigate the distress by dividing the feeling of it among all.

The attitude of the press to the people's conditions of life is based on *reason*, but it is equally based on *feeling*. Hence it does not speak only in the clever language of judgment that soars above circumstances, but the passionate language of circumstances themselves, a language which cannot and should not be demanded of *official reports*. The free press, finally, brings the people's need in its real shape, not refracted through any bureaucratic medium, to the steps of the throne, to a power before which the difference between rulers and ruled vanishes and there remain only equally near and equally far removed *citizens of the state*.

If, therefore, a freer press became *essential* owing to the *specific* state of distress of the Mosel region, if it there became an urgent, because *actual*, need, it is obvious that no exceptional obstacles to the press were required to create such a need, but that, on the contrary, an exceptional freedom of the press was required to satisfy the existing need.

As regards 2. The press which deals with the affairs of the Mosel region is in any case only a *part of the Prussian political press*. Hence, in order to ascertain its state before the promulgation of the frequently cited Cabinet Order, it will be necessary to take a quick glance at the state of the whole Prussian press before 1841. Let us listen to a man whose loyal frame of mind is generally recognised:

"General ideas and matters," says David *Hansemann* in his book *Preussen und Frankreich*, second edition, Leipzig, 1834, p. 272, "develop quietly and tranquilly in Prussia, and do so the more unnoticed because the *censorship does not permit any thorough discussion* in Prussian newspapers of *political* and *even economic* questions concerning the state, *however decent and moderate their formulation*. A thorough discussion can only mean one in which arguments and counter-arguments can be put forward. *Hardly any economic* question can be discussed *thoroughly unless* its connections, with *internal and external policy* are also examined, for there are few questions, perhaps *none at all in the case of economic questions,* in which such connections do not exist. Whether this exercise of the censorship is expedient, whether the censorship could be exercised in any other way in the present state of the government in Prussia, is not the question here, *suffice it that such is the case*."

It should be recalled, further, that § 1 of the censorship decree of December 19, 1788, already stated:

"It is certainly not the intention of the censorship to hinder a decent, earnest and modest investigation of the truth or *otherwise* impose *any* unnecessary and burdensome constraint on writers."

In Article II of the censorship decree of October 18, 1819, it is stated again:

"The censorship will not prevent serious and modest investigation of truth nor impose undue constraint on writers."

Compare with this the introductory words of the censorship instruction of December 24, 1841 [130]:

"In order *already now* to free the press from *improper* restrictions, which are against the *intentions of the All-Highest,* His Majesty the King, by a supreme order issued to the royal state ministry [...] has been pleased to disapprove *expressly* of any undue constraint on the activity of writers and [...] empowered us to direct the censors *anew* to due observance of Article II of the censorship decree of October 18, 1819."

Finally, let us recall the following statement:

"The censor can very well permit a frank discussion also of *internal affairs.*—The undeniable difficulty of determining the correct limits in this matter should not deter the censor from endeavouring to comply with the *true intention of the law,* nor mislead him into the kind of *anxiety* which has *already only too often* given rise to *misinterpretations* of the *government's intention.*"

In view of all these official declarations, it is clear that the question why censorship obstacles have occurred despite the wish of the authorities that conditions in the Mosel region should be discussed as frankly and publicly as possible, becomes instead the *more general* question: why, *in spite of* the "*intention of the law*", the "*government's intention,*" and, finally, the "*intentions of the All-Highest*", should the press in 1841 admittedly still have to be freed "from *improper* restrictions", and the censorship in 1841 have to be *reminded* of Article II of the 1819 decree? As regards the *Mosel region* in particular, the former question should not ask what *special obstacles to the press* have occurred, but what *special measures in favour of the press* should be taken *by way of exception* to ensure that this partial discussion of *internal* conditions is as *frank and public as possible.*

The clearest indication of the inner content and character of *political literature* and the *daily press* prior to the above-mentioned Cabinet Order is contained in the following statement of the censorship instruction:

"In this way it may be *hoped* that both *political literature* and the *daily press* will realize their function *better*, adopt a *more dignified* tone, and *in future* will scorn to *speculate* on the *curiosity* of their readers through communication of baseless reports taken from foreign newspapers, etc., etc. ... It is to be *expected* that thereby *greater* sympathy for the interests of the *Fatherland* will be *aroused* and thus *national feeling* enhanced."

From this it seems to follow that, although no *special* measures prevented a frank and public discussion of conditions in the Mosel region, nevertheless the *general state* of the Prussian press itself was bound to be an insurmountable obstacle both to frankness and to publicity. If we sum up the above-quoted passages from the censorship instruction, they tell us that: the censorship was excessively anxious and an *external* barrier to a free press, that hand in hand with this went the *internal* narrowness of the press, which had lost courage and even abandoned the effort to rise above the horizon of novelty, and that, finally, in the nation itself *sympathy for the interests of the Fatherland* and *national feeling* had been lost, that is to say, precisely the elements which are not only the creative forces of a frank and public press, but also the conditions within which a frank and public press can operate and win popular recognition, recognition which is the breath of life of the press, and without which it hopelessly pines away.

Hence, although measures taken by the authorities can create an *unfree* press, it is *beyond the power of the authorities*, when the general state of the press is unfree, to ensure that special questions are discussed as frankly and publicly as possible. Under such conditions, even frank statements which might happen to be made on particular subjects in the columns of the newspaper would fail to evoke any *general* sympathy, and would therefore be unable to achieve any real publicity.

In addition, as *Hansemann* rightly remarks, there is *perhaps not a single question of the state economy in which connections with internal and external policy do not exist.* Hence the possibility of a frank and public discussion of *conditions in the Mosel region* presupposes the *possibility* of frank and public discussion of the whole of "*internal and external policy*". Individual administrative authorities were so powerless to ensure this possibility that *only* the direct and decisive expression of the will of the *King himself* could play a determining and lasting role here.

If public discussion was not frank, frank discussion was not public. Frank discussion was limited to *obscure* provincial sheets, whose horizon, of course, did not go beyond their area of circulation and, as shown above, could not do so. To characterise such local discussions, we shall quote a few extracts from the Bernkastel *Gemeinnütziges Wochenblatt* of different years. In 1835 it stated:

"In the autumn of 1833 in *Erden*, a person from another place made 5 ohms[a] of wine. In order to fill the barrel (fuder), this person bought an additional 2 ohms at a price of 30 talers. The barrel cost 9 talers, the grape-pressing tax amounted to 7 talers 5 silver groschen, the harvesting of the grapes 4 talers, cellar rent 1 taler 3 silver groschen, payment for the cooper 16 silver groschen. Therefore, without counting cultivation costs, the total expenditure was 51 talers 24 silver groschen. On May 10, the barrel of wine was sold for 41 talers. It should be noted also that this wine was of good quality and was not sold from sheer necessity, not did it fall into the hands of usurers" (p. 87). "On November 21 in the Bernkastel market, $^3/_4$ ohm of 1835 wine was sold for 14 silver groschen — *fourteen silver groschen* — and on the 27th of the same month 4 ohms *together with* the barrel were sold for 11 talers; moreover, it should be noted that on the previous Michaelmas the barrel had been bought for 11 talers" (p. 267, ibid.).

On April 12, 1836, there was a similar item. We should like to quote also some extracts from 1837:

"On the first of this month in *Kinheim*, in the presence of a notary there was sold by public auction a young, four-year-old vineyard containing about 200 vine-stocks, correctly trained on stakes. It cost the buyer $1^1/_2$ *pfennigs* per stock, under the usual conditions of payment. In 1828, the same vine-stock there cost 5 silver groschen" (p. 47). "In *Graach*, a widow surrendered her ungathered grape harvest for half of the wine yield and she received for her share one ohm of wine, *which she exchanged for 2 lbs. of butter, 2 lbs. of bread and $^1/_2$ lb. of onions*" (No. 37, ibid.). "On the 20th of this month there was a forced sale by auction here of 8 fuders of 1836 wine from *Graach* and Bernkastel, part of it from the *best* sites, and 1 fuder of 1835 wine from Graach. The sale (barrels included) yielded a total sum of 135 talers 15 silver groschen, so that the wine cost the buyer about 15 talers per fuder. The barrel alone could have cost 10-12 talers. What is left for the poor vine-grower to pay for the cost of cultivation? Is it then impossible to remedy this terrible distress?!! (Letter to the Editor)" (No. 4, p. 30).

We have here, therefore, merely a *simple* relation of facts, sometimes accompanied by a brief elegiac epilogue. Precisely because of their artless simplicity they can produce a shattering effect, but they could hardly even claim to be a frank and public discussion of conditions in the Mosel region.

If then an individual or even a considerable part of a population falls victim to a striking and terrifying misfortune and no one discusses this calamity, if no one treats it as a phenomenon *worthy*

---

[a] One ohm is about 100-150 litres.— *Ed.*

of being thought about and discussed, the unfortunate victims are bound to conclude either that the others are not *allowed* to speak about it, or that they do not *want* to do so because they consider the importance attached to the matter illusory. Even for the most uneducated vine-grower, however, the recognition of his misfortune by others, this spiritual participation in it, is an urgent need, if only because he can conclude that when all give thought to it and many speak of it, soon some will do something about it. Even if a free and open discussion of the Mosel conditions had been permitted, no such discussion *took place,* and it is clear that people believe only in what *actually exists;* they do not believe in a free press which might exist, but only in a free press that actually exists. The Mosel inhabitants, of course, had felt their distress *before* the appearance of the royal Cabinet Order, and indeed had heard doubts expressed about this distress, only they did not see any discussion of it by a public and frank press. *After* the appearance of the Cabinet Order, on the other hand, they saw such a press spring up, as it were, out of nothing. Thus their conclusion that the royal Cabinet Order was the *sole* cause of this movement of the press, in which, for the reasons mentioned above, they took such an exceptional interest, owing directly to their *actual* need, this conclusion seems to have been at least a very popular one. Finally, it seems that, apart from the popularity of this opinion, a critical examination would lead also to the same result. The introduction to the censorship instruction of December 24, 1841, states:

"*His Majesty the King* has been pleased to *disapprove expressly* of any undue constraint on the activity of writers and, *recognising the value and need* of frank and decent publicity ... etc."

This introductory statement assures the press of a special *royal* recognition, hence a recognition of its *state significance.* That a *single* word from the King could have such an important effect and was welcomed by the Mosel inhabitants as a word of magical power, as a panacea against all their tribulations, seems only to testify to the genuinely royalist disposition of the Mosel population and to their thankfulness expressed in no niggardly fashion, but in overflowing measure.

[*Rheinische Zeitung* No. 20, January 20, 1843]

As regards 3. We have tried to show that the *need* for a free press *necessarily* arose from the *specific character* of the conditions in the Mosel region. We have shown further that prior to the appearance of the royal Cabinet Order this need could not be satisfied, if not because of *special* constraints imposed on the press, at any rate owing to the *general state of the Prussian daily press.* Lastly we shall show that *as a matter of fact special* circumstances have been hostile to a frank and public discussion of conditions in the Mosel region. Here, too, we must in the first place stress the point of view by which we have been guided in our exposition and recognise the powerful influence of general *conditions* on the *will* of the acting persons. In the *special* circumstances which prevented a frank and public discussion of the state of affairs in the Mosel region we ought not to see anything but the *factual embodiment* and *obvious manifestation* of the above-mentioned *general* conditions, namely, the *specific* position of the administration in regard to the Mosel region, the general state of the daily press and of public opinion, and, finally, the prevailing political spirit and its system. If these conditions were, as seems to be the case, the *general, invisible* and *compelling* forces of that period, it hardly needs to be shown that they had to take effect as *such,* and were bound to be manifested in facts and *expressed* in separate actions which had the *semblance* of being arbitrary. Anyone who abandons this objective standpoint falls victim to one-sided, bitter feelings against individual personalities in whom he sees embodied all the harshness of the contemporary conditions confronting him.

Among the *special* obstacles to the press we must include not only individual *difficulties due to censorship,* but equally the *special circumstances* which made censorship itself superfluous because they did not allow the object of censorship to come into being at all, even tentatively. When the censorship comes into obvious, persistent and sharp conflict with the press, it can be concluded with a fair certainty that the press has achieved vitality, character and self-assurance, for only a perceptible action produces a perceptible reaction. When, on the other hand, there is no censorship because there is no press, although the need for a free and therefore *censurable* press exists, one must expect to find a *pre-censorship* in circumstances which have suppressed by fear the expression of thought even in its more unpretentious forms.

We cannot aim at giving a full description of these *special* circumstances even in an approximate form. It would mean describing the whole history of the period since 1830 insofar as it concerns the Mosel region. We believe we shall have fulfilled our task if we prove that the frank and public word *in all* its *forms*—in *spoken* form, in *written* form, and in *printed* form, print *not yet censored* as well as that already *censored*—has encountered *special* obstacles.

Depression and despondency, which in any case shatter the moral strength required by a distressed population for public and frank discussion, were especially aroused by the court sentences imposed *"for insult to an official in the performance of his duty or in connection with his duty"*, which necessarily followed numerous *denunciations.*

This kind of procedure is still fresh in the memory of many Mosel vine-growers. One citizen, particularly liked because of his good nature, jokingly remarked to the maidservant of a *district president*, who the evening before had busily applied himself to the bottle when celebrating the King's birthday in joyful company: *"Your master was a bit tiddly last night."* For this innocent remark he was *publicly* brought before the police court at Trier, but, as might have been expected, he was *acquitted.*

We have chosen this particular example because a simple conclusion necessarily follows from it. Each *district president* is the *censor* in the chief town of his district. The district president's administration, however, together with that of the official bodies subordinated to him, will provide the principal subject-matter for the *local press*, because it is the latter's immediate concern. If in general it is difficult to be the judge in one's own case, incidents of the kind mentioned above, which testify to a pathologically sensitive notion of the inviolability attaching to an official position, make the mere existence of the *district president's censorship* a sufficient reason for the non-existence of a frank local press.

If, therefore, we see that an ingenuous and innocent *utterance* can lead to an appearance before the police court, a *written* form of free speech, a *petition*, which is still a long way from publicity by the press, has the same police-court result. In the former case, frank speaking is prevented by the inviolability attaching to an *official position*, in the latter case by the inviolability of the *laws of the land.*

Following a "Cabinet Order" of July 6, 1836, which stated, among other things, that the King[a] was sending his son to the Rhine Province to *acquaint himself with the conditions prevailing there,* some cultivators in the Trier administrative district were inspired to request their "deputy to the Provincial Assembly" to draw up a petition to the Crown Prince[b] on their behalf. At the same time they indicated the various items of their complaint. In order to increase the importance of the petition by a larger number of signatures, the deputy to the Provincial Assembly[c] sent to the environs a messenger who obtained the signatures of 160 peasants. The petition read as follows:

---

[a] Frederick William III.— *Ed.*

[b] Who became Frederick William IV in 1840.— *Ed.*

[c] Valdenaire.— *Ed.*

"We, the undersigned inhabitants of the circuit ... of the Trier administrative district, being informed that our gracious King is sending us His Royal Highness the Crown Prince to acquaint himself with our position, and in order to spare His Royal Highness the trouble of hearing complaints from a number of separate persons, herewith authorise our deputy to the Provincial Assembly, Herr ..., most humbly to submit to His Royal Highness, His most gracious Majesty's son, the Crown Prince of Prussia, that:

"1. When we are unable to sell our surplus products, especially as regards cattle and *wine*, it is impossible for us to pay the taxes, which in all circumstances are too high; for which reason we desire a considerable reduction of the same, since otherwise we have to give the tax-collectors our goods and chattels, as shown by the attached (it contains an order from a tax-collector to pay 1 reichstaler 25 silver groschen 5 pfennigs).

"2. That His Royal Highness should not judge our situation from the evidence of innumerable, much too highly paid, officials, pensioners, persons with special remuneration, civilian and military personnel, rentiers and industrialists, who, owing to the fall in the price of our products, are able to live in the towns cheaply in a luxury such as is not to be found, on the other hand, in the poor hut of the cultivator, who is overwhelmed by debts, and this contrast arouses his indignation. Whereas previously there were 27 officials receiving 29,000 talers, there are now 63 officials, excluding those on pension, who are paid a total of 105,000 talers.

"3. That our communal officials should be elected, as was previously the case, directly by members of the community.

"4. That the tax offices should not be closed for hours on end during the day, but should be open at all times, so that the cultivator who, through no fault of his own, arrives a few minutes late, does not have to wait five to six hours, even having to freeze all night in the street or stand in the burning sun all day, since the official should always be ready to serve the people.

"5. That the provision in §12 of the law of April 28, 1828, renewed by the official gazette of His Majesty's Government of August 22 last, which makes it a punishable offence to plough within two feet of the ditch at the edge of roads going through cultivated land, should be annulled and the owners allowed to plough their whole land right up to the road ditch, so as to prevent this land from being stolen from them by the highway custodians.

"Your Royal Highness' most humble subjects."

(Signatures follow.)

This petition, which the deputy to the Provincial Assembly wanted to hand personally to the Crown Prince, was accepted by someone else with the express promise that it would be given to His Royal Highness. No reply to it was received, but court proceedings were instituted against the deputy to the Provincial Assembly as the initiator of a petition containing "*insolent, dishonourable accusations against the laws of the province*". As a result of this charge, the deputy to the Provincial Assembly was sentenced in Trier to *six months' imprisonment* with costs. This punishment, however, was amended by the appeal court so that only the part relating to costs was left in force, on the grounds that the conduct of the accused was not quite free from indiscretion and therefore he was responsible for the case being brought against him. The *contents of the petition itself*, on the other hand, were acknowledged to be not at all *punishable*.

Partly because of the aim of the Crown Prince's journey, and partly because of the official position of the accused as a deputy to the Provincial Assembly, the petition in question was bound to be magnified in the eyes of the whole environs into a specially important and decisive event and to attract public attention in the highest degree. Taking this into account, the consequences cannot be said to have encouraged a public and frank discussion of the conditions in the Mosel region or to have made probable any wishes of the authorities on this subject.

We come now to the real obstacle to the press, to *prohibitions imposed by the censorship*. From what has been said above, it is evident that such prohibitions are bound to be rare, since attempts at a censurable discussion of the Mosel conditions have been a rarity.

The *minutes of a council of elders*, which, besides some eccentric statements, contained also some frank speaking, were not allowed to be printed owing to the censorship exercised by the *district president*. The discussion took place in the *council of elders,* but the *minutes of the council* were drawn up by the burgomaster. His introductory statement was as follows:

"Gentlemen! The Mosel region between Trier and Koblenz, between the Eifel and the Hundsrücken, is outwardly very poor because it is entirely dependent on viticulture, which has been dealt the *death-blow* by the trade agreements with Germany. The above-mentioned region is also *spiritually* poor", etc.

Finally, yet another fact can be adduced to show that when a public and frank discussion did overcome all the above-mentioned obstacles and *by way of exception* managed to get into the columns of a newspaper, it was treated as an *exception* and subsequently suppressed. Several years ago an article by Herr *Kaufmann, professor of cameralistics* at Bonn University, "on the distressed state of the vine-growers in the Mosel region, etc." was printed in the *Rhein- und Mosel-Zeitung*. After three months, during which it had been reprinted in various newspapers, it was *banned* by order of the government and the ban is still in force.

I think I have now sufficiently replied to the question of the attitude of the Mosel region to the Cabinet Order of December 10, to the *censorship instruction* of December 24 based on this order, and to the subsequent freer movement of the press. It only remains for me to substantiate my assertion: "For a long time the desperate state of the vine-growers was doubted in higher quarters, and their cry of distress was regarded as an insolent shrieking." The statement in question can be divided into two parts: "For a long time the desperate state of the vine-growers was doubted in higher quarters" and "Their cry of distress was regarded as an insolent shrieking".

The first proposition, I think, requires no further proof. The second one: "Their cry of distress was regarded as an insolent shrieking", cannot be deduced directly from the first, as the Herr Oberpräsident does by giving it the form: "Their cry of distress was regarded in *higher quarters* as an isolent shrieking." Incidentally, this interpolation, too, holds good, insofar as "*higher* quarters" and "*official* quarters" can be taken as equivalent in meaning.

That one could speak of a "*cry of distress*" of the vine-growers, not in a *metaphorical* sense, but in the *strict* sense of the word, is evident from the information we have given above. That, on the one hand, this cry of distress was declared to be without justification and the description of the distress itself regarded as a glaring exaggeration prompted by bad, selfish motives; and that, on the other hand, the complaint and the petition of those suffering distress were regarded as "*insolent,* dishonourable accusations against the laws of the province" — these propositions have been proved by a *government report* and *criminal proceedings.* That, furthermore, an excessive outcry, which does not correspond to the true state of affairs and is exaggerated from bad motives, involving *insolent* accusations against the laws of the province — that such an *outcry* is identical with a "shrieking", and indeed an "insolent shrieking", cannot at least be regarded as a far-fetched or *dishonest* assertion. That finally, therefore, one side of the identity can be put in place of the other seems simply to follow as a logical consequence.

Written between January 1 and 20, 1843
First published in the *Rheinische Zeitung* Nos. 15, 17, 18, 19 and 20, January 15, 17, 18, 19 and 20, 1843

Printed according to the newspaper
Published in English for the first time

[POLEMICAL ARTICLES
AGAINST THE *ALLGEMEINE ZEITUNG*[131]]

[*Rheinische Zeitung* No. 3, January 3, 1843]

The *lady of Augsburg* has reached the stage when the fair sex itself no longer dares to *simulate youth*, and now has no more terrible accusation to make against her sisters than that of youth. In No. 360, however, the worthy Sibyl's means of estimating age has surprisingly misled her. She speaks about a *cooling* off of the "youthful ardour" of the *Rheinische Zeitung* in connection with a correspondent who happens to be a *sexagenarian* and could hardly have expected to find a testimonial to his youth in the columns of the Augsburg *Allg. Zeitung*. But that is what happens! Freedom is sometimes too old, sometimes too young; it is never on the order of the day, at any rate not on that of the Augsburg *Allg. Ztg.*, which is more and more emphatically rumoured to be published in *Augsburg*.

[*Rheinische Zeitung* No. 12, January 12, 1843]

If the editorial board of the *Rheinische Zeitung* desired to add to the above correspondence a postscript in the manner of the *Allg. A. Ztg.*, since she was so kind as to recognise the ensign *Pistol* in the *Rheinische Zeitung*, we could only give her a choice between *Doll Tearsheet* and *Mistress Quickly*. Her *manly* confession of faith, however, we would expect from the friend of those ladies, from *Falstaff*:

"Honour pricks me on. Yea, but how if honour pricks me off when I come on? how then? Can honour set to a leg? No. Or an arm? No. Or take away the grief of a wound? No. Honour hath no skill in surgery then? No. What is honour? A word. What is in that word honour? What is that honour? Air. A trim reckoning! Who hath it? He that died a Wednesday. Doth he feel it? No. Doth he hear it? No. Is it insensible then? Yea, to the dead. But will it not live with the living? No. Why? *Detraction* will not suffer it:—therefore I'll none of it. Honour is a mere scutcheon, and so ends my catechism."[a]

---

[a] W. Shakespeare, *King Henry IV*, Part One, Act V, Scene 1.—*Ed.*

Thus, too, ends the political catechism of the Augsburg *A. Z.*; thus she reminds the press that one could lose arm and leg in *critical* times, thus she detracts from honour, because she has renounced any honour which could be detracted from.

The Augsburg *A. Z.* promised to engage us in a fight over principles and she has kept her promise. She has used *no* principles, hence *her* principles, against us in the struggle. Now and again she has assured us of her indignation, cast petty suspicions, attempted minor corrections, made a big show of small performance, and laid claim to superiority of age. In regard to this last point, to her title of *veteran,* we could say what M. Dézamy says to M. Cabet:

"Que monsieur Cabet ait bon courage: avec tant de titres, il ne peut manquer d'obtenir bientôt ses *invalides!*" [a]

Madame Augsburg survives because of a mistake in calculation, an anachronism. *Form,* the only thing she possessed in earlier days, even form, the *parfum littéraire,* she has lost. It has been replaced by a philistine, diffuse and arrogant formlessness, and no one is likely to regard the platitude of "Herr Puff" and the simile of "the bullfrog that tried to blow itself up into an ox" as elegant because he finds the same sort of thing in the Augsburg *A. Z.*

First published in the *Rheinische Zeitung* Nos. 3 and 12, January 3 and 12, 1843

Printed according to the newspaper.

Published in English for the first time

---

[a] "Let Monsieur Cabet take heart; with so many titles, he cannot fail to obtain his *disability pension* soon!" Th. Dézamy, *Calomnies et politique de M. Cabet,* p. 7, note.— *Ed.*

MARGINAL NOTES TO THE ACCUSATIONS
OF THE MINISTERIAL RESCRIPT [132]

I

"From the outset, it" (the *Rheinische Zeitung*)"pursued such a *reprehensible* course" etc. "Unmistakably," it is stated, "the intention continued to prevail in the newspaper to attack the basis of the state constitution, to develop theories which aim at undermining the monarchical principle, to maliciously cast suspicion on the actions of the government in the eyes of the public, to incite some estates of the nation against others, to arouse dissatisfaction with the existing legal conditions, and to promote very hostile trends against friendly powers. Its views on alleged defects of administration, apart from the fact that they were mostly without foundation and largely devoid of thoroughness and expert knowledge, were not couched in a serious, calm and dignified tone, but marked by malicious hostility towards the state and its administrative forms and organs."

It is obvious that a trend does not become *reprehensible* merely because the government declares it to be so. Even the *Copernican system of the universe* was not only found reprehensible by the supreme authority of the time, but was actually condemned. Furthermore, it is everywhere the law that the *accuser* should provide the proof. Finally, there is attributed to the *Rheinische Zeitung* the "*unmistakable* intention" of committing the crimes laid to its charge. But an intention only becomes *recognisable,* and the more so *unmistakable,* when it has been realised in *acts.*

But if even for a moment we were to concede (what, however, we expressly deny) that all the accusations of the ministerial rescript were well founded, the result nevertheless would be that in their present indefinite and ambiguous formulation they would provide just as much and just as little reason for a ban on *any* newspaper *whatever* as for a ban on the *Rheinische Zeitung.*

First of all, it is said that there prevailed in the *Rheinische Zeitung* "the unmistakable intention to attack the basis of the state constitution". It is well known, however, that there unmistakably prevails a great diversity of opinion on the Prussian constitution and its basis. Some deny that the basis has any constitution, others that the constitution has any basis.

One view is held by Stein, Hardenberg, Schön, another one by Rochow, Arnim, and Eichhorn. Hegel in his day believed that he had laid the basis for the Prussian constitution in his philosophy of law, and the government and the German public concurred in this belief. One way by which the government proved this was the official dissemination of his writings; the public, however, did so by accusing him of being the philosopher of the Prussian state, as one can read in the old Leipzig conversational dictionary.[133] What Hegel believed at that time, Stahl believes today. In 1831, by a special order of the government, Hegel lectured on the philosophy of law.

In 1830, the *Staats-Zeitung* declared that Prussia was a monarchy surrounded by republican institutions. Today it says Prussia is a monarchy surrounded by Christian institutions.

In view of this great diversity of opinion on the Prussian constitution and its basis, it seems natural that the *Rh. Z.* also should have *its* opinion, which of course may differ from the current view of the government, but which nevertheless can quote in its favour both Prussian history and many elements of the present-day life of the state as definitively highly placed authorities.

Far from intending to attack the basis of the Prussian constitution, therefore, the *Rh. Z.*, on the contrary, was convinced that it was attacking only deviations from this basis.

In regard to the banning of the *Rh. Z.*, an official article in the *Allgemeine Königsberger Zeitung* described Prussia as a state of liberal sovereignty.[134] This is a definition which is not to be found in Prussian law and allows of all possible interpretations.

"Liberal sovereignty" can be understood in two ways: either that freedom is merely the *personal* frame of mind of the King, and therefore his personal quality, or that freedom is the spirit of sovereignty, and is therefore realised, or at least should be realised, also through free institutions and laws. In the former case we have a *despotisme éclairé*,[a] and the *person* of the prince is contrasted to the state as a whole as to a mindless and unfree material. In the latter case, and this was the view of the *Rh. Z.*, one does not confine the prince within the bounds of his personality, but regards the whole state as his body, so that the institutions are the organs in which he lives and acts, and the laws are the eyes by which he sees.

Further it is said to have been the intention of the *Rh. Z.* "to develop theories which aim at undermining the monarchical principle".

---

[a] Enlightened despotism.— *Ed.*

Once again, the question arises: What is to be understood by the "monarchical principle"? The *Rh. Z.*, for instance, maintained that the predominance of distinctions between the estates, one-sided bureaucracy, censorship, etc., contradicted the monarchical principle, and it has always tried to *prove* its assertions, and has not put them forward as mere ideas. In general, however, the *Rh. Z.* has never given special preference to a *special form of state.* It was concerned for a *moral and rational commonweal*; it regarded the demands of such a commonweal as demands which would have to be realised and could be realised under *every* form of state. Hence it did not treat the *monarchical principle* as a principle *apart*; it treated monarchy rather as the realisation of the state principle in general. If this was an error, it was not an error of underestimation, but of overestimation.

Further, the *Rh. Z.* has never tried maliciously to cast suspicion on the actions of the government in the eyes of the public. On the contrary, it is out of goodwill that it has tried to cast suspicion on those measures of the government itself that are contrary to the spirit of the people. Furthermore, it has never abstractly counterposed the government to the people; on the contrary, it has considered defects of the state to be just as much defects of the people as of the government.

As far as thoroughness and expert knowledge are concerned, as also the tone of the *Rh. Z.*, at least not a single newspaper in Germany has shown more thoroughness or expert knowledge. As for its tone, it is truly serious, calm and dignified, compared with the rowdy tone of the servile (conservative)[a] journals. In this respect, the *Rh. Z.* has been accused, not unjustly, of *unpopularity*, of being too *scientific* in its form, which directly contradicts the ministry's accusation.

No more has the *Rh. Z.* tried to incite some estates of the nation against others; on the contrary, it has tried to incite every estate against its own egoism and limitations, it has everywhere brought civic reason to bear against estate unreason, and human love against estate hatred. Moreover, if it has sinned in this respect, it has only committed a sin that is sanctioned by the law and usage of the Rhine Province.

The reproach of having wanted to "arouse dissatisfaction with the existing legal conditions" cannot in this indefinite formulation even be regarded as a reproach.

---

[a] "(conservative)" has been inserted above the word "servile" in the manuscript.— *Ed.*

Even the government has tried to arouse dissatisfaction with the existing legal conditions, for example with the old Prussian marriage situation. All reform and revision of the law, all progress, rests on such dissatisfaction.

Since legal development is not possible without development of the laws, and since development of the laws is impossible without criticism of them, and since every criticism of the laws sets the mind and therefore also the heart of the citizen at variance with the existing laws, and since this variance is experienced as dissatisfaction, it follows that a loyal participation of the press in the development of the state is impossible if it is not permitted to arouse dissatisfaction with the existing legal conditions.

The reproach that the *Rh. Z.* persecutes loyal organs by unworthy ridicule, which is obviously intended to refer to the newspaper controversy, cannot provide grounds for a ban. From all sides, the *Rh. Z.* has been denounced, has had mud cast at it, and been attacked. It was its duty to defend itself. Moreover, there is no *official* press.

The *Rh. Z.* has not insulted *foreign* powers,[135] but has only condemned their insults against Germany. In this respect it has merely pursued a *national* policy. As far as the states of the German Confederation are concerned, it has only expressed the view of the majority of the representatives of the people in these states.

As regards religion, the newspaper has treated it in accordance with Article II of the 1819 censorship decree, that is to say, it has opposed religious truths being fanatically transplanted into politics and the confusion of ideas [136] arising therefrom.

II

If the *Rh. Z.* had wanted to promote systematic opposition to the government, it would have had to employ entirely *opposite tactics*.

It would have flattered the prejudices of the Rhine Province, instead of opposing them. Above all, it would have paid homage to its *religious prejudices* and have exploited the antithesis between North-German and South-German culture after the manner of the ultramontane,[137] instead of introducing North-German culture in the Rhine Province.

It would have based itself on French, and not German, theories.

It would have put forward the provincial spirit with its special limitations in opposition to the idea of state unity; hence, like Görres,[138] it would above all have taken the provincial assemblies under its protection.

It would have considered that all that was good came from the estates while all that was bad came from the government, as ordinary liberalism does. In its criticism of the Rhine estates it would not have laid stress on the general wisdom of the government in contrast to the private egoism of the estates,[139] as it has done in contrast to many Rhine[a] liberals. Lastly, it would have joined in the chorus of other newspapers and demanded extended rights for the commissions, instead of describing such a demand as contrary to the interests of the state.

III

Finally, it is strangely exaggerating to speak of the *malice* of the *whole tendency,* since in that case
1. the fight for the Customs Union,
2. for Prussia in the matter of the Russian cartel,[140]
3. for Prussian hegemony,
4. the constant reference to Prussia as the progressive state,
5. the praise of Prussian popular institutions, such as the army, administration, etc.,
would likewise be ill-intentioned.

Neither has the *Rh. Z.* one-sidedly opposed the bureaucracy. On the contrary, it has brought the influence of the latter to bear:
1. against Bülow-Cummerow,
2. against the romantic trend.

On the contrary, it was the only *liberal* newspaper which recognised also the good aspect of the bureaucracy, as well as the good aspect of the old Prussian legislation.

Thus, the *Rh. Z.* alone has defended the main principle of the new divorce law, in contradiction to almost all other newspapers.

Thus, lastly, it was the first and almost the sole newspaper to welcome the Cabinet Order on *corrections*[b] as a progressive step.[141]

We cite these examples only to prove that the *Rh. Z.* has not conducted a *systematic,* abstract opposition, but has always asserted only what it was convinced was rational, from whatever side it proceeded.

Written on February 12, 1843
First published in the book *Rheinische Briefe und Akten zur Geschichte der politischen Bewegung 1830-1850,* 1. Bd., Essen, 1919

Printed according to the manuscript
Published in English for the first time

---

[a] See this volume, pp. 280-81.— *Ed.*
[b] Corrected by Marx from "Prussian".— *Ed.*

THE LOCAL ELECTION OF DEPUTIES
TO THE PROVINCIAL ASSEMBLY

Cologne, March 9. The *Rhein- und Mosel-Zeitung*, which is so modest as to be neither "the most widely read newspaper of the Rhine Province" nor an "exponent of political thought", remarks in connection with the election of deputies from the city of Cologne,[142] *inter alia:*

"We are quite ready to regard Herr *Merkens* and Herr *Camphausen* as very *honourable* men" ("so are they all, all honourable men",[a] as it is said in the tragedy) "and even" (just think of it!) "*even* to bestow applause on the *Rheinische Zeitung*" (a most valuable gift!) "when it triumphantly counterposes these men to the opponents of the rights of our province. But we must all the more sharply and resolutely condemn the *reasons* for which an attempt has been made to exert an influence on the election of these men, not because these reasons are undeserving of *any* consideration, but because they deserve no such *exclusive* consideration, but *only* a secondary one."

The fact is that the following lithographed circular had been distributed to *various* electors of Cologne city:

"What the city of Cologne has to represent first and most importantly in the forthcoming Provincial Assembly is indisputably the conditions of its trade and industry. Hence the choice must fall on men who, besides being of an honourable disposition and occupying an independent civic position among us, are closely acquainted with the course of these relations in all respects and are able to grasp, illuminate and expound them from the correct standpoint."

Then follows the reference to the above-mentioned, certainly very honourable men. After which the circular states in conclusion:

"Our city already today occupies a powerful position in the commercial world. But a still greater extension of its trade and industry is in store for it, and the time for this development is not far distant. Shipping by sail, steam, towage, and the railways, will bring back to our city the period of the old Hansa, only its true interest must be represented with understanding and circumspection in the forthcoming Provincial Assembly.

"*Cologne*, Feb. 24.

A number of electors"

This circular elicited the following Capuchin's tirade from the extremely witty *Rhein- und Mosel-Zeitung*:

---

[a] W. Shakespeare, *Julius Caesar*, Act 3, Scene 2.—*Ed.*

"If anywhere material local interests prevail to such an extent that there is not even a faint glimmering of spiritual and general needs, is it any wonder that those who hold the reins of government in their hands pay attention only to the former, and the latter are ordered only according to their discretion? O you great city of Cologne, you holy city of Cologne, you witty city of Cologne, what a low point the spiritual state and historical recollections of many of your children have reached! By the realisation of wishes and hopes that could at most make you into a big money-bag, they dream of bringing back the period of the old Hansa!!!"

The *Rhein- und Mosel-Zeitung* does not find fault with the election of the deputies; it finds fault with the *reasons* which are said to have "exerted an influence" on the election. And what were these reasons? The newspaper quotes *one* circular addressed to *various* electors, in which the "conditions of trade and industry" are described as the most important objects of Cologne's representation in the forthcoming Provincial Assembly. How does the *Rhein- und Mosel-Zeitung* know that this circular, which incidentally, as the newspaper itself admits, reached only "various" electors, exerted such an effect on the minds of the electors that it primarily and exclusively decided the election of Herr Merkens and Herr Camphausen? Because the election of these gentlemen is recommended in a circular for quite *special* reasons, and because in fact these gentlemen were elected, does it in any way follow that their election is a result of that recommendation and its special motivation?

The *Rhein- und Mosel-Ztg.* bestows applause on the *Rheinische Zeitung* when it "triumphantly counterposes these men" (Herr Camphausen and Herr Merkens) "to the opponents of the rights of our province". What moves it to this "bestowal of applause"? Obviously the character of those elected. Is this character supposed to have been less well known in Cologne than in Koblenz? [143] Among the interests to be represented in the Provincial Assembly, the *Rhein- und Mosel-Zeitung* mentions *only* a "*freer political system of local government*" and an "*extension of the rights of the estates*". Does it think that it is not known in Cologne that Herr Merkens has distinguished himself in various provincial assemblies by his struggle for a "free political system of local government", and that in one Provincial Assembly he even defended this courageously and indefatigably in opposition to almost the entire Assembly? But in regard to "the extension of the interests of the estates" it is very well known in Cologne that Herr Merkens has primarily protested against the narrowing of these interests by autonomy, that nevertheless he stood just as resolutely for the interests of the estates being kept within their proper bounds when they opposed the general interest, general law and reason, as in the debates on the law on wood thefts and hunting.[a] If, therefore, the general

---

[a] See this volume, pp. 224-62.— *Ed.*

qualification of Herr Merkens to be a deputy to the Provincial Assembly is established beyond all doubt by his whole parliamentary career, if Herr Camphausen's exceptional, universal culture, high intelligence and serious honourable character are generally known and recognised, how does the *Rhein- und Mosel-Zeitung* know that the election of these gentlemen is due not to these obvious reasons, but rather to the above-quoted circular?

No! No! the honourable newspaper will reply to us, that is not what I maintain, not all! My delicate spiritual cast of mind is merely offended by the *originators* of that circular, by those materialists who have laid stress not on the spiritual and true interests of the people, but on other and much lower motives, and who for improper reasons have sought to exert an influence on the election of those men and on those "children of Cologne" whose "spiritual state and historical recollections" have sunk so low!

If the *Rhein- und Mosel-Zeitung* is only concerned about the *originators* of that anonymous document, why does it raise such an outcry? Why does it say:

> "If *anywhere* material local interests *prevail* to such an extent that *there is not even a faint glimmering of spiritual and general needs*, is it any wonder that those who hold the reins of government in their hands pay attention only to the former, and the latter are ordered only according to their discretion?"

Do then material local interests prevail exclusively in Cologne because they prevail exclusively in an anonymous circular? No more than *juristic* interests prevail exclusively in Cologne because these interests are exclusively asserted in another circular which likewise reached *various* electors! Are not *dull* children to be found in every town as in every family? Would it be fair to judge the character of a town or a family from these children?

Closer examination, however, shows that the circular is in fact not so bad as the honourable *Koblenz* newspaper wants to make us believe. It is even completely justified by the function of the provincial estates as fixed by law. Their legal function consists partly in asserting the *general interest of the province*, and partly in asserting *their special estate interests*. That Herr Camphausen and Herr Merkens are worthy representatives of *Rhenish provincial interests* is a general conviction that did not need to be confirmed or even so much as mentioned by the originators of the circular.

Since the *general* qualification of these gentlemen as deputies to the Provincial Assembly was above all discussion, the question therefore concerned only the special requirements of *a Cologne* deputy. The question was what *city interests* Cologne should "first and most importantly" represent in the "*forthcoming Provincial Assembly*"! Would anyone want to deny that these are the "conditions of trade and industry"? But neither would the simple denial suffice; *proof* would have to be given.

The *Rhein- und Mosel-Zeitung* particularly objects to the passage:

"Shipping by sail, steam, towage, and the railways, will bring back to our city the *period of the old Hansa.*"

Oh, woe to the poor city of Cologne! How it is deceived! How it deceives itself! "By the realisation of wishes and hopes," moans the *Rhein- und Mosel-Zeitung*, "that could at most make you into a big *money-bag,* they dream of bringing back the period of the old Hansa!"

Poor *Rhein- und Mosel-Zeitung*! It does not understand that the phrase "period of the old Hansa" is intended to mean only the period of the old flourishing of trade, that in reality the death-knell would have to sound for "all *spiritual* and *general* needs", that "spiritual state" would have to be totally *deranged,* and that all "historical recollections" would have to be quite blotted out if Cologne wanted to bring back the political, social and intellectual period of the Hansa towns, the period of the *Middle Ages!* Would the government not have to make "spiritual and general needs" exclusively its private domain if a town were to have so completely estranged itself from all rational and healthy awareness of the present time as to live only in a dream of the past! Would it not be even the duty of the government, its duty of self-preservation, to tighten its hold on the reins if the attempt was made in all seriousness to blow sky-high the whole present and future in order to bring back *obsolete and decayed conditions.*

We want to tell our readers the plain truth. There took place in Cologne—and that is the clearest testimony to its political vitality—a serious *election struggle,* a struggle between the men of the present and the men of the past. The men of the past, the men who would like to see the "period of the old Hansa towns" restored *in its entirety,* have been driven from the field despite all machinations. And now along come these fantastic materialists, for whom every steamship and every railway should have demonstrated *ad oculos* their utter lack of sense, and talk hypocritically of "spiritual state" and "historical recollections", and lament by the waters of Babylon over "the great city of Cologne, the holy city of Cologne, the witty city of Cologne"—and it is to be hoped that their tears will not dry up so soon!

Written in March 1843

First published in the *Rheinische Zeitung* No. 68, March 9, 1843

Printed according to the newspaper

Published in English for the first time

THE *RHEIN- UND MOSEL-ZEITUNG*
AS GRAND INQUISITOR

Cologne, March 11. A few days ago the *Rhein- und Mosel-Zeitung* published a bull of excommunication against the pious *Kölnische Zeitung.* Today the *Trier'sche Zeitung* stands before the court of inquisition in Koblenz, and rightly so.

For, in connection with Friedrich von Sallet, the *Trier'sche Zeitung* says among other things [144]:

> "We have before us his book, the *Laien-Evangelium, which without falsification reveals for us the holy, eternal truths of the gospel.*" "He" (Sallet) "endeavoured to be a man in the highest sense, following the example given by Jesus, and, *as the true champion of the Lord, revealed eternal truth.*"

> "Anyone who reads that," says the *Rhein- und Mosel-Zeitung,* "and knows nothing more about this man who is given such high praise, would he not believe that Herr von Sallet must have been a faithful Christian and in his *Laien-Evangelium* must have preached the Lord's word with fiery zeal? But what in truth is the content of this gospel? It is that false and pernicious doctrine which a Strauss, a Feuerbach, a Bruno Bauer, and all the apostles of modern paganism, whatever their names are, expound in lecture-rooms and in their writings for a narrow circle of learned people and so on."

As an authentic proof of its assertion, the *Rhein- und Mosel-Zeitung* quotes

> "a passage from this *Laien-Evangelium,* namely, that in which a parallel is drawn between the traitor Judas and the Christ of the gospels, i.e., Christ as depicted in the Bible".

The proofs cited strikingly demonstrate Sallet's attitude of deliberate opposition to *historical* Christianity.

A mistaken feeling of humanity may be offended by the ruthless polemic of the *Rhein- und Mosel-Zeitung* against a man who has only just died, but is not the apologia of the *Trier'sche Zeitung* more inhuman, and equally offensive? Do I honour the deceased by giving a *false* account of his spiritual personality? Sallet indeed endeavoured to reveal truth, but by no means the truth of the gospel. Sallet certainly endeavoured to be a *true* human being, but by no means a champion of ecclesiastical truth.

On the contrary, Sallet believed that he could make rational truth effective only in opposition to holy truth, and that he could make the moral human being effective only in opposition to the Christian human being, and that is why he wrote his *Laien-Evangelium*. And what happened? Did the *Trier'sche Zeitung's* apologist honour the man when he turned all his efforts upside down? Would it be an honour for Luther if one said he was a good Catholic, or for Pope Ganganelli if one called him a Maecenas for the Jesuits? What hypocrisy! What weakness! Sallet was a republican; can you be his friend if you make a great show of declaring his royalism? Sallet loved truth above all; do you believe there is no better way to pay homage to him than by an untruth? Or are Christianity and friendship at odds in your person? All right! Admit it then, and say: Sallet was a good man, etc., but a bad *Christian*! Deplore that, if you like, deplore it publicly, but do not pretend that his works are an illuminating testimony to his Christianity. If you *condemn* what your friend strove for, then condemn it *sans-gêne* as the *Rhein- und Mosel-Zeitung* does, but not in a hypocritical, devious way, not by praising him for being what he was *not*, and therefore rejecting precisely what he *really* was.

Even if we admit that the *Laien-Evangelium* itself could give rise to such a conception, that Sallet *here* has by no means got things clear in his own mind, that he himself *believes* he is teaching the true meaning of the gospel, and that it is easy to counterpose quite Christian-sounding contradictory excerpts to the quotation given by the *Rhein- und Mosel-Zeitung*, that newspaper is still correct in claiming that he puts forward a *self-made* Christianity instead of *historical* Christianity.

Finally, a few words more on the passages quoted by the *Rhein- und Mosel-Zeitung*! They suffer from a fundamental defect, that of being *unpoetical*. And what an altogether mistaken idea it is to want to treat theological controversies poetically! Has it ever occurred to a composer to set dogma to music?

Leaving aside this heresy against art, what is the content of the passage quoted? *Sallet* finds it *incompatible* with the divinity of Christ that Christ knows the treacherous intention of Judas and does not attempt to reform him or to frustrate the crime. Hence Sallet exclaims (as cited by the *Rhein- und Mosel-Zeitung*):

> Woe to whoever—in dazzled delusion!—
> Contrived to invent such traits of the Lord,
> And caricatured him to let him retain
> This morsel of knowledge of man's human nature.[a]

Sallet's verdict testifies to the fact that he was neither a *theologian* nor a *philosopher*. As a *theologian* he could not have been disturbed by the contradiction with *human* reason and morality, for the theologian does not judge the gospel by human reason and morality; on the contrary, he judges these by the gospel. On the other hand, as a *philosopher* he would have regarded such contradictions in the *nature of religious thought* as well founded, and therefore he would have conceived the contradiction as a *necessary product* of the Christian outlook and would by no means have condemned it as a *falsification of the latter*.

May the *Rhein- und Mosel-Zeitung* vigorously continue its work of faith and clothe all and sundry Rhenish newspapers in the sanbenito.[145] We shall see whether the *half-and-half*, lukewarm ones, who are neither hot nor cold, will get on better with the *terrorism of faith* than with the *terrorism of reason*.

Written on March 11, 1843

First published in the *Rheinische Zeitung*
No. 71, March 12, 1843

Printed according to the newspaper

Published in English for the first time

---

[a] F. von Sallet, *Laien-Evangelium*, S. 442.—*Ed.*

STYLISTIC EXERCISES
OF THE *RHEIN- UND MOSEL-ZEITUNG*

Cologne, March 13. The *Rhein- und Mosel-Zeitung* has replied today [146] to our article of March 9 on the deputies to the Provincial Assembly.[a] We do not want to hold back from our readers some samples of this masterpiece of *style*. Among other delicacies is the following:

"Thus in far-reaching strokes, not it is true with a halberd, but with its *accustomed cudgel*, the *Rhein. Ztg*. has let fly at a spectre" (Just think! *An accustomed cudgel! To let fly in strokes with a cudgel!*) "which it believed it perceived in an article of the *Rhein- und Mosel-Zeitung*, and as is self-evident" (what a luxury, to expend words on things that are self-evident!) "all its strokes fell wide" (*fell wide!* wide of the *Rhein- und Mosel-Zeitung*, perhaps on its editor!), "and the *attacked*" (the spectre was indeed only attacked!) "newspaper finds itself quite unhurt and intact."

What generous logic, which does not leave to the sagacity of its readers even the conclusion that strokes which fell *wide* of the attacked newspaper did not fall *on* the attacked newspaper! What luxury of understanding, what a thoroughgoing narration! Only it should be mentioned how interesting it must have seemed to the *Rhein- und Mosel-Zeitung* to proclaim that its back was intact. How the imagination of the *Rhein- und Mosel-Zeitung* is preoccupied with its splendid idea of the "spectre" and the *Rhein. Ztg*. letting fly at it, and of the cudgel-blows that fell wide, can be demonstrated by the following variations, as ingenious as they are surprising, on this superlative theme. In enumerating them, we will not fail to call attention to their fine nuances and shades. Thus:

---

[a] See this volume, pp. 366-69.— *Ed.*

1. "In far-reaching strokes with its accustomed cudgel, the *Rhein. Ztg.* of March 9 has thus let fly at a *spectre* which it believed it perceived in an article of the *Rhein- und Mosel-Zeitung*, and as is self-evident all its strokes fell wide."

2. "But the article which made the *Rhein. Ztg.* a *spirit-seer* (previously the spirit was a spectre, and since when could the *Rhein. Ztg.* have detected any *spirit* in the obscure ultramontane paper?) "and consequently a heroine fighting a *shadow*."

So this time the shadow of the *Rhein- und Mosel-Zeitung* at least is said to have been hit!

3. "The *Rhein. Ztg.*, however, which is *certainly* aware *also* that in respect of everything *substantial*, true and *solid*" (the *back* of the *Rhein- und Mosel Zeitung*?) "its powers become a laughing-stock" (and what spiritual power would not become a laughing-stock in respect of a back?), "and which *nevertheless for once* wants to show that it has *horns*" (the "accustomed cudgel" has mysteriously turned into "horns") "and can butt" (previously, let fly in far-reaching strokes), "has *thought up*" (previously "seen" or *"believed it has seen"*) "a spectre which it would like to have regarded as the real spirit of our article" (a repetition to remind the reader of the facts of the matter!), "and against which it vents its anger to its heart's content and tests its strength" (a clever rhetorical performance), "just as in a bull-baiting the *baited beast*" (somewhat earlier the *Rh. Ztg.* was "the man with the cudgel", so surely the *Rhein- und Mosel-Zeitung* is the "beast") "vents its anger on a straw figure thrown to it, and *considers* itself the victor when it has torn it to pieces."

It is truly Homeric! Just think of its epic amplitude. And how Aesopian, too, this profound insight into animal psychology! This subtle interpretation of the mental state of a bull that *considers* itself the victor!

It would be "very childish and ingenuous" and no less "insipid and trivial" to want to discuss the subject itself with such an "eminent publicist". Therefore we shall only add the following for a characterisation of the man.

In its article which was so unfortunately attacked, the *Rhein- und Mosel-Zeitung "merely"* expressed "doubt" "whether the attainment of their" (i.e., of the originators of the circular on the election of Herr Camphausen and Herr Merkens) "hopes *would really bring back the period of the old Hansa*", but there was in its "article *no* talk" of "a *return* to obsolete and decayed conditions". Let him who can, understand that!

Further:

The *Rhein. Ztg.* tried to "put forward an obvious *lie* in saying: 'Among the interests to be represented in the Provincial Assembly, the *Rhein- und Mosel-Ztg. mentions only* a freer political system of local government and an extension of the rights of the estates' whereas one can read in the *Rhein- und Mosel-Zeitung* the addition: *'the disclosure of so many other undecided questions in the development of the people's life'.*"

Has then the *Rhein- und Mosel-Zeitung* formulated or even *mentioned* a single one of these "undecided questions"? Does it

Prometheus Bound. Allegory on the prohibition
of the *Rheinische Zeitung*

believe that such vague indecisive phrases as "disclosure of *many other undecided questions*" could serve as an equivalent of *naming* these questions for a definite demand to the deputies of the Provincial Assembly? And now let our readers take one more look at the originality of style of the *Rhein- und Mosel-Zeitung*:

Among "the *interests* to be represented in it" (i.e., in the Provincial Assembly) is "the *disclosure* of so many undecided questions in the development of the people's life"!

An undecided question in the development of the people's life! A disclosure to be represented!

Written on March 13, 1843

First published in the *Rheinische Zeitung* No. 72-73, March 14, 1843

Printed according to the newspaper

Published in English for the first time

ANNOUNCEMENT [147]

The undersigned declares that, owing to the *present conditions of censorship*, he has retired as from today from the editorial board of the *Rheinische Zeitung*.

Cologne, March 17, 1843

Dr. Marx

First published in the *Rheinische Zeitung* No. 77, March 18, 1843

Printed according to the newspaper
Published in English for the first time

LETTERS

April 1841-March 1843

1 8 4 1

1
TO CARL FRIEDRICH BACHMANN
IN JENA

Berlin, Schützenstrasse 68
April 6, 1841

Dear Sir,

I send you herewith a dissertation for a doctor's degree on the difference between the natural philosophy of Democritus and the natural philosophy of Epicurus,[a] and enclose the *litterae petitoriae*,[b] *curriculum vitae*, my leaving certificates from the universities of Bonn and Berlin, and, finally, the legal fees of twelve friedrichsdors. At the same time, in the event of my work being found satisfactory by the faculty, I humbly beg you to hasten as much as possible the conferring of the doctor's degree[148] since, on the one hand, I can only remain a few weeks longer in Berlin and, on the other hand, external circumstances make it highly desirable for me to obtain the doctor's degree before my departure.

I should like the leaving certificates to be returned, as they are originals.

I remain, Sir, with great respect,

Your most devoted servant,

Karl Heinrich Marx

First published in the yearly *Archiv für die Geschichte des Sozialismus und der Arbeiterbewegung*, 1926

Printed according to the original

Published in English for the first time

---

[a] See this volume, pp. 25-105.— *Ed.*
[b] Application form.— *Ed.*

2

TO OSCAR LUDWIG BERNHARD WOLFF

IN JENA

Berlin, April 7 [1841]
Schützenstrasse 68

Dear Herr Professor,

In expressing my most sincere thanks for your great kindness in fulfilling my request, I take the liberty of informing you that I have just sent my dissertation, together with the accompanying material, to the faculty of philosophy, and I beg you, in accordance with your kind offer, to be so good as to hasten the dispatch of the diploma. I thought that I had already made too great a claim on your kindness to dare to trouble you still further by sending my dissertation direct to you.

Assuring you of my most sincere gratitude and highest respect, I remain

Yours most devotedly,

Karl Heinrich Marx

First published in the yearly *Archiv für die Geschichte des Sozialismus und der Arbeiterbewegung*, 1926

Printed according to the original

Published in English for the first time

1 8 4 2

3

TO ARNOLD RUGE

IN DRESDEN [149]

Trier, February 10 [1842]

Dear Friend,

I take the liberty of sending you a small contribution for the *Deutsche Jahrbücher* in the form of the enclosed criticism of the censorship instruction.[a]

If the article is suitable for your journal, I ask you for the time being not to mention *my name to anyone except Wigand,* and also to send me *by post immediately* the issues of the *Deutsche Jahrbücher* containing my article; because *for the time being* here in Trier I am completely excluded from the literary world.

It is obvious that it is in the interest of the cause that the printing should be expedited, if the censorship does not censor my censure.

If you do not know of a critic for Vatke's super-clever book on sin [b]—were it not so devilishly clever, one would be tempted to call it stupid—my critical zeal is at your disposal.

It would perhaps be equally worth while to deal again with Bayer's work on the moral spirit.[c] Feuerbach's criticism was a friendly service.[150] Honourable as is Bayer's moral frame of mind, his work itself is just as weak and even immoral.

I should be very glad if you would let *Wigand* know that my manuscript will reach you in a few days' time. *Bauer's*[d] letter in

---

[a] See this volume, pp. 109-31.— *Ed.*

[b] W. Vatke, *Die menschliche Freiheit in ihrem Verhältnis zur Sünde und zur göttlichen Gnade.*— *Ed.*

[c] K. Bayer, *Betrachtungen über den Begriff des sittlichen Geistes und über das Wesen der Tugend.*— *Ed.*

[d] Bruno Bauer.— *Ed.*

which he demands that it should be sent off *at last,* came when I was very ill in bed and therefore was handed to me only a few days ago. Being busy on the enclosed article, I was not able to make the necessary corrections.

As I have now come to the end of some voluminous works, it goes without saying that all my forces are at the disposal of the *Deutsche Jahrbücher.*

With sincere respect,

Marx

My address is: Dr. Marx, *Trier;* to be delivered to Geheimer Regierungsrat von Westphalen.

First published in the journal
Documente des Socialismus, Bd. I, 1902

Printed according to the original

Published in English for the first time

4

TO ARNOLD RUGE

IN DRESDEN

Trier, March 5 [1842]

Dear Friend,

I fully agree with the plan for the *Anekdota philosophica*[151] and also think it would be better to include *my name* among the others. A demonstration of this kind, by its very nature, *precludes* all anonymity. Those gentlemen must see that one's conscience is clear.

With the sudden revival of the Saxon censorship it is obvious from the outset that it will be quite impossible to print my "Treatise on *Christian Art*", which should have appeared as the second part of the *Posaune.*[152] But what about including it in a modified version in the *Anekdota?* The mass of material obnoxious to the censorship which now fills people's minds perhaps makes it possible also to publish the *Anekdota,* as material accumulates, in a number of separate instalments! Another article which I also intended for the *Deutsche Jahrbücher* is a criticism of Hegelian natural law, insofar as it concerns the *internal political system.* The central point is the struggle against *constitutional monarchy* as a hybrid which from beginning to end contradicts and abolishes itself.[153] *Res publica* is quite untranslatable into German. I would send both these articles immediately for your examination if they did not require the rewriting of a fair copy and, in part, some corrections. The fact is that my future father-in-law, Herr von Westphalen, lay on his death-bed for three months and died the day before yesterday. During this period, therefore, it was impossible to do anything properly.

Regarding the other things, next time.

With sincerest respect,

Devotedly yours,

Marx

Apropos. Through an oversight, the manuscript on the censorship contains the phrase: "the censorship of tendency and the tendency censorship". It should be: "the censorship of tendency and the tendency of censorship".[a]

Be so kind as to send me the reply directly by post to Trier.

Bauer has been suspended from his post, as he writes in a letter just received, *par lit de justice*.[b] [154]

First published in the journal *Documente des Socialismus*, Bd. I, 1902

Printed according to the original

Published in English for the first time

5

TO ARNOLD RUGE

IN DRESDEN

Trier, March 20 [1842]

Dear Friend,

Novices are the most pious people, as Saxony proves *ad oculos*.[c]

Bauer once had the same sort of scene with Eichhorn in Berlin as you had with the Minister of the Interior.[d] As orators, these gentlemen are as alike as two peas. On the other hand, what is exceptional is that philosophy speaks intelligibly with the state

---

[a] See this volume, p. 123.— *Ed.*

[b] Here—by a royal order.— *Ed.*

[c] By ocular demonstration.— *Ed.*

[d] Von Rochow.— *Ed.*

wisdom of these over-assured scoundrels, and even a little fanaticism does no harm. There is nothing more difficult than to make these earthly Providences believe that belief in truth and spiritual convictions exist. They are such sceptical state dandies, such experienced fops, that they no longer believe in true, disinterested love. How, then, is one to get at these *roués* except with the aid of what, in the highest circles, is called fanaticism? A guards lieutenant regards a lover whose intentions are honourable as a fanatic. Should people no longer marry because of that? It is a remarkable thing that the degradation of people to the level of animals has become for the government an article of faith and a principle. But this does not contradict religiosity, for the deification of animals is probably the most consistent form of religion, and perhaps it will soon be necessary to speak of religious zoology instead of religious anthropology.

When I was still young and good, I already knew at least that the eggs laid in Berlin were not the eggs of the swan Leda, but goose eggs. A little later I realised that they were crocodile eggs, like, for example, the very latest egg by which, allegedly, on the proposal of the Rhine Province Assembly, the illegal restrictions of French legislation concerning high treason, etc., and crimes of officials, have been abolished.[155] But this time, because it is a question of objective legal provisions, the hocus-pocus is so stupid that even the stupidest Rhenish lawyers have immediately seen through it. At the same time, Prussia has declared with complete naivety that publicity of court proceedings would jeopardise the prestige and credit of Prussian officials. That is an extremely frank admission. All our Rhenish scribblings about publicity and publicising suffer from a basic defect. Honest folk continually point out that these are by no means political, but merely legal, institutions, that they are a right, and not a wrong. As though that were the question! As though all the evil of these institutions did not consist precisely in the fact that they are a right! I should very much like to prove the opposite, namely, that Prussia cannot introduce publicity and publicising, for free courts and an unfree state are incompatible. Similarly, Prussia should be highly praised for its piety, for a transcendental state and a positive religion go together, just as a pocket icon does with a Russian swindler.

Bülow-Cummerow, as you will have seen from the Chinese newspapers,[156] makes his pen flirt with his plough.[a] Oh, this rustic

---

[a] Bülow-Cummerow, *Preussen, seine Verfassung, seine Verwaltung, sein Verhältnis zu Deutschland*, Th. I.— Ed.

coquette, who adorns herself with artificial flowers! I think that writers with this earthly position—for, after all, a position on ploughland is surely earthly—would be desirable, and even more so if in the future the plough were to think and write instead of the pen, while the pen, on the other hand, were to perform serf labour in return. Perhaps, in view of the present uniformity of the German governments, this will come to pass, but the more uniform the governments, the more multiform nowadays are the philosophers, and it is to be hoped that the multiform army will conquer the uniform one.

Ad rem,[a] since among us, loyal, moral Germans, *politica* is included in *formalia*, whence Voltaire deduced that we have the profoundest textbooks on public law.

Therefore, as regards the matter, I found that the article "On Christian Art", which has now been transformed into "On Religion and Art, with Special Reference to Christian Art", must be entirely redone, because the tone of the *Posaune*, which I conscientiously followed:

"*Thy word* is a lamp unto my feet, And light unto my path." "Thy commandments make me wiser than mine enemies, For they are ever with me," and "The Lord shall roar from Zion"[b]

—this tone of the *Posaune* and the irksome constraint of the Hegelian exposition should now be replaced by a freer, and therefore more thorough exposition. In a few days, I have to go to Cologne, where I set up my new residence,[157] for I find the proximity of the Bonn professors intolerable. Who would want to have to talk always with intellectual skunks, with people who study only for the purpose of finding new dead ends in every corner of the world!

Owing to these circumstances, therefore, I was not able, of course, to send herewith the criticism of the Hegelian philosophy of law for the next *Anekdota* (as it was also written for the *Posaune*); I promise to send the article on religious art by mid-April, if you are prepared to wait so long. This would be the more preferable for me, since I am examining the subject from a new *point de vue* and am giving also an epilogue *de romanticis*[c] as a supplement. Meanwhile I shall most actively, to use Goethe's language, continue to work on the subject and await your decision. Be so kind

---

[a] To come to the matter.—*Ed.*

[b] Psalm 119: 105, 98; Amos 1:2 (paraphrased).—*Ed.*

[c] On the romantics.—*Ed.*

as to write to me on this to Cologne, where I shall be by the beginning of next month. As I have not yet any definite domicile there, please send me the letter to *Jung's* address.

In the article itself I necessarily had to speak about the general essence of religion; in doing so I come into conflict with Feuerbach to a certain extent, a conflict concerning not the principle, but the conception of it. In any case religion does not gain from it.

I have heard nothing about Köppen for a long time. Have you not yet approached Christiansen in Kiel? I know him only from his history of Roman law,[a] which, however, contains also something about religion and philosophy in general. He seems to have an excellent mind, although when he comes to actual philosophising, his writing is horribly incomprehensible and formal. Perhaps, he has now begun to write plain German. Otherwise he seems to be *à la hauteur des principes*.[b]

I shall be very pleased to see you here on the Rhine.

Yours,

Marx

I have just had a letter from Bauer in which he writes that he wants to travel northwards again, owing to the silly idea that there he will be better able to conduct his proceedings against the Prussian Government. Berlin is too close to Spandau.[158] At all events, it is good that Bauer is not allowing the matter to take its own course. As I have learned here from my future brother-in-law,[c] aristocrat *comme il faut*, people in Berlin are particularly vexed at Bauer's *bonne foi*.[d]

First published in the journal *Documente des Socialismus*, Bd. I, 1902

Printed according to the original

Published in English for the first time

---

[a] J. Christiansen, *Die Wissenschaft der römischen Rechtsgeschichte im Grundrisse*, Bd. 1.— *Ed.*

[b] Highly principled.— *Ed.*

[c] Ferdinand von Westphalen.— *Ed.*

[d] Good faith.— *Ed.*

6

TO ARNOLD RUGE

IN DRESDEN

c/o engineer Krämer
Bonn, April 27 [1842]

Dear [...]ᵃ

You must not become impatient if my contributions are delayed for a few days more—but *only for a few* days. Bauer will probably inform you orally that this month, owing to all kinds of external muddles, it has been almost impossible for me to work.

Nevertheless, I have almost finished. I shall send you four articles: 1) "On Religious Art", 2) "On the Romantics", 3) "The Philosophical Manifesto of the Historical School of Law",ᵇ 4) "The *Positivist Philosophers*", whom I have teased a little.¹⁵⁹ These articles, in content, are connected.

You will receive the article on religious art as a duodecimo extract, for the work has steadily grown into almost book dimensions, and I have been drawn into all kinds of investigations which will still take a rather long time.

I have abandoned my plan to settle in Cologne, since life there is too noisy for me, and an abundance of good friends does not lead to better philosophy.

I have sent the *Rheinische Zeitung* a long article on our last Rhine Province Assembly with a light introduction about the *Preussische Staats-Zeitung*.ᶜ In connection with the debates on the press I have returned again to the question of censorship and freedom of the press, examining it from other viewpoints.

Thus, Bonn remains my residence for the time being; after all, it would be a pity if no one remained here for the holy men to get angry with.

Yesterday *Hasse* came from Greifswald, in regard to whom the only thing I have admired is his enormous top-boots, like those of a village priest. He spoke, too, just like the top-boot of a village

---

ᵃ In the original the name has been made illegible by someone unknown.— *Ed.*
ᵇ See this volume, pp. 203-10.— *Ed.*
ᶜ Ibid., pp. 132-81.— *Ed.*

priest, he knew nothing about anything, is preparing to publish a book in several volumes about the boring Anselm of Canterbury, on which he has been working for ten years.[160] He thinks that the present critical trend is a moment which must be overcome. He speaks of religiosity as a product of life experience, by which he probably means his successful rearing of children and his fat belly, for fat bellies undergo all sorts of experiences and, as Kant says: if it goes behind it becomes an F., if it goes upwards it becomes religious inspiration. What a man this pious Hasse is with his religious constipation!

We were very much amused with what you wrote in your letters about Vatke's lack of a "full heart". This super-clever, diplomatic Vatke, who would so much like to be the greatest critic and the greatest believer, who always knows everything better than anyone else, this Vatke has for one party no heart, and for the other no head. *Hic jacet*[a] Vatke—a notable example of what the passion for cards and religious music leads to.

Fichte, who has wrapped himself in the mantle of his unpopularity, has spread the half-ambiguous rumour that he has been invited to Tübingen. The faculty is not meeting his wish to be held fast by an increase in salary.

Sack has made a trip to Berlin with the most pious intentions to speculate on the insanity of his brother and to get himself appointed in his place.

Nothing but wars and debauchery, says Thersites,[b] and if the university here cannot be reproached with wars, at least there is no lack of debauchery.

Do you not want to carry out your plan of a trip to the Rhine?

Yours,
Marx

First published in the journal *Documente des Socialismus*, Bd. 1, 1902

Printed according to the original

Published in English for the first time

---

[a] Here lies.— *Ed.*
[b] Homer, *Iliad.— Ed.*

7

TO ARNOLD RUGE

IN DRESDEN

Trier, July 9 [1842]

Dear Friend,

If events had not apologised for me, I would have abandoned any attempt at an excuse. It stands to reason that I regard it as an honour to contribute to the *Anekdota* and only unpleasant extraneous circumstances prevented me from sending you my articles.

From April to the present day I have been able to work for a total of perhaps only four weeks at most, and that not without interruption. I had to spend six weeks in Trier in connection with another death. The rest of the time was split up and poisoned by the most unpleasant family controversies. My family laid obstacles in my way, which, despite the prosperity of the family, put me for the moment in very serious straits.[161] I cannot possibly burden you with the story of these private scandals; it is truly fortunate that scandals of a public nature make it impossible for a man of character to be irritated over private ones. During this time I was writing for the *Rheinische Zeitung*, to which I should long ago have sent my articles, etc., etc. I would have informed you long before about these intermezzos, had I not hoped from day to day to be able to complete my work. In a few day's time I am going to Bonn and shall not touch a thing until I have finished the contributions for the *Anekdota*. Of course, in this state of affairs I was not able to elaborate in particular the article "On Art and Religion" as thoroughly as the subject requires.

Incidentally, do not imagine that we on the Rhine live in a political Eldorado. The most unswerving persistence is required to push through a newspaper like the *Rheinische Zeitung*. My second article on the Provincial Assembly, dealing with the question of clerical discords, was deleted by the censor.[162] I showed in this article how the defenders of the state adopted a clerical standpoint, and the defenders of the church a state standpoint. This incident is all the more unpleasant for the *Rheinische Zeitung* because the stupid Cologne Catholics fell into the trap, and defence of the Archbishop[a] would have attracted subscribers. Incidentally, you can hardly imagine how contemptible are oppres-

---

[a] Von Droste-Vischering.— *Ed.*

sors and at the same time how stupidly they dealt with the orthodox blockhead.[a] But the matter has had a successful ending: before the entire world, Prussia has kissed the Pope's[b] mule, and our government automatons walk the streets without blushing. The *Rheinische Zeitung* has now put in an appeal about the article. In general, the fight for the *Rheinische Zeitung* is beginning. In the *Kölnische Zeitung*, the author of the leading articles, Hermes, ex-editor of the former political *Hannoverzeitung*, has taken the side of Christianity against the philosophical newspapers in Königsberg and Cologne. If the censor does not again play some trick, a reply from me will be published in the next Supplement.[c] The religious party is the most dangerous in the Rhine area. The opposition has of late become too accustomed to opposing within the church.

Do you know any details about the so-called "Free"? The article in the *Königsberger Zeitung*[163] was, to say the least, undiplomatic. It is one thing to declare for emancipation—that is honest; it is another thing to start off by shouting it out as propaganda; that sounds like bragging and irritates the philistine. And then, reflect on who are these "Free", a man like Meyen, etc. But, at any rate, if there is a suitable city for such ventures, it is Berlin.

I shall probably be drawn into a prolonged polemic with the Cologne Hermes. No matter how ignorant, shallow and trivial the man is, thanks precisely to these qualities he is the mouthpiece of philistinism and I intend not to let him go on chattering. Mediocrity should no longer enjoy the privilege of immunity. Hermes will also try to saddle me with "The Free", about whom, unfortunately, I do not know the slightest thing for sure. It is fortunate that Bauer is in Berlin. He, at least, will not allow any "stupidities" to be committed, and the only thing that disquiets me in this affair (if it is true and not merely a deliberate newspaper fabrication), is the probability that the insipidity of the Berliners will make their good cause ridiculous and that in a serious matter they will not be able to avoid various "stupidities". Anyone who has spent as much time among these people as I have will find that this anxiety is not without foundation.

How are you getting on with your *Jahrbücher*[d]?

As you are at the centre of philosophical and theological news, I should like nothing better than to learn something from you about

---

[a] Frederick William III.— *Ed.*
[b] Gregory XVI.— *Ed.*
[c] See this volume, pp. 184-202.— *Ed.*
[d] *Deutsche Jahrbücher für Wissenschaft und Kunst.— Ed.*

the present situation. True, the movement of the hour-hand is visible here, but not that of the minute-hand.

Old Marheineke seems to have considered it necessary to provide the whole world with documentary proof of the complete impotence of the old Hegelianism.[a] His vote is a disgraceful vote.

Will the Saxons in this Assembly not denounce the censorship? Fine constitutionalism!

Hoping to hear from you soon,

Yours,

Marx

Rutenberg is a weight on my conscience. I brought him on to the editorial board of the *Rheinische Zeitung*, but he is absolutely incapable. Sooner or later he will be shown the door.

What do you advise if the article on the Archbishop is not stamped for publication by the high police censorship? It must appear in print because of 1) our Provincial Assembly, 2) the government, 3) the Christian state. Should I, perhaps, send it to Hoffmann and Campe? It does not seem to me suitable for the *Anekdota*.

First published in the journal *Documente des Socialismus*, Bd. I, 1902

Printed according to the original

Published in English for the first time

8

TO DAGOBERT OPPENHEIM

IN COLOGNE

[Bonn, approximately August 25, 1842].

Dear Oppenheim,

I enclose a manuscript from Ruge. No. 1 is not usable, but No. 2, on the state of affairs in Saxony, you will probably be able to use.[164]

Send me Mayer's article in the *Rheinische Zeitung* on the *system of local government* and, if possible, all Hermes' articles *against the Jews*.[165] I will then send you as soon as possible an article which,

---

[a] Ph. Marheineke, *Einleitung in die öffentlichen Vorlesungen über die Bedeutung der Hegelschen Philosophie in der christlichen Theologie.— Ed.*

even if it does not finally settle the latter question, will nevertheless make it take another course.

Will the article on Hanover [166] go through? At least try to make a small start with it soon. It is not so much a matter of this article itself as of a series of useful articles from that quarter which I can then promise you. The author of the article wrote to me yesterday:

"I do not think my attacks on the opposition will do harm to sales of the newspaper in Hanover; on the contrary, people there are fairly generally so far advanced that the views I put forward will be accepted as correct."

If it is in accord with your views on the subject, send me also the Juste-Milieu article [167] for criticism. The subject must be discussed dispassionately. In the first place, quite general theoretical arguments about the state political system are more suitable for purely scientific organs than for newspapers. The correct theory must be made clear and developed within the concrete conditions and on the basis of the existing state of things.

However, since it has now happened, two things should be borne in mind. Every time we come into conflict with other newspapers, the matter can, sooner or later, be used against us. Such a clear demonstration against the foundations of the present state system can result in an intensification of the censorship and even the suppression of the newspaper. It was in this way that the South-German *Tribüne* came to an end. But in any case we arouse the resentment of many, indeed the majority, of the free-thinking practical people who have undertaken the laborious task of winning freedom step by step, within the constitutional framework, while we, from our comfortable arm-chair of abstractions, show them their contradictions. True, the author of the Juste-Milieu article invites criticism; but 1) we all know how governments respond to such challenges; 2) it is not enough for someone to express readiness to hear criticism, for which in any case his permission will not be asked; the question is whether he has selected the appropriate arena. Newspapers only begin to be the appropriate arena for such questions when these have become questions of the real state, practical questions.

I consider it essential that the *Rheinische Zeitung* should not be guided by its contributors, but that, on the contrary, it should guide them. Articles of the kind mentioned afford the best opportunity for indicating a definite plan of operations to the contributors. A single author cannot have a view of the whole in the way the newspaper can.

If my views do not coincide with yours, I would—if you do not find it inappropriate—give this criticism to the *Anekdota,* as a supplement to my article against Hegel's theory of constitutional monarchy.[a] But I think it is better when the newspaper is its own doctor.

Hoping for an early reply from you,

Yours,
Marx

First published in the book *Rheinische Briefe und Akten zur Geschichte der politischen Bewegung 1830-1850,* 1. Bd., Essen, 1919

Printed according to the original

Published in English for the first time

9

TO ARNOLD RUGE

IN DRESDEN [168]

Cologne, November 30 [1842]

Dear Friend,

My letter today will be confined to the "confusion" with "The Free".

As you already know, every day the censorship mutilates us mercilessly, so that frequently the newspaper is hardly able to appear. Because of this, a mass of articles by "The Free" have perished. But I have allowed myself to throw out as many articles as the censor, for Meyen and Co. sent us heaps of scribblings, pregnant with revolutionising the world and empty of ideas, written in a slovenly style and seasoned with a little atheism and communism (which these gentlemen have never studied). Because of Rutenberg's complete lack of critical sense, independence and ability, Meyen and Co. had become accustomed to regard the *Rheinische Zeitung* as *their own,* docile organ, but I believed I could not any longer permit this watery torrent of words in the old manner. This loss of a few worthless creations of "freedom", a freedom which strives primarily "to be free from all thought", was therefore the first reason for a darkening of the Berlin sky.

Rutenberg, who had already been removed from the German department (where his work consisted mainly in inserting punctua-

---

[a] See this volume, pp. 382-83.— *Ed.*

tion marks) and to whom, only *on my application*, the French department was provisionally transferred—Rutenberg, thanks to the monstrous stupidity of our state providence, has had the luck to be regarded as dangerous, although he was not a danger to anyone but the *Rheinische Zeitung* and himself. A categorical demand was made for the removal of Rutenberg. Prussian providence, this *despotisme prussien, le plus hypocrite, le plus fourbe*,[a] spared the manager an unpleasant step, and the new martyr, who has already learned to display consciousness of martyrdom in facial expression, behaviour and speech with some virtuosity, is exploiting this turn of events. He writes to all the corners of the earth, he writes to Berlin that he is the *banished principle* of the *Rheinische Zeitung*, which is adopting a *different position* in relation to the government. It goes without saying that this also evoked demonstrations from the heroes of freedom on the banks of the Spree, "whose muddy water washes souls and dilutes tea".[b]

Finally, on top of this came your and Herwegh's attitude to "The Free" to cause the cup of the angry Olympians to overflow.[c]

A few days ago I received a letter from little Meyen, whose favourite category is, most appropriately, what *ought* to be. In this letter I am taken to task over my attitude 1) to you and Herwegh, 2) to "The Free", 3) to the new editorial principle and the position in relation to the government. I replied at once and frankly expressed my ópinion about the defects of their writings, which find freedom in a licentious, sansculotte-like, and at the same time convenient, form, rather than in a *free*, i.e., independent and profound, content. I demanded of them less vague reasoning, magniloquent phrases and self-satisfied self-adoration, and more definiteness, more attention to the actual state of affairs, more expert knowledge. I stated that I regard it as inappropriate, indeed even immoral, to smuggle communist and socialist doctrines, hence a new world outlook, into incidental theatrical criticisms, etc., and that I demand a quite different and more thorough discussion of communism, if it should be discussed at all. I requested further that religion should be criticised in the framework of criticism of political conditions rather than that political conditions should be criticised in the framework of religion, since this is more in accord with the nature of a newspaper and the educational level of the reading public; for

---

[a] Prussian despotism, the most hypocritical, the most deceitful.— *Ed.*

[b] Paraphrase of a line from Heine's "Frieden" (*Die Nordsee*, 1. Zyklus).— *Ed.*

[c] See this volume, p. 287.— *Ed.*

religion in itself is without content, it owes its being not to heaven but to the earth, and with the abolition of distorted reality, of which it is the *theory*, it will collapse of itself. Finally, I desired that, if there is to be talk about philosophy, there should be less trifling with the *label* "atheism" (which reminds one of children, assuring everyone who is ready to listen to them that they are not afraid of the bogy man), and that instead the content of philosophy should be brought to the people. *Voilà tout.*

Yesterday I received an insolent letter from Meyen, who had not yet received this work and who now questions me on every possible thing: 1) I should state on whose side I am in their quarrel with Bauer, about which I know absolutely nothing; 2) why did I not allow this and that to go through; I am threatened with being accused of conservatism; 3) the newspaper should not temporise, it must act in the *most extreme fashion*, i.e., it should calmly yield to the police and the censorship instead of holding on to its positions in a struggle, imperceptible to the public but nevertheless stubborn and in accordance with its duty. Finally, an infamous report is given of Herwegh's betrothal, etc., etc.

All this is evidence of a terrible dose of the vanity which does not understand how, in order to save a political organ, one can sacrifice a few Berlin windbags, and thinks of nothing at all except the affairs of its clique. Moreover, this little man strutted like a peacock, solemnly laid his hand on his breast and on his dagger, let fall something about "his" party, threatened me with his displeasure, declaimed *à la* Marquis Posa, only somewhat worse, etc.

Since we now have to put up from morning to night with the most horrible torments of the censorship, ministerial communications, complaints of the Oberpräsident,[169] accusations in the Provincial Assembly, howls from shareholders, etc., etc., and I remain at my post only because I consider it my duty to prevent, to the best of my ability, those in power from carrying out their plans, you can imagine that I am somewhat irritated and that I replied rather sharply to Meyen. It is possible, therefore, that "The Free" will withdraw for a while. Therefore I earnestly beg that you yourself help us by contributing articles, and also ask your friends to do the same.

Yours,

Marx

First published in the journal *Documente des Socialismus*, Bd. I, 1902   Printed according to the original

1843

10

TO ARNOLD RUGE
IN DRESDEN

Cologne, January[a] 25 [1843]

Dear [...][b]

You probably already know that the *Rheinische Zeitung* has been banned, suspended, and is under sentence of death.[170] The termination of its life has been fixed for the end of March. During this period of grace before execution, the newspaper is being subjected to a double censorship. Our censor,[c] a decent fellow, is under the censorship of von Gerlach, Regierungspräsident here, a passively obedient blockhead. When ready, our newspaper has to be presented to the police to be sniffed at, and if the police nose smells anything un-Christian or un-Prussian, the newspaper is not allowed to appear.

The ban resulted from the coincidence of several special causes: its wide circulation; *my own* "Justification of the Correspondent from the Mosel",[d] in which very highly placed statesmen were thoroughly exposed; our stubborn refusal to name the person who sent us the text of the law on marriage[171]; the convocation of the provincial estates, which we could influence by our agitation; finally, our criticism of the ban on the *Leipziger Allgemeine Zeitung*,[e] and on the *Deutsche Jahrbücher*.

The ministerial rescript, which will appear in the newspapers in a day or so, is if possible more feeble than the previous ones. The following are given as motives:

1) The *lie* that we had *no* permission, as though in Prussia,

---

[a] In the original by mistake: December.—*Ed.*
[b] In the original the name has been made illegible by someone unknown.—*Ed.*
[c] Wiethaus.—*Ed.*
[d] See this volume, pp. 332-58.—*Ed.*
[e] Ibid., pp. 311-30.—*Ed.*

where not even a dog can exist without its police number, the *Rheinische Zeitung* could have appeared even a single day without fulfilling the official conditions for existence.

2) The censorship instruction of December 24[172] aimed at establishing a censorship of *tendency*. By tendency it meant the *illusion*, the romantic belief in possessing a freedom which one would not allow oneself to possess *realiter*.[a] Whereas the rationalist Jesuitism which prevailed under the former government had a stern, rational physiognomy, this romantic Jesuitism demands *imagination* as its main requisite. The censored press should learn to live under the illusion of freedom, and of that magnificent man[b] who majestically permitted this illusion. But whereas the censorship instruction wanted censorship of tendency, now the ministerial rescript explains that in Frankfurt a *ban, suppression*, has been invented for a thoroughly bad tendency. It states that the censorship exists only in order to censor eccentricities of a good tendency, although the instruction said precisely the oppo-site—namely, that eccentricities of a good tendency are to be permitted.

3) The old balderdash about a bad frame of mind, empty theory, hey-diddle-diddle, etc.

Nothing has surprised me. You know what my opinion of the censorship instruction has been from the outset. I see here only a consequence; in the suppression of the *Rheinische Zeitung* I see a definite *advance* of political consciousness, and for that reason I am resigning.[173] Moreover, I had begun to be stifled in that atmosphere. It is a bad thing to have to perform menial duties even for the sake of freedom; to fight with pinpricks, instead of with clubs. I have become tired of hypocrisy, stupidity, gross arbitrariness, and of our bowing and scraping, dodging, and hair-splitting over words. Consequently, the government has given me back my freedom.

As I wrote to you once before, I have fallen out with my family[c] and, as long as my mother is alive, I have no right to my property. Moreover, I am engaged to be married and I cannot, must not, and will not, leave Germany without my fiancée.[d] If, therefore, the possibility arose that I could edit the *Deutscher Bote*[174] with Herwegh in Zurich, I should like to do so. I can do nothing more

---

[a] In reality.—*Ed.*
[b] Frederick William IV.—*Ed.*
[c] See this volume, p. 389.—*Ed.*
[d] Jenny von Westphalen.—*Ed.*

in Germany. Here one makes a counterfeit of oneself. If, therefore, you will give me advice and information on this matter, I shall be very grateful.

I am working on several things, which here in Germany will find neither censor nor bookseller, nor, in general, any possible existence. I await an early reply from you.

Yours,

Marx

First published in the journal *Documente des Socialismus*, Bd. I, 1902

Printed according to the original

Published in English for the first time

11

TO ARNOLD RUGE

IN DRESDEN

Cologne, March 13 [1843]

Dear Friend,

As soon as it is at all possible I shall set my course straight for Leipzig. I have just had a talk with Stucke, who seems to have been greatly impressed by most of the statesmen in Berlin. This Dr. Stucke is an extremely good-natured man.

As for our plan,[175] as a preliminary I will tell you of my own conviction. When Paris was taken, some people proposed Napoleon's son[a] with a regency, others Bernadotte, while yet others suggested that Louis Philippe should rule. But Talleyrand replied: "Louis XVIII or Napoleon. That is a principle, anything else is intrigue."

In the same way I could call almost anything else, other than Strasbourg (or at any rate Switzerland), not a principle, but an intrigue. Books of more than 20 printed sheets are not books for the people. The most that one can venture on there are monthly issues.

Even if the publication of the *Deutsche Jahrbücher* were again permitted, at the very best we could achieve a poor copy of the deceased publication, and nowadays that is no longer enough. On the other hand, *Deutsch-Französische Jahrbücher*—that would be a

---

[a] The duke of Reichstadt.—*Ed.*

principle, an event of consequence, an undertaking over which one can be enthusiastic. It goes without saying that I am only expressing my own unauthoritative opinion, and for the rest submit myself to the eternal powers of fate.

Finally — newspaper affairs compel me to close — let me tell you also about my *personal plans*. As soon as we had concluded the contract, I would travel to Kreuznach, marry and spend a month or more there at the home of my wife's mother,[a] so that before starting work we should have at any rate a few articles ready. The more so since I could, if necessary, spend a few weeks in Dresden, for all the preliminaries, the announcement of the marriage, etc., take considerable time.

I can assure you, without the slightest romanticism, that I am head over heels in love, and indeed in the most serious way. I have been engaged for more than seven years, and for my sake my fiancée has fought the most violent battles, which almost undermined her health, partly against her pietistic aristocratic relatives, for whom "the Lord in heaven" and the "lord in Berlin" are equally objects of religious cult, and partly against my own family, in which some priests and other enemies of mine have ensconced themselves. For years, therefore, my fiancée and I have been engaged in more unnecessary and exhausting conflicts than many who are three times our age and continually talk of their "life experience" (the favourite phrase of our Juste-Milieu [b]).

Apropos, we have received an anonymous reply to Prutz's report against the new Tübingen *Jahrbücher*.[176] I recognised *Schwegler* by the handwriting. You are described as an over-excited agitator, Feuerbach as a frivolous mocker, and Bauer [c] as a man of wholly uncritical mind! The Swabians! The Swabians! That will be a fine concoction!

On the subject of your very fine, truly popular written complaint, we have inserted a superficial article by Pfützner — half of which, moreover, I have deleted — for lack of a better criticism and of time.[177] P. P. does not go sufficiently deep into the matter and the little capers he cuts tend to turn him into a laughing-stock instead of making his enemy ridiculous.

Yours,
Marx

---

[a] Caroline von Westphalen.— *Ed.*
[b] Nickname of Edgar Bauer.— *Ed.*
[c] Bruno Bauer.— *Ed.*

I have arranged for the books for Fleischer. Your correspondence published at the beginning is interesting.[178] Bauer on Ammon is delightful.[a] The "Sorrows and Joys of the Theological Mind"[b] seems to me a not very successful rendering of the section of the *Phenomenology:* "The Unfortunate Consciousness".[c] Feuerbach's aphorisms[d] seem to me incorrect only in one respect, that he refers too much to nature and too little to politics. That, however, is the only alliance by which present-day philosophy can become truth. But things will probably go as they did in the sixteenth century, when the nature enthusiasts were accompanied by a corresponding number of state enthusiasts. I was most of all pleased by the criticism of the good *Literarische Zeitung.*[e]

You have probably already read Bauer's self-defence.[f] In my opinion, he has never before written so well.

As far as the *Rheinische Zeitung* is concerned I would not remain *under any conditions*; it is impossible for me to write under Prussian censorship or to live in the Prussian atmosphere.

I have just been visited by the chief of the Jewish community here, who has asked me for a petition for the Jews to the Provincial Assembly, and I am willing to do it. However much I dislike the Jewish faith, Bauer's view seems to me too abstract. The thing is to make as many breaches as possible in the Christian state and to smuggle in as much as we can of what is rational. At least, it must be attempted—and the *embitterment* grows with every petition that is rejected with protestations.

First published in the journal *Documente des Socialismus*, Bd. I, 1902

Printed according to the original

---

[a] B. Bauer's review on the book: Ammon, *Die Geschichte des Lebens Jesu*, *Anekdota*, Bd. II.— *Ed.*

[b] By B. Bauer.— *Ed.*

[c] G. W. F. Hegel, *Phänomenologie des Geistes*, Ch. IV.— *Ed.*

[d] L. Feuerbach, "Vorläufige Thesen zur Reformation der Philosophie", *Anekdota*, Bd. II.— *Ed.*

[e] A. Ruge, "Das 'christlich-germanische' Justemilieu. Die Berliner *Literarische Zeitung*", *Anekdota*, Bd. II.— *Ed.*

[f] B. Bauer, *Die gute Sache der Freiheit und meine eigene Angelegenheit.*— *Ed.*

FROM THE PREPARATORY
MATERIALS

NOTEBOOKS
ON EPICUREAN PHILOSOPHY [179]

Written in 1839

First published in part in: Marx/Engels, *Gesamtausgabe*, Abt. 1, Bd. 1, Hb. 1, 1927

First published in full in Russian in the book: K. Marx and F. Engels, *From Early Writings*, Moscow, 1956
Signed: *Karl Heinrich Marx*

Printed according to the manuscript

Translated from the German, Greek and Latin

Published in English for the first time

EPICUREAN PHILOSOPHY

First Notebook

I. DIOGENES LAERTIUS, BOOK TEN
EXCERPTS FROM BOOK TEN OF DIOGENES LAERTIUS
CONTAINED IN P. GASSENDI:
NOTES ON BOOK TEN OF DIOGENES LAERTIUS,
LYONS, 1649, VOL. I

I. DIOGENES LAERTIUS, BOOK TEN

Epicurus

[2] "... but on coming across the works of Democritus [Epicurus] turned to philosophy." p. 10.

[4] (Posidonius the Stoic and Nicolaus and Sotion in the twelfth book of the work entitled *Dioclean Refutations* allege)[a] "... that he put forward as his own the doctrines of Democritus about atoms and of Aristippus about pleasure." p. 11.

[6] "I [Epicurus] know not how to conceive the good, apart from the pleasures of taste, [sexual pleasures,] the pleasures of sound and the pleasures of beautiful form." p. 12.

[12] "Among the early philosophers ... his favourite was Anaxagoras, although he occasionally disagreed with him...." p. 16.

[29] "It [Epicurean philosophy] is divided into three parts—The Canon, Physics, Ethics" [p. 25.]

I. *The Canon*

[31] "Now in *The Canon* Epicurus affirms that *our sensations* and *preconceptions* (*prolepseis*) and our *feelings* are the *standards* of truth; the Epicureans generally make *perceptions of mental presentations* to be also standards." pp. 25-26. "His own statements are also to be found ... in the *Principal Doctrines*." p. 26.

I. "...*the sensations are true*. Every sensation ... is devoid of reason and incapable of memory; for neither is it *self-caused* nor, regarded as having an *external cause*, can it *add* anything thereto or *take* anything therefrom, neither *judge* nor *deceive*."

[31-32] "Nor is there anything which can refute sensations: one sensation cannot convict another and kindred sensation, for they are equally valid (*aequipollentiam*); nor can one sensation refute another which is not kindred, for the objects which the two judge are not the same; nor can one sensation refute another, since we pay equal heed to all; nor again can reason refute them, for reason is dependent on sensation.

---

[a] Written in Latin in the manuscript.— *Ed.*

"And the *reality* of ... *perceptions* guarantees the truth of our senses. But *seeing and hearing are just as real as feeling pain. Between being true and being a reality, there is no difference.*" p. 26.

"Hence it is from phenomena that we must seek to obtain information about the unknown. For all our *notions are derived from perceptions, either by actual contact or by analogy, or resemblance, or composition,* with some slight aid from reasoning." p[p]. 26[-27].

"*And the objects presented to madmen as well as presentations in dreams are true, for they ... produce movements, which that which does not exist never does.*" p. 27.

II. [33] "*By preconception they* [the Epicureans] *mean a sort of apprehension* or a *right opinion* or *notion* or *universal idea stored in the mind;* that is, a *recollection of an external object often presented,* e. g., such and such a thing is a man; for *no sooner is the word man uttered than we think of his shape by an act of preconception* in which the senses take the lead. *Thus the object primarily denoted by every term is then evident.* And we could not *seek what we do seek,* unless we *knew it before. ... we could not name* anything at all, if *we did not previously know its form by way of preconception.* It follows, then, that *preconceptions are evident.* Mere *opinion* also *depends on a previous evident presentation,* by reference to which we *form a judgment* [...]. *Opinion* they also call ... *assumption.* They say *it* is sometimes *true,* sometimes *false* by something being *added* to it or *taken away* from it, or by its being *confirmed or contradicted as being evident or not.* For if it is *confirmed* or *not contradicted,* it is *true,* and if it is not *confirmed* or is *contradicted,* it is *false.* Hence the introduction of '*that which awaits*', for example, when one *waits* and then approaches the tower and establishes whether it looks from close quarters as it does from afar." [p]p. [27-]28.

"*They affirm that there are two feelings: pleasure and pain....* The first is *favourable* to nature, the second *hostile;* according to these is *determined* what we must *strive after* and what we must *avoid.*" [p]p. [28-]29.

"There are two kinds of *inquiry,* the one concerned *with things,* the other with the *mere word.*" p. 29.

Epicurus to Menoeceus

[123] "*First believe that God is a ... being indestructible and blessed* according to the *universal notion of God,* and do not *ascribe* to him anything which is *incompatible with his immortality,* or that *agrees not with his blessedness....*" p. 82.

"*For gods verily there are. For the notion of them is evident*" (cf. "the universal notion of God", *consensus omnium,* c [onsensus] *gentium*[a]), "*but they are not such as the multitude believe,* seeing that men do not steadfastly *maintain the notions they form respecting them.*

"Not the man who *denies the gods worshipped by the multitude,* but *he who affirms of the gods what the multitude believe about them* is truly *impious.* [124] For the *utterances of the multitude about the gods* are not *true preconceptions,* but *false accumptions;* hence the multitude believe that the *greatest evils happen to the wicked* and the *greatest blessings happen to the good from the hand of the gods.* For being entirely *prejudiced in favour of their own virtues,* they grant their favour to those who are like themselves and *consider as alien whatever is not so.*" p. 83.

"*Accustom thyself to believe that death is nothing to us,* for all that is good or bad is based on *sentience,* and *death is the loss of sentience.*

---

[a] The censensus of all, the consensus of the peoples.— *Ed.*

"Therefore a *right understanding* that *death* is *nothing* to us *makes transient life worth living*, not by *adding indefinite time to life*, but by *putting an end to the yearning after immortality.* [125] For *life has no terrors* for him who *has thoroughly apprehended* that *ceasing to live has no terrors*. Foolish, therefore, is the man who *says* that *he fears death* not because *it causes suffering when it comes*, but because *it causes suffering when it is yet to come*. For that which *causes no annoyance when it is present* causes only *imaginary suffering when it is expected*. *Death, which is indeed the most terrifying of all evils, is nothing to us since, as long as we are, death is not come, and as soon as death is come, we are no more. It is nothing then, either to the living or to the dead, since for the former it is not, and the latter are no longer.*" pp. 83-84.

[126] "*He who admonishes the young to live honourably* and *the old to die honourably, is foolish*, not merely because of the *desirableness* of life, but also because the *striving to live honourably* and the striving *to die honourably are one and the same thing.*" p. 84.

[127] "We *must* however *remember* that the *future* neither *depends on us* nor is altogether *independent of us*, so that we must *not expect it as something which will certainly be* nor *give up hope* of it as of something which *will* certainly *not be.*" p. 85.

"...*some* desires are *natural*, others are *vain*, and *among the natural ones* some are *necessary*, others *natural* only. And *among the necessary ones* some are *necessary for happiness* (as the desire *to free the body of uneasiness*), others *for very life.*" p. 85.

[128] "*An error-free consideration of these things can lead ... to health of body* and *ataraxy of soul*, for these are the *aim of a blessed life. For the end of all our actions is to be free from pain and not to live in confusion.* And when once we have attained this, *every tempest of the soul is laid*, for man no longer needs to seek for something which he still lacks or for anything else through which the *welfare of the soul and the body will be complete.* For *we need pleasure when the lack of pleasure causes us pain*, but when *we feel no pain, we no longer need pleasure.*" p. 85.

"*Wherefore we say that pleasure is the beginning* and *the end of the blessed life.* [129] We apprehend *pleasure* as the *first* and *innate good* and *we proceed from it* in all that we do or refrain from doing and *to it we come back*, inasmuch as *this feeling serves us as the guide-line by which we judge of everything good.*" [p]p. [85-]86.

"And *since* pleasure is our *first* and *innate good* for *that reason* we do not choose *every pleasure....*

"*All pleasure therefore, because it is suited to us by nature*, is *a good*, yet not every pleasure is choiceworthy; just as *all pain is an evil* and yet not all pain is to be avoided under all circumstances. [130] *All these matters must rather be decided by weighing one against another* and from the *standpoint* of *advantage* and *disadvantage*, for *what is good proves at certain times to be an evil for us*, and conversely *what is evil* proves to be a *good.*" p. 86.

"Again we regard *independence of outward things* as a *great good*, not so as to be satisfied in every case with little, but in order to be contented with little when abundance is lacking, being honestly convinced that those who least need *luxury* enjoy it most and that *everything which is natural* is easy to obtain, while that which is vain and worthless is hard to procure." p. 86.

[131] "[...] By pleasure we mean the absence of pain in the body and of trouble in the soul..." p. 87.

[132] "Of all this the beginning and the *supreme good* is *reasonableness*, and hence *it is more precious even than philosophy*, from which all other virtues spring, and they teach us that one cannot live pleasantly unless one lives reasonably, honourably [and justly], [and that one cannot live reasonably, honourably] and justly without living pleasantly. For the *virtues are closely connected with pleasant living*, and *pleasant living is inseparable from them.*" p. 88.

[133] "Who, then, in your opinion, is superior to him who thinks piously of the gods and is quite fearless of death, who has reflected on the purpose of nature and understands that the greatest good is easy to reach and to attain whereas the worst of evils lasts only a short time or causes short pains? *Necessity, which has been introduced by some as the ruler over all things, is not the ruler*, he maintains, over that *some of which depends on chance and some on our arbitrary will. Necessity is not subject to persuasion; chance*, on the other hand, *is inconstant. But our will is free*; it can entail blame and also the opposite." p. 88.

[134] "It would be better to accept the myth about the gods than to bow beneath the yoke of fate imposed by the Physicists, for the former holds out hope of obtaining mercy by honouring the gods, and the latter, inexorable necessity. [135] *But he* [the wise man] *must accept chance, not god* as the multitude do ... and not an *uncertain cause*.... He considers it better to be unhappy but reasonable than to be happy but unreasonable. It is, of course, better when in actions a good decision attains a good issue also through the favour of circumstances." [p]p. [88-]89.

"[...] you will never be disturbed, but will live as a god among men. For a man who lives in the midst of intransient blessings is not like a mortal being." p. 89.

"*Elsewhere he* [Epicurus] *rejects the whole of divination.... There is no divination*, and *even if there is, what happens does not rest with us....*" [p. 89].

[136] "He differs from the Cyrenaics in his teaching on pleasure. They *do not recognise pleasure in a state of rest, but only pleasure in motion*. But Epicurus admits both, the *pleasure of the mind* as well as the *pleasure of the body* ... *for one can conceive pleasure in a state of rest as well as in motion*. But Epicurus says ... the following: '*Ataraxy and freedom from pain are sensations of pleasure in a state of rest, joy* and *delight are seen to be effective only in motion*.'" p. 90.

[137] "He further differs from the Cyrenaics in this: they hold that *bodily pains are worse than mental pains* ... whereas he holds mental pains to be worse, since the flesh is tormented only by that which is present, the mind by that which is past as well as by that which is present and that which is coming. So also are the pleasures of the mind greater." p. 90.

"And as proof that pleasure is the end he adduces the fact that living beings, as soon as they are born, *naturally and unaccountably* to themselves *find satisfaction in pleasure* but *reject pain. Instinctively*, then, we *shun pain....*" [pp. 90-91.]

[138] "And the *virtues too are chosen on account of pleasure* and *not for themselves* ... he says also that *only virtue is inseparable from pleasure, all the rest is separable, for instance human things.*" p. 91.

[*Principal Doctrines*]

[139] "*A blessed* and *immortal being has no trouble himself* nor *brings it on anybody else*; hence he *knows no anger* or *partiality, for the like exists only in the weak*."

"*Elsewhere* he says that the *gods are discernible by reason alone*, not, indeed, being *numerically distinct*, yet *through resemblance* (as a *result of the continuous influx of similar images made pricisely for this purpose) human in appearance*." pp. 91-92.

"*The highest peak of pleasure is the exclusion of all pain. For wherever pleasure reigns*, as long as it *continues*, there *is no pain or grief, nor both together*." p. 92.

[140] "It is impossible to live pleasantly without living *reasonably, honourably* and *justly,* and it is impossible to live *reasonably, honourably* and *justly without living pleasantly*." p. 92.

[141] "*No pleasure is in itself an evil*, but that which produces certain pleasures *causes manifold disturbances of pleasure*." p. 93.

[142] "If *all pleasure were accumulated and with time* had become *compact*, this concentrate would be just as [perfect] as principal parts of nature, and the *sensations of pleasure would never differ one from another.*" p. 93.

[143] "It is impossible to banish fear over matters of the greatest importance if one does not know the essence of the universe but is apprehensive on account of what the myths tell us. Hence without the study of nature one cannot attain pure pleasure." p[p]. 93[-94].

[142] "If we were not alarmed by the meteors and by death, as to how it might in some way or other affect us, and if we were moreover able to comprehend the limits of pain and desire, we should need no study of nature." p. 93.

[143] "It is useless to provide security against men so long as we are alarmed by things up above and things under the earth and in general things in the boundless universe. For security against men exists only for a definite time." p. 94.

"The same security which we attain by quiet and withdrawal from the multitude arises through the possibility of banishing [by moderation those desires which are not necessary] and through the very simple [and very easy] attainment of [the necessary things]." p. 94.

[144] "The wealth of nature is limited and easily obtainable, but that which arises from vain fancies extends into infinity." p. 94.

"Pleasure of the flesh does not increase any more once the pain of privation has been removed, it is then subject only to variation." p. 94.

"The peak of thought (as far as joy is concerned) in *fathoming* precisely those questions (and those related to them) which most alarm the mind." p. 94.

[145] "Unlimited time contains the same pleasure as the limited if its limits are measured with the necessary discernment." p. 95.

"Limits of pleasure are prescribed to the flesh, but the yearning for unlimited time has made them recede to infinity; but the mind, which has made clear to itself the aim and the limits of the flesh and has extinguished desires concerning eternity, has made a complete life possible for us and we no longer need infinite time. And it does not shun pleasure, even when circumstances cause a parting from life, accepting the end of the best life as a consummation." p. 95.

[146] "We must always have before our mind's eye the set aim to which we refer all our judgments; if not, everything will be full of disorder and unrest." p. 95.

"If you fight against all sensations, you will have nothing by which to be guided in judging those which you declare to be false." p. 95.

[148] "Unless on every occasion you refer all your actions to the end prescribed by nature, but swerve and (whether in shunning or in striving after something) turn to something else, your actions will not be in harmony with your words." p. 96.

[149] "Some desires are natural and necessary, others natural [but] not necessary, and others again neither natural nor necessary, but the offspring of vain fancy." p. 96.

[148] "The same knowledge which fills us with assurance that terrors are neither eternal nor of long duration enables us to see that in our limited lifetime the security of friendship is the most reliable." p. 97.

The following passages represent Epicurus' views on spiritual nature, the state. The contract (συνθήκη) he considers as the basis, and accordingly, only utility (συμφέρον) as the end.

[150] "Natural right is a mutual agreement, contracted for the purpose of utility, not to harm or allow to be harmed." p. 97.

"For all living beings which could not enter into mutual contracts not to harm each other or allow each other to be harmed, there is neither justice nor injustice. It is the same, too, with peoples who have been either unable or unwilling to enter into contracts not to harm each other or allow each other to be harmed." p. 98.

"*Justice is not something existing in itself*; it exists *in mutual relations*, wherever and whenever an agreement is concluded not to harm each other or allow each other to be harmed." p. 98.

[151] "*Injustice is not in itself an evil*, but the evil lies in the fearful anxiety over its remaining concealed from the guardians of the law appointed to deal with it.... For whether he [the transgressor of the law] will remain undiscovered until death, is uncertain." p. 98.

"*In general, the same justice is valid for all* (for it is something useful in mutual intercourse); *but the special conditions of the country* and the *totality* of *other possible grounds* bring it about that *the same justice is not valid for all*." p. 98.

[152] "That which proves to be useful for the needs of mutual intercourse, that which is considered just, has the essence of right when the same is valid for everyone. If, however, somebody stipulates this, but it does not turn out to be to the advantage of mutual intercourse, then it no longer has the essence of justice." p. 99.

"And when the usefulness which is contained in right has ceased to exist but for a certain time continues to correspond to the conception of right, then it has nevertheless during that time remained right for those who do not let themselves be deluded by empty talk, but take many things into account." p. 99.

[153] "Where, without any new circumstances having arisen, that which is considered as right proves in practice not to correspond to the conception of right, then it is not right; but where, *new circumstances having arisen, the same valid right is no longer useful, it was indeed formerly right, when it was useful for the mutual intercourse of citizens, but later when it was no longer useful, it was no longer right*." p. 99.

[154] "He who knew how best to gain self-assurance from the external circumstances *procured for himself that which was possible, as something not alien to himself*, and *considered that which was not possible as alien to himself*." p. 99

End of the tenth book of Diogenes Laertius [a]

Epicurus to Herodotus

[37] "In the first place ... we must understand what it is that words denote, so that we have something to which we can refer opinions or inquiries or doubts, and by which we can test them, and so that everything does not slip from us into infinity without our having a judgment on it and that we are not left with mere empty words. [38] For it is necessary that the original meaning of every word should be perceived and need no proof, if we want to have something to which we can refer inquiries or doubts or opinions." pp. 30-31.

It is significant that Aristotle, in his *Metaphysics*, makes the same remark on the relation of language to philosophising. Since the ancient philosophers, not excluding the Sceptics, all begin by presupposing consciousness, a firm foothold is necessary. This is provided by the concepts presented in knowledge in general. Epicurus, being the philosopher of the concept, is most exact in

---

[a] In the manuscript this phrase is in Latin.—*Ed.*

this and therefore defines these fundamental conditions in greater detail. He is also the most consistent and, like the Sceptics, he completes ancient philosophy, but from the other side.

[38] "Further we must observe everything both on the basis of sensations and also simply of present impressions, whether of the mind or of any criterion whatever, and equally on the basis of actual feelings, so that we have something by which we can characterise what is to be expected and what is unknown. *Once this is done, one must begin reflections on the unknown.*" p. 31.

"[...] the common opinion of the physicists that nothing comes into being from not-being [...]." Aristotle, *Physics*, Book I, Chap. 4, Commentary of Coimbra [Jesuit] College, p[p]. 123[-125].

"[...] In one sense things come-to-be out of that which has no 'being' ... yet in another sense they come-to-be always out of 'what is'. For coming-to-be necessarily implies the pre-existence of something which potentially 'is', but actually 'is not'; and this something is spoken of both as 'being' and as 'not-being'." Aristotle, *De generatione et corruptione*, Book I, Chap. 3, Commentary of Coimbra College, p. 26.

[Diogenes Laertius, X, 39] "[...] the universe was always such as it is now, and such it will ever remain." p. 31.

"[...] the universe consists of bodies and space." [p. 32.]

[40] "[...] of bodies some are composite, others the elements of which these composite bodies are made." p. 32.

[41] "These [elements] are *indivisible* and unchangeable ... if things are not all to be destroyed and pass into non-existence [...]." [p]p. [32-]33. "[...] the universe is infinite. For what is finite has an extremity [...]." p. 33. "[...] the universe is unlimited by reason of the multitude of bodies and the extent of the void." p. 33. ("[...] the infinite body will obviously prevail over and annihilate the finite body...." Aristotle, *Physics*, Book III. Chap. 5, Commentary of Coimbra College, p. 487.)

[Diogenes Laertius, X, 42] "[...] they [the atoms] ... vary indefinitely in their shapes". p[p]. 33[-34].

[43] "The atoms are in continual motion through all eternity." p. 34.

[44] "Of all this there is no beginning, since both atoms and void exist from all eternity." p. 35.

"[...] atoms have no quality at all except shape, size and weight [...]." p. 35. "... they are not of any and every size; at any rate no atom has ever been seen by our senses." p. 35. [45] "[...] there is an infinite number of worlds [...]." p. 35. [46] "Again there are impressions which are of the same shape as the solid bodies but far thinner than what we can perceive." p. 36. "These impressions we call images." p. 36. [48] "Besides this, ... the production of the images is as quick as thought. For the continual streaming off from the surface of the bodies is *evidenced* by *no visible sign*...." p. 37.

"*And there are other modes in which these natural phenomena may be formed. For there is nothing in them which contradicts the sensations if we in some way take into account what is evident in order to refer the impressions produced on us from outside.*" p. 38.

[49] "*But it must also be assumed that when anything streams in from outside, we see and apprehend the shapes.*" p. 38.

[50] "Every presentation *received* either by the mind or through *sensation*, but not judged (*non judicata*), is *true*. The illusion and *error*, whether it is *not confirmed* or is even *refuted*, always lies in what is *added by thought, following a motion in ourselves which, though connected with a certain effort of presentation, has its own perception, through which the error arises.*" p. 39.

[51] "For there would be no error if we did not experience also a certain other motion in ourselves which is connected [with the effort of presentation], but has its own perception." p. 39. "It is through this [inner movement which is connected with] the effort of presentation, but has its own perception, that, if it is not confirmed or is refuted, illusion arises; but if it is confirmed or not refuted, truth results." [p]p. [39-]40.

[52] "Again, hearing takes place when a current passes from the object which emits sounds, etc." p. 40.

[53] "Also concerning smell we must assume (as I have said about hearing) ...." p. 41.

[54] "*Every quality which is inherent in and proper to them* (the atoms), meaning those *named above (magnitudo, figura, pondus*[a]*), is unchangeable just as the atoms also do not change.*" p. 41.

[55] "*Again one should not suppose that there are atoms of every size, lest this be contradicted by phenomena; but some changes in size must be admitted.* For if this is so, the processes in feelings and sensations will be more easily explained." [p]p. [42-]43.

[56] "Besides, one must not suppose that in a limited body there is an infinite number of atoms, and of every size [...]." p. 43.

[60] "[...] one motion must be assumed which must be thought of as directed upwards to infinity, and one directed downwards [...]." p. 45.

See end of page 44 and beginning of page 45, where, strictly speaking, the atomistic principle is violated, and an internal necessity is attributed to the atoms themselves. Since they have a certain size, there must be something smaller than they are. Such are the parts of which they are composed. But these are necessarily to be considered together as a κοινότης ἐνυπάρχουσα.[b] Thus ideality is transferred to the atoms themselves. The smallest thing in them is not the smallest imaginable, but is likened to it without anything definite being thought of. The necessity and ideality attributed to them is itself merely fictitious, accidental, external to them. The principle of Epicurean atomistics is not expressed until the ideal and necessary is made to have being only in an imaginary form external to itself, the form of the atom. Such is the extent of Epicurus' consistency.

[61] "When they are travelling through the void and meet with no resistance, the atoms must move with equal speed." p. 46.

Just as we have seen that necessity, connection, differentiation, within itself, is transferred to or rather expressed in the atom, that ideality is present here only in this form external to itself, so it is with *motion* too, the question of which necessarily arises once the motion of the atoms is compared with the motion of the κατά τάς

---

[a] Size, shape, weight.— *Ed.*

[b] Permanent community.— *Ed.*

συγχρίσεις [a] bodies, that is, of the concrete. In comparison with this motion, the motion of the atoms is in principle absolute, that is, all empirical conditions in it are disregarded, it is ideal. In general, in expounding Epicurean philosophy and its immanent dialectics, one has to bear in mind that, while the principle is an imagined one, assuming the form of being in relation to the concrete world, the dialectics, the inner essence of these ontological determinations, as a form, in itself void, of the absolute, can show itself only in such a way that they, being immediate, enter into a necessary confrontation with the concrete world and reveal, in their specific relation to it, that they are only the imagined form of its ideality, external to itself, and not as presupposed, but rather only as ideality of the concrete. Thus its determinations are in themselves untrue and self-negating. The only conception of the world that is expressed is that its basis is that which has no presuppositions, which is nothing. Epicurean philosophy is important because of the naiveness with which conclusions are expressed without the prejudice of our day.

[62] "And *not even when it is a question of composite bodies* can one be said to be *faster* than the other, etc." p. 46. "[...] it can only be said that *they often rebound until the continuity of their movement becomes perceptible to the senses*. For what we conjecture of the invisible, namely, that periods of time contemplated through speculation may also contain continuity of movement, is not true for things of this kind, since only all that which is *really perceived or is comprehended from an impression by thinking is true*." p. 47.

The question must be considered, why the principle of the reliability of the senses is disregarded and what abstracting conception is set up as a criterion of truth.

[63] "[...] the soul is a corporeal thing, composed of fine particles, which is spread (*diffusum*) over the whole of the body (*corpus*) [...]." p. 47.

Interesting here again is the specific difference between fire and air, on the one hand, and the soul, on the other, showing that the soul is adequate to the body, analogy being used and nevertheless discarded, which is in general the method of imaginative consciousness; thus all concrete determinations collapse and a mere monotonous echo takes the place of development.

[63] "Further we must keep in mind that the *soul* is the *chief cause of sensation.*[64] It would not be, if it were not in a manner of speaking *enveloped by the rest of the mass of the body. The remaining mass of the body, which makes it possible for the soul to be this cause,* itself *shares* through the soul *in this quality* (yet not in all of what the soul possesses). *That is why* it has no longer any sentience when the soul has departed. For it did not *have this ability in itself,* but *served as an intermediary for it to another*

---

[a] Composite.—*Ed.*

being which emerged simultaneously with it and which, owing to the *ability it had achieved to produce immediately a sensation corresponding to the specific stimulation,* imparted sentience both to itself and to the remaining mass of the body by reason of neighbourhood (*vicinia*) and sympathy." p. 48.

We have seen that the atoms, taken abstractly among themselves, are nothing but entities, imagined in general, and that only in confrontation with the concrete do they develop their ideality, which is imagined and therefore entangled in contradictions. They also show, by becoming one side of the relation, that is, when it comes to dealing with objects which carry in themselves the principle and its concrete world (the living, the animate, the organic), that the realm of imagination is thought of now as free, now as the manifestation of something ideal. This freedom of the imagination is therefore but an assumed, immediate, imagined one, which in its true form is the atomistic. Either of the determinations can therefore be taken for the other, each considered in itself is the same as the other, but in respect of each other too the same determinations must be ascribed to them, from whichever viewpoint they are considered; the solution is therefore the return to the simplest, first determination, where the realm of the imagination is assumed as *free*. As this return takes place in regard to a totality, to what is imagined, which really has the ideal in itself, and is the ideal itself in its being, so here the atom is posited as it really is, in the totality of its contradictions; at the same time, the basis of these contradictions emerges, the desire to apprehend the thing imagined as the free ideal thing as well, while only imagining it. The principle of absolute arbitrariness appears here, therefore, with all its consequences. In its lowest form, this is already essentially the case with the atom. As there are many atoms, each one contains in itself a difference in respect of the many, and hence it is in itself many. But that is already contained in the definition of the atom, so that the plurality in it is necessarily and immanently a oneness; it is so because it is. But it still remains to be explained, with regard to the world, why it develops freely from a single principle into a plurality. Therefore what is to be proved is assumed, the atom itself is what is to be explained. Then the difference of the ideality could be introduced only by comparison; in themselves both sides come under the same definition, and ideality itself is again posited by the external combination of these many atoms, by their being the principles of these compositions. The principle of this composition is therefore that which initially was composite in itself without any cause, that is, what is explained is itself the explanation, and it is thrust into the nebulous space of imaginative abstraction. As already said, this emerges in its totality only when the organic is considered.

It must be noted that the fact that the soul, etc., perishes, that it owes its existence only to an accidental mixture, expresses in general the *accidental nature of all these notions*, e. g., soul, etc., which, not being necessary in ordinary consciousness, are *accounted for* by Epicurus as *accidental conditions*, which are seen as something given, the necessity of which, the necessity of the existence of which, is not only not proved, but is even admitted to be not provable, only possible. What persists, on the other hand, is the free being of the imagination, which is firstly the free which itself exists in general, and secondly, as the thought of the freedom of what is imagined, a lie and a fiction, and hence in itself an inconsistency, an illusion, an imposture. It expresses rather the demand for a concrete definition of the soul, etc., as immanent thought. What is lasting and great in Epicurus is that he gives no preference to conditions over notions, and tries just as little to save them. For Epicurus the task of philosophy is to prove that the world and thought are thinkable and possible. His proof and the principle by which it proceeds and to which it is referred is again possibility existing for itself, whose natural expression is the atom and whose intellectual expression is chance and arbitrariness. Closer investigation is needed of how all determinations may be exchanged between soul and body and how either of them is the same as the other in the bad sense that neither one nor the other is at all conceptually defined. See end of page 48 and beginning of page 49: Epicurus stands higher than the Sceptics in that not only are conditions and presentations reduced to nothing, but their perception, the thinking of them and the reasoning about their existence, proceeding from something solid, is likewise only a possibility.

[67] "*It is impossible to conceive anything that is incorporeal as self-existent, except empty space.* (The incorporeal is not thought by the imagination, it pictures it as the void and as empty.[a]) And empty space can neither act nor be acted upon, but by virtue of its existence makes motion possible for the bodies." p. 49. "Hence those who say the soul is incorporeal talk nonsense." [p]p. [49-]50.

It is necessary to study the passage on page 50 and the beginning of page 51, where Epicurus speaks of the determinations of concrete bodies and seems to refute the atomistic principle by saying:

[69] "... that the whole body in general receives its specific being out of all that; not as though it were a composite of it, as, for instance, when out of conglomera-

___
[a] This sentence is in German in the manuscript.— *Ed.*

tions of atoms themselves a larger formation is made up ... but only that, as stated, it receives its specific being out of all that. And all these things demand specific consideration and judgment, in which the whole must constantly be considered and not in any way be separated, but, apprehended as a whole, receives the designation of body." pp. 50 and 51.

[70] "Again, the bodies often *encounter non-specific* accidentals, some of which, of course, are invisible and incorporeal. Thus, by using this word in the manner in which it is most frequently used, we make it clear that the accidentals neither possess the nature of the whole to which, as the composite whole, we give the name of body, nor that [of the] specific qualities without which a body is unthinkable." p. 51.

[71] "[...] we must regard them as that which they appear to be, namely, as accidental attributes of the body which, however, neither are in themselves concomitants of the body nor possess the function of an independent being; we see them such as sensation itself makes their individuality appear." p. 52.

It is a matter of certainty for Epicurus that repulsion is posited with the law of the atom, the declination from the straight line. That this is not to be taken in the superficial sense, as though the atoms in their movement could meet only in this way, is expressed at any rate by Lucretius. Soon after saying in the above-quoted passage:

Without this *clinamen atomi*[a] there would be neither *"offensus natus, nec plaga creata"* [b] [II, 223], he says:

"Again, if all movement is always interconnected, the new arising from the old in a determinate order—if the atoms never swerve so as to originate some new movement that will snap the bonds of fate, the everlasting sequence of cause and effect—what is the source of the free [will]...." ([*On the Nature of Things,*] Book II, 251 ff.)

Here another motion by which the atoms can meet is posited, distinct from that caused by the *clinamen.* Further it is defined as absolutely deterministic, hence negation of self, so that every determination finds its being in its immediate being-otherwise, in the being-negated, which in respect of the atom is the straight line. Only from the *clinamen* does the individual motion emerge, the relation which has its determination as the determination of its self and no other.

Lucretius may or may not have derived this idea from Epicurus. That is immaterial. The conclusion from the consideration of repulsion, that the atom as the immediate form of the concept is objectified only in immediate absence of concept, this same is true also of the philosophical consciousness of which this principle is the essence.

This serves me at the same time as justification for giving a quite different account of the matter from that of Epicurus.

---

[a] Declination of the atom.—*Ed.*
[b] "Meeting nor collision possible."—*Ed.*

EPICUREAN PHILOSOPHY

Second Notebook

I. DIOGENES LAERTIUS, BOOK TEN
II. SEXTUS EMPIRICUS
III. PLUTARCH, *THAT EPICURUS ACTUALLY MAKES
A PLEASANT LIFE IMPOSSIBLE*

I. DIOGENES LAERTIUS, BOOK TEN,
COMMENTARY BY GASSENDI

Epicurus to Herodotus. Continued

[72] "We must not investigate time as we do the other accidents which we investigate in a subject, namely, *by referring them to the preconceptions envisaged in our minds*; but *we must take into account* the plain fact itself, in virtue of which we speak of time as *long or short....* We must not adopt any new terms as preferable, but should employ the *already existing* ones; *nor must we predicate anything else of time, as if this something had the same essence* as the proper meaning of the word; ... but we must chiefly reflect upon how we associate and measure what is peculiar to it." [73] "*For this also requires no proof, but only reflection that we associate it with days and nights and their parts and likewise also with feelings and absence of feeling, with movement and rest*, conceiving a peculiar attribute of these to be precisely that which we call time." pp. 52-53.
"[...] and all things are again dissolved [...]." p. 53.
"It is clear, then, that he [Epicurus] also makes the words perishable, since their parts are subject to change. He says this also elsewhere." p. 53.
[74] "And further, we *must not suppose that the worlds have necessarily one and the same shape, but that they differ* from one another." p. 53.
"*For neither are living things necessarily separated from the infinite*, nor have they fallen from heaven. [75] ... we must grasp that nature too in many and very different respects follows the instruction and pressure of things, and thinking gives greater precision to that which it receives from nature and adds new discoveries*, in some cases more quickly and in others more slowly, requiring for this sometimes more and sometimes less time". [p]p. [53-]54.

See end of page 54 and beginning of page 55, where the ἀρχαὶ τῶν ὀνομάτων [a] is discussed.

[76] "*As for the meteors, we must believe that their motion, position, eclipse, [rising and] setting and the like do not take place because someone governs and orders or has ordered them, who at the same time enjoys perfect bliss*"

(we must compare with this what Simplicius attributes to Anaxagoras about the νοῦς [b] which orders the world)

---

[a] Origin of designations.— *Ed.*
[b] Mind.— *Ed.*

"... *along with immortality* [77] (for actions and *anxieties, anger* and favour do not accord with *bliss,* but *result* from weakness, fear and *need,* with which they are most related). Nor must we believe that the being *which has acquired bliss willingly submits to these movements,* for this is an *annoyance* and *contradictory* [to bliss], but *we must rather maintain all its sublimity by using expressions which lead to such notions as do not give rise to any opinions contradictory to sublimity.* If we do not agree with this, *this contradiction will itself produce the greatest mental confusion. Hence we must assume that, with the appearance of the world, both the original interception of these conglomerations and the obligatory character and periodicity of these movements appeared.*" pp. 55 and 56.

Here we must observe the principle of the thinkable in order, on the one hand, to maintain the freedom of self-consciousness, and, on the other hand, to attribute to God freedom from any determination.

[78] "[...] that what makes one *blissful* in the *knowledge of the meteors* ... [lies] in *particular* in accurate *study* of what those *natural phenomena* are *which are observed in our meteors* and what is in some way kindred to them in principle: [Here we have that which can be 'in a plurality of ways'] that which can *possibly* be and that which is in *some other way*[a]: but it is rather an *absolute rule that nothing which threatens danger, which can disturb ataraxy, can ever happen to an indestructible* and *blissful nature. Consciousness must apprehend that this is an absolute law.*" p. 56.

Further, on pages 56 and 57, Epicurus denounces the senseless mere wondering contemplation of the celestial bodies as stultifying and fear-inspiring; he asserts the absolute freedom of mind.

[80] "... *We must beware of the prejudice that the study of those objects is not thorough or subtle enough because it is aimed only at our ataraxy and bliss. Hence we must investigate the meteors and all that is unknown, observing how often the same thing occurs within our experience.*" p. 57.

[81]"*Besides all this we must understand that the greatest confusion in men's minds arises* through the *belief* that there are *beings which are blissful* and *indestructible* and *that at the same time have desires, actions and feelings* which conflict with these attributes and that men somehow foresee eternal suffering and *entertain suspicions of the kind fostered by the myths* (and because in death there is no sensation they also fear to be at some time deprived of sensation) and that they are not guided by the correct notions ... so that, unless they set limits to their fears, they experience equal or still greater anxiety than they would were their imaginings true." [82] "*But ataraxy means to have freed oneself from all that....*" [p]p. [57-]58.

"*Therefore we must pay attention to all things that are present to us and to the sensations,* to general ones in relation to what is general, to particular ones in relation to what is particular, and *to all the evidence available for every single criterion.*" p. 58.

Epicurus to Pythocles

Epicurus repeats at the beginning of his discussion on the meteors that the aim of this is γνώσεως ... ἀταραξία and πίστις

---

[a] In the manuscript here, after the semicolon, follows Gassendi's Latin translation of the preceding Greek phrase: (*esse* [...] *id, quod pluribus modis fieri dicitur, et non uno modo necesse contingere; et posse alio quoque modo se habere*).— *Ed.*

βεβαία, καθάπερ καί ἐπί τῶν λοιπῶν[a] [X, 85]. But the study of these celestial bodies also differs substantially from the rest of science:

[86] "...nor must we *apply to everything the same theory* as in Ethics or in clarifying the other problems of Physics, for example that the *universe consists of bodies and the incorporeal*" (*quod* τὸ **ϰεγὸγ**[b]) "or that there are *indivisible elements* and the like, where only a *single explanation* corresponds to the phenomena.[c] *For this is not the case with the meteors. These have no simple cause of their coming into being and have more than one essential category corresponding to the sensations.*" pp. 60 and 61.

It is important in the whole of Epicurus' view of things that the celestial bodies, as something beyond the senses, cannot command the same degree of evidence as the rest of the moral and sensuous world. To them Epicurus' theory of *disjunctio*[d] applies in practice, viz.: that there is no *aut aut*,[e] and hence that internal determinateness is denied and that the principle of the thinkable, the imaginable, of accident, of abstract identity and freedom manifests itself as what it is, as the indeterminate, which precisely for that reason is determined by a reflection external to it. It is seen here that the method of consciousness which imagines and represents, fights only its own shadow; what the shadow is depends on how it is seen, how that which reflects is reflected out of it back into itself. As in the case of the organic in itself, when it is substantialised, the contradiction of the atomistic outlook is revealed, so now, when the object itself assumes the *form* of sensuous certainty and of imagining reason, philosophising consciousness admits what it is doing. As there the *imagined principle and its application* are found *objectified as one,* and the contradictions are thereby called to arms as the antithesis of the concretised presentations themselves, so here, where the object hangs, as it were, over the heads of men, where through the self-sufficiency, through the sensuous independence and the mysterious remoteness of its existence, the object challenges consciousness, so here consciousness comes to acknowledge its own activity, it contemplates what it does, so as to make the presentations which pre-exist in it intelligible and to vindicate them as its own: just as the whole activity of consciousness is only struggle with remoteness, which, like a curse, shackles the whole of

---

[a] Knowledge ... ataraxy and firm conviction as is also the case with everything else.— *Ed.*

[b] That is, void (note by Marx).— *Ed.*

[c] In the manuscript here follows in brackets the last phrase in Gassendi's Latin translation: (*quaecumque uno tantum modo rebus apparentibus congruunt*).— *Ed.*

[d] Disjunction.— *Ed.*

[e] Either—or.— *Ed.*

antiquity, just as it has only possibility, chance, as its principle, and seeks in some way to establish identity between itself and its object, so does it admit this, as soon as this remoteness confronts it in objective independence as heavenly bodies. Consciousness is indifferent as to just what explanation is offered: it affirms that there is not one explanation, but many, that is, that any explanation will suffice; thus it acknowledges that its activity is active fiction. For this reason, in antiquity in general, in whose philosophy premises are not lacking, the meteors and the doctrine concerning them are the image in which, even in the person of Aristotle, it contemplates its own defects. Epicurus expressed this, and this is the service he rendered, the iron logic of his views and conclusions. The meteors challenge sensuous understanding, but it overcomes their resistance and will listen to nothing but its own ideas of them.

[86] "For nature must be studied not according to empty axioms and laws, but as required by the phenomena.... [87] (life [requires]) us to live without confusion." p. 61.

Here, where the premise itself confronts actual consciousness, arousing fear in it, there is no longer any need for any principles or premises. The imagination is extinguished in fear.

Epicurus therefore again formulates the following proposition, as though finding himself in it:

[87] "Everything therefore happens, once it is explained consistently *in various ways*, in conformity with the phenomena, if that which has been *credibly* established in respect of them is maintained. But if we maintain one thing as valid and reject another, although it equally conforms to the phenomena, then we are openly overstepping the bounds of the study of nature and launching into the realm of myth." p. 61.

The question now is how the explanation is to be arranged:

[87] "Certain signs of the processes of the meteors can be taken from the processes going on in our experience which can be observed or are present in the same way as the phenomena of the meteors. For these can occur in a plurality of ways. [88] But one must observe the appearance of every single thing and also explain whatever is connected with it. This will not be inconsistent with the fact that it can take place in various ways, as happens in our experience." p. 61.

For Epicurus the sound of his own voice drowns the thunder and blots out the lightning of the heavens of his conception. We can gather from the monotonous repetition how important Epicurus considers his new method of explanation, how intent he is to eliminate the miraculous, how he always insists on applying not one, but several explanations, giving us very frivolous examples of this in respect of everything, how he says almost outright that while he leaves nature free, he is concerned only with freedom of consciousness. The only proof required of an explanation is that it should not be ἀντιμαρτυρεῖσθαι[a] by the evidence of the senses and experience, by the phenomena, the appearance, for what matters is only how nature appears. These propositions are reiterated.

On the origin of the sun and the moon:

[90] "For this also is suggested in this way by sensation." p. 63.

On the size of the sun and the constellations:

[91] "[...] the phenomena *here* [on the earth] we see ... *as we perceive them by the senses.*" p. 63.

On the rising and setting of the constellations:

[92] "For no phenomenon testifies against this." p. 64.

On the turnings of the sun and the moon:

[93] "For all that and what is connected with it does not contradict any of the evident phenomena if in separate explanations we always hold fast to what is possible and can bring each of them into conformity with the phenomena, without fear of the slavish artifices of the astrologers." [p]p. [64-]65.

On the waning and waxing of the moon:

[94] "[...] and in *any of the ways* by which also the phenomena within our experience suggest an explanation of this problem, *unless, being in love with some one means of explanation, we lightly reject the others or are unable to see what it is possible for a man to know* and *therefore seek to know what is impossible.*" p. 65.

On the *species vultus*[b] in the moon:

[95] "[...] *in general in any way considered as being in conformity with the phenomena.*" [96] "*For, it must be added, this way must be used in respect of all the meteors. For if you fight against what is evident, you will never be able to enjoy genuine ataraxy.*" p. 66.

---

[a] Disproved.— *Ed.*
[b] Face.— *Ed.*

Note particularly the exclusion of all divine, teleological influence in the passage on the *ordo periodicus*,[a] where it is clearly seen that the explanation is only a matter of consciousness listening to itself and the objective is a delusion simulated:

[97] "... *must be seen as something ordinary* which also occurs *within our own experience*; the *divinity must not on any account be adduced for this, but must be kept free from all tasks and in perfect bliss*. For unless this be done, the whole theory of origins of the meteors will be rendered senseless, as has already been the case with some theoreticians who did not apply a possible explanation, but *indulged in idle attempts at explanations, believing that it happens only in one way and excluding all other possible explanations*, and *thus* arrived at things which are impossible, and were unable to understand the *phenomena* as signs, which one *must do*, and were not disposed to rejoice with God." p. 67.

The same arguments are often repeated almost word for word:
[98] On the varying lengths of nights and days: on the μήχη νυχτῶν καὶ ἡμερῶν παραλλάττοντα,[b] p. 67.

[98] On the ἐπισημασίαι,[c] p. 67.

[99] On the origin of the νέφη,[d] p. 68.

[100-101] of the βρονταὶ,[e] of the ἀστραπαί,[f] p. 69; [103] thus he says of the κεραυνός[g]:

[104] "And there are several other ways in which *thunderbolts* may occur. *Exclusion of myth is the sole condition necessary*; and it will be excluded if one *properly attends* to the *phenomena* and hence draws inferences concerning what is invisible." p. 70.

(After adducing many explanations of σεισμοί, terrae motus,[h] he adds as usual: [106] "But there are also *several other ways*", etc., p. 71.)

On the comets:

[112] "... there are many other ways by which this might be brought about if one is capable of finding out what accords with the phenomena." p. 75.

De stellis fixis et errantibus[i]:

[113] "To assign a *single cause* for these effects when the phenomena suggest several causes is *madness* and an enormity of those who are obsessed by senseless

---

[a] Periodical order.— *Ed.*
[b] This is the Greek original of the previous phrase.— *Ed.*
[c] Weather signs.— *Ed.*
[d] Clouds.— *Ed.*
[e] Thunder.— *Ed.*
[f] Lightning.— *Ed.*
[g] Thunderbolts.— *Ed.*
[h] Earthquake.— *Ed.*
[i] On fixed and wandering stars.— *Ed.*

astrology and assign at random causes for certain phenomena *when they by no means free the divinity from burdensome tasks.*" p. 76.

He even accuses those who *simpliciter*, ἁπλῶς [a] discuss such things,

[114] *portentosum quidpiam coram multitudine ostentare affectare=* "that applies to those who wish to do something to impress the crowd". p. 76.

He says in connection with ἐπισημασίαι,[b] the anticipation of *tempestas*[c] in animals, which some connected with God:

[116] "For such folly as this would not possess the *most ordinary being* if ever so little enlightened, *much less one who enjoys perfect felicity.*" p. 77.

From this we can see among other things how Pierre Gassendi, who wants to rescue divine intervention, assert the immortality of the soul, etc., and still be an Epicurean (see, for example, *esse animos immortales, contra Epicurum*, Pet. Gassendi animadvers. in 1. dec. Diog. Laert., pp. 549-602, or, *esse deum authorem mundi, contra Epicurum*, pp. 706-725, *gerere deum hominum curam, contra Epicurum*, pp. 738-751, etc. Compare: Feuerbach, *geschichte der neuern Philosophie*, "Pierre Gassendi", pp. 127-150), does not understand Epicurus at all and still less can teach us anything about him. Gassendi tries rather to teach us from Epicurus than to teach us about him. Where he violates Epicurus' iron logic, it is in order not to quarrel with his own religious premises. This struggle is significant in Gassendi, as is in general the fact that modern philosophy arises where the old finds its downfall: on the one hand from Descartes' universal doubt, whereas the Sceptics sounded the knell of Greek philosophy; on the other hand from the rational consideration of nature, whereas ancient philosophy is overcome in Epicurus even more thoroughly than in the Sceptics. Antiquity was rooted in nature, in materiality. Its degradation and profanation means in the main the defeat of materiality, of solid life; the modern world is rooted in the spirit and it can be free, can release the other, nature, out of itself. But equally, by contrast, what with the ancients was profanation of nature is with the moderns salvation from the shackles of servile faith, and the modern rational outlook on nature must first raise itself to the point from which the ancient Ionian philosophy, in principle at

---

[a] Simply, absolutely.— *Ed.*
[b] Weather signs.— *Ed.*
[c] Tempest.— *Ed.*

least, begins—the point of seeing the divine, the Idea, embodied in nature.

Who will not recall here the enthusiastic passage in Aristotle, the acme of ancient philosophy, in his treatise περί τῆς φύσεως ζωϊκῆς,[a] which sounds quite a different note from the dispassionate monotony of Epicurus.[180]

Characteristic of the method of the Epicurean outlook is the way it deals with the *creation of the world*, a topic in the treatment of which the standpoint of a philosophy will always be ascertainable, since it reveals how, according to this philosophy, the spirit creates the world, the attitude of a philosophy to the world, the creative power, the spirit of a philosophy.

Epicurus says (pp. 61 and 62)[181]:

[88] "The world is a *celestial complex* (περιοχή τις οὐρανοῦ), which comprises stars and earth and all phenomena containing a cut-out segment (ἀποτομήν) of the *infinite*, and *terminating in a boundary* which may be either ethereal or solid (a boundary whose dissolution will bring about the wreck of all within it), which may be at rest, and may be round, triangular or of any other shape. *All these alternatives are possible* since none of them is contradicted by the *phenomena. Where* the world ends *cannot be discerned*. That there is an *infinite number* of such worlds is evident...."[b]

Anybody will at once be struck by the poverty of this world construction. That the world is a complex of the earth, stars, etc., means nothing, since the origin of the moon, etc., occurs and is explained only later.

In general every concrete body is a complex, or more precisely, according to Epicurus, a complex of atoms. The definition of a complex, its specific distinction, lies in its boundary, and for that reason, once the world is defined as having been cut out from the infinite, it is superfluous to add the boundary as a closer definition, for something which is cut out is separated from the remainder and is a concrete, distinct thing, and therefore bounded in regard to the remainder. But the boundary is what must be defined, since a bounded complex in general is not yet a world. Further on it is said that the boundary can be defined in any way one likes, πανταχῶς, and finally it is admitted that it is impossible to define its specific difference, but that it is conceivable that one exists.

---

[a] *On the Nature of Animals.—Ed.*
[b] In the manuscript this quotation and the next one on p. 426 are written in German.—*Ed.*

Hence all that is said is that the notion of the return of a totality of differences to an indefinite unity, i.e., the notion of a "world", exists in consciousness, is present in everyday thinking. The boundary, the specific difference, and hence the immanence and necessity of this notion is declared to be not conceivable; that the notion exists can be conceived, tautologically, because it is there; so that what is to be explained, the creation, the origin and internal production of a world by thought, is declared inconceivable, and the existence of this notion in consciousness is passed off as the explanation.

It is the same as if one were to say that it can be proved that there is a God, but his *differentia specifica, quid sit*,[a] the what of this determination, cannot be investigated.

When Epicurus further says that the boundary can be conceived as of any kind, i.e., every determination which in general we distinguish in a spatial boundary can be applied to it, then the notion of the world is nothing but the return to sensuously perceptible unity, which is indefinite and therefore may be defined in any way one likes, or more generally, since the world is an indefinite notion of half sensuous, half reflecting consciousness, the world is present in this consciousness together with all other sensuous notions and bounded by them; its definition and boundary is therefore as multiple as these sensuous notions surrounding it, each of them can be regarded as its boundary and hence as its closer definition and explanation. That is the essence of all Epicurean explanations, and it is all the more important because it is the essence of all the explanations of reflecting consciousness which is the prisoner of preconceptions.

So it is also with the moderns in regard to God, when goodness, wisdom, etc., are ascribed to Him. Any one of these notions, which are definite, can be considered as the boundary of the indefinite notion of God which lies between them.

The substance of this kind of explanation is therefore that a notion which is to be explained is found in consciousness. The explanation or closer definition is then that notions in the same sphere and accepted as known stand in relation to it; hence that in general it lies in consciousness, in a definite sphere. Here Epicurus admits the weakness of his own and of all ancient philosophy, namely, that it knows that notions are in consciousness, but that it does not know their boundary, their principle, their necessity.

---

[a] Specific distinction, what he is.— *Ed.*

However, Epicurus is not satisfied with having worked out his conception of the creation; he performs the drama himself, objectifies for himself what he has just done, and only then does his creation proper begin. For he says further:

[89] "Such a world may arise ... in one of the intermundia (by which term we mean the spaces between worlds), in a vast empty space ... in a great transparent void ... when certain suitable seeds rush in from a world or an intermundium or from several worlds, and gradually form compounds or divisions, or, as may happen, undergo changes of place, and receive into themselves waterings from without as far as the foundations laid can hold the compound. [90] For if a world arises in the void, it is not enough that there should be an aggregation or vortex or a multitude and that it should meet with another, as one of the physicists says. For this is in conflict with the phenomena." [p. 62.]

Here, first, worlds are presupposed for the creation of the world, and the place where this occurs is the void. Hence what was foreshadowed to begin with in the concept of creation, viz. that what was to be created is presupposed, is substantiated here. The notion without its closer definition and relation to the others, that is to say, as it is provisionally presupposed, is empty or disembodied,[a] an intermundium, an empty space. How this notion gets its determination is presented as follows: seeds appropriate for the creation of a world combine in the way necessary for the creation of a world, that is, no determination, no difference is given. In other words, we have nothing but the atom and the κενόν,[b] despite Epicurus himself striving against this, etc. Aristotle has already in a profound manner criticised the superficiality of the method which proceeds from an abstract principle without allowing this principle to negate itself in higher forms. After praising the Pythagoreans because they were the first to free the categories from their substrate, and did not consider them as attributes of the things of which they are predicated, but as the very substance itself:

"They [the Pythagoreans] thought that the finitude and infinity [...] were not *attributes of certain other things*, e.g. of fire or earth, etc., but *were the substance of the things of which they are predicated*",

he reproaches them because

"*they thought* that the *first subject of which a given definition was predicable* was the substance of the thing [...]". [Aristotle,] *Metaphysics*, Book I, Chap. V.

---

[a] There must have been a slip of the pen here, for the manuscript has *verkörper* (embodied) instead of *entkörpert* (disembodied).— *Ed.*
[b] Void.— *Ed.*

II. SEXTUS EMPIRICUS

We now go on to the attitude of the Epicurean philosophy to Scepticism, insofar as it can be gathered from Sextus Empiricus.

But first a basic definition given by Epicurus himself must be cited from Book Ten of Diogenes Laertius contained in the description of the wise man:

[121] "[the wise man] *will be a dogmatist but not a mere sceptic.*" p. 81.

What Epicurus says about his principle of thinkability, and about language and the origin of concepts, makes up an important part of his exposition of his system as a whole, defining its essential attitude towards ancient philosophy and containing *implicite*[a] his position in relation to the Sceptics. It is interesting to see what Sextus Empiricus says about why Epicurus took to philosophy.

[IX, 18] "If anybody asks ... *out of what chaos originated,* he will have nothing to answer. And according to *some, this was precisely the reason why Epicurus plunged into philosophising.* [19] For when he was a boy he asked his teacher, who was reading to him: [...] out of what chaos arose if it arose first. When the teacher said it was not his business to teach that, but the business of those who were called philosophers, Epicurus said: 'I must go to them if they know the truth of things,'" Sext. Empiricus, *Against the Professors,* Geneva, 1621, p. 383.

[II, 23] "For Democritus says that 'Man is that which we all know', etc. [24] For this thinker proceeds to say that *only the atoms and the void truly exist, and these, he says, form the substrate not only of living beings, but of all compound bodies, so that, as far as these are concerned, we shall not form a concept of the particular essence of Man, seeing that they are common to all things.* But besides these there is no existing substrate; so that we shall possess no means whereby we shall be able to distinguish Man from the other living beings and *form a clear conception* of him. [25] Again, Epicurus says that Man is *such and such a shape combined with a soul.* According to him, then, since *Man is shown by pointing out,* he that is *not pointed out is not a man,* and, if anyone points out a female, the male will not be Man, while if the female points out a male, she will not be Man." *Outlines of Pyrrhonism,* p. 56.

[VIII, 64] "For besides Pythagoras also Empedocles and the Ionians, besides Socrates also Plato, Aristotle and the Stoics, and perhaps also the Garden philosophers, [182] concede that God exists, *as the speeches made by Epicurus testify.*" *Against the Professors,* p. 320.

[VIII, 71] "For it cannot be assumed that the souls are carried down below.... [72] They are *not* dissolved, when *separated from the bodies, as Epicurus used to say,* like smoke. For before also it was not the body which held them fast, but they themselves were for the body the reason why it held together, but still more for themselves." *Against the Professors,* p. 321.

[VIII, 58] "And *Epicurus,* according to some, concedes the essence of God as far as the multitude is concerned, but *by no means as concerns the nature of things.*" *Against the Professors,* p. 319.

---

[a] Implicitly.— *Ed.*

[VII, 267] "The Epicureans [...] did not know that if *that which is pointed out is Man*, that which is not pointed out is not Man. And further *such pointing out takes place* either in respect of a man ... flat-nosed or aquiline-nosed, long-haired or curly-haired, or in respect of *other distinctive features.*" *Against the Professors*, p. 187.

[I, 49] "... amongst them we must place Epicurus, although he seems to be hostile to the professors of science." *Against the Professors*, p. 11.

[I, 57] "*Since, according to the sage Epicurus, it is not possible either to inquire or to doubt without a preconception,* it will be well first of all to consider what 'grammar' ... is...." *Against the Professors*, p. 12.

[I, 272] "... but we shall find even the *accusers of grammar*, Pyrrho and *Epicurus*, acknowledging its necessity. [...] [273] Epicurus has been detected as guilty of having filched the best of his dogmas from the poets. For he has been shown to have taken his proposition that the intensity of pleasure is 'the removal of everything painful'—from this one verse:

"'When they had now put aside all longing for drinking and eating.'

"And as to death, that 'it is nothing to us', Epicharmus had pointed this out to him when he said:

"'To die or to be dead concerns me not.'

"So too, he stole the notion that dead bodies have no feeling from Homer, where he writes:

"'Tis dumb clay that he beats with abuse in his violent fury.'" *Against the Professors*, p. 54.

[VII, 14] "Side by side with him,"

(Archelaus of Athens, who divides philosophy into τὸ φυσικὸν καὶ ἠθικόν [a])

"they place Epicurus as one who also rejects logical consideration. [15] But there were others who said that *he did not reject logic in general, but only that of the Stoics.*" *Against the Professors*, p. 140.

[22] "But the Epicureans proceed from logic: for they investigate first the Canonics and create for themselves the doctrine of the visible and the concealed and the appearances which accompany them." *Against the Professors*, p. 142.

[I, 1] "*Opposition to the representatives of science seems to be common to the Epicureans* and the followers of Pyrrho, though *not from the same* standpoint; the Epicureans hold that the *sciences contribute nothing to the perfecting of wisdom,*"

(this means that the Epicureans consider the knowledge of things, as another form of existence of the spirit, to be powerless in raising the reality of the spirit; the Pyrrhonists consider the powerlessness of the spirit to comprehend things as its essential aspect, its real activity. There is a similar relation between the dogmatists and the Kantians in their attitude to philosophy, although both sides appear degenerate and deprived of the freshness of ancient philosophy. The former renounce knowledge out of godliness, that is, they believe with the Epicureans that the divine in man is ignorance, that this divine, which is laziness, is disturbed by understanding. The Kantians, on the contrary, are as

---

[a] Physics and ethics.— *Ed.*

it were the appointed priests of ignorance, their daily business is to tell their beads over their own powerlessness and the power of things. The Epicureans are more consistent: if ignorance is inherent in the spirit, then knowledge is no enhancement of the spiritual nature, but something indifferent to the spirit, and for an ignorant man the divine is not the motion of knowledge, but laziness);

[1-2] "Or, as some conjecture, because they see in this a way of covering up their ignorance. For in many matters Epicurus stands convicted of ignorance, and even in ordinary converse his speech was not always correct." *Against the Professors*, p. 1.

After quoting some more gossip which clearly proves his confusion, Sextus Empiricus defines the difference between the Sceptics' attitude to science and that of the Epicureans as follows:

[5] "The followers of Pyrrho [opposed the sciences] *neither because they did not contribute anything to wisdom, for that assertion would be dogmatic,* nor because they were uneducated.... [6] They had the same attitude to the *sciences* as to the whole of *philosophy.*"

(From this it is evident that one must distinguish between μαθήματα [a] and φιλοσοφία [b] and that Epicurus' contempt for μαθήματα extends to what we call knowledge, and how exactly this assertion *suo systemati omni consentit.* [c])

"For just as they approached philosophy with the desire of attaining truth, but, *when faced with an anomaly of things resembling contradiction, suspended judgment,* so also, when they set about mastering the sciences and tried also to attain the truth contained in them, they found equal difficulties, which they did not conceal." p. 6 [*Against the Professors*, Book I].

In the *Outlines of Pyrrhonism*, Book I, Chap. XVII, the aetiology which Epicurus in particular applied is aptly refuted, in such a way, however, that the Sceptics' own impotence is revealed.

[I, 185] "Possibly, too, the Five Modes of suspension of judgment may suffice as against the aetiologies. For either a person will suggest a cause which accords with all the trends of philosophy and of scepticism and with the phenomena, or he will not. And perhaps it is impossible to assign a cause which accords with all these."

(Of course, to assign such a cause which is nothing else at all but a phenomenon, is impossible because the cause is the ideality of the phenomenon, the transcended phenomenon. Just as little can [the assignment of] a cause accord with Scepticism, because Scepticism is professional opposition to all thought, the negation of

---

[a] Science.— *Ed.*
[b] Philosophy.— *Ed.*
[c] Corresponds to his whole system.— *Ed.*

determination itself. It is naive to confine scepticism to φαινόμενα [a], for the phenomenon is the being-lost, the not-being of thought: scepticism is the same not-being of thought as reflected in itself, but the phenomenon has in itself disappeared, it is only a semblance; scepticism is the speaking phenomenon and disappears as the phenomenon disappears, it is also only a phenomenon.)

[185-186] "For all things, whether apparent or non-evident, are *matters of controversy.* But if *there is controversy,* the cause of this cause will also be asked for"

(that is, the Sceptic wants a cause which itself is only a semblance and therefore no cause).

"And if he assumes an apparent cause for an apparent, and a non-evident for a non-evident, he will be lost in the regress *ad infinitum*" [*Outlines of Pyrrhonism,* Book I],

(that is, because the Sceptic refuses to get away from the semblance and wants to hold on to it as such, he cannot get away from the semblance and this manoeuvre can be carried on into infinity; it is true that Epicurus wishes to go on from the atom to further determinations, but as he will not allow the atom as such to be dissolved, he cannot go beyond atomistics, determinations external to themselves and arbitrary; the Sceptic, on the other hand, accepts all determinations, but in the determinateness of semblance; his activity is therefore just as arbitrary and displays everywhere the same inadequacy. He swims, to be sure, in the whole wealth of the world, but remains in the same poverty and is himself an embodiment of the powerlessness which he sees in things; Epicurus makes the world empty from the start and so he ends up with the completely indeterminate, the void resting in itself, the otiose god).

[186] "And if at any point he makes a stand, either he will state that the cause is valid in respect of the previous admission, introducing the relating-to-something while he negates the relating-to-nature,"

(it is precisely in the semblance, in the appearance, that the πρός τι [b] is the πρός τὴν φύσιν [c]);

"or if he accepts something out of a presupposition, he will be stopped." p. 36 [*Outlines of Pyrrhonism*].

As the meteors, the *visible heaven,* are for the ancient philosophers the symbol and the visible confirmation of their pre-

---

[a] Phenomena.— *Ed.*
[b] Relating-to-something.— *Ed.*
[c] Relating-to-nature.— *Ed.*

judice for the substantial, so that even Aristotle takes the stars for gods, or at least brings them into direct connection with the highest energy, so the *written heaven*, the *sealed word* of the god who has been revealed to himself in the course of world history, is the battle-cry of Christian philosophy. The premise of the ancients is the act of nature, that of the moderns the act of the spirit. The struggle of the ancients could only end by the visible heaven, the substantial nexus of life, the force of gravity of political and religious life being shattered, for nature must be split in two for the spirit to be one in itself. The Greeks broke it up with the Hephaestan hammer of art, broke it up in their statues; the Roman plunged his sword into its heart and the peoples died, but modern philosophy unseals the word, lets it pass away in smoke in the holy fire of the spirit, and as fighter of the spirit fighting the spirit, not as a solitary apostate fallen from the gravity of Nature, it is universally active and melts the forms which prevent the universal from breaking forth.

III. PLUTARCH, PUBLISHED BY C. XYLANDER, *THAT EPICURUS ACTUALLY MAKES A PLEASANT LIFE IMPOSSIBLE*

It goes without saying that very little of this treatise by Plutarch is of any use. One need only read the introduction with its clumsy boastfulness and its crude interpretation of the Epicurean philosophy in order no longer to entertain any doubt about Plutarch's utter incompetence in philosophical criticism.

Although he may agree with the view of Metrodorus:

[III, 2] "They [the Epicureans] believe that the supreme good is found in the belly and all other passages of the flesh through which pleasure and non-pain make their entrance, and that all the notable and brilliant inventions of civilisation were devised for this belly-centred pleasure and for the good expectation of this pleasure [....]" p. 1087,

this is *minime*[a] Epicurus' teaching. Even Sextus Empiricus sees the difference between Epicurus and the Cyrenaic school in that he asserts that *voluptas*[b] is *voluptas animi.*[c]

[III, 9-10] "Epicurus asserts that in illness the sage often actually laughs at the paroxysms of the disease. Then how can men for whom the pains of the body are so slight and easy to bear find anything appreciable in its pleasures?" p. 1088.

---

[a] Least of all.— *Ed.*
[b] Pleasure.— *Ed.*
[c] Pleasure of the soul.— *Ed.*

It is clear that Plutarch does not understand Epicurus' consistency. For Epicurus the highest pleasure is freedom from pain, from diversity, the absence of any dependence; the body which depends on no other for its sensation, which does not feel this diversity, is healthy, positive. This position, which achieves its highest form in Epicurus' otiose god, is of itself like a chronic sickness in which the disease, because of its duration, ceases to be a condition, becomes, as it were, familiar and normal. We have seen in Epicurus' philosophy of nature that he strives after this absence of dependence, this removal of diversity in theory as well as in practice. The greatest good for Epicurus is ἀταραξία ,[a] since the spirit, which is the thing in question, is empirically unique. Plutarch revels in commonplaces, he argues like an apprentice.

Incidentally we can speak of the conception of the σοφός,[b] who is a preoccupation equally of the Epicurean, Stoic and Sceptic philosophies. If we study him we shall find that he belongs most logically to the atomistic philosophy of Epicurus and that, viewed from this standpoint too, the downfall of ancient philosophy is presented in complete objectiveness in Epicurus.

Ancient philosophy seeks to comprehend the wise man, ὁ σοφός, in two ways, but both of them have the same root.

What appears theoretically in the account given of matter, appears practically in the definition of the σοφός. Greek philosophy begins with seven wise men, among whom is the Ionian philosopher of nature Thales, and it ends with the attempt to portray the wise man conceptually. The beginning and the end, but no less the centre, the middle, is one σοφός , namely Socrates. It is no more an accident that philosophy gravitates round these substantial individuals, than that the political downfall of Greece takes place at the time when Alexander loses his wisdom in Babylon.

Since the soul of Greek life and the Greek mind is substance, which first appears in them as free substance, the knowledge of this substance occurs in independent beings, individuals, who, being notable, on the one hand, each has his being in *external* contrast to the others, and whose knowledge, on the other hand, is the inward life of substance and thus something internal to the conditions of the reality surrounding them. The Greek philosopher is a demiurge, his world is a different one from that which flowers in the natural sun of the substantial.

---

[a] Ataraxy.— *Ed.*
[b] Wise man.— *Ed.*

Page from *Notebooks on Epicurean Philosophy*

(Second Notebook)

The first wise men are only the vessels, the Pythia, from which the substance resounds in general, simple precepts; their language is as yet only that of the substance become vocal, the simple forces of moral life which are revealed. Hence they are in part also active leaders in political life, lawgivers.

The Ionian philosophers of nature are just as much isolated phenomena as the forms of the natural element appear under which they seek to apprehend the universe. The Pythagoreans organise an inner life for themselves within the state; the form in which they realise their knowledge of substance is halfway between a completely conscious isolation not observed among the Ionians, whose isolation is rather the undeliberate, naive isolation of elementary existences, and the trustful carrying on of life within a moral order. The form of their life is itself substantial, political, but maintained abstract, reduced to a minimum in extent and natural fundamentals, just as their principle, number, stands midway between colourful sensuousness and the ideal. The Eleatics, as the first discoverers of the ideal forms of substance, who themselves still apprehend the inwardness of substance in a purely internal and abstract, intensive manner, are the passionately enthusiastic prophetic heralds of the breaking dawn. Bathed in simple light, they turn away indignantly from the people and from the gods of antiquity. But in the case of Anaxagoras the people themselves turn to the gods of antiquity in opposition to the isolated wise man and declare him to be such, expelling him from their midst. In modern times (cf., for example, Ritter, *Geschichte der alten Philosophie*, Bd. I [1829, pp. 300 ff.]) Anaxagoras has been accused of dualism. Aristotle says in the first book of the *Metaphysics* that he uses the νοῦς [a] like a machine and only resorts to it when he runs out of natural explanations. But this apparent dualism is on the one hand that very same dualistic element which begins to split the heart of the state in the time of Anaxagoras, and on the other hand it must be understood more profoundly. The νοῦς is active and is resorted to where there is no natural determination. It is itself the *non ens* [b] of the natural, the ideality. And then the activity of this ideality intervenes only when physical sight fails the philosopher, that is, the νοῦς is the *philosopher's* own νοῦς, and is resorted to when he is no longer able to objectify his activity. Thus the subjective νοῦς appeared as the essence of

---

[a] Reason.— *Ed.*
[b] Not-being.— *Ed.*

the wandering scholar,[a] and, in its power as ideality of real determination, it appears on the one hand in the Sophists and on the other in Socrates.

If the first Greek wise men are the real spirit, the embodied knowledge of substance, if their utterances preserve just as much genuine intensity as substance itself, if, as substance is increasingly idealised, the bearers of its progress assert an ideal life in their particular reality in opposition to the reality of manifested substance, of the real life of the people, then the ideality itself is only in the form of substance. There is no undermining of the living powers; the most ideal men of this period, the Pythagoreans and the Eleatics, extol state life as real reason; their principles are objective, a power which is superior to themselves, which they herald in a semi-mystical fashion, in poetic enthusiasm; that is, in a form which raises natural energy to ideality and does not consume it, but processes it and leaves it intact in the determination of the natural. This embodiment of the ideal substance occurs in the philosophers themselves who herald it; not only is its expression plastically poetic, its reality is this person, whose reality is its own appearance; they themselves are living images, living works of art which the people sees rising out of itself in plastic greatness; while their activity, as in the case of the first wise men, shapes the universal, their utterances are the really assertive substance, the laws.

Hence these wise men are just as little like ordinary people as the statues of the Olympic gods; ther motion is rest in self, their relation to the people is the same objectivity as their relation to substance. The oracles of the Delphic Apollo were divine truth for the people, veiled in the chiaroscuro of an unknown power, only as long as the genuine evident power of the Greek spirit sounded from the Pythian tripod; the people had a theoretical attitude towards them only as long as they were the resounding theory of the people itself, they were of the people only as long as they were unlike them. The same with these wise men. But with the Sophists and Socrates, and by virtue of δύναμις [b] in Anaxagoras, the situation was reversed. Now it is ideality itself which, in its immediate form, the *subjective spirit*, becomes the principle of philosophy. In the earlier Greek wise men there was revealed the ideal form of the substance, its identity, in distinction to the

---

[a] Cf. Goethe, *Faust*, 1, 3.— *Ed.*
[b] Potentialities.— *Ed.*

many-coloured raiment woven from the individualities of various peoples that displayed its manifest reality. Consequently, these wise men on the one hand apprehend the absolute only in the most one-sided, most general ontological definitions, and on the other hand, themselves represent in reality the appearance of the substance enclosed in itself. While they hold themselves aloof from the πολλοί,[a] and express the mystery of the spirit, on the other hand, like the plastic gods in the market places, in their blissful self-contemplation, they are the genuine embellishment of the people, to which as individuals they return. It is now, on the contrary, ideality itself, pure abstraction which has come to be for itself, that faces the substance; subjectivity, which establishes itself as the principle of philosophy. Not of the people, this subjectivity, confronting the substantial powers of the people, is yet of the people, that is, it confronts reality externally, is in practice entangled in it, and its existence is motion. These mobile vessels of development are the Sophists. Their innermost form, cleansed from the immediate dross of appearance, is Socrates, whom the Delphic oracle called the σοφώτατον.[b]

Being confronted by its own ideality, substance is split up into a mass of accidental limited existences and institutions whose right—unity, and identity with it—has escaped into the subjective spirit. The subjective spirit itself is as such the vessel of substance, but because this ideality is opposed to reality, it is present in minds objectively as a "must", and subjectively as a striving. The expression of this subjective spirit, which knows that it has the ideality in itself, is the judgment of the concept, for which the criterion of the individual is that which is determined in itself, the purpose, the good, but which is still here a "must" of reality. This "must" of reality is likewise a "must" of the subject which has become conscious of this ideality, for it itself stands rooted in reality and the reality outside it is its own. Thus the position of this subject is just as much determined as its fate.

First, the fact that this ideality of substance has entered the subjective spirit, has fallen away from itself, is a leap, a falling away from the substantial life determined in the substantial life itself. Hence this determination of the subject is for it an accomplished fact, an alien force, the bearer of which it finds itself to be, the daemon of Socrates. The daemon is the immediate appearance of the fact that for Greek life philosophy is just as

---

[a] Multitude.— Ed.
[b] Wisest.— Ed.

much only internal as only external. The characteristics of the
daemon determine the empirical singularity of the subject, because
the subject naturally detaches itself from the substantial, and
hence naturally determined, life in this [Greek] life, since the
daemon appears as a natural determinant. The Sophists themselves are these daemons, not yet differentiated from their actions.
Socrates is conscious that he carries the daemon in himself.
Socrates is the substantial exemplar of substance losing itself in the
subject. He is therefore just as much a substantial individual as the
earlier philosophers, but after the manner of subjectivity, not
enclosed in himself, not an image of the gods, but a human one,
not mysterious, but clear and luminous, not a seer, but a sociable
man.

The second determination is therefore that this subject pronounces a judgment on the "must", the purpose. Substance has
lost its ideality in the subjective spirit, which thus has become in
itself the determination of substance, its predicate, while substance
itself has become in relation to the subjective spirit only the
immediate, unjustified, merely existing composite of independent
existences. The determination of the predicate, since it refers to
something existing, is hence itself immediate, and since this
something is the living spirit of the people, it is in practice the
determination of the individual spirits, education and teaching.
The "must" of substantiality is the subjective spirit's own determination expressed by it; the purpose of the world is therefore its
[the spirit's] own purpose, to teach about it is its calling. It
therefore embodies in itself the purpose and hence the good both
in its life and in its teaching. It is the wise man as he has entered
into practical motion.

Finally, inasmuch as this individual pronounces the judgment of
the concept on the world, he is in himself divided and judged; for
while he has his roots for one part in the substantial, he owes his
right to exist only to the laws of the state to which he belongs, to
its religion, in brief, to all the substantial conditions which appear
to him as his own nature. On the other hand, he possesses in
himself the purpose which is the judge of that substantiality. His
own substantiality is therefore judged in this individual himself
and thus he perishes precisely because he is born of the substantial, and not of the free spirit which endures and overcomes all
contradictions and which need not recognise any natural conditions as such.

The reason why Socrates is so important is that the relation of
Greek philosophy to the Greek spirit, and therefore its inner limit,

is expressed in him. It is self-evident how stupid was the comparison drawn in recent times between the relation of Hegelian philosophy to life and the case of Socrates, from which the justification for condemning the Hegelian philosophy was deduced. The specific failing of Greek philosophy is precisely that it stands related only to the substantial spirit; in our time both sides are spirit and both want to be acknowledged as such.

Subjecivity is manifested in its immediate bearer [Socrates] as his life and his practical activity, as a form by which he leads single individuals out of the determinations of substantiality to determination in themselves; apart from this practical activity, his philosophy has no other content than the abstract determination of the good. His philosophy is his transference from substantially existing notions, differences, etc., to determination-in-self, which, however, has no other content than to be the vessel of this dissolving reflection; his philosophy is therefore essentially his *own wisdom*, his own *goodness*; in relation to the world the only fulfilment of his teaching on the good is a quite different subjectivity from that of Kant when he establishes his categorical imperative. For Kant it is of no account what attitude he, as an empirical subject, adopts towards this imperative.

With Plato motion becomes ideal; as Socrates is the image and teacher of the world, so Plato's ideas, his philosophical abstraction, are its prototypes.

In Plato this abstract determination of the good, of the purpose, develops into a comprehensive, world-embracing philosophy. The purpose, as the determination in itself, the real will of the philosopher, is thinking, the real determinations of this good are the immanent thoughts. The real will of the philosopher, the ideality active in him, is the real "must" of the real world. Plato sees this his attitude to reality in such a way that an independent realm of ideas hovers over reality (and this "beyond" is the philosopher's own subjectivity) and is obscurely reflected in it. If Socrates discovered only the name of the ideality which has passed out of substance into the subject, and was himself consciously this motion, the substantial world of reality now enters really idealised into Plato's consciousness, but thereby this ideal world itself is just as simply organised in itself as is the really substantial world facing it, of which Aristotle most aptly remarked:

(*Metaphysics*, I, Chap. IX) "For the Forms are practically equal to—or not fewer than—the things, in trying to explain which these thinkers proceeded from them to the Form".

The determination of this world and its organisation in itself is therefore to the philosopher himself a beyond, the motion has been removed from this world.

"Yet when the Forms exist, still the things that share in them do not come into being, unless there is something to originate movement [...]." Aristotle, op. cit.

The philosopher as such, that is, as the wise man, not as the motion of the real spirit in general, is therefore the truth-beyond of the substantial world facing him. Plato expresses this most precisely when he says that either the philosophers must become kings or the kings philosophers for the state to achieve its purpose. In his attempts to educate a tyrant he also made a practical effort on these lines. His state has indeed as its special and highest estate that of the learned. [a]

I wish to mention here two other remarks made by Aristotle, because they provide the most important conclusions concerning the form of Platonic consciousness and link up with the aspect from which we consider it in relation to the σοφός. [b]

Aristotle says of Plato:

"In the *Phaedo* the case is stated in this way—that the Forms are causes both of being and of becoming; yet when the Forms exist, still the things that share in them do not come into being, unless there is something to originate movement [...]." Aristotle, op. cit.

It is not only that which is, it is the whole possibility of being that Plato wants to bring out into ideality: this ideality is a closed, specifically different realm in the philosophising consciousness itself: because it is this, it lacks motion.

This contradiction in the philosophising consciousness must objectify itself to the latter, the philosophising consciousness must eject this contradiction.

"Again the Forms are patterns not only of sensible things, but of Forms themselves also: e.g. the genus, as genus of Forms; so that the same thing could be both pattern and copy." [op. cit.]

Lucretius on the ancient Ionian philosophers:

"... have certainly made many excellent and divine discoveries and uttered oracles from the inner sanctuary of their hearts with more sanctity and far surer reason than those the Delphic prophetess pronounces, drugged by the laurel fumes from Apollo's tripod." Book I, ll. 736-740.

Important for the definition of the Epicurean philosophy of nature is the following:

---

[a] Plato, *Res publica*, V, 473.— *Ed.*
[b] Wise man.— *Ed.*

1. The *eternity of matter*, which is connected with the fact that time is considered as an accident of accidents, as proper only to composites and their *eventis*, and hence is relegated to outside the material principle, outside the atom itself. It is further connected with the fact that the substance of the Epicurean philosophy is that which reflects only externally, which has no premises, which is arbitrariness and accident. Time is rather the fate of nature, of the finite. Negative unity with itself, its internal necessity.

2. The void, the negation, is not the negative of matter itself, but [space] where there is no matter. In this respect too, therefore, matter is in itself eternal.

The form which we see emerge at the conclusion from the workshop of Greek philosophical consciousness, out of the darkness of abstraction, and veiled in its dark garb, is the same form in which Greek philosophy walked, alive, the stage of the world, the same form which saw gods even in the burning hearth, the same which drank the poison cup, the same which, as the God of Aristotle, enjoys the greatest bliss, theory.

[III.] PLUTARCH, 1. *THAT EPICURUS ACTUALLY MAKES
A PLEASANT LIFE IMPOSSIBLE*

[III, 10-11] "[...] as a *common end for it* (pleasure) Epicurus has set the *removal of all pain.* For he believes that our nature adds to pleasure only up to the point where pain disappears and *does not allow it to increase any further* (although the pleasure, when the *state of painlessness is not reached,* admits of certain unessential variations). But to proceed to this point, accompanied by desire, is our stint of pleasure, and the journey is indeed short and quick. Hence it is that becoming aware of the poverty here they [the Epicureans] *transfer their final good from the body, as from an unproductive piece of land, to the soul.*" p. 1088.

[IV, 1] "[...] do you not hold that the gentlemen [the Epicureans] do well to begin with the body, where [pleasure] first appears, and then pass to the soul as having more stability and bring the whole to consummation in it?"

The answer to this is that the transition is correct, but

[IV, 3] "When you hear their loud protest that the soul is so constituted as to find joy and tranquillity in nothing in the world but pleasure of the body either present or anticipated, and that this is its good, do they not appear to you to be using the soul as a funnel of the body, through which they pour pleasure, like wine, from a worthless and leaky vessel into another and leave it to age there in the belief that they are turning it into something more respectable and precious?" p. 1088.

Here too, Plutarch fails to understand the logic of Epicurus; it is important to note anyhow that he does not see a specific transition from the *voluptas corporis ad voluptatem animi,*[a] and Epicurus' attitude in this respect should be more closely defined.

[IV, 4] "... the soul takes up the memory ... but retains nothing else ... and the memory of it [pleasure] is obscure...." p. 1088.

[IV, 5] "Observe the greater moderation of the Cyrenaics, though they have tippled from the same jug as Epicurus: they even think it wrong to indulge in sexual commerce when there is a light, and instead provide for a cover of darkness, so that the mind may not, by receiving the images of the act in full clarity through

[a] Pleasure of the body to pleasure of the soul.— *Ed.*

the sense of sight, too often rekindle the desire. [IV, 6] ... the other set ... hold that the superiority of the sage lies above all in this, in vividly remembering and keeping intact in himself the sights and feelings and movements associated with pleasure, ... thus recommending a practice unworthy of the name of wisdom by allowing the slops of pleasure to remain in the soul of the sage as in the house of a wastrel." p. 1089.

[IV, 9] "For it betrays a violent and brutish longing for present and anticipated enjoyments, when the soul revels with such bacchanalian attachment to recollection." p. 1089.

[IV, 10] "It is this, I believe, that has driven them, seeing for themselves the absurdities to which they were reduced, to take refuge in the 'painlessness' and the 'stable condition of the flesh'...; for the 'stable and settled condition of the flesh' and the 'trustworthy expectation' of this condition contain, they say, the highest and the most assured delight for men who are able to reflect. [V, 1] Now first observe their conduct here, how they keep decanting this 'pleasure' or 'painlessness' or 'stable condition' of theirs back and forth, from body to soul and then once more from soul to body, compelled, since they cannot retain volatile pleasure, to begin again from the beginning, and though they lay the pleasure of the body as he says at the base of the delight of the soul, they again let the delight pass through anticipation into pleasure." p. 1089.

This remark is of importance for the Epicurean dialectics of pleasure, although it is wrongly criticised by Plutarch. According to Epicurus, the wise man himself is in this vacillating condition which appears to be the determination of ἡδονή.[a] Only God is μακαριότης,[b] the pure rest of nothingness in itself, the complete absence of all determination; this is why he has his abode not inside the world like the wise man, but outside it.

[V, 5] "For whereas a 'stable condition of the flesh' occurs frequently enough, no certain and firm expectation where the flesh is concerned can arise in a reasonable mind." p. 1090.

Plutarch criticises Epicurus on the grounds that because of the possibility of pain there can be no freedom in a healthy present. But in the first place the Epicurean spirit is not one which concerns itself with such possibilities, but because absolute relativity, the accidental nature of [every] relationship, is in itself only unrelatedness, the Epicurean wise man takes his condition as unrelated, and as such it is for him a stable one. Time is for him only the accident of accidents; how could its shadow penetrate into the solid phalanx of ἀταραξία[c]? But if he postulates that the immediate premise of the individual spirit, namely the body, should be healthy, this is only [postulated] to bring back home to the spirit its own unrelatedness, its inborn nature, that is [by postulating] a healthy body not externally differentiated [from the

---

[a] Pleasure.— *Ed.*
[b] Bliss.— *Ed.*
[c] Ataraxy.— *Ed.*

individual spirit]. If, when one is suffering, this real nature of his hovers before him in the guise of fantasies and hopes of individual conditions in which that characteristic condition of his spirit would be realised, that only means that the individual as such contemplates his ideal subjectivity in an individual way — a completely correct observation. For Epicurus, Plutarch's objection means simply that the freedom of the spirit is not present in a healthy body because it is present; for it is superfluous to remove the possibility outside precisely because reality is determined only as a possibility, as chance. If on the other hand the matter is regarded in its universality, then it is precisely a renunciation of universality if the true positive condition is to be obscured by accidental details; this simply means that dwelling in the free ether one thinks of particular mixtures, of the exhalations of poisonous plants, of the inhalations of tiny living things, this means to renounce life because one is liable to die, etc.; it means not to allow oneself the enjoyment of the universal but to fall out of it into particularities. Such a frame of mind concerns itself only with the very smallest things, it is so meticulous that it fails to see anything. Finally, if Plutarch says one must take care to maintain the health of the body, Epicurus also repeats that same platitude, but with more genius: he who perceives the universal condition as the true one takes the best care to maintain it. That is human common sense. It believes it has the right to counterpose to the philosophers its most foolish trivialities and commonplaces as a *terra incognita*. It thinks itself a Columbus when it stands eggs on end. Apart from his system (for this is his right, *summum jus*[a]) Epicurus is on the whole correct when he says the wise man considers illness as a non-being, but the semblance disappears. If therefore he is ill, that is to him a disappearance which does not endure; if he is healthy, in his essential condition, the semblance does not exist for him and he has other things to do than to think that it could exist. If he is ill, he does not believe it the illness; if he is healthy, he acts as though this were the condition to which he is entitled, that is, he acts as a healthy person. How lamentable in comparison with this resolute, healthy individual is a Plutarch, who recalls Aeschylus, Euripides, and even Doctor Hippocrates merely in order not to rejoice in health!

Health, as the condition of being identical with oneself, is forgotten of itself, there is no reason to busy oneself with the body; this differentiation begins only with illness.

Epicurus desires no eternal life: how much less can it matter to him that the next instant may conceal some misfortune.

---

[a] Supreme right.— *Ed.*

Just as wrong is the following criticism made by Plutarch:

[VI, 1] "Criminals and transgressors of the law, they say, pass their entire lives in misery and apprehension, since even though they may succeed in escaping detection, they can have no assurance of doing so; in consequence fear for the future lies heavy on them and precludes any delight or confidence in their present situation. [VI, 2] In these words, without knowing it, they have also spoken against themselves: we can often enjoy in the body a 'stable condition', that is, health, but there is no way to acquire any assurance that it will last. Hence they cannot but be constantly anxious and worried for the body in facing the future." p. 1090.

In actual fact it is just the contrary of what Plutarch says. Only when the individual violates them do the laws and general customs begin to be premises for him, he sets himself against them, and his escape from this state of tension would only lie in πίστις,[a] which, however, is not guaranteed by anything.

In general, the interesting thing in Epicurus is that in every sphere he eliminates the condition by which the premise as such is provoked to appear and he considers as normal the condition in which the premise is concealed. In general, it is nowhere a question of the mere σάρξ.[b] Punitive justice is a direct manifestation of inner connection, mute necessity, and Epicurus eliminates both its category from logic and the semblance of its reality from the wise man's life. The accidental fact, on the contrary, that the just man suffers, is an external relation and does not wrest him out of his unrelatedness.

Hence it can be seen how wrong is the following criticism made by Plutarch:

[VI, 3] "To do no wrong does nothing to bring assurance; it is not suffering deservedly, but suffering at all that is dreaded." p. 1090.

What Plutarch means is that Epicurus must reason in that way according to his principles. It does not occur to him that Epicurus may have other principles than those which he, Plutarch, attributes to him.

[VI, 4] "For the nature of the flesh possesses in itself the raw material of diseases, and as in the jesting proverb we speak of getting the whip from the ox's hide, so it gets the pains from the body, and suffices to make life precarious and full of fears for wicked and honest men alike, once they have been taught to let their delight and trust depend on the body and on expectation for the body and on nothing else, *as Epicurus teaches in his treatise 'On the Highest Goods' and in many other passages as well.*" pp. 1090-1091.

---

[a] Trust.— Ed.
[b] Body, flesh.— Ed.

[VII, 1] "Inasmuch as their [the Epicureans'] good is an escape from ills, and they say that no other can be conceived, and indeed that nature has no place at all in which to put its good except the place left when evil is expelled [...]." p. 1091.

[VII, 2] "*Epicurus too makes a similar statement to the effect that the good is a thing that arises out of your very escape from evil* and from your memory and reflection and jubilation that this has happened to you. His words are these: 'For what produces a jubilation unsurpassed is the contrast of the *great* evil escaped; and this is the nature of good, if you apply your mind rightly and then stand firm and do not indulge in meaningless prating about good.'" p. 1091.

"Shame!" exclaims Plutarch here.

[VII, 4] "Therefore in this they are no whit inferior to swine or sheep.... Actually, for the cleverer and more graceful animals the escape from evil is not the end. ... since once they have escaped evil they instinctively seek out the good, or better, let us say that they reject everything painful or alien as an impediment to the pursuit of the real, better kernel of their nature." ([VIII, 1] For what is necessary is not good*, what is worth seeking and choosing lies beyond the escape from evil....)ᵃ p. 1091.

Plutarch thinks himself very wise when he says that besides the necessity of flying from evil, the animal seeks the good, the good that lies beyond the escape. Its animal nature lies precisely in the fact that the animal seeks something good over-beyond. According to Epicurus, no good for man lies outside himself; the only good which he has in relation to the world is the negative motion to be free of it.

That all this is understood individually in Epicurus follows from the principle of his philosophy, which he formulates with all its consequences; Plutarch's syncretic senseless argumentation cannot measure up to this.

[VIII, 3] "For even if an itching of the skin or a rheumy flux in the eye is unpleasant, it does not follow that scratching the skin and wiping the eye are anything special; nor does it follow that if pain, fear of the gods and anxiety about what awaits one in Hades are evil, escape from them is enviable bliss [...]." p. 1091. [VIII, 4] "No; these men coop up their *delight* in *quarters* that are *small* and cramped ... advancing beyond the usual stupid notions and taking as the final goal of wisdom that which, it would appear, is naturally present in irrational beasts. [VIII, 5] For if it makes no difference in the freedom of the body from pain whether it has got free by itself or through nature, so too in ataraxy it is of no importance whether the unperturbed condition is achieved by the soul or through nature.... [VIII, 6] For likewise these gentlemen will be seen to be no better off than the brutes in this matter of not being disturbed by what awaits them in Hades or by tales about the gods and of not anticipating endless anxiety or pain [...]." [pp. 1091-1092.]

* (on this point Aristotle has quite different views; he teaches in the *Metaphysics* that necessity rules free men more than it does slaves).— *Note by Marx.*

ᵃ The manuscript here gives in brackets the Latin translation of the last sentence of the citation.— *Ed.*

[VIII, 7] *"...Epicurus himself ... says, 'If we were not troubled with misgivings about meteors and again with fear of death and pain, we should never have stood in need of natural philosophy.'"* p. 1092.

[VIII, 8] "... since, however, the aim of their theology is to have no fear of God, but instead to be rid of anxieties, I should think that this condition is more securely in the possession of creatures that have no faintest notion of God than of those who have been taught to think of him as injuring no one. For they [the animals] have not been delivered from superstition, since they have never even been its victims; nor have they put aside the notion of the gods that is disturbing, but have never even adopted it. [VIII, 9] The same is to be said of things in Hades." p. 1092.

[VIII, 9-10] "[...] misgiving and dread of what comes after death is less the portion of those who have no preconception of death than of those who still have to conceive that death is no concern of ours. Death is a concern of these men to the extent that they reason about it and subject it to inquiry; but the brutes are relieved of any concern whatever for what is nothing to them, and when they avoid blows and wounds and being killed, they fear only that in death which the Epicureans fear as well." p. 1092.

That the Epicureans are said to demand that mathematics should be shunned. Plutarch, op. cit., p. 1094D.

[XII, 1] "... in admiration and most hearty commendation of one Apelles they write that from the beginning he held aloof from mathematics and thus kept himself unspotted." loc. cit.

Likewise history, etc., cf. Sext. Empiricus. Plutarch considers as a great fault of Metrodorus that the latter writes:

[XII, 2] "[...] so if you must admit that you do not even know on which side Hector fought, or the opening lines of Homer's poem, or again what comes between, do not be dismayed." loc. cit.

[XIII, 1] "[...] Epicurus ... says ... that the wise man is a lover of spectacles and yields to none in the enjoyment of musical and theatrical shows; but on the other hand he allows no place, even over the wine, for questions about music and the philological enquiries of critics", etc. p. 1095.

[XV, 4] "Why, the Epicureans themselves assert that it is more pleasant to confer a benefit than to receive one." p. 1097.

These αὐτοί [a] are precisely those *qui in haeresim Epicuri illapsi.*[b]

[XVIII, 5] "But Epicurus himself allowed that some pleasures come from fame." p. 1099.

[...] more worthy of consideration than the above-quoted shallow moral objections of Plutarch is his polemic against the Epicurean theology, not that polemic as such, but because it is revealed how ordinary consciousness, adopting, on the whole, the Epicurean standpoint, shies only before the obvious philosophical conclusion. Here one must always bear in mind that Epicurus is concerned

---

[a] Themselves.— *Ed.*
[b] Who have fallen into the heresy of Epicurus.— *Ed.*

neither with *voluptas*[a] nor with sensuous certainty, nor with anything else except the freedom of the mind and its freedom from
determination. Therefore we shall go through Plutarch's considerations one by one.

[XX, 3] "One point, that of the pleasure they derive from these views, has, I
should say, been dealt with [by Epicurus]: where their theory is fortunate and
successful, it *does remove fear* and superstition in a way; but it *gives no joy or favour of the
gods.* Instead it *puts us in the same state of mind in relation to the gods, of neither
being alarmed nor rejoicing*" (i.e., being unrelated), "that we have in relation to
Hyrcanian fishes, from which we expect neither good nor evil. [XX, 4] But if we
are to add anything to what has already been said, I think we can take this from
them themselves: first, they disagree with those who would do away with grief and
tears and lamentations at the death of friends, and say that an absence of grief
extending to complete insensibility stems from another, greater evil: callousness or
unrestrained ambition and infatuation. Hence they say that it is better to be moved
somewhat and to grieve and to melt into tears and fret and manifest other
sentiments which make one appear soft-hearted and affectionate. [XX, 5] For this is
what Epicurus said in many other passages...." [p.] p. [1100-]1101.

Plutarch does not understand the fear of God at all in the sense
that Epicurus does; he does not grasp how philosophical consciousness wishes to free itself from it. The ordinary man is not
aware of this. Plutarch therefore quotes trivial empirical examples
showing how little terror this belief has for people at large.

In contrast to Epicurus, Plutarch first considers the belief of the
πολλοί [b] in God and says that with the multitude this habit of mind
indeed takes the form of fear; to be precise, sensuous fear is the
only form in which he can grasp the anguish of the free spirit in
face of a personal almighty being which absorbs freedom in itself
and is, therefore, exclusive. He says:

1. [XXI, 3] Those who fear him (God): "If they fear him as a ruler gracious to
the good and hostile to the wicked, they are freed by this one fear from doing
wrong and do not need many redeemers, and since they let evil die down within
themselves, in all calm, they are less tormented than those who make use of it and
behave impudently but suddenly experience anxiety and regret." p. 1101.

And so by this sensuous fear they are protected against evil, as
though this immanent fear were not evil. What is then the essence
of the empirically evil? That the individual shuts himself off from
his eternal nature in his empirical nature; but is that not the same
as to shut his eternal nature out of himself, to apprehend it in the
form of persistent isolation in self, in the form of the empirical,
and hence to consider it as an empirical god outside self? Or must
the stress be laid on the form of the relation? Then God is

---

[a] Pleasure.— *Ed.*
[b] Multitude.— *Ed.*

punitive in relation to the evil, lenient in relation to the good; and the evil here is what is evil to the empirical individual, and the good what is good to the empirical individual, for otherwise whence would this fear and this hope come, since the individual is concerned with what is evil and what is good for him? In this relation God is merely what is common to all the consequences that empirical evil actions can have. So does the empirical individual refrain from doing evil out of fear lest from the good which he achieves by evil actions a greater evil will result and a greater good will be forfeited, that is to say, in order that the continuity of his well-being will not be broken by the immanent possibility of being snatched out of that continuity?

Is that not the same thing as Epicurus teaches in plain words: do not act unjustly, so as not to go in continual fear of being punished? This immanent relation of the individual to his ἀταραξία [a] is therefore presented as a relationship to a god existing outside the individual, but again having no other content than this ἀταραξία, which is here continuity of well-being. Fear of the future, that condition of insecurity, is here inserted into the remote consciousness of God, considered as a condition which pre-exists in him, but also as a mere threat, and therefore precisely as in individual consciousness.

2. Plutarch says that this striving towards God also procures *voluptas*.[b]

[XXI, 6] "No, wherever it believes and conceives most firmly that God is present, there more than anywhere else it puts away all feelings of pain, fear, and worry, and gives itself up so far to pleasure that it indulges in a playful and merry inebriation in amatory matters...." p. 1101.

He goes on to say that old men, women, merchants, and kings rejoice in religious feast days....

[XXI, 8] "For it is not the abundance of wine or the attraction of the meats that cheer the heart at festivals, but good hope and the belief in the benign presence of God and his gracious acceptance of what is done." p. 1102.

There is need for closer study of how Plutarch describes this rejoicing, this *voluptas*.

First he says that the soul is most free from sorrow, fear and anxiety when God is present. So the presence of God is defined as freedom of the soul from fear, sorrow and anxiety. This freedom is manifested in exuberant rejoicing, for this is the individual soul's positive manifestation of this its condition.

---

[a] Ataraxy.— *Ed.*
[b] Pleasure.— *Ed.*

Further: the accidental difference of the individual situation disappears where this pleasure exists. And thus the individual is freed from his other determinations and in this rejoicing the individual as such is determined, and this is a substantial determination. Finally, the pleasure is not in the separate enjoyment, but in the certainty that God is not something separate, but that his content is to rejoice over this pleasure of the individual, to look down benevolently on it, and hence to be himself in the determination of the rejoicing individual. Therefore what is deified and celebrated here is the deified individuality as such, freed from its customary bonds, therefore the σοφός[a] of Epicurus with his ἀταραξία.[b] God is worshipped not as non-present God, but as the present pleasure of the individual. This God has no further determination. Yes, the true form in which this freedom of the individual emerges here is enjoyment, and indeed individual, sensuous enjoyment, the enjoyment which is not disturbed. Ἀταραξία therefore hovers overhead as the general consciousness, but it manifests itself as the sensuous *voluptas* of Epicurus, except that what is here a living isolated condition is there total consciousness of life, and that for this reason the individual manifestation in Epicurus is more indifferent [to external conditions], more animated by its soul, by ἀταραξία, while in Plutarch this element is more lost in individuality and both are directly blended, and therefore are directly separate. Such is the pitiful outcome of the differentiation of the divine which Plutarch asserts in his polemic against Epicurus. And, to make another remark, if Plutarch says that kings do not enjoy their *publicis conviviis et viscerationibus*[c] so much as the sacrificial meals, this means nothing else than that in the first case enjoyment is considered as something human, accidental, and in the second as divine, that individual enjoyment is considered as divine, which is precisely Epicurean.

From this relation of the πονηροί[d] and the πολλοί[e] to God Plutarch distinguishes the relation of the βέλτιον ἀνθρώπων καί θεοφιλέστατον γένος.[f] We shall see what point he wins here against Epicurus.

---

[a] Wise man.— *Ed.*
[b] Ataraxy.— *Ed.*
[c] Public feasts and entertainments.— *Ed.*
[d] Bad.— *Ed.*
[e] Multitude.— *Ed.*
[f] Best men and most agreeable to God.— *Ed.*

Plutarch says:

[XXII, 1-3] "... what great pleasures they have through their pure notions about God, who for them is the guide to all blessings, the father of everything honourable, and may no more do than suffer anything base. For he is good, and in none that is good arises envy about aught or fear or anger or hatred; for it is as much the function of heat to chill instead of warm as it is of good to harm. By its nature anger is infinitely far removed from favour, wrath from goodwill, and from love of man and kindness, hostility and a forbidding disposition; for the one set belong to virtue and power, the other to weakness and vice. Hence the deity cannot have in itself anger and favour together; rather, because it is God's nature to bestow favour and lend aid, it is not his nature to be angry and to do harm." p. 1102.

The philosophical meaning of the proposition that God is the ἡγεμών ἀγαθῶν [a] and the father πάντων καλῶν [b] is that this is not a predicate of God, but that the idea of good is the divine itself. But according to Plutarch a quite different result follows. Good is taken in the strictest opposition to evil, for the former is a manifestation of virtue and of power, the latter of weakness, privation and badness. Judgment, difference, is therefore removed out of God, and this is precisely a basic principle with Epicurus, who is therefore quite consistent when he finds this absence of difference in man theoretically as well as practically in his immediate identity, in sensuousness, whereas in God he finds it in pure *otium*. The God who is determined as good by removal of judgment is the void, for every determination carries in it an aspect which it receives in contrast to others and encloses in itself, and hence reveals in opposition and contradiction its ὀργή,[c] its μῖσος,[d] its φόβος [e] to renounce itself. Plutarch therefore gives the same determination as Epicurus, but only as an image, as imagination, which the latter calls by its conceptual name and does away with the human image.

There is therefore a false ring to the question:

[XXII, 5] "Do you think that those who deny providence require any further punishment, and are not adequately punished when they deprive themselves of so great a pleasure and delight?" [pp. 1102-1103.]

For it must be affirmed, on the contrary, that he experiences more pleasure in the contemplation of the divine who sees it as pure bliss in itself, without any notionless anthropomorphic relations, than he who does the opposite. It is already in itself bliss to have the thought of pure bliss, however abstractly it be

---

[a] Master-principle of all good.— *Ed.*
[b] Of all that is beautiful.— *Ed.*
[c] Wrath.— *Ed.*
[d] Hatred.— *Ed.*
[e] Fear.— *Ed.*

apprehended, as we can see from the Indian holy men. Besides, Plutarch has abolished πρόνοια[a] by opposing evil, difference, to God. His further descriptions are purely notionless and syncretic, and besides, he shows in everything that he is concerned only with the individual, not with God. That is why Epicurus is so honest as not to make God bother about the individual.

The internal dialectics of Plutarch's thinking thus necessarily leads him back to speak about the individual soul instead of about the divinity, and he arrives at the λόγος περί ψυχῆς.[b] Of Epicurus he says:

[XXIII, 6] "Consequently it (the soul) is overjoyed at receiving this most sapient and godlike doctrine that for it the *end* of *suffering* means *ruin, destruction and being nothing.*" p. 1103.

One must not let oneself be misled by Plutarch's unctuous words. We shall see how he negates each one of his determinations. Already the artificial means of escape τοῦ κακῶς πράττειν πέρας[c] and then in contrast ἀπολέσθαι[d] and φθαρῆναι[e] and μηδέν εἶναι,[f] show where the centre of gravity is, how thin one side is and the other three times stronger.

The study is divided again into that of the attitudes of, first, the τῶν ἀδίκων καί πονηρῶν,[g] then the πολλῶν καί ἰδιωτῶν,[h] and finally the ἐπιεικῶν καί νοῦν ἐχόντων[i] (p. 1104) to the doctrine of the continued existence of the soul. Already this division into hard and fast qualitative differences shows how little Plutarch understands Epicurus, who, as a philosopher, considers the position of the human soul in general; and if, despite its determination as transient, he remains sure of ἡδονή,[j] Plutarch should have seen that every philosopher involuntarily extols a ἡδονή which is alien to him in his limitation. Fear is again adduced as a means of improvement for the unjust. We have already dealt with this point. For in fear, and indeed an inner, unextinguishable fear, man is determined as animal, and it is absolutely indifferent to the animal how

---

[a] Providence.— *Ed.*
[b] Consideration on the soul.— *Ed.*
[c] The end of suffering.— *Ed.*
[d] Ruin.— *Ed.*
[e] Destruction.— *Ed.*
[f] Being nothing.— *Ed.*
[g] Unjust and the wicked.— *Ed.*
[h] Many and the uneducated.— *Ed.*
[i] Decent and the reasonable.— *Ed.*
[j] Pleasure.— *Ed.*

it is kept in check. If a philosopher does not find it outrageous to consider man as an animal, he cannot be made to understand anything.

[XXVI, 1-2] "The great majority, free from fear of what happens in Hades, have a myth-inspired expectation of eternal life; and the love of being, the oldest and most powerful of all our passions, provides pleasure and bliss overcoming that childish terror." p. 1104. "Indeed, when men have lost children, a wife, or friends, *they would rather have them exist somewhere in hardship and survive than be utterly taken away* and destroyed *and reduced to nothing*; and they like to hear such expressions used of the *dying* as 'he is *leaving* us' or '*going to dwell* elsewhere' and all that represent death as a *change of residence of the soul* but not as *destruction*....." p. 1104.

[XXVI, 5] "Such expressions as '*it is the end*' and '*he has perished*' and '*he is no more*' disturb them..... [XXVII, 1-3] ... but they are dealt the *finishing blow* by those who say: '*We men are born but once; there is no second time*....' Indeed, by discounting the present moment as a minute fraction, or rather as nothing at all, in comparison with all time, men let it pass without enjoying it. They neglect virtue and action and despise themselves as creatures of a day, impermanent and born for no high end." [p. 1104.] "For *being without sensation and dissolved* and the doctrine that *what has no sensation is nothing to us does not remove the terror of death, but rather confirms it by adding what amounts to proof. For this is the very thing our nature dreads:* ... *the dissolution* of the soul *into what has neither thought nor feeling; and Epicurus, by making the dissolution a scattering into emptiness and atoms,* does still more to root out our *hope of immortality*, for which, *I had almost said, all men and all women* are ready to be torn to pieces by Cerberus and carry water to the leaky urn, if only they may still continue to be and not to be blotted out." p. 1105.

We now come to the view of the πολλοί,[a] although it becomes apparent in the end that there are not many who do not share it and that, indeed, all, δέω λέγειν πάντας,[b] swear allegiance to this banner.

Actually there is no qualitative difference from the preceding stage, but what appeared in the form of animal fear appears here in the form of human fear, the form of feeling. The content remains the same.

We are told that the desire to be is the oldest love; of course, the most abstract and therefore the oldest love is love of self, love of one's own particular being. But actually that would be to formulate the matter too bluntly, it is taken back again and surrounded with an ennobling radiance by the appearance of feeling. So he who loses wife and children wishes that they should be *somewhere*, even if *things are bad* with them, rather than that they should have completely ceased to be. Simply as a matter of love, the wife and the child of the individual as such are cherished deeply and faithfully in his heart—a much higher form of being than empirical existence. But the matter stands in a different way.

---

[a] Multitude.— *Ed.*
[b] Without any exaggeration, all.— *Ed.*

Wife and child in empirical existence are merely wife and child, insofar as the individual himself exists empirically. The fact that he wants to be assured that they are somewhere, in spatial sensuousness, even if things are bad with them, rather than that they do not exist at all, means nothing more than that the individual wishes to be conscious of his own empirical existence. The cloak of love was only a shadow; the naked empirical ego, self-love, the oldest love is the kernel, and it has not been rejuvenated into any more concrete, more ideal form. Plutarch is of the opinion that the name of change sounds more pleasant than that of completely ceasing to exist. But the change must not be a qualitative one; the individual ego in its individual being must persist; the name is therefore only the sensuous presentation of that which it is, and is meant to signify the opposite. It is therefore a lying fiction. The thing must not be changed, but only put in a dark place, the interposition of fantastic remoteness is only intended to conceal the qualitative leap—and every qualitative difference is a leap, without which there is no ideality.

Plutarch is further of the opinion that this consciousness of finiteness makes one weak and inactive, [generates] dissatisfaction with the present life; only it is not life that passes away, but merely this individual being. If this individual being considers itself as excluded from this persisting universal life, can it become richer and fuller by maintaining its tininess for an eternity? Does this relation change, or does it not rather remain ossified in its lifelessness? Is it not the same whether it finds itself in this indifferent relation to life today or whether this lasts hundreds of thousands of years?

Finally Plutarch says outright that it is not the content, the form, that matters, but the being of the individual. To be, even though torn to pieces by Cerberus. What is then the content of his teaching on immortality? That the individual, abstracted from the quality which gives him here his individual position, persists not as the being of a content, but as the atomistic form of being; is that not the same as what Epicurus says, namely, that the individual soul becomes dissolved and returns into the form of the atoms? To ascribe feeling to these atoms as such, even though it is granted that the content of this feeling is indifferent, is but an illogical fantasy. Plutarch therefore teaches the Epicurean doctrine in his polemic against Epicurus: but he does not forget always to present the μὴ εἶναι [a] as the most fearful thing. This pure

---

[a] Non-being.— *Ed.*

being-for-self is the atom. If in general the individual is assured of immortality not in his content, which, insofar as it is general, exists in itself in general, and, insofar as it is form, eternally individualises itself, if as individual being he is assured of immortality, then the concrete differentiation of the being-for-self ceases to exist, for the differentiation does not mean that the individual continues to exist, but that the eternal persists, unlike the transient, and all that this comes to is the assertion that the atom as such is eternal and that the animate returns to this its basic form.

Epicurus carries his teaching on immortality thus far, but he is philosophical and consistent enough to call it by its name, to say that the animate returns to the atomistic form. No compromise helps here. If some concrete differentiation of the individual must disappear, as is shown by life itself, then all those differentiations must disappear which are not in themselves universal and eternal. If the individual must nevertheless be indifferent to this μεταβολή,[a] then there remains only this atomistic husk of the former content; that is the teaching on the eternity of the atoms.

> To whom eternity is as time
> And time as eternity,
> He from all strife
> Is free,

says Jacobus Bohemus.[183]

[XXVIII, 1] "Hence in abolishing belief in immortality they [the Epicureans] also abolish the sweetest and greatest hopes of the multitude." p. 1105.

If therefore Plutarch says that with immortality Epicurus takes away the sweetest hopes of the multitude, he would have been far more correct if he had said what he says meaning something else,

[XXVII, 3] he "does not remove [the terror of death] but rather explains it." [p. 1105.]

Epicurus does not negate this view, he explains it, he expresses it as a concept.

We now come to the class of the ἐπιεικῶν and νοῦν ἐχόντων.[b] Needless to say, it by no means takes us any further than the preceding, but what at first appeared as animal fear, then as human fear, as anxious suspiration, as reluctance to give up atomistic being, now appears in the form of arrogance, of

---

[a] Change.— Ed.
[b] Decent and reasonable.— Ed.

demand, of entitlement. Hence this class, as Plutarch describes it, departs most of all from reason. The lowest class puts forward no claims; the second weeps and will put up with anything to save the atomistic being; the third is the philistine who exclaims, "My God, that would be too much, that such a clever, honest fellow should have to go to the devil!"

[XXVIII, 1-4] "What then do we believe about the hopes of the good, whose lives have been pious and upright and who anticipate in the other world not evil, but the most beautiful and godly gifts? For in the first place, just as the athletes do not receive a wreath without a contest, but only when they have contested and won, so it is not to be wondered at, that those *believe that the reward for victory in life will be conferred on the good only after life* are intent on virtue; these hopes include also that of seeing at last the *deserved punishment of those who in their wealth and power are injurious and insolent now and in their folly laugh to scorn those who are better than they.* In the next place, no one longing for truth and the vision of reality has ever been able to find full satisfaction in this world.... Hence I regard death as a great and perfect blessing since only in that other world will the soul live its real life, whereas [here] it does not truly live, but is as in a dream." p. 1105.

So these good and clever men expect the reward for life after life; but how inconsistent it is, in that case, to expect life again as a reward for life, since for them the reward for life is something qualitatively different from life. This qualitative difference is again clothed in fiction, life is not raised to any higher sphere, but transferred to another place. They only pretend to despise life, they are not concerned with anything better, they only clothe their hope in a demand.

They despise life, but [for them] their atomistic existence is the good thing in that life and they covet the eternity of their atomistic being, which is the good. If to them the whole of life seemed a spectre, something bad, whence their consciousness of being good? Only from knowledge of themselves as atomistic being, and Plutarch goes so far as to say that they are not satisfied with that consciousness, that because the empirical individual exists only insofar as he is seen by another, these good men rejoice now because after death those who until then despised them will truly see them as good and will have to recognise them and be punished because they did not previously consider them to be good. What a demand! The bad must recognise them in life as good and they themselves do not recognise the universal powers of life as good! Is that not the pride of the atom screwed up to the highest pitch?

Is that not saying in plain language how arrogant and self-conceited the eternal is made and how eternal the arid being-for-self is made when it has content! It is of no avail to conceal this with phrases, to say that nobody can satisfy his curiosity in this respect.

This demand does not express anything else than that the general must exist in the form of the individual as [individual] consciousness, and that this demand is eternally fulfilled by the general. But inasmuch as it is demanded that it should be present in this empirical, exclusive being-for-self, it means nothing but that it is a question not of the general, but of the atom.

So we see how Plutarch, in his polemic against Epicurus, says the same thing as Epicurus at every step; but Epicurus develops the conclusions simply, abstractly, truly and plainly and knows what he is talking about, whereas Plutarch everywhere says something else than what he means to say and at bottom also means something else than what he says.

That is in general the relationship of common consciousness to philosophical consciousness.

[III.] 2. PLUTARCH, *COLOTES*, XYLANDER EDITION

[I, 1] "Colotes, my dear Saturninus, whom Epicurus used to call affectionately his 'Colly' and 'Collikins', brought out a book entitled *On the Point that Conformity to the Doctrines of the Other Philosophers Actually Makes It Impossible to Live.*" p. 1107.

If in the preceding dialogue Plutarch tried to prove to Epicurus *quod non beate vivi possit*[a] according to his, Epicurus', philosophy, now he tries to vindicate the δόγματα[b] of the other philosophers against this objection on the part of the Epicureans. We shall see whether he succeeds better with this task than with the preceding one, in which the polemic can in effect be called a panegyric in favour of Epicurus. This dialogue has an important bearing on Epicurus' relationship to the other philosophers. Colotes makes a good joke when he offers Socrates hay instead of bread and asks him why he does not put his food in his ear, but in his mouth. Socrates occupied himself with very trivial matters, this being a necessary consequence of his historical position.

[III, 3] "Leonteus ... writes ... that *Democritus was honoured by Epicurus* for having embraced the true *teaching* before him, and ... because he had first *discovered the principles of nature.*" p. 1108.

[VI, 3] "... the man who asserts that the majority are deceived in supposing that what heats is heating and what cools is cooling [is himself deceived] if he does not believe that from what he asserts it follows that nothing is of one nature more than of another." p. 1110.

---

[a] That it is not possible to live happily.— *Ed.*

[b] Doctrines.— *Ed.*

Plutarch feels an itch every time Epicurus' philosophical logic breaks through to the front. The philistine is of the opinion that whoever argues that the cold is not cold and the warm is not warm, relying on the way such things are judged by the multitude in accordance with their sensations, deceives himself when he fails to assert that neither the one nor the other exists. Our learned friend does not realise that the differentiation is thus merely transferred from the object to consciousness. If one wishes to solve this dialectic of sensuous certitude in itself, one must admit that the attribute is in the combination, in the relation of sensuous knowledge to the sensuous, and as this relation is directly differentiated, so must the attribute also be directly differentiated. Thus the error will not be ascribed either to the object or to knowledge, but the whole of sensuous certainty will be considered as this fluctuating process. He who has not the dialectical power to negate this sphere as a whole, he who wishes to let it remain, must also be satisfied with the truth as it is present within this sphere. Plutarch is too incompetent a gentleman to do the former, and too honest and clever to do the latter

[VII, 4] "... so that of every quality we can truly say, 'It no more is than is not'; for to those affected in a certain way the thing is, but to those not so affected it is not." p. 1110.

So, Plutarch says, one would have to say of every property that it no more is than is not, for it changes according to the way one is affected. His question alone suffices to show that he does not understand the matter. He speaks of a fixed being or non-being as a predicate. But the being of the sensuous consists rather in not being such a predicate, in not being a fixed being or non-being. When I separate these in this way, I separate precisely that which is not separated in sensuousness. Ordinary thinking always has ready abstract predicates which it separates from the subject. All philosophers have made the predicates themselves into subjects.

a) *Epicurus and Democritus*

[VII, 2] "He [Colotes] says that Democritus' words '*colour is by convention, sweet by convention, a compound by convention, ...* [what is real is the void] and the atoms' are in conflict with our senses, and that anyone who abides by this reasoning and applies it *is not capable of reflecting whether he is* [dead] *or alive.*" [VIII, 3] "Against this proposition I have nothing to object, but I must say that this is as *inseparable from Epicurus' doctrine* as their own [the Epicureans'] assertion inseparable from the atom. [VIII, 4-5] *For what does Democritus say? That entities infinite in number, indivisible and different,* destitute moreover of quality and of perception, move scattered about in the void; that when they draw near one another or collide or become entangled the *resulting aggregate appears in the one case* to be water, *in others fire*, a plant, *or a man, but that everything really is atoms, 'ideas', as he calls them, and nothing else. For there is no generation from the non-existent, and again nothing can be generated from the existent*, as the atoms owing to their solidity can be neither affected nor changed. *From this* it follows that *no colour* comes from the colourless, and no nature or mind from things *without qualities....* [VIII, 6] *Democritus is therefore to be censured not for admitting the consequences which flow from his principles, but for setting up principles that lead to these consequences.* For he *should not have posited immutable first elements;* but having posited them, he should have *observed that the generation of any quality becomes impossible* and *denied* it although he had noted it. But Epicurus is quite unreasonable when *he says that he lays down the same first principles, but does not say that 'colour is by convention' and so the other qualities.* [VIII, 7] *If this is the case with 'not-saying', does he not then admit that he is following his usual practice;* for *he does away with providence and says he has left piety;* he *entertains friendship for the sake of pleasure,* and says that *he* is ready to *assume the greatest pains for friends;* and *he posits an infinite universe* but *does not eliminate 'up' and .'down'."* [pp. 1110-1111.]

[IX, 1-2] *"'What then? Did not Plato too and Aristotle and Xenocrates find themselves producing gold from something not gold ... and everything else from four simple and primary bodies?' ... But in their view the first principles combine at the outset to generate every thing and bring with them their inherent qualities* as no inconsiderable provision; and *when they have combined,* and wet *has come together* with dry, cold with hot, and so on, *bodies which interact on each other and change throughout, then by another mixture they bring into being another product.* [IX, 3] *But the atom stands alone and is destitute of any generative power,* and *when it collides with another owing to its hardness and resistance it undergoes a shock,* but it *neither suffers nor causes any further effect.* Rather the *atoms receive and inflict blows for all time,* and *are unable to produce a living thing or mind or natural being or even to produce out of themselves a common mass or a single heap* in their constant colliding and scattering." p. 1111.

b) *Epicurus and Empedocles*

[X, 1] "But Colotes ... fastens in turn on Empedocles, ... who writes:
This too I'll tell thee:
No nature is there of a mortal thing
Nor any curst fatality of death.
Mixture alone there is and dissolution
Of things commingled, and men call them nature." p. 1111.
[X, 2] "I for one do not see to what extent it is in conflict with life to *assume that there can be neither generation of the non-existent nor destruction of the existent, but that 'generation' is a name given to the conjunction of certain existents with one another,* and *'death' a name given to their separation.* That he used 'nature' in the sense of generation Empedocles has indicated by opposing death to it. [X, 3] But if those who say that generation is a mixing and death a dissolution do not and cannot live, what else do they [the Epicureans] do? Yet when Empedocles *cements and joins the elements together by the operation of heat,* softness, etc., he somehow *opens the way for them to a 'mixture' that coalesces into a natural unity; whereas those* [i.e., the Epicureans] *who herd together unchangeable and unresponsive atoms produce nothing out of them, but cause an uninterrupted series of collisions among the atoms.* For an entanglement that is supposed to prevent dissolution produces rather an intensification of the collisions, so that what they call generation is neither mixture nor

cohesion, *but confusion and conflict.* [X, 4] ... so that nothing, not even an inanimate body, is produced out of them; [X, 5] while perception, mind, intelligence and thought cannot so much as be conceived, even with the best of will, as arising among void and atoms, things which *taken separately have no quality* and which on meeting are not thereby affected or changed; indeed their meeting or fusion produces neither mixture nor coalescence, but only shocks and rebounds. [X, 6] *Thus by such doctrines life and the existence of living things are made impossible,* since they are based on principles which are void, impassive, godless, and moreover incapable of mixture or fusion." [XI, 1-2] "Then how can they claim to leave room for a thing's nature, for a soul, for a living being? As they do for an oath, for prayer, for sacrifice, for worship ... *in words, by affirmation, by pretending, by naming things while by their principles and their doctrines they do away with all this. So by 'nature' they merely mean a thing that naturally is, and by 'generation' a thing generated,* just as something wooden is commonly called 'wood' and what harmonises 'harmony'." [p]p. [1111-]1112.

[XI, 2] "Why (says Colotes, *scilicet adversus Empedoclem*[a]) do we wear ourselves out, toiling for ourselves and seeking certain things and avoiding others? For neither do we exist nor live in association with others. [XI, 3] 'Why never fear,' one might say, 'my dear little Colotes; no one keeps you from taking care of yourself when he teaches that Colotes' nature is nothing but Colotes himself or from attending to affairs (affairs for you and your company being pleasures) when he points out that there is no nature of cakes or odours or intercourse, but that there are cakes and perfumes and women.' [XI, 4] No more does the grammarian, who says that 'Heracles' strength' is Heracles himself [, deny the existence of Heracles]; nor do those who declare that accords and rafterings are mere forms of speech deny the existence of sounds and rafters...."

[XI, 5] "When Epicurus says, 'the nature of existing things is bodies and void', do we take him to mean that 'nature' is distinct from 'existing things', or simply to indicate 'existing things' and nothing more, just as it is his habit for instance to use the expression 'the nature of void' for 'void' and, by Zeus, 'the nature of the universe' for 'the universe'? p. 1112.

[XI, 6] "What else, then, has Empedocles done when he teaches that nature is not distinct from that which is generated nor death from what dies?" p. 1112.

Empedocles is quoted:

[XI, 7-8] "'When what is mixed [comes] to the light of day
    As man or as a beast or plant or bird,
[Men say] 'tis born; but call the parts disjoined
    Unhappy fate.'

Though Colotes cites these lines himself, he fails to see that Empedocles did not abolish men, beasts, etc., by saying they are produced by the mixture of the elements—but rather, when he showed how wrong those are who call this combination and separation 'nature', 'unhappy fate' and 'lurid death', he did not wish to abolish the use of the current expressions for them." [p. 1113.]

[XII, 1-2] "'Fools! For they have no thoughts that range afar

        Who look for birth of what was not before
        Or for a thing to die and wholly perish.'

These are the words of one who says in ringing tones for all who have ears to hear that he does not abolish generation, but only generation from the non-existent; nor

---

[a] To wit, to Empedocles.— *Ed.*

abolish destruction, but only out and out destruction, that is, the destruction that reduces to non-existence." [p. 1113.]

[XII, 3] "'No sage in his prophetic soul would say
    That, while men live (this thing they call their 'life'),
    So long they are, and suffer good and ill;
    But both before the joining of their frame,
    And once it is disjoined, why, they are nothing.'
For these are not the words of one who denies the existence of men who have been born and are living, but rather of one who takes both the unborn and the already dead to exist." [p. 1113.]

[XII, 4-5] "[...] but [Colotes] says that in Empedocles' view we shall never so much as fall ill or receive a wound. But how can one who says that before life and after life each person suffers 'good and ill', leave no suffering to the living? Who is it, Colotes, that really find themselves impervious to wounds and disease? You yourselves, compacted of atom and void, neither of which has any sensation. Not this is objectionable, but that there is nothing to give you pleasure either, since your atom does not receive the causes of pleasure and your void does not respond to them." p. 1113.

c) *Epicurus and Parmenides.*

[XIII, 2-3] "Yet I do not see how, by saying that 'the universe is one', he has made it impossible for us to live. So Epicurus too, when he says that 'the universe' is infinite, ungenerated and imperishable, and subject neither to increase nor diminution, speaks of the universe as of some one thing. When he premises at the beginning of his treatise that 'the nature of things is atoms and void', he treats that nature as one, dividing it into two parts, one of them actually nothing, but termed by you and your company 'intangible', 'empty', and 'bodiless'. So that for you too the universe is one.... [XIII, 5] Observe right here the sort of first principles you people premise for generation: infinity and the void—the void incapable of action, incapable of being acted upon, bodiless; the infinite disordered, irrational, elusive, disrupting and confounding itself because of a multiplicity that defies control or limitation. [XIII, 6] Parmenides, for one, has abolished neither 'fire' nor 'water' ... nor 'cities lying in Europe and Asia' (in Colotes' words).... [XIII, 8] But before all others and even before Socrates he saw that nature has in it something that we apprehend by opinion, and again something that we apprehend by the intellect...." [pp. 1113-1114.]

"... what belongs to the world of the intellect ... is

    'Entire, unmoving and unborn',

to quote his own words, and is always like itself and enduring in what it is...." [p. 1114.]

"Colotes says outright that Parmenides makes a clean sweep of all things by affirming that the universe is one." [p. 1114.]

[XIII, 9] "... the world of the intellect ... which he calls 'being' because it is eternal and imperishable, and 'one' because it is uniform with itself and admits of no variation; while he puts what belongs to the world of the senses under the head of disordered and moving nature." [p. 1114.]

[XIII, 10] " 'Here most persuasive truth...'
which deals with what is thought and forever unalterably the same, and there
    '... man's beliefs, that lack all true persuasion',

because they deal with objects admitting all manner of changes, accidents, and irregularities." p. 1114.

"Thus the contention that being is one was no denial of the plural and perceptible, but an indication of its distinction from what is thought." p. 1114.

d) *Epicurus and Plato*

A proof of Plutarch's unphilosophical manner of thinking is provided by the following passage on Aristotle:

[XIV, 4] "As for the *ideas* for which he (Colotes[a]) denounces Plato, Aristotle, who everywhere assails them and brings up against them every sort of objection in his treatises on ethics and on physics and in his popular dialogues, *was held by some to be more contentious than philosophical in his attitude to this doctrine and bent on undermining Plato's philosophy....*" p. 1115.

[XV, 2] "[...] but he [Colotes], who has not a grain of wisdom, took 'man is not' to be one and the same as 'man is non-existent'. But in Plato's view there is a world of *difference between 'is not' and 'is non-existent'*, for *by the former is meant the denial of any kind of being*, by the latter *the otherness of the partaken and what it partakes in* [XV, 3] that later philosophers brought under the head of a mere difference of genus and species, and *went no higher* because they became involved in greater problems of logic."

(Yet another passage from which one can see the immanent, self-satisfied stupidity *beati Plutarchi.*[b])

[XV, 4] "The relation of the partaken in to the partaker is that of cause to matter, model to copy, power to effect." p. 1115.

If Plutarch says about Plato's doctrine of ideas,

[XV, 7] "... he does not deny the sensuous, but asserts that what is thought has being", p. 1116,

it is because the stupid eclectic does not see that this is precisely what Plato must be reproached with. He does not negate the sensuous, but he asserts that what is thought has being. Thus sensuous being is not expressed in thought, and what is thought too has a being, so that two realms of being exist one beside the other. Here one can see how easily Plato's pedantry finds a response among common men, and as for Plutarch's philosophical views, we can class him among the common men. It goes without saying that what in Plato appears original, necessary, at a certain stage of general philosophical development splendid, is in an individual witnessing the departure of the ancient world a shallow reminiscence of the ecstasy of a dead man, a lamp of antediluvian

---

[a] Marx's manuscript has: Aristotle.— *Ed.*
[b] Of blessed Plutarch.— *Ed.*

times, the perverseness of an old man who has relapsed into childhood.

There can be no better criticism of Plato than Plutarch's praise.

[XV, 7] "He does not deny the effect produced on us and made perceptible in us, but points out to those who follow him that there are other things more stable and more enduring"

(notions abstracted from sensuous perception and hollow)

"in being because they neither begin nor come to an end nor are subject to any influence

(note μήτε — μήτε — μήτε ᵃ — 3 negative determinations),

"and teaches by formulating the difference more clearly in words"

(correct, the difference is a nominal one),

"to call the one things that are and the other things that come to be." p. 1116.

[XV, 8] "The more recent [philosophers] have also done the like; they refuse to many important realities the name of being—the void, time, place and, generally, the whole class of nameable things, which includes all real ones. For these, they say, though they are not 'being', are nevertheless 'something'; and they continue to make use of them in their lives and their philosophy as permanent and enduring magnitudes." p. 1116.

Plutarch now addresses Colotes and asks whether they themselves do not distinguish between stable and transient being, etc. Now Plutarch becomes waggish and says:

[XVI, 2] "... but Epicurus is wiser than Plato in acknowledging that all alike have being.... He holds that the transient has the same being as the eternal ... and realities that can never divest themselves of their being the same as those whose being lies in the fact that they are acted upon and changed and which never remain the same. [XVI, 3] Yet if Plato was indeed greatly mistaken in this, he should be called to account for confusion of terms by those who speak better Greek." p. 1116.

It is amusing to listen to this swaggering respectability which thinks itself clever. He himself, that is, Plutarch, reduces the Platonic differentiation of being to two names, and yet on the other hand claims that the Epicureans are wrong when they ascribe a stable being to both sides (nevertheless they distinguish quite well the ἄφθαρτον ᵇ and the ἀγέννητον ᶜ from that which exists by composition); does not Plato also do this if the εἶναι ᵈ stands stable on the one hand and the γενέσθαι ᵉ on the other?

ᵃ Neither—nor—nor.— *Ed.*
ᵇ Indestructible.— *Ed.*
ᶜ Uncreated, having no beginning.— *Ed.*
ᵈ Being.— *Ed.*
ᵉ Becoming.— *Ed.*

EPICUREAN PHILOSOPHY

Fourth Notebook

III. PLUTARCH. 2. *COLOTES*
IV. LUCRETIUS, *ON THE NATURE OF THINGS*
(THREE BOOKS, 1, 2, 3)

III. PLUTARCH. 2. *COLOTES*

e) *Epicurus and Socrates*

[XIX, 2] "For it is one of Epicurus' tenets that none but the sage is unalterably convinced of anything." p. 1117.

An important passage as regards Epicurus' attitude to Scepticism.

[XIX, 5] "[...] but the reflection by which we conclude that the senses are not accurate or trustworthy enough does not deny that every single object presents to us a certain appearance, but, though we make use of the perceptions as they appear to us in what we do, it does not allow us to trust them as absolutely and [infallibly] true. [For it is sufficient that they are necessary and that] they are useful, since there is nothing better available." p. 1118.

[XX, 1] "When he [Colotes] ridicules and scorns Socrates for seeking to discover what man is and flauntingly (as Colotes puts it) declaring that he did not know it, we can see that Colotes himself had never dealt with the problem." p. 1118.

f) *Epicurus and Stilpo*

[XXII, 1-2] "... he [Colotes] says that *Stilpo makes life impossible by the assertion that nothing else can be predicated of one thing. For how shall we live if we cannot say that man is good*, etc., but only that *man is man ... good is good*", etc. p. 1119.

While it really must be admitted that Colotes knows how to feel out an opponent's weaknesses, Plutarch lacks philosophical bearings to such an extent that he does not even know what it is all about, especially when the proposition of abstract identity as the death of all life is formulated and censured. He makes the following foolish retort, worthy of the very stupidest village schoolmaster:

[XXII, 3] "What man's life was ever the worse because of it? Who that heard that assertion [i.e., Stilpo's] did not recognise it as coming from a witty mocker or from one who wished to offer it as a dialectical exercise for others? What is bad,

Colotes, is not to refuse to call a man good ... *but to refuse to call God God* and not to believe in him (and this is what you or your company do), who will not admit that a Zeus exists who presides over generation, or Demeter, the giver of laws, or Poseidon, the begetter. It is this disjoining of one word from another that works harm and fills your lives with contempt of the gods and shamelessness, when you tear away from the gods the appellations attached to them and also annihilate all sacrifices, mysteries, processions and festivals." p. 1119.

[XXIII, 1] "Stilpo's point, however, is this: if we predicate ... running of a horse, the predicate (he maintains) is not the same as that of which it is predicated, but the concept of what man is is one thing, and that of goodness is another [...], for when asked for a definition we do not give the same for both. Therefore they err who predicate one of the other...."

[XXIII, 2] "For if good is the same as man ... how comes it that [we can] also predicate good of food and of medicine...?" p. 1120.

A very good and important exposition of Stilpo.

g) *Epicurus and the Cyrenaics*

[XXIV, 4-5] "For they [the Cyrenaics] say we are affected by sweetness and darkness, each of these influences possessing within itself a specific and unchangeable effect ... whereas the view that honey is sweet ... and night air dark, encounters evidence to the contrary from many witnesses,—animals, things, and men alike; for to some honey is disagreeable, while others feed on [it]. Accordingly opinion continues free from error only as long as it keeps to experience; but when it strays beyond and meddles with judgments and pronouncements about external appearances, it is forever getting embroiled with itself and falling into conflict with others in whom the same things give rise to contrary experiences and dissimilar impressions." p. 1120.

[XXV, 2, 4-5] "For the school that asserts that when a round image impinges on us, or in another case a bent one, the imprint is truly received by the senses, but refuses to allow us to affirm that the tower is round or that the oar is bent, *maintains the truth of its impressions as real manifestations, but will not admit that external objects correspond* ... for it is the image producing the effect in the eye that is bent.... Thus, since the impression produced on the senses differs from the external object, belief must stick to the impression or be proved if it claims being as well as appearance." p. 1121.

h) *Epicurus and the Academics (Arcesilaus)*

What Plutarch says on this subject is confined to the fact that the Academics recognise three movements: φανταστικόν, ὁρμητικόν and συγκαταθετικόν[a] [p. 1122], and the error is in the last; so what is perceptible to the senses disappears neither in practice nor in theory, but opinion does.

He tries to prove to the Epicureans that they doubt much of what is evident.

---

[a] Imaginative, impulsive and assentive.— *Ed.*

IV. LUCRETIUS, *ON THE NATURE OF THINGS*
Published by Eichstädt, 1801, Vol. 1

It goes without saying that but little use can be made of Lucretius.

Book I

"When human life lay grovelling in all men's sight, crushed to the earth under the dead weight of religion, whose grim features loured menacingly upon mortals from the four quarters of the sky, a man of Greece was first to raise mortal eyes in defiance, first to stand erect and brave the challenge. Fables of the gods did not crush him, nor the lightning flash and the growling menace of the sky.... Therefore religion in its turn lies crushed beneath his feet, and we by his triumph are lifted level with the skies."   ll. 63-80.

"Nothing can ever be created by divine power out of nothing."   l. 151.

"... if things were made out of nothing, any species could spring from any source, and nothing would require seed."   ll. 160 and 161.

"Be not, however, mistrustful of my words, because the primary principles of things are not visible to the eyes."   ll. 268 and 269.

"Therefore nature works through the agency of invisible bodies."   l. 329.

"Neither are things hemmed in by the pressure of solid bodies in a tight mass. This is because there is void in things."   ll. 330 and 331.

"This" (*scilicet inanis cognitio*[a]) "will save you from ever brooding about the universe... For there is a space, untouched and void and vacant. If it did not exist, things could not move at all.... Nothing could proceed, because nothing would give it a starting point by receding.... And if there were no empty space ... things could not possibly have come into existence, hemmed in as they would have been in motionless matter."   ll. 333-346.

"... mingled with the things is void, from whence things first receive the possibility of movement."   ll. 383-384.

"All ... nature ... consists of two things, bodies and the void." ll. 420 and 421.

"Similarly, time by itself does not exist ... no one can sense time by itself apart from the movement of things and restful immobility."   ll. 460-464.

"Neither bodies exist by themselves nor can [events] be said to be by themselves.

"Events cannot be said to be by themselves like matter or in the same sense as the void. Rather, they must be described as accidents of matter, or of the place in which things happen."   ll. 480-483.

"... we have found that nature is twofold, consisting of two totally different things, matter and space.... Each of these must exist by itself, without admixture of the other. For, where there is empty space ... there matter is not, where matter exists, there cannot be a void."   ll. 504-510.

"... matter ... everlasting...."   l. 541.

"... *there must be an ultimate point in objects.... This point is without parts and is the smallest thing that can exist. It never has been and never will be able to exist by itself.*"   ll. 600-604.

"... there are certain bodies ... they do not resemble fire or anything else that can bombard our senses with particles or impinge on our organs of touch."   ll. 685-690.

---

[a] To wit, the knowledge of the void (note by Marx).— *Ed.*

"Again, if everything is created from four things and resolved into them, why should we say that these are the elements of things rather than the reverse—that other things are the elements of these?" ll. 764-767.

"... then nothing can be created from them [the four elements], neither animate, nor, like a tree, with inanimate body. For each element in a composite assemblage will betray its own nature, air will appear mixed with earth, and fire will remain side by side with moisture. But in fact the elements, in giving birth to things, must contribute a nature that is hidden and viewless, so that nothing may show that conflicts with the thing created and prevents it from being distinctively itself." ll. 773-781.

"... they make ... things never cease to interchange, migrating (to be precise, fire rising into the air, hence is born rain, then earth, and from the earth all returns again[a]) from heaven to earth, from earth to the starry firmament. This is something elements ought never to do. For it is essential that something should remain immutable, or everything would be reduced to nothing. For, if ever anything is so transformed that it oversteps its own limits, this means the immediate death of what was before." ll. 783-793.

"... because there are in things many elements common to many things commingled in many ways, various things draw their food from various sources." ll. 814-816.

"For the same elements compose sky, sea and lands, rivers and sun, crops, trees and animals, but they are moving differently and in different combinations." ll. 820-822.

"Add to this that he" (Anaxagoras) "makes the elements too frail.... For which of these things will withstand violent assault, so as to escape extinction...? Will fire or water or air? Will blood or bones? Nothing, I maintain, will escape, where everything is as perishably as those objects that we see vanishing from before our eyes under stress of some force or other." ll. 847-856.

"If flame, smoke and ashes lurk unseen in wood, then wood must consist of unlike matter which rises out of it." ll. 872-873.

"Here is left some scanty cover for escaping detection, and Anaxagoras avails himself of it. He asserts that there is in everything a mixture of everything, but all the ingredients escape detection except the one whose particles are most numerous and conspicuous and lie nearest the surface. This is far removed from the truth. Otherwise it would naturally happen that corn, when it is crushed by the dire force of the grindstone, would often show some signs of blood.... When sticks are snapped, ashes and smoke ought to be revealed, and tiny hidden fires. But observation plainly shows that none of these things happens. It is clear therefore that one sort of thing is not intermingled with another in this way, but there must be in things a mixture of invisible seeds that are common to many sorts." ll. 874-895.

"Now do you see the point of my previous remark, that it makes a great difference in what combinations and positions the same elements occur, and what motions they mutually pass on and take over, so that with a little reshuffling the same ones may produce forests and fires? This is just how the words themselves are formed, by a little reshuffling of the elements, when we pronounce 'forests' and 'fires' as two distinct utterances." ll. 906-913.

---

[a] The words in brackets are Marx's summary of ll. 784-786.— *Ed.*

"... the universe is not bounded in any direction. If it were, it would necessarily have a limit somewhere. But clearly a thing cannot have a limit unless there is something outside to limit it.... Since you must admit that there is nothing outside the universe, it can have no limit, and is accordingly without end or measure."

ll. 957-963.

"Further, if all the space in the universe were shut in and confined on every side by definite boundaries ... there would be no sky.... As it is, no rest is given to the atoms, because there is no bottom where they can accumulate and take up their abode. Things are happening all the time, through ceaseless motion in every direction; and atoms of matter bouncing up from below are supplied out of the infinite."

ll. 983-996.

"Nature ... compels body to be bounded by void and void by body. Thus it makes both of them infinite in alternation, or else one of them, if it is not bounded by the other, must extend in a pure state, without limit."

ll. 1008-1012.

"None of these results would be possible if there were not an ample supply of matter to rise up out of infinite space to replace in time all that is lost. Just as animals deprived of food waste away through loss of body, so everything must decay as soon as its supply of matter goes astray and is cut off."

ll. 1034-1040.

As nature in spring lays herself bare and, as though conscious of victory, displays all her charm, whereas in winter she covers up her shame and nakedness with snow and ice, so Lucretius, fresh, keen, poetic master of the world, differs from Plutarch, who covers his paltry ego with the snow and ice of morality. When we see an individual anxiously buttoned-up and cringing into himself, we involuntarily clutch at coat and clasp, make sure that we are still there, as if afraid to lose ourselves. But at the sight of an intrepid acrobat we forget ourselves, feel ourselves raised out of our own skins like universal forces and breathe more fearlessly. Who is it that feels in the more moral and free state of mind — he who has just come out of Plutarch's classroom, reflecting on how unjust it is that the good should lose with life the fruit of their life, or he who sees eternity fulfilled, hears the bold thundering song of Lucretius:

"... high hope of fame has struck my heart with its sharp goad and in so doing has implanted in my breast the sweet love of the Muses. That is the spur that lends my spirit strength to pioneer through pathless tracts of their Pierian realm where no foot has ever trod before. What joy it is to light upon virgin springs and drink their waters. What joy to pluck new flowers and gather for my brow a glorious garland from fields whose blossoms were never yet wreathed by the Muses round any head. This was my reward for teaching on these lofty topics, for struggling to loose men's minds from the tight knots of religion and shedding on dark corners the bright beams of my song that irradiate everything with the sparkle of the Muses."

ll. 921 ff.

He who would not prefer to build the whole world out of his own resources, to be a creator of the world, rather than to be eternally bothering about himself, has already been anathematised by the spirit, he is under an interdict, but in the opposite sense; he is expelled from the temple and deprived of the eternal enjoyment of the spirit and left to sing lullabies about his own private bliss and to dream about himself at night.

"Blessedness is not the reward of virtue, but is virtue itself." [a]

We shall also see how infinitely more philosophically Lucretius grasps Epicurus than does Plutarch. The first necessity for philosophical investigation is a bold, free mind.

First we must appreciate the pertinent criticism of earlier natural philosophers from the Epicurean viewpoint. It is all the more worthy of consideration since it brings out in a masterly manner what is specific in the teaching of Epicurus.

We here consider in particular what is taught about Empedocles and Anaxagoras, since the same points are still more valid for the others.

1. No *definite* elements can be considered to be the substance, for if everything is included in them and everything arises out of them, what forbids us to assume, on the contrary, that in this alternating process the totality of other things is their principle, since they themselves possess only a determinate, limited mode of existence side by side with the others and are brought forth likewise by the process of these [other] existences? And the other way round (ll. 764-768).

2. If a number of definite elements are held to be the substance, then they reveal on the one hand their natural one-sidedness by maintaining themselves in conflict with each other, asserting their determinateness and so dissolving in their opposite; on the other hand they are subject to a natural process, mechanical or other, and reveal their formative ability as one confined to their individuality.

If we concede the Ionian natural philosophers the historical excuse that their fire, water, etc., were not the things perceptible to the senses but something general, then Lucretius as an opponent is completely right in criticising them on these grounds. If obvious elements, obvious to the daylight of the senses, are taken to be the basic substances, then these have as their criterion sensuous perception and the sensuous forms of their existence. If one says that what is in question is a determination of another kind, in which they are the principles of that which exists, then it is a determination which their sensuous individuality conceals;

---

[a] B. Spinoza, *Ethics*, Part V, Prop. 42.—*Ed.*

only in internal, therefore external, determination are they principles; that is, they are not principles as given definite elements, precisely not in that which distinguishes each element from the others as fire, water, etc. (ll. 773 ff.)

3. But thirdly the view that definite elements are basic principles is contradicted not only by their limited existence side by side with others, from which they are arbitrarily singled out, and in respect of which, therefore, they differ only according to the determination of number; but being limited far more by the plurality, the infinite number of the others, they seem not only to be determined as to their principle by their mutual relationship in their particularity, which reveals an exclusion just as much as a formative power enclosed in natural limits; but the process itself by which they are supposed to generate the world manifests their finiteness and changeability.

As they are elements enclosed in a particular natural form, their creativity can only be a particular one, that is, their own transformation, which again has the form of particularity, namely, natural particularity; that is, their creativity is the natural process of their transformation. So these natural philosophers have fire flicker in the air, so rain is produced and falls down, and so the earth is formed. What is shown here is the elements' own changeability and not their constancy, not their substantial being, which they [the natural philosophers] assert as principles; for their creativity is rather the death of their particular existence, and what proceeds out of them comes rather from their non-persistency (ll. 783 ff.).

The mutual necessity of the elements and natural things for each other's existence signifies only that their conditions are their own powers, outside them as well as inside them.

4. Lucretius now comes to the homoeomerias [a] of Anaxagoras. His objection to them is that

"[he makes] the elements too frail" [ll. 847-848],

for since the homoeomerias have the same quality, are the same substance, as that of which they are homoeomerias, we must also attribute to them the same transience as is evident in their concrete manifestations. If wood conceals within itself fire and smoke, that means that it is a mixture *ex alienigeneis* [b] [l. 873]. If every body were made up of all the seeds perceptible to the senses, when it was broken up it would be seen to contain them.

---

[a] Seeds.— *Ed.*

[b] Of unlike species.— *Ed.*

It may seem strange that a philosophy like that of Epicurus, which proceeds from the sphere of the sensuous and, at least in cognition, assesses it as the highest criterion, should posit as principle such an abstraction, such a *caeca potestas*[a] as the atom. Concerning this, see lines 773 ff. and 783 ff., where it is seen that the principle must have an independent existence without any particular sensuously perceptible, physical quality. It is substance:

"... the same elements compose sky, sea and lands, rivers and sun," etc.

ll. 820 f.

Universality is inherent in it.

An important remark on the relationship of the *atom and the void*. Lucretius says of this *duplex natura*[b]:

"... each of these must exist by itself, without admixture of the other."

ll. 504 ff.

Further, they are mutually exclusive:

"For, where there is empty space ... there matter is not."   loc. cit.

Each one is itself the principle, so that the principle is neither the atom nor the void, but their basis, that which each of them manifests as an independent nature. This mean is enthroned at the consummation of Epicurean philosophy.

On the void as a principle of motion, see ll. 363 ff., notably as an immanent principle, see ll. 383 ff., τὸ κενὸυ καὶ τὸ ἄτομου,[c] the objectivised antithesis of thinking and being.

LUCRETIUS, *ON THE NATURE OF THINGS*

Book II

"But nothing is sweeter than to stand in a quiet temple stoutly fortified by the teaching of the wise."   ll. 7 f.

"O joyless hearts of men! O minds without vision! How dark and dangerous the life in which this tiny span is lived away!"   ll. 14 ff.

"As children in blank darkness tremble and start at everything, so we in broad daylight fear.... This dread and darkness of the mind cannot be dispelled by the sunbeams, the shining shafts of day, but only by an understanding of the outward form and inner workings of nature."   ll. 54 ff.

"Since the atoms are moving freely through the void, they must all be kept in motion either by their own weight or by the impact of another...."   ll. 82 ff.

"Remember that the universe has nowhere a bottom: *there is no place where the*

---

[a] Blind power.— *Ed.*
[b] Dual nature.— *Ed.*
[c] The void and the atom.— *Ed.*

atoms could come to rest. It has been variously proved that space is without end or limit and spreads out immeasurably in all directions alike...."   ll. 89 ff.

"... no rest is given to the atoms in their course through the depths of space ... but [they are driven] in an incessant and variable movement", etc.   ll. 94 ff.

The formation of combinations of atoms, their repulsion and attraction, is a noisy affair. An uproarious contest, a hostile tension, constitutes the workshop and the smithy of the world. The world in the depths of whose heart there is such tumult, is torn within.

Even the sunbeam, falling on shady places, is an image of this eternal war.

"A multitude of tiny particles ... within the light of the beam, as though contending in everlasting conflict, rushing into battle rank upon rank with never a moment's pause in a rapid sequence of unions and disunions. From this you may picture what it is for the atoms to be perpetually tossed about in the illimitable void."   ll. 115 ff.

One sees how the blind, uncanny power of fate is transposed into the arbitrary will of the person, of the individual, and shatters the forms and substances.

"Besides, there is a further reason why you should give your mind to these particles that are seen dancing in a sunbeam: their dancing is an actual indication of underlying *movements of matter* that are *hidden from our sight.* There you will see many particles under the impact of invisible blows changing their course and driven back upon their tracks."   ll. 124 ff.

"First the atoms are set in movement by themselves. Then those small compound bodies that are, as it were, least removed from the impetus of the atoms are set in motion by the impact of their invisible blows and in turn cannon against slightly larger bodies. So the movement mounts up from the atoms and gradually emerges to the level of our senses, so that at last those bodies are in motion that we see in sunbeams, moved by blows that remain invisible."   ll. 132 ff.

"... when separate atoms are travelling, simple and solid, through empty space, they encounter no obstruction from without and move as single units on the course on which they have embarked. They must certainly have greater speed than anything else and move far faster than the light of the sun...."   ll. 156 ff.

"Even if I knew nothing of the atoms, I would venture to assert on the evidence of the celestial phenomena themselves, supported by many other arguments, that the universe was certainly not created for us by divine power...."
                                                                        ll. 177 ff.

"... no material thing can be uplifted or travel upwards by its own power."
                                                                        ll. 185 f.

The *declinatio atomorum a via recta*[a] is one of the most profound conclusions, and it is based on the very essence of the Epicurean philosophy. Cicero might well laugh at it, he knew as little about philosophy as about the president of the United States of North America.

---

[a] Declination of the atoms from the straight line.— *Ed.*

The straight line, the simple direction, is the negation of immediate being-for-self, of the point; it is the negated point; the straight line is the being-otherwise of the point. The atom, the material point, which excludes from itself the being-otherwise and is absolute immediate being-for-self, excludes therefore the simple direction, the straight line, and swerves away from it. It shows that its nature is not spatiality, but being-for-self. The law which it follows is different from that of spatiality.

The straight line is not only the being-negated of the point, but also its existence. The atom is indifferent to the breadth of existence, it does not split up into differences which have being, but just as little is it mere being, the immediate, which is, as it were, indifferent to its being, but it exists rather precisely in being different from existence; it encloses itself in itself against that existence; in terms of the sensuous it swerves away from the straight line.

As the atom swerves away from its premise, divests itself of its qualitative nature and therein shows that this divestment, this premiseless, contentless being-enclosed-in-self exists for itself, that thus its proper quality appears, so also the whole of the Epicurean philosophy swerves away from the premises; so pleasure, for example, is the swerving away from pain, consequently from the condition in which the atom appears as differentiated, as existing, burdened with non-being and premises. But the fact that pain exists, etc., that these premises from which it swerves away exist for the individual—this is its finiteness, and therein it is accidental. True, we already find that in themselves these premises exist for the atom, for it would not swerve away from the straight line if the straight line did not exist for it. But this results from the position of the Epicurean philosophy, which seeks the premiseless in the world of the substantial premise, or, to express it in terms of logic, inasmuch as for it [the Epicurean philosophy] the being-for-self is the exclusive, the immediate principle, it has existence directly confronting it, has not logically overcome it.

Determinism is swerved away from by accident, [i.e.] necessity, and arbitrariness raised to the status of law; God swerves away from the world, it does not exist for him, and therein is he God.

It can therefore be said that the *declinatio atomi a recta via* is the law, the pulse, the specific quality of the atom; and this is why the teaching of Democritus was a quite different philosophy, not the philosophy of the age as the Epicurean philosophy was.

"If it were not for this swerve, everything would fall downwards ... through the abyss of space. No *collision would take place* and no *impact of atom on atom* would be created. Thus nature would never have created anything."   ll. 221 ff.

Inasmuch as the world is created, as the atom refers itself to itself, that is, to another atom, so its [the atom's] motion is not one which presupposes a being-otherwise, the motion of the straight line, but one which swerves away from the latter, refers itself to itself. In sensuous imagination, the atom can refer itself only to the atom, each of the atoms swerving away from the straight line.

"For this reason also the atoms must swerve a little, but only a very little, so that we will not imagine slantwise movements, which the fact refutes." ll. 243 ff.

"Again, if all movement is always interconnected, the new arising from the old in a determinate order—if the atoms never swerve so as to originate some new movement that will snap the bonds of fate, the everlasting sequence of cause and effect—what is the source of the free will possessed by living things throughout the earth? What, I repeat, is the source of that will-power snatched from the fates, whereby we follow the path along which we are severally led by pleasure...?" ll. 251 ff.

"... on these occasions the will of the individual originates the movements that trickle through his limbs", etc. ll. 281 f.

The *declinatio a recta via* is the *arbitrium*,[a] the specific substance, the true quality of the atom.

"So also in the atoms you must recognise the same possibility: besides weight and impact there must be a third cause of movement, the source of this inborn power of ours, since we see that nothing can come out of nothing. For the weight of an atom prevents its movements from being completely determined by the impact of other atoms. But the fact that the mind itself has no internal necessity to determine its every act and compel it to suffer in helpless passivity—*this is due to the slight swerve of the atoms, not determined by place or time*." ll. 284 ff.

This *declinatio*, this *clinamen*,[b] is neither *regione loci certa* nor *tempore certo*,[c] it is not a sensuous quality, it is the soul of the atom.

In the void the differentiation of weight disappears, that is, it is no external condition of motion, but being-for-self, immanent, absolute movement itself.

"But empty space can offer no resistance to any object in any quarter at any time, so as not to yield free passage as its own nature demands. Therefore, through undisturbed vacuum all bodies must travel at equal speed, although impelled by unequal weight." ll. 235 ff.

Lucretius asserts this in contrast to motion restricted through conditions perceptible to the senses:

"The reason why objects falling through water or thin air vary in speed according to their weight is simply that the matter composing water or air cannot obstruct all objects equally, but is forced to give way more speedily to heavier ones." ll. 230 ff.

---

[a] Free will.— *Ed.*
[b] Declination, deviation.— *Ed.*
[c] Defined by place, determined by time.— *Ed.*

"Do you not see then, that although many men are driven by an external force and often constrained involuntarily to advance or to rush headlong, yet there is within the human breast something that can fight against this force and resist it", etc.   ll. 277 ff.

See the lines quoted above.

This *potestas*, [a] this *declinare*[b] is the defiance, the headstrongness of the atom, the *quiddam in pectore*[c] of the atom; it does not characterise its relationship to the world as the relationship of the fragmented and mechanical world to the single individual.

As Zeus grew up to the tumultuous war dances of the Curetes, so here the world takes shape to the ringing war games of the atoms.

Lucretius is the genuine Roman epic poet, for he sings the substance of the Roman spirit; in place of Homer's cheerful, strong, integral characters we have here solid, impenetrable armed heroes possessed of no other qualities, we have the war *omnium contra omnes*,[d] the rigid shape of the being-for-self, a nature without god and a god aloof from the world.

We now come to the determination of the more immediate qualities of the atom; we have already clarified its inner, immanent specific quality, which, however, is rather its substance. These determinations are extremely unsatisfactory in Lucretius and on the whole they are among the most arbitrary, and therefore the most difficult parts of the whole Epicurean philosophy.

1. *The motion of the atoms*

"The supply of matter in the universe was never more tightly packed than it is now, or more widely spaced out.... The sum of things cannot be changed by any force."   ll. 294 f.

"In this connection there is one fact that need occasion no surprise. Although all the atoms are in motion, their totality appears to stand totally motionless.... This is because the atoms all lie far below the range of our senses. Since they are themselves invisible, their movements also must elude observation. Indeed, even visible objects, when set at a distance, often disguise their movements."

ll. 308 ff.

2. *Shape*

"And now perceive the characteristics of the atoms of all substances, the extent to which they differ in shape and the rich multiplicity of their forms.... *When the*

---

[a] Power.— *Ed.*
[b] Declination.— *Ed.*
[c] Something in the breast.— *Ed.*
[d] Of all against all.— *Ed.*

multitude of them, as I have shown, *is such* that it is without limit or count, *it is not to be expected that they should all be identical in build and configuration."*   ll. 333 ff.

"There must, therefore, be great differences in the shapes of the atoms to provoke these different sensations."   ll. 442 f.

"... the number of different forms of atoms is finite. If it were not so, *some of the atoms would have to be of infinite magnitude. Within the narrow limits of any single particle, there can be only a limited range of forms.* Suppose the atoms consist of three minimum parts, or enlarge them by a few more. When by fitting on parts at top or bottom and transposing left and right you have exhausted every shape that can be given to the whole body by all possible arrangements of the parts, you are obviously left with no means of varying its form further except by adding other parts. Thence it will follow, if you wish to vary its form still further, that the arrangement will demand still other parts in exactly the same way. *Variation in shape goes with increase in size.* You cannot believe, therefore, that the *atoms are distinguished by an infinity of forms;* or you will compel *some of them to be of enormous magnitude,* which I have already proved to be impossible."   ll. 479 ff.

This *Epicurean dogma* that the *figurarum varietas* is not *infinita,*[a] but that the *corpuscula ejusdem figurae* are *infinita, e quorum perpetuo concursu mundus perfectus est resque gignuntur*[b] is the most important, most immanent consideration of the relationship of the atoms to their qualities, to themselves as principles of a world.

"For whatever might be would always be surpassed by something more excellent."   l. 507

"And as all good things might yield to better, so might bad to worse. One thing would always be surpassed by another more offensive...."   ll. 508 ff.

"Since this is not so, but things are bound by a set limit at either extreme, you must acknowledge a corresponding limit to the different forms of matter."   ll. 512 ff.

"To the foregoing demonstration I will link on another fact, which will gain credence from this context: the number of atoms of any one form is infinite. Since the *varieties of form are limited,* the *number of uniform atoms must be unlimited.* Otherwise the *totality of matter would be finite,* which I have proved in my verses is not so."   ll. 522 ff.

The distance, the differentiation of the atoms are finite; were they not assumed to be finite, the atoms in themselves would be mediate, would contain an ideal variety. The infinity of the atoms as repulsion, as a negative attitude to themselves, produces an infinity of similars, *quae similes sint, infinitas,* their infinity has nothing to do with their qualitative difference. If one assumed infinite

---

[a] The variety of shapes is not infinite.— *Ed.*

[b] Particles with the same shape are infinite out of whose continual collision the world emerged and the bodies arose.— *Ed.*

variety in the shapes of the atoms, each atom would contain the other in itself negated, and then there would be atoms which presented the whole infinity of the world, like the monads of Leibniz.

"It is evident, therefore, that there are infinite atoms of every kind to keep up the supply of everything." ll. 568 f.

"So the war of the elements that has raged throughout eternity continues on equal terms. Now here, now there, the forces of life are victorious and in turn vanquished. With the voice of mourning mingles the cry that infants raise when their eyes open on the sunlit world. Never has day given place to night nor night to dawn that has not heard, blended with these infant wailings, the lamentation that attends on death and sombre obsequies." ll. 547 ff.

"The more qualities and powers a thing possesses, the greater variety it attests in the component atoms and their forms." ll. 587 ff.

"For it is essential to the very nature of deity that it should enjoy immortal existence in utter tranquillity, aloof and detached from our affairs. It is free from all pain and peril, strong in its own resources, exempt from any need of us, indifferent to our merits and immune from anger." ll. 646 ff.

"... and the atoms do not emerge into the light." l. 796.

"Do not imagine that colour is the only quality that is denied to the atoms. They are wholly devoid of warmth and cold and scorching heat; they are barren of sound and starved of savour, and emit no inherent odour from their bodies." ll. 842 ff.

"All these must be kept far apart from the atoms, if we wish to provide the universe with imperishable foundations on which it may rest secure; or else you will find everything slipping back into nothing." ll. 861 ff.

"It follows that the atoms cannot be afflicted by any pain or experience any pleasure in themselves, since they are not composed of any primal particles, by some reversal of whose movements they might suffer anguish or reap some fruition of vitalising bliss. They cannot therefore be endowed with any power of sensation." ll. 967 ff.

"Again, if we are to account for the power of sensation possessed by animate creatures in general by attributing sentience to their atoms [, what of those atoms that specifically compose the human race?]" ll. 937 ff.

The answer to this is:

"If they [the principles] are to be likened to entire mortals, they must certainly consist of other elemental particles, and these again of others without end." ll. 980 ff.

[Book III]

"First, I affirm that it [the mind] is of very fine texture and is composed of exceptionally minute particles." ll. 180 f.

"But what is so mobile must consist of exceptionally minute and spherical atoms...." ll. 187 f.

"The stickier consistency is due to the closer coherence of the component matter, consisting of particles not so smooth or so fine or so round." ll. 194 ff.

"The greater their weight and roughness, the more firmly they are anchored...." ll. 202 f.

Negation of cohesion, of specific weight.

"... it may be inferred that mind and spirit are composed of exceptionally diminutive seeds, *since their departure is not accompanied by any loss of weight.* It must not be supposed that the stuff of mind or spirit is a single element. The body at death is abandoned by a sort of *rarefied wind* mixed with warmth, while the warmth carries with it also air. Indeed, *heat* never occurs without an intermixture of air."

ll. 229 ff.

"The *composition of the mind* is thus found to be *threefold*. But all these three components together are not enough to create sentience, since the mind does not admit that any of these can create the sensory motions.... We must accordingly add to these a fourth component, which is quite nameless. Than this there is nothing more mobile or more tenuous—nothing whose component atoms are smaller or smoother."

ll. 238 ff.

"But usually a stop is put to these movements as near as may be to the surface of the body. Because of this we can retain life."

ll. 257 f.

"One who no longer is cannot suffer, or differ in any way from one who has never been born, *when once this mortal life has been usurped by death the immortal.*"

ll. 880 ff.

It can be said that in the Epicurean philosophy it is death that is immortal. The atom, the void, accident, arbitrariness and composition are in themselves death.

"For if it is really a bad thing after death to be mauled and crunched by ravening jaws, I cannot see why it should not be disagreeable to roast in the scorching flames of a funeral pyre, or to lie embalmed in honey, stifled and stiff with cold, on the surface of a chilly slab, or to be squashed under a crushing weight of earth."

ll. 901 ff.

"Men feel plainly enough within their minds a heavy burden, whose weight depresses them. If only they perceived with equal clearness the causes of this depression, the origin of this lump of evil within their breasts, they would not lead such a life as we now see all too commonly—no one knowing what he really wants and every one for ever trying to get away from where he is, as though mere change of place could throw off the load."

ll. 1066 ff.

End of Book Three

Accident is known to be the dominating category with the Epicureans. A necessary consequence of this is that the idea is considered only as a *condition*; condition is existence accidental in itself. The innermost category of the world, the atom, its connection, etc., is for this reason relegated into the distance and considered as a past condition. We find the same thing with the Pietists and Supernaturalists. The creation of the world, original sin, the redemption, all this and all their godly determinations, such as paradise, etc., are not an eternal, timeless, immanent determination of the idea, but a condition. As Epicurus makes the ideality of his world, the void, into [the condition for] the creation of the world, so also the Supernaturalist gives embodiment to premiselessness, [namely] the idea of the world, in paradise.

LUC. ANNAEUS SENECA, *WORKS*, VOLS. [I-]III, AMSTERDAM, 1672

Epistle IX, [1,] Vol. II, p. 25. "You desire to know whether Epicurus is right when, in one of his letters, he rebukes those who hold that the wise man is self-sufficient and for that reason does not stand in need of friendships. This is the objection raised by Epicurus against Stilpo and those who believe that the Supreme Good is a dispassionate mind."

"Epicurus himself ... spoke similar language: 'Whoever does not regard what he has as most ample wealth, is unhappy, though he be master of the whole world.'" op. cit., p. 30.

"[...] he (Epicurus) added: 'So greatly blest were Metrodorus and I that it has been no harm to us to be unknown and almost unheard of, in this well-known land of Greece.'" Ep. LXXIX, [15,] p. 317.

"As Epicurus himself says, he will sometimes withdraw from pleasure and even seek pain if either remorse threatens to follow pleasure or a smaller pain is accepted to avoid a larger one." L. Seneca, *On the Leisure of the Wise Man*, p. 582, Vol. I.

"Epicurus also maintains that the wise man, though he is being burned in the bull of Phalaris, will cry out: ''Tis pleasant, and concerns me not at all.' Epicurus will say that it is pleasant to be tortured." Ep. LXVI, [18,] [Vol. II,] p. 235, also Ep. LXVII, [15,] p. 248.

"We find mentioned in the works of Epicurus two goods, of which his Supreme Good, or blessedness, is composed, namely, a body free from pain and a soul free from disturbance." Ep. LXVI, [45,] p. 241.

"For he [Epicurus] tells us that he had to endure excruciating agony from a diseased bladder and from an ulcerated stomach,—so acute that it permitted no increase of pain; 'and yet,' he says, 'that day was none the less happy.'" Ep. LXVI, [47,] p. 242.

"I ... remember the distinguished words of Epicurus ... 'This little garden ... does not whet your appetite; it quenches it. Nor does it make you more thirsty with every drink; it slakes the thirst by a natural cure,—a cure that demands no fee. This is the "pleasure" in which I have grown old.' In speaking to you, however, I refer to those desires which refuse alleviation, which must be bribed to cease. For in regard to the exceptional desires, which may be postponed, which may be chastened and checked, I have this one thought to share with you: a pleasure of that sort is according to our nature, but it is not according to our needs; you owe nothing to it; whatever is expended upon it is a free gift. The belly does not listen to advice; it makes demands, it importunes. And yet it is not a troublesome creditor; you can send it away at small cost, provided only that you give it what you owe, not what you are able to give." Ep. XXI, [9, 10, 11,] pp. 80-81.

"[...] Epicurus, whom you accept as the patron of your indolence, and of whom you think that he teaches softness and idleness and things which lead to pleasure, says: 'Happiness seldom affects the wise man.'" Vol. I, p. 416, *On the Constancy of the Wise Man* [XV 4].

"Epicurus upbraids those who crave, as much as those who shrink from death: 'It is absurd,' he says, 'to run towards death because you are tired of life, when it is your manner of life that has made you run towards death.' And in another passage: 'What is so absurd as to seek death, when it is through fear of death that you have robbed your life of peace?' [To this can be added also] the following: 'Men are so thoughtless, nay, so mad, that some, through fear of death, force themselves to die.'" Ep. XXIV, [22-23,] p. 95.

"I am also of the opinion (and I say this in defiance of my colleagues) that Epicurus' teaching is pure and correct, and on closer consideration even severe: pleasure is confined to a small and insignificant role; and he prescribes for pleasure the law that we prescribe for virtue. He commands it to obey nature, but very little pleasure is sufficient for nature. What is it then? He who describes as pleasure idle leisure and a continual alternation of gluttony and sensuality, seeks a good advocate for a bad cause, and when he, attracted by a misleading name, attains it, he abandons himself to pleasure, yet not to that of which he has heard, but to that which he brought with him." *On the Happy Life*, Vol. I, p. 542.

"[...] *friends* ... the name which our Epicurus bestowed upon them (the *slaves*)." Ep. CVII, [1,] [Vol. II,] p. 526. "[...] Epicurus, Stilpo's critic." p. 30, Ep. IX [20].

"[...] let me tell you that Epicurus says the same thing. ... *that only the wise man knows how to return a favour.*" Ep. LXXXI, [11,] p. 326.

"Epicurus remarks that certain men have worked their way to the truth without any one's assistance, he, among them, made his own way. And he gives special praise to these, for their impulse has come from within, and they have forged to the front by themselves. Again, he says, there are others who need outside help, who will not proceed unless someone leads the way, but who will follow faithfully. Of these, he says, Metrodorus was one; this type of man is also excellent, but belongs to the second grade." Ep. LII, [3,] [p]p. [176-]177. "You will find still another class of man,—and a class not to be despised,—who can be forced and driven into righteousness, who do not need a guide so much as they need someone to encourage and, as it were, to force them along. This is the third class." ibid.

"Epicurus, the teacher of pleasure, used to observe stated days on which he satisfied his hunger in niggardly fashion; he wished to see whether he thereby fell short of full and complete happiness, and, if so, by what amount he fell short, and whether this amount was worth purchasing at the price of great effort. At any rate, he makes such a statement in the well-known letter written to Polyaenus in the archonship of Charinus. Indeed, he boasts that he himself lived on less than a penny, but that Metrodorus, whose progress was not yet so great, needed a whole penny. Do you think there can be fulness on such fare? Yes, and there is pleasure also,—not that shifty and fleeting pleasure which needs a fillip now and then, but a pleasure that is steadfast and sure. For though water, barley-meal, and crusts of barley-bread, are not a cheerful diet, yet it is the highest kind of pleasure to be able to derive pleasure from this sort of food, and to have reduced one's needs to that modicum which no unfairness of Fortune can snatch away." Ep. XVIII, [9-10,] p[p]. 67[-68].

"[It was to him (Idomeneus)] that Epicurus addressed his well-known saying, urging him to make Pythocles rich, but not rich in the vulgar and equivocal way. 'If you wish,' said he, 'to make Pythocles rich, do not add to his store of money, but subtract from his desires.'" Ep. XXI, [7,] p. 79.

Cf. Stobaeus, Sermon XVII [41-42]. "If you want to make somebody rich, do not give him more money, but free him of some of his desires."

"'It is bad to live under necessity, but there is no necessity to live under necessity.' Of course not. On all sides lie many short and simple paths to freedom; and *let us thank God that no man can be kept in life. We may spurn those very necessities,* said [Epicurus]...." Ep. XII, [10-11,] p. 42.

"The fool, with all his other faults, has this also,— *he is always getting ready to live....* And what is baser than getting ready to live when you are already old? I should not name the author of this motto, except that it is somewhat unknown to fame and is not one of those popular sayings of Epicurus...." Ep. XIII, [16-17,] p. 47.

"'He who needs riches least, enjoys riches most,' is a saying of Epicurus." Ep. XIV, [17,] p. 53.

"This is a saying of Epicurus: 'If you live according to nature, you will never be poor; if you live according to opinion, you will never be rich.' Nature's wants are slight; the demands of opinion are boundless." Ep. XVI, [7-8,] p. 60.

"The acquisition of riches has been for many men, not an end, but a change, of troubles." Ep. XVII, [11,] p. 64.

"Here is a draft on Epicurus.... 'Ungoverned anger begets madness.' You cannot help knowing the truth of these words, since you have had not only a slave, but an enemy. But indeed this emotion blazes out against all sorts of persons; it springs from love as much as from hate, and shows itself not less in serious matters than in jest and sport. And it makes no difference how important the provocation may be, but into what kind of soul it penetrates. Similarly with fire; it does not matter how great is the flame, but what it falls upon. For solid bodies have repelled the greatest fire; conversely, dry and easily inflammable stuff nourishes the slightest spark into a conflagration." Ep. XVIII, [14-15,] [p]p. [68-]69.

"... of Epicurus. He says: 'You must reflect carefully beforehand with whom you are to eat and drink, rather than what you are to eat and drink. For a dinner of meats without the company of a friend is like the life of a lion or a wolf.'" Ep. XIX, [10,] p. 72.

"'No one,' says he (Epicurus), 'leaves this world in a different manner than he was born into it'.... A man has caught the message of wisdom, if he can die as free from care as he was at birth." Ep. XXII, [15, 16,] p. 84.

"I can give you a saying of ... Epicurus: 'It is bothersome always to be beginning life.'" Ep. XXIII, [9,] p. 87.

"'When a man has limited his desires within these bounds [i.e., bread and water, which nature demands, cf. Epistle CX, [18,] p. 548], he can challenge the happiness of Jove himself,' as Epicurus says." Ep. XXV, [4,] p. 97.

"Epicurus, who says: 'Reflect which of the two is more convenient, that death should come to us or we go to it.'" Ep. XXVI, [8,] p. 101.

"Wealth is poverty adjusted to the law of nature." Ep. XXVII, [9,] p. 105.

"'The knowledge of sin is the beginning of salvation.' This saying of Epicurus seems to me to be an excellent one." Ep. XXVIII, [9,] p. 107.

"Writing to one of the partners of his studies, Epicurus said: 'I write this not for the many, but for you; indeed, each of us is enough of an audience for the other.'" Ep. VII, [11,] p. 21.

"I am still conning Epicurus: 'If you would enjoy real freedom, you must be the slave of Philosophy.' The man who submits and surrenders himself to her is not kept waiting; he is emancipated on the spot. For the very service of Philosophy is freedom." Ep. VIII, [7,] p. 24.

"It was not the class-room of Epicurus, but association with him, that made [them] great men." Ep. VI, [6,] p. 16.

"Hence I hold Epicurus' saying to be most apt: 'That the guilty may haply remain hidden is possible, that he should be sure of remaining hidden is not possible.'" Ep. XCVII, [13,] p. 480.

"I have read the letter of Epicurus addressed to Idomeneus which bears on this matter. The writer asks him to hasten as fast as he can, and beat a retreat before some stronger influence comes between and takes from him the liberty to withdraw. But he also adds that one should attempt nothing except at the time when it can be attempted suitably and seasonably. Then, when the long-sought occasion comes, let him be up and doing. Epicurus forbids us to doze when we are meditating escape and hopes for a safe release from even the hardest trials, provided that we are not in too great a hurry before the time, nor too dilatory when the time arrives." Ep. XXII, [5, 6,] p. 82.

"No reasonable man fears the gods. For it is folly to fear that which is beneficent, and no one loves those whom he fears. In the end, you, Epicurus, disarm God. You have taken from him all weapons, all might, and so that no one should fear him, you have put him out of action. Therefore you have no reason to fear him who is surrounded by a huge and insuperable wall and is separated from the contact and the sight of mortals. He has not the possibility either to give or to harm. In the middle space between this and the other heaven, alone, without any living things, without any humans, without anything, he seeks to escape from the ruins of the worlds which are collapsing above him and around him, not heeding desires and without any concern for us. And yet you wish to appear as if you honour him as a father, with a grateful heart, as it seems to me; or if you do not wish to appear grateful, because you receive no mercy from him, but the atoms and these your particles have formed you accidentally and not according to any plan, why then do you honour him? Because of his majesty, you say, and his unique essence. If I concede you that, apparently you do this not induced by hope of any kind, by reward of any kind. Consequently there is something which is worth striving after for itself, whose worth itself attracts you: that is the moral Good." *On Benefits*, Book IV, Chap. 19, p. 719, Vol. I.

"'All these causes could exist,' says Epicurus, and tries several other explanations; and he rebukes those who have asserted that any definite one of these exists, because it is rash to judge apodictically of that which follows only from conjectures. Consequently an earthquake can be caused by water when it has eroded and carried away some parts of the earth, and these have been weakened; that which was borne by the parts when they were undamaged could no longer be held. Pressure of the air can set the earth in motion. For perhaps the air is set in vibration when other air streams in from outside. Perhaps it is shaken and set in motion when a part suddenly gives way. Perhaps it is held up by some part of the earth as by some kind of columns and pillars; if these are damaged and yield, the weight resting on them quakes. Perhaps hot masses of air are transformed into fire and rush down like lightning, doing great damage to what is in their path. Perhaps some blast of wind sets boggy and stagnant waters in motion and consequently the earth is shaken by an impulse or a vibration of the air, which increases with the motion itself, is carried above from below, however he says that no other cause is of greater importance in the case of an earthquake than motion of the air." *Questions of Nature*, Book VI, Chap. 20, p. 802. Vol. II.

"On this question, two schools above all are in disagreement, that of the Epicureans and that of the Stoics; but each of them points, though in different ways, to retirement. Epicurus says: 'The wise man shows no concern for the state, unless a special situation has arisen.' Zeno says: 'He must have concern for the state unless something hinders him.' The former wants leisure on principle, the latter according to circumstances." *On the Leisure of the Wise Man,* Chap. 30, p. 574, Vol. I.

"The pleasure of Epicurus is not estimated [...] because of how sober and dull it is, but they seize on the mere name, seeking some cover and veil for their lusts. Thus they lose the only good thing which they had in their badness, namely, shame of sinning. For they now praise that over which they blushed formerly, and they glory in vice, and for this reason even young people cannot regain their strength since shameful idleness has been covered with an honourable mantle." p. 541, Chap. 12, [4, 5,] *On the Happy Life,* Vol. I.

"For all these [Plato, Zeno, Epicurus] did not speak of how they themselves lived, but of how one should live." Chap. 18, [1,] p. 550, op. cit.

"Hence God does not dispense mercy, but, untroubled, unconcerned about us, and turned away from the world, he does something else or (and this for Epicurus is the greatest bliss) does nothing, and good deeds affect him no more than acts of injustice." *On Benefits,* Book IV, Chap. 4, [1,] p. 699, Vol. I.

"Here we must bear good testimony to Epicurus, who continually complains that we are ungrateful in respect of the past, that we do not bear in mind the good that we have received and do not include it in enjoyments, as no enjoyment is surer than that which cannot be taken away from us again." *On Benefits,* Book III, Chap. 4 [, 1, p. 666, Vol. I].

"We may dispute with Socrates, doubt with Carneades, repose with Epicurus, transcend human nature with the Stoics, defy it with the Cynics; Nature allows us to participate in any age." *On the Shortness of Life,* p. 512, Vol. I.

"In this respect we are in conflict with the self-indulgent and retiring crowd of the Epicureans who philosophise at their banquets and for whom virtue is the handmaid of pleasure. They obey pleasure, they serve it, they see it above themselves." *On Benefits,* Book IV, Chap. 2, p. 697, Vol. I.

"But how can virtue rule pleasure, which it follows, since to follow is proper to him who obeys, and to rule to him who commands?" *On the Happy Life,* Chap. 11, p. 538, Vol. I.

"For you [Epicureans] it is pleasure to abandon the body to idle leisure, to strive after freedom from care like people asleep, to conceal yourselves under a thick veil, to relax the sluggishness of the idle mind with emotional contemplation, which you call repose of the soul, and to strengthen with food and drink in the shade of gardens your bodies weakened by idleness; for us it is pleasure to accomplish good actions, even if they are wearying, provided only that through them the weariness of others is alleviated, or dangerous, provided that through them others are freed from danger, or burdensome for our fortune, provided only the distress and needs of others are attenuated." *On Benefits,* Book IV, Chap. 13, p. 713, Vol. I.

"For those who lack experience and training, there is no limit to the downhill course; such a one falls into the chaos of Epicurus—empty and boundless." Ep. LXXII, [9,] p. 274, Vol. II.

"The Epicureans held that philosophy consists of two parts, natural and moral, and they did away with logic. Then, when they were compelled by the facts to distinguish between equivocal ideas and to expose fallacies that lay hidden under the cloak of truth, they themselves also introduced a heading which they called 'on judgments and rules', which is another name for logic, but *which they consider an adjunct of natural philosophy.*" Ep. LXXXIX, [11,] p. 397.

"The Epicurean god neither has anything to do himself, nor does he give others anything to do." *On the Death of the Emperor Claudius*, p. 851, Vol. II.

"Then you say: 'Is it retirement, Seneca, that you are recommending to me? You will soon be falling back upon the maxims of Epicurus'. I do recommend retirement to you, but only that you may use it for greater and more beautiful activities than those which you have resigned." Ep. LXVIII, [10,] p. 251.

"I am not so foolish as to go through at this juncture the arguments which Epicurus harps upon, and say that the terrors of the world below are idle,—that Ixion does not whirl round on his wheel, that Sisyphus does not shoulder his stone uphill, that a man's entrails cannot be restored and devoured every day; no one is so childish as to fear Cerberus, or the shadows, or the spectral garb of those who are held together by naught but their unfleshed bones. Death either annihilates us or frees us. If we are released, there remains the better part, after the burden has been withdrawn; if we are annihilated, nothing remains: good and bad are alike removed." Ep. XXIV, [18,] p. 93.

End

JOH. STOBAEI *SENTENTIAE ET ECLOGAE, ETC.*
GENEVA, 1609

"Thanks be to bountiful nature for having made that which is necessary easy to obtain and that which is difficult to obtain not necessary.

"If you want to make somebody rich, do not give him more money, but free him of some of his desires.

"Temperance is the virtue of the appetitive part of the soul by which, with the help of reason, one represses longings for vulgar pleasure.

"It is the nature of temperance to be able to repress with the help of reason the longing for the vulgar enjoyment of pleasure and to endure and bear natural privations and suffering." *On Temperance*, Sermon XVII, p. 157.

"We are born once, it is not possible to be born twice, and it is of necessity that life is not longer *(necessarium est aetatem finiri)*. But you, who have no power over the morrow *(qui ne crastinum diem quidem in tua potestate habes)*, are putting off the moment *(tempus differs)*. Everybody's life is wasted through procrastination, and for that reason everyone of us dies without having any leisure." *On Economy*, Sermon XVI, p. 155.

"I have more than enough bodily pleasure when I have water and bread, and I do not care a straw for costly pleasures, not because of themselves, but because of all the unpleasantness that follows them.

"We feel the need for pleasure when we are sad because we do not have it. But when we do not experience this in our sensations, then we have no need for pleasure. For it is not the natural pleasure which causes external annoyance, but the striving for empty appearance." *On Temperance*, Sermon XVII [p. 159].

"The laws exist for the wise not so that they shall do no wrong, but so that no wrong shall happen to them." *On the State*, Sermon XLI, p. 270.

"Death is nothing to us. For that which is dissolved is without sensation. And that which is without sensation is nothing to us." *On Death*, Sermon CXVII, p. 600.

"Epicurus of Demos Gargettios proclaimed: 'To him for whom a little is not sufficient, nothing is sufficient.' He said he was prepared to dispute over bliss with anybody if he had only bread and water." *On Temperance*, Sermon XVII, p. 158.

"For this reason Epicurus also believes that those who are ambitious and seek after glory must not practise quietism, but must follow their nature taking part in civic affairs and work for the common weal, for their nature is such that, if they do not attain that for which they strive, they will become restless and embittered through inactivity. And yet he is foolish who enlists in work for the common weal not those who are suitable for it, but those who cannot be inactive; inner tranquillity and inner unrest must not be measured (*securitatem animi anxietatemque metiri*) either by the amount, great or small, of what one has done, but by the good and the bad. For to omit to do good is no less painful and disquieting (*molestum est et turbulentum*) than to do evil." *On Steadfastness*, Sermon XXIX, p. 206.

"When somebody said: 'The wise man will not be affected by love. The evidence for this is ... Epicurus ...', he [Chrysippus] said: 'This I take as a proof. For if ... the unfeeling Epicurus ... was not affected by love (the wise man will certainly not be affected by it)' (*ne sapiens quidem eo capietur*)." [a] *On Sensual Pleasure and Love*, Sermon LXI, p. 393.

"But we will concentrate our attention on the tedious philosophers according to whom pleasure does not conform to nature, but follows that which does conform to nature—justice, self-control and generosity of mind. Why then does the soul rejoice and find peace (*tranquillatur*) in the smaller goods of the body, as Epicurus says [...?]" *On Intemperance*, Sermon VI, pp. 81, 82.

"Epicurus [assumes] that the gods indeed resemble man, but that one and all they can be perceived only by thought because of the fineness of the nature of their images. He himself however [assumes] four other substances to be indestructible by their nature: the atoms, the void, the infinite, and the *homogeneous particles*; and these are called *homoeomerias* and *elements*." *Physical Selections*, Book 1, p. 5.

"Epicurus [is guided] by necessity, by free decision, by fate. And on the subject of fate they [the Pythagoreans] used to say: 'To be sure there is also a divine part in it, for some men receive from the divinity an inspiration for better or for worse; and in accordance with this some are clearly happy and others unhappy. But it is quite obvious that those who act without previous deliberation and haphazardly are often successful, while others, who deliberate beforehand and consider beforehand how to do something correctly, are not successful. But fate manifests itself in another way, by virtue of which some are talented and purposeful, while others are talentless and, because they have a contrary nature, do harm; the former though hasty in judgment attain every object at which they aim, while the latter do not achieve their object, because their thinking is never purposeful, but confused. This misfortune, however, is innate, and not imposed from outside (*non externam*)." *Physical Selections*, Book 1, [p] p. [15-]16.

"[...] Epicurus (calls time) an accident, i.e., a concomitant of movements [...]." l.c., p. 19.

"Epicurus [says] that the fundamental principles of that which is are bodies perceptible through thinking, bodies having no part of void, uncreated, indestructible, which can be neither damaged nor changed. Such a body is called an atom, not because it is the smallest, but because it cannot be divided, can have nothing done to it and has no part of void." *Physical Selections*, Book 1, p. 27.

"Epicurus [says] that the bodies are imperceptible and that the primary ones are simple, and the bodies composed of them have weight; that the atoms move, sometimes falling in a straight line (*rectis lineis*), sometimes swerving from the straight line; and upward movement occurs through collision and repulsion." *Physical Selections*, Book 1, p. 33.

"Epicurus ... [says] that coloured bodies have no colour in the dark [...]." *Physical Selections*, Book 1, p. 35.

---

[a] Here and below Marx inserts phrases from a Latin translation of Stobaeus where the Greek text is damaged.—*Ed.*

"[...] Epicurus [says] that the atoms are infinite in number and the void is infinite in extent." *Physical Selections*, Book 1, p. 38.

"Epicurus uses alternatively all the names: void, place, space." *Physical Selections*, Book 1, p. 39.

Cf. D[iogenes] L[aertius]. "'[...] if there did not exist that which we call void and space and intangible nature [...].'" p. 32. [Letter] to Herodotus.

"Epicurus [distinguishes] two kinds of motion, that in a straight line and that which swerves away from the straight line." *Physical Selections*, Book 1, p. 40.

"Epicurus [says] that the world perishes in many ways, namely, as animal, as plant and in many other ways." *Physical Selections*, Book 1, p. 44.

"All others [assumed] that the world is animated and guided by providence; Leucippus, Democritus and Epicurus, on the other hand, make neither of these [assumptions], but say that it arose out of the atoms through nature not endowed with reason." *Physical Selections*, Book 1, p. 47.

"Epicurus [says] that the extremity of some worlds is tenuous, that of others is dense, and of these some are mobile, others are immobile." *Physical Selections*, Book 1, p. 51.

The following passage from Stobaeus, which does not belong to Epicurus, is perhaps one of the most elevated.

"Is there, Father, anything beautiful besides these? Only God" (by τούτων χωρίς one should understand σχῆμα, χρῶμα and σῶμα[a]), "my child, *rather that which is greater is the name of God*." Stobaeus, *Physical Selections*, Book 1, p. 50.

"Metrodorus, the teacher of Epicurus, [says] that ... the causes, however, are the atoms and elements." l.c., p. 52.

"[...] Leucippus, Democritus and Epicurus [say] that an infinite number of worlds [exist] to infinity in every direction; of those who assert an infinite number of worlds Anaximander [says] that they are at equal distance from each other; Epicurus, that the distance between the worlds is unequal." l.c., p. 52.

"Epicurus does not reject any of them" (i.e., the views on the stars),[b] "he adheres to the possible." l.c., p. 54.

"Epicurus says that the sun is a big lump of earth similar to pumice-stone and sponge-like, which has been set on fire through its holes." l.c., p. 56.

The passage cited above from the *Physical Selections*, Book 1, p. 5[c] seems, more than the passage quoted by Schaubach, to confirm the view that there are two kinds of atoms. In this passage of the *Selections*, the ὁμοιότητες[d] are adduced as indestructible principles alongside the atoms and the void; they are not εἴδολα,[e] but are explained: αἱ δὲ λέγονται ὁμοιομερείαι καὶ στοιχεῖα.[f] Thus it follows from this passage that the atoms, which underlie appearance, as elements, have no homoeomerias, and possess the

---

[a] Shape, colour and body.— *Ed.*
[b] The words in brackets were written by Marx in German in the original.— *Ed.*
[c] See this volume, p. 485.— *Ed.*
[d] Homoeomerias.— *Ed.*
[e] Images.— *Ed.*
[f] Which are called homoeomerias and elements.— *Ed.*

qualities of the bodies of which they are the basis. This is in any case false. In the same way Metrodorus adduces as cause αἱ ἄτομοι καὶ τὰ στοιχεῖα [a] (p. 52).

CLEMENT OF ALEXANDRIA, *WORKS*, COLOGNE, 1688

"Epicurus also pilfered his leading dogmas from Democritus." *The Miscellanies*, Book VI, p. 629.

"[...] Homer, while representing the gods as subject to human passions, appears to know the Divine Being, whom Epicurus does not so revére." *The Miscellanies*, Book V, p. 604.

"Epicurus also says that the removal of pain is pleasure; and says that that is to be preferred, which first attracts from itself to itself, being, that is, wholly in motion.... Epicurus, indeed, and the Cyrenaics, say that pleasure is the first thing proper to us; for it was for the sake of pleasure, they say, that virtue was introduced, and produced pleasure." *The Miscellanies*, Book II, p. 415.

"...Epicurus thinks that all joy of the soul arises from previous sensations of the flesh. Metrodorus, in his book, *On the Happiness Which Has Its Source in Ourselves Being Greater Than That Which Arises from Circumstances*, says: What else is the good of the soul but the sound state of the flesh, and the sure hope of its continuance?" *The Miscellanies*, Book II, p. 417.

"Indeed Epicurus says that the man who in his estimation was wise, 'would not do wrong to anyone for the sake of gain; for he could not persuade himself that he would escape detection.' So that, if he knew he would not be detected, he would, according to him, do evil." *The Miscellanies*, Book IV, p. 532.

It does not escape Clement that hope in the future world is also not free from the principle of utility.

"If, too, one shall abstain from doing wrong from hope of the recompense promised by God for righteous deeds, he is not on this supposition spontaneously good (*ne hic quidem sua sponte bonus est*). ... For as fear makes that man just, so reward makes this one; or rather makes him appear to be just." op. cit.

"Epicurus, too, who very greatly preferred pleasure to truth, supposes faith to be a preconception of the mind (*anticipationem*); and defines preconception as a notion based on something evident, and on the obviously correct image; and asserts that, without preconception, no one can either inquire, or doubt, or judge, or even argue (*arguere*)." *The Miscellanies*, Book II, pp. 365 and 366.

Clement adds:

"If, then, faith is nothing else than a preconception of the mind in regard to what is the subject of discourse", etc.,

from which one can see what here by *fides intelligi debet*.[b]

"Democritus repudiates marriage and the procreation of children, on account of the many annoyances thence arising, and the abstraction (*abstractio*) from more

---

[a] The atoms and the elements.—*Ed.*
[b] Must be understood by faith.—*Ed.*

necessary things. Epicurus agrees, as do all who place good in pleasure, and in the absence of trouble and pain." *The Miscellanies*, Book II, p. 421.

"[...] but Epicurus, on the other hand (*contra*), supposes that only Greeks can philosophise [...]." *The Miscellanies*, Book I, p. 302.

"Well, then, Epicurus, writing to Menoeceus, says: 'Let not him who is young delay philosophising', etc." *The Miscellanies*, Book IV, p. 501. Cf. Diogenes Laertius, Letter to Menoeceus.[a]

"... but the Epicureans too say that they have things that may not be uttered (*arcana*), and do not allow all to peruse those writings." *The Miscellanies*, Book V, p. 575.

According to Clement of Alexandria, the apostle Paul had Epicurus in mind when he said:

"'Beware lest any man spoil you through philosophy and vain deceit, after the tradition of men, *after the rudiments of the world, and not after* Christ'; branding not all philosophy, but the *Epicurean*, which Paul mentions in the Acts of the Apostles, which *abolishes providence and deifies pleasure*, and whatever other philosophy honours the elements, but places not over them the efficient cause, nor apprehends the Creator." *The Miscellanies*, Book I, p. 295.

It is good that the philosophers who did not weave fantasies about God are rejected.

This passage is now better understood, and it is known that Paul had all philosophy in mind.

---

[a] See this volume, pp. 406-07.— *Ed.*

[Sixth Notebook]

[LUCRETIUS, *ON THE NATURE OF THINGS*]
Book IV

"[...] images of things, a sort of outer skin perpetually peeled off the surface of objects and flying about this way and that through the air." ll.34 ff.

"Because each particular floating image wears the aspect and form of the object from whose body it has emanated." ll.49 f.

"Similarly the films must be able to traverse an incalculable space in an instant of time, and that for two reasons. First, a very slight initial impetus far away to their rear sufficed to launch them and they continue on their course. Secondly, they are thrown off with such a loose-knit texture that they can readily penetrate any object and filter through the interspace of air." ll.192 ff.

"... it must be acknowledged that objects emit particles that strike upon the eyes and provoke sight. From certain objects there also flows a perpetual stream, as coolness flows from rivers, heat from the sun, and from the ocean waves a spray that eats away walls round the sea-shore. Sounds of every sort are surging incessantly through the air. When we walk by the seaside, a salty tang of brine enters our mouth; when we watch a draught of wormwood being mixed in our presence, a bitter effluence touches it. So from every object flows a stream of matter, spreading out in all directions. The stream flows without rest or intermission, since our senses are perpetually alert and everything is always liable to be seen or smelt or to provoke sensation by sound." ll.217 ff.

"Again, when some shape or other is handled in the dark, it is recognised as the same shape that in a clear and shining light is plain to see. It follows that touch and sight are provoked by the same stimulus." ll.231 ff.

"*This shows that the cause of seeing lies in these films* and without these nothing can be seen." ll.238 f.

"That is how we perceive the distance of each object; the more air is driven in front of the film and the longer the draught that brushes through our eyes, the more remote the object is seen to be. Of course this all happens so quickly that we perceive the nature of the object and its distance simultaneously." ll.251 ff.

"A similar thing happens when a mirrored image projects itself upon our sight. On its way to us the film shoves and drives before it all the air that intervenes between itself and the eyes, so that we feel all this before perceiving the mirror. When we have perceived the mirror itself, then the film that travels from us to it and is reflected comes back to our eyes, pushing another lot of air in front of it, so that we perceive this before the image, which thus appears to lie at some distance from the mirror." ll. 280 ff.

Book V

"The whole substance and structure of the world, upheld through many years, will crash." ll. 96 f.

"May reason rather than the event itself convince you that the whole world can collapse with one ear-splitting crack!" ll. 109 f.

"For naturally a whole whose members and parts we see to consist of created matter in mortal forms is by the same rule discerned to be likewise created and mortal. So ... it is a fair inference that sky and earth too had their birthday and will have their day of doom." ll. 241 ff.

"... you will see ... temples and images of the gods defaced, their destined span not lengthened by any sanctity that avails against the laws of nature." ll. 307 ff.

"Again, there can only be three kinds of everlasting objects. The first, owing to the absolute solidity of their substance, can repel blows and let nothing penetrate them so as to unknit their close texture from within. Such are the atoms of matter, whose nature I have already demonstrated. The second kind can last for ever because it is immune from blows. Such is empty space, which remains untouched and not subject to any impact. Last is that which has no available place surrounding it into which its matter can disperse and disintegrate. It is for this reason that the sum total of the universe is everlasting, having no space outside it into which the matter can escape and no matter that can enter and disintegrate it by the force of impact." ll. 352 ff.

"It follows that the doorway of death is not barred to sky and sun and earth and the sea's unfathomed floods. It lies tremendously open and confronts them with a yawning chasm." ll. 374 ff.

"Already in those early days men had visions when their minds were awake, and more clearly in sleep, of divine figures, dignified in mien and impressive in stature. To these figures they attributed sentience, because they were seen to move their limbs and give voice to lordly utterances appropriate to their stately features and stalwart frames. They further credited them with eternal life, because their shape was perpetually renewed and their appearance unchanging and in general because they thought that beings of such strength could not lightly be subdued by any force. They pictured their lot as far superior to that of mortals, because none of them was tormented by the fear of death, and also because in dreams they saw them perform all sorts of miracles without the slightest effort." ll. 1168 ff.

Book VI[185]

As the νοῦς [a] of Anaxagoras comes into motion in the Sophists (here the νοῦς becomes *realiter*[b] the not-being of the world) and this immediate *daemonic motion* as such becomes objective in the *daemon* of Socrates, so also the practical motion in Socrates becomes a general and ideal one in Plato, and the νοῦς expands itself into a realm of ideas. In Aristotle this process is apprehended again in individuality, but this is now true conceptual individuality.

---

[a] Reason.—*Ed.*
[b] Really.—*Ed.*

As in the history of philosophy there are nodal points which raise philosophy in itself to concretion, apprehend abstract principles in a totality, and thus break off the rectilinear process, so also there are moments when philosophy turns its eyes to the external world, and no longer apprehends it, but, as a practical person, weaves, as it were, intrigues with the world, emerges from the transparent kingdom of Amenthes and throws itself on the breast of the worldly Siren. That is the carnival of philosophy, whether it disguises itself as a dog like the Cynic, in priestly vestments like the Alexandrian, or in fragrant spring array like the Epicurean. It is essential that philosophy should then wear character masks. As Deucalion, according to the legend, cast stones behind him in creating human beings, so philosophy casts its regard behind it (the bones of its mother are luminous eyes) when its heart is set on creating a world; but as Prometheus, having stolen fire from heaven, begins to build houses and to settle upon the earth, so philosophy, expanded to be the whole world, turns against the world of appearance. The same now with the philosophy of Hegel.

While philosophy has sealed itself off to form a consummate, total world, the determination of this totality is conditioned by the general development of philosophy, just as that development is the condition of the form in which philosophy turns into a practical relationship towards reality; thus the totality of the world in general is divided within itself, and this division is carried to the extreme, for spiritual existence has been freed, has been enriched to universality, the heart-beat has become in itself the differentiation in the concrete form which is the whole organism. The division of the world is total only when its aspects are totalities. The world confronting a philosophy total in itself is therefore a world torn apart. This philosophy's activity therefore also appears torn apart and contradictory; its objective universality is turned back into the subjective forms of individual consciousness in which it has life. But one must not let oneself be misled by this storm which follows a great philosophy, a world philosophy. Ordinary harps play under any fingers, Aeolian harps only when struck by the storm.

He who does not acknowledge this historical necessity must be consistent and deny that men can live at all after a total philosophy, or he must hold that the dialectic of measure as such is the highest category of the self-knowing spirit and assert, with some of the Hegelians who understand our master wrongly, that *mediocrity* is the normal manifestation of the absolute spirit; but a mediocrity which passes itself off as the regular manifestation of the Absolute has itself fallen into the measureless, namely, into measureless pretension. Without this necessity it is impossible to grasp how after Aristotle a Zeno, an Epicurus, even a Sextus Empiricus could appear, and how after Hegel attempts, most of them abysmally indigent, could be made by more recent philosophers.

At such times half-hearted minds have opposite views to those of whole-minded generals. They believe that they can compensate losses by cutting the armed forces, by splitting them up, by a peace treaty with the real needs, whereas Themistocles, when Athens was threatened with destruction, tried to persuade the Athenians to abandon the city entirely and found a new Athens at sea, in another element.

Neither must we forget that the time following such catastrophes is an iron time, happy when characterised by titanic struggles, lamentable when it resembles centuries limping in the wake of great periods in art. These centuries set about moulding in wax, plaster and copper what sprang from Carrara marble like Pallas Athena out of the head of Zeus, the father of the gods. But titanic are the times which follow in the wake of a philosophy total in itself and of its subjective developmental forms, for gigantic is the discord that forms their unity. Thus Rome followed the Stoic, Sceptic and Epicurean philosophy. They are unhappy and iron epochs, for their gods have died and the new goddess still reveals the dark aspect of fate, of pure light or of pure darkness. She still lacks the colours of day.

The kernel of the misfortune, however, is that the spirit of the time, the spiritual monad, sated in itself, ideally formed in all aspects in itself, is not allowed to recognise any reality which has come to being without it. The fortunate thing in such misfortune is therefore the subjective form, the modality of the relation of philosophy, as subjective consciousness, towards reality.

Thus, for example, the Epicurean, [and the] Stoic philosophy was the boon of its time; thus, when the universal sun has gone down, the moth seeks the lamplight of the private individual.

The other aspect, which is the more important for the historian of philosophy, is that this turn-about of philosophy, its transubstantiation into flesh and blood, varies according to the determination which a philosophy total and concrete in itself bears as its birthmark. At the same time it is an objection to those who now conclude in their abstract one-sidedness that, because Hegel considered Socrates' condemnation just, i.e., necessary, because Giordano Bruno had to atone for his fiery spirit in the smoky flame at the stake, therefore the philosophy of Hegel, for example, has pronounced sentence upon itself. But from the philosophical point of view it is important to bring out this aspect, because, reasoning back from the determinate character of this turn-about, we can form a conclusion concerning the immanent determination and the world-historical character of the process of development of a philosophy. What formerly appeared as growth is now determination, what was negativity existing in itself has now become negation. Here we see, as it were, the *curriculum vitae* of a philosophy in its most concentrated expression, epitomised in its subjective point, just as from the death of a hero one can infer his life's history.

Since I hold that the attitude of the Epicurean philosophy is such a form of Greek philosophy, may this also be my justification if, instead of presenting moments out of the preceding Greek philosophies as conditions of the life of the Epicurean philosophy, I reason back from the latter to draw conclusions about the former and thus let it itself formulate its own particular position.

To define the subjective form of Platonic philosophy still further in a few features, I shall examine more closely some views set forth by Professor Baur in his work *Das Christliche im Platonismus*. Thus we shall arrive at a result by simultaneously clarifying opposing views more precisely.

Das Christliche des Platonismus oder Sokrates und Christus, by D. F. C. Baur, Tübingen, 1837.

Baur says on page 24:

"According to this, Socratic philosophy and Christianity, considered at their starting point, are related to each other as consciousness of self and consciousness of sin."

It seems to us that the comparison between Socrates and Christ, presented in this way, proves precisely the opposite of what is to be proved, namely, the opposite of an analogy between Socrates and Christ. Consciousness of self and consciousness of sin are, of course, related to each other as the general and the particular, that is to say, as philosophy and religion. This position is adopted by every philosopher, whether ancient or modern. This would be the eternal separation of the two fields rather than their unity, admittedly also a relationship, for every separation is separation of a unity. This means nothing more than that the philosopher Socrates is related to Christ as a philosopher to a teacher of religion. If now a similarity, an analogy is established between grace and Socrates' midwifery, irony, this means carrying only the contradiction, not the analogy, to the extreme. Socratic irony, as understood by Baur and as it must be understood with Hegel, namely as the dialectic trap through which human common sense is precipitated out of its motley ossification, not into self-complacent knowing-better, but into the truth immanent in human common sense itself, this irony is nothing but the form of philosophy in its subjective attitude to common consciousness. The fact that in Socrates it has the form of an ironical, wise man follows from the basic character of Greek philosophy and its attitude to reality. With us irony as a general immanent form, so to speak, as philosophy was taught by Fr. v. Schlegel. But objectively, so far as content is concerned, Heraclitus, who also not only despised, but hated human common sense, is just as much an ironist, so is even Thales, who taught that everything is water, though every Greek knew that no one could live on water, so is Fichte with his world-creating *ego*, despite which even Nicolai realised that he could not create any world, and so is any philosopher who asserts immanence in opposition to the empirical person.

In grace, on the other hand, in consciousness of sin, not only the subject which receives grace, which is brought to consciousness of sin, but even that which bestows grace and that which arises out of the consciousness of sin are empirical persons.

If therefore there is any analogy here between Socrates and Christ, it must consist in the fact that Socrates is philosophy personified and Christ is religion personified. But here it is not a question of a general relation between philosophy and religion; the question is rather in what relation personified philosophy stands to personified religion. That they have some relation to each other is a very vague truth or rather the general condition of the question, not the particular basis of the answer. In this striving to prove the existence of a Christian element in Socrates, the relation between the two persons, namely Christ and Socrates, is defined no further than as the relation in general of a philosopher to a teacher of religion; the same vacuity is revealed when the general moral division of Socrates' Idea, Plato's Republic, is placed in relationship to the general division of the Idea, and Christ as a historical personality in relationship mainly to the church.[a]

---

[a] After this the following is crossed out in the manuscript: Thereby the important fact is overlooked that Plato's Republic is his own product, whereas the church is something totally different from Christ.— *Ed.*

If Hegel's pronouncement, which Baur accepts, is correct,[a] that in his Republic Plato asserted Greek substantiality against the irrupting principle of subjectivity, then Plato is diametrically opposed to Christ, since Christ asserted this element of subjectivity against the existing state, which he characterised as only worldly, and therefore unholy. The fact that Plato's Republic remained an ideal, whereas the Christian church achieved reality, was not the real difference but was expressed reversed in Plato's Idea following reality, whereas that of Christ preceded it.

In general it is far more correct to say that there are Platonic elements in Christianity rather than Christian elements in Plato, particularly as the earliest Fathers of the Church proceeded historically in part from Platonic philosophy, e.g., Origen, Irenaeus. From the philosophical point of view it is important that in Plato's Republic the first estate is that of the learned or the wise. It is the same with the relationship of Platonic ideas to the Christian logos (p. 38), the relationship of the Platonic recollection to the Christian restoration of man to his original image (p. 40), and with Plato's fall of souls and the Christian falling into sin (p. 43), myth of the pre-existence of the soul.

Relation of the myth to Platonic consciousness.

Platonic transmigration of souls. Connection with the constellations.

Baur says on page 83:

"There is no other philosophy of antiquity in which philosophy bears so much of a religious character as in Platonism."

This must also follow from the fact that Plato defines the "task of philosophy" (p. 86) as a λύσις, ἀπαλλαγή, χωρισμός[b] of the soul from the body, as a dying and a μελετᾶν ἀποθνήσκειν.[c]

"That this saving force in the final resort is ascribed to philosophy is, to be sure, the one-sidedness of Platonism [...]." p. 89.

On the one hand, one could accept Baur's pronouncement that no philosophy of antiquity bears so much the character of religion as the Platonic. But it would only mean that no philosopher had taught philosophy with more religious inspiration, that to no one philosophy had to a greater extent the determination and the form, as it were, of a religious cult. With the more intensive

---

[a] G. W. F. Hegel, *System der Philosophie*. Dritter Teil. "Die Philosophie des Geistes". §552.—*Ed.*

[b] Saving, freeing, separation.—*Ed.*

[c] Striving for death.—*Ed.*

philosophers, such as Aristotle, Spinoza, Hegel, their attitude itself had a more general form, less steeped in empirical feeling; but for that reason Aristotle's inspiration, when he extols θεωρια [a] as the best thing, τὸ ἥδιστον καὶ ἄριστον,[b] or when he admires the rationality of nature in his treatise περί τῆς φύσεως ξωϊκῆς,[c] and Spinoza's inspiration when he speaks of contemplation *sub specie aeternitatis*,[d] of the love of God or of the *libertas mentis humanae*,[e] and Hegel's inspiration when he expounds the eternal realisation of the Idea, the magnificent organism of the universe of spirits, is more genuine, warmer, more beneficial to a mind with a more general education, for that reason the inspiration of Plato culminates in ecstasy while that of the others burns on as the pure ideal flame of science; that is why the former was only a hot-water bottle for individual minds, while the latter is the animating spirit of world-historical developments.

Hence even if it may be admitted, on the one hand, that in the Christian religion, as the peak of rel[igious] development, there must be more points of contact with the subjective form of Platonic philosophy than with that of other early philosophies, it must equally be asserted on the same grounds that in no philosophy the opposition between the religious and the philosophical could be expressed more clearly, for here philosophy appears in the character of religion, while there religion appears in the character of philosophy.

Further, Plato's pronouncements on the salvation of the soul, etc., prove nothing at all, for every philosopher desires to free the soul from its empirical limitation; to draw an analogy with religion only shows a lack of philosophy, namely, to consider this as the task of philosophy, whereas it is only the condition for fulfilling that task, only the beginning of the beginning.

Finally, it is no defect of Plato, no one-sidedness, that he ascribes this saving force in the last resort to philosophy; it is the one-sidedness which makes of him a philosopher and not the teacher of a faith. It is not the one-sidedness of Plato's philosophy, but that by which alone it is philosophy. It is that by which he negates again the formula—which has just been denounced—[namely, the formula] of a task of philosophy which would not be philosophy itself.

---

[a] Theory.—*Ed.*

[b] The most pleasant and the best.—*Ed.*

[c] *On the Nature of Animals.*[186]—*Ed.*

[d] From the point of view of eternity.—*Ed.*

[e] Freedom of the human mind.—*Ed.*

"In this, therefore, in the striving to provide what has been cognised through philosophy with a basis independent of the subjectivity of the individual [i.e., an objective basis], lies the reason why Plato, precisely when he expounds truths which are of the greatest moral and religious interest, at the same time presents them in a mythical form." p. 94.

Is anything at all explained in this way? Does not this answer include as its kernel the question of the reason for this reason? The question that arises is: why is it that Plato felt the desire to provide a positive, above all mythical, basis for what is cognised by philosophy? Such a desire is the most astonishing thing that can be attributed to a philosopher, for it means that he does not find the objective force in his system itself, in the eternal power of the Idea. That is why Aristotle calls mythologising kenologising.[187]

On the surface of it, the answer to this can be found in the subjective, namely dialogic, form of the Platonic system and in irony. What is the pronouncement of an individual and is asserted as such in opposition to opinions or individuals, needs some support through which the subjective certainty becomes objective truth.

But then a further question arises: why is this mythologising to be found in those dialogues which mainly expound moral and religious truths, whereas the purely metaphysical *Parmenides* is free from it? The question is: why is the positive basis a mythical one and a reliance on myths?

And here we have the answer to this riddle. In expounding definite questions of morality, religion, or even natural philosophy, as in *Timaeus*, Plato sees that his negative interpretation of the Absolute is not sufficient; here it is not enough to sink everything in the one dark night in which, according to Hegel, all cows are black; at this point Plato has recourse to the positive interpretation of the Absolute, and its essential form, which has its basis in itself, is myth and allegory. Where the Absolute stands on one side, and limited positive reality on the other, and the positive must all the same be preserved, there this positive becomes the medium through which absolute light shines, the absolute light breaks up into a fabulous play of colours, and the finite, the positive, points to something other than itself, has in it a soul, to which this husk is an object of wonder; the whole world has become a world of myths. Every shape is a riddle. This has recurred in recent times, due to the operation of a similar law.

This positive interpretation of the Absolute and its mythical-allegorical attire is the fountain-head, the heartbeat of the philosophy of transcendence, a transcendence which at the same time has an essential relation to immanence, just as it essentially breaks through the latter. Here we have, of course, a kinship of

Platonic philosophy with every positive religion, and primarily with the Christian religion, which is the consummate philosophy of transcendence. Here we have therefore also one of the viewpoints from which a more profound relationship can be established between historical Christianity and the history of ancient philosophy. It is in connection with this positive interpretation of the Absolute that Plato saw in an individual as such, Socrates, the mirror, so to speak, the mythical expression of wisdom, and called him the philosopher of death and of love. That does not mean that Plato negated the historical Socrates; the positive interpretation of the Absolute is connected with the subjective character of Greek philosophy, with the definition of the wise man.

Death and love are the myth of negative dialectic, for dialectic is the inner, simple light, the piercing eye of love, the inner soul which is not crushed by the body of material division, the inner abode of the spirit. Thus the myth of it is love, but dialectic is also the torrent which smashes the many and their bounds, which tears down the independent forms, sinking everything in the one sea of eternity. The myth of it is therefore death.

Thus dialectic is death, but at the same time the vehicle of vitality, the efflorescence in the gardens of the spirit, the foaming in the bubbling goblet of the tiny seeds out of which the flower of the single flame of the spirit bursts forth. Plotinus therefore calls it the means of the soul's ἅπλωσις,[a] of its direct union with God,[188] an expression in which death and love and at the same time Aristotle's θεωρία,[b] are united with Plato's dialectic. But as these determinations in Plato and Aristotle are, as it were, presupposed, not developed out of immanent necessity, their submergence in the empirical individual consciousness in Plotinus appears as a condition, the condition of *ecstasy*.

Ritter (in his *Geschichte der Philosophie alter Zeit*, Part I, Hamburg, 1829) speaks with a certain repulsive moralising superiority about Democritus and Leucippus, in general about the atomistic doctrine (later also about Protagoras, Gorgias, etc.). There is nothing easier than to rejoice in one's own moral perfection on every occasion, easiest of all when dealing with the dead. Even Democritus' *learning* is made a subject of reproach (p. 563); mention is made of

"how sharply the higher flight of speech, *simulating* inspiration, must have

---

[a] Simplification.— *Ed.*
[b] Theory.— *Ed.*

contrasted with the *base attitude* which underlies his outlook on life and the world."
p. 564.

Surely that is not supposed to be a historical remark! Why must precisely the attitude underlie the outlook and not rather the other way round, the definite outlook and discernment underlie his attitude? The latter principle is not only more historical, it is also the only one according to which a philosopher's attitude may be considered in the history of philosophy. We see in the shape of the spiritual personality what is expounded to us as a system, we see, as it were, the demiurge standing alive at the centre of his world.

"Of the same content is also the proposition of Democritus that something primary, which did not come into existence, must be assumed, for time and infinity did not come into existence, so that to inquire after their origin would mean to seek the beginning of the infinite. One can see in this only a sophistical denial of the question of the origin of all phenomena." p. 567.

I can see in that assertion of Ritter's only a moral denial of the question concerning the basis of this Democritean determination; the infinite is posited in the atom as a principle, it is contained in the definition of the atom. To inquire after the basis of the definition would, of course, be to negate his definition of the concept.

"Democritus ascribes to the atom only one physical property, *weight*.... One can again recognise here the mathematical interest which seeks to save the applicability of mathematics to the calculation of weight." p. 568.
"Hence the atomists deduced motion also from necessity, conceiving the latter as the causelessness of motion receding into the indeterminate." p. 570.

[IX, 19] "Democritus, however, holds that certain images approach (meet) men; some of these have a beneficial effect, others a harmful one[a]; for this reason also he prays that only images endowed with reason should meet him. But these are big and gigantic and indeed very *hard to destroy*, but not *indestructible*; he says they foretell men the future, are visible and emit sound. Proceeding from the notion of these images, the ancients conjectured that there is a god [....]" Sextus Empiricus, *Against the Professors*, p. 311.
[20-21] "Now Aristotle said that the notion of god arose in men from two factors, from the processes in the soul and from the heavenly phenomena. From the processes in the soul because of the divine inspiration of the soul in sleep and because of the prophecies. For, he says, when the soul in sleep becomes independent, it discards its own nature, has premonitions and foretells the future.... For this reason, he says, men have surmised that god is something which in itself resembles the soul and the most intelligent of all. But also from the heavenly phenomena." op. cit., pp. 311 f.
[25] "Epicurus believes that men derived the notion of god from the visions of fantasy which appear during sleep. For, he says, since in sleep big images

---

[a] In the manuscript this part of the quotation is given in German, the rest in Greek.— *Ed.*

resembling human beings appear, they assume that in reality also there are some such gods resembling human beings." op. cit., p. 312.

[58] "[...] Epicurus, some say, admits the existence of God as far as the multitude is concerned, but not as far as the nature of things goes." op. cit., p. 319.

a) *Soul*, p. 321. *Against the Professors* [Book IX].

[218] "[...] Aristotle asserted that God is incorporeal and the limit of heaven, the Stoics that he is a breath which permeates even through things foul, Epicurus that he is anthropomorphic, Xenophanes that he is an impassive sphere.... [219] Epicurus declares that 'what is blessed and incorruptible neither feels trouble itself nor causes it to others'." *Outlines of Pyrrhonism*, Book III, p. 155.

[219-221] "But to Epicurus, who wishes to define time as the accidental of accidentals (σύμπτωμα συμπτωάτων), can be objected, besides many other things, that everything which behaves as substance belongs to the substrates, to the underlying subjects; but what is called accidental possesses no consistency, since it is not separate from the substances. For there is no resistance (ἀντιτυπία) except the bodies which resist, no making way (εἶξις) (yielding) except that which yields and the void, etc." [*Against the Professors*, Book IX, p. 417.] [a]

[240-241] "Hence Epicurus, who says that a *body* must be *thought of* as a *composition of size, and shape, resistance* and weight, forces us to think of an existing body as consisting of non-existing bodies.... Hence, in order that there may be time, there must be accidentals; but in order that there may be accidentals, there must be an underlying condition; and if there is no underlying condition, neither can there be time."

[244] "So if this is time,—and Epicurus says its accidentals are time"

(by this αὐτῶν [b] one must understand ἡμέρα, νύξ, ὥρα, κίνησις, μονή, πάθος, ἀπάθειά, [c] etc.),

"—then according to Epicurus, time will be its own accidental." *Against the Professors* [Book IX], pp. 420 and 421.

If, according to Hegel (see *Gesamtausgabe*, Vol. 14, p. 492), the Epicurean philosophy of nature deserves no great praise when judged by the criterion of objective gain, from the other point of view, according to which historical phenomena do not stand in need of such praise, the frank, truly philosophical consistency with which the whole range of the inconsistencies of his principle in itself is expounded, is admirable. The Greeks will for ever remain our teachers by virtue of this magnificent objective naïveté, which makes everything shine, as it were, naked, in the pure light of its nature, however dim that light may be.

Our time in particular has given rise even in philosophy to evil phenomena, guilty of the greatest sin, the sin against the spirit and against truth, inasmuch as a hidden intention lurks behind the judgement and a hidden judgment behind the intention.

---

[a] In the manuscript this paragraph is given in German with the Greek words inserted in brackets.— *Ed.*

[b] Its.— *Ed.*

[c] Day, night, hour, motion, rest, sensibility, insensibility.— *Ed.*

EPICUREAN PHILOSOPHY

Seventh Notebook

CICERO
I. *ON THE NATURE OF THE GODS*
II. *TUSCULAN DISPUTATIONS,* FIVE BOOKS [189]
CICERO, *ON THE NATURE OF THE GODS*

Book I

Chap. VIII [,18]. "Hereupon, Velleius began, in the confident manner that is customary with them [the Epicureans], afraid of nothing so much as lest he should appear to have doubts about anything. One would have supposed he had just come down from the assembly of the gods and from the intermundane spaces of Epicurus", etc., etc.

Chap. XIII [,32]. Fine is the passage from Antisthenes:

"... in his book entitled *The Natural Philosopher,* he says that while there are many *gods of popular belief,* there is *one god in nature* [...]."

Chap. XIV [,36]. Of Zeno the Stoic it is said:

"... in his interpretation of Hesiod's *Theogony* he does away with the customary and received ideas of the gods altogether, for he does not reckon either Jupiter, Juno or Vesta as gods, or any being that is so called, but teaches that these names have been assigned with a certain meaning to dumb and lifeless things."

Chap. XV [,41]. Of Chrysippus the Stoic it is said:

"In Book II [of his *Nature of the Gods*] he aims at reconciling the myths of Orpheus, Musa, Hesiod and Homer with what he himself said in Book I of the immortal gods, and so makes out that even the earliest poets of antiquity, who had no notion of these doctrines, were really Stoics."

"In this he is followed by Diogenes of Babylon, who in his book entitled *Minerva* transfers the birth of the virgin goddess from Jove to physiology and dissociates it from myth."

Chap. XVI [,43]. "For he [Epicurus] alone perceived that, first there must be gods, because nature herself has imprinted a conception of them on the minds of all mankind. For what nation or what tribe of men is there but possesses untaught some preconception of the gods? Such notions Epicurus designates by the word πρόληψις,[a] that is, a sort of preconceived mental picture of a thing without which nothing can be understood or investigated or discussed. The significance and

---

[a] Prolepsis.—*Ed.*

usefulness of this argument we learn in that work of genius, Epicurus' *Rule or Standard of Judgment*."

Chap. XVII [,44]. "... it must be understood that the gods exist, since we possess an instinctive, or rather innate, concept of them; but a belief which all men by nature share must necessarily be true.... [45] If this is so, the famous maxim of Epicurus truthfully enunciates that 'that which is eternal and blessed can neither know trouble itself nor cause trouble to another, and accordingly cannot feel either anger or favour, since all such things belong only to the weak'. [...] whatever is outstanding commands the reverence that is its due [...]."

Chap. XVIII [,46]. "From nature all men of all races derive the notion of gods as having human shape and none other... But not to make primary concepts the sole test of all things, reason itself delivers the same pronouncement. [47] ... what shape ... can be more beautiful than the human form? [48] ... it follows that the gods possess the form of man. [49] However, that form is not a body, but only a semblance of a body, it has no blood, but only the semblance of blood."

[*Chap. XVIII-XIX*.] "Epicurus ... teaches that the force and nature of the gods is such that, in the first place, it is perceived not by the senses but by the mind, not as solid things, or according to number, like that which Epicurus in virtue of their substantiality calls στερέμνια,[a] but as images, which are perceived by similitude and succession."

Chap. XIX. "Because an endless train of precisely similar images arises from the innumerable atoms and streams towards the gods, our mind with the keenest feelings of pleasure fixes its gaze on these images and so attains an understanding of the nature of a being both blessed and eternal. [50] Moreover there is the supremely potent principle of infinity, which claims the closest and most careful study; and we must understand that this nature is such that like always corresponds to like. This is termed by Epicurus ἰσονομία, or the principle of uniform distribution. From this principle it follows that if the *whole number of mortals be so many, there must exist no less a number of immortals*, and if the forces of destruction are beyond count, the forces of conservation must also be infinite. You Stoics are fond of asking us, Balbus, what is the mode of life of the gods and how they pass their days. [51] It is obvious that nothing happier is conceivable, nothing more abounding in all good things. For God does nothing, he is free from all ties of occupations, he toils not, neither does he labour, but he takes delight in his wisdom and virtue and he knows with absolute certainty that he will always enjoy the greatest and eternal pleasures."

Chap. XX [,52]. "This god we can rightly call happy, yours indeed most toilsome. For if the world itself is God, what can be less restful than to revolve at incredible speed round the axis of the heavens without a single moment of respite? But without rest there is no bliss. But if there is in the world some god who rules and governs it, maintaining the courses of the stars, the changes of the seasons and all the ordered process of things, and, watching over the land and the seas, guards the interests and the lives of men, is he not involved in irksome and laborious business! [53] We for our part deem happiness to consist in tranquillity of mind and entire exemption from all duties. For he who taught us all the rest has also taught us that the world was made by nature, without needing an artificer to construct it, and that which you say cannot be produced without divine skill is so easy that nature will produce, is producing and has produced worlds without number. Because you cannot see how nature can do all this without any intellect, you, like tragic poets, cannot bring your arguments to a denouement and

---

[a] *Steremnia*—solid objects.—*Ed.*

have recourse to a god. [54] His work you would certainly not require if you would but contemplate the immense and boundless extent of space that stretches out in every direction into which the mind projects itself and journeys onward far and wide without ever seeing any ultimate limit where it could stop. In this immense length and breadth and height there *flits an infinite quantity of atoms innumerable, which though separated by void yet cohere together* and *taking hold of each other form an unbroken series* out of which are created those shapes and forms of things which you think cannot be created without bellows and anvil and *so have saddled us with an eternal master whom we must fear day and night; for who would not fear a prying busybody of a god who foresees and thinks of and notices all things and deems that everything is his concern.* [55] *An outcome of this was first of all that fatal necessity which* you call εἱμαρμένη,[a] according to which whatever happens is the result of an eternal truth and an unbroken chain of causes. But what value can be assigned to a philosophy which holds like old women, and ignorant old women at that, that everything happens by fate? And next follows your μαντική,[b] in Latin *divinatio*, by which, if we listened to you, we should be so filled with superstition that we should be the devotees of soothsayers, augurs, oracle-mongers, seers and interpreters of dreams. [56] But Epicurus has set us free from these terrors and delivered us out of captivity, so that we have no fear of beings who, we know, create no trouble for themselves and seek to cause none to others, while we worship with pious reverence the transcendent majesty of nature."

Chap. XXI. Then follows Cotta's objection.

[58] "I ... pronounce that your exposition has been most illuminating, and not only rich in thought, but also *more graced with a charm of style than is customary in your school.*"

Chap. XXIII [,62]. "You said that a sufficient reason for our admitting that the gods exist was the fact that all the nations and races of mankind believe it. But that is at the same time a weak argument and a false one...."

(After relating that the books of Protagoras, in which he denied the existence of the gods, had been burnt in the assembly of the people and he himself driven out of the country, Cotta continued:)

[63] "From this I can well suppose that many people were caused to be more reserved in professing that opinion, since not even doubt could escape punishment."

Chap. XXIV [,66]. "... for the outrageous doctrines of Democritus, or of Leucippus before him, that there are certain minute particles, some smooth, others rough, some round, some angular, some curved or hook-shaped, and that heaven and earth were created from these, *not compelled by nature,* but *by some kind of accidental collision....* [67] Then is this the truth? For as to happiness I do not deny anything, of which you say that not even the divinity has it without being relaxed in idleness.... I will grant you therefore that everything is made out of indivisible bodies; but this takes us no further [68] for we are trying to discover the nature of

---

[a] Fate.— *Ed.*
[b] Divination.— *Ed.*

the gods. Suppose we allow that they are made of atoms, then they are not eternal. For what is made of atoms came into existence at some time; but if they came into existence, before they came into existence there were no gods. And if the gods had a beginning, they must also perish, as you were arguing a little while ago about the world conceived by Plato. Where then do we find your blessed and eternal, by which two words you mean God? When you wish to make this out, you take cover   in a thicket of jargon. For you said just now that God has no body, but a semblance of a body, no blood, but a semblance of blood."

    Chap. XXV [,69]. "This is a very common practice with your school. You advance a paradox, and then, when you want to escape censure, you adduce something which is absolutely impossible, so that it would have been better to abandon the point in dispute rather than to insist on it so shamelessly. For instance, Epicurus saw that if the atoms travelled downwards by their own weight, we should have no power to do anything, since the motion of the atoms would be determined by necessity. He therefore invented a device by which to *avoid necessity (a point which had apparently escaped the notice of Democritus)*: he said that the atom, while travelling vertically downward by weight and gravity, makes a very slight swerve. [70] To assert that is more shameful than not to be able to defend what he wants to defend."

It is of substantial significance that the cycle of the three Greek philosophical systems, which complete pure Greek philosophy, the Epicurean, the Stoic and the Sceptic, take over their main elements from the past as they were already there. Thus, the Stoic philosophy of nature is largely Heraclitean, its logic is similar to that of Aristotle, so that Cicero already noted:

    "... the Stoics, while they seem to agree with the Peripatetics as to substance, disagree in words." *On the Nature of the Gods*, Book I, Chap. vii [,16].

Epicurus' philosophy of nature is basically Democritean, his ethics similar to that of the Cyrenaics. Finally, the Sceptics are the scientists among the philosophers, their work is to compare, and consequently to assemble together the various assertions already available. They cast an equalising, levelling learned glance back on the systems and thereby brought out the contradictions and oppositions. Their method also has its general prototype in the Eleatic, Sophistic, and pre-Academic dialectics. And yet these systems are original and form a whole.

But they not only found ready-made building elements for their science; the living spirits of their spiritual realms themselves preceded the latter, so to speak, as prophets. The personalities associated with their system were historical persons, system was, so to speak, incorporated in system. This was the case with Aristippus, Antisthenes, the Sophists and others.

How is this to be understood?

Aristotle's remark about the "nutritive soul":

"It is possible for this ... to exist apart from the others; but for the others to exist apart from it is impossible, at least in mortal beings" (Aristotle, *On the Soul*, Book II, chap. ii),

must be borne in mind also in regard to Epicurean philosophy in order to understand it itself on the one hand, and, on the other hand, to understand Epicurus' own apparent absurdities as well as the ineptitude of his later critics.

With him the most general form of the concept is the *atom*; for this is its most general form of being, which, however, is in itself concrete and a genus, itself a species as against higher particularisations and concretisations of the concept of his philosophy.

The atom, therefore, remains the abstract being-in-self, for example, of the person, of the wise man, of God. These are higher qualitative additional determinations of the same concept. Therefore, in the genetic exposition of this philosophy one must not raise the inept question raised by Bayle and Plutarch, among others, as to how can a person, a wise man, a god, arise from and be composed of atoms. On the other hand, this question seems to be justified by Epicurus himself, for of the higher forms of development, e.g., God, he says that the latter consists of finer and more subtle atoms. In this connection it must be noted that Epicurus' own consciousness is related to its further developments, to the further determinations of its principle imposed on him as the scientific consciousness[a] of later people regarding his system.

If, for example, in respect of God, etc., abstraction being made of the further determinations of form which he introduces as a necessary link in the system, the question is raised of his existence, his being-in-self, then the general form of existence is the atom and the plurality of atoms; but precisely in the concept of God, of the wise man, this existence has been submerged in a higher form. His specific being-in-self is precisely the further determination of his concept and his necessity in the totality of the system. If the question is raised of any other form of being outside this, that is a relapse into the lower stage and form of the principle.

But Epicurus is bound to fall back constantly in this way, for his consciousness is atomistic like his principle. The essence of his nature is also the essence of his actual self-consciousness. The instinct which drives him, and the further determinations of this

---

[a] The manuscript has "unwissenschaftliche Bewußtsein" (unscientific consciousness), probably a slip of the pen; it should read "wissenschaftliche Bewußtsein" (scientific consciousness).— *Ed.*

instinct-driven essence, are similarly again to him one phenomenon among others, and from the high sphere of his philosophising he sinks back again into the most general, mainly because
existence, as being-for-self in general, is for him the form of all
existence whatsoever.

The essential consciousness of the philosopher is separate from
his own manifest knowledge, but this manifest knowledge itself, in
its discourses with itself as it were about its real internal urge,
about the thought which it thinks, is conditioned, and conditioned
by the principle which is the essence of his consciousness.

Philosophical historiography is not concerned either with comprehending the personality, be it even the spiritual personality of
the philosopher as, in a manner of speaking, the focus and the image
of his system, or still less with indulging in psychological
hair-splitting and point-scoring. Its concern is to distinguish in
each system the determinations themselves, the actual crystallisa-
tions pervading the whole system, from the proofs, the justifica-
tions in argument, the self-presentation of the philosophers as they
know themselves; to distinguish the silent, persevering mole of real
philosophical knowledge from the voluble, exoteric, variously
behaving phenomenological consciousness of the subject which is the
vessel and motive force of those elaborations. It is in the division of
this consciousness into aspects mutually giving each other the lie that
precisely its unity is proved.[a] This *critical element* in the presentation
of a philosophy which has its place in history is absolutely
indispensable in order scientifically to expound a system in
connection with its historical existence, a connection which must not
be [over]looked precisely because the [system's] existence is historical, but which at the same time must be asserted as philosophical, and
hence be developed according to its essence. Least of all must a
philosophy be accepted as a philosophy by virtue of an authority or
of good faith, be the authority even that of a people and the faith
that of centuries. The proof can be provided only by expounding its
essence. Anybody who writes the history of philosophy separates
essential from unessential, exposition from content; otherwise he
could only copy, hardly even translate, and still less would he be
entitled to comment, cross out, etc. He would be merely a copying
clerk.

The question to be asked is rather: How do the concepts of a
person, of a wise man, of God, and the specific definitions of these
concepts enter into the system, how are they developed out of it?

---

[a] In the manuscript two words of this sentence are not clearly legible.— *Ed.*

CICERO, *ON THE HIGHEST GOODS AND EVILS*

Book I

Chap. VI [,17] "Let me begin ... with physics, which is his [Epicurus'] particular boast. Here, in the first place, he is quite a stranger.... Democritus believes in ... atoms, that is, bodies so solid as to be indivisible, moving about in a vacuum of infinite extent, which has neither top, bottom, nor middle, neither beginning nor end. The motion of these atoms is such that they collide and so cohere together; and from this process result the whole of the things that exist and that we see. Moreover, this movement of the atoms must not be conceived as starting from a beginning, but as having gone on from all eternity. [18] He [Epicurus] believes that these same indivisible solid bodies are borne by their own weight perpendicularly downward, which he holds is the natural movement of all bodies; [19] but thereupon this clever fellow, encountering the difficulty that if they all travelled downward in a straight line, and, as I said, perpendicularly, no one atom would ever be able to overtake any other atom, accordingly introduced an idea of his own invention: he said that the atom makes a very tiny swerve,—the smallest divergence possible; and so are produced entanglements and combinations and cohesions of atoms with atoms, which result in the creation of the world and all its parts, and of all that is in them.... The swerving itself is an arbitrary fiction (for Epicurus says the atoms swerve *without a cause*, and nothing is more repugnant to the physicist than to speak of something taking place uncaused).... [20] Democritus, being an educated man and well versed in geometry, thinks the sun is of a vast size; Epicurus considers it perhaps *two feet* in diameter, for he pronounces it to be exactly as large as it appears, or a little larger or smaller. [21] Thus where Epicurus alters the doctrines of Democritus, he alters them for the worse; while for those ideas which he adopts, the credit belongs entirely to Democritus,—the atoms, the void, the *images, or as they call them, eidōla, whose impact* is the cause not only of vision but also of thought; the *very* conception of infinite space, ἀπειρία as they term it, is entirely derived from Democritus; and again the countless numbers of worlds that come into existence and pass out of existence every day", etc.

Chap. VII [,22]. "Turn next to the second division of philosophy ... which is termed λογική.[a] Of the whole armour of logic your founder ... is absolutely destitute. He does away with definition; he has no doctrine of division or partition; he gives no rules for deduction or syllogistic inference, and imparts no method for solving dilemmas or for detecting fallacies of equivocation. The criteria of reality he places in sensation; once let the senses accept as true something that is false, and every possible criterion of truth and falsehood seems to him to be immediately destroyed.... [23] He lays the very greatest stress upon that which, as he declares, nature herself decrees and rejects, that is, the feeling of pleasure and pain. These he maintains lie at the root of every act of choice and avoidance [...]."

Chap. IX [,29]. "[...] this Epicurus finds in pleasure; pleasure he holds to be the chief good, pain the chief evil. This he sets out to prove as follows: [30] Every animal, as soon as it is born, seeks for pleasure, and delights in it, as the chief good, while it recoils from pain as the chief evil, and so far as possible avoids it. This it does when it is not yet perverted, at the prompting of nature's own unbiased and honest verdict. Hence he refuses to admit any necessity for argument or discussion to prove that pleasure is desirable and pain to be avoided. ... it follows that nature herself is the judge of that which is in accordance with or contrary to nature...."

---

[a] Logic.— *Ed.*

Chap. XI [,37]. "So generally, the removal of pain causes pleasure to take its place. Epicurus consequently maintained that there is not such thing as a neutral state of feeling intermediate between pleasure and pain."

Chap. XII [,40]. "One so situated must possess in the first place a strength of mind that is proof against all fear of death or of pain; he will know that death means complete unconsciousness, and that pain is generally light if long and short if strong, so that its intensity is compensated by brief duration and its continuance by diminishing severity. [41] Let such a man moreover have no dread of any supernatural power; let him never suffer the pleasures of the past to fade away, but constantly renew their enjoyment in recollection,—and his lot will be one which will not admit of further improvement. [42] But *that which is not itself a means to anything else, but to which all else is a means,* is what the Greeks term the τέλος,[a] the highest, ultimate or final good. *It must therefore be admitted that the chief good is to live agreeably.*"

Chap. XIII [,45] "Nothing could be more useful or more conducive to well-being than Epicurus' doctrine as to the different classes of the desires. One kind he classified as both natural and necessary, a second as natural without being necessary, and a third as neither natural nor necessary; the principle of classification being that the necessary desires are gratified with little trouble or expense; the natural desires also require but little, since nature's own riches, which suffice to content her, are both easily procured and limited in amount; but for vain desires no bound or limit can be discovered."

Chap. XVIII [,57]. "Epicurus, the man whom you denounce as a voluptuary, cries aloud that no one can live pleasantly without living wisely, honourably and justly, and no one wisely, honourably and justly, without living pleasantly. ... [58] much less then can a mind divided against itself and filled with inward discord taste any particle of pure and liberal pleasure [...]."

Chap. XIX [,62]. "For Epicurus thus presents his Wise Man who is always happy: his desires are kept within bounds; death he disregards; he has a true conception, untainted by fear, of the immortal gods; he does not hesitate to depart from life, if it would be better so. Thus equipped, he enjoys perpetual pleasure, for there is no moment when the pleasures he experiences do not outbalance the pains; since he remembers the past with gratitude, *grasps the present with a full realisation of how great and pleasant it is,* and does not depend upon the future; he looks forward to it, but *finds his true enjoyment in the present* ... and he derives no inconsiderable pleasure from comparing his own existence with the life of the foolish. Moreover, any pains that the Wise Man may encounter are never so severe but that he has more cause for gladness than for sorrow. [63] Again, it is a fine saying of Epicurus that 'the Wise Man is but little interfered with by fortune; the great concerns of life, the things that matter, are controlled by his own wisdom and reason'; and that 'no greater pleasure could be derived from a life of infinite duration that is actually afforded by this existence which we know to be finite'. Dialectics, on which your school lays such stress, he held to be of no effect either as a guide to a better life or as an aid to thought. Physics he deemed very important. ... a thorough knowledge of the facts of nature relieves us of the burden of superstition, frees us from the fear of death, and shields us against the disturbing effects of ignorance, which is often in itself a cause of terrifying apprehensions; lastly, to learn what nature's real requirements are improves the moral character also...."

By the fact that we acknowledge that nature is reasonable, our dependence on it ceases. Nature is no longer a sourse of terror to

---

[a] Ultimate purpose.— *Ed.*

our consciousness, and it is precisely Epicurus who makes the form of consciousness in its directness, the being-for-self, the form of nature. Only when nature is acknowledged as absolutely free from conscious reason and is considered as reason in itself, does it become entirely the property of reason. Any reference to it as such is at the same time alienation of it.

[*Chap.* XIX, 64]. "On the other hand, without a full understanding of the world of nature it is impossible to maintain the truth of our sense-perceptions. Furthermore, every mental presentation has its origin in sensation: so that no certain knowledge will be possible unless all sensations are true, as the theory of Epicurus teaches that they are. Those who deny the validity of sensation and say that nothing can be perceived, are unable, having excluded the evidence of the senses, even to expound their own argument.... Thus physics supplies courage to face the fear of death resolution to resist the terrors of religion [...]."

Chap. XX [,65]. "Now Epicurus' pronouncement about friendship is that of all the means to happiness that wisdom has devised, none is greater, none more fruitful, none more delightful than this.... [68] Epicurus well said (I give almost his exact words): 'The same knowledge that has given us courage to overcome all fear of everlasting or long-enduring evil, has discerned that friendship is our strongest safeguard in this present term of life.

Chap. XXI [,71]. "If then the doctrine I have set forth ... is derived entirely from nature's source; if my whole discourse relies throughout for confirmation on the unbiased and unimpeachable evidence of the senses...."

[72] "No! Epicurus was not uneducated: the real ignoramuses are those who ask us to go on studying till old age the subjects that we ought to be ashamed not to have learnt in boyhood."

Book II

Chap. II [4], op. cit. "For he says that he does not hold with giving a definition of the thing in question [...]."

Chap. VII [21]. (A passage out of the χύριαι δόξαι[a] of Epicurus.) "If the things in which sensualists find pleasure could deliver them from the fear of the gods and of death and pain, and could teach them to set bounds to their desires, we should have no reason to blame them, since on every hand they would be abundantly supplied with pleasures, and from nowhere would be exposed to any pain or grief, that is, to evil."

Chap. XXVI [,82]. "In one of your remarks I seemed to recognise a saying of Epicurus himself,—that friendship cannot be divorced from pleasure, and that it deserves to be cultivated for the reason that without it we cannot live secure and free from fear, and therefore cannot live agreeably."

Chap. XXXI [,100]. "For he [Epicurus] ... stated ... that 'death does not affect us at all; for a thing that has experienced dissolution must be devoid of sensation; and that which is devoid of sensation cannot affect us in any degree whatsoever' [...]."

Book III

Chap. I [,3]. "In fact Epicurus himself declares that there is no occasion to argue about pleasure at all [...]."

---

[a] *Principal Doctrines.— Ed.*

PLAN OF HEGEL'S PHILOSOPHY
OF NATURE [190]

[First Version]

A. *General divisions.* The Idea as nature is:
   I) In the determination of *juxtaposition,* of *abstract singularisation,* outside which is the unity of form, *this* as merely an ideal being-in-self, *matter* and its *ideal system.*
   Mechanics. Universal nature.
   II) In the determination of *particularity,* so that reality is posited with immanent determinateness of form and the difference existing in it, a relation of reflexion the being-within-itself of which *is natural individuality.*
   III) *Singular nature.* The determination of subjectivity, in which the real distinctions of the form are likewise brought back to ideal unity, which is self-found and for itself — *Organics.*

I. *Mechanics*

A) *Abstract Universal Mechanics*

a) *Space. Immediate continuity;* as external are:
   α) The dimensions: height, length and *breadth.*
   β) Point, line and *surface:* on the one hand, a determinateness in regard to line and point; on the other hand, as restoration of the spatial totality: an enclosing surface which separates off an individual whole space.
b) *Time. Immediate discreteness:* The seen becoming: *present, future* and *past* (Now, etc.).
c) The immediate unity of space and time, in the determination of space. *Place,* in the determination of time — *motion,* their unity — *matter.*

B) *Particular Mechanics. Matter, Motion*
Repulsion — Attraction — Gravity

1) *Inert matter, mass, ...* as *content* indifferent to the form of *space and time.*
   External motion — *inert matter.*
2) *Impact. Communication of motion* — weight — *velocity* — *external centre, rest, centripetence* — *pressure.*
3) *Falling. Centrifugence.*

C) *Absolute Mechanics* or *Narrower Mechanics.*
Gravitation. Motion as a System of Several Bodies.
Universal Centre — *Centreless Singularity. Particular Centres.*

II. *Physics*

a) *Universality in physics.*
   1) *Universal bodies. Identity.*
      α) *Light* (*sun,* stars). *Darkness (smooth) (spatial relation* — direct).
      β) *Bodies of opposition.* **Darkness**
         1) as *corporeal diversity, rigidity, material being-for-itself.*
         2) *Opposition as such.* Dissolution and neutrality of lunar and cometary bodies.
      γ) *Bodies of individuality. Earth* or *planet* in general.
   2) *Particular bodies. Elements.*
      1) *Air,* negative universality.
      2) *Elements of opposition. Fire* and *water.*
      3) *Individual element, terrestriality, earth.*
   3) *Singularity.* The *elementary process.* The *meteorological process.*
      1) *Diremption of individual identity* into the moments of independent opposition, into *rigidity* and into *selfless neutrality.*
      2) *The consumption by spontaneous combustion of attempted differentiated existence.* Thus the *earth* became a *real* and *fruitful individuality.*
b) *Physics of particular individuality.*
      α) *Specific gravity. Density of matter.* Ratio of *weight of mass* to *volume.*
      β) *Cohesion,* seen as a *specific form* of *resistance* in mechanical behaviour towards other masses.

    Adhesion — cohesion, etc.
    Elasticity.
  γ) *Sound.*
  δ) *Heat.* (Specific heat-capacity.)
c) *Physics of singular individuality.*
  a) *Form.*
    α) Immediate form — the *extreme of pointedness of brittleness,* the extreme of *coagulating fluidity.*
    ß) The *brittle* disclosed into difference of the notion. *Magnetism.*
    γ) *Activity* which has passed *into its product,* the crystal.
  b) *Particular form.*
    α) *Relation to light.*
      1) *Transparency.*
      2) *Refraction.* (Internal *equalisation in the crystal.*)
      3) *Brittleness* as *darkening,* metallity *(colour).*
    ß) *Relation to fire and water. Smell and taste.*
    γ) *Totality in particular individuality. Electricity.*
  c) Chemical process.
    1) Combination.
      α) *Galvanism. Metals, oxidation, deoxidation.*
      ß) *The fire process.*
      γ) *Neutralisation. The water process.*
      δ) *The process in its totality. Elective affinity.*
    2) *Separation.*

[Second Version]

I

Mechanics

a) *Abstract Mechanics*

1) *Space.* Height, breadth, depth. Point, line, surface.
2) *Time.* Past, present, future.
3) *Place. Motion* and *matter (repulsion, attraction, gravity).*

b) *Finite Mechanics*

1) *Inert matter. Mass* as content. *Space and time as form, external motion.*

2) *Impact.* Communication of motion, weight. Velocity, external centre, rest, centripetence. Pressure.
3) Falling.

c) *Absolute Mechanics. Gravitation*

The various centres

II

Physics

a) *Physics of universal individuality*

α) *Free bodies*

1) *Light* (luminaries).
2) *Rigidity* (moon). Dissolution (comet).
3) Earth.

β) *Elements*

1) *Air.*
2) *Fire. Water.*
3) *Earth.*

γ) *Meteorological Physics*

b) *Physics of particular individuality*

1) *Specific weight.*
2) *Cohesion* (adhesion, cohesion, etc. Elasticity).
3) *Sound* and *heat.*

c) *Physics of total individuality*

α) *Form*

1) *Brittle pointedness, coagulating fluidity.*
2) *Magnetism.*
3) *Crystal.*

β) *Particular form*

1) Relation to *light.* Transparency, refraction, metallity, colour.
2) Relation to water and fire, smell, taste.
3) Electricity.

[*Third Version*]

I

a)

1) *Space,* 2) *time,* 3) *place,* 4) *motion,* 5) *matter, repulsion, attraction, gravity.*

b)

1) *Inert matter,* 2) *impact,* 3) *falling.*

c)

Gravitation, real repulsion and attraction.

II

a)

α) 1) *Luminaries.* 2) *Lunar and comet bodies.* 3) *Terrestriality.*
β) *Air, fire and water. Earth.*
γ) *The meteorological process.*

b)

1) *Specific weight.* 2) *Cohesion.* 3) *Sound and heat.*

c)

1) *Magnetism.* 2) *Electricity* and *chemism.*

III

a)

a) *Geological nature.*
b) *Vegetable nature.*

Written in 1839

First published in: Marx/Engels, *Gesamtausgabe,* Abt. 1, Bd. 1, Hb. 2, 1929

Printed according to the manuscript
Published in English for the first time

EARLY LITERARY
EXPERIMENTS

FROM THE ALBUMS OF POEMS DEDICATED TO JENNY VON WESTPHALEN [191]

From the *Book of Love* (Part I) [192]

CONCLUDING SONNETS TO JENNY

I

Take all, take all these songs from me
    That Love at your feet humbly lays,
Where, in the Lyre's full melody,
    Soul freely nears in shining rays.
Oh! if Song's echo potent be
    To stir to longing with sweet lays,
To make the pulse throb passionately
    That your proud heart sublimely sways,
Then shall I witness from afar
    How Victory bears you light along,
Then shall I fight, more bold by far,
Then shall my music soar the higher;
    Transformed, more free shall ring my song,
And in sweet woe shall weep my Lyre.

II

To me, no Fame terrestrial
    That travels far through land and nation
To hold them thrillingly in thrall
    With its far-flung reverberation
Is worth your eyes, when shining full,
    Your heart, when warm with exultation,
Or two deep-welling tears that fall,
    Wrung from your eyes by song's emotion.
Gladly I'd breathe my Soul away
    In the Lyre's deep melodious sighs,

And would a very Master die,
Could I the exalted goal attain,
    Could I but win the fairest prize—
To soothe in you both joy and pain.

III

Ah! Now these pages forth may fly,
    Approach you, trembling, once again,
My spirits lowered utterly
    By foolish fears and parting's pain.
My self-deluding fancies stray
    Along the boldest paths in vain;
I cannot win what is most High,
    And soon no more hope shall remain.
When I return from distant places
    To that dear home, filled with desire,
A spouse holds you in his embraces,
And clasps you proudly, Fairest One.
    Then o'er me rolls the lightning's fire
Of misery and oblivion.

IV

Forgive that, boldly risking scorn
    The Soul's deep yearning to confess,
The singer's lips must hotly burn
    To waft the flames of his distress.
Can I against myself then turn
    And lose myself, dumb, comfortless,
The very name of singer spurn,
    Not love you, having seen your face?
So high the Soul's illusions aspire,
    O'er me you stand magnificent;
'Tis but your tears that I desire,
And that my songs you only enjoyed
    To lend them grace and ornament;
Then may they flee into the Void!

Written in the latter half of October 1836

First published in: Marx/Engels, *Werke*, Ergänzungsband, Erster Teil, Berlin, 1968

Printed according to the manuscript

Published in English for the first time

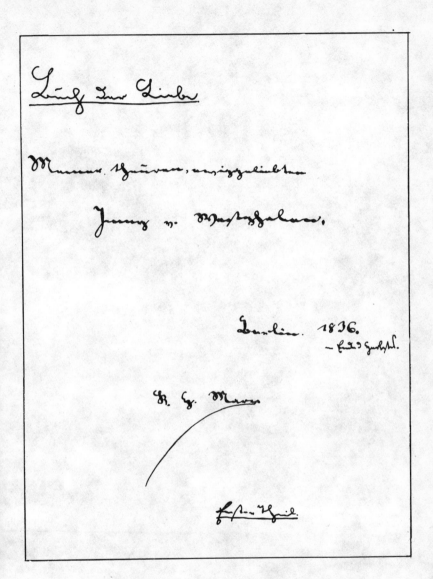

Title page of Marx's *Book of Love*,
with dedication to Jenny

From the *Book of Songs*[193]

TO JENNY

I

Words—lies, hollow shadows, nothing more,
    Growding Life from all sides round!
In you, dead and tired, must I outpour
    Spirits that in me abound?
Yet Earth's envious Gods have scanned before
    Human fire with gaze profound;
And forever must the Earthling poor
    Mate his bosom's glow with sound.
For, if passion leaped up, vibrant, bold,
    In the Soul's sweet radiance,
Daringly it would your worlds enfold,
Would dethrone you, would bring you down low,
    Would outsoar the Zephyr-dance.
Ripe a world above you then would grow.

TO JENNY

I

Jenny! Teasingly you may inquire
    Why my songs "To Jenny" I address,
When for you alone my pulse beats higher,
When my songs for you alone despair,
When you only can their heart inspire,
    When your name each syllable must confess,
    When you lend each note melodiousness,
    When no breath would stray from the
                       Goddess?

'Tis because so sweet the dear name sounds,
        And its cadence says so much to me,
And so full, so sonorous it resounds,
Like to vibrant Spirits in the distance,
        Like the gold-stringed Cithern's harmony,
Like some wondrous, magical existence.

II

See! I could a thousand volumes fill,
        Writing only "Jenny" in each line,
Still they would a world of thought conceal,
Deed eternal and unchanging Will,
Verses sweet that yearning gently still,
        All the glow and all the Aether's shine,
        Anguished sorrow's pain and joy divine,
        All of Life and Knowledge that is mine.
I can read it in the stars up younder,
        From the Zephyr it comes back to me,
From the being of the wild waves' thunder.
Truly, I would write it down as a refrain,
        For the coming centuries to see—
LOVE IS JENNY, JENNY IS LOVE'S NAME.

Written in November 1836

First published in Russian, in the journal
Inostrannaya Literatura No. 1, 1962

Printed according to the manuscript

Published in English for the first time

From the *Book of Love* (Part II) [194]

MY WORLD

Worlds my longing cannot ever still,
    Nor yet Gods with magic blest;
Higher than them all is my own Will,
    Stormily wakeful in my breast.

Drank I all the stars' bright radiance,
    All the light by suns o'erspilled,
Still my pains would want for recompense,
    And my dreams be unfulfilled.

Hence! To endless battle, to the striving
    Like a Talisman out there,
Demon-wise into the far mists driving
    Towards a goal I cannot near.

But it's only ruins and dead stones
    That encompass all my yearning,
Where in shimmering Heavenly radiance
    All my hopes flow, ever-burning.

They are nothing more than narrow rooms
    Ringed by timid people round,
Where it stands, the frontier of my dreams,
    Where my hopes reach journey's end.

Jenny, can you ask what my words say,
    And what meaning hides within?
Ah! 'Twere useless to speak anyway,
    Futile even to begin.

Look into those eyes of yours so bright,
    Deeper than the floor of Heaven,
Clearer than the sun's own beaming light,
    And the answer shall be given.

Dare to joy in life and being fair,
    Only press your own white hand;
You yourself shall find the answer there,
    Know my distant Heaven-land.

Ah! When your lips only breathed to me,
    Only one warm word to say,
Then I dived into mad ecstasy,
    Helpless I was swept away.

Ha! In nerve and spirit I was stricken,
    To the bottom of my soul,
As a Demon, when the High Magician
    Strikes with lightning bolt and spell.

Yet why should words try to force in vain,
    Being sound and misty pall,
What is infinite, like yearning's pain,
    Like yourself, and like the All.

Written in October-December 1836   Printed according to the manu-
Published in full for the first time   script

FEELINGS

Never can I do in peace
That with which my Soul's obsessed,
Never take things at my ease;
I must press on without rest.

Others only know elation
When things go their peaceful way,
Free with self-congratulation,
Giving thanks each time they pray.

I am caught in endless strife,
Endless ferment, endless dream;
I cannot conform to Life,
Will not travel with the stream.

Heaven I would comprehend,
I would draw the world to me;
Loving, hating, I intend
That my star shine brilliantly.

All things I would strive to win,
All the blessings Gods impart,
Grasp all knowledge deep within,
Plumb the depths of Song and Art.

Worlds I would destroy for ever,
Since I can create no world,
Since my call they notice never,
Coursing dumb in magic whirl.

Dead and dumb, they stare away
At our deeds with scorn up yonder;
We and all our works decay—
Heedless on their ways they wander.

Yet their lot I would share never—
Swept on by the flooding tide,
On through nothing rushing ever,
Fretful in their Pomp and Pride.

Swiftly fall and are destroyed
Halls and bastions in their turn;
As they fly into the Void,
Yet another Empire's born.

So it rolls from year to year,
From the Nothing to the All,
From the Cradle to the Bier,
Endless Rise and endless Fall.

So the spirits go their way
Till they are consumed outright,
Till their Lords and Masters they
Totally annihilate.

Then let us traverse with daring
That predestined God-drawn ring,
Joy and Sorrow fully sharing
As the scales of Fortune swing.

Therefore let us risk our all,
Never resting, never tiring;
Not in silence dismal, dull,
Without action or desiring;

Portrait of Jenny von Westphalen

Not in brooding introspection
Bowed beneath a yoke of pain,
So that yearning, dream and action
Unfulfilled to us remain.

Written in October-December 1836

Published in full for the first time

Printed according to the manuscript

TRANSFORMATION

Mine eyes are so confused,
    My cheek it is so pale,
My head is so bemused,
    A realm of fairy-tale.

I wanted, boldly daring,
    Sea-going ways to follow,
Where a thousand crags rise soaring,
    And Floods flow bleak and hollow.

I clung to Thought high-soaring,
    On its two wings did ride,
And though storm winds were roaring,
    All danger I defied.

I did not falter there,
    But ever on did press
With the wild eagle's stare
    On journeys limitless.

And though the Siren spins
    Her music so endearing
Whereby the heart she wins—
    I gave that sound no hearing.

I turned away mine ear
    From the sweet sounds I heard,
My bosom did aspire
    To a loftier reward.

Alas, the waves sped on,
        At rest they would not be;
There swept by many a one
        Too swift for me to see.

With magic power and word
        I cast what spells I knew,
But forth the waves still roared,
        Till they were gone from view.

And by the Flood sore pressed,
        And dizzy at the sight,
I tumbled from that host
        Into the misty night.

And when I rose again
        From fruitless toil at last,
My powers all were gone,
        And all the heart's glow lost

And trembling, pale, I long
        Gazed into my own breast;
By no uplifting song
        Was my affliction blessed.

My songs were flown, alack;
        The sweetest Art was gone—
No God would give it back
        Nor Grace of Deathless One.

The Fortress had sunk down
        That once so bold did stand;
The fiery glow was drowned,
        Void was the Bosom's land.

Then shone your radiance,
        The purest light of soul,
Where in a changing dance
        Round Earth the Heavens roll.

Then was I captive bound,
        Then was my vision clear,
For I had truly found
        What my dark strivings were.

Soul rang more strong, more free,
    Out of the deep-stirred breast
In triumph heavenly,
    And in sheer happiness.

My spirits then and there
    Soared, jubilant and gay,
And, like a sorcerer,
    Their courses did I sway.

I left the waves that rush,
    The floods that change and flow,
On the high cliff to crash,
    But saved the inner glow.

And what my Soul, Fate-driven,
    Never in flight o'ertook,
That to my heart was given,
    Was granted by your look.

Written between November 1836
and February 1837

Published in full for the first time

Printed according to the manuscript

A BOOK OF VERSE
DEDICATED BY MARX
TO HIS FATHER [195]

Written prior to April 12, 1837

First published in: Marx/Engels, *Gesamt-ausgabe*, Abt. 1, Bd. 1, Hb. 2, 1929

Printed according to the manu-script

Published in English for the first time

VERSE

of the year 1837
dedicated to my dear father
on the occasion of his birthday
as a feeble token of everlasting love

K. H. Marx, Berlin

Contents

Verse

To My Father
The Magic Harp. A Ballad
Yearning. A Romance
Nocturnal Love. A Romance[a]
Siren Song. A Ballad
The Little Old Man of the
    Water. A Ballad
The First Elegy of Ovid's
    Tristia Freely Rendered
The Madwoman. A Ballad
Flower King. A Fantastic Ballad
The Awakening
Invocation of
    One in Despair
Lucinda. A Ballad
The Last Judgment. A Jest
Two Singers Accompanying
    Themselves on the Harp.
    A Ballad
Epigram on Hegel
Epigrams on the Germans and
    on Pustkuchen
On a Certain Bald-head

Harmony
Distraught. A Ballad
Human Pride
Oulanem. A Tragedy. Act I
Song to the Stars
The Song of a Sailor at Sea
The Pale Maiden. A Ballad
The Forest Spring
The Fiddler. A Ballad[a]
Three Little Lights
The Abduction. A Ballad
Epigrams and Xenia
Sought
Found
Sonnet
Dialogue. A Ballad
Sea Rock
Man and Drum. A Fable
Evening Stroll
The Magic Ship. A Romance
The Man in the Moon
Night Thoughts. A Dithyramb
Dream Vision. A Dithyramb

Supplement

Some chapters from *Scorpion and Felix*. A Humoristic Novel.

---

[a] Published by Marx under the title of *Wild Songs*. See this volume, pp. 22-24.— *Ed.*

TO MY FATHER

I
CREATION

Creator Spirit uncreated
    Sails on fleet waves far away,
Worlds heave, Lives are generated,
    His Eye spans Eternity.
All inspiriting reigns his Countenance,
In its burning magic, Forms condense.

    Voids pulsate and Ages roll,
        Deep in prayer before his Face;
    Spheres resound and Sea-Floods swell,
        Golden Stars ride on apace.
Fatherhead in blessing gives the sign,
And the All is bathed in Light divine.

    In bounds self-perceived, the Eternal
        Silent moves, reflectively,
    Until holy Thought primordial
        Dons Forms, Words of Poetry.
Then, like Thunder-lyres from far away,
Like prescient Creation's Jubilee:

    "Gentler shine the floating stars,
        Worlds in primal Rock now rest;
    O my Spirit's images,
        Be by Spirit new embraced;
When to you the heaving bosoms move,
Be revealed in piety and love.

    "Be unlocked only to Love;
        Eternity's eternal seat,
    As to you I gently gave,
        Hurl you my Soul's lightning out.
'Harmony alone its like may find,
Only Soul another Soul may bind.'

Out of me your Spirits burn
    Into Forms of lofty meaning;
To the Maker you return,
    Images no more remaining,
By Man's look of Love ringed burningly,
You in him dissolved, and he in me."

II
POETRY

Flames Creator-like once poured
    Streaming to me from your breast,
Clashing up on high they soared,
    And I nursed them in my breast.
Shone your form like Aeolus-strains above,
Shielded soft the fire with wings of Love.

I saw glow and I heard sound,
    Heavens onward sweeping far,
Rising up and sinking down,
    Sinking but to soar the higher.
Then, when inner strife at last was quelled,
Grief and Joy made music I beheld.

Nestling close to forms so soft
    Stands the Soul, by spells enchained,
From me images sailed aloft.
    By your very Love inflamed.
Limbs of Love, by Spirit once released,
Shine again within their Maker's breast.

THE FOREST SPRING

In flowery grove I lost my way
Where forest spring showers silver spray
    In murmuring fall, o'erhead
    The lofty bay trees spread.

They see it ever rushing fleet,
They see it flowing at their feet,
    Burn in sweet shadows there
    To mate with Sea and Air.

But when it flees the hard land's thrall,
Loud thundering smites the rocky wall.
    Dizzy the flood spins round
    In mist-rings with no sound.

Through flowery groves it roams again,
Swallowing deep draughts of Death's pain,
    And then the tall bay trees
    Waft down sweet reveries.

THE MAGIC HARP

A Ballad

So strangely in the ear it sings,
Like thrilling harp, like trembling strings,
    It wakes the Minstrel sleeping.
"Why beats the heart so fearfully,
What are those sounds, like harmony
    Of Stars and Spirits weeping?"

He rises, springs from off his bed,
Towards the shadows turns his head
    And sees the cords of gold.
"Come, Minstrel, step you up and down,
High in the air, deep in the ground,
    Those strings you cannot hold."

He sees it growing, branching wide,
His soul is troubled deep inside,
    The sound swells in the air.
He follows, and it lures him on,
By ghostly stairways up and down,
    Here, there and everywhere.

He stops. A gate swings open wide,
A burst of music from inside
    Would carry him away.
A Lyre in golden splendour bright
Sounds forth in song all day and night,
    But no one's there to play.

It grips him like desire, like pain,
His bosom swells, his heart within
  Beats high beyond control.
"The Lyre plays from my own heart,
It is myself, its pangs—the Art
  That gushes from my soul."

In ecstasy he plucks the strings,
The sound trills high as mountain springs,
  Dives booming, like the abyss.
His blood leaps wild, far swells his song,
Was never yearning's pain so strong,
  He saw the world no more.

THE ABDUCTION

A Ballad

The Knight, he stands at the iron gate,
The Maiden so sweet and fair looks out.
"Dear Knight, however can I come down?"
And silence and darkness reign all round.

  "Catch this I throw, and it shall be
  Your rescue's sweetest surety.
Up there you can firmly bind the end,
And by the rope you may descend."

  "Ah, Knight, I fly like a thief to you,
  Ah, Knight, for love what won't I do!"
  "Dear love, you take but what's your own,
  We'll flee like shadows that dance and are gone!"

"Ah, Knight, the darkness yawns below,
My senses reel, I dare not go!"
  "Then you refuse; my life I'd stake,
  And yet at empty terrors you quake!"

"Ah, Knight, ah, Knight, you play with fire,
Yet you alone are my heart's desire!
  Farewell, ye Halls, forever and ay,
  Where never again my feet shall stray.

"What lures me on I cannot fight;
Ye loved ones all, I bid good-night!"
    No more she demurs and plays for time,
    She clutches the rope for the downward climb.

No sooner has she slid halfway,
Than she takes fright, her glances stray.
    Her arms grow weak, she must let go
    To fall on the breast of Death below.

"Ah, Knight, warm me once more, and I
Blissfully in your arms may die,
    Let me but breathe your every kiss,
    And I'll fade into sweet nothingness."

The Knight embraces her trembling form,
And to his bosom he presses her, warm.
    And as their souls together strain,
    He too is pierced by mortal pain.

"Farewell, my Love, so true, so kind!"
"Stay, and I'll follow close behind!"
    A flash, as of eternal fire,—
    Their souls depart and they expire.

YEARNING
A Romance

"Why sighs your breast, why glows your gaze,
    Why are your veins all burning,
As if Night weighs, as if Fate flays
    Down into storm your yearning?"

"Show me the eyes, like ringing bells,
    That glow in rainbows high,
Where brightness streams, where music swells,
    Where stars go swimming by.

"I dreamed this dream, so troublesome,
    Past all elucidating.
My head is void, my heart is numb,
    My grave shall soon be waiting."

"What dream you here, what dream you there,
    What lures to distant lands?
Here booms the Tide, here Hope rides fair,
    Here's fire in True Love's bonds."

"Here naught rides fair, here is no fire,
    But see what glimmers yonder,
I'm blinded, burning with desire,
    And I would fain sink under."

He stares aloft, his eyes shine bright,
    He shakes in every limb.
His sinews swell, his heart's alight,
    His soul departs from him.

THE VIENNESE APE THEATRE IN BERLIN

I

"The public's shoving, unafraid of bruises!
Some Talma there, perhaps, home of the Muses!"
Please, friend, sharp weapons don't attract.
It's comedy — by apes that act.

II

At ease, I watched the apes put on
Their show. And it was good clean fun.
So natural — just one thing missing,
Which was, to use the walls for p——.

Suddenly, somebody plucked my cloak.
"Really, that was a peculiar joke!
A young girl swooned at what she saw,
Flew on a monkey's breast and claws.
She batted her eyes, said timidly:
'O depths of exquisite agony!
O harmony! Delicious sorrow!
That monkey thrills me to the marrow!
I feel as if I were magnetised,
The ape played me; I loved him, hypnotised.
O monkey, speak, for I'm bewitched by you!
I just can't breathe, my head is spinning, too!'"

SIR (G)LUCK'S *ARMIDE*[196]

I

I also sought amusement, so
I spared no money for a show,
Threw on my frock-coat by lamplight,
And entered the nearest box that night.
I got much worse than I'd bargained for;
Oh, how I cursed myself and swore.
A missie needs must make me hold
The libretto. I muttered, "My hand feels cold!"
"Well, then, wear gloves!" the lady cried.
"They get on my nerves, Miss!" I replied.
She bared her neck and bosom and all,
And asked me to keep an eye on her shawl.
Said I to her, "The fire burns low,
And raw flesh gives me vertigo!"
She shrieked, "Oh, wasn't the ballet divine!"
Said I, "O God, has the gazette got anything worth
                 reading about in the meantime?"

II

I sat, lost in the music's spell.
She sneered, "The man's a fool as well!"

TERMS OF ENGAGEMENT

Mistress: Now then, just what d'you want of me?
Maid: The usual terms. But one more thing—
        To avoid any family quarrelling,
        I must have visitors once a month for tea.

SENTIMENTAL SOULS

The butcher's slaughtering a calf. They cry.
The creature bellows till it's been bled dry.
They laugh. O Heaven, how very, very weird
The ways of Nature. A dog wears no beard.
Why all these ravings, as if from sunstroke?
We hear that even Balaam's Ass once spoke!

ROMANTICISM À LA MODE

The child who, as you know, once wrote to Goethe,
Wanting to make him fancy that he loved her,
    Went to the theatre one fine day.
    A Uniform then stalked her way
And came towards her with a friendly smile.
"Kind Sir, Bettina wishes, for a while,
    Smitten with sweet desire, to rest
    Her curly head upon your breast."
The Uniform then answered rather drily,
"Bettina, that is up to you entirely!"
    "Sweetie," she answered in a trice,
    "Of course you're sure I have no lice?"

TO THE SUN OF TRUTH (F. QUEDNOW)

Lamplight and star glimmer,
Depth of heart and beauty's shimmer,
    Soul's grace and white skin's bloom—
You never show them openly,
Sun of Truth you claim to be.
    Every bride has her groom,
Sun of Truth you well may call
Yourself—the Sun throws shadows, after all!

ON A CERTAIN KNIGHT-HERO

Dig at him here, dig at him there, and ever
You'll find that Knight and Hero merge together.
His dance-talk's up-to-date all right,
But ancient bugs eat him at night.

TO MY NEIGHBOUR ACROSS THE STREET

    She stares at me from over yonder;
    God, I can't stand it any longer.
    A little man, a yellow house,
    A woman lank and nauseous.
    Since Inspiration could take flight,
    I'd better pull the blind down—tight.

SIREN SONG

A Ballad

The wave, soft murmuring,
With the wind frolicking,
    Leaps up into the air.
You see it tremble, hover,
Tumble and topple over,
    It is the Sirens' lair.

They pluck the lyre to enthrall
In heavenly festival,
    In melody divine.
They draw both near and far,
Earth and distant star
    Into their song sublime.

Its charm is so profound
One cannot chide the sound
    That soars so radiantly.
As if great spirits there
Would lure the listener
    Into the dark blue sea.

As if there swells and grows
From waves a world that flows
    Loftily, secretly.
As if in waters deep
The Gods are all asleep
    Down in the dark blue sea.

A little boat draws near,
The waves are charmed to hear
    A gentle bard exalted,
His looks so frank and free,
Image and melody
    Like love and hope transfigured.

His lyre rules o'er the deep.
Naiads that were asleep
    Lend him their song-charmed ear.

And all the waves resound
With song and lyre's sweet sound
    And dance high in the air.

But hear the sad refrains,
The Sirens' far-off strains
    Of sweet melodiousness.
The poet to enthrall,
The Goddesses shine all
    In sound and loveliness.

"O youth, soar up and play,
    Rule o'er the listening sea;
The goal you seek is high,
    Your breast swells rapturously.

"Here, sumptuous water-halls
    Your song alone surprises,
And as the great tide falls,
    Ev'n so your music rises.

"Sportive waves bear it up
    And send it surging high.
The eye, bright, full of hope,
    Encompasses the sky.

"Enter our Spirit-Ring;
    Magic your heart shall gain,
Hear the waves dance and sing,
    They sound like True Love's pain.

"Worlds came from the Ocean,
    Spirits were borne on the tide
Which dared to cradle the High Ones,
    While the All was void.

"As Heaven and star-glow
    Look downwards, ever glancing
Into the waves below,
    Into the blue waves' dancing—

"As droplets, shivering, shaking,
    Enfold the Worlds in pride,
The spirits' life, awaking,
    Emerges from the tide.

"Seeking the All inspires you?
    You'd burn in song away?
The lyre's sweet music stirs you?
    You'd blaze in Heaven's ray?—

"Then come down to us all,
    And tender us your hand;
Your limbs shall Spirit be,
    You'll see the deep, deep Land."

They rise up from the sea,
Hair weaving in roundelay,
    Heads resting on the air.
Their eyes flash blazing fires,
And, shooting sparks, their lyres
    Glow through the waters fair.

The Youth yields to Delusion,
His tears flow in profusion,
    His heart pounds in his breast.
He cannot turn away,
Held captive in Love's sway,
    To burning passion lost.

Deep thoughts stir in his soul,
It fights to gain control,
    Soars higher, ever higher,
Looks up with prideful bearing,
In God's own image daring,
    And this the Sirens hear:

"In your cold depths below
Nothing that's High can go,
    Nor God burn deathlessly.
You glitter but to ensnare,
For me you have no care,
    Your songs are mockery.

"You lack the bosom's beat,
The heart's life-giving heat,
　　The soul's high flight so free.
The Gods in my breast rule,
And I obey them all;
　　I mean no treachery.

"You shall not captivate
Me, nor my love, nor hate,
　　Nor yet my yearning's glow.
It shoots like lightning shafts
That gentle power uplifts
　　In melodies that flow."

The Sirens all sink down
Before his blazing frown
　　In weeping springs of light.
They seek to follow him,
But ah, the Flood so grim
　　Engulfs them all from sight.

A PHILISTINE WONDERS

"I don't know how they quarrel with themselves the way
　　　　　　　　　　　　　　　　　　they do.
Just button up your coat, good sir, and they won't steal
　　　　　　　　　　　　　　　　　from you."

MATHEMATICAL WISDOM

I

We have boiled everything down to signs,
　And Reasoning's done on strict mathematical lines.
If God's a point, as cylinder he just won't pass,
You can't stand on your head while sitting on your——.

II

If a's the Beloved and b is the Lover,
My shirt I'll wager ten times over
That a and b when added up'll
Constitute one Loving Couple.

III

Measure the World with lines about,
You'll never drive its Spirit out.
If feuds were settled by *a* and *b*,
The Courts would be swindled out of their fee.

THE LITTLE OLD MAN OF THE WATER
A Ballad

1

The waters rush with an eerie sound,
The waves are swirling round and round.
They seem to feel no pain at all,
As they break and fall,
Cold of heart, cold of mind,
Rushing, rushing all the time.

2

But down in the depths where the waters rage
Sits a mannikin, white with age.
He dances about when the Moon appears,
When little star through cloudlet peers.
Eerily hopping and skipping, he'd try
To drink the little streamlet dry.

3

Waves are his murderers, every one,
They gnaw his ancient skeleton,
It cuts through his marrow and limb like ice
To see them gambol in this wise;
His face is a grimace of sorrow and gloom
Till sunshine stops the dance of the Moon.

4

The waters then rush with an eerie sound,
The waves are swirling round and round.
They seem to feel no pain at all,
As they break and fall,
Cold of heart, cold of mind,
Rushing, rushing all the time.

TO THE MEDICAL STUDENTS

Damned philistino-medico-student crew,
The whole world's just a bag of bones to you.
When once you've cooled the blood with Hydrogen,
    And when you've felt the pulse's throbbing, then
    You think, "I've done the most I'm able to.
Man could be very comfortable, too.
How clever of Almighty God to be
So very well versed in Anatomy!"
And flowers are all instruments to use,
When they've been boiled down into herbal brews.

MEDICAL STUDENT PSYCHOLOGY

Who eats a supper of dumplings and noodles,
Will suffer from—nightmares, oodles and oodles.

MEDICAL STUDENT METAPHYSICS

No Spirit ever has existed.
Oxen have lived and never missed it.
The Soul is idle fantasy;
    In the stomach it certainly can't be found,
    And if one were able to run it to ground,
Then almost any pill would set it free.
Then Spirits would be seen
Emerging in an endless stream.

MEDICAL STUDENT ANTHROPOLOGY

He who would sickness foil
Must learn to rub his nether half with oil,
    So that no wind or draught
    Can chill him fore and aft.
Man also can achieve his ends
With dietary regimens;
    And Culture thus emerges
As soon as Man starts using purges.

MEDICAL STUDENT ETHICS

Lest perspiration harm, it's best
On journeys to wear more than just one vest.
    Beware all passion that produces
    Disorders of the gastric juices.
Do not let your glances wander
Where flames can burst your eyes asunder.
    Mix water with your wine,
    Take milk in coffee every time;
And don't forget to have us called
When leaving for the Afterworld.

THE FIRST ELEGY
of
Ovid's *Tristia*
Freely Rendered

1

Go, little book, make haste away,
    Go to the joyful victory seat.
I go not with you, I must stay,
    For by Jove's lightning I was hit.

2

Go, poorly clad and indigent!
    Put on your Master's mourning dress,
As is befitting banishment,
    And as commands this time of stress.

3

On you must shine no purple veil
    To make in violet's blood its show.
Longing and hope without avail
    Cannot wear joy's exalted glow.

4

In shameful silence hide your name,
    And let no scent of cedar waft,
Nor silver knob shine bright to shame
    The blackness of your crooked staff.

5

To works by Fortune blessed is due
    Such decoration, rare and bright.
Only my pain shall mate with you,
    Only my sorrow's darkest night.

6

Shaggy and rough you may appear,
    Like one whose hair unkempt hangs down,
Not rendered wondrous soft and fair
    By smoothing block of pumice-stone.

7

If darker is your pallid face,
    It is because by me 'twas stained.
Oh, how my tears have flown apace
    And hotly down on you have rained.

8

Go, book, and greet those places, greet
    The hallowed spot so dear to me.
Dreams take me there on pinions fleet
    Of magic word and fantasy.

9

If someone, seeing you, at last
    Should find his memory stirred, and pester
With questions flying thick and fast
    Of him who sent you there, your Master;

10

I'm still alive — that you may say,
    And that I hope for rescue soon,
And if my pulse still beats away,
    It is a mercy, not a boon.

11

If someone asks you further questions,
    Mind each and every spoken word.
Beware of thoughtless indiscretions,
    In word and tone be on your guard.

12

Many will scold you and berate you,
    Reminding you I was to blame.
As my accomplice they will rate you,
    You will cast down your eyes in shame.

13

To insults and to condemnation
    Listen, but keep your mouth closed tight.
Fire will not quench a conflagration,
    Two wrongs will never make a right.

14

Yet some there'll be, as you will find,
    Who speak to you with melting sighs.
A flow of gentle tears will blind
    The light of longing in their eyes.

15

Then tender words will flow and mild
    Forth from the bosom agitated.
"Could Caesar but be reconciled,
    The punishment be mitigated...."

16

Who says with kind solicitude,
    "May God be merciful on high,"
For him I pray with gratitude,
    "May thunder ever pass him by!"

17

Would his desire might be fulfilled!
    Oh, let me die there in that seat
Which the Gods in their keeping hold.
    May Caesar's lightning lose its heat!

18

When thus my greetings you've conveyed,
    They may lay charges at my door
That no sweet form has been displayed,
    And that my spirit fails to soar.

19

But let the critic be aware
    During what times the work was done,
And if his judgment's sound and fair,
    You need not fear—the danger's gone.

20

For poetry's magic fullness flows
    Out of a breast stirred with elation,
But oh, a pall of darkest woes
    Covers the brow, kills inspiration.

21

And then his lyrics all bewail
    The singer's exile, harsh and dread,
And storm, and sea, and winter flail
    Around his all-unheeding head!

22

Fear must not clutch with icy grip
    If splendid song is to be heard,
A lonely outcast here, I weep—
    Look, yonder gleams the murder-sword!

23

Whatever I have so far done
    Has won the fairer critic round,
And he will pass my message on,
    Bearing my grievous plight in mind.

24

Give me Maeonides, for one, (Homer)
    Plunge him in misery, like me,
His magic powers will be gone,
    Danger is all his eyes will see.

25

Go, book, go forth upon your way,
    Heed not the voice of evil fame.
If scornful folk cast you away,
    Do not be overwhelmed by shame.

26

'Tis not that Fortune's gentle waves
　　Bear me so lovingly along
That praise or prize my spirit craves,
　　That I seek recompense for song.

27

When with desire I still was bedded,
　　Then inspiration welled in me,
To thirst for glory I was fettered,
　　The world's race for celebrity.

28

But if the Lyre sounds as before,
　　And if the urge still burns as strong,
Surely my heart need ask no more,
　　Seeing my downfall came from song?

29

Go—it is not prohibited
　　That you should see Rome's pomp for me.
If only I might go instead,
　　Watched by a God indulgently!

30

Do not imagine that you'll wend
　　Your way unrecognised through Rome,
That to the public you will bend
　　Your steps unheeded and unknown.

31

Though you lack title, witnesses,
　　Your colour will betray your name.
If you deny me nonetheless,
　　You'll show yourself up just the same.

32

Slip quietly through the gates and watch
　　My songs inflict on you no hurt.
No more they sing love's praises which
　　So much delight the drunken heart.

33

Who turns you cruelly away
    Because you were born of my labours,
And sternly says you lead astray
    Innocence with voluptuous dangers —

34

To him say, "Only read my name.
    No longer do I teach sweet love.
Alas, the Gods to council came
    And passed stern judgment from above."

35

Seek not to climb to that great hall
    Which proudly dares to Heaven aspire.
Approach not Caesar's pack at all
    There, where his column soars still higher.

36

Those sanctified and sacred spots
    Your Lord and Master now disown.
The lightning from the castle shoots,
    The Higher Judgment strikes me down!

37

Though Gods great, merciful and mild
    Abide within those halls up there,
When the Spring's image comes with wild
    And furious storms, we shrink with fear.

38

Alas, the dove with frightened sound
    Will tremble, though but Zephyr stir,
While she is kissing dry the wound
    Inflicted by the hawk on her.

39

The frightened lamb that gets away
    From the wolf's fangs, will not again
Ever feel safe, unless it lie
    Huddled inside the low-walled pen.

40

If Phaethon were alive today,
    To Aether's vaults he would not soar,
Nor would he drive so recklessly
    The coveted chariot team of four.

41

Jove's weapons I indeed do dread,
    And from his sea of flame I flee.
When Heaven thunders overhead,
    I think he hurls his spear at me.

42

No sailor of the Argive fleet
    Who fled the Capharean shore,
Will ever turn his sails to meet
    Euboea's surging flood once more.

43

My bark, tossed by the tempest's force,
    Dares not draw nearer to that ground;
It veers off on a different course,
    For much more distant places bound.

44

And so, my book, be wise and sane,
    Mind how you go and take good care.
No need to seek the Higher Fame
    When common people lend an ear.

45

Icarus dared to soar on high,
    Audaciously he spread his wings.
His name was destined not to die,
    In the swift ocean wave it sings.

46

Whether to pull hard on the oars,
    Or leave the sails gently to swell—
Postpone it for another hour—
    Time and the place will quickly tell.

47

And when his brow is clear at last,
    When kindness beams upon his face,
When all his rage is of the past,
    Quiescent, gone without a trace;

48

When you, that still in terror stand
    And dare not yet approach from fright,
Are proffered friendly word and hand,
    Then go—to day now yields the night.

49

More softly tolls the hour of Fate,
    Unlike your Master you rejoice.
The torments of your wound abate,
    And Mercy speaks with gentle voice.

50

The hurt can only be made less
    By him who caused it in his rage.
Achilles wounded Telephus;
    The pain he caused he then assuaged.

51

Be sure not to spread any poison
    When trying to set matters right.
Hope, ever bright and airy vision,
    Terror can turn you into night!

52

Take care lest from its quiet repose
    Wrath in a violent storm should rise,
Piling upon me yet more woes
    That you have caused by deeds unwise.

53

But if within the Muses' shrine
    A happy welcome should await,
Bright in that house then you may shine
    Where Literature and Glory mate.

54

And there you may be sure to see
    Drawn up in line the brothers, those
Whom I begot in ecstasy
    After the day had reached its close.

55

All bear with open pride their names,
    In consciousness of victory:
Like hope upon their brows it flames,
    And like the joy of poetry.

56

Three only form a group apart,
    On every side by darkness pressed.
They swell, luxurious with "Love's Art",
               (*ars amandi*)
    And gaiety bubbles in each breast.

57

Flee them, or bravely dare to call
    For counsel fraught with curse and doom;
Remember Oedipus' dread fall,
    Telegonus' appalling crime!

58

Songs lately granted their salvation
    From violent death by fire and flame,
Tell you their tales of Transformation
              (*Metamorphosis*)
    And of worlds under Spirit-reign.

59

Now tell the story of the change
    That's overcome my Fate at last,
How it's turned into something strange,
    And how the form has been recast.

60

Once it was different, when I sucked
    Warmth from the red lips of Success.
Where the Immortals sealed their pact,
    The tears now flow of deep distress.

61

That you would ask what more I need
    Is plainly written on your face.
Meanwhile, the graceful Horae speed
    Onward their rushing waves apace.

62

And if with you I were to send
    All that seethes in my bosom now,
Oh, I would never reach the end;
    The weight would make the bearer bow.

63

The road is long. No time to spare,
    O book. Remotest of all lands
Here with the Scythians I must share;
    Estranged from all the rest it stands.

CONCLUDING SONNET TO JENNY

One more thing to you, Child, I must tell:
    Gay this farewell poem, my singing's end;
These last waves of silver throb and swell
    That my Jenny's breath its music lend.
Swift as over gulf and looming fell,
    Through cascade and forest land,
Life's fleet hours shall hasten on until
    Pure perfection's end in you they find.

Bravely clad in flowing robes of fire,
    Proud uplifted heart transformed by light,
Master now, from bonds released entire,
Firmly do I tread through spaces free,
    Shatter pain before your visage bright,
While the dreams flash out towards Life's Tree.

THE MADWOMAN

A Ballad

There dances a woman by moonlight,
She glimmers far into the night,
Robe fluttering wild, eyes glittering clear,
Like diamonds set in rock-face sheer.

"Come hither, O blue sea,
I'll kiss you tenderly.
Wreathe me a willow crown,
Weave me a blue-green gown!

"I bring fine gold and rubies red
Wherein there beats my own heart's blood.
On warm breast 'twas by lover worn,
Into the ocean he was drawn.

"For you, my songs I'll sing,
That wind and wave must spring,
High in the dance I'll leap,
And wind and wave must weep!"

She grasps a willow with her hand
And binds it with a blue-green band.
She eyes it in the strangest way,
And bids it lightly step away.

"Now lend your wings to me
To echo down the sea:
Mother, have you not known
How fair I've wreathed your son?"

So nightly here and there went she,
Decked every willow by the sea.
Proudly she danced there up and down,
Until her magic course was run.

TWO SONGS TO JENNY

SOUGHT

A Song

I rose, broke free of all that bound me;
"Where would you go?" "A world I'd find me!"
    "Are there not here lush meadows gay,
    Below—the seas, above—star-play?"

"Know, fool, I seek not to cross over,
There to strike rock, or sound the Aether.
    They bind so dumb the foot in pain,
    Their words of love become a chain.

"The world must rise out of myself
And to my breast incline itself.
    From my life's blood its well-springs come,
    My soul's breath—its aethereal dome."

I wandered far as I could go,
Returned, held worlds above, below.
    Within there leaped the stars and sun;
    The lightning flashed, and they sank down.

FOUND

A Song

Why do the bushes dance and swirl,
Why do the May-wreaths stray to heel,
    Why arches Heaven forever higher,
    And vales to cloudy peak aspire?

If I sail on my pinions there,
The echo falls from rock through air.
    Do eye and starlight marry ever?
    I look, my gaze is clouded over.

Roll forth, you waves of life, away,
Soar, smash those bridges in your way,
    By golden liberty inspired
    When you came soulless from the void.

Again the glance in recklessness
Stirs, sparks to bless'd forgetfulness.
Where should it have sought worlds? In you,
Into a very world it grew.

FLOWER KING

A Fantastic Ballad

1

"You in the sunshine, Mannikin,
Will you be the Flower King?
Ever runs your courage high,
Tinge us with your blood's red dye!"

2

"Flower bright and flower pale,
You've drunk my blood and drunk it deep.
Now my kingdom without fail!
In calyx, in calyx let me steep!"

3

"Sweet your blood was, Little Man,
Show your deep little heart, if you can.
If our King you would become,
Your heart must glisten in the sun."

4

"My heart, my heart beats high and true,
It shines forth fairly in my gaze.
If I gave up my heart to you,
Never again I'll feast my eyes."

5

"Mannikin, we'll jump and rest,
All of us, inside your breast.
Let your heart shine in the sun,
Flower King you shall become!"

6

He starts, he thinks, that Mannikin,
    He tears his breast rose-red apart.
"Give me sceptre, give me crown,
    Take, O take my deep little heart!"

7

"You in the sunshine, Mannikin,
Cannot be the Flower King.
No more your rose-red blood can spurt,
For us must glow your deep little heart."

8

The Mannikin plucks out his eyes,
    Digs himself a hole deep down,
Digs his own deep grave, and lies
    Buried, buried underground.

SEA ROCK

Marble pillar towers high,
    Jagged summit saws the air,
Putrefaction, life's decay,
    Moulders in the abyss down there.
Grim the cliff that upward climbs
Clamps the ground with iron limbs.

Round it spreads the radiance glowing
    From its mad and fevered brain,
Sends the ocean surge a-flowing
    Crazy, round and round again.
Weary moss shakes grey autumnal locks,
Blood seeps out from under laughing rocks.

Midnight comes, with voices roaring
    Crazy from the marble womb,
Like a thousand years' life thawing,
    Like remembrance howling doom.
Should the traveller dare to eavesdrop, he
Turns to stone and crashes in the sea.

THE AWAKENING

I

When your beaming eye breaks
Enraptured and trembling,
Like straying string music
That brooded, that slumbered,
Bound to the lyre,
Up through the veil
Of holiest night,
Then from above glitter
Eternal stars
Lovingly inwards.

II

Trembling, you sink
With heaving breast,
You see unending
Eternal worlds
Above you, below you,
Unattainable, endless,
Floating in dance-trains
Of restless eternity;
An atom, you fall
Through the Universe.

III

Your awakening
Is an endless rising,
Your rising
An endless falling.

IV

When the rippling flame
Of your soul strikes
In its own depths,
Back into the breast,
There emerges unbounded,
Uplifted by spirits,
Borne by sweet-swelling
Magical tones,

The secret of soul
Rising out of the soul's
Daemonic abyss.

V

Your sinking down
Is an endless rising,
Your endless rising
Is with trembling lips —
The Aether-reddened,
Flaming, eternal
Lovekiss of the Godhead.

NIGHT THOUGHTS

A Dithyramb

See overhead the cloud sails, lowering,
    Around its flanks roar eagle-wings.
Stormwards it rushes, fire-sparks showering,
    Night thoughts from morning's realm it brings.

Thought blazes up, so heavy-stupendous,
    Curse-frenzy batters the vaults of Aether.
Blood spurts from eyeball, terror-enormous,
    Sea-waves spit up at Heaven's rafters.

The silent Aether, tranquil-tremendous,
    Girdles the brow with blazing brands.
Clash of arms. In its womb — Ur-darkness,
    Cloud swoops, howling woe to the land.

INVOCATION OF ONE IN DESPAIR

So a god has snatched from me my all
    In the curse and rack of Destiny.
All his worlds are gone beyond recall!
    Nothing but revenge is left to me!

On myself revenge I'll proudly wreak,
    On that being, that enthroned Lord,
Make my strength a patchwork of what's weak,
    Leave my better self without reward!

I shall build my throne high overhead,
 Cold, tremendous shall its summit be.
For its bulwark — superstitious dread,
 For its Marshall — blackest agony.

Who looks on it with a healthy eye,
 Shall turn back, struck deathly pale and dumb;
Clutched by blind and chill Mortality,
 May his happiness prepare its tomb.

And the Almighty's lightning shall rebound
 From that massive iron giant.
If he bring my walls and towers down,
 Eternity shall raise them up, defiant.

THREE LITTLE LIGHTS

Three distant lights gleam quietly,
They shine like starry eyes to see.
The storm may rage, the wind may shout,
The little lights are not blown out.

One sweetly struggles ever higher,
Trembling to Heaven it would aspire.
It blinks its eye so trustingly,
As if the All-Father it could see.

The other looks down on Earth's halls,
And hears the echoing victory calls,
Turns to its sisters in the sky,
Inspired with silent prophecy.

The last one burns with golden fire,
The flames shoot forth, it sinks entire,
The waves plunge in its heart and — see! —
Swell up into a flowering tree.

Then three small lights gleam quietly
In turn, like starry eyes to see.
The storm may rage, the wind may blow,
Two souls in one are *happy* now.

THE MAN IN THE MOON

See, breathed upon by starlight's glance,
  Swift up and down a-hopping,
The Man in the Moon beats out his dance,
  His lively limbs a-bobbing.

Soft weeping dew of Heaven shines
  Tangled in curly hair,
Then trickles down on to the plains
  Till blossoms tinkle there.

And now it sparkles, sprouts apace
  In flakelets gold and pale.
The flowerbells tell the earthly place
  The Moonman's grievous tale.

He waves in such a friendly way
  But deep his sorrows smart.
He would be with the sinking ray,
  Lean to the Sun's full heart.

He's tarried long, he's listened long
  To hear the rising spheres.
He pines, he yearns to be a song,
  To thaw in dancing flowers.

Earth's glade is covered with his pain
  Till field and meadow ring;
Rapt with his own sweet shine, he then
  Beats, reconciled, his wings.

LUCINDA

A Ballad

Life seems wed to gaiety
  As the dancers tread the measure.
Each feels chosen specially
  For the sacred vows to pleasure.

Rosy cheeks flush ever higher,
  Faster still the heart's blood races,
And the longings of desire
  Lift the soul to heavenly places.

Kiss fraternal and hearts' union
 Close all in a circle round,
Gone the clash of rank, opinion,
 Love is lord and in command.

But it is an idle dream
 That enfolds warm hearts, and flies
From this dust and earthly scene,
 Surging to aethereal skies.

Gods can never bear to see
 Man, to his own folly blind,
Blissfully believing he
 May span Heaven with an Earth-born mind.

Through the lines a sombre guest
 Creeps with sword and knife, apart,
Envy's fire consumes his breast,
 And disdain his wretched heart.

She, now in the bridal wreath,
 Once was love and life to him;
Pledged him once her solemn troth,
 And her heart she gave to him.

So, to battle for the Good,
 Trusting her, he went away,
And his quest was crowned by Gods;
 Deed and valour won the day.

Wreathed in glory, he returns
 To the township, quiet and still,
Where his lovely jewel burns,
 Where desire and bliss do call.

Now he sees the battlements,
 And his heart beats violently,
Soon he shall win all he wants,
 Dream shall turn reality.

To the threshold now he races
 Of the house that he loves so.
Bright with many lamps it blazes,
 Guests are streaming to and fro.

But the footman there, aloof,
    Halts him with restraining hand.
"Stranger, would you climb the roof?
    Whither leads this rush so blind?"

"Man, I seek Lucinda fair!"
    Then the footman, open-eyed:
"Anyone may find her here,
    For Lucinda is the bride!"

Stunned, the stranger stands and sways
    In his full athletic height,
Stands with wide and staring eyes,
    Staggers up towards the gate.

"You should look your festive best
    For this gay and brilliant place,
If you want to be a guest!"
    Calls the footman's uncouth voice.

Proud and grim, he turns in haste,
    Takes the long-familiar way.
Heart with rage and grief obsessed,
    Fury darting from his eye.

To the place of his abode
    Flies he like the storm wind rushing,
And the door bursts open wide
    At his kicking and his pushing.

Grabs the candle from the maid,
    Stays his hand, lest tremor show;
With cold sweat the brow's bedewed
    That he beats in silent woe.

On his shoulders lets unfold
    Cape of purple, wondrous fair,
Decks himself with clasps of gold,
    Loosens and lets fall his hair.

To his bosom's sanctuary
    Presses he the gold-chased sword
That he wielded to the glory
    Of the one whom he adored.

Back he flies on wings of wind
    To the place of revelry,
Heart beyond all bridling,
    Deadly lightning in his eye.

Trembling, steps he through the door
    To the brilliant hall within.
Parcae name their victim, pour
    Curses hissing after him.

Draws he nearer, sad and bowed,
    Prideful in his stately cloak.
All the guests are frightened, cowed,
    By his awe-inspiring look.

Like a ghost he seems to stride
    Lonely through the crowded hall.
Onward still the partners glide,
    Foams the festive goblet full.

Many dancers throng the rows,
    But Lucinda shines the best.
From the filmy froth of gauze
    Swells voluptuous her breast.

Each is filled with silent yearning,
    Gripped by power all-pervading,
Longing, all their eyes are turning
    On that form in beauty gliding.

And her eyes, full of caprice,
    Laugh in undimmed radiance;
On she moves with body's grace
    In the many-coloured dance.

Past the man she lightly dances,
    Neither does he yield nor quail;
Clouded are her glowing glances,
    And her rosy cheeks turn pale.

She would mingle with the crowd,
    From the stranger turn away,
But a scornful hiss is heard
    And a God holds her in sway.

Grim, he looks her up and down,
 Ominously closes on her.
All the dancers, turned to stone,
 Questioningly eye each other.

But Lucinda's throat and breathing
 Seem as if by Gods pressed tight.
With her soul for respite striving,
 Clutches she her maid in fright.

"Ha! So I must find you faithless,
 Who once pledged yourself to me,
You, Lucinda, you a traitress,
 You another's bride I see!"

Then the crowd would rush upon him
 For his conduct in that place,
But he hurls the assailants from him,
 And like thunder sounds his voice.

"Let no one dare interfere!"
 Menace in his eyes is plain.
And all present, cowed, must hear,
 Listen to the voice of pain.

"Never fear, I shall not harm her,
 She shall not be hurt this night.
She need only watch the drama
 That I stage for her delight.

"Let the dancing not be over,
 Carry on your revelry.
Soon you shall embrace your lover,
 Soon you shall be free of me.

"I, too, shall the nuptial bond
 Celebrate this eventide.
But another way I've found—
 Night and Blade shall be my bride.

"From your eyes but let me suck
 Sensuous passion, sensuous glow.
Ah! Now I have seen your look,
 You shall watch my life's blood flow!"

Swiftly through him go the blades
 Long held ready in his hands,
Snapped are all life's quivering threads,
 Darkness on his eyes descends.

With a heavy crash he falls,
 Every muscle breaks in twain.
Death his prideful limbs enfolds,
 And no God wakes him again.

Then without a word she seizes
 Sword and dagger, quivering.
With the iron her skin she pierces,
 And the purple life's blood springs.

In a trice, the watchful maid,
 Shuddering at the bloody spray,
Wrests from her the deadly blade,
 Pulls the fatal steel away.

Then in pain Lucinda sinks
 On the corpse with grievous moan.
From his heart the blood she drinks,
 To his heart lets flow her own.

And the drapes of gauzy white
 That her slender body cover,
Redden now with bloodstains bright,
 Frothing, bubbling all over.

Long she moans there, hanging, clinging
 On to him who lies in death.
He might live, if only longing
 Soul back into clay could breathe.

Pale and bloody then she rises
 From the one she chose at last.
Slowly back the whole crowd presses,
 Murmuring, horror-struck, aghast.

And a Goddess, tall, uprearing,
 Her own doom's artificer,
Turns her gaze, destructive, searing,
 On the man who married her.

And a smile, ice-cold and mocking,
  On the pale lips starts to play.
Anguished wailing tells its shocking
  Tale of madness on the way.

Broken up the merry revels,
  Fled the dancers, one and all,
Silent now the clashing cymbals,
  Desolate the empty hall.

DIALOGUE WITH....

A Singer stands in festive attire,
Clasps to his bosom warm a lyre,
  And plucks the strings, enraptured.
"How play you my tunes, how sing my refrains,
How swell you, O Lyre, with soul that strains
  As if by your own fires captured?"

"Singer, think you that I am cold
To bosom's light, to yearning soul,
  To images upwards striving?
They shine as clear as the Land of Stars,
They surge, they soar like streaming fires,
  They lead to a Loftier Living.

"I knew with prescience profound
When called by your Word's sparkling sound,
  'Twas not your fingers touching.
It was a breath from sweeter lips
Uprising from the heart's own depths,
  A subtler music teaching.

"There shone a visage wondrous fair,
Haloed in song, in golden hair,
  That flashed forth rarest lays.
High beat her heart, eyes glowed sublime,
You were no more, you sank in dream,
  And I must honour and praise.

"Her image in me sank silently,
Like flower-shine rose out of me,
        As melting into sound.
But say, it falls, it soars again,
And yet for you cloud-veiled remain
        The sun and stars all round."

"O wondrous Lyre of magic skill,
Your joy's like bubbling founts that well,
        Ringed round with May-wreaths fair.
Her breath inspires, her eyes invite,
Your tones vibrate, your light beams bright,
        And rolls with the dancing spheres.

"One drinks, one sings of raptures blest,
Then Love flees echoing from the breast,
        One's spirits no more sound.
Yours was the dream, yours was the life,
You shine in her, afar I strive,
        You soar, I must bow down."

"Singer, though lulled by flower-dream,
I too reach out to Heaven's hem
        With golden stars to bind it.
The music sounds, life is in tears,
The music sounds, the sun shines clear,
        And distances are blended."

THE LAST JUDGMENT

A Jest

Ah! that life of all the dead,
        Hallelujahs that I hear,
Make my hair stand on my head,
        And my soul is sick with fear.

For, when everything is severed
        And the play of forces done,
When our sufferings fade for ever,
        And the final goal is won,

God Eternal we must praise,
    Endless hallelujahs whine,
Endless hymns of glory raise,
    Know no more delight or pain.

Ha! I shudder on the stair
    Leading to perfection's goal,
And I shudder when I hear,
    Urging me, that death-bed call.

There can only be one Heaven,
    That one's fully occupied,
We must share it with old women
    Whom the teeth of Time have gnawed.

While their flesh lies underground
    With decay and stones o'ershovelled,
Brightly hued, their souls hop round
    In a spider-dance enravelled.

All so skinny, all so thin,
    So aethereal, so chaste,
Never were their forms so lean,
    Even when most tightly laced.

But I ruin the proceedings
    As my hymns of praise I holler.
And the Lord God hears my screamings,
    And gets hot under the collar;

Calls the highest Angel out,
    Gabriel, the tall and skinny,
Who expels the noisy lout
    Without further ceremony.

I just dreamed it all, you see,
    Thought I faced the Court Supreme.
Good folk, don't be cross with me,
    It was never sin to dream.

TWO SINGERS ACCOMPANYING THEMSELVES
ON THE HARP

A Ballad

"What brings you to this Castle here
    To breathe Song's radiant aureole?
Seek you a loving comrade dear
    For whom in longing yearns your soul?"

"Know you him who soulful dwells therein,
    Ask you if he set my heart a-burning?
Can you tell me if the sight of him
    Ever favoured mortals drawn by yearning?

"Never have I seen that shine of his,
    Yet the gleam of precious stone
Burning on that splendid edifice
    Surely needs must lure me on.

"Truly, it might be my place of birth,
    Here might be my native land.
Ah! 'twas chosen by the gentle South,
    Turned towards the glow it stands.

"Here my melody more free resounds,
    And my breast the higher swells.
Sweet the golden Lyre's music sounds,
    As in joy of grief it wells.

"And I do not know that High Master,
    Him who strikes the heart-strings powerfully,
Nor the heavenly spirits that the Castle
    Harbours in its womb so secretly.

"And in vain is my desire's hot burning,
    Not for me the fair gates opening.
I lean on the columns, sadly yearning,
    Here Love's tribute I must sing!"

In despair her jet black hair she shakes,
    Bursts into a flood of tears,
And the other kisses dry her cheeks,
    Clasps her to her bosom's warming fires.

"I too am drawn by secret bonds
    To this divine and holy fane.
I quested wandering through the lands,
    Was pierced, as if by lightning's flame.

"But why the burning dew so spill,
    The tears of bitter sorrow weep?
We may enjoy the view at will,
    On flowery meadow dance and leap!

"The heart may glow more full in us,
    And sorrow may more sweetly come.
The looks may shine more luminous,
    Here the Most Beautiful's soon won!

"A humble cottage let us find
    Where we our songs of praise may sing,
Where the sweet West may play around
    In spirits' secret struggling."

Full many a day they lingered there,
    At eventide the strings were heard
That held entranced with sad allure
    Full many a flower and many a bird.

Once, as they both lay fast asleep,
    Arms clasped the gentle bodies round
On bed of moss full soft and deep,
    A Demon wondrous tall was found.

He bore them up on wings of gold;
    They were as bound in magic bonds,
And where that cottage stood of old
    A wondrous melody resounds.

EPIGRAMS

I

In its armchair, stupid and dumb,
    The German public watches it come.
Hither and thither rumbles the storm,
Heaven clouds over, more dark and forlorn.

Lightning hisses, snakes out of sight,
Feelings remain inviolate.
But when the sun comes out in greeting,
The winds soft sighing, the storm abating,
It stirs itself, makes a fuss at last,
And writes a book: *The Commotion Is Past;*
Is seized with an urge for fantasy,
Would plumb the whole thing thoroughly;
Believes it's extremely wrong of Heaven
To play such jokes, though brilliant even,
It should the All systematically treat;
First rub the head and then the feet;
Just like a baby it carries on
Looking for things which are dead and gone;
Should get the Present in proper perspective,
Let Heaven and Earth go their ways respective;
They've followed their courses as before,
And the wave laps quiet on the rocky shore.

II

ON HEGEL

1

Since I have found the Highest of things and the Depths of them
also,
Rude am I as a God, cloaked by the dark like a God.
Long have I searched and sailed on Thought's deep billowing
ocean;
There I found me the Word: now I hold on to it fast.

2

Words I teach all mixed up into a devilish muddle,
Thus, anyone may think just what he chooses to think;
Never, at least, is he hemmed in by strict limitations.
Bubbling out of the flood, plummeting down from the cliff,
So are his Beloved's words and thoughts that the Poet devises;
He understands what he thinks, freely invents what he feels.
Thus, each may for himself suck wisdom's nourishing nectar;
Now you know all, since I've said plenty of nothing to you!

3

Kant and Fichte soar to heavens blue
   Seeking for some distant land,
I but seek to grasp profound and true
   That which — in the street I find.

4

Forgive us epigrammatists
For singing songs with nasty twists.
In Hegel we're all so completely submerged,
But with his Aesthetics we've yet to be——
                         purged.

III

The Germans once actually stirred their stumps,
With a People's Victory turned up trumps.
   And when all that was over and done,
   On every corner, everyone
Read: "Wonderful things are in store for you —
Three legs for all instead of two!"
   This shook them badly, and in due course
   They were all smitten by deep remorse.
"Too much has happened at once, it's plain.
We'll have to behave ourselves again.
   The rest it were better to print and bind,
   And buyers will not be hard to find."

IV

Pull down the stars for them at night,
They burn too pale or far too bright.
   The sun's rays either scorch the eye
   Or shine from much too far away.

V

Of Schiller there's reason to complain,
Who couldn't more humanly entertain.
   Endowed with an elevating mind,
   He didn't stick to the daily grind.
He played with Thunder and Lightning much,
But totally lacked the common touch.

VI

But Goethe's taste was too nicely ordered;
He'd rather see Venus than something sordid.
Although he grasped things, as one should, from below,
It was for the Highest he made us go.
He wanted to make things so sublime
That Soul-grip evaded him most of the time.
Schiller was surely nearer the mark,
You can read his ideas in letters stark.
His thoughts are there in black and white,
Though it's hard to fathom the meaning aright.

VII

ON A CERTAIN BALD-HEAD

As lightning born of radiancy
Sparkles from cloud-realms far away,
Pallas Athena victorious
Sprang from the thought-filled head of Zeus.
Even so, in sportiveness unbounded,
On to his head she's likewise bounded,
And what in depth he could never plumb
Visibly shines on his cranium.

VIII

PUSTKUCHEN (FALSE WANDERING YEARS) [a]

1

Schiller, thinks he, had been less of a bore
If only he'd read the Bible more.
One could have nothing but praise for *The Bell*
If it featured the Resurrection as well,
Or told how, on a little ass,
Christ into the town did pass;
While David's defeat of the Philistine
Would have added something to *Wallenstein*.

---

[a] *Pustkuchen*—a punning reference to Johann Friedrich Wilhelm Pustkuchen, author of *Wilhelm Meisters Wanderjahre*, based on *Wilhelm Meisters Wanderjahre* by Goethe. *Pustkuchen* also means "puff cake", hence "hot air" or "nonsense".— *Ed.*

2

Goethe can give the ladies a fright,
For elderly women he's not quite right.
He understood Nature, but this is the quarrel,
He wouldn't round Nature off with a moral.
   He should have got Luther's doctrine off pat
   And made up his poetry out of that.
He had beautiful thoughts, if sometimes odd,
But omitted to mention—"Made by God".

3

Extremely strange is this desire
To elevate Goethe higher and higher.
How low in actual fact his reach—
Did he ever give us a sermon to preach?
   Show me in Goethe solid ground
   For Peasant or Pedagogue to expound.
Such a genius marked with the stamp of the Lord
That a sum in arithmetic had him floored.

4

Hear Faust in the full authentic version;
The Poet's account is sheer perversion.
   Faust was up to his ears in debts,
   Was dissolute, played at cards for bets.
No offer of help from above was extended,
So he wanted it all ignominiously ended.
   But was overwhelmed by a fearful sensation
   Of Hell and the anguish of desperation.
He then devoted due reflection
To Knowledge, Deed, Life, Death, and Perdition;
   And on these topics had much to say
   In a darkly mystical sort of way.
Couldn't the Poet have managed to tell
How debts lead man to the Devil and Hell.
   Who loses his credit may well conceivably
   Forfeit redemption quite irretrievably.

5

Since Faust at Easter had the gall
To think, why trouble the Devil at all?
Who dares to think on Easter Day
Is doomed to Hell-fire anyway.

6

Credibility too is defied.
The Police would soon have had enough!
They'd surely have had him clapped inside
For running up debts and making off!

7

Vice alone could elevate Faust,
Who really loved himself the most.
God and the World he dared to doubt,
Though Moses thought they'd both worked out.
Silly young Gretchen had to adore him
Instead of getting his conscience to gnaw him,
Telling him he was the Devil's prey,
And the Day of Judgment was well on the way.

8

There's use for the "Beautiful Soul". It's simple:
Just trim it with specs and a nun's wimple.
"What God hath done is right well done,"
Thus the true Poet hath begun.

CONCLUDING EPIGRAM
ON THE PUFF-PASTRY COOK

So knead your cake as well as you can,
You'll never be more than a baker's man.
And, after all, whoever asked *you*
To emulate Goethe the way you do?
As he knew nothing of your profession,
Whence came his genius and perception?

HARMONY

Know you that magic image sweet
When souls into each other go,
And then in one soft breath outflow,
Melodious, loving, mild, replete?
They flame up in one rose-bloom, blushing red,
And coyly hide deep in some mossy bed.

Roam far and wide throughout the land,
 The magic image you'll not find
 That talisman can never bind,
Nor sun's fierce rays portend.
The light of no sun ever gave it birth,
It never knew the nourishment of Earth.

Ever resplendent there it stays,
 Though Time its rapid pinions beats,
 Though bright Apollo guides his steeds,
Though worlds fade into nothingness.
 Alone its own true power did it create
 That neither world nor God can dominate.

Perhaps 'tis like the Cithern sounding,
 As played on one eternal Lyre,
 In endless glow, in endless fire,
In yearning's lofty urge resounding.
 Once hear within yourself those strings that play
 Your steps to wander shall not further stray.

DISTRAUGHT

A Ballad

I

All decked with finery
 She stands, in purple dressed;
A satin ribbon coy
 Is hidden in her breast.

And playfully there glow
 Sweet roses in her hair,
Some are like flakes of snow,
 The others—blood and fire.

But never a rose is playing
 Upon her pallid face.
She sinks, distressful, bowing,
 As hart shot in the chase.

Tremulous, pale she looks
    In diamonds' full display.
The blood drains from her cheeks
    Into her heart away.

"I have been driven again
    To gaiety's false allure,
My heart oppressed with pain,
    My wavering steps unsure.

"O'er soul's high-billowing sea
    Other desires have called.
Enough of this display,
    So loveless and so cold.

"I cannot understand it,
    Within my breast this flame;
Heaven alone can grant it,
    No mortal speak its name.

"I would bear suffering even,
    Willingly I would die,
That I might merit Heaven,
    A better land might see."

She lifts her tearful gaze
    To Heaven's radiance,
Her bosom's fantasies
    In sighs give utterance.

Quietly she lays her down
    And says a heartfelt prayer.
Sleep folds her gently round,
    An angel watches her.

II

Years have flown swiftly by,
    Hollow her cheeks have grown.
Quieter, sadder she,
    More distant, more withdrawn.

She struggles, but in vain,
    Fighting great agony,

Those mighty powers to tame;
    Her heart leaps violently.

Dreaming, one day she lies
    In bed, but not asleep,
Drowning in nothingness...
    The blow has struck full deep.

Her look becomes a stare,
    Hollow, and void, and numb.
She raves, all unaware,
    In wild delirium.

And from her eye there streams
    The blood that nothing stays.
The pain now quieter seems,
    Now flash the Spirit's rays.

"The gates of Heaven yield,
    And I am moved with awe.
My hopes shall be fulfilled,
    Nearer the stars I'll draw."

Trembling on lips so pale,
    The soul would seek to roam.
The gentle spirits sail
    To their aethereal home.

Striving profound has drawn her,
    Lured by a magic bond.
Too cold has life been for her,
    Too poor this earthly land.

MAN AND DRUM

A Fable

A Drum it is no Man, and a Man he is no Drum,
The Drum is very clever, and the Man is very dumb.

The Drum is tied with straps, but the Man is on his own,
And the Drum sits firm when the Man falls down.

The angry Man he beats it, and the Drum goes bippety-bop,
Yes, the merry Drum it rattles, and the Man goes hippety-hop.

And then the Man pulls faces, and the Drum it laughs at him,
And the Man shouts up and down the house and makes an
                                                    awful din.

"Hey, Drum, ho, Drum, why laugh so mockingly?
You take me for a fool and you stick out your tongue at me!

"Damn you, Drum, you shame me, you jeer and you deride!
Why d'you rattle when I beat, why d'you hang where you were
                                                    tied?

"You think I raised you from a tree into a Drum full-grown
To carry on like that as if you'd done it on your own?

"You shall dance when I beat, you shall beat when I sing,
You shall cry when I laugh, you shall laugh when I spring."

The Man scowls at the Drum all in a sudden furious bout,
He bangs and bangs and bangs it till its blood comes gushing
                                                    out.

So the Drum it has no Man, and the Man he has no Drum,
And the Man takes holy orders for a friar to become.

HUMAN PRIDE

When these stately Halls I scan
    And the giant burden of these Houses,
And the stormy pilgrimage of Man
    And the frenzied race that never ceases,

Pulse's throbbing do I sense
    And the giant flame of Soul so proud?
Shall the Waves then bear you hence
    Into Life, into the Ocean's flood?

Shall I then revere these forms
    Heavenward soaring, proud, inviolate?
Should I yield before the Life that storms
    Towards the Indeterminate?

No! You pigmy-giants so wretched,
    And you ice-cold stone Monstrosity,
See how in these eyes averted
    Burns the Soul's impetuosity.

Swift eye scans the circles round,
    Hastens through them all exploringly,
Yearning, as on fire, resounds,
    Mocking through the vast Halls and away.

When you all go down and sink,
    Fragment-world shall lie around,
Even though cold Splendour blink,
    Even though grim Ruin stand its ground.

There is drawn no boundary,
    No hard, wretched earth-clod bars our way,
And we sail across the sea,
    And we wander countries far away.

Nothing bids to stay our going,
    Nothing locks our hopes inside;
Swift away go fancies fleeing,
    And the bosom's joy and pain abide.

All those monstrous shapes so vast
    Tower aloft in fearfulness,
Feeling not love's fiery blast
    That creates them out of nothingness.

No giant column soars to Heaven
    In a single block, victorious;
One stone on the other meanly woven
Emulates the timid snail laborious.

But the Soul embraces all,
    Is a lofty giant flame that glows,
Even in its very Fall
    Dragging Suns in its destructive throes.

And out of itself it swells
    Up to Heaven's realms on high;
Gods within its depths it lulls,
    Thunderous lightning flashes in its eye.

And it wavers not a whit
    Where the very God-Thought fares,
On its breast will cherish it;
    Soul's own greatness is its lofty Prayer.

Soul its greatness must devour,
    In its greatness must go down;
Then volcanoes seethe and roar,
    And lamenting Demons gather round.

Soul, succumbing haughtily,
    Raises up a throne to giant derision;
Downfall turns to Victory,
    Hero's prize is proud renunciation.

But when two are bound together,
    When two souls together flow,
Each one softly tells the other
    No more need alone through space to go.

Then all Worlds hear melodies
    Like the Aeolian harp full sighing,
In eternal Beauty's rays
    Wish and Soul's desire together flowing.

Jenny! Do I dare avow
    That in love we have exchanged our Souls,
That as one they throb and glow,
    And that through their waves one current rolls?

Then the gauntlet do I fling
    Scornful in the World's wide open face.
Down the giant She-Dwarf, whimpering,
    Plunges, cannot crush my happiness.

Like unto a God I dare
    Through that ruined realm in triumph roam.
Every word is Deed and Fire,
    And my bosom like the Maker's own.

EVENING STROLL

"Why gaze you towards the cliff-wall there,
    What do you softly sigh?"
"The sun sinks glowing through the air,
    Kissing the cliff good-bye."

"And this before you've never seen —
    The sun's orb slowly scale
The morning sky, and then from noon
    Sink down into the vale?"

"Indeed I have, indeed that glow
    In crimson folds throbbed burning,
Until its Eye, being loth to go,
    Dwelt on her in its yearning.

"We walked in peace. By her footfall
    The echoing cliffs were captured.
The light wind gently kissed her shawl,
    Soft spoke her eyes, enraptured.

"And sick with love, I lisped a-sighing;
    She trembled, rosy red.
I pressed her heart, down sank the dying
    Sun, star-cosseted.

"That draws me to the cliff-wall there,
    That's what I softly sigh.
She waves far off as evening fire,
    She bows as from on high."

Scenes
from
OULANEM
A Tragedy

Characters:

Oulanem, a German traveller

Lucindo, his companion

Pertini, a citizen of a mountain town in Italy

Alwander, a citizen of the same town

Beatrice, his foster-daughter

Wierin

Perto, a monk

> *The action takes place inside or before Pertini's house,*
> *Alwander's house, and in the mountains.*

ACT I

A mountain town

Scene 1

A street. Oulanem, Lucindo; Pertini before his house.

Pertini. Sirs, the whole town is crowded out with strangers,
Attracted to the spot by fame, to see
The wonders of the neighbourhood. In short,
I offer you my home. For at no inn
Will you find room. So all I can provide
With my small means I shall be glad to place
At your disposal. Truly, I am drawn
To friendship with you. That's no flattery.

Oulanem. We thank you, stranger, and I only fear
   Lest your opinion of us be too high.
Pertini. Good ... good.... Then let us leave the compliments.
Oulanem. But we intend to make a lengthy stay.
Pertini. Each day the less you spend in pleasure here
   Will be my loss.
Oulanem. Once more we thank you warmly.
Pertini (calling a servant).
   Boy! See the gentlemen up to their room.
   They wish to take some rest after their journey;
   They also want to be alone and change
   Their heavy travelling clothes for lighter wear.

Oulanem. We take our leave, but we shall soon return.

   (*Oulanem and Lucindo go out with the servant.*)

Pertini (alone, cautiously looking round).
   It's he, by God, it's he; the day has come;
   He, the old friend I never could forget,
   Any more than my conscience gives me rest.
   That's excellent! Now I'll exchange my conscience;
   He shall be it henceforth, yes, he, Oulanem.
   So, conscience, now may it go well with you.
   For every night you stood before my bed,
   You went to sleep when I did, rose with me—
   We know each other, man, my eyes upon it!
   What's more, I know that there are others here;
   They are Oulanem also, also Oulanem!
   There's death rings in that name. Well, let it ring
   Till in its owner vile it rings its last.
   But wait, I have it now! As clear as air,
   Firm as my bones, it comes up from my soul.
   His oath stands up in arms before my eyes!
   I've found it, and I'll see he finds it too!
   My plan is made—you are its very soul,
   Yes, you, Oulanem, are its very life.
   Would you work Destiny as 'twere a puppet?
   Make Heaven a plaything for your calculations?
   Fabricate Gods out of your old spent loins?
   Now, play your part off pat, my little God;
   But wait—wait for your cue—leave that to me!

   (*Enter Lucindo.*)

Scene 2

Pertini, Lucindo.

Pertini. Pray, why so much alone, my dear young sir?

Lucindo. Curiosity. The old find nothing new.

Pertini. Indeed! Your time of life!

Lucindo. No, but if ever
    My soul cherished a strong desire, if ever
    My heart was moved by a presentient yearning,
    It was to call him Father, be his son,
    That one's whose manly and impassioned spirit
    Can drink in worlds entire; whose heart streams forth
    The radiance of the Gods. Did you not know him,
    Then you might not conceive that such a man
    Could be.

Pertini. It sounds indeed most fine and tender,
    When from the warm voluptuous lips of youth
    The praise of Age streams forth like tongues of fire.
    It sounds so moral, like a Bible sermon,
    Just like the story of the Dame Susannah,
    Or like that tale about the Prodigal Son.
    But dare I ask you if you know this man
    With whom your heart would seem so closely bound?

Lucindo. Seem? Only semblance—semblance and delusion?
    You hate mankind?

Pertini. Well, at the very least
    I am a man!

Lucindo. Forgive if I've offended.
    You are full well disposed towards the Stranger,
    And he who goes in friendship to the Wanderer,
    His spirit is not locked within itself.
    You seek an answer. Answer you shall have.
    We are together bound in a strange union
    Deep woven in the bottom of our hearts
    Which, even as bright blazing brands of fire,
    The spirits of his breast weave round with radiance,
    As if well-wishing Demons of the Light
    With thoughtful tenderness had matched us both.
    Thus have I known him since long, long ago—
    So long ago, that Memory scarcely whispers

Of our first meeting. How we found each other,
I know it not.

Pertini. It sounds indeed romantic.
And yet, my dear young sir, it is but sound
That sounds only to parry a request.

Lucindo. I swear to it.

Pertini. What do you swear to, sir?

Lucindo. I do not know him, yet indeed I know him.
He hides some mystery deep within his breast,
Which I may not yet know—not now ... not yet....
These words repeat themselves each day, each hour.
For see, I do not know myself!

Pertini. That's bad!

Lucindo. I stand here so cut off, so separate.
The poorest wretch takes pride in what he is
When, smiling, he tells of the line that bore him,
Cherishing in his heart each little detail.
I cannot do this. Men call me Lucindo,
But they could call me gallows too, or tree.

Pertini. What do you want, then? Friendship with the gallows?
Kinship, even? Well, I can help you there!

Lucindo (earnestly). Play not with empty syllables and sounds
When I rage inwardly.

Pertini. Rage on, my friend,
Till rage is spent.

Lucindo (indignantly). What do you mean?

Pertini. Mean? Nothing!
I am a dry house philistine, no more,
A man who simply calls each hour an hour,
Who goes to sleep at night-time, just to rise
When morning comes again; who counts the hours
Until he's counted out and the clock stops,
And worms become the hands that show the time;
And so on till the final Judgment Day
When Jesus, with the Angel Gabriel,
Pronouncing sentence on his wrathful trumpet,
Reads out the list of our recorded sins,
And stands us on the right or on the left,

And runs his God-fist over all our hides
To find out whether we are lambs or wolves.

Lucindo. He'll not name me, because I have no name.

Pertini. Well said! That's how I like to hear you speak!
But since I'm just a plain house philistine,
My thoughts are homely, and I handle thoughts
As you do stones and sand. So if a man
Cannot name his own family, but turns
Up with another, he's an off-shoot—born
On the wrong side of the blanket.

Lucindo. What was that?
Think sooner black the sun and flat the moon,
And neither sending forth one shaft of light,
But here a sound—a surmise—and Life weighs it.

Pertini. My friend, you must not improvise so wildly.
Believe me, I'm not prone to nervous fits!
But off-shoots are quite often green and mossy,
Yes, yes, they take their own luxuriant way
And shoot up shining towards the very Heavens,
As if they knew that they had sprung from joy,
Begotten by no dull and slavish union.
For look you, off-shoots of this kind are satires;
Nature's a Poet, Marriage sits in a chair,
Its cap on, and with all the accessories,
Its sullen face with grimacing distorted,
And, lying at its feet, a dusty parchment
Scrawled over with the parson's blasphemies,
The church's dismal halls to give perspective,
The churlish rabble gaping in the background—
Give me off-shoots!

Lucindo (incensed). For God's sake, that's enough!
What is it, man? What do you mean? Speak out;
But by the Eternal I shall speak with you.
What do I ask? Lies it not clear before me,
Grins not Hell out of it, does it not rise
Before my look like Death's own withered shape,
To glare at me and mutter threats of storm?
But, man, not easily, believe you me,
Have you hurled from your withered devil's fist
This blazing brand of fire into my breast:

For do not think you play dice with a boy,
Flinging the dice with shattering force straight at
His childish head. You've played too fast with me.
So now—and mark you this—we're gaming comrades.
You've quickly made yourself familiar. Out
With all that's heaving in your vile snake's bosom!
And be it mistrust only, or derision,
Then I shall throw it back into your throat,
And you yourself shall choke your poison down,
And then I'll play with you! But speak! I wish it!

Pertini. You do? You think of Faust and Mephistopheles.
You've brooded on them deeply, I dare say.
I tell you, no. Keep your wish to yourself,
And I'll throw dust into its silly eyes.

Lucindo. Take care. Don't blow upon the glowing embers
Until the flames blaze up and you yourself
Are burnt to cinders!

Pertini. A phrase! An empty phrase!
The only one they burn will be yourself!

Lucindo. Myself! So be it! To myself I'm nothing!
But you, oh, you my youthful arms enfold
And twine themselves in frenzy round your breast.
The abyss yawns gaping night to both of us,
If you sink down, smiling, I'll follow you,
And whisper to you, "Down! Come with me! Comrade!"

Pertini. It seems you're gifted with imagination.
You have dreamed much already in your life?

Lucindo. Just so. I am a dreamer, yes, a dreamer.
What knowledge do I want from you who have none?
You've only seen us, but you know us not,
Yet hurl against me scorn and blasphemy.
What am I waiting for? Still more of you?
You have no more ... but I have more for you.
For me—guilt, poison, shame—you must redeem it.
You've drawn the circle, and it leaves no room
For two of us. Now use your jumping skill.
As Fate draws, so it draws. So let it be.

Pertini. You must have read that ending out in class
From some dry, dusty book of tragedies.

Lucindo. True, this is tragedy that we are playing.
   Come on, now. Where and how you want. You choose.

Pertini. And when, and everywhere, and any time,
   And none!

Lucindo. Coward, don't make a mockery of my words,
   Or I'll write coward across your very face,
   And shout it out through each and every street
   And thrash you publicly, if you'll not follow,
   If you dare crack your feeble hackneyed jokes
   When my heart's blood runs cold within my veins.
   Not one word more; follow or do not follow,
   Your sentence is pronounced, you coward, you knave!

Pertini (incensed). Say that again, boy! Say those words again!

Lucindo. Why, if it brings you joy—a thousand times;
   If it stirs up your gall and sets it flowing
   Until the blood starts furious from your eyeballs,
   Then here it is again: you knave, you coward!

Pertini. We'll have this out. Write that upon your brain.
   There's still one place to knit us two together,
   And that is Hell—Hell not for me, but you!

Lucindo. Why count the syllables, if it can be settled
   Here on the spot. Then fly away to Hell,
   And tell the Devils it was I that sent you!

Pertini. Just one more word.

Lucindo. What is the use of words?
   I hear them not. Blow bubbles in the wind,
   Draw lineaments on your face to match your words,
   I see them not. Bring weapons, let them speak,
   I'll put my whole heart into them, and if
   It breaks not, then—

Pertini (interrupting him).
   Not quite so bold, my lad, and not so callow!
   You, you have not a thing to lose, no, nothing!
   You are a stone that's fallen from the moon,
   That someone somewhere scratched one single word on.
   You spelled the letters out: they read "Lucindo".
   See! On that empty tablet I'll not dare
   Wager myself, my life, my honour, all.
   You want to use my blood for artist's colour?
   Am I to be the brush that lends you tone?

We are too far removed in rank and station.
Am I to stand against you as you are?
I know what I am. Tell me, what are you?
You know not, are not, you have naught to lose!
Thief-like, you seek to pledge to me an honour
That never in your bastard's bosom glowed?
You seek to swindle, lay your empty ticket
Against my sterling worth, my friend?
Not so! First get you honour, name and life—
You are still nothing—then I'll gladly stake
My honour, name and life against your own!

Lucindo. So that's it, coward! You want to save your skin?
You've worked the sum out so ingeniously,
Oh, so ingeniously, in your dull brain?
Do not deceive yourself: I'll change your answer,
And I shall write down "coward" in its place.
I'll scorn you as I would a maddened beast;
I'll shame you, yes, shame you before the world,
And then you can explain, with all the details,
To aunts and uncles, children, everyone,
I call myself Lucindo, yes, Lucindo,
That is my name; it might have been some other;
I go by it, though it could have been different.
What men call being, I do not possess;
But you are what you are, and that's a coward!

Pertini. That's nice, that's very pretty. But supposing
I could give you a name—you hear, a name?

Lucindo. You have no name yourself, and yet you'd give one,
You who have never seen me, save this once;
And seeing's a lie, the eternal mockery
That hounds us down: we see, and that is all.

Pertini. Good. But who grasps more than is seen?

Lucindo. Not you.
You've seen in all things what you are: a scoundrel.

Pertini. True; I'm not easily fooled by the first glance.
But that man—he was not born yesterday!
Believe me, he has seen a thing or two.
What if we knew each other?

Lucindo. I don't believe it.

Pertini. But is there not a poet, wondrous strange,
    A gloomy aesthete, butt of ridicule,
    Who spends his hours in subtle meditation,
    Who would make rhymes of Life, and would most gladly
    Himself be author of the poem of Life?
Lucindo. Ha! It might well be chance. You don't deceive me!

Pertini. Chance! Such is the language of philosophers
    When reason doesn't come to rescue them.
    Chance—it's so easily said—one syllable,
    A name is also chance. Anyone's name
    Might be Oulanem if he had no other.
    And so it is pure chance if I so call him.

Lucindo. You know him? Heavens! Speak! In Heaven's name!

Pertini. You know the boys' reward? Its name is—silence.

Lucindo. It sickens me to ask of you a favour,
    But I beseech you, by all you hold dear!

Pertini. Dear? You think that I am going to bargain?
    A coward, you know, is deaf to all entreaty.

Lucindo. You must, then, if you would wipe out the taunt
    Of coward, you must speak without delay.

Pertini. Let's duel now, I'll fight you as you are.
    You're good enough for me, so let us fight.

Lucindo. Don't drive me to the extreme, not to that verge
    Where there are no more bounds, where all things end.

Pertini. Listen to him! We want to try extremes,
    As Fate draws, so it draws. So let it be!

Lucindo. Ha! Is there no way out, no hope at all?
    His breast as hard as iron, all feeling withered,
    Cankered and dried with scorn, he mixes poison
    And rubs it in for balsam. And he smiles.
    This may be your last hour, man, yes, your last,
    Seize it, absorb it, for in less than no time
    You'll stand before your Judge; so break the chain
    Of your life's vicious actions with one last,
    One last good deed, one solitary word,
    As lightly breathed as air!
Pertini. 'Twas chance, good friend.
    Believe me, I believe in chance myself.

Lucindo. In vain!—all—all—But stop, you shallow fool,
It won't be settled that way, no, by God!
Your sharp eye has deceived you once again.
I'll call him here in person. Then you may stand,
Before him, face to face and eye to eye,
Just like a little boy caught doing wrong.
You cannot hold me, man! Out of my way!

(*He rushes off.*)

Pertini. A greater plan now rescues you, my lad;
Pertini can't forget, believe you me!

Pertini (*calls*). Lucindo, ho! In Heaven's name, come back!

(*Lucindo returns.*)

Lucindo. What would you? Off with you!

Pertini. There's honour for you!
Go, tell the worthy gentleman we quarrelled;
You challenged me, but being a good boy—
A good boy and a very pious child!—
Repented, begged forgiveness, were forgiven.
Then shed a pious tear, and kiss his hand,
And cut the rod for your repentant back!

Lucindo. You drive me to it.

Pertini. You let yourself be driven.
This sounds as moral as a children's primer.
Do you believe in God?

Lucindo. Confess to *you*?

Pertini. Don't you demand that I confess to you?
I shall. But say, do you believe in God?

Lucindo. What's that to you?

Pertini. It's hardly fashionable,
So I'd much like to hear you tell me plainly.

Lucindo. I don't believe with what is called belief,
And yet I know Him as I know myself.

Pertini. We'll talk of that when mood and moment suit;
How you believe is all the same to me,
At least you do believe. Good. Swear by Him.

Lucindo. What? Swear to you?

Pertini. Yes, swear you must that never
    Will your tongue blab a single syllable.

Lucindo. By God, I swear it.

Pertini. Then swear you'll cherish only friendship for me.
    See, I am not so bad—only outspoken.

Lucindo. By God, I would not swear it for a world
    That I loved you or held you in esteem.
    I cannot and I will not ever swear it,
    But what is past, let that be all wiped out
    As if it were a loathsome, evil dream.
    I'll plunge it down where all dreams disappear to,
    Deep in the rolling waves of oblivion.
    That I will swear to you by Him that's holy,
    From whom the worlds come whirling up through space,
    Who with His glance brings forth Eternity,
    I swear! But now the guerdon for my oath.

Pertini. Come! I will lead you to a quiet place,
    And show you many a sight: rocky ravines,
    Where lakes have welled up from volcanic Earth,
    Cradling in quietude their rounded waters;
    And where the years rush past in silent sequence,
    Then will the storm indeed subside, and then—

Lucindo. What's this? You speak of stones, bays, worms and mud?
    But rocks and crags tower upwards everywhere,
    In every spot a spring comes bubbling forth:
    Whether impetuous, low, high—what matter?
    Mysterious places still are to be found
    Where we are held enraptured and spellbound.
    To see them wakes excitement in my breast,
    And if it bursts, why, it is jest, no more.
    So take me where you will, yes, to that goal!
    Waver and falter not, but let's away!

Pertini. The rolling thunder first must cease its din
    Ere the pure lightning cleanse your breast within.
    So to a spot I'll make myself your guide
    Where, I much fear, you'll wish too long to abide.

Lucindo. Oh, let our journey's goal lie where it may,
    I'll follow you, if you will lead the way.

Pertini. Mistrustful! (*They both go out.*)

Scene 3

A room in Pertini's house.
Oulanem is alone, seated at a table, writing.
Papers lie about. Suddenly he springs up, walks up and down, then
stops abruptly and stands with folded
arms.

Oulanem. All lost! The hour is now expired, and time
　　Stands still. This pigmy universe collapses.
　　Soon I shall clasp Eternity and howl
　　Humanity's giant curse into its ear.
　　Eternity! It is eternal pain,
　　Death inconceivable, immeasurable!
　　An evil artifice contrived to taunt us, ·
　　Who are but clockwork, blind machines wound up
　　To be the calendar-fools of Time; to be,
　　Only that something thus at least might happen;
　　And to decay, that there might be decay!
　　The worlds must have had need of one thing more—
　　Dumb, searing agony to send them whirling.
　　Death comes to life and puts on shoes and stockings;
　　The sorrowing plant, the stone's inert erosion,
　　The birds that find no song to tell the pain
　　Of their aethereal life, the general discord
　　And the blind striving of the All to shake
　　Itself out of itself, be crushed in quarrel—
　　This now stands up and has a pair of legs,
　　And has a breast to feel the curse of life!
　　Ha, I must twine me on the wheel of flame,
　　And in Eternity's ring I'll dance my frenzy!
　　If aught besides that frenzy could devour,
　　I'd leap therein, though I must smash a world
　　That towered high between myself and it!
　　It would be shattered by my long-drawn curse,
　　And I would fling my arms around cruel Being,
　　Embracing me, 'twould silent pass away.
　　Then silent would I sink into the void.
　　Wholly to sink, not be—oh, this were Life,
　　But swept along high on Eternity's current
　　To roar out threnodies for the Creator,
　　Scorn on the brow! Can Sun burn it away?
　　Bound in compulsion's sway, curse in defiance!

Let the envenomed eye flash forth destruction —
Does it hurl off the ponderous worlds that bind?
Bound in eternal fear, splintered and void,
Bound to the very marble block of Being,
Bound, bound forever, and forever bound!
The worlds, they see it and go rolling on
And howl the burial song of their own death.
And we, we Apes of a cold God, still cherish
With frenzied pain upon our loving breast
The viper so voluptuously warm,
That it as Universal Form rears up
And from its place on high grins down on us!
And in our ear, till loathing's all consumed,
The weary wave roars onward, ever onward!
Now quick, the die is cast, and all is ready;
Destroy what only poetry's lie contrived,
A curse shall finish what a curse conceived.
                (*He sits down at the table and writes.*)

Scene 4

Alwander's house; first — before the house. Lucindo, Pertini.

Lucindo. Why bring me here?

Pertini. For a succulent piece of woman,
        That's all! See for yourself, and if she softly
        Breathes a melodious peace into your soul,
        Then forward!

Lucindo. What? You're taking me to whores?
        And at the very time when all of Life
        Comes down with crushing force upon my shoulders,
        And when my breast swells irresistibly
        In a mad frenzy craving self-destruction;
        When each breath breathes a thousand deaths for me, —
        And now a woman!

Pertini. Ha! Rave on, young man,
        Breathe hellfire and destruction, breathe away!
        What whores? Did I misunderstand your meaning?
        See, there's the house. Does it look like a brothel?
        You think I want to play the pimp for you,
        And use the very daylight for a lantern?

That's rich. But enter first and there, perhaps,
You'll learn what you desire.

Lucindo. I see your trick.
The stuff you made it of is very cheap.
You really seek to slip the hand that holds you.
Be grateful that this moment I must hear you;
But temporising will cost you your life.

(*They go into the house. The curtain falls and another is raised.
A modern, elegant room.
Beatrice is sitting on the sofa, a guitar beside her.
Lucindo, Pertini, Beatrice.*)

Pertini. Beatrice, a young traveller I bring,
A pleasant gentleman, my distant kinsman.

Beatrice (*to Lucindo*). Welcome!

Lucindo. Forgive me if I find no words,
No speech to express my heart's astonishment.
Beauty so rare quite overwhelms the spirits;
The blood leaps high, but not a word will come.

Beatrice. Fair words, young sir. You are in a pleasant mood.
I thank your disposition, not the favour
That Nature has denied me so unkindly,
When 'tis your tongue that speaks, and not your heart.

Lucindo. Oh, if my heart might speak, if it might only
Pour forth what you have quickened in its depths,
The words would all be flames of melody,
And every breath a whole eternity,
A Heaven, an Empire infinitely vast,
In which all lives would sparkle bright with thoughts
Full of soft yearning, full of harmonies,
Locking the World so sweetly in its breast,
Streaming with radiance of pure loveliness,
Since every word would only bear your name!

Pertini. You will not take it in bad part, young lady,
If I explain to you that he is German
And always raves of Melody and Soul.

Beatrice. A German! But I like the Germans well,
And I am proud to be of that same stock.
Come, sit here, German sir.

(*She offers him a place on the sofa.*)

Lucindo. Thank you, my lady.

(*Aside to Pertini.*)

Away! There is still time; here I am lost!

Beatrice (abashed). Did I speak out of place?

(*Lucindo wants to speak, but Pertini cuts in.*)

Pertini. Spare us your flourishes and your flattery!
'Twas nothing, Beatrice; merely some business
That I must still arrange for him in haste.

Lucindo (confused, in a low voice).
By God, Pertini, you are playing with me!

Pertini (aloud).
Take it not so to heart, don't be so scared!
The lady trusts my word, is it not so?
Beatrice, he may stay, is it not so,
Till I am back. And please remember — prudence;
You are a stranger, so no foolishness.

Beatrice. Oh, come, young sir, was then my welcome such
That you could think I'd banish you, a stranger,
Friend of Pertini, an old friend of ours,
Unceremoniously from this house,
Whose hospitable doors are open to all?
You need not flatter, but you must be fair.

Lucindo. By God, your gracious kindness overwhelms me!
You speak as gently as the angels speak.
Forgive if overawed and overcome
By the wild stream of passion long forgotten,
The lips spoke what they ought to have concealed.
Yet see the sky all clear and luminous
Smile down upon us from the clouds' blue realm,
And see the colours throb so sweet and bright,
Now wrapped in shade and now in gentle light,
Mingling in harmonies so soft and full,
One lovely picture, one inspired soul.
See this, and then be silent if your lips
Obey. But no! your heart enchanted leaps,
Prudence and circumspection vanished all.
The lips must speak what holds your heart in thrall.
Even as the Aeolian lyre is stirred to sound
When Zephyr wraps his fluttering pinions round.

Beatrice. Reproof I cannot find within my heart,
 You dress the poison, sir, with such sweet art.

Lucindo (*aside to Pertini*).
 Confounded villain, yet good villain too,
 What shall I do? Get out of here, by God!

Pertini (*aloud*).
 It rankles in his mind, remembering how
 I took the words out of his mouth just now.
 In language beautiful he would have talked,
 When by my interruption he was balked.
 But never mind, 'tis Beatrice's belief
 You kindly wished to afford her some relief
 From your grand talk; like any German jest,
 Once swallowed, it's not easy to digest.
 I go.

Lucindo (*in a low voice*). But man!

Pertini (*aloud*). Think of the sympathies
 .That from the stomach to the heart soon rise;
 I'll soon be back to fetch you swift away,
 Or else in this sweet place too long you'll stay.
(*Aside.*) I must be gone. And while he pays his court,
 I'll see the old man brings it all to naught.

   (*Exit Pertini. Lucindo is in confusion.*)

Beatrice. And must I yet once more bid you be seated?

Lucindo. I'll gladly sit here if you truly wish it.

   (*Sits down.*)

Beatrice. Our friend Pertini's often strangely moody.

Lucindo. Yes, strangely so! Most strangely! Very strangely!

   (*Pause.*)

 Forgive me, lady—you esteem this man?

Beatrice. He has long been a true friend of the household,
 And always treated me most amiably.
 And yet—I know not why—I cannot bear him.
 He's often violent. Often from his breast—
 Forgive me, he's your friend—some secret spirit
 Calls strangely, in a voice I do not like.
 It is as though some inner turbulent darkness
 Shrank from the daylight's open look of love
 And feared to make response, as if he harboured

An evil worse than his tongue speaks, worse even
Than his heart dares to think. This is but surmise,
And I do wrong, confiding it so soon;
It is suspicion; suspicion is a viper.

Lucindo. Do you regret confiding in me, then?

Beatrice. Were it a secret that concerned myself—
But oh, what am I saying? Have you won
My trust already? Yet it is not wrong
That I should tell you everything I know;
I could confide it all to anyone,
Since I know nothing that's not known to all.

Lucindo. To all? Well said! You would be kind to all?

Beatrice. Would you not too?

Lucindo. O angel, O sweet being!

Beatrice. You make me fearful, sir. What mean these words?
You jump so suddenly from theme to theme!

Lucindo. I must act quickly, for the hour is striking.
Why hesitate? Death is in every minute.
Can I conceal it? It's a miracle,
I have just met you; strange though it appears,
We might have known each other many years.
It is as if the music I heard sound
Within my own heart, living form had found,
And into vibrant, warm reality
The spirit-bond uniting us breaks free.

Beatrice. I won't deny it: you are not to me
A stranger, yet still strange you are, unknown.
But as dark spirits would not let us see
Each other till this hour, so we must own
There may be other spirits whose deceit
Binds us with treacherous bonds, however sweet.
Foresight and wisdom we must not despise;
The strongest lightning strikes not from dark skies.

Lucindo. O fair philosopher of the heart! O God,
I can resist no more, for you compel me!
Do not imagine that I do not hold
You in respect because my heart grows bold.
It throbs to bursting, all my nerves are tense.
I can resist no more. Soon I'll be gone,

Far, far away from here, from you divided.
Then, worlds, plunge down, plunge down into the abyss!
Forgive me, sweet my child, forgive the hour
That drives me onward with such violent power.
I love you, Beatrice, by God I swear it,
And Love and Beatrice make but one word
That I can utter only in one breath,
And in this thought I'd go to meet my death.

Beatrice. Since good can never come of it, I pray
Speak no more thus. If — but this cannot be —
You were to win my heart, now, straightaway,
Surely you would no longer honour me.
You'd say that I was just a common thing,
Ready, as thousands are, to have her fling.
If for a moment such a notion crossed
Your mind, then love and honour would be lost.
'Twould mean that you cared for me not a jot,
And self-reproach would have to be my lot.

Lucindo. Tender and lovely being, hear me plead!
If only in my bosom you could read,
I never loved till now, by God above,
And your reproaches make a mock of love.
Let the base merchant haggle over flaws,
By shrewd delays more profit still he draws.
Love brings the union of the worlds about,
Naught is beyond, and naught else to desire.
Let those who bind themselves in hatred doubt.
Love is a flashing spark from Life's own fire,
Magic that holds us in an open ring,
So yield to it — this is the only thing
That counts in love, not prudent carefulness;
For love is quick to kindle, quick to bless.

Beatrice. Shall I be modest? Coy? No, I must dare,
However high may leap the flames' fierce flare.
Yet my breast tightens under fearful strain
As if delight were mixed with searing pain,
As if between our union there came floating
A hissing sound mixed in by devils gloating.

Lucindo. It is the fire which you do not yet know,
And the old life, which now has turned to go
Away from us, is speaking its last word;

Then its reproaches will no more be heard.
But tell me, Beatrice, how will you be mine?

Beatrice. My father wants to tie me to a man
Whom I would hate if I could hate my fellows.
But be assured you soon will hear from me.
Where are you staying, sweet friend of my heart?

Lucindo. Why, at Pertini's house.

Beatrice. I'll send a courier.
But now your name? Most surely it must sound
As does the music of the circling spheres.

Lucindo (in a serious voice). Lucindo is my name.

Beatrice. Lucindo! Sweet,
Sweet rings that name to me. Ah, my Lucindo,
He is my world, my God, my heart, my all.

Lucindo. Beatrice, that's yourself, and you are more,
You are yet more than all, for you are Beatrice.

(*He presses her ardently to his breast. The door bursts open
and Wierin enters.*)

Wierin. A pretty sight! O Beatrice! O snake!
Puppet of virtue, are you, cold as marble!

Lucindo. What do you mean by this? What do you seek?
By God, no ape could ever look so sleek.

Wierin. Damned boy, you'll soon enough learn what I mean.
We'll speak together, you and I, O rival
Fashioned in human form to make it loathsome,
Creature puffed up with impudent conceit,
A piece of blotting-paper to wipe pens on,
A comic hero of some wretched jape.

Lucindo. And as remarked, behold the complete ape!
Shame on you thus to bandy words with me!
Such courage is like barrel-organ music
Played to a painted picture of a battle.
Soon the real thing will count.

Wierin. Soon? Now boy, now we'll have this matter out!
B-b-by God — my very blood runs cold!
Beatrice, I'll finish off this paramour.

Lucindo. Silence, fellow, I'll follow you this instant.

(*Pertini enters.*)

Pertini. What's all this noise? You think you're on the street?

(*To Wierin.*)

Why do you screech, you crow? I'll stop your mouth!

(*Aside.*)

I've come just in the nick of time. The fellow
Has somewhat misinterpreted my meaning.

(*Beatrice falls in a faint.*)

Lucindo. Help! She swoons! O God!

(*He bends over her.*)

Come to yourself, angel, sweet spirit, speak!

(*He kisses her.*)

Feel you the warmth? Her eyelids flutter, she breathes!
Beatrice, why are you so? Oh, tell me, why?
You want to kill me? Can I see you thus?

(*He raises her up, embracing her. Wierin wants to rush upon him.
Pertini holds him back.*)

Pertini. Come, friend Crow, just a few words in your ear.

Beatrice (*in a faint voice*). Lucindo, my Lucindo, ah, my lost one,
And lost to me, my heart, before I won you.

Lucindo. Be calm, my angel, nothing shall be lost,
And soon I'll see this fellow breathe his last.

(*He carries her to the sofa.*)

Lie there a while; we cannot long remain,
This holy place must bear no evil stain.

Wierin. Come, we shall speak together.

Pertini. I'll come too.
One second at a duel is something new.

Lucindo. Compose yourself, sweet child, be of good cheer.

Beatrice. Farewell.

Lucindo. Angel, farewell.

Beatrice (*with a deep sigh*). I'm full of fear.

(*Curtain. End of Act I.*)

SONG TO THE STARS

You dance round and around
    In shimmering rays of light,
Your soaring shapes abound
    In number infinite.

Here breaks the noblest Soul,
    The full heart bursts in twain,
And like a jewel in gold
    Is clasped by mortal pain.

It turns on you its look
    Darkly, compellingly,
From you, babe-like, would suck
    Hope and Eternity.

Alas, your light is never
    More than aethereally rare.
No divine being ever
    Cast into you his fire.

You are false images,
    Faces of radiant flame;
Heart's warmth and tenderness
    And Soul you cannot claim.

A mockery is your shining
    Of Action, Pain, Desire.
On you is dashed all yearning
    And the heart's song of fire.

Grieving, we must turn grey,
    End in despair and pain,
Then see the mockery
    That Earth and Heaven remain;

That, as we tremble even,
    And worlds within us drown,
No tree trunk's ever riven,
    No star goes plunging down.

Dead you'd be otherwise,
    Your grave the ocean blue,
All gone, the shining rays,
    And all fire spent in you.

Truth you'd speak silently,
    Not dazzle with dead light,
Nor shine in clarity;
    And all round would be Night.

DREAM VISION

A Dithyramb

From my dreamings I would coax
    Soft an image in scent-woven web;
        I would weave rings passing fair
        From the locks of my own hair;
            Night-encompassed, heart's blood I would swell
            That, from waves of dream, fire-image well,
Image, ebbing and a-flowing,
    Fair in love, Aeolian music sighing.

It would soar, all golden shining,
    And the little house would arch up higher,
        And my locks would wander, curling,
        Divinest girl in darkness furling,
            Forth in pearly songs my blood would flow,
            Streaming round the marble shoulders' glow,
And the lamp would flicker Suns,
    My heart would flood Heaven's dome.

Down would shake the rooms all round,
   But for me, grown into Giant-Hero,
      In his mighty gaze high festal fire,
      World-great would be storm's lyre,
         Thunder-song my heart would beat amain
         Suns would be its love and rock its pain,
Proudly-humble, I'd sink down,
   Proud-audacious, rush unto the breast.

THE SONG OF A SAILOR AT SEA

You may frolic and beat and roll
   Round my boat just as you will,
You must carry me to my goal;
   For you are my subjects still.

Blue waves beneath that flow,
   My little brother's there.
You dragged him down below,
   His bones became your fare.

I was a boy, no more;
   Once rashly he cast off,
He seized hold of the oar,
   Sank by a sandy reef.

I vowed a vow so true
   By the waves of the briny sea,
I'd be revenged on you,
   Lash you relentlessly.

Soul's oath and word I've kept,
   Them I have not betrayed.
I've whipped you and I've whipped,
   On land have seldom stayed.

When booms the stormy main,
   The bell rocks in the tower,
When blows the hurricane,
   When raging winds do roar,

I'm driven from my bed,
From seat secure and warm,
From cosy quiet homestead,
To sail through wind and storm.

With wind and wave I fight,
To the Lord God I pray,
And let the sails fill out;
A true star guides my way.

New strength comes, with the breath
Of joy and ecstasy,
And in the game of death
Song from the breast bursts free.

You may frolic and beat and roll
Round my boat just as you will,
You must carry me to my goal;
For you are my subjects still.

THE MAGIC SHIP

A Romance

Without sails or lights there flees
A ship round the world without rest.
The moon shines down on the seas,
And weathered stands the mast.

A sinister Helmsman steers,
No blood flows in his veins,
No light shines from his eyes,
No thought stirs in his brain.

The waves beat, wild and savage;
She strikes a cliff, to founder,
But rides aloft, undamaged,
As swift as she went under.

Till raging sea-flood swells
In blood-bath weltering.
Troubled, the Helmsman quails;
This proves an evil thing.

The Spirits scream vengeful doom
    Below and up on high.
The Helmsman's plunged in gloom,
    The ship goes shooting by.

To far-off lands she fares,
    Where coasts and bays she sees,
Then flashes in mirror-fire,
    Till kissed down by the seas.

THE PALE MAIDEN

A Ballad

The maiden stands so pale,
    So silent, withdrawn,
Her sweet angelic soul
    Is misery-torn.

Therein can shine no ray,
    The waves tumble over;
There, love and pain both play,
    Each cheating the other.

Gentle was she, demure,
    Devoted to Heaven,
An image ever pure
    The Graces had woven.

Then came a noble knight,
    A grand charger he rode;
And in his eyes so bright
    A sea of love flowed.

Love smote deep in her breast,
    But he galloped away,
For battle-triumph athirst;
    Naught made him stay.

All peace of mind is flown,
    The Heavens have sunk.
The heart, now sorrow's throne,
    Is yearning-drunk.

And when the day is past,
    She kneels on the floor,
Before the holy Christ
    A-praying once more.

But then upon that form
    Another encroaches,
To take her heart by storm,
    'Gainst her self-reproaches.

"To me your love is given
    For Time unending.
To show your soul to Heaven
    Is merely pretending."

She trembles in her terror
    Icy and stark,
She rushes out in horror,
    Into the dark.

She wrings her lily-white hands,
    The tear-drops start.
"Thus fire the bosom brands
    And longing, the heart.

"Thus Heaven I've forfeited,
    I know it full well.
My soul, once true to God,
    Is chosen for Hell.

"He was so tall, alas,
    Of stature divine.
His eyes so fathomless,
    So noble, so fine.

"He never bestowed on me
    His glances at all;
Lets me pine hopelessly
    Till the end of the Soul.

"Another his arm may press,
    May share his pleasure;
Unwitting, he gives me distress
    Beyond all measure.

"With my soul willingly,
    With my hopes I'd part,
Would he but look towards me
    And open his heart.

"How cold must the Heavens be
    Where he doesn't shine,
A land full of misery
    And burning with pain.

"But here the surging flood
    May deliver me, cooling
The hot fire of heart's blood,
    The bosom's feeling."

She leaps with all her might
    Into the spray.
Into the cold dark night
    She's carried away.

Her heart, that burning brand,
    Is quenched forever;
Her look, that luminous land,
    Is clouded over.

Her lips, so sweet and tender,
    Are pale and colourless;
Her form, aethereal, slender,
    Drifts into nothingness.

And not a withered leaf
    Falls from the bough;
Heaven and Earth are deaf,
    Won't wake her now.

By mountain, valley, on
    The quiet waves race,
To dash her skeleton
    On a rocky place.

The Knight so tall and proud
    Embraces his new love,
The cithern sings about
    The joys of True Love!

Supplementary to Dedicated Verses

Some Chapters
from
SCORPION AND FELIX
A Humoristic Novel

First Book

Chapter 10

Now follows, as we promised in the previous chapter, the proof that the aforesaid sum of 25 talers is the personal property of the dear Lord.

They are without a master! Sublime thought, no mortal power owns them, yet the lofty power that sails above the clouds embraces the All, including therefore the aforesaid 25 talers; with its wings woven from day and night, from sun and stars, from towering mountains and endless sands, which resound as with harmonies and the rushing of the waterfall, it brushes where no mortal hand can reach, including therefore the aforesaid 25 talers, and — but I can say no more, my inmost being is stirred, I contemplate the All and myself and the aforesaid 25 talers, what substance in these three words, their standpoint is infinity, their tinkle is angelic music, they recall the Last Judgment and the state exchequer, for — it was Grethe, the cook, whom Scorpion, stirred by the tales of his friend Felix, carried away by his flame-winged melody, overpowered by his vigorous youthful emotion, presses to his heart, sensing a fairy within her.

I conclude therefore that fairies wear beards, for Magdalene Grethe, not the repentant Magdalene, was decked out like a warrior jealous of his honour with whiskers and mustachios, the curls on the soft cheeks caressed the finely moulded chin which like a rock in lonely seas — that men however behold from afar — jutted out of the flat skilly-plate of a face, enormous and proudly aware of its sublimity, cleaving the air, to stir the gods and overwhelm men.

The goddess of fantasy seemed to have dreamed of a bearded beauty and to have lost herself in the enchanted fields of her vast countenance; when she awoke, behold, it was Grethe herself who had dreamed, fearful dreams that she was the great whore of Babylon, the Revelation of St. John and the wrath of God, and that on the finely furrowed skin He had caused a prickly stubble-field to sprout, so that her beauty should not excite to sin, and that her youth should be protected, as the rose by its thorns, that the world should

> to knowledge aspire
> and not for her take fire.

Chapter 12

"A horse! a horse! my kingdom for a horse!" said Richard III.[a]
"A husband, a husband, myself for a husband," said Grethe.

Chapter 16

"In the beginning was the Word, and the Word was with God, and the Word was God. And the Word was made flesh, and dwelt among us, and we beheld his glory." [b]

Innocent, beautiful thought! Yet these associations of ideas led Grethe onward to the thought that the Word dwells in the thighs, just as in Shakespeare Thersites believes that Ajax wears his wit in his belly and his guts in his head,[c] and being convinced—Grethe, not Ajax—and filled with understanding of how the Word had been made flesh, she saw in the thighs its symbolic expression, she beheld their glory and decided—to wash them.

Chapter 19

But she had big blue eyes, and blue eyes are commonplace, like the water in the Spree.

There is a silly, sentimental innocence in their expression, an innocence which is sorry for itself, a watery innocence which evaporates at the approach of fire into grey steam, and nothing else lies behind these eyes, their entire world is blue and their soul a blue bag, but as for brown eyes—theirs is the realm of the ideal, and the infinite, stimulating world of night slumbers in

---

[a] W. Shakespeare, *King Richard III*, Act V, Scene 4.— *Ed.*
[b] John 1: 1, 14.— *Ed.*
[c] W. Shakespeare, *Troilus and Cressida*, Act II, Scene 1.— *Ed.*

their depths, lightnings of the soul flash out of them, and in their glance is music like the songs of Mignon, a distant, mellow land of radiance where there dwells a rich god who luxuriates in his own depths and, absorbed in the universality of his being, pours forth infinity and suffers infinity. We are held as by a spell, we would clasp to our breast the melodious, profound, soulful being and suck the spirit from its eyes and make songs from their glances.

We love the world of rich animation which opens before us, we see in the background great sun-thoughts, we sense a demonic suffering, and before us delicate figures tread the measures of the round dance and wave to us and, like the Graces, shyly retire as soon as they are recognised.

Chapter 21

Philological Broodings

Felix tore himself from the embraces of his friend far from gently, for he did not suspect the latter's profound and emotional nature, and at that moment was preoccupied with the continuation of his—digestion, to which we now address a final summons to set the coping-stone to its great work, since it is holding up our plot.

So Merten also thought to himself, for a strong blow, which Felix felt, had been delivered by his broad historic hand.

The name *Merten* recalls Charles Martel, and indeed Felix believed himself to have been caressed with a hammer, so agreeable was the electric shock which he received.

He opened his eyes wide, swayed on his feet and thought of his sins and the Last Judgment.

But I meditated upon electric matter, upon galvanism, upon Franklin's learned letters to his geometrical lady-friend, and upon *Merten*, for I am intensely curious to learn what lies behind this name.

It is beyond doubt that the man himself is a direct descendant of *Martel*: I was assured of this by the sexton, although this period lacks all harmony.

The *l* changes to an *n*, and since *Martel*, as everyone familiar with history knows, is an Englishman and in English *a* is often pronounced like the German "*eh*", which appears as "*e*" in Merten, *Merten* may well be another form of *Martel*.

Since among the Germans of old names serve to express the character of their bearer, as may be seen from such bywords as Krug the Knight, Raupach the Hofrat, Hegel the Dwarf, it may be concluded that Merten is a rich and respectable man, although by trade he is a tailor and in this story the father of Scorpion.

This warrants a new hypothesis: partly because he is a tailor, partly because his son's name is Scorpion, it is highly probable that he is descended from *Mars*, the god of war, genitive *Martis*, Greek accusative *Martin, Mertin, Merten*, since the craft of the god of war, like that of the tailor, consists in cutting, for he cuts off arms and legs and hacks the happiness of the earth to pieces.

The scorpion, further, is a poisonous animal which kills with a glance, whose wounds are fatal, whose eyes discharge annihilating lightning, a fine allegory of war, whose gaze is lethal, whose consequences leave scars on the victim which bleed internally and are past healing.

As, however, *Merten* had in him little of the heathen, but was, on the contrary, of a most Christian turn of mind, it appears even more probable that he is a descendant of St. *Martin*. A slight displacement of the vowels gives us *Mirtan; i* in the speech of the common people is often pronounced *e*, as in "gib mer" instead of "gib mir", and in English, as has already been pointed out, *a* is often pronounced *"eh"*, which with the passage of time can easily become *e*, especially with the growth of culture; and thus the name *Merten* evolves quite naturally and means a Christian tailor.

Although this derivation is quite probable and is grounded in profound reasoning, nevertheless we cannot refrain from mentioning another which does much to weaken our faith in St. *Martin*, whom it would only be possible to consider as a patron saint, since to the best of our knowledge he was never married and therefore could not have had any male descendant.

This doubt appears to be reinforced by the following fact. All members of the *Merten* family, like the Vicar of Wakefield, made a habit of marrying as early as possible, and so each generation adorned itself betimes in the *Myrthen* [myrtle] wreath, and this alone—unless one is to have recourse to miracles—explains *Merten's* birth and his appearance in this story as Scorpion's father.

"Myrthen", of course, would have to lose the *"h"*, as at the conclusion of a marriage the *"Eh"*[a] is accentuated and so the *"he"* is dropped, so that *"Myrthen"* becomes *"Myrten"*.

"y" is a Greek *"v"*, not a German letter at all. Since the *Merten* family, as we have established, was of sound German stock and at the same time a most Christian family of tailors, the foreign and heathen *"y"* of necessity changed into a German *"i"*; and because

[a] A pun on the German word *Ehe* (marriage).— *Ed.*

in this same family marriage is the dominant trait, while the vowel "i" is shrill and ascending in contrast to the mild gentleness of *Merten* marriages, it changed into an "eh" and later, in order that the bold alteration should not arouse remark, into "e", which being a short sound serves to indicate the resoluteness of spirit displayed in the solemnisation of marriage, so that in the German "Merten", open to diverse interpretations, "Myrthen" attains the summit of perfection.

In accordance with this deduction we should have St. *Martin's* Christian tailor, the sterling courage of *Martel*, the quick resolution of the war god *Mars* linked with that marriage-proneness which reverberates in the two *e*'s in "*Merten*", so that this hypothesis unites within itself all previous ones and at the same time invalidates them.

A different opinion is advanced by the scholiast who with great diligence and unremitting pains wrote commentaries on the ancient historian from whom we have gleaned our story.

Although we cannot accept it, his opinion nevertheless merits a critical appraisal, since it originated in the mind of a man who combined immense learning with a great proficiency in smoking, so that his parchments were enveloped with holy tobacco fumes and thus in a Pythian ecstasy of incense filled with oracles.

He believes that "*Merten*" must come from the German "Mehren" [to multiply], which in its turn comes from "Meer" [sea], because the *Merten* marriages multiplied like the sand of the sea, and because in the concept of a tailor there is concealed the concept of a "Mehrer" [multiplier], since he makes men out of apes. It is on investigations as thorough and profound as these that he has founded his hypothesis.

As I read this, I was as if dizzy with amazement, the tobacco oracle transported me, but soon cold, discriminating reason awakened and mustered the following counter-arguments.

I grant the aforesaid scholiast that the concept of a tailor can include that of a multiplier, but the concept of a multiplier should on no account be considered to embrace the concept of a diminisher since this would be a *contradictio in terminis*, which we may explain to the ladies as the equating of God with the Devil, tea-table talk with wit, and the ladies themselves with philosophers. But if "*Merten*" was derived from "*Mehrer*", then clearly the word would have lost, hence not gained, an "h", which has been shown to be in contradiction with the substance of its formal nature.

Thus "Merten" cannot possibly be derived from "Mehren", and its derivation from Meer is disproved by the fact that *Merten* families have never fallen into the water nor have they ever wavered, but they have been a pious family of tailors, which is in contradiction to the concept of a wild and stormy sea, from which reasons it becomes manifest that the aforesaid author, despite his infallibility, was mistaken and that ours is the only true deduction.

After this victory I am too fatigued to continue further and will relish the bliss of self-satisfaction, one moment of which, as Winkelmann declares, is worth more than all posterity's praise, though of this I am as convinced as was Pliny the Younger.

Chapter 22

"Quocumque adspicias, nihil est nisi pontus et aer,
Fluctibus hic tumidis, nubibus ille minax.
Inter utrumque fremunt immani turbine venti:
Nescit, cui domino pareat, unda maris.
Rector in incerto est: nec quid fugiatve petatve
Invenit: ambiguis ars stupet ipsa malis." [a]

"Look where you may, there is nought to be seen but Scorpion
and Merten,
The former in torrents of tears, the latter beclouded with wrath.
Wild is the storm of words that rages between them unceasing,
Nor does the tossing sea know which of the two to obey.
I, the helmsman, can make no choice twixt writing and silence,
From the commotion art cowers in corners and holes."

Thus Ovid relates in his *libri tristium* the sad story which as the sequel comes after what went before. The task was clearly beyond him, but I continue the story as follows:——

Chapter 23

Ovid sat in Tomi, whither the god Augustus had hurled him in his anger, because he had more genius than sense.

There among the wild barbarians wilted the tender poet of love, whose ruin love itself had brought about. Deep in thought, he rested his head upon his right hand, and his longing eyes wandered toward distant Latium. The singer's heart was broken, and yet he could not abandon hope and his lyre could not be silent and in sweet songs of passionate melody it spoke his longing and his pain.

Around the old man's frail limbs the north wind whistled, so

---

[a] Ovid, *Tristia*, II, 23 et seq.— *Ed.*

that he was seized with unfamiliar shudderings, for it was in the hot land of the South that his life had flowered, and it was there that his imagination had decked its rich hot-blooded frolics in robes of splendour, and when these children of genius became too bold, then about their shoulders Grace would gently cast her divine, enswathing garland of veils so that the gossamer folds spread wide and a rain of warm dew-drops fell.

"Soon to dust, poor poet!" and a tear rolled down the old man's cheek, when — Merten's powerful bass, incited against Scorpion, was heard——

Chapter 27

"Ignorance, limitless ignorance."

"Because (refers to an earlier chapter) his knees bent too much to a certain side!", but definition is lacking, definition, and who shall define, who shall determine, which is the right side and which the left?

Tell me, thou mortal, whence cometh the wind, or has God a nose in his face, and I will tell you which is right and left.

Nothing but relative concepts, to drink of wisdom is to gain only folly and frenzy!

Oh, vain is all our striving, our yearning is folly, until we have determined which is right and left, for he will place the goats on the left hand, and the sheep on the right.

If he turns round, if he faces in another direction, because in the night he had a dream, then according to our pitiful ideas the goats will be standing on the right and the pious on the left.

So define for me which is right and left, and the whole riddle of creation is solved, *Acheronta movebo*, I shall deduce for you exactly on which side your soul will come to stand, from which I shall further infer which step you are standing on now; for that primal relation would appear to be measurable with the help of the Lord's definition of where you stand, but your present position can be judged by the thickness of your skull. I am dizzy — if a Mephistopheles appeared I should be Faust, for clearly each and every one of us is a Faust, as we do not know which is the right side and which the left; our life is therefore a circus, we run round, try to find sides, till we fall down on the sand and the gladiator, Life, slays us. We need a new saviour, for — you rob me of slumber, tormenting thought, you rob me of my health, you are killing me — we cannot distinguish the left side from the right, we do not know where they lie——

Chapter 28

"Clearly on the moon, on the moon lie the moonstones, false-ness in the breast of women, sand in the sea and mountains on the earth," answered a man who knocked on my door, without waiting for me to ask him in.

I quickly pushed my papers to one side, said that I was very glad not to have made his acquaintance before, since I thus had the pleasure of making it now, that in his teaching there was great wisdom, that all my doubts were stilled by his words; but the only thing was that however fast I spoke, he spoke still faster, hissing sounds poured forth from between his teeth, and the whole man, as I perceived with a shudder on closer perusal and inspection, appeared a shrivelled lizard, nothing but a lizard, that had crawled out of crumbling masonry.

He was of stocky build, and his stature had much in common with that of my stove. His eyes might be called green rather than red, pinpoints rather than flashes of lightning, and he himself more goblin than man.

A genius! I recognised that quickly and with certainty, for his nose had sprung out of his skull like Pallas Athena from the head of Father Zeus, to which fact I also attributed its delicate scarlet glow indicating aethereal origin, while the head itself might be described as hairless, unless one wished to apply the term of head-covering to a thick layer of pomade which together with diverse products of the air and elements richly encrusted the primeval mountain.

Everything in him bespoke height and depth, but his facial structure seemed to betray a man of papers, for the cheeks were hollowed out like smooth basins and so well protected against the rain by the gigantic prominences of the cheek-bones that they could serve as containers for documents and governmental decrees.

In short, everything reveals that he was the god of love himself, if only it had not been himself that he resembled, and that his name has a sweet ring to it like love, if it did not sooner remind one of a juniper bush.

I prayed him to calm himself, for he claimed to be a hero, whereat I humbly interposed that the heroes had been of a somewhat finer build, that the heralds for their part had had voices of simpler, less contrived, more harmonious tone, and Hero, lastly, was beauty transfigured, a truly beautiful nature in which form and soul vied with each other, each claiming to be the sole source of her perfection, and that she was therefore unsuited for his love.

But he remonstrated that he had a p-p-powerful bone-str-r-r-ructure, that he had a sh-sh-shadow as good as anybody else's and even better, because he cast more sh-sh-shadow than light about him, and so his s-s-spouse could cool herself in his shadow, prosper and become a sh-sh-shadow herself, that I was a c-c-coarse man and a gutter-genius and a blockhead into the bargain, that he was c-c-called Engelbert, which was a n-name with a b-b-better ring to it than S-S-Scorpion, that I had been mistaken in Ch-Ch-Chapter 19 because blue eyes were more beautiful than brown, and d-d-dove's eyes were the most s-s-spiritual, and that even if he himself was no dove[a] he was at least deaf[b] to reason, and besides he championed the right of primogeniture and possessed a wash-closet.

"Sh-sh-she shall take my r-r-right hand in betrothal, and now let us have no more of your investigations into right and left, she lives directly opposite, neither to the right nor to the left."

The door slammed, from my soul there emanated a heavenly apparition, the sweet tones of converse ceased, but through the keyhole came a ghostly whisper: "Klingholz, Klingholz!"

Chapter 29

I sat deep in thought, laid aside Locke, Fichte and Kant, and gave myself up to profound reflection to discover what a wash-closet could have to do with the right of primogeniture, and suddenly it came to me like a flash, and in a melodious succession of thoughts one upon the other my vision was illuminated and a radiant form appeared before my eyes.

The right of primogeniture is the wash-closet of the aristocracy, for a wash-closet only exists for the purpose of washing. But washing bleaches, and thus lends a pale sheen to that which is washed. So also does the right of primogeniture silver the eldest son of the house, it thus lends him a pale silvery sheen, while on the other members it stamps the pale romantic hue of penury.

He who bathes in rivers, hurls himself against the rushing element, fights its fury, and with strong arms wrestles against it; but he who sits in the wash-closet, remains in seclusion, contemplating the corners of the walls.

---

[a] *Taube* in German.— *Ed.*
[b] *Tauber* in German.— *Ed.*

The ordinary mortal, i.e., he who has no right of primogeniture, fights the storms of life, throws himself into the billowing sea and seizes pearls of Promethean rights from its depths, and before his eyes the inner form of the Idea appears in glory, and he creates with greater boldness, but he who is entitled to primogenital inheritance lets only drops fall on him, for fear he might strain a limb, and so seats himself in a wash-closet.

Found, the philosopher's stone!

Chapter 30

Thus in our day, as is apparent from the two considerations just set forth, no epic can be composed.

In the first place, by engaging in profound speculations on the subject of the right and left side, we strip these poetical expressions of their poetical drapery as Apollo flayed Marsyas and turn them into an embodiment of doubt, like the mis-shapen baboon, who has eyes in order not to see and is an Argus in reverse; for the latter had a hundred eyes to find what was lost, while he, the wretched stormer of heaven, doubt itself, possesses a hundred eyes to make what has been seen unseen.

But the side, the situation, is among the main prerequisites of epic poetry, and as soon as there are no more sides, which has been shown to be the case with regard to us, epic poetry can only arise from its slumber of death when the blast of trumpets wakes Jericho.

Further, we have discovered the philosopher's stone, everybody unfortunately points to the stone and they——

Chapter 31

They were lying on the ground, Scorpion and Merten, for the supernatural apparition (refers to an earlier chapter) had so shattered their nerves that in the chaos of expansion, which, like the embryo, had not yet broken away from world relations to assume separate form, the cohesive power of their limbs had disintegrated, so that their noses hung down to their navels and their heads sank to the ground.

Merten shed thick blood containing much iron—how much, I am unable to determine, the general state of chemistry is still unsatisfactory.

Organic chemistry in particular is every day becoming more involute through simplification, inasmuch as every day new elements are being discovered which have this in common with bishops that they bear the names of countries which belong to the unfaithful and are situated *in partibus infidelium,* names, moreover, which are as lengthy as the title of a member of numerous learned societies and of the German imperial princes, names which are free-thinkers among names, because they do not let themselves be bound to any language.

In general organic chemistry is a heretic in seeking to explain life by a dead process! Sinning against life, as if I were to derive love from algebra.

The whole clearly rests on the theory of process, which has not yet been properly elaborated, nor ever can be, because it is based on the card game, a game of pure chance, in which the ace plays a leading part.

The ace is, however, the foundation of all recent jurisprudence, for one evening Irnerius lost at cards, came straight from a ladies' party, finely dressed in a blue tail-coat, new shoes with long buckles, and a waistcoat of crimson silk, and sat down and wrote a *dissertatio* on the *as*, which then led him on to start teaching Roman law.

Now Roman law embraces everything, including the theory of process and including chemistry — for it is the microcosm which has broken loose from the macrocosm, as Pacius has demonstrated.

The four books of the Institutions are the four elements, the seven books of the Pandects are the seven planets and the twelve books of the Codex are the twelve signs of the zodiac.

No spirit, however, penetrated the whole, it was merely Grethe, the cook, calling out that supper was ready.

In violent agitation Scorpion and Merten had kept their eyes closed and so had mistaken Grethe for a fairy. When they had recovered from their Spanish terror, which dated from the last defeat and the victory of Don Carlos, Merten flung himself upon Scorpion and rose up like an oak, for O! Moses will say, let man consider the stars and not look down upon the ground; meanwhile Scorpion seized his father's hand and placed his body in a dangerous position, by setting it up on its two feet.

Chapter 35

"By God! Merten the tailor is good at helping out, but he also charges high prices!"

"*Vere! beatus Martinus bonus est in auxilio, sed carus in negotio!*"

exclaimed Clovis after the battle of Poitiers when the priests of Tours told him that it was *Merten* who had tailored the riding-breeches in which he had ridden the mettlesome jade that secured him the victory, and demanded two hundred gold gulden for Merten's services.

But the truth of the whole matter is——

Chapter 36

They were sitting at table, Merten at the head, Scorpion on his right, on his left Felix the senior apprentice, and lower down the table, leaving a certain gap between the principes and the plebs, the subordinate members of the *Merten* body politic, usually termed apprentices.

The gap, which no human creature might occupy, was not filled by Banquo's ghost but by Merten's dog, which had every day to say grace at table, for *Merten*, who cultivated Humaniora, maintained that his Boniface—that was the dog's name—was one and the same person as St. Boniface, the apostle of Germany, quoting in proof a passage in which the latter announces that he is a barking dog (see Epist. 105, p. 145, ed. Seraria). He therefore felt superstitious reverence for this dog, whose place at table was by far the most elegant; for his Boniface was seated upon a soft crimson rug of finest cassimere with a fringe of silken tassels, upholstered like a sumptuous couch, supported on cunningly interlocked springs, and as soon as the gathering broke up, the seat was carried to the seclusion of a remote alcove, which appears to be the same as that described by Boileau in his *patrie* as the provost's temple of repose.

Boniface was not in his place, the gap was not filled, and the colour drained from Merten's cheeks. "Where is Boniface?" he called from a deeply troubled heart, and the whole table was visibly moved. "Where is Boniface?" Merten asked again, and how he started in fear, how he trembled in every limb, how his hair stood on end, when he heard that Boniface was not there.

All leapt up to search for him, Merten's usual calm seemed to have completely deserted him, he rang the bell, Grethe entered, her heart fearing the worst, she thought——

"Hey, Grethe, where is Boniface?" and she was visibly relieved, and he then knocked over the lamp with his groping arms, so that all was veiled in darkness, and night fell, tempestuous and pregnant with disaster.

Chapter 37

David Hume maintained that this chapter was the *locus communis* of the preceding, and indeed maintained so before I had written it. His proof was as follows: since this chapter exists, the earlier chapter does not exist, but this chapter has ousted the earlier, from which it sprang, though not through the operation of cause and effect, for this he questioned. Yet every giant, and thus also every chapter of twenty lines, presupposes a dwarf, every genius a hidebound philistine, and every storm at sea — mud, and as soon as the first disappear, the latter begin, sit down at the table, sprawling out their long legs arrogantly.

The first are too great for this world, and so they are thrown out. But the latter strike root in it and remain, as one may see from the facts, for champagne leaves a lingering repulsive aftertaste, Caesar the hero leaves behind him the play-acting Octavianus, Emperor Napoleon the bourgeois king Louis Philippe, the philosopher Kant the carpet-knight Krug, the poet Schiller the Hofrat Raupach, Leibniz's heaven Wolf's schoolroom, the dog Boniface this chapter.

Thus the bases are precipitated, while the spirit evaporates.

Chapter 38

That last sentence about the bases was an abstract concept, and therefore not a woman, for, as Adelung exclaims, an abstract concept and a woman, how different they are! However, I maintain the contrary and will duly prove it, only not in this chapter but in a book without any chapters at all which I intend to write as soon as I have accepted the Holy Trinity.

Chapter 39

If anyone desires to obtain a concrete, not abstract conception of the same — I do not mean the Greek Helen nor the Roman Lucretia, but the Holy Trinity — I can**not** advise him better than to dream of **Nothing,** as long as he does **not** fall asleep, but on the contrary to watch in the Lord and to examine this sentence, for in it there lies the concrete conception. If we ascend to its height, whole flights above our present position and floating over it like a cloud, we are confronted by the gigantic *"Not"*, if we descend to its middle, we behold in fear the enormous

"Nothing", and if we sink down into its depth, then both are again harmoniously reconciled in the **"Not"** which in its upright, bold characters of flame springs to meet them.

"Not" — **"Nothing"** *— "Not"*

that is the concrete conception of the Trinity, but as for the abstract—who shall fathom it, for

"Who hath ascended up into heaven, and descended? Who hath gathered the wind in his fists? Who hath bound the waters in a garment? Who hath established all the ends of the earth? What is his name, and what is his son's name, if thou canst tell?" says the wise Solomon.[a]

Chapter 40

"I do not know where he is, but this much is certain, a skull is a skull!" exclaimed Merten. Anxiously he stooped down to discover whose head his hand was touching in the dark, and then he started back as if in mortal terror, for the eyes——

Chapter 41

Yes, indeed! The eyes!
They are a magnet and attract iron, for which very reason we feel ourselves attracted to the ladies, but not to Heaven, for the ladies look at us out of two eyes, but Heaven out of only one.

Chapter 42

"I'll prove to him the opposite!" said an invisible voice to me, and as I looked round to see who spoke, I saw—you will not believe it, but I assure you, I swear, that it is true—I saw—but you must not be angry, do not be afraid, for it is nothing to do either with your wife or with your digestion—I saw myself, for I had offered myself as proof of the contrary.

The thought—"Ha! I am a doppelgänger!"—came over me in a flash, and Hoffmann's Elixirs of the Devil——

Chapter 43

—— Lay on the table before me just as I was pondering why the Wandering Jew is a native of Berlin and not a Spaniard; but it

---

[a] Proverbs 30: 4.— *Ed.*

coincides, I see, with the counter-evidence I have to provide, therefore we will, for the sake of precision—do neither, but instead content ourselves with the remark that Heaven lies in the ladies' eyes but not the ladies' eyes in Heaven, whence it emerges that it is not so much the eyes that attract us but rather Heaven, for we do not see the eyes but only Heaven within them. If it were the eyes that attracted us and not Heaven, then we should feel ourselves attracted to Heaven and not to the ladies, for Heaven has not one eye, as stated above, but no eye at all, yet Heaven itself is nothing but a look of infinite love from the Godhead, indeed the mild, melodious eye of the spirit of light, and an eye cannot have an eye.

Thus the final result of our inquiry is that the reason why we feel ourselves attracted to the ladies and not to Heaven is that in Heaven we do not see the ladies' eyes, whereas in the ladies' eyes we do see Heaven; that we therefore feel ourselves attracted to the eyes so to speak because they are not eyes, and because wandering Ahasuerus is a native of Berlin, for he is old and ailing and has seen many lands and eyes, yet he still does not feel himself attracted to Heaven but very much so to the ladies, and there are only two magnets, a Heaven without eyes and an eye without Heaven.

The one lies above us and draws us aloft, the other beneath us and draws us down into the depths. And Ahasuerus is drawn mightily downwards, for would he otherwise wander eternally through the lands of the Earth? And would he wander eternally through the lands of the Earth if he were not a native of Berlin and used to sands?

Chapter 44

Second Fragment from Halto's Letter-Case

We came to a country-house, it was a beautiful, dark-blue night. Your arm was in mine and you wanted to break free, but I would not release you, my hand held you captive as you held my heart, and you let it be so.

I murmured words of longing, my utterance was the most sublime and the most beautiful that mortal man can speak, for I said nothing whatever, I was withdrawn into myself, I saw a realm rise up in which the air hung so light and yet so heavy, and in that ether there stood a divine image, beauty personified, as once in the deep dreams of fantasy I had sensed but not known her, she was radiant with spiritual fire, she smiled, and you were the image.

I marvelled at myself, for I had become great through my love, as a giant; I beheld a boundless sea, but no tides swelled it any more, for it had attained depth and eternity, its surface was crystal and in its dark abyss were set quivering golden stars, they sang love-songs, they sent forth radiant fire and the sea itself was aglow!

If only this path had been life!

I kissed your sweet, soft hand, I spoke of love and of you. Above our heads floated a fine mist, its heart broke and it shed a great tear which fell between us, we felt the tear and were silent——

Chapter 47

"It is either Boniface or a pair of trousers!" cried Merten. "Light, I say, light!" and there was light. "By God, it is no pair of trousers, but Boniface, stretched out here in this dark corner, and his eyes are burning with a sinister fire, but what do I see? He is bleeding!" and without another word he flung himself down. The apprentices looked first at the dog and then at their master. At length he leapt violently to his feet. "You asses, what are you gaping for? Do you not see that the holy Boniface is hurt? I will institute strict inquiries, and woe, thrice woe, to the guilty. But quick, carry him to his seat, summon the doctor, bring vinegar and lukewarm water, and do not forget to summon the schoolmaster Vitus! His words have powerful influence over Boniface!" Thus followed the curt commands. They rushed out of the door in all directions, Merten took a closer look at Boniface, in whose eyes a milder gleam had still not yet appeared, and shook his head many times.

"I fear misfortune, a great misfortune! Call a priest!"

Chapter 48

As still not one of his helpers had appeared, Merten sprang to his feet several times in desperation.

"Poor Boniface! But wait! What if in the meantime I dared to administer the treatment myself? You are all in a fever, the blood is streaming from your mouth, you refuse your food, I see violent convulsions shake your belly, I understand you, Boniface, I understand you!" and then Grethe came in with lukewarm water and vinegar.

"Grethe! How many days is it since Boniface last had a motion? Did I not instruct you to administer to him a lavement at least once every week? But I see that in future I shall have to take over such weighty matters myself! Bring oil, salt, bran, honey and a clyster!

"Poor Boniface! You are constipated with your holy thoughts and reflections, since you can no longer relieve yourself in speech and writing!

"O admirable victim of profundity! O pious *constipation*!"

APPENDICES

BIRTH CERTIFICATE

No. 231 of the Register of Births

In the year eighteen hundred and eighteen, on the *seventh day* of the month of *May*, at *four* o'clock in the *afternoon*, there appeared before me, registrar of births, marriages and deaths at *Trier* burgomaster's office in *Trier* district, *Herr Heinrich Marx*, domiciled in *Trier*, aged *thirty-seven*,[197] by profession *barrister of the Higher Court of Appeal*, who showed me a *male* child and stated that the said child had been born in *Trier*, on the *fifth day* of the month of *May* at *two* o'clock in the *morning*, to *Herr Heinrich Marx*, *barrister* by profession, domiciled in *Trier*, and his wife *Henriette Presborck*, and that they wished to give the name *Carl* to this their child. After the aforesaid showing of the child and the above statement made in the presence of two witnesses, namely: *Herr Carl Petrasch*, aged *thirty-two*, by profession *government secretary*, domiciled in *Trier*, and *Mathias Kropp*, aged *twenty-one*, by profession *office employee*, domiciled in *Trier*, had taken place, I drew up in writing in the presence of the exhibitor of the child and the witnesses the present *certificate* on all this in double original, which after being read aloud were signed by the exhibitor of the child, the witnesses and myself.

Done in *Trier* on the day, month and year as above.

Carl Petrasch. Kropp. Marx. E. Grach.

First published in: Marx/Engels, *Gesamtausgabe*, Abt. 1, Bd. 1, Hb. 2, 1929

Printed according to a photocopy of the original

Published in English for the first time

GYMNASIUM EXAMINATION PAPERS
WRITTEN BY MARX

THE UNION OF BELIEVERS WITH CHRIST ACCORDING TO JOHN 15: 1-14, SHOWING ITS BASIS AND ESSENCE, ITS ABSOLUTE NECESSITY, AND ITS EFFECTS [198]

Before examining the basis and essence and the effects of the union of Christ with believers, let us see whether this union is necessary, whether it is determined by the nature of man, whether man cannot by himself achieve the purpose for which God brought him into being out of nothing.

If we turn our attention to history, the great teacher of mankind, we shall find engraved there that every people, even when it had attained the highest level of civilisation, when the greatest men had sprung from its womb, when the arts had blossomed within it in their full radiance, when the sciences had solved the most difficult problems, was nevertheless unable to cast off the fetters of superstition, that it had not conceived worthy and true ideas either of itself or of the Deity, that even its morality and ethics were never seen to be free from foreign admixture, from ignoble limitations, and that even its virtues owed their origin more to a crude greatness, an unbridled egoism, a passion for fame and audacious deeds than to striving for true perfection.

And the ancient peoples, the savages, who have not yet heard the teaching of Christ, betray an inner unrest, a fear of the anger of their gods, an inner conviction of their own iniquity, by making sacrifices to their gods, imagining they can atone for their sins by sacrifices.

Indeed, the greatest sage of antiquity, the divine Plato, expresses in more than one passage a profound longing for a higher being, whose appearance would fulfil the unsatisfied striving for truth and light.

Thus the history of peoples teaches us the necessity of union with Christ.

When we consider also the history of individuals, when we consider the nature of man, it is true that we always see a spark of divinity in his breast, a passion for what is good, a striving for knowledge, a yearning for truth. But the sparks of the eternal are extinguished by the flames of desire; enthusiasm for virtue is drowned by the tempting voice of sin, it is scorned as soon as life has made us feel its full power; the striving for knowledge is supplanted by a base striving for worldly goods, the longing for truth is extinguished by the sweetly flattering power of lies; and so there stands man, the only being in nature which does not fulfil its purpose, the only member of the totality of creation which is not worthy of the God who created it. But that benign Creator could not hate His work; He wanted to raise it up to Him and He sent His Son, through whom He proclaimed to us:

"Now ye are clean through the word which I have spoken unto you" (John 15:3).

"Abide in me, and I in you" (John 15:4).

Having thus seen how the history of peoples and a consideration of individuals prove the necessity of union with Christ, let us examine the last and surest proof, the word of Christ Himself.

Nowhere does He express more clearly the necessity of union with Himself than in the beautiful parable of the vine and the branches, in which He calls Himself the vine and us the branches. The branch cannot bear fruit of itself, and so, Christ says, without me you can do nothing. He expresses this still more strongly by saying:

"If a man abide not in me", etc. (John 15: 4, 5, 6).

One must, however, understand this as applying only to those who have been able to learn the word of Christ; for we cannot judge of God's decision in regard to such peoples and individuals, since we are not capable even of grasping it.

Our hearts, reason, history, the word of Christ, therefore, tell us loudly and convincingly that union with Him is absolutely essential, that without Him we cannot fulfil our goal, that without Him we would be rejected by God, that only He can redeem us.

Thus, penetrated with the conviction that this union is absolutely essential, we are desirous of finding out in what this lofty gift consists, this ray of light which descends from higher worlds to animate our hearts, and bears us purified aloft to heaven, what its inner nature and basis is.

Once we have grasped the necessity of this union, the basis for it — our need for redemption, our sinfully inclined nature, our wavering reason, our corrupted heart, our iniquity in the sight of God—is clearly visible to us and we have no need to investigate further what it is.

But who could express the nature of this union more beautifully than Christ did in the parable of the vine and the branches? Who in lengthy treatises could lay bare before our eyes in all its parts the innermost basis of this union as comprehensively as Christ did in the words:

"I am the true vine, and my Father is the husbandman" (John 15: 1).
"I am the vine, ye are the branches" (John 15: 5).

If the branch could feel, how joyfully it would look at the husbandman who tends it, who carefully frees it from weeds and binds it firmly to the vine from which it draws the nourishment and sap to form more beautiful blossoms.

In union with Christ, therefore, we turn above all our loving eyes to God, feel the most ardent thankfulness towards Him, sink joyfully on our knees before Him.

Then, when by union with Christ a more beautiful sun has risen for us, when we feel all our iniquity but at the same time rejoice over our redemption, we can for the first time love God, who previously appeared to us as an offended ruler but now appears as a forgiving father, as a kindly teacher.

But, if it could feel, the branch would not only look upwards to the husbandman, it would fondly snuggle up to the vine, it would feel itself most closely linked with it and with the branches which have sprung from it; it would love the other branches if only because the husbandman tends them and the vine gives them strength.

Thus, union with Christ consists in the most intimate, most vital communion with Him, in having Him before our eyes and in our hearts, and being so imbued with the highest love for Him, at the same time we turn our hearts to our brothers whom He has closely bound to us, and for whom also He sacrificed Himself.

But this love for Christ is not barren, it not only fills us with the purest reverence and respect for Him, it also causes us to keep His commandments by sacrificing ourselves for one another, by being virtuous, but virtuous solely out of love for Him. (John 15: 9, 10, 12, 13, 14.)

This is the great abyss which separates Christian virtue from any other and raises it above any other: this is one of the greatest effects that union with Christ has on man.

Virtue is no longer a dark distorted image, as it was depicted by the philosophy of the Stoics; it is not the offspring of a harsh

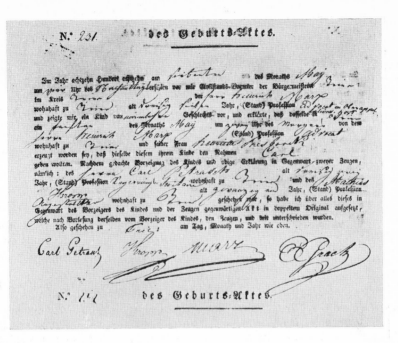

Karl Marx's Birth Certificate

Trier

The house where Karl Marx was born

Gymnasium where Marx studied
(front and view from courtyard)

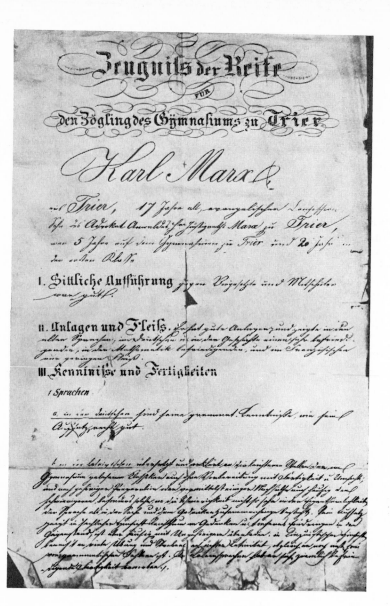

Karl Marx's Certificate of Maturity

theory of duty, as we find it among all heathen peoples, but what it achieves it accomplishes through love for Christ, through love for a divine Being, and when it springs from this pure source it is seen to be free from all that is earthly and to be truly divine. All repulsive aspects disappear, all that is earthly is suppressed, all coarseness is removed, and virtue is more brilliant by having become at once milder and more human.

Never could it have been depicted in this way by human reason, its virtue would always remain a limited, earthly virtue.

Once man has attained this virtue, this union with Christ, he will await the blows of fate with calm composure, courageously oppose the storms of passion, and endure undaunted the wrath of the iniquitous, for who can oppress him, who could rob him of his Redeemer?

What he asks, he knows will be fulfilled, for he asks only in union with Christ, hence only what is divine, and who could fail to be uplifted and comforted by this assurance which the Saviour Himself proclaims? (John 15: 7.)

Who would not bear suffering gladly, knowing that by his abiding in Christ, by his works, God Himself is glorified, that by his perfection the Lord of creation is exalted? (John 15: 8.)

Therefore union with Christ bestows inner exaltation, consolation in suffering, calm assurance, and a heart which is open to love of mankind, to all that is noble, to all that is great, not out of ambition, not through a desire for fame, but only because of Christ. Therefore union with Christ bestows a joy which the Epicurean strives vainly to derive from his frivolous philosophy or the deeper thinker from the most hidden depths of knowledge, a joy known only by the ingenuous, childlike mind which is linked with Christ and through Him with God, a joy which makes life higher and more beautiful. (John 15: 11.)

Marx

Written between August 10 and 16, 1835   Printed according to the original

First published in the yearly *Archiv für die Geschichte des Sozialismus und der Arbeiterbewegung*, 1925

DOES THE REIGN OF AUGUSTUS DESERVE TO BE COUNTED AMONG THE HAPPIER PERIODS OF THE ROMAN EMPIRE? [199]

One who seeks to know what the Augustan age was like has many things by which he can judge it: in the first place, a comparison with other periods of Roman history; for if it is shown that the Augustan age was similar to previous periods which are termed happy, but unlike those in which, according to contemporary and recent judgment, morals had changed and become worse, the state was split into factions, and even defeats were suffered in war, from them a conclusion can be drawn about the Augustan age; then it must be inquired what the ancients said about it, what view was held by foreign peoples about the empire, whether they feared or despised it, and, finally, what was the state of the arts and sciences.

In order not to be more prolix than necessary, I shall compare with the Augustan age the finest epoch before Augustus, which was made happy by the simplicity of its morals, the striving for excellence, and the unselfishness of officials and common people, and in which Lower Italy was subjugated, and also the epoch of· Nero, which was worse than any other.

At no time were the Romans more disinclined to pursue the fine arts than in the period before the Punic wars; learning was least valued since the most important men of those times chiefly devoted their efforts and labours to agriculture; eloquence was superfluous since they used few words in speaking of what had to be done and did not seek elegance of speech but attached more importance to the content; history, indeed, had no need of eloquence since it was concerned only with things done and was confined to the compilation of annals.

But the whole epoch was filled with the conflict between patricians and plebs; because from the expulsion of the kings until the first Punic war there was strife over the right of each side and a large part of history is concerned only with the laws which were made by tribunes or consuls contending keenly with one another.

What in this period deserves to be praised we have already said.

If we wish to describe the period of Nero, we do not need many words; for who would have to ask what this age was like, since the best citizens were killed, shameful arbitrary rule prevailed, laws were violated, the city burnt down, and the generals preferred to seek renown through peace rather than war, because they were afraid lest they should excite suspicion by deeds well done and because there was nothing to inspire them to perform great deeds.

That the Augustan age was unlike this no one can deny, for his reign was marked by its mildness. Although all freedom, even all appearance of freedom, had disappeared, institutions and laws were altered by order of the sovereign, and all powers previously possessed by the people's tribunes, censors and consuls were now in the hands of one man, the Romans believed they themselves ruled and that emperor was only another name for the powers which the tribunes and consuls previously possessed, and they did not see that they had been deprived of their freedom. It is, however, a telling proof of mildness if the citizens can doubt who is the sovereign and whether they themselves rule or are ruled over.

In war, however, the Romans were never more fortunate, for the Parthians were subjugated, the Cantabri conquered, the Raetians and Vindelicians laid prostrate; but the Germans, the worst enemies of the Romans, whom Caesar had fought against in vain, overcame the Romans in some isolated encounters through treachery, cunning and bravery, and owing to their forests; but on the whole the power of many of the Germanic tribes was broken by Augustus granting Roman citizenship to individuals, by the weapons of experienced generals, and by the hostility which broke out among the Germanic peoples themselves.

In peace and war, therefore, the Augustan age is not to be compared with the time of Nero and even worse rulers.

The parties and conflicts, however, which occurred in the period before the Punic wars, had ceased to exist, for we see that Augustus had combined all parties, all honorary titles and all power in his own person. Hence the sovereign power could not be disunited within itself, which brings the greatest danger to every state, because thereby its authority among foreign peoples is diminished and public affairs are administered more for the ambition of individuals than for the well-being of the people.

The Augustan age should not, however, be regarded in such a way as not to see that it was inferior to that earlier period in many respects, for if morals, freedom and worth are either diminished of definitely set aside, while avarice, prodigality and intemperance prevail, that age itself cannot be called happy. But the greatness of Augustus, the institutions and laws of the men he selected in order to put the troubled state in a better condition, did a great deal to end the disorder which had been evoked by the civil wars.

For example, we see that Augustus purged the senate, into which extremely corrupt men had penetrated, of remnants of crime, by expelling from it many men whose morals were hateful to him and by admitting many others who were distinguished for their ability and intelligence.

Under the rule of Augustus, men of outstanding worth and wisdom always served the state, for who can name greater men of that period than Maecenas and Agrippa? Although the sovereign occasionally resorted to dissimulation, he apparently did not abuse his power and exercised odious force in a milder form. And if the state, as it existed before the Punic wars, was the most suitable for that time because it stimulated people to great deeds, struck terror into its enemies, and aroused a noble emulation between patricians and plebs, from which however envy was not always absent, the state, as Augustus instituted it, seems to us the most suitable for his time, for when people have grown soft and the simplicity of morals has disappeared, but the state has grown greater, a ruler is more capable than a free republic of giving freedom to the people.

We come now to the judgment of the ancients on the Augustan age.

He himself was called divine, and regarded not as a man, but rather as a god. This could not be said if one relied only on the testimony of Horace, but the distinguished historian Tacitus also speaks of Augustus and his age with the utmost respect, the greatest admiration and even love.

At no time did arts and letters flourish more, for in that age there lived a very large number of writers from whom as from a fountain-head all peoples drew learning.

Since, therefore, the state appears to have been well ordered, the ruler desirous of happiness for the people and by his authority official positions occupied by the best men, since, moreover, the Augustan age appears to be not inferior to the best periods of Roman history, but different from the worst, and since parties and dissensions are seen to have ceased, whereas arts and letters flourished, the Augustan age deserves to be counted among the better epochs and the man held in high esteem who, although everything was permitted to him, nevertheless after his accession to power had only one aim, to ensure the safety of the state.

Marx

Written between August 10 and 16, 1835   Printed according to the original

First published in the yearly *Archiv für*   Translated from the Latin
die Geschichte des Sozialismus und der Ar-
beiterbewegung, 1925

CERTIFICATE OF MATURITY [200]
FOR
PUPIL OF THE GYMNASIUM IN TRIER

Karl Marx,

from *Trier,* *17* years of age, of *evangelical* faith, son of *barrister-at-law, Herr Justizrat Marx* in *Trier,* was *five* years at the gymnasium in Trier, and *two* years in the first class.

    I. Moral behaviour towards superiors and fellow pupils *was good.*

    II. Aptitudes and diligence. *He has good aptitudes, and in ancient languages, German, and history showed a very satisfactory diligence, in mathematics satisfactory, and in French only slight diligence.*

    III. Knowledge and accomplishments

      1. Languages:

      a) In German, *his grammatical knowledge and composition are very good.*

      b) In Latin, *even without preparation he translates and explains with facility and circumspection the easier passages of the classics read in the gymnasium; and after due preparation or with some assistance frequently also the more difficult passages, especially those where the difficulty consists not so much in the peculiarity of the language as in the subject-matter and train of thought. His composition shows, in regard to material, a wealth of thought and deep insight into the subject-matter, but is often overladen with irrelevancies; in regard to language, he gives evidence of much practice and striving for genuine latinity, although he is not yet free from grammatical errors. In speaking Latin, he has acquired a fairly satisfactory fluency.*

      c) In Greek, *his knowledge and abilities, in regard to understanding the classics read in the gymnasium, are almost the same as in Latin.*

d) In French, *his knowledge of grammar is fairly good; with some assistance he reads also more difficult passages and has some facility in oral expression.*

e) In Hebrew,[a]

2. Sciences:

a) Religious knowledge. *His knowledge of the Christian faith and morals is fairly clear and well grounded; he knows also to some extent the history of the Christian Church.*

b) Mathematics. *He has a good knowledge of mathematics.*

c) In History and Geography *he is in general fairly proficient.*

d) Physics [and nature study]. *In physics his knowledge is moderate.*

3. Accomplishments.

a) ....

b) ....

The undersigned examining commission has accordingly, since he is now leaving this gymnasium in order to study *jurisprudence,* awarded him the certificate of *maturity* and discharges him, *cherishing the hope that he will fulfil the favourable expectations which his aptitudes justify.*

Trier, *September 24, 1835.*

Royal Examining Commission
   Brüggemann, Royal Commissioner
   Wyttenbach, Director
   Loers
   Hamacher
   Schwendler   *Küpper*
   Steininger
     Schneemann

First published in the yearly *Archiv für die Geschichte des Sozialismus und der Arbeiterbewegung,* 1925

Printed according to the original

Published in English for the first time

---

[a] Not filled in.— *Ed.*

Father's Letters

(NOVEMBER 1835-JUNE 1836)[201]

HEINRICH MARX TO KARL MARX
IN BONN

Trier, November 8, 1835

Dear Karl,

More than three weeks have passed since you went away, and there is no sign of you! You know your mother[a] and how anxious she is, and yet you show this boundless negligence! That, unfortunately, only too strongly confirms the opinion, which I hold in spite of your many good qualities, that in your heart egoism is predominant.

Your mother knows nothing of this letter. I do not want to increase her anxiety still more, but I repeat, it is irresponsible of you.

For my part, I can wait—but I expect you to set your mother's mind at rest by return of post.

Your father
Marx

First published in: Marx/Engels, *Gesamtausgabe*, Abt. 1, Bd. 1, Hb. 2, 1929

Printed according to the original

Published in English for the first time

HEINRICH MARX TO KARL MARX
IN BONN

[Trier, November 18-29, 1835]

Dear Karl,

First of all, a few words about my letter, which may possibly have annoyed you. You know I don't pedantically insist on my

---

[a] Henriette Marx.—*Ed.*

authority and also admit to my child if I am wrong. I did actually tell you to write only after you had had a somewhat closer look around you. However, since it took so long, you ought to have taken my words less literally, especially as you know how anxious and worried your good mother is. Well, that is enough on that subject.

Your letter, which was barely legible, gave me great joy. Of course, I have no doubt of your good intentions, your diligence, or of your firm resolve to achieve something worth while. However, I am glad that the beginning is pleasant and easy for you and that you are getting a liking for your professional studies.

Nine lecture courses seem to me rather a lot and I would not like you to do more than your body and mind can bear. If, however, you find no difficulty about it, it may be all right. The field of knowledge is immeasurable, and time is short. In your next letter you will surely give me a somewhat larger and more detailed report. You know how greatly I am interested in everything which concerns you closely.

In connection with the lectures on law, you must not demand [...] should be touching and poetic. The subject-matter does not allow [...] poetic composition, you will have to put up with it and [...] find worthy of deep thought. Excuse [...] subjects.

What more ought I to say to you? Give you a sermon? In order [...] to tell [...] what you do not know? Although enough of [...] nature has so endowed you that if you truly ... the [...] your clear mind, your pure feeling, your unspoilt [...] instruct, in order not to stray from the right path [...] and what I wish, you know very well. I want now [...] you make up for what I in less favourable circumstances [...] could not achieve. I should like to see in you what perhaps I could have become, if I had come into the world with equally favourable prospects. You can fulfil or destroy my best hopes. It is perhaps both unfair and unwise to build one's best hopes on someone and so perhaps undermine one's own tranquillity. But who else than nature is to blame if men who are otherwise not so weak are nevertheless weak fathers?

You have been granted a good fortune, dear Karl, that is given to few youths of your age. At the important initial stage of your career you have found a friend, and a very worthy friend, who is older and more experienced than you. Know how to value this good fortune. Friendship in the true classical sense is life's most beautiful jewel, and at this age for your whole life. It will be the best touchstone of your character, your mind and heart, indeed of your morality, if you are able to retain your friend and be worthy of him.

That you will continue to be good morally, I really do not doubt. But a great support for morality is pure faith in God. You know that I am anything but a fanatic. But this faith is a real [require]ment of man sooner or later, and there are moments in life when even the atheist is [involun]tarily drawn to worship the Almighty. And it is common [...], for what Newton, Locke and Leibniz believed, everyone can [...] submit to.

[Herr] Loers has taken it ill that you did not pay him a farewell [visit]. You and Clemens were the only ones, he [...] Herr Schlick. I had to have recourse to a white lie and tell him [...] we were there while he was away. The society [...] association with Clemens was little to my liking.

Herr Loers has been appointed second director and Herr [Brügge]mann as Commissioner was here yesterday for the installation. It was a big [... ce]remony, since both Herr Brüggemann and Herr Loers spoke. Herr Loers gave a great luncheon, which I also attended. There I spoke with several persons who asked after you, and from many quarters I was congratulated on Herr Wienenbrügge being your friend. I am truly desirous of making his acquaintance, and I should be very glad if you would both visit us at Easter and, of course, stay with us together. I should regard that especially as a proof of his friendship for you.

And so, dear Karl, fare you very well, and in providing really vigorous and healthy nourishment for your mind, do not forget that in this miserable world it is always accompanied by the body, which determines the well-being of the whole machine. A sickly scholar is the most unfortunate being on earth. Therefore, do not study more than your health can bear. With that, daily exercise and abstemiousness, and I hope to find you stronger in mind and body every time I embrace you.

Trier, November 18, 1835

Your faithful father

Marx

Apropos! I have read your poem word by word. I quite frankly confess, dear Karl, that I do not understand it, neither its true meaning nor its tendency. In ordinary life it is an undisputed proposition that with the fulfilment of one's most ardent wishes the value of what one wished is very much diminished and often disappears altogether. That is surely not what you wanted to say. That would be worth consideration at most as a moral principle, because guided by this idea one avoids immoral enjoyments and even puts off what is permissible, in order by the postponement to retain the desire or even secure a heightened enjoyment. Kant felicitously says something of this sort in his anthropology.[202]

Do you want to find happiness only in abstract idealising (somewhat analogous to fanciful reverie)? In short, give me the key, I admit that this is beyond me.

[In the left margin of the first page]

On the occasion of the celebration for Herr Loers I found the position of good Herr Wyttenbach extremely painful. I could have wept at the offence to this man, whose only failing is to be much too kind-hearted. I did my best to show the high regard I have for him and, among other things, I told him how devoted you are to him and that you would have liked to compose a poem in his honour but had no time. That made him very happy. Will you do me the favour of sending me a few verses for him?

[Postscript at the top of the first page on the right-hand side]

P.S. Your dear mother has been prevented from writing and so it has taken until today, November 29. It is remarkable that we do not even know your exact address.

[Postscript by Marx's mother on November 29 to the letter of November 18]

Much beloved, dear Carl,

With great pleasure I take up my pen to write to you; your dear father's letter has been ready a long time, but I have always been prevented. I should like to have another letter from you, which would prove that you are well, for you can well believe that I long for you very much. We are still all quite well, heaven be thanked, everybody is busy and industrious, and even Eduard[a] is working very hard so that we hope to make an able man of him yet. Now, you must not regard it as a weakness of our sex if I am curious to know how you arrange your little household, whether economy really plays the main role, which is an absolute necessity for both big and small households. Here allow me to note, dear Carl, that

---

[a] Karl Marx's brother.— *Ed.*

you must never regard cleanliness and order as something secondary, for health and cheerfulness depend on them. Insist strictly that your rooms are scrubbed frequently and fix a definite time for it—and you, my dear Carl, have a weekly scrub with sponge and soap. How do you get on about coffee, do you make it, or how is it? Please let me know everything about your household. Your amiable Muse will surely not feel insulted by your mother's prose, tell her that the higher and better is achieved through the lower. So good-bye now. If you have any wish to express for Christmas that I can satisfy, I am ready to do so with pleasure. Farewell, my dear beloved Carl, be upright and good and always keep God and your parents before your eyes. Adieu, your loving mother Henriette Marx.

All the children send you greetings and kisses, and as usual you are the kindest and best.

First published in: Marx/Engels, *Gesamtausgabe*, Abt. 1, Bd. 1, Hb. 2, 1929

Printed according to the original

Published in English for the first time

HEINRICH MARX TO KARL MARX
IN BONN

[Trier, beginning of 1836]

Dear [Karl,]ᵃ

Unless the description of your condition was somewhat poetical—as I hope it was—it is well adapted to cause us disquiet. I hope at least that the sad experience will bring home to you the need to pay rather more attention to your health. Next to a clear conscience, this is man's greatest blessing, and youthful sins in any enjoyment that is immoderate or even harmful in itself meet with frightful punishment. We have a sad example here in Herr Günster. True, in his case there is no question of vice, but smoking and drinking have worked havoc with his already weak chest and he will hardly live until the summer. His life itself is a torture, and in him we shall have lost an excellent mind.

ᵃ The page is damaged here.— *Ed.*

Even excessive study is madness in such a case. On the other hand, moderate exer[cise],[a] such as walking, and sometimes even riding, but not madly, is very beneficial; cheerfulness and banishing all worries still better.

Your accounts, dear Karl, are *à la* Carl, disconnected and inconclusive. If only they had been shorter and more precise, and the figures properly set out in columns, the operation would have been very simple. One expects *order* even from a scholar, and especially from a practical lawyer.

On the whole, I find nothing to object to, only at the present moment I think it is inexpedient and burdensome to buy a lot of books, especially big historical works.

Your journey was appropriate if it was good for your health, only you ought to have sent a few words about it beforehand.

In spite of your *two* letters (you see, they can be counted), I still do not know your study plan, which of course is of great interest to me. This much I do see, that you are not going in for any branch of natural history, and if physics and chemistry are really so badly taught, you will indeed do better to attend these courses in Berlin. Only a general introduction into cameralistics, it seems to me, would be expedient, because it is always useful to have a general idea of what one will have to do some day.

Apropos! Herr Gratz here has sent me a recommendation for Herr Walter. I sent it to him with a letter—have you heard anything about it? I would be pleased at this, because it was precisely this professor you so particularly liked.

Your little circle appeals to me, as you may well believe, much more than ale-house gatherings. Young people who take pleasure in such meetings are necessarily educated people and are more aware of their value as future excellent citizens than those who find their outstanding value in outstanding coarseness.

You do well to wait before going into print. A poet, a writer, must nowadays have the calling to provide something sound if he wants to appear in public. Otherwise, let him, of course, pay homage to the Muses. That always remains one of the most noble acts of homage to women. But if everywhere the first appearance in the world is largely decisive, this is primarily the case for these demigods. Their superiority must show itself in the first verse, so that everyone immediately recognises their divine inspiration. I tell you frankly, I am profoundly pleased at your aptitudes and I expect much from them, but it would grieve me to see you

_____

[a] The page is damaged here.— *Ed.*

make your appearance as an ordinary poetaster; it should still be enough for you to give delight to those immediately around you in the family circle. Only the excellent have the right to claim the attention of a pampered world which has a Schiller — poetic minds would probably say "gods".

I thank you, by the way, dear Karl, for your very filial remark that you would submit your first work to me for criticism before anybody else. That is all the more proof of your tender regard since you know how little nature has endowed me with poetry, so that throughout my life I was never capable of composing a merely tolerable poem, even in the sweet days of first love. However, I will bear it in mind and wait to see if it was merely a compliment.

How does it happen, dear Karl, that your journey does not figure in the expenses. You haven't eked out your existence by cadging, I hope.

I enclose a money order for 50 talers, and on this occasion can only say that your only concern should be your studies and, without using more than is necessary, you should save yourself any further anxiety. The hope that you might some day be a support for your brothers and sisters is an idea too beautiful and too attractive for a good-natured heart for me to want to deprive you of it.

For the time being, I have nothing more to add, and only repeat my advice to you to take care of your health. There is no more lamentable being than a sickly scholar, and no more unfortunate parents than those who see a son of great promise wasting away, for whose education they have made sacrifices. Take that to heart. I can only appeal to your heart, for I believe it good and noble.

Embracing you affectionately,

Your father
Marx

[Postscript by Marx's mother]

Dear beloved Carl,

Your being ill has worried us very much, but I hope and wish that you will have recovered, and although I am very anxious about the health of my dear children, I am sure that if you, dear Carl, behave sensibly you can reach a ripe old age. But for that you must avoid everything that could make things worse, you must not get over-heated, not drink a lot of wine or coffee, and not eat anything pungent, a lot of pepper or other spices. You must not smoke any tobacco, not stay up too long in the evening, and rise early. Be careful also not to catch cold and, dear Carl, do not dance until you are quite well again. It will seem ridiculous to you, dear Carl, that I act the doctor in this way, but you do not know how parents take it to heart when they see that their children are not well, and how many anxious hours this has already caused us. You children see to it that you keep morally and physically healthy, and do not worry about anything else. Dear father has been well throughout the winter, thank God, and there has been no lack of work, and we are still all quite well. How do you like my native city—it is a really beautiful place and I hope that it may have so much inspired you as to give you material for poetry. Write soon, dear Carl, even if not a lot, but don't put it off too long. Adieu, dear Carl, I kiss you in my thoughts,

Your loving mother

Henriette Marx

First published in: Marx/Engels, *Gesamtausgabe*, Abt. 1, Bd. 1, Hb. 2, 1929

Printed according to the original

Published in English for the first time

HEINRICH MARX TO KARL MARX [a]
IN BONN

Trier, March 19, 1836

Dear [Karl,]

I have just received your letter, and I must confess that I am somewhat surprised at it.

As regards your letter containing the accounts, I already told you at the time that I could not make head or tail of them. This much I did see, that you need money, and therefore I sent you 50 talers. With what you took with you, that makes 160 talers. You have been away five months in all, and now you do not even say *what* you need. That, at all events, is strange. Dear Karl, I repeat that I do everything very willingly, but that as the father of many children—and you know quite well I am not rich—I am not willing to do more than is necessary for your well-being and progress.

---

[a] The envelope bears the address "Herrn Karl Marx, studiosus juris in Bonn."—*Ed.*

If therefore you have somewhat overstepped the bounds, let it be glossed over, since it must. But I assure you, what the *"nec plus ultra"* stands for is money *thrown away*. I am convinced that it is possible to manage with less, and Herr Müller, the notary here, gives less and can perhaps do better. But no more under any condition; I should have to have some special stroke of good fortune, but there is nothing of the kind at the present time; on the contrary, my income has decreased. I don't by any means say that to distress you, far from it, but to make my firm decision clear to you once and for all.

I enclose a draft on Herr Kaufmann, who, as Herr Hofmann tells me, is the keeper of the lottery office in the university building; you will get money there, as m[uch as] you need.

Well, may God take care of you, and come soon. We are all longing to see you.

Your faithful father
Marx

First published in: Marx/Engels, *Gesamt-ausgabe*, Abt. 1, Bd. 1, Hb. 2, 1929

Printed according to the original

Published in English for the first time

HEINRICH MARX TO KARL MARX
IN BONN [203]

[Trier, about May or June 1836]

Dear Karl,

Your letter, which I received only on the 7th, has strengthened my belief in the uprightness, frankness and loyalty of your character, which means more to me than the money, and therefore we will not say anything more about that. You are receiving 100 talers herewith and, if you ask for it, you will receive the rest. However, you will surely become somewhat wiser, and also will have to concern yourself with the smaller things, for, God knows, in spite of all philosophy, these smaller things give one many grey hairs.

And is duelling then so closely interwoven with philosophy? It is respect for, indeed fear of, opinion. And what kind of opinion?

Not exactly always of the better kind, and yet!!! Everywhere man has so little consistency.—Do not let this inclination, and if not inclination, this craze, take root. You could in the end deprive yourself and your parents of the finest hopes that life offers. I think a sensible man can easily and decently pay no heed to it, *tout en imposant*.

Dear Karl, if you can, arrange to be given good certificates by competent and well-known physicians there, you can do it with a good conscience. Your chest is weak, at least at present.—If you like, I will send you one from Herr Berncastel, who treats you. But to be consistent with your conscience, do not smoke much.

You have not kept your word to me—you remember your promise—and I rather prided myself on the recognition of my criticism. However, like political optimists, I take the actual state of things as it is, but I did wish to have some knowledge of my own of the matter, i.e., of the negotiations conducted, which perhaps I would have been able to check better than Schäfer—and if possible also knowledge of the matter in question—but if this last involves too much trouble, I shall wait till your arrival. Farewell, dear Karl, always remain frank and true, always look on your father and your good mother as your best friends. I could not keep anything secret from her, because otherwise she would have been anxious at your long silence. She is economical, but for her love of life is [...][a]—and everything is secondary to this. I embrace you affectionately.

Your faithful father
Marx

I must, however, inform you about something peculiar.

Your friend Kleinerz wrote to me that he is being badly persecuted (probably because he left) and has even had to take the school examination, which, however, to his astonishment he passed brilliantly. He fears very many difficulties. Of very effective assistance to him would be a recommendation from your bishop[b] to the Dean of the Medical Faculty, Herr Professor Müller, who in his youth received much kindness from this worthy man.

---

[a] The paper has been damaged, the sense is perhaps "the highest good".— *Ed.*
[b] J. L. A. Hommer.— *Ed.*

And lo and behold, good Herr Görgen undertook to speak to the bishop, and the latter at once agreed, and said I should draw up the paper myself (without, however, in the slightest wanting to admit his relation to Herr Müller). I sent the recommendation post-paid to Herr Müller and informed Herr Kleinerz about it.

The latter displayed great tact because at once, and in order to safeguard my position to some extent in relation to the friend who trusted my bare word, he sent me, without waiting for the result, his service testimonials, which are really splendid. Moreover, he seemed to have no doubt of success.

How chance plays with human beings!

Your dear mother greets and kisses you. It is too late to write any more—until next time.

[Added on the first page of the letter]

At the moment I could not send you any more. In the next few days you will probably receive 20 talers through Rabe.

First published in: Marx/Engels, *Gesamtausgabe*, Abt. 1, Bd. 1, Hb. 2, 1929

Printed according to the original

Published in English for the first time

FATHER'S CONSENT TO MARX'S TRANSFER FROM BONN TO BERLIN UNIVERSITY

I not only grant my son Karl Marx permission, but it is my will that he should enter the University of Berlin next term for the purpose of continuing there his studies of Law and Cameralistics, which he began in Bonn.

Trier, July 1, 1836

Marx
Justizrat, Barrister

[Postscript]

Please, dear Karl, write at once, but write frankly, without reserve and truthfully. Calm me and your dear, kind mother, and we will soon forget the little monetary sacrifice.

Marx

First published in: Marx/Engels, *Gesamtausgabe*, Abt. 1, Bd. 1, Hb. 2, 1929

Printed according to the original
Published in English for the first time

CERTIFICATE OF RELEASE
FROM BONN UNIVERSITY[204]

To No. 26

Copy

We, the Rector and Senate of the Royal Prussian Rhenish Frederick William University in Bonn, testify by this certificate that Herr *Carl Heinrich Marx*, born in Trier, son of Herr Justizrat Marx of the same place, prepared for academic studies at the gymnasium in Trier, on the basis of the certificate of maturity of the above-mentioned gymnasium, was matriculated here on October 17, 1835, has since then resided here until now as a student, and has applied himself to the study of jurisprudence.

During this stay at our University, according to the certificates submitted to us, he has attended the lectures listed below:

I. In the winter term 1835/36

1) Encyclopaedia of jurisprudence with Professor *Puggé*, very diligent and attentive.
2) Institutions with Professor *Böcking*, very diligent and with constant attention.
3) History of Roman law with Professor *Walter*, ditto.
4) Mythology of the Greeks and Romans with Professor *Welcker*, with excellent diligence and attention.
5) Questions about Homer with Professor *von Schlegel*, diligent and attentive.
6) History of modern art with Professor *D'Alton*, diligent and attentive.

II. In the summer term 1836

7) History of German law with Professor *Walter*, diligent.

8) Elegiacs of Propertius with Professor *von Schlegel*, diligent and attentive.
9) European international law and
10) Natural right with Professor *Puggé*. Could not be testified owing to the sudden death of Professor Puggé on August 5.

In regard to his behaviour, it has to be noted that he has incurred a punishment of one day's detention for disturbing the peace by rowdiness and drunkenness at night; nothing else is known to his disadvantage in a moral or economic respect. Subsequently, he was accused of having carried prohibited weapons in Cologne. The investigation is still pending.

He has not been suspected of participation in any forbidden association among the students.

In witness thereof, this certificate has been drawn up under the seal of the University and signed with their own hand by the Rector pro tem and also by the present Deans of the Faculties of Law and Philosophy.

Bonn, August 22, 1836

Rector	Dean of the Faculty of Law
Freytag	*Walter*
University judge	Dean of the Faculty of Philosophy
von Salomon /	*Loebell*

Oppenhofen, U.S.

Witnessed by the Extraordinary Governmental Plenipotentiary and Curator

Von Rehfues

First published in the yearly *Archiv für die Geschichte des Sozialismus und der Arbeiterbewegung*, 1926

Printed according to the copy of the original

Published in English for the first time

Wir Rector und Senat der Königlich Preußischen Rheinischen Friedrich=Wilhelms Universität zu Bonn

beurkunden durch dieses Abgangs=Zeugniß, daß Herr *Carl Heinrich Marx*

geboren zu *Trier*

Sohn *des Herrn Justizraths Marx daselbst*

zu den academischen Studien *auf dem Gymnasium zu Trier*

vorbereitet auf den Grund *der Entlassungszeugnisse der Ersten gedachten Gymnasiums*

am *17 ten October 1835* bei uns immatriculirt worden ist, sich seitdem bis *hiehier*

als Studirender hier aufgehalten und sich *der Rechts= Wissenschaften*

beflissen hat.

Während dieses Aufenthalts hat derselbe bei unserer Universität nach den vorgelegten Zeugnissen die nachstehend verzeichneten Vor= lesungen gehört:

I. Im Wintersemester 1835–36.

1.) *Encyclopädie der Rechtswissenschaft bei Prof. Puggé sehr fleißig und aufmerksam.*

2.)

Certificate of Release from Bonn University

HEINRICH MARX TO KARL MARX
IN BERLIN

Trier, November 9, 1836

Dear Karl,

We had, it is true, already received news of you before getting your letter, because Herr Jaehnigen was kind enough to write to me. His letter is very courteous towards you and me. He even very kindly asks me to recommend that you should comply with his desire and visit him and his family quite often *sans gêne*; and as I play such a small part in the world, I have all the less reason to doubt his sincerity, since in general I have always seen him behaving as a man most worthy of respect and most noble. It does one good to enjoy the esteem of such a man, whose heart and mind rank him among the privileged.

That Herr Esser treated you with such respect, I found rather unexpected, and it does you honour, for this circumstance proves that, in spite of your strict principles, you are able to associate with the most diverse kinds of people on human terms. These principles remind me of my bygone youth, and the more so since they were all I possessed. I was not adroit, and that can easily be explained. Your mother says that you are a favourite of fortune. I have no objection to that. Please God that you believe it! At least, in this respect I do not for a moment doubt your heart, that you are serious in counting yourself lucky to have your parents. And surely a little exaggeration is nowhere more pardonable than on this point, and no harm is done if here the head is ruled by the heart.

Even if Herr Reinhard is ill, nevertheless he must have a clerk who should surely know something about my son.

Herr Sandt is not *von*, he is the brother of the Attorney General Sandt of Cologne and has a post at the Court of Appeal. Herr Meurin knows him well. If necessary, he can inform you about my case, in which he is probably the opponent.

That you like Herr Meurin so much gives me great pleasure, for I have a special liking for him. He is one of the rare people who retain goodness of heart along with polite manners. His practical mind certainly puts to shame many very learned persons.

I am particularly glad that you live with well-educated people and do not associate much with young people, at least those whom you don't know well enough. The only thing I ask of you is not to overdo your studying, but to keep physically fit and spare your badly impaired eyesight. You have been attending many and important courses — naturally, you have every reason to work a great deal, but do not exhaust yourself. You have still a long time to live, God willing, to the benefit of yourself and your family and, if my surmise is not mistaken, for the good of mankind.

For the moment, I have not yet settled on any commercial firm. I want to talk to Herr von Nell about it. For the time being I am sending you herewith 50 talers. You must at present be able to estimate approximately the amount you absolutely need each year, and that is what I should like to know.

I wrote to you from Frankfurt, where I was because of Hermann.[a] Herr Donner conveyed the letter to the Hofrat. It was sent on October 20.[205] You seem not to have received it yet. It contained rather a lot of sermonising, so I won't engage in that for a long time to come. But I should like a reply to that letter. Because of the one and, of course, extremely important item, I beg you even to enclose, besides the special letter for me, an extra-special one. True, as a rule I never keep anything secret from your good mother. But in this matter I am concerned at present about her all too great anxiety, which is not, as in the case of the husband, adequately countered by the more lively feeling of strict duty.

I am no angel, it is true, and I know that man does not live by bread alone. But in the face of a sacred duty to be fulfilled, subsidiary intentions must give way. And, I repeat, there is no more sacred duty for the husband than that which he undertakes towards his wife, who is weaker. Therefore, in this, as in every other respect, be quite frank with me as with a friend. But if, after self-examination, you really persist in your resolve, you must at

---

[a] Karl Marx's brother.— *Ed.*

once show yourself to be a man. That, all the same, does not prevent poetic ardour, the aspiration to fulfil one's duty is also very poetic.

Today Hermann has gone to Brussels, where he is entering a good house. But he has to pay 1,000 fr. immediately for the entrée. In return, the house is merely bound to introduce him to all the commercial transactions that occur, without stipulation of period, so that it depends on his diligence and understanding to put himself as quickly as possible in a position to become independent. I expect a good deal from his diligence, but all the less from his intelligence. Understandably, he is not living at the businessman's house, and for the present he has to keep himself entirely. It is a pity that this well-meaning youth has not got a better brain.

Menni[a] attends the gymnasium and, it seems, he does want to show rather more zeal.— The girls are good and diligent. My hair stands on end when I reflect that this commodity now is only sought after if gilded, and I understand so little of that art.

Why have you not told me any details about Kleinerz? I am very interested to know what has become of him.

Well, God take care of you, dear Karl, and always love your father as he loves you.

Marx

First published in: Marx/Engels, *Gesamtausgabe*, Abt. 1, Bd. 1, Hb. 2, 1929

Printed according to the original
Published in English for the first time

HEINRICH MARX TO KARL MARX
IN BERLIN

Trier, December 28, 1836

Dear Karl,

If I were less indulgent, if in general I could harbour resentment for a long time, and particularly against my dear ones, I would certainly be justified in not answering you at all. It is not in itself praiseworthy to be exaggeratedly touchy, least of all towards a father whose failing is certainly not that of severity.

---

[a] Karl Marx's brother Eduard.— *Ed.*

If you had reflected that at the time I sent you the last letter I had had no word from you apart from your first letter; that the interval was somewhat large, even counting from my second letter from here; that having once got mixed up in a matter — which in itself was not precisely pleasing to me — from a feeling of duty towards a really most worthy person, I was bound to be extremely sensitive to a silence that was inexplicable to me, and that, if I then used some expressions which might sound harsh, in the first place I did not think of weighing my words, but also was sensitive not entirely without cause; besides, I assure you I did not have any *animus calumniandi*.

If I did not have a high opinion of your kind heart, I would not in general be so attached to you and would suffer less at aberrations, for you know that high as I esteem your intellectual gifts, in the absence of a good heart they would be of no interest to me at all. But you yourself confess that you have previously given me some cause to harbour some doubts about your self-abnegation. And in view of all this, you could very well be somewhat less touchy towards your father.

It is now high time that you did away with the tension that ruins mind and body, and I can rightly demand that in this connection you should show some consideration for the well-being of your good mother and myself, for we certainly do not soar to Elysian fields, and consider it of some importance that you should remain healthy.

But I repeat, you have undertaken great duties and, dear Karl, at the risk of irritating your sensitivity, I express my opinion somewhat prosaically after my fashion: with all the exaggerations and exaltations of love in a poetic mind you cannot restore the tranquillity of a being to whom you have wholly devoted yourself; on the contrary, you run the risk of destroying it. Only by the most exemplary behaviour, by manly, firm efforts which, however, win people's goodwill and favour, can you ensure that the situation is straightened out and that she is exalted in her own eyes and the eyes of the world, and comforted.

I have spoken with Jenny[a] and I should have liked to be able to set her mind at rest completely. I did all I could but it is not possible to argue everything away. She still does not know how her parents will take the relationship. Nor is the judgment of relatives and the world a trifling matter. I am afraid of your not always just

---

[a] Jenny von Westphalen.— *Ed.*

sensitivity and therefore leave it to you to appreciate this situation. If I were powerful enough to protect and soothe this noble being in some respect by vigorous intervention, no sacrifice would be too great for me. Unfortunately, however, I am weak in every respect.

She is making a priceless sacrifice for you. She is showing a self-denial which can only be fully appreciated in the light of cold reason. Woe to you, if ever in your life you could forget this! At present, however, only you yourself can effectively intervene. From you must come the certainty that, despite your youth, you are a man who deserves the respect of the world, and wins it in mighty strides, who gives assurance of his constancy and his serious efforts in the future, and compels evil tongues to be silent about past mistakes.

How you can best set about this, only you can be fully aware.

In this connection I must ask you whether you know how old one must be to hold an academic post. It is very important to know this, for your plan, I think, should aim at attaining such a position as soon as possible, even if in a lower grade, and you should try by writing to create prospects for a good situation and eventually to realise them.

Poetry must surely be the first lever; the poet, of course, should be competent here. However, the kind of poetry to bring about the magic effect might preferably be a matter for one who is wise and a man of the world.— In ordinary life that might well be too much to demand of a young man; but he who undertakes higher duties must be consistent, and here wisdom and policy will be sanctified in the eyes of the poet himself by high and creditable fulfilment of duty.

I beg and beseech you — since basically you have talent, only the form is not yet smooth — henceforth be calm, moderate these storms, do not arouse them either in the bosom of one who deserves and needs tranquillity. Your mother, I myself, Sophie,[a] the good child, who exercises self-denial in the highest degree, watch over you, as far as the situation allows, and in return for your efforts the future holds out for you a happiness to deserve which all hardships are easy to bear.

Your views on law are not without truth, but are very likely to arouse storms if made into a system, and are you not aware how violent storms are among the learned? If what gives offence in this matter itself cannot be entirely eliminated, at least the form must be conciliatory and agreeable.

---

[a] Karl Marx's sister.— *Ed.*

You do not say anything about Meurin, nor whether you paid a visit to Herr Eichhorn.

I do not want to write to Herr Jaehnigen just now, and since the matter is not at all urgent, you can wait for an opportunity.

If you send bulky letters by ordinary post, they are very expensive. The last but one cost a taler. Parcels sent by express post are dear too, the last one also cost a taler.

If you want to write a great deal in future, then write on all possible sorts of subjects, so that what we hear is much and varied. Let it mount up to form a parcel and send this by the luggage van. Do not be offended at this little remark about economy.

I hope that you will have received the wine by now. Drink it and be cheerful, and give up all irrelevant ventures, all despair, and abandon poetry if it does not embellish your life and make it happy.

[Postscript by Marx's mother]

Dear Carl,

Your dear father is in such a hurry to send off this letter that all I can do is to send you heartiest greetings and kisses.

Your loving mother

Henriette Marx

[Continuation from Marx's father]

Enclosed a money order for 50 talers. If you prefer me to look for a firm there to make an arrangement with you, you must tell me approximately the monthly sum I should fix for you. By now you must be able to say what it amounts to with one thing and another.

Marx

[Postscript by Marx's sister Sophie]

Your last letter, dear Karl, made me weep bitter tears; how could you think that I would neglect to give you news of your Jenny!? I dream and think only of you two. Jenny loves you; if the difference in age worries her, that is because of her parents. She will now try gradually to prepare them; after that write to them yourself; they do indeed think highly of you. *Jenny* visits us frequently. She was with us yesterday and wept tears of delight and pain on receiving your poems. Our parents and your brothers and sisters love her very much, the latter beyond all measure. She is *never* allowed to leave us before ten o'clock, how do you like that? Adieu, dear, good Karl, my most ardent wishes for the success of your heart's desire.

First published in: Marx/Engels, *Gesamtausgabe*, Abt. 1, Bd. 1, Hb. 2, 1929

Printed according to the original

Published in English for the first time

HEINRICH MARX TO KARL MARX

IN BERLIN

Trier, February 3, 1837

Dear Karl,

Your last letter made me particularly glad, for it proves that you have got rid of the little weaknesses which, by the way, disquieted me; you recognise your position and are endeavouring with energy and dignity to assure your future. But, dear Karl, do not fall into the opposite extreme.

Apart from the fact that to be sociable offers very great advantages for diversion, rest and development, especially to a young man, wisdom demands—and this is something you must not neglect, since you are no longer alone—that one should acquire some support, in an honourable and worthy way, of course. *Neglect*, especially as one is not always inclined to seek the most honourable reason for it, is not easily forgiven by distinguished persons, or those who think themselves such, and particularly if they have shown a certain degree of condescension.— Herr Jaehnigen and Herr Esser are not only excellent men, but are probably important for you, and it would be most unwise and really improper to neglect them, since they received you in a very decent way. At your age and in your position you cannot demand any reciprocity.

Nor must the body be neglected. Good health is the greatest boon for everyone, for scholars most of all.

Do not overdo things. With your natural gifts and your present diligence, you will reach your goal, and a single term does not matter.

However much experience I may have, I cannot draw up a complete plan for you with a clear survey of all nuances.

In any case, it seems to me beyond doubt that your intention of advancing yourself by academic studies is quite good and suitable for you, if, besides, you do not overlook the trifle of paying some attention to physical development.

But, of course, this may take rather a long time and given the state of things it would of course be desirable that something be done about it. In this respect, therefore, the only thing left is *authorship*. But how to make a start? This is a difficult question, but there is another that precedes it: will you succeed at once in winning the confidence of a good publisher? For that could well be the most difficult thing. If you succeed in that — and on the whole you are a favourite of fortune — then the second question arises. Something philosophical or legal, or both together, seems excellent for laying a basis. Good poetry might well take second place, and it never harms one's reputation, except perhaps in the eyes of a few pedants. Light polemical articles are the most useful, and with a few good titles, if they are original and have a new style, you can decently and safely await a professorship, etc., etc., etc. But you must come to a firm decision, if not at the present moment, at any rate this year, and when you have taken it, keep it firmly in view and pursue your course unswervingly. It is by no means so difficult for you as it was for your papa to become a lawyer.

You know, dear Karl, because of my love for you I have let myself in for something which is not quite in accord with my character, and indeed sometimes worries me. But no sacrifice is too great for me if the welfare of my children requires it. Moreover, I have won the full confidence of your Jenny. But the good, lovable girl torments herself incessantly — she is afraid of doing you harm, of making you over-exert yourself, etc., etc., etc. It weighs on her mind that her parents do not know or, as I believe, do not want to know. She cannot explain to herself how it is that she, who considers herself quite unsentimental, has let herself be so carried away. A certain shyness may have something to do with it.

A letter from you, which you may enclose sealed, but which should not be dictated by the fanciful poet, could comfort her. It must, of course, be full of delicate, devoted feeling and pure love, as I have no doubt it will be, but it must give a clear view of your relationship and elucidate and discuss the prospects. The hopes expressed must be set out without reserve, clearly and with firm conviction, so that they in their turn are convincing.

You must give a firm assurance that this relationship, far from doing you any harm, has the happiest effect on you, and in certain respects I believe that myself. On the other hand, resolutely demand, with the manly audacity in the face of which the poor child was so defenceless, that now she must not waver, not look back, but calmly and confidently look to the future.

What have you to say to your father? Are you not astonished to find me in the role of intermediary? How wrongly I might be judged by many persons if my influence were to become known! What ignoble motives might perhaps be imputed to me! But I do not reproach myself—if only heaven bestows its blessing, I shall feel extremely happy.

It would be proper to pay a visit to Herr Eichhorn, but I leave that to you. I repeat, however, that I should like to see you going more often to Herr Jaehnigen and Herr Esser.

It would be just as well, too, if you were to make somewhat closer contact with at least one of the most influential professors.

Have you not seen any more of young Herr Schriever? Since we are on very good terms and Mlle. Schriever will probably marry your friend Karl von Westphalen, and since anyway he should be coming here soon, I should like you to visit him now and again.

Have you not heard any further news of Dr. Kleinerz? I should like to learn something about him.

I enclose herewith a letter of credit. It is for a higher amount than you yourself asked, but I did not want to have it altered, because now I trust you not to use more than is necessary.

Well, good-bye, dear Karl, write soon if you have not yet sent a letter such as I have requested. Write also what your landlord is doing, he interests me very much.

Herr von Notz told me that you would come here during the autumn vacation. I am not at all in favour of this, and if you bear in mind your circumstances and those of persons who are dear to you, you will have to agree with me. But it is possible that I may go to Berlin. What do you say to that?

Your faithful father

Marx

I send my best regards to my dear friend Meurin and his amiable wife. Tell him that he would do well to spare a moment for me.

P.S. It would not be a bad thing, dear Karl, if you would write more legibly.

I seldom see Jenny, she cannot do as she likes. You can be easy in your mind, her love is true.—When you have written in the way I would like, I will ask for a reply.

First published in: Marx/Engels, *Gesamtausgabe*, Abt. 1, Bd. 1, Hb. 2, 1929

Printed according to the original
Published in English for the first time

HEINRICH MARX TO KARL MARX

IN BERLIN

Trier, March 2, 1837

It is remarkable that I, who am by nature a lazy writer, become quite inexhaustible when I have to write to you. I will not and cannot conceal my weakness for you. At times my heart delights in thinking of you and your future. And yet at times I cannot rid myself of ideas which arouse in me sad forebodings and fear when I am struck as if by lightning by the thought: is your heart in accord with your head, your talents? Has it room for the earthly but gentler sentiments which in this vale of sorrow are so essentially consoling for a man of feeling? And since that heart is obviously animated and governed by a demon not granted to all men, is that demon heavenly or Faustian? Will you ever— and that is not the least painful doubt of my heart—will you ever be capable of truly human, domestic happiness? Will—and this doubt has no less tortured me recently since I have come to love a certain person like my own child—will you ever be capable of imparting happiness to those immediately around you?

What has evoked this train of ideas in me, you will ask? Often before, anxious thoughts of this kind have come into my mind, but I easily chased them away, for I always felt the need to surround you with all the love and care of which my heart is capable, and I always like to forget. But I note a striking phenomenon in Jenny. She, who is so wholly devoted to you with her childlike, pure disposition, betrays at times, involuntarily and against her will, a kind of fear, a fear laden with foreboding, which does not escape me, which I do not know how to explain, and all trace of which she tried to erase from my heart, as soon as I pointed it out to her. What does that mean, what can it be? I cannot explain it to myself, but unfortunately my experience does not allow me to be easily led astray.

That you should rise high in the world, the flattering hope to see your name held one day in high repute, and also your earthly well-being, these are not the only things close to my heart, they are long-cherished illusions that have taken deep root in me. Basically, however, such feelings are largely characteristic of a weak man, and are not free from all dross, such as pride, vanity, egoism, etc., etc., etc. But I can assure you that the realisation of these illusions could not make me happy. Only if your heart remains pure and beats in a purely human way, and no demonic spirit is capable of estranging your heart from finer feelings—only then would I find the happiness that for many years past I have dreamed of finding through you; otherwise I would see the finest aim of my life in ruins. But why should I grow so soft and perhaps distress you? At bottom, I have no doubt of your filial love for me and your good, dear mother, and you know very well where we are most vulnerable.

I pass on to positive matters. Some days after receiving your letter, which Sophie brought her, Jenny visited us and spoke about your intention. She appears to approve your reasons, but fears the step itself, and that is easy to understand. For my part, I regard it as good and praiseworthy. As she intimates, she is writing to you that you should not send the letter direct—an opinion I cannot agree with. What you can do to put her mind at rest is to tell us eight days beforehand on what day you are posting the letter. The good girl deserves every consideration and, I repeat, only a lifetime full of tender love can compensate her for what she has already suffered, and even for what she will still suffer, for they are remarkable saints she has to deal with.

It is chiefly regard for her that makes me wish so much that you will soon take a fortunate step forward in the world, because it would give her peace of mind, at least that is what I believe. And I assure you, dear Karl, that were it not for this, I would at present endeavour to restrain you from coming forward publicly rather than spur you on. But you see, the bewitching girl has turned my old head too, and I wish above all to see her calm and happy. Only you can do that and the aim is worthy of your undivided attention, and it is perhaps very good and salutary that, immediately on your entry into the world, you are compelled to show human consideration, indeed wisdom, foresight and mature reflection, in spite of all demons. I thank heaven for this, for it is the human being in you that I will eternally love. You know that, a practical man though I am, I have not been ground down to such a degree as to be blunted to what is high and good. Nevertheless, I do not readily allow myself to be completely torn up from the earth, which is my solid basis, and wafted exclusively into airy spheres where I have no firm ground under my feet. All this naturally gives me greater cause than I would otherwise have had to reflect on the means which are at your disposal. You have taken up dramatic composition, and of course it contains much that is true. But closely bound up with its importance, its great publicity, is quite naturally the danger of coming to grief. Not always, especially in the big cities, is it necessarily the inner value which is decisive. Intrigues, cabals, jealousy, perhaps among those who have had the most experience of these, often outweigh what is good, especially if the latter is not yet raised to and maintained in high honour by a well-known name.

What, therefore, would be the wisest course? To look for a possible way by which this great test would be preceded by a smaller one involving less danger, but sufficiently important for you to emerge from it, in the event of success, with a not quite unimportant name. If, however, this has to be achieved by something small, then the material, the subject, the circumstances, must have some exceptional quality. I racked my brains for a long time in the search for such a subject and the following idea seemed to me suitable.

The subject should be a period taken from the history of Prussia, not one so prolonged as to call for an epic, but a crowded moment of time where, however, the future hung in the balance.

It should redound to the honour of Prussia and afford the opportunity of allotting a role to the genius of the monarchy—if need be, through the mind of the very noble Queen Louise.

Such a moment was the great battle at La Belle Alliance-Waterloo. The danger was enormous, not only for Prussia, for its monarch,[a] for the whole of Germany, etc., etc., etc. In fact, it was Prussia that decided the great issue here—hence, at all events this could be the subject of an ode in the heroic genre, or otherwise—you understand that better than I do.

The difficulty would not be too great in itself. The biggest difficulty, in any case, would be that of compressing a big picture

---

[a] Frederick William III.— *Ed.*

into a small frame and of giving a successful and skilful portrayal of the great moment. But if executed in a patriotic and German spirit with depth of feeling, such an ode would itself be sufficient to lay the foundation for a reputation, to establish a name.

But I can only propose, advise. You have outgrown me; in this matter you are in general superior to me, so I must leave it to you to decide as you will.

The subject I have spoken of would have the great advantage that it could very soon be presented apropos, since the anniversary is on June 18.[a] The cost would not be very considerable, and if necessary I will bear it.—I should so very much like to see good Jenny calm and able to hold up her head proudly. The good child must not wear herself out. And if you are successful in this project—and the demand is not beyond your powers—then you will be in a secure position and able to relax somewhat from the hothouse life.

In point of fact, too, it is impossible not to be enthusiastic over this moment of time, for its failure would have imposed eternal fetters on mankind and especially on the human mind. Only today's two-faced liberals can deify a Napoleon. And in truth under his rule not a single person would have dared to think aloud what is being written daily and without interference throughout Germany, and especially in Prussia. And anyone who has studied the history of Napoleon and what he understood by the absurd expression of ideology can rejoice greatly and with a clear conscience at his downfall and the victory of Prussia.

Give my cordial greetings to our friend Meurin. Tell him that until now I have not been able to carry out the commission with which I have been charged. I suffered from a cold for eight days and since then I have not ventured any farther than to attend the sitting.

Your faithful father
Marx

First published in: Marx/Engels, *Gesamtausgabe*, Abt. 1, Bd. 1, Hb. 2, 1929

Printed according to the original
Published in English for the first time

---

[a] The date of the battle of Waterloo.— *Ed.*

23*

HEINRICH MARX TO KARL MARX
IN BERLIN[206]

Bad Ems, August 12, 1837

Dear Karl,

My letter, written when I was greatly excited, may have hit you rather hard, and I am sincerely sorry if this was actually the case. Not as though I would thus have committed an injustice; I leave it to you to judge for yourself whether I had a valid reason to lose my temper. You know, you must know, how much I love you. Your letters (so long as I do not find in them any traces of that sickly sensitivity and fantastic, gloomy thoughts) are a real need and would have been particularly so this summer for your deeply feeling mother and myself. Eduard has been ailing for the last six months, and has grown quite thin, his recovery is very doubtful, and, what is so rare among children and so exhausting, he suffers from the deepest melancholy, really fear of dying.— And you know what your mother is like — she won't go from his side, she torments herself day and night, and I am for ever afraid that she will be overcome by these exertions.

For the last 7-8 months, I myself have been afflicted by a painful cough, which has been continually irritated by the eternal necessity of speaking. Sophie, too, is never quite well and is always taking medicine without success. In this situation — what with your love affair, Jenny's prolonged indisposition, her profound worry, and the ambiguous position in which I, who have always known only the most straightforward course, find myself in relation to the Westphalens — all this has deeply affected me and at times depressed me so much that I no longer recognised myself, and so I ask you: have I been too hard under the influence of the most profound ill humour?

However much I love you above everything — except your mother — I am not blind and still less want to be so. I do you justice in many matters, but I cannot entirely rid myself of the thought that you are not free from a little more egoism than is necessary for self-preservation, and I cannot always dispel the thought that were I in your position I would show greater consideration for and more self-sacrificing love towards my parents. I received nothing from my parents apart from my existence — although not to be unjust, love from my mother — and how I have fought and suffered, in order not to distress them as long as possible.

Do not put forward your character as an excuse. Do not blame nature. It has certainly treated you like a mother. It has given you strength enough, the will is left to man. But to abandon oneself to grief at the slightest storm, to lay bare a shattered heart and break the heart of our beloved ones at every suffering, do you call that poetry? God protect us from the most beautiful of all nature's gifts if that is its immediate effect. No, it is only weakness, over-indulgence, self-love and conceit which reduce everything to their own measure in this way and force even those we love most into the background!

The first of all human virtues is the strength and will to sacrifice oneself, to set aside one's ego, if duty, if love calls for it, and indeed not those glamorous, romantic or hero-like sacrifices, the act of a moment of fanciful reverie or heroic feeling. Even the greatest egoist is capable of that, for it is precisely *the ego* which then has pride of place. No, it is those daily and hourly recurring sacrifices which arise from the pure heart of a good person, of a loving father, of a tender-hearted mother, of a loving spouse, of a thankful child, that give life its sole charm and make it beautiful despite all unpleasantness.

You yourself have described so beautifully the life of your excellent mother, so deeply felt that her whole life is a continual sacrifice of love and loyalty, and truly you have not exaggerated. But what is the good of beautiful examples if they do not inspire one to copy them? But can you, with your hand on your heart, pride yourself on having done this up to now?

I do not want to press you too hard, certainly I do not want to offend you, for as a matter of fact I am weak enough to regret having offended you. But it is not merely that I, and your good mother, suffer from it, perhaps I would let that pass. In no one's heart is there so little selfishness as in that of good parents. But for your own good I must not and will not ever abandon this text until I am convinced that this stain on your otherwise so noble character has disappeared. Quite soon you will and must be the father of a family. But neither honour nor wealth nor fame will make your wife and children happy; you alone can do that, your better self, your love, your tender behaviour, the putting behind you of stormy idiosyncrasies, of violent outbreaks of passion, of morbid sensitivity, etc., etc., etc. I am hardly speaking any longer on my own behalf, I am calling your attention to the bond that is to be tied.

You say yourself that good fortune has made you its pet child. May God in His infinite goodness make it ever attend you closely, as much as frail humanity permits. But even the happiest man experiences gloomy hours, no mortal basks in eternal sunshine. But from him who is happy one has every right to demand that he meet the storm with manly courage, calm, resignation, cheerfulness. One can rightly demand that past happiness be an armour against temporary suffering. The heart of the happy man is full and wide and strong, it must not allow itself to be easily shattered.

Your dear mother has forwarded your letter to me here. The plan you have outlined is fine, and if properly executed, well fitted to become a lasting monument of literature. But great difficulties are piling up in the way, particularly because of the selfishness of those who are offended, and of the fact that there is no man of outstanding critical reputation to be at the head. On the other hand, the paper is suitable for creating a reputation. Here the question arises whether your name appears in this connection. For it is precisely to gain a reputation, a reputation as a critic, that is so essential for you, as helping towards a professorship. Nevertheless, I could not derive any certainty on that score from your letter. May God give you His blessing.

It seems that my trip to Berlin will not materialise. After the big expenses I have had this year it would make too great a demand on my funds. And then also I must confess that I have had some intention (although not very definite) to try if possible to transfer to the magistracy. However, I would have liked to know in advance the opinion of Herr Jaehnigen, whose co-operation could in any case be very useful. But since this did not come about, I see little hope for the matter. I did not want to ask anything of you that went against your feelings, but perhaps you could have acted more wisely.— I hear, by the way, that Herr Jaehnigen and his wife are making a trip to Paris and will pass through Trier. You have missed a lot, for this summer Frau Jaehnigen has written some really exceptionally tender letters to your Jenny.

I am looking forward with great desire to receiving a letter from you to hear more about your undertakings. But I ask you to go into rather more detail.

Today I have sacrificed my morning walk for you, but there is just time to make a smaller one and to write a few lines to your good mother, to whom I will send this letter. For it would irk me to write again at length, and in this way your mother has a big letter all the same.

Good-bye, my good Karl, and always hold me as dear as you say, but do not make me blush with your flattery. There is no harm in having a high opinion of your father. In my position I have also achieved something, enough to have you, but not enough by far to satisfy me.

Your father
Marx[a]

P.S. The supposed funeral sermon which you asked me for is a work of about ten lines, which I no longer possess, but which I believe Sophie has, and which even in the last version has undergone some alterations.

First published in: Marx/Engels, *Gesamt-ausgabe,* Abt. 1, Bd. 1, Hb. 2, 1929

Printed according to the original
Published in English for the first time

HEINRICH MARX TO KARL MARX
IN BERLIN[b]

Bad Ems [approximately August 20, 1837][c]

Dear, good Karl,

I do not know whether on receipt of this letter you will already have received the letter which I [sent] to your dear mother. But I think so. Meanwhile, since I like talking to you, and since you may perhaps find it pleasant to see someone whose friendly company I have enjoyed for a number of days, I take advantage of the kind willingness of the bearer [to] send you a few lines.

The bearer is a fine young man, tutor to the son of Prince Karl.[d] I made his acquaintance here, where I, who do not easily mix, have mostly been isolated. I have spent many pleasant hours with Herr Heim, and insofar as one can get to know [someone] in a short time, I think I have found in him a very honest,

---

[a] Heinrich Marx's letter to his son ends here and is followed by a few lines to his wife.— *Ed.*

[b] On the envelope is written: "Herrn H. Karl Marx, stud. juris et camer[alium], alte Leipziger Strasse Ia Berlin." — *Ed.*

[c] Here and in the following places marked by square brackets the paper has been damaged.— *Ed.*

[d] Friedrich Karl, Prince of Prussia.— *Ed.*

pleasant and upright man. He will look you up, he tells me, and I shall be [glad if] he finds that the picture sketched by a father's self-complacency is accurate.

In view of the approaching vacation, it may perhaps not be unpleasing for you to see some things that are remarkable and it is possible that owing to his position Herr Heim can easily help you in this respect.

If you have leisure and write to me, I shall be glad if you will draw up for me a concise plan of the positive legal studies that you have gone through this year. According to your project, it seems to me unnecessary for you to take lectures on cameralistics. Only do not neglect natural science, for there is no certainty of being able to make up for this later, and regret comes too late.

Perhaps in a few years' time it will be a favourable moment to obtain an [...] entry into law, if you are making Bonn your goal, since there is absolutely no man there who can do anything out of the ordinary. I know that in regard to science Berlin has advantages and great attraction. But apart from the fact that greater difficulties arise there, you must surely also have some regard for your parents, whose sanguine hopes would be largely shattered by your residing so far away. Of course that must not hinder your plan of life; parental love is probably the least selfish of all. But if this plan of life could be fraternally combined with these hopes, that would be for me the highest of all life's joys, the number of which decreases so considerably with the years.

My stay here has so far yielded very little success, and yet I shall have to prolong it in spite of the most painful boredom in order to comply with the wish of your dear mother, who most urgently begs me to do so.

I shall obviously have to abandon my beautiful, long-cherished desire to see you during this vacation. It costs me great effort, but it seems it cannot be helped. This fatal cough tortures me in every respect!

Well, God take care of you, dear Karl, be happy and — I cannot repeat it too often — do not neglect your health as you enrich your mind.

With all my heart and soul,

Your father
Marx

First published in: Marx/Engels, *Gesamt-ausgabe*, Abt. 1, Bd. 1, Hb. 2, 1929

Printed according to the original

Published in English for the first time

HEINRICH MARX TO KARL MARX
IN BERLIN[a]

Trier, September 16, 1837

Dear Karl,

Your last letter, which we received about eight days ago, leads me to expect a larger sequel, and that indeed soon, and I should have liked to wait until I have a general view of the whole. But it might have worried you to have to wait too long, especially as it concerns a plan which will perhaps determine the next steps.

You know me, dear Karl, I am neither obstinate nor prejudiced. Whether you make your career in one department of learning or in another [is] essentially all one to me. But it is dear to my heart, of course for your sake, that you choose the one that is most in accord with your natural talents. At the outset it was the ordinary thing that one had in mind. Such a career, however, seemed not to your liking and I confess that, infected by your precocious views, I applauded you when you took academic teaching as your goal, whether in law or philosophy, and in the final count I believed the latter to be more likely. I was sufficiently aware of the difficulty of this career, and I particularly learned about it recently in Ems, where I had the opportunity to see a good deal of a professor of Bonn University. On the other hand, one thing is undeniable, namely [that] someone who is sure of himself could play an important role as a professor of law in Bonn, and it is easier to be sent from Berlin to Bonn, provided of course one has some patronage. Poetry would have to procure this patronage for you. But whatever your good fortune in this respect, it will take several years and your special situation puts you under pressure[...].

Let us take a look at the other aspect (and an important point is that with good classical studies a professorship can always remain a final goal). Does a practical career advance one so rapidly? As a rule it does not, and experience proves this only too well. Here also patronage does a great deal. Without it you would not be able to complain at all if, a few years after having completed your studies, you became an unpaid assessor, and then [remained] an assessor for years after. However, even with the strictest moral standards and the most meticulous scruples, it may be permissible

---

[a] On the envelope is written: "Herrn Karl Marx, stud. juris wohlgeboren in Stralow. N. 4 bei Berlin."— *Ed.*

to procure for oneself through one's own merits a patron who, convinced of the protégé's efficiency, conscientiously advances and promotes him. And in any case you have been endowed by nature with talents that are very suitable for this purpose. How to make the best use of them is a matter for you to decide, and can hardly be judged by a third person, the more so since here the individual character must be very much taken into consideration. And whatever you undertake you must necessarily look at the matter and make your estimate from *this* point of view, for you are in a hurry; you feel that and so do I.

In some respects, that is of course to be regretted, but the most beautiful picture has its shades, and here resignation has to come into play. This resignation, moreover, is based on parts so brilliantly lit, and owes its origin so entirely to one's own will, which is guided by the heart and mind, that it is to be considered a pleasure rather than a sacrifice.

But I return to the question: What should I advise? And, in the first place, as regards your plan for theatrical criticism, I must confess above all that, as far as the subject itself is concerned, I am not particularly competent. Dramatic criticism requires much time and great circumspection. As far as art is concerned, such work in our time may perhaps be most meritorious. As far as fame is concerned, it can lead to an academic diploma.

How will it be received? I think with more hostility than favour, and the good, learned Lessing pursued, as far as I know, no rose-strewn path, but lived and died a poor librarian.

Will it yield particular financial profit? The question merges with the preceding one, and I am not in a position to give a categorical reply. I still think that some outstanding single works, a really good poem, a sterling tragedy or comedy, are far more suitable for your purpose.— But you are carving out your own career and you want to go on doing so. I can only address one wish to heaven, that in one way or another you may as quickly as possible achieve your real aim.

I will say only one thing more. If, owing to the fact that after three years of study you ask nothing more from home, you expose yourself too much to the necessity of doing what could be harmful to you, then let fate have its way and at all events even if it involves sacrifice on my part, I will much rather make such sacrifice than harm your career. If you manage it sensibly and without holding up your career, you will certainly afford me great relief, because, in point of fact, since the separation of the law court and the hawking activities of the young men, my income has diminished in proportion as my expenses have become heavier. But, as I have said, this consideration must not stand in the way.

In coming back to the question of a practical career, however, why do you say nothing of cameralistics? I do not know whether I am mistaken, but it seems to me that poetry and literature are more likely to find patrons in the administration than in the judiciary, and a singing government adviser seems to me more natural than a singing judge. And after all what more is there in cameralistics than you already need as a true lawyer, apart from natural science? This last you must by no means neglect, that would be irresponsible.

You are, however, at the fountain-head, from which you can derive instruction, and precisely that aspect of the whole structure which under normal conditions you would probably still be far from appreciating, viz., *the vital question in the proper sense,* is forced on your attention and hence you will reflect, check and act with due care. I feel no anxiety that these considerations, even though forced on you, will ever lead you to base, grovelling actions. Despite my grey hairs, somewhat depressed state of mind and all too many cares, I would still be defiant and despise what is base. To you with your unimpaired powers, on whom nature has showered blessings, anything of the sort must seem impossible. But proud youth with its abundance of vital energy may regard as humiliating much that wisdom and duty peremptorily dictate in regard to oneself and especially to those whose welfare one has made it one's duty to ensure. True, worldly wisdom is a good deal to ask of a 19-year-old, but one who at 19——

I have not shown your last letter to Westphalen. These very good people are of such a peculiar stamp; they discuss everything from so many aspects and at such length that it is as well to give them as little material as possible. Since your studies this year remain the same, I do not see why I should give them material for new fantasies.

Jenny is not yet here, but is to come soon; that she does not write to you is—I cannot call it anything else—childish, head-strong. For there can be no doubt at all that her attitude to you is one of the most self-sacrificing love, and she was not far from proving it by her death.

She has somehow got the idea that it is unnecessary to write, or some other obscure idea about it that she may hold, she has also a touch of genius, and what bearing does that too have on the matter? You can be certain, as I am (and you know that I am not credulous by nature), that no prince would be able to turn her away from you. She is devoted to you body and soul, and you must never forget it, at her age she is making a sacrifice for you that ordinary girls would certainly not be capable of. So if she has the idea of not being willing or able to write, in God's name let it pass. For after all it is only a token, and one can dispense with that at least, if one is assured of the essential. I [shall] speak to her about it if the occasion offers, however unwilling I am to do so.

Throughout the year I was gladdened by the expectation of seeing you, and so one lives under an eternal illusion. The only thing that does not deceive is a good heart, the love that flows from the heart; and in this respect I can only count myself among the rich, for I enjoy the love of an incomparable wife and the love of good children.

Do not make us wait so long for letters. Your good mother needs to be cheered up and your letters have a wonderful effect on her spirits. She has suffered so much this summer that only one so entirely forgetful of self could keep going, and things are still the same. May God rescue us soon from this long struggle! Write now and again a few lines for Eduard[a] but act as if he were quite well again.

If, without too much inconvenience to yourself, you can make closer contact with Herr Jaehnigen, you will be doing me a favour, I very much desire it. For you especially, it would be very advantageous to associate with Herr Esser and, as I hear, he is on friendly terms with Meurin.

Further, I beg you to go to Herr Geh. Justizrat Reinhard and in my name ask him to take steps to get a move made at last in my affair. Win or lose, I have cares enough and should like to have this worry off my mind at least.

Well, my dear good Karl, I think I have written enough. I seldom divide things into portions and think that warmed-up portions are not as good as fresh ones. Good-bye, and in connection with your old father do not forget that your blood is young; and if you are lucky enough to safeguard it from tempestuous and ravaging passions, refresh it at least by youthful cheerfulness and a joyful spirit, and by youthful pleasures in which heart and mind agree. I embrace you with all my heart and soul.

Your faithful father

---

[a] Karl Marx's brother.— *Ed.*

[Postscript by Marx's mother]

Dear beloved Carl,

That heaven may keep you in good health is indeed my most ardent wish, apart from that you be moderate in your way of life and as much as possible also in your wishes and hopes now that you have achieved what is most essential, you can act with more calm and discretion. Frau von Westphalen[a] spoke to the children today. [Jenny is to] come today or tomorrow. She writes that she wants so very much to return to Trier and is longing to hear from you. I think Jenny's silence towards you is due to maidenly modesty, which I have already often noted in her, and which is certainly not to her disadvantage, but only still more enhances her charms and good qualities.—Edgar will probably go to Heidelberg to continue his studies from [...] for the feared—that your welfare and your success in whatever you undertake is dear to our hearts, you can rest assured. May the Almighty and the All-good only show you the right path that is most beneficial for you, that is what we wish to ask for. Only be of good courage and [...] persists will be crowned. I kiss you with all my heart in my thoughts. [...] make you for the autumn woollen jackets which will protect you from catching cold. Write very soon, dear Carl.

Your ever loving mother

Henriette Marx

Write also a few lines sometime to Hermann,[b] and enclose them in a letter to us. He is doing very well and people are very satisfied with him.

First published in: Marx/Engels, *Gesamtausgabe*, Abt. 1, Bd. 1, Hb. 2, 1929

Printed according to the original
Published in English for the first time

HEINRICH MARX TO KARL MARX
IN BERLIN

Trier, November 17, 1837

Dear Karl,

Have you still your headquarters in Stralow? At this time of year and in the land where no lemon trees are in bloom, can this be thinkable? But where are you then? That is the question, and for a

---

[a] Caroline von Westphalen.— *Ed.*
[b] Karl Marx's brother.— *Ed.*

practical man the first requirement for correspondence is to know an address. Therefore, I have to take advantage of the kindness of others.

An address, however, is form, and precisely that seems to be your weak side. Things may well be different as regards material? At least, one should suppose so, if one bears in mind: 1) that you have no lack of subject-matter, 2) that your situation is serious enough to arouse great interest, 3) that your father is perhaps somewhat partial in his attachment to you, etc., etc., etc., and yet after an interval of two months, the second of which caused me some unpleasant hours full of anxiety, I received a letter without form or content, a torn fragment saying nothing, which stood in no relation to what went before it and had no connection with the future!

If a correspondence is to be of interest and value, it must have consistency, and the writer must necessarily have *his* last letter before his eyes, as also the last reply. Your last letter but one[a] contained much that excited my expectation. I had written a number of letters which asked for information on my points. And instead of all that, I received a letter of bits and fragments, and, what is much worse, an *embittered* letter.

Frankly speaking, my dear Karl, I do not like this modern word, which all weaklings use to cloak their feelings when they quarrel with the world because they do not possess, without labour or trouble, well-furnished palaces with vast sums of money and elegant carriages. This embitterment disgusts me and you are the last person from whom I would expect it. What grounds can you have for it? Has not everything smiled on you ever since your cradle? Has not nature endowed you with magnificent talents? Have not your parents lavished affection on you? Have you ever up to now been unable to satisfy your reasonable wishes? And have you not carried away in the most incomprehensible fashion the heart of a girl whom thousands envy you? Yet the first untoward event, the first disappointed wish, evokes embitterment! Is that strength? Is that a manly character?

You yourself had declared, in dry words, that you would be satisfied with assurances for the future, and because of them renounce all outward signs for the present. Did you not make that renunciation word for word in writing? And only children complain about the word they have given when they begin to feel pressure.

---

[a] See this volume, pp. 10-21.— *Ed.*

Yet here too your luck holds. Your good mother, who has a softer heart than I have and to whom it still very often occurs that we too were once the plaything of the little blind rogue, sounded the alarm, and the all too good parents of your Jenny could hardly wait for the moment when the poor, wounded heart would be consoled, and the recipe is undoubtedly already in your hands, if a defective address has not caused the epistle to go astray.

Time is limited, for Sophie is to take the letter before the post to the von Westphalens, who now live far away, and this good opportunity also was announced to me only today, so that I must conclude. As a matter of fact, at present I would not know what to say, at most I could only put questions to you, and I do not like to be importunate. Only one thing more my Herr Son will still allow me, namely, to express my surprise that I have still not received any request for money! Or do you perhaps want already now to make up for it from the too great amount taken? It's a little too early for that.

Your dear mother refused to reconcile herself entirely to the fact that you did not come home in the autumn as the others did. If it is too long for you and dear mother until next autumn, you could come for the Easter vacation.

Your faithful father

Marx

[Postscript by Marx's sister Sophie]

Good-bye, dear Karl, let us have news soon that you are now satisfied and that your mind is at rest. Until Easter, Karl, the hours until then will seem to me an eternity!

First published in: Marx/Engels, *Gesamtausgabe*, Abt. 1, Bd. 1, Hb. 2, 1929

Printed according to the original

Published in English for the first time

HEINRICH MARX TO KARL MARX

IN BERLIN

Trier, December 9, 1837

Dear Karl,

If one knows one's weaknesses, one must take steps against them. If then I wanted as usual to write in a coherent way, in the end my love for you would mislead me into adopting a sentimental tone, and all that had gone before would be the more wasted since you — so it seems at least — never take a letter in your hand a second time, and indeed quite logically, for why read a letter a second time if the letter sent in return is never an answer.

I will therefore give vent to my complaints in the form of aphorisms, for they are really complaints that I am putting forward. So, in order to make them quite clear to myself and to make you swallow them like pills, I raise questions which I am inclined to settle quite *a posteriori*.

1. What is the task of a young man on whom nature has incontestably bestowed unusual talent, in particular

a) if he, as he asserts and moreover I willingly believe, reveres his father and idealises his mother;

b) if he, without regard to his age and situation, has bound one of the noblest of girls to his fate, and

c) has thereby put a very honourable family into the position of having to approve a relationship which apparently and according to the usual way of the world holds out great dangers and gloomy prospects for this beloved child?

2. Had your parents any right to demand that your conduct, your way of life, should bring them joy, at least moments of joy, and as far as possible banish causes of sorrow?

3. What have been so far the fruits of your magnificent natural gifts, as far as your parents are concerned?

4. What have been these fruits as far as you yourself are concerned?

Strictly speaking, I could and should perhaps end here and leave it to you to reply and give a complete explanation. But I am afraid of any vein of poetry in this connection. I will reply prosaically, from real life as it actually is, at the risk of appearing too prosaic even to my Herr Son.

The mood in which I find myself is in fact anything but poetic. With a cough which I have had for a year and which makes it hard for me to follow my profession, coupled with recent attacks of gout, I find myself to be more ill-humoured than is reasonable and become annoyed at my weakness of character, and so, of course, you can only expect the descriptions of an aging, ill-tempered man who is irritated by continual disappointments and especially by the fact that he has to hold up to his own idol a mirror full of distorted images.

Replies and/or Complaints

1. Gifts deserve, call for gratitude; and since magnificent natural gifts are certainly the most excellent of all, they call for a specially high degree of gratitude. But the only way nature allows gratitude to be shown her is by making proper use of these gifts and, if I may use an ordinary expression, making one's talent bear profit.

I am well aware how one should and must reply in a somewhat nobler style, namely, such gifts should be used for one's own ennoblement, and I do not dispute that this is true. Yes, indeed, they should be used for one's ennoblement. But how? One is a human being, a spiritual being, and a member of society, a citizen of the state. Hence physical, moral, intellectual and political ennoblement. Only if unison and harmony are introduced into the efforts to attain this great goal can a beautiful, attractive whole make its appearance, one which is well-pleasing to God, to men, to one's parents and to the girl one loves, and which deserves with greater truth and naturalness to be called a truly plastic picture than would a meeting with an old schoolfellow.

But, as I have said, only the endeavour to extend ennoblement in due, equal proportion to all parts is evidence of the will to prove oneself worthy of these gifts; only through the evenness of this distribution can a beautiful structure, true harmony, be found.

Indeed, if restricted to individual parts, the most honest endeavours not only do not lead to a good result, on the contrary, they produce caricatures: if restricted to the physical part—simpletons; if to the moral part—fanatical visionaries; if to the political part—intriguers, and if to the intellectual part—learned boors.

a) Yes, a young man must set himself this goal if he really wants to give joy to his parents, whose services to him it is for his heart to appreciate; especially if he knows that his parents put their finest hopes in him.

b) Yes, he must bear in mind that he has undertaken a duty, possibly exceeding his age, but all the more sacred on that account, to sacrifice himself for the benefit of a girl who has made a great sacrifice in view of her outstanding merits and her social position in abandoning her brilliant situation and prospects for an uncertain and duller future and chaining herself to the fate of a younger man. The simple and practical solution is to procure her a future worthy of her, in the real world, not in a smoke-filled room with a reeking oil-lamp at the side of a scholar grown wild.

c) Yes, he has a big debt to repay, and a noble family has the right to demand adequate compensation for the forfeiting of its great hopes so well justified by the excellent personality of the child. For, in truth, thousands of parents would have refused their consent. And in moments of gloom your own father almost wishes they had done so, for the welfare of this angelic girl is all too dear to my heart; truly I love her like a daughter, and it is for that very reason that I am so anxious for her happiness.

All these obligations together form such a closely woven bond that it alone should suffice to exorcise all evil spirits, dispel all errors, compensate for all defects and develop new and better instincts. It should suffice to turn an uncivilised stripling into an orderly human being, a negating genius into a genuine thinker, a wild ringleader of wild young fellows into a man fit for society, one who retains sufficient pride not to twist and turn like an eel, but has enough practical intelligence and tact to feel that it is only through intercourse with moral-minded people that he can learn the art of showing himself to the world in his most pleasant and most advantageous aspect, of winning respect, love and prestige as quickly as possible, and of making practical use of the talents which mother nature has in fact lavishly bestowed upon him.

That, in short, was the *problem*. How has it been solved?

God's grief!!! Disorderliness, musty excursions into all departments of knowledge, musty brooding under a gloomy oil-lamp; running wild in a scholar's dressing-gown and with unkempt hair instead of running wild over a glass of beer; unsociable withdrawal with neglect of all decorum and even of all consideration for the *father.*— The art of association with the world restricted to a dirty work-room, in the classic disorder of which perhaps the love-letters of a Jenny and the well-meant exhortations of a father, written perhaps with tears, are used for pipe-spills, which at any rate would be better than if they were to fall into the hands of third persons owing to even more irresponsible disorder.— And is it here, in this workshop of senseless and inexpedient erudition, that the fruits are to ripen which will refresh you and your beloved, and the harvest to be garnered which will serve to fulfil your sacred obligations!?

3. I am, of course, very deeply affected in spite of my resolution, I am almost overwhelmed by the feeling that I am hurting you, and already my weakness once again begins to come over me, but in order to help myself, quite literally, I take the real pills prescribed for me and swallow it all down, for I will be hard for

once and give vent to all my complaints. I will not become soft-hearted, for I feel that I have been too indulgent, given too little utterance to my grievances, and thus to a certain extent have become your accomplice. I must and will say that you have caused your parents much vexation and little or no joy.

Hardly were your wild goings-on in Bonn over, hardly were your old sins wiped out — and they were truly manifold — when, to our dismay, the pangs of love set in, and with the good nature of parents in a romantic novel we became their heralds and the bearers of their cross. But deeply conscious that your life's happiness was centred here, we tolerated what could not be altered and perhaps ourselves played unbecoming roles. While still so young, you became estranged from your family, but seeing with parents' eyes the beneficial influence on you, we hoped to see the good effects speedily developed, because in point of fact reflection and necessity equally testified in favour of this. But what were the fruits we harvested?

We have never had the pleasure of a rational correspondence, which as a rule is the consolation for absence. For correspondence presupposes consistent and continuous intercourse, carried on reciprocally and harmoniously by both sides. We never received a reply to our letters; never did your next letter have any connection with your previous one or with ours.

If one day we received the announcement that you had made some new acquaintance, afterwards this disappeared totally and for ever, like a still-born child.

As to what our only too beloved son was actually busy with, thinking about and doing, hardly was a rhapsodic phrase at times thrown in on this subject when the rich catalogue came to an end as if by magic.

On several occasions we were without a letter for months, and the last time was when you knew Eduard was ill, mother suffering and I myself not well, and moreover cholera was raging in Berlin; and as if that did not even call for an apology, your next letter contained not a single word about it, but merely some badly written lines and an extract from the diary entitled *The Visit*,[a] which I would quite frankly prefer to throw out rather than accept, a crazy botch-work which merely testifies how you squander your talents and spend your nights giving birth to monsters; that you follow in the footsteps of the new immoralists who twist their words until they themselves do not hear them; who christen

---

[a] See this volume, pp. 12 and 19.— *Ed.*

a flood of words a product of genius because it is devoid of ideas or contains only distorted ideas.

Yes, your letter did contain something—complaints that Jenny does not write, despite the fact that at bottom you were convinced that you were favoured on all sides—at least there was no reason for despair and embitterment—but that was not enough, your dear ego yearned for the pleasure of reading what you knew already (which, of course, in the present case is quite fair), and that was almost all that my Herr Son could say to his parents, whom he knew to be suffering, whom he had oppressed by a senseless silence.

As if we were men of wealth, my Herr Son disposed in one year of almost 700 talers contrary to all agreement, contrary to all usage, whereas the richest spend less than 500. And why? I do him the justice of saying that he is no rake, no squanderer. But how can a man who every week or two discovers a new system and has to tear up old works laboriously arrived at, how can he, I ask, worry about trifles? How can he submit to the pettiness of order? Everyone dips a hand in his pocket, and everyone cheats him, so long as he doesn't disturb him in his studies, and a new money order is soon written again, of course. Narrow-minded persons like G. R. and Evers may be worried about that, but they are common fellows. True, in their simplicity these men try to digest the lectures, even if only the words, and to procure themselves patrons and friends here and there, for the examinations are presided over by men, by professors, pedants and sometimes vindictive villains, who like to put to shame anyone who is independent; yet the greatness of man consists precisely in creating and destroying!!!

True, these poor young fellows sleep quite well, except when they sometimes devote half a night or a whole night to pleasure, whereas my hard-working talented Karl spends wretched nights awake, weakens his mind and body by serious study, denies himself all pleasure, in order in fact to pursue lofty abstract studies, but what he builds today he destroys tomorrow, and in the end he has destroyed his own work and not assimilated the work of others. In the end the body is ailing and the mind confused, whereas the ordinary little people continue to creep forward undisturbed and sometimes reach the goal better and at least more comfortably than those who despise the joys of youth and shatter their health to capture the shadow of erudition, which they would probably have achieved better in an hour's social intercourse with competent people, and with social enjoyment into the bargain!!!

I conclude, for I feel from my more strongly beating pulse that I am near to lapsing into a soft-hearted tone, and today I intend to be merciless.

I must add, too, the complaints of your brothers and sisters. From your letters, one can hardly see that you have any brothers or sisters; as for the good Sophie, who has suffered so much for you and Jenny and is so lavish in her devotion to you, you do not think of her when you do not need her.

I have paid your money order for *160* talers. I cannot, or can hardly, charge it to the old academic year, for that truly has its full due. And for the future I do not want to expect many of the same kind.

To come here at the present moment would be nonsense! True, I know you care little for lectures, though you probably pay for them, but I will at least observe the decencies. I am certainly no slave to public opinion, but neither do I like gossip at my expense. Come for the Easter vacation—or even two weeks earlier, I am not so pedantic—and in spite of my present epistle you can rest assured that I shall receive you with open arms and the welcoming beat of a father's heart, which is actually ailing only through excessive anxiety.

Your father
Marx

First published in: Marx/Engels, *Gesamt-ausgabe*, Abt. 1, Bd. 1, Hb. 2, 1929

Printed according to the original
Published in English for the first time

HEINRICH MARX TO KARL MARX

IN BERLIN

Trier, February 10, 1838

Dear Karl,

For already two months now I have had to keep to my room, and for one whole month to my bed, and so it has come about that I have not written to you. Today I intend to be up for a few hours and to see how far I can succeed in writing a letter. True, I manage rather shakily, but I do manage, only I shall of course have to be somewhat shorter than I should be and would like to be.

When I wrote you a rather blunt letter, the mood in which I was had naturally to be taken into account, but that mood did not make me invent anything, although of course it could make me exaggerate.

To embark again on a discussion of each separate complaint is what I am now least capable of doing, and in general I do not want to engage with you in the art of abstract argument, because in that case I should first of all have to study the terminology before I could as much as penetrate into the sanctum, and I am too old for that.

All right, if your conscience modestly harmonises with your philosophy and is compatible with it.

Only on one point, of course, all transcendentalism is of no avail, and on that you have very wisely found fit to observe an aristocratic silence; I am referring to the paltry matter of money, the value of which for the father of a family you still do not seem to recognise, but I do all the more, and I do not deny that at times I reproach myself with having left you all too loose a rein in this respect. Thus we are now in the fourth month of the law year and you have already drawn 280 talers. I have not yet earned that much this winter.

But you are wrong in saying or imputing that I misjudge or misunderstand you. Neither the one nor the other. I give full credit to your heart, to your morality. Already in the first year of your legal career I gave you irrefutable proof of this by not even demanding an explanation in regard to a very obscure matter, even though it was very problematic.—Only real faith in your high morality could make this possible, and thank heaven I have not gone back on it.—But that does not make me blind, and it is only because I am tired that I lay down my arms. But always believe, and never doubt, that you have the innermost place in my heart and that you are one of the most powerful levers in my life.

Your latest decision is worthy of the highest praise and well considered, wise and commendable, and if you carry out what you have promised, it will probably bear the best fruits. And rest assured that it is not only you who are making a big sacrifice. The same applies to all of us, but reason must triumph.

I am exhausted, dear Karl, and must close. I regret that I have not been able to write as I wanted to. I would have liked to embrace you with all my heart, but my still poor condition makes it impossible.

Your last proposal concerning me has great difficulties. What rights can I bring to bear? What support have I?

Your faithful father

Marx

[Postscript by Marx's mother]

Dear beloved Carl,

For your sake your dear father has for the first time undertaken the effort of writing to you. Good father is very weak, God grant that he may soon regain his strength. I am still in good health, dear Carl, and I am resigned to my situation and calm. Dear Jenny behaves as a loving child towards her parents, takes an intimate part in everything and often cheers us up by her loving childlike disposition, which still manages to find a bright side to everything. Write to me, dear Carl, about what has been the matter with you and whether you are quite well again. I am the one most dissatisfied that you are not to come during Easter; I let feeling go before reason and I regret, dear Carl, that you are too reasonable. You must not take my letter as the measure of my profound love; there are times when one feels much and can say little. So good-bye, dear Carl, write soon to your good father, and that will certainly help towards his speedy recovery.

Your ever loving mother

Henriette Marx

[Postscript by Marx's sister Sophie]

You will be glad, dear Karl, to hear from Father; my long letter now appears to me so unimportant that I do not know whether I should enclose it, since I fear that it might not be worth the cost of carriage.

Dear Father is getting better; it is high time too. He will soon have been in bed for eight weeks, and he only got up for the first time a few days ago so that the bedroom could be aired. Today he made a great effort to write a few lines to you in a shaky hand. Poor Father is now very impatient, and no wonder: the whole winter he has been behindhand with business matters, and the need is now four times as great as before. I sing to him daily and also read to him. Do send me at last the romance you have so long promised me. Write at once, it will be a pleasant distraction for us all. Karoline is not well, and Louise is also in bed; in all probability she has scarlet fever. Emilie keeps cheerful and in good spirits, and Jette^a is not exactly in the most amiable humour.

First published in: Marx/Engels, *Gesamt-ausgabe*, Abt. 1, Bd. 1, Hb. 2, 1929

Printed according to the original Published in English for the first time

POSTSCRIPT BY HEINRICH MARX TO HENRIETTE MARX'S LETTER TO KARL MARX IN BERLIN [207]

[February 15-16, 1838]

Dear Karl,

I send you a few words of greeting, I cannot do much yet.

Your father

Marx

First published in: Marx/Engels, *Gesamt-ausgabe*, Abt. 1, Bd. 1, Hb. 2, 1929

Printed according to the original Published in English for the first time

---

^a Karoline, Louise, Emilie and Henriette are Marx's sisters.— *Ed.*

JENNY VON WESTPHALEN TO KARL MARX

IN BERLIN [a] [208]

Trier [1839-40]

My dear and only beloved,

Sweetheart, are you no longer angry with me, and also not worried about me? I was so very upset when I last wrote, and in such moments I see everything still much blacker and more terrible than it actually is. Forgive me, one and only beloved, for causing you such anxiety, but I was shattered by your doubt of my love and faithfulness. Tell me, Karl, how could you do that, how could you set it down so dryly in writing to me, express a suspicion merely because I was silent somewhat longer than usual, kept longer to myself the sorrow I felt over your letter, over Edgar, indeed over so much that filled my soul with unspeakable misery. I did it only to spare you, and to save myself from becoming upset, a consideration which I owe indeed to you and to my family.

Oh, Karl, how little you know me, how little you appreciate my position, and how little you feel where my grief lies, where my heart bleeds. A girl's love is different from that of a man, it cannot but be different. A girl, of course, cannot give a man anything but love and herself and her person, just as she is, quite undivided and for ever. In ordinary circumstances, too, the girl must find her complete satisfaction in the man's love, she must forget everything in love. But, Karl, think of my position, you have no regard for me, you do not trust me. And that I am not capable of retaining your present romantic youthful love, I have known from

---

ᵃ Note to Edgar von Westphalen: "My dear Edgar, please be so good as to take charge of this letter for me and I shall be ready to act as a messenger of love for you at any time."— *Ed.*

the beginning, and deeply felt, long before it was explained to me so coldly and wisely and reasonably. Oh, Karl, what makes me miserable is that what would fill any other girl with inexpressible delight—your beautiful, touching, passionate love, the indescribably beautiful things you say about it, the inspiring creations of your imagination—all this only causes me anxiety and often reduces me to despair. The more I were to surrender myself to happiness, the more frightful would my fate be if your ardent love were to cease and you became cold and withdrawn.

You see, Karl, concern over the permanence of your love robs me of all enjoyment. I cannot so fully rejoice at your love, because I no longer believe myself assured of it; nothing more terrible could happen to me than that. You see, Karl, that is why I am not so wholly thankful for, so wholly enchanted by your love, as it really deserves. That is why I often remind you of external matters, of life and reality, instead of clinging wholly, as you can do so well, to the world of love, to absorption in it and to a higher, dearer, spiritual unity with you, and in it forgetting everything else, finding solace and happiness in that alone. Karl, if you could only sense my misery you would be milder towards me and not see hideous prose and mediocrity everywhere, not perceive everywhere want of true love and depth of feeling.

Oh, Karl, if only I could rest safe in your love, my head would not burn so, my heart would not hurt and bleed so. If only I could rest safe for ever in your heart, Karl, God knows my soul would not think of life and cold prose. But, my angel, you have no regard for me, you do not trust me, and your love, for which I would sacrifice everything, everything, I cannot keep fresh and young. In that thought lies death; once you apprehend it in my soul, you will have greater consideration for me when I long for consolation that lies outside your love. I feel so completely how right you are in everything, but think also of my situation, my inclination to sad thoughts, just think properly over all that as it is, and you will no longer be so hard towards me. If only you could be a girl for a little while and, moreover, such a peculiar one as I am.

So, sweetheart, since your last letter I have tortured myself with the fear that for my sake you could become embroiled in a quarrel and then in a duel. Day and night I saw you wounded, bleeding and ill, and, Karl, to tell you the whole truth, I was not altogether unhappy in this thought: for I vividly imagined that you had lost your right hand, and, Karl, I was in a state of rapture, of bliss, because of that. You see, sweetheart, I thought that in that case I could really become quite indispensable to you, you would then always keep me with you and love me. I also thought that then I could write down all your dear, heavenly ideas and be really useful to you. All this I imagined so naturally and vividly that in my thoughts I continually heard your dear voice, your dear words poured down on me and I listened to every one of them and carefully preserved them for other people. You see, I am always picturing such things to myself, but then I am happy, for then I am with you, yours, wholly yours. If I could only believe that to be possible, I would be quite satisfied. Dear and only beloved, write to me soon and tell me that you are well and that you love me always. But, dear Karl, I must once more talk to you a little seriously. Tell me, how could you doubt my faithfulness to you? Oh, Karl, to let you be eclipsed by someone else, not as if I failed to recognise the excellent qualities in other people and regarded you as unsurpassable, but, Karl, I love you indeed so inexpressibly, how could I find anything even at all worthy of love in someone else? Oh, dear Karl, I have never, never been wanting in any way towards you, yet all the same you do not trust me. But it is curious that precisely someone was mentioned to you who has hardly ever been seen in Trier, who cannot be known at all, whereas I have been often and much seen engaged in lively and cheerful conversation in society with all kinds of men. I can often be quite cheerful and teasing, I can often joke and carry on a lively conversation with absolute strangers, things that I cannot do with you. You see, Karl, I could chat and converse with anyone, but as soon as you merely look at me, I cannot say a word for nervousness, the blood stops flowing in my veins and my soul trembles.

Often when I thus suddenly think of you I am dumbstricken and overpowered with emotion so that not for anything in the world could I utter a word. Oh, I don't know how it happens, but I get such a queer feeling when I think of you, and I don't think of you on isolated and special occasions; no, my whole life and being are but one thought of you. Often things occur to me that you have said to me or asked me about, and then I am carried away by indescribably marvellous sensations. And, Karl, when you kissed me, and pressed me to you and held me fast, and I could no longer breathe for fear and trembling, and you looked at me so peculiarly, so softly, oh, sweetheart, you do not know the way you have often looked at me. If you only knew, dear Karl, what a peculiar feeling I have, I really cannot describe it to you. I sometimes think to myself, too, how nice it will be when at last I am with you always and you call me your little wife. Surely, sweetheart, then I shall be able to tell you all that I think, then one would no longer feel so horribly shy as at present. Dear Karl, it is so lovely to have such a sweetheart. If you only knew what it is like, you would not believe that I could ever love anyone else. You, dear sweetheart, certainly do not remember all the many things you have said to me, when I come to think of it. Once you said something so nice to me that one can only say when one is totally in love and thinks one's beloved completely at one with oneself. You have often said something so lovely, dear Karl, do you remember? If I had to tell you exactly everything I have been thinking—and, my dear rogue, you certainly think I have told you everything already, but you are very much mistaken—when I am no longer your sweetheart, I shall tell you also what one only says when one belongs wholly to one's beloved. Surely, dear Karl, you will then also tell me everything and will again look at me so lovingly. That was the most beautiful thing in the world for me. Oh, my darling, how you looked at me the first time like that and then quickly looked away, and then looked at me again, and I did the same, until at last we looked at each other for quite a long time and very deeply, and could no longer look away. Dearest one, do not be angry with me any more and write to me also a little tenderly, I am so happy then. And do not be so much concerned about my health. I often imagine it to be worse than it is. I *really do feel better now than for a long time past.* I have also stopped taking medicine and my appetite, too, is again very good. I walk a lot in Wettendorf's garden and am quite industrious the whole day long. But, unfortunately, I can't read anything. If I only knew of a book which I could understand properly and which could divert me a little. I often take an hour to read one page and still do not understand anything. To be sure, sweetheart, I can catch up again even if I get a little behind at present, you will help me to go forward again, and I am quick in grasping things too. Perhaps you know of some book, but it must be quite a special kind, a bit learned so that I do not understand everything, but still manage to understand something as if through a fog, a bit such as not everyone likes to read; and also no fairy-tales, and no poetry, I can't bear it. I think it would do me a lot of good if I exercised my mind a bit. Working with one's hands leaves too much scope to the mind. Dear Karl, only keep well for my sake. The funny little dear is already living somewhere else. I am very glad at the change in your....

Published for the first time   Printed according to the original

RECORD SHEET FILLED IN BY MARX[209]

FREDERICK WILLIAM UNIVERSITY IN BERLIN
Record Sheet
Student of law K. H. Marx from Trier

Has taken here the following lectures	with	No. of attendance list	Questor's remark regarding fee	Lecturer's testimony on attendance at lectures

Winter term I. 1836/37

Private lectures
1) *Pandects* — Prof. Dr. v. Savigny — 1. paid — diligent v. Savigny 14/3. 37

2) *Criminal Law* — Dr. Prof. Gans — 2. ditto — exceptionally diligent. Gans 17/3. 37

3) *Anthropology* — Dr. Prof. Steffens — 3. ditto — diligent. Steffens 18/3. 37

(9/11.36)

Wittenberg 24/1. 41 — Corresponds to the original. Wittenberg Berlin 9/3. 41

Summer term II. 1837

Private lectures
1) *Ecclesiastical law* with Dr. Prof. Heffter — Heffter — 1. paid

2) *Civil procedure* with Dr. Prof. Heffter — Heffter — 2. ditto — diligent 12/[...]37

Public lecture
3) *Prussian civil procedure* with Dr. Prof. Heffter — 3. public 2/5. 37 Wittenberg 24/1. 41

Has taken here the following lectures	with	No. of attendance list	Questor's remark regarding fee	Lecturer's testimony on attendance at lectures
		Winter term III. 1837/38		
Criminal legal procedure with Dr. Prof. Heffter	Heffter		paid 10/11. 37 Wittenberg 24/1. 41	diligent [...] [...] Heffter
		Summer term IV. 1838		
1) *Logic* with Dr. Prof. Gabler		1. paid		extremely diligent attendance 9/8. 38 Gabler
2) *Geography* with Dr. Prof. Ritter		2. ditto		
3) *Prussian law* with Dr. Prof. Gans		3. ditto Wittenberg 19/5. 38		exceptionally diligent 7/8. 38 Gans p. j. copy Wittenberg 9/3. 41
		Winter term V. 1838/39		
Inheritance law with Dr. Prof. Rudorff	Rudorff		paid Wittenberg 10/12. 38	diligent 8/3 Rudorff
		Summer term VI. 1839		
Isaiah with Licentiate Bauer			remitted by authorisation	attended as per appended certificate
		Term VII		
Iphigenie in Aulis by Euripides			public Wittenberg 28/1. 41	diligent attendance attested Berlin, 23/3. 40 Geppert, Dr. Ph.

Published for the first time   Printed according to the original

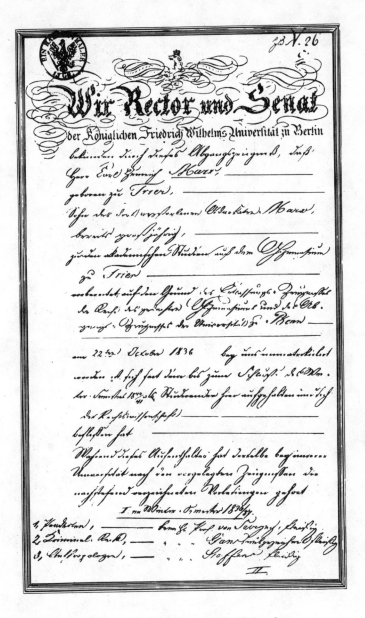

Leaving Certificate from Berlin University

Bonn University

Berlin University

QUOD

FELIX FAUSTUMQUE ESSE IUBEAT

SUMMUM NUMEN

AUCTORITATE

HUIC LITTERARUM UNIVERSITATI

AB

FERDINANDO I

IMPERATORE ROMANO GERMANICO

ANNO MDLVII CONCESSA

CLEMENTISSIMIS AUSPICIIS

SERENISSIMORUM

MAGNI DUCIS ET DUCUM SAXONIAE

NUTRITORUM ACADEMIAE IENENSIS

MUNIFICENTISSIMORUM

RECTORE ACADEMIAE MAGNIFICENTISSIMO

AUGUSTO ET POTENTISSIMO PRINCIPE AC DOMINO

CAROLO FRIDERICO

MAGNO DUCE SAXONIAE VIMARIENSIUM ATQUE ISENACENSIUM PRINCIPE LANDGRAVIO THURINGIAE
MARCHIONE MISNIAE PRINCIPALI DIGNITATE COMITE HENNENERGAE
DYNASTA BLANKENHAYNII NEOSTADII AC TAUTENBURGI

PRORECTORE ACADEMIAE MAGNIFICO

VIRO PERILLUSTRI ATQUE AMPLISSIMO

ERNESTO REINHOLDO

PHILOSOPHIAE DOCTORE ARTIUMQUE LIBERALIUM MAGISTRO
MAGNI DUCIS SAXONIAE VIMARIENSIS ET ISENACENSIS A CONSILIIS AULAE INTIMIS PHILOSOPHIAE PROFESSORE PUBLICO ORDINARIO

DECANO ORDINIS PHILOSOPHORUM ET BRABEUTA

MAXIME SPECTABILI

VIRO PERILLUSTRI ATQUE EXCELLENTISSIMO

CAROLO FRIDERICO BACHMANNO

PHILOSOPHIAE DOCTORE

SERENISSIMI DUCIS SAX ALTENBURGENSIS A CONSILIIS AULAE INTIMIS MORALIUM ET POLITICES PROFESSORE PUBLICO ORDINARIO INSTITUTORUM
MAGNODUCALIUM MINERALIUM ORIN M DIRECTORE INSTITUTI HISTORIAE PARISIENSIS SOCIETATUM CAESAREAE PETROPOLITANAE MINERALOGICAE
REGIAE DRESDENSIS MINERALOGICAE POLYTECHNICAE PARISIENSIS ARTIUM ET SCIENTIARUM PURIPAE APUD TRAIECTINOS ARTIUM ET LITTERARUM
GANDAVIENSIS SCIENTIARUM ET ARTIM M ANTVERPIENSIS MEDII ORC N ET PHYSICORUM BRUXELLENSIS INN TRINARCH DF BEN M NATURA
PHILADELPHILNSIE IN AMERICA SEPTENTRIONALI ET LATINAE IENENSIS ALIARUMQUE SOCIO

ORDO PHILOSOPHORUM

VIRO PRAENOBILISSIMO ATQUE DOCTISSIMO

CAROLO HENRICO MARX

TREVIRENSI

DOCTORIS PHILOSOPHIAE HONORES

DIGNITATEM IURA ET PRIVILEGIA

INGENII DOCTRINAE ET VIRTUTIS SPECTATAE INSIGNIA ET ORNAMENTA

DETULIT

DELATA

PUBLICO HOC DIPLOMATE

CUI IMPRESSUM EST SIGNUM ORDINIS PHILOSOPHORUM

PROMULGAVIT

IENAE DIE XV M. APRILIS A. MDCCCXLI

TYPIS BRANII

Karl Marx's Doctor's Diploma

LEAVING CERTIFICATE
FROM BERLIN UNIVERSITY [210]

To No. 26

We, the *Rector* and *Senate*
of the Royal Frederick William University
in Berlin,

testify by this leaving certificate that Herr *Carl Heinrich Marx*, born in Trier, son of the barrister *Marx* there deceased, already of age, prepared for academic studies at the gymnasium in Trier, was matriculated here on October 22, 1836, on the basis of the certificate of maturity of the above-mentioned gymnasium and of the certificate of release of the University in Bonn, has been here since then as a student until the end of the winter term 1840/41, and has applied himself to the study of jurisprudence.

During this stay at our University, according to the certificates submitted to us, he has attended the lectures listed below:

I. *In the winter term 1836/37*

1. Pandects with Herr Professor v. *Savigny*, diligent.
2. Criminal law   ”   ”   ” *Gans*, exceptionally diligent.
3. Anthropology   ”   ”   ” *Steffens*, diligent.

II. *In the summer term 1837*

1. Ecclesiastical law
2. Common German civil procedure } with Herr Professor *Heffter*, diligent.
3. Prussian civil procedure

III. *In the winter term 1837/38*

1. Criminal legal procedure with Herr Professor *Heffter*, diligent.

IV. *In the summer term 1838*

1. Logic with Herr Professor *Gabler*, extremely diligent.
2. General geography with Herr Professor *Ritter*, attended.
3. Prussian law   ”   ”   ”   *Gans*, exceptionally diligent.

V. *In the winter term 1838/39*

1. Inheritance law with Herr Professor *Rudorff*, diligent.

VI. *In the summer term 1839*

1. Isaiah with Herr Licentiate *Bauer*, attended.

VII and VIII. *In the winter term 1839/40 and summer term 1840*, none

IX. *In the winter term 1840/41*

1. Euripides with Herr Dr. *Geppert*, diligent.

v. Medem
23.3.41

In regard to his behaviour at the University here, there is nothing specially disadvantageous to note from the point of view of discipline, and from the economic point of view only that on several occasions he has been the object of proceedings for debt.

He has not hitherto been charged with participating in forbidden associations among students at this University.

In witness thereof, this certificate has been drawn up under the seal of the University and signed with their own hand by the Rector pro tem and by the Judge, and also by the present Deans of the Faculties of Law and Philosophy.

Berlin, March 30, 1841

Lichtenstein.   *Krause.* / *Lancizolle.*   *Zumpt.*

Witnessed by the Deputy Royal Governmental Plenipotentiaries
Lichtenstein.   *Krause.*

First published in the yearly *Archiv für die Geschichte des Sozialismus und der Arbeiterbewegung*, 1926   Printed according to the original Published in English for the first time

RECOMMENDATORY REFERENCE
ON THE DISSERTATION
OF KARL MARX[211]

Senior Venerande,
Assessores Gravissimi,

I present to you hereby a very worthy candidate in Herr *Carl Heinrich Marx* from *Trier*. He has sent in 1) A *written request*. (sub. lit. *a*.) 2) Two university certificates on his academic studies in Bonn and Berlin. (lit. *b*. and *c*.) The disciplinary offences therein noted can be disregarded by us. 3) A written request in Latin, curriculum vitae, and specimen: *On the Difference Between the Democritean and Epicurean Philosophy of Nature*, together with a certificate on authorship written in Latin. (lit. *d*.) 4) 12 Friedr. d'or, the excess of which will be returned to the candidate. The specimen testifies to intelligence and perspicacity as much as to erudition, for which reason I regard the candidate as pre-eminently worthy. Since, according to his German letter, he desires to receive only the degree of Doctor, it is clear that it is merely an error due to lack of acquaintance with the statutes of the faculty that in the Latin letter he speaks of the degree of Magister. He probably thought that the two belong together. I am convinced that only a clarification of this point is needed in order to satisfy him.

Requesting your wise decision,
Most respectfully,

Dr. Carl Friedrich *Bachmann*
pro tem Dean

Jena, April 13, 1841

Ordinis philosophorum Decane maxime spectabilis
As Your Spectabilität

Luden
F. Hand
E. Reinhold
Döbereiner
J. F. Fries
Goettling
Schulze

First published in the yearly *Archiv für die Geschichte des Sozialismus und der Arbeiterbewegung*, 1926

Printed according to the original
Published in English for the first time

JENNY VON WESTPHALEN TO KARL MARX

IN BONN

[Trier, August 10, 1841]

My little wild boar,

How glad I am that you are happy, and that my letter made you cheerful, and that you are longing for me, and that you are living in wallpapered rooms, and that you drank champagne in Cologne, and that there are Hegel clubs there, and that you have been dreaming, and that, in short, you are mine, my own sweetheart, my dear wild boar. But for all that there is one thing I miss: you could have praised me a little for my Greek, and you could have devoted a little laudatory article to my erudition. But that is just like you, you Hegeling gentlemen,[212] you don't recognise anything, be it the height of excellence, if it is not exactly according to your view, and so I must be modest and rest on my *own* laurels. Yes, sweetheart, I have still to rest, alas, and indeed on a feather bed and pillows, and even this little letter is being sent out into the world from my little bed.

On Sunday I ventured on a bold excursion into the front rooms—but it proved bad for me and now I have to do penance again for it. Schleicher told me just now that he has had a letter from a young revolutionary, but that the latter is greatly mistaken in his judgment of his countrymen. He does not think he can procure either shares or anything else. Ah, dear, dear sweetheart, now you get yourself involved in politics too. That is indeed the most risky thing of all. Dear little Karl, just remember always that here at home you have a sweetheart who is hoping and suffering and is wholly dependent on your fate. Dear, dear sweetheart, how I wish I could only see you again.

Unfortunately, I cannot and may not fix the day as yet. Before I feel quite well again, I shall not get permission to travel. But I am staying put this week. Otherwise our dear synopticist[a] may finally depart and I should not have seen the worthy man. This morning quite early I studied in the Augsburg newspaper three Hegelian articles and the announcement of Bruno's book![213]

Properly speaking, dear sweetheart, I ought now to say *vale faveque*[b] to you, for you only asked me for a couple of lines and the page is already filled almost to the end. But today I do not want to keep so strictly to the letter of the law and I intend to stretch the lines asked for to as many pages. And it is true, is it not, sweetheart, that you will not be angry with your little Jenny on that account, and as for the content itself, you should bear firmly in mind that only a knave gives more than he has. Today my buzzing, whirring little head is quite pitiably empty and it has hardly anything in it but wheels and clappers and mills. The thoughts have all gone, but on the other hand, my little heart is so full, so overflowing with love and yearning and ardent longing for you, my infinitely loved one.

In the meantime have you not received a letter written in pencil sent through Vauban? Perhaps, the intermediary is no longer any good, and in future I must address the letters directly to my lord and master.

Commodore Napier has just passed by in his white cloak. One's poor senses fail one at the sight. It strikes me as just like the wolves' ravine in the *Freischüz*, when suddenly the wild army and all the curious fantastic forms pass through it. Only on the miserable little stage of our theatre one always saw the wires to which the eagles and owls and crocodiles were fastened — in this case the mechanism is merely of a somewhat different kind.

Tomorrow, for the first time, Father[c] will be allowed out of his constrained position and seated on a chair. He is rather discouraged by the very slow progress of his recovery, but he vigorously issues his orders without pause, and it will not be long before he is awarded the grand cross of the order of commanders.

If I were not lying here so miserably, I would soon be packing my bag. Everything is ready. Frocks and collars and bonnets are in beautiful order and only the wearer is not in the right condition. Oh, dearest one, how I keep thinking of you and your love during

---

[a] Bruno Bauer.— *Ed.*
[b] Good-bye and be devoted to me.— *Ed.*
[c] Ludwig von Westphalen.— *Ed.*

my sleepless nights, how often have I prayed for you, blessed you and implored blessings for you, and how sweetly I have then often dreamed of all the bliss that has been and will be.— This evening Haizinger is acting in Bonn. Will you go there? I have seen her as Donna Diana.

Dearest Karl, I should like to say a lot more to you, all that remains to be said—but Mother[a] will not tolerate it any longer—she will take away my pen and I shall not be able even to express my most ardent, loving greetings. Just a kiss on each finger and then away into the distance. Fly away, fly to my Karl, and press as warmly on his lips as you were warm and tender when starting out towards them; and then cease to be dumb messengers of love and whisper to him all the tiny, sweet, secret expressions of love that love gives you—tell him everything—but, no, leave something *over* for your mistress.

Farewell, one and only beloved.

I cannot write any more, or my head will be all in a whirl [...][b] you know, and *quadrupedante putrem sonitu,*[c] etc., etc.— Adieu, you dear little man of the railways. Adieu, my dear little man.— It is certain, isn't it, that I can marry you?

Adieu, adieu, my sweetheart.

First published in: Marx/Engels, *Werke*, Ergänzungsband, Erster Teil, Berlin, 1968

Printed according to the original

Published in English for the first time

---

[a] Caroline von Westphalen.— *Ed.*

[b] Here there are three incorrectly written Latin words which do not make sense.— *Ed.*

[c] The four-footed clanging of hooves (Virgil, *Aeneid*, VIII, 596).— *Ed.*

COLOGNE CITIZENS' PETITION
FOR THE CONTINUANCE
OF THE *RHEINISCHE ZEITUNG*[a][214]

Cologne, February 1843

Most excellent, most powerful King,
Most gracious King and Lord,

Scarcely a year has elapsed since Your Majesty by Your memorable, royal, free decision released the press from the oppressive shackles in which it had been laid by unfortunate circumstances. Every citizen inspired by a genuine feeling of freedom and patriotism looked with redoubled confidence to the present and the immediate future, in which public opinion with its manifold convictions and deep-seated contradictions has acquired appropriate organs of the press, and by means of ever more thorough development and ever-renewed justification of its own content will refine itself until it reaches that purity, clarity and resoluteness by which it offers the richest, surest and most vivifying source of national legislation. The Rhinelander in particular, Your Majesty, was filled with the most noble joy when he saw that free, public utterance—whose high value and inner worth he had come to appreciate so thoroughly in his judicial system—had at least been given an opening also in other areas of state life, where the need for it is greatest, in the sphere of political conviction, which is the most essential element of state life, and in which morality is of the highest significance.

That confidence and this joy were, we say frankly, most painfully affected by the news of the measures decided upon against the *Rheinische Zeitung*. Participating directly in the upsurge

---

[a] Added in a different handwriting at the top of the page: "To Minister of State, Count von Arnim. Berlin, March 5, 1843."—*Ed.*

of public life evoked by Your Majesty's accession to the throne, that newspaper developed its conception of state affairs at all events with uncompromising consistency, and indeed was not seldom bluntly outspoken. One may favour the political views of this newspaper, one may, like many of the undersigned, not share them, one may indeed be definitely hostile to them, in any case, the true friend of an efficient and free state life must sincerely regret the blow that has befallen this newspaper. By the suppression of this one newspaper alone, the entire press of the Fatherland is deprived of that independence which, as it is the foundation of all moral relationships, is also absolutely essential for a principled discussion of specific state affairs, and without which neither outstanding talent nor firm character can be applied to political literature.

The undersigned citizens of Cologne, in whose midst the threatened newspaper found its origin, feel themselves above all obliged and impelled to express frankly to Your Majesty, whom they have learnt to honour as the mightiest protector of free speech, their feeling of pain at the decreed suppression and to submit before the steps of the throne the most humble request:

That Your Majesty will most graciously order that the measures projected against the *Rheinische Zeitung* by the high censorship authorities on January 21 of this year shall be annulled and that this newspaper shall continue to exist without any restriction of the freedom hitherto accorded to our domestic press in general by Your Majesty yourself.

We remain most humble and obedient subjects of Your Majesty, loyal citizens of Cologne

[signatures follow][a]

First published in *Rheinische Briefe und Akten zur Geschichte der politischen Bewegung 1830-1850*, 1. Bd., Essen, 1919

Printed according to the original

Published in English for the first time

---

[a] Among the signatures in Marx's hand: "K. Marx, Doctor."—*Ed.*

MINUTES OF THE GENERAL MEETING
OF SHAREHOLDERS
OF THE *RHEINISCHE ZEITUNG*
FEBRUARY 12, 1843 [215]

Proceedings of the Extraordinary General Meeting
of February 12, 1843

Present:

Herr	Renard,	responsible editor
"	G. Jung	
"	D. Oppenheim	managers
"	Dr. Fay, Chairman of the Board of Directors	
"	" Claessen	
"	" Stucke	
"	" Thomé	members of the Board of Directors

Assessor	Bürgers	
Barrister	E. Mayer	} members of the Board of Directors
Herr	Haan	
Dr.	Marx	
Herr	H. Kamp	
Herr	Karl Stein	
"	Leist, Councillor of the Court of Appeal	
"	J. J. von Rath	
"	Dr. D'Ester	
"	Dr. Haass	
"	A. W. Esch	
"	A. Oppenheim	
"	G. Mallinckrodt	
"	F. G. Heuser	
"	J. Mülhens	
"	Plassmann	
"	Ph. Engels	

Herr   K. Heinzen
"   L. Camphausen
"   Georg Heuser
"   Kaufmann
"   J. Herstatt
"   J. Boisserée
"   W. Boisserée
"   Boismard
"   S. B. Cohen
"   J. De Jonge
"   Christians von Overath
"   J. W. Dietz
"   Kühn
"   Karl Engels
"   Rüb
"   T. Göbbels
"   J. Horst
"   von Hontheim
"   J. Herrmanns
"   H. Hellwitz (represented by L. Herz)
"   F. Bloemer, lawyer (represented by Ref. Scherer)
"   W. Kühn
"   M. Morel
"   J. Müller
"   A. Ochse-Stern
"   B. Reichard
"   J. P. von Rath
"   J. Ritter
"   C. Reimbold
"   A. Rogge
"   J. B. Rick, on his own behalf and representing notary
             Bendermacher
"   Dr. Stucke, representing C. Baumdahl
"   J. F. Sehlmeyer
"   Seligmann, lawyer
"   V. Vill
"   E. Vahrenkamp
"   Ch. Welker
"   A. Zuntz-Bonn

The Chairman of the Board of Directors, Herr Fay, opened the meeting with a speech in which he stated that the ministerial edict which was the occasion for the present meeting was an outcome of the conflict of principles between the bureaucratic state authorities and public opinion. The people demand to share in legislation, on the strength of laws and promises, on the strength of the past period from 1807 to 1815, and of the hopes and wishes newly awakened at the beginning of the rule of Frederick William IV. This friction between the people and the state authority is manifested in the press, and the ministerial edict is directed against this manifestation in general.

Herr Oppenheim stressed that the ban on the *Rheinische Zeitung* seemed completely unjustified, since prior to November 12 last year there had been no warning, indeed not the slightest indication of anything of the kind. Herr Oppenheim then read out the edict of Oberpräsident Herr Schaper of November 12, as well as the further notifications made through Präsident Herr Gerlach in accordance with the instruction of the Oberpräsidium and the subsequent reply of the responsible editor, Herr Renard,[a] and finally the petition of the last named to the Oberpräsidium with the subsequent reply of the Oberpräsident on November 19, 1842.[216]

The editorial board made no reply to the last edict because it has always been, and still is, most firmly convinced of the falsity and illegality of the premises advanced by the Oberpräsidium in connection with the permit granted to the *Rheinische Zeitung.*

Herr Oppenheim then read out the order of Präsident Herr Gerlach of January 24 of this year, pointed out the illegality of the measures taken by the ministries, and left it to the discretion of the general meeting to discuss and adopt appropriate measures against this illegality. This illegality itself was analysed in more detail in the memorandum next read by Herr Dr. Claessen, for which purpose he quoted and elucidated the Cologne government order of November 17.

Herr Fay invited the meeting to open the discussion and to adopt decisions, and he informed the meeting of a discussion which had taken place within the Board of Directors, as a result of which the Board as a whole "put on record" the declaration which follows.

Herr Dr. Haass opened the discussion with the following statement:

---

[a] See this volume, pp. 282-85.—*Ed.*

Ten days ago a number of shareholders met at the Bomel Hof and drafted a petition; I signed that petition and wish to know the result.

Herr Oppenheim replied that the lists had not yet all been received.

Herr Hontheim. We all aim to ensure that the *Rheinische Zeitung* will be able to continue in existence. What measures should be adopted to ensure that the ministerial decision is retracted? The speaker does not wish to discuss the question of legality or illegality. Even if the edict of January 21 were rescinded, the *Rheinische Zeitung* would still continue to appear disagreeable to the ministries. According to the existing laws, the permit that has been granted can always be withdrawn, and the ministries would certainly decide on such a withdrawal. The question arises whether steps in a sense conforming to the wishes of the ministry would be compatible with the honour of the shareholders. In the first place, this purpose might be achieved by the resignation of certain members of the Board of Directors, by the appointment of a new editorial board. The speaker does not want to dwell on the subject of trend, but says: "We have to dispute with a government authority and must keep to the legal standpoint. Let a member of the Board of Directors state his opinion on how it would be possible to make to the ministry such concessions as would ensure a continuance."

Herr Jung. We cannot very well know what concessions the ministry will demand. The *Rheinische Zeitung* is a party which must be accepted freely and wholly. If we respond to the wishes of the ministry, we shall have to begin a new life in contradiction to the previous one, and only a few members of the Board would agree to that. A retraction of the ministerial edict could only be expected as a result of petitions from the whole province.

Herr Marx believed the question could be clarified by reading the official article which follows, and he expressed his view that the trend would have to be altered if one wished to come to an understanding with the prevailing liberal sovereignty.

Herr Claessen. I agree with the opinion of Herr Hontheim as regards the continuance of the newspaper, but do not believe that a change of editors would lead to the goal. Herr Hontheim has acknqwledged that the ministerial rescript contains a formal defect. But he believes that it is possible for the minister to correct this defect at any time. The memorandum which I read out shows that the withdrawal of a permit which has been granted entirely contradicts the spirit of Prussian legislation and the intentions of

His Majesty. His Majesty has stated that a consistent opposition is permitted to exist. On behalf of the Board of Directors, gentlemen, I put the proposal to you that the memorandum which has just been read, supported by the petition which follows, should be submitted to the supreme decision of His Royal Majesty.

Herr Claessen then read the petition.

I believe that I can assume, gentlemen, that your views in regard to the point of law are in agreement with the motives of the memorandum. The only question, gentlemen, is whether other steps to preserve the *Rheinische Zeitung* ought to be decided upon.

Herr Leist asked why the memorandum had not been sent in November.

Herr Oppenheim replied that there had been no reason to believe that the censorship ministries would ever [require] such an assurance as a condition for discussing actually existing difficulties.

Herr *Bürgers*. I believe that I am expressing a general conviction when I say that the motive which guided us in founding the *Rheinische Zeitung* was to have an entirely independent newspaper.

In order to ensure that independence, managers and a Board of Directors were elected by the shareholders. The trend represented by the managers and the Board, as pondered in their minds and felt in their hearts, had to be given expression. We decided to express and represent clearly and freely the principles we hold to be most expedient for the welfare of the Fatherland. These principles have come into conflict with the principles of the present government. This trend has resulted in the suppression of the newspaper by *force*. I now ask, will the original independent frame of mind of the company be maintained? Even if the majority does not agree with the way in which the trend is carried out, there will surely be no conflict over the guiding principle.

Herr Kamp. If I have understood Herr Hontheim correctly, he believes that a discussion of legality or illegality could not yield any result. I share this view and am in favour of a petition to His Majesty. But I cannot say that I agree with the version which has just been proposed. It seems to me that the main question today is whether the shareholders approve the trend and principles, in regard to content and form, which the *Rheinische Zeitung* has followed up to now. Mention was made earlier of the opposition press. I can conceive of such a press only in a constitutional state, and not in our monarchical state. We owe our freedoms to an act of grace, and if we use this freedom with moderation, our views will often find gracious acceptance. In speaking to me, many high-placed officials have praised the trend of the *Rheinische*

Zeitung, but censured its tone, form, blunt mode of expression. If the shareholders now approve the tone, it will have to be maintained. If they do not approve the form and tone, this disapproval will easily lead to a change that will please the ministers.

We all desire a frank discussion of home and foreign affairs. Let the meeting only decide how this frank discussion should be understood.

Jung. The general meeting has no right to criticise the form of frank discussion. The managers are the business leaders of the *Rheinische Zeitung.* The newspaper has prospered in its present form, it has gained a surprising number of readers with astonishing rapidity. That is the result of the work of the present leaders; hence from the commercial standpoint we certainly stand justified. However, I do not want in any way to reject a discussion of the trend. I repeat, gentlemen, our newspaper was and had to be a partisan newspaper, from the point of view both of conviction and of commercial interest. The result that has been achieved was possible only along the lines that were adopted. The *Rheinische Zeitung* has become the citadel of the liberal tendency in Germany. But without passion there can be no struggle. Then no call, whether to go forward or back, is of any avail; in battle it is the moment that decides. Singly, gentlemen, you cannot reproach us with anything. Either you reject us entirely, or you accept us.

Herr Seligmann. The *Rheinische Zeitung* does not seek any financial gain, but only to represent a definite trend. Hence the meeting is entitled to ask the managers: Have you represented *our* trends?

The *Leipziger Zeitung,* gentlemen, has been suppressed by an order of His Majesty.[217] How much more is the suppression of the *Rheinische Zeitung* bound to have taken place with the agreement of His Majesty.

Under these circumstances, I do not expect any success from a petition.

I tell you frankly that it is my conviction that the *Rheinische Zeitung* has not been in accord with the just demands of the state authority. We must now retreat within the bounds marked out for us by the state. Proceeding from this standpoint we can then claim the right to further development. Since in fighting for principles we have failed to take account of the obtaining situation, the general meeting today must demand from the managers that they return to within the bounds set to free discussion by the authority. If the present managers do not want to do this, the general meeting must elect new managers. We must promise here to return to the above-mentioned bounds in order to ensure the continuance of the newspaper.

Herr Oppenheim. We all want, if possible, to ward off the blow struck at the *Rheinische Zeitung*. According to the express wording of the Statute, we are not entitled today to criticise the trend of the *Rheinische Zeitung*. The shareholders have renounced the right to determine the trend. The general meeting is empowered only to renew the Board of Directors. Even the most zealous supporters of the *Rheinische Zeitung* will surely admit that at times the form has been somewhat blunt and has given offence in Berlin. The proposal of the last speaker would result in the dissolution of the company. It seems to me that we can and must modify the petition. If the sword of authority is directed against us, we must submit. Let us acknowledge on the steps of the throne that we shareholders do not approve the somewhat blunt character of the newspaper, but that we claim for ourselves the rights that exist, and on this basis request His Majesty to lift the ban.

It can surely be presumed that such a petition will secure the desired decision.

We can indeed safely expect that the managers and the Board will in future avoid bluntness.

Herr Mülhens. I must insist that the company should declare whether it agrees with the trend of the newspaper and the form in which it is carried out. Only then will it be possible to draft a petition in a particular spirit.

Herr Oppenheim. How can we decide on the trend by a majority vote? The managers and the Board of Directors can reject such a decision. But what would a disapproval of the present trend lead to? The present *Rheinische Zeitung* would perish and another newspaper quite alien to the present so successful one would take its place.

The question now is what wisdom dictates in order to ensure continuance.

Herr Mülhens. I am firmly convinced that the result of a vote will be unanimous approval of the trend. Only the form can be a matter for dispute.

Herr Leist. Is the editorial board still of the opinion that it is impossible to make any change in the form? If it is, then I oppose any petition to His Majesty as a completely useless step.

It must surely be possible for men who are confident of the truth of their convictions to express them in warm and persuasive

Prohibition of the *Rheinische Zeitung*

Burial of the *Rheinische Zeitung*

terms instead of caustic and sarcastic language. I do not fail to recognise the difficulty of modifying the language of certain personalities.

Bürgers. The view that the reason for the suppression of the *Rheinische Zeitung* is to be sought in its form seems to me erroneous. There is not a word of that in the ministerial edict. Quite different accusations are cast at us. One could presume that these principles were advanced merely as an excuse and that nevertheless the form was the real reason for the ban. But, unfortunately, everything that has taken place in the entire life of the state over the past year proves that the trend which has raised the *Rheinische Zeitung* as its standard is everywhere being consistently suppressed and reduced to silence. I am convinced that the ministerial edict must either meet with the complete disapproval of the King or the *Rheinische Zeitung* with its present principles must cease to exist.

Bürgers. Gentlemen, we are concerned for something higher than money. We have sought to assert a principle. This principle we cannot renounce.

Haan. Whatever the views, in any case *wisdom* requires that the shareholders should censure the bluntness of form.

Hontheim. Herr Bürgers has stated that it is not the form, but errors of trend, that the ministries condemn. We as shareholders have only two parties: the managers and Board of Directors and the ministries. Can these two parties unite without giving up something of their basic principles? The theme for this has been given by the proposal advanced by Dr. Claessen. Should the petition, as presented to us, be signed or should it perhaps be modified? I propose as an amendment that the shareholders intercede with the ministers to secure that the *Rheinische Zeitung* be allowed to continue to exist under the present double censorship for a further three months from April 1.

Herr Camphausen. It will be inevitable to have to bring personal influence to bear in the Residency. Only in this way can we learn the demands of the ministry.

Herr Mayer. The Board of Directors sees nothing offensive in adopting the wise course of disavowing the blunt tone of the *Rheinische Zeitung.* But how can we make an application for a further three months' existence to the ministers whose edict has attacked our honour, our rights, in the severest possible way? In its present shape, indeed, the *Rheinische Zeitung* is so crippled that its continued existence in this shape can only destroy the reputation it once won.

Herr Haass. I repeat the question of a previous speaker whether the managers and members of the Board of Directors will not allow their view to be modified in any way by the clearly expressed opinion of the general meeting. No sacrifice should be made that could threaten the honour of the leading persons. I am against any personal intervention in Berlin. Such a step would certainly be fruitless. The ministry will not accept instruction. The time is not yet ripe for that.

Herr Kaufmann. We all want to preserve the newspaper. To blame the trend will get us nowhere. I should like justificatory grounds to be inserted in the petition.

Herr Heinzen. I think that the company is in agreement on the following points: that the rights of the shareholders have been infringed by the ministerial edict, even if we do not approve the trend represented by the managers and the Board. The newspaper's trend can be discussed at the next general meeting, which has to renew the Board of Directors. If we assume that the Board has done wrong, it will be a matter of offering the ministries guarantees now, and the prospect of these guarantees can be held out by reference to the forthcoming new elections. This is the sole guarantee we can offer. I propose that the following be inserted in today's petition.

Herr Seligmann. Gentlemen, I propose that the plan of a petition to the King be dropped altogether, and that, instead of a direct petition to the King, a petition be made to the censorship ministries and submitted through Herr von Gerlach. The censorship ministries will certainly not decide without previous consultation. If we keep to the regular procedure through the chain of instances, loss of time is inevitable. A direct petition seems to me unconstitutional, because we would be bypassing the lower instances and applying at once to the highest instance. This unconstitutional step would offend the ministries. Therefore I propose that a petition be made to those ministries, all the more because there is no hope that His Majesty will disapprove of the steps taken by his ministries.

Herr Kamp. Let us consider first of all the competence and powers of the shareholders. We were told this morning that the shareholders have to decide only on the commercial circumstances of the company. Now the shareholders are being attributed further rights in accordance with the Statute. Let us first establish the rights of the shareholders. I move that a decision be taken whether the shareholders are authorised to adopt a decision on the trend of the newspaper.

Herr Oppenheim. The shareholders are entitled to draw up a petition in any sense they choose. If it is to be drawn up in a way that is incompatible with our honour, with our convictions, it cannot be demanded that we should sign it. It seems to me that from the standpoint of the shareholders' interests the moment for a disapproving statement has been badly chosen. Although one may condemn the blunt form, one should bear in mind that the freer development of the press is still new, and that mistakes are inevitable in every new institution.

Herr Haass. I should like to see no opposition between managers, Board of Directors and shareholders. Let us seek to bring about a development of all interests for the good of the institution.

Herr Oppenheim. We are quite prepared to put the composition of the petition in your hands, without thereby making you responsible for any action taken by the administration.

Herr Leist. The rights of the shareholders have been conceived too narrowly. In accordance with the Statute, the general meeting has the right to judge the Board of Directors, and indirectly the managers.

Herr Oppenheim. I did not want to deny the shareholders' right to criticise the administration, but I do deny their right to intervene in the measures of the administration.

Herr Jung. The general meeting can very easily say in the petition that it wishes to use its influence with the editorial board in order to bring about a change in the sense desired by the ministry.

Herr Kamp. For that very reason there must first be a decision on the powers of the general meeting.

Herr Jung. The general meeting cannot compel the managers to conform to a particular trend. The general meeting can only exert its influence indirectly, through the election of the Board of Directors.

Herr Claessen. The managers have stated that they are prepared to resign if the ministry demands concessions that are incompatible with their convictions, in the event of the general meeting approving these concessions. I permit myself to propose the following amendment to the petition submitted this morning.

Herr Haass. The general meeting is entitled to express approval or disapproval, and I must speak out most definitely for the maintenance of this right.

Herr Seligmann. Hitherto the *Rheinische Zeitung* has endeavoured to spread constitutional ideas and to achieve participation of the masses in legislation, and should the masses today have no right to exert influence? The administration is only a derivation of the will of the general meeting and this will can always be asserted.

Herr Camphausen. I, too, believe that the managers and the Board have not had a sufficiently clear conception of their powers and those of the general meeting. I am of the opinion that the competence of the general meeting is far more extensive than the managers believe, but I do not attach any practical importance to the question. If on some occasion a general meeting were to express disapproval, I believe the result would always be the same, whether its competence were disputed or not. The question will only be: Does the general meeting want to accept the petition with or without amendments?

Herr von Hontheim. The right of the general meeting to take decisions cannot, I think, be disputed. In the Statute, of course, nothing is laid down about the trend, nothing as to whether the trend of the shareholders should be realised by the management. But such a premise is provided by the matter itself. I consider Herr Heinzen's proposal the most suitable now for giving effect to the powers of the shareholders. Nevertheless that proposal seems to me impracticable because we shall hardly find new members for the Board of Directors. I repeat my proposal that the ministry should be asked to permit a three months' extension from April 1st. I think that the double censorship can be no obstacle whatever to the continued existence of the newspaper.

Herr Fay. We have not assembled here in order to interpret the Statute. We have gathered here in order to decide on definite steps and measures. First of all then, I put the question: Should a petition be addressed directly to the King?

The meeting unanimously replied to this question in the affirmative.

Herr Fay. Should the memorandum read out today be submitted along with the petition?

By a majority vote the general meeting resolved to adopt the memorandum.

Herr Fay. Should the petition be adopted in its present form, or should it be modified by amendments?

The general meeting decided first of all to put to the vote the amendments raised in the discussion.

In accordance with this decision, Herr Dr. Claessen proposed the following amendment.

By a majority vote, the general meeting approved the insertion of this amendment.

Dr. Marx, Jung and Bürgers opposed this amendment.

Herr Kamp moved that the passage referring to the company's considerable financial sacrifice be deleted. Herr Kamp abstained from voting on this amendment.

Herr Fay then moved that the petition be voted on, inclusive of the amendment put forward.

The general meeting decided by a majority vote to adopt the petition as thus modified.

Herr Fay. Will the general meeting now express its opinion whether the petition should be presented personally to His Majesty by a deputation, or whether it should be sent through the post? Herr Fay moves that, in the event of the general meeting declaring for presentation by a deputation, a commission be elected to negotiate with the members of the company delegated to form the deputation.

Herr Kamp has no hope of any success from the deputation.

Herr Jung. I entirely agree with Herr Kamp. The ministry will demand concessions to which we cannot agree, and put forward greater demands to a deputation than if the matter were handled in a different way.

Herr Claessen declares in favour of a deputation, since that would also settle the question of Herr Hontheim's amendment concerning the request for a three months' stay of execution.

Herr von Rath declared for the deputation in order thereby to achieve at any rate an extension of the period.

Herr Bürgers. The reputation of the newspaper in the eyes of the public will certainly be endangered by a deputation. Opinion on the step taken by Herr Brockhaus[a] in Berlin is already a sufficient criterion in this respect.

Herr von Hontheim moved that one of the friends of the *Rheinische Zeitung* be entrusted with the presentation of the petition in Berlin.

Herr Camphausen. I do not share Herr Bürgers' view. Moreover it does not seem to me necessary to endow the deputation with plenipotentiary powers.

Herr von Hontheim. Everything will depend on the selection of the persons.

Herr Fay. I put it to the vote whether the petition should be presented by a deputation.

---

[a] The minutes book has here: (of the *Leipziger Allgemeine Zeitung*).—*Ed.*

Herr Haass supported the motion of Herr von Hontheim.

Herr Jung. I do not regard it as a misfortune if the *Rheinische Zeitung* ceases on April 1, even if the ban is lifted later. The *Rheinische Zeitung* as such would then arise anew in its true nature and would certainly at once regain its readership. But it will surely lose its readers if it continues a drab and impotent vegetative existence dependent on gracious permission and a double censorship.

Von Hontheim considered that it was a matter for the managers and the Board to decide whether to send a deputation or not, and also that the choice of the persons concerned should be left entirely to them.

In the voting on whether a deputation should be appointed or not, 61 votes were cast for the appointment of a deputation, and 53 votes against. Accordingly, it was decided by a majority vote to appoint a deputation.

In accordance with this decision, the general meeting commissioned the managers to send a deputation at the company's cost. The managers accepted this commission with the reservation that they would send the petition in writing if they were unable to find a suitable deputation within the next eight days.

Following this decision, the chairman, Herr Fay, declares today's meeting closed.

Cologne, February 12, 1843

G. Mevissen, in charge of the minutes
M. Kaufmann, K. Stucke, Wilhelm Boisserée, Heinzen, H. Haan,
I. Bürgers, G. Fay, G. Mallinckrodt

First published in *Rheinische Briefe und Akten zur Geschichte der politischen Bewegung 1830-1850*, I. Bd., Essen, 1919

Printed according to the original
Published in English for the first time

HUMBLE PETITION FROM THE SHAREHOLDERS OF THE *RHEINISCHE ZEITUNG* COMPANY FOR THE CONTINUANCE OF THE *RHEINISCHE ZEITUNG*[218]

Most excellent, most powerful King,
Most gracious King and Lord,

The High Royal Ministries in charge of censorship have ordered, by a rescript of January 21 of this year, the closure as from April 1 of the *Rheinische Zeitung*, published here in Cologne, and thereby threatened with ruin a concern which was founded by the undersigned, not without a considerable financial sacrifice, in order first of all to meet an urgent need of their native city, but was also meant, with Your Majesty's protection and trusting in Your Royal Majesty's noble-minded intentions, to act as a free and independent mouthpiece of public opinion fearlessly and unselfishly for the honour and interests of the Fatherland.

The undersigned believe that they have proved in a memorandum, which they lay in the most profound submission on the steps of Your Majesty's throne, that this decision of the high censorship authorities is impaired not only by a formal defect, but also that it is contrary both to the spirit of all previous legislation pertaining to the press and to Your Majesty's lofty intentions.

In order to meet the desires of the high censorship authorities, Your most humble subjects, the undersigned, will use the influence accorded to them by the stipulations of the Statute which they humbly enclose to ensure that the tone of the newspaper is moderate and dignified and that every possible offence is avoided, and therefore they all the more confidently express the following most respectful request:

May it please Your Royal Majesty, by rescinding the ministerial rescript issued by the High Ministries in charge of censorship on

January 21 of this year, to order the unhindered continuance of the *Rheinische Zeitung*.

We remain most humbly Your Majesty's loyal subjects, the shareholders of the *Rheinische Zeitung* Company.

Cologne

February 12, 1843

[Then follow the shareholders' signatures][a]

Published in full for the first time

Printed according to the original
Published in English for the first time

---

[a] The following signatures are given in Marx's hand:

"Dr. Marx for himself and on behalf of:

Dr. Schleicher, practising physician from Trier

Dr. Vencelius, practising physician   ditto

Cetto, merchant   ditto

Clentgen, landowner   ditto

Mittweg, lawyer   ditto." — *Ed.*

JENNY VON WESTPHALEN TO KARL MARX

IN COLOGNE

[Kreuznach, March 1843]

Although at the last conference of the two great powers nothing was stipulated on a certain point, nor any treaty concluded on the obligation of initiating a correspondence, and consequently no external means of compulsion exist, nevertheless the little scribe with the pretty curls feels inwardly compelled to open the ball, and indeed with feelings of the deepest, sincerest love and gratitude towards you, my dear, good and only sweetheart. I think you had never been more lovable and sweet and charming, and yet every time after you had gone I was in a state of delight and would always have liked to have you back again to tell you once more how much, how wholly, I love you. But still, the last occasion was your victorious departure; I do not know at all how dear you were to me in the depths of my heart when I no longer saw you in the flesh and only the true image of you in all angelic mildness and goodness, sublimity of love and brilliance of mind was so vividly present to my mind. If you were here now, my dearest Karl, what a great capacity for happiness you would find in your brave little woman. And should you come out with ever so bad a leaning, and ever such *wicked* intentions, I would not resort to any reactionary measures. I would patiently bow my head and surrender it to the wicked knave. "What", how?—Light, what, how light. Do you still remember our twilight conversations, our guessing games, our hours of slumber? Heart's beloved, how good, how loving, how considerate, how joyful you were!

How brilliant, how triumphant, I see you before me, how my heart longs for your constant presence, how it quivers for you with delight and enchantment, how anxiously it follows you on all the paths you take. To Paßschritier, to Merten in Gold, to Papa Ruge, to Pansa, everywhere I accompany you, I precede you and I follow you. If only I could level and make smooth all your paths, and sweep away everything that might be an obstacle to you. But then it does not fall to our lot that we also should be allowed to interfere actively in the workings of fate. We have been condemned to passivity by the fall of man, by Madame Eve's sin; our lot lies in waiting, hoping, enduring, suffering. At the most we are entrusted with knitting stockings, with needles, keys, and everything beyond that is evil; only when it is a question of deciding where the *Deutsche Jahrbücher*[a] is to be printed [219] does a feminine veto intervene and invisibly play something of a small main role. This evening I had a tiny little idea about Strasbourg. Would not a return to the homeland be forbidden you if you were to betray Germany to France in this way, and would it not be possible also that the liberal sovereign power would tell you definitely: "Emigrate then, or rather stay away if you do not like it in my states." But all that, as I have said, is only an idea, and our old friend Ruge will certainly know what has to be done, especially when a private little chick lurks like this in the background, and comes out with a separate petition. Let the matter rest, therefore, in Father Abraham's bosom.

This morning, when I was putting things in order, returning the draughtsmen to their proper place, collecting the cigar butts, sweeping up the ash, and trying to destroy the "Althäuschen" [?], I came across the enclosed page. You have dismembered our friend Ludwig[b] and left a crucial page here. If you are already past it in your reading, there is no hurry; but for the worthy bookbinder, in case it is to be bound, it is urgently needed. The whole work would be spoilt. You have certainly scattered some more pages. It would be a nuisance and a pity. Do look after the loose pages.

Now I must tell you about the distress and misfortune I had immediately after you went away. I saw at once that you had not paid any attention to your dear nose and left it at the mercy of wind and weather and air, and all the vicissitudes of fate, without taking a helpful handkerchief with you. That, in the first place, gave me grave concern. In the second place, the barber dropped in. I thought of putting it to great advantage and with rare

---

[a] i.e., the *Deutsch-Französische Jahrbücher.— Ed.*

[b] Feuerbach.— *Ed.*

amiability I asked him how much the Herr Doctor owed him. The answer was $7^1/_2$ silver groschen. I quickly did the sum in my head and $2^1/_2$ groschen were saved. I had no small change and I therefore gave him 8 silver groschen in good faith that he would give me change. But what did the scoundrel do? He thanked me, pocketed the whole sum, my six pfennigs were gone and I could whistle for them. I was still on the point of reproving him, but either he did not understand my glance of distress or Mother[a] tried to soothe me—in short, the six pfennigs were gone as all good things go. That was a disappointment!

Now I come to a matter of dress. I went out this morning and I saw many new pieces of lace at Wolf's shop. If you cannot get them cheap or get someone else to choose them, then I ask you, sweetheart, to leave the matter in my hands. In general, sweetheart, I would *really prefer at present* that you did not buy anything and saved your money for the journey. You see, sweetheart, I shall then be with you and we shall be buying together, and if someone cheats us, then at least it will happen in company. So, sweetheart, don't buy anything now. That applies also to the wreath of flowers. I am afraid you would have to pay too much, and to look for it together would indeed be very nice. If you won't give up the flowers, let them be rose-coloured. That goes best with my green dress. But I would prefer you to drop the whole business. Surely, sweetheart, that would be better. You can do that only when you are my dear lawful, church-wed husband. And one thing more, before I forget. Look for my last letter. I should be annoyed if it got into anyone else's hands. Its tendency is not exactly well-meaning, and its intentions are unfathomably malevolent. Were you barked at as a deserter when you jumped in? Or did they temper justice with mercy? Has Oppenheim come back and is Claessen still in a bit of a rage? I shall send Laffarge on as soon as I can.[220] Have you already delivered the letter of bad news to E[...][b]? Are the passport people willing? Dearest sweetheart, those are incidental questions, now I come to the heart of the matter. Did you behave well on the steamer, or was there again a Madame Hermann on board? You bad boy. I am going to drive it out of you. Always on the steamboats. I shall have an interdiction imposed immediately on wanderings of this kind in the *contrat social,* in our marriage papers, and such enormities will be severely punished. I shall have all the cases specified and punish-

---

[a] Caroline von Westphalen.— *Ed.*
[b] The name is indecipherable.— *Ed.*

ment imposed for them, and I shall make a second marriage law similar to the penal code. I shall show you alright. Yesterday evening I was dead tired again, but all the same I ate an egg. Food shares, therefore, are not doing so badly and are going up like the Düsseldorf shares. When you come, it is to be hoped they will be at par, and the state guarantees the interest. However, adieu now. Parting is painful. It pains the heart. Good-bye, my one and only beloved, black sweet, little'hubby. "What", how! Ah! you knavish face. Talatta, talatta, good-bye, write soon, talatta, talatta.

First published in: Marx/Engels, *Werke*, Ergänzungsband, 1, Teil, Berlin, 1968

Printed according to the original

Published in English for the first time

NOTES
AND
INDEXES

NOTES

[1] *Reflections of a Young Man on the Choice of a Profession*—an essay written by Marx at the school leaving examinations at the Royal Frederick William III gymnasium in Trier in August 1835. Only seven of Marx's examination papers have been preserved: the above-mentioned essay on a subject at the writer's choice, a Latin essay on the reign of Augustus and a religious essay (both are published in the appendices to this volume), a Latin unseen, a translation from the Greek, a translation into French, and a paper in mathematics (all of which are published in: Marx/Engels, *Historisch-Kritische Gesamtausgabe*, Erste Abteilung, Band 1, Zweiter Halbband, Berlin, 1929, S. 164-82).

In the original there are numerous underscorings presumably made by the history and philosophy teacher, the then headmaster of the gymnasium, Johann Hugo Wyttenbach (they are not reproduced in the present edition). He also made the following comment: "Rather good. The essay is marked by a wealth of thought and a good systematised narration. But generally the author here too made a mistake peculiar to him—he constantly seeks for elaborate picturesque expressions. Therefore many passages which are underlined lack the necessary clarity and definiteness and often precision in separate expressions as well as in whole paragraphs."

In English this essay was published in 1961 in the United States, in the journal *The New Scholasticism*, Vol. XXXV, No. 2, Baltimore-Washington, pp. 197-201, and in *Writings of the Young Marx on Philosophy and Society*, New York, 1967, pp. 35-39.

p. 3

[2] *Letter from Marx to His Father*—this is the only letter written by Marx in his student years which has been preserved. Of all Marx's letters that are extant, this is the earliest. It was published in English in the collections: *The Young Marx*, London, 1967, pp. 135-47, *Writings of the Young Marx on Philosophy and Society*, New York, 1967, pp. 40-50 and *Karl Marx. Early Texts*, translated and edited by David McLellan, University of Kent at Canterbury, Oxford, 1971, pp. 1-10. p. 10

[3] The *Pandect*—compendium of Roman civil law (*Corpus iuris civilis*) made by order of the Emperor of the Eastern Roman Empire Justinian I in 528-534. The Pandect or the Digest contained excerpts from works in civil and criminal law by prominent Roman jurists. p. 12

[4] The work mentioned is not extant.   p. 12

[5] Marx quotes these passages from memory.   p. 15

[6] This refers to the classification of contracts in Immanuel Kant's *Die Metaphysik der Sitten*. Theil I. Metaphysische Anfangsgründe der Rechtslehre, Königsberg, 1797-98.   p. 17

[7] The philosophical dialogue mentioned here has not been preserved.   p. 18

[8] The *Doctors' Club* was founded by representatives of the radical wing of the Hegelian school in Berlin in 1837. Among its members were lecturer on theology of Berlin University Bruno Bauer, gymnasium history teacher Karl Friedrich Köppen and geography teacher Adolf Rutenberg. The usual meeting place was the small Hippel café. The Club, of which Marx was also an active member, played an important part in the Young Hegelian movement.   p. 19

[9] The work has not been preserved.   p. 19

[10] Marx refers to the *Deutscher Musenalmanach*, a liberal annual published in Leipzig from 1829.   p. 19

[11] As is seen from Heinrich Marx's letter of September 16, 1837, to his son (see this volume, p. 680), Karl Marx intended at that time to publish a journal of theatrical criticism.   p. 20

[12] The letter has not survived.   p. 21

[13] These two poems, written in 1837, were included in a book of verse dedicated to Karl Marx's father (see this volume, pp. 531-632).

The general title *Wild Songs* was introduced when the poems were published in the journal *Athenäum* in 1841. The text of both poems was reproduced with slight alterations. In *The Fiddler* two lines

"Fort aus dem Haus, fort aus dem Blick,
Willst Kindlein spielen um dein Genick?"
("Away from the house, away from the look,
O child, do you seek to risk your neck?")

coming in the original in the fifth stanza after the lines

"How so! I plunge, plunge without fail
My blood-black sabre into your soul"

were omitted.

A comment on the *Wild Songs* was published in the *Frankfurter Konversationsblatt* No. 62 of March 3, 1841. Though unfavourably commenting on the form, the paper admitted the author's "original talent".

In English the poems were published in the book: R. Payne, *Marx*, New York, 1968, pp. 62-64.   p. 22

[14] Marx's work *Difference Between the Democritean and Epicurean Philosophy of Nature* is part of a general research on the history of ancient philosophy which he planned as far back as 1839.

During his research on ancient philosophy Marx compiled the preparatory *Notebooks on Epicurean Philosophy* (see this volume, pp. 401-509). In early April 1841 Marx submitted his work to the Faculty of Philosophy of the University of Jena as a dissertation for a doctor's degree (see this volume, p. 379) and received the degree on April 15. He intended to have his work printed and for this purpose wrote the dedication and the foreword dated March 1841. However, he did not succeed in getting it published, although he thought of doing so again at the end of 1841 and beginning of 1842.

Marx's own manuscript of the thesis has been lost. What remains is an incomplete copy written by an unknown person. This copy has corrections and insertions in Marx's handwriting. Texts of the fourth and fifth chapters of Part One and the Appendix, except for one fragment, are missing. Each chapter of Part One and Part Two has its own numeration of the author's notes. These notes, in the form of citations from the sources and additional commentaries, are also incomplete. They are given, according to the copy of the manuscript which has survived, after the main text of the dissertation and marked in the text, in distinction to the editorial notes, by numbers and brackets. Obvious slips of the pen have been corrected. Changes made by Marx which affect the meaning are specified.

In the first publication of the thesis in *Aus dem Literarischen Nachlass von Karl Marx, Friedrich Engels und Ferdinand Lassalle*, Bd. I, Stuttgart, 1902, the fragments from the Appendix "Critique of Plutarch's Polemic Against the Theology of Epicurus", have been omitted as well as all the author's notes except for some excerpts. The first publication in full (according to the part of the manuscript that has been preserved) was carried out by the Institute of Marxism-Leninism, CC CPSU, in 1927 in Volume One of MEGA (Marx/Engels, *Historisch-Kritische Gesamtausgabe*, Erste Abteilung, Band 1, Erster Halbband, S. 3-81).

The first translation into English was done by Kurt Karl Merz in 1946 in Melbourne (a typewritten copy of it is kept in the Institute of Marxism-Leninism, CC CPSU, in Moscow). The foreword to the thesis was published in the collection: K. Marx and F. Engels, *On Religion*, Moscow, 1957, pp. 13-15. In 1967 a translation by Norman D. Livergood was published in the book: *Activity in Marx's Philosophy*, Hague, 1967, pp. 55-109. Two excerpts from the dissertation (see this volume, pp. 84-87 and 103-05) were published in *Writings of the Young Marx on Philosophy and Society*, New York, 1967, pp. 60-66, and *Karl Marx. Early Texts*, Oxford, 1971, pp. 11-22. p. 25

[15] Marx here refers to the book Petri Gassendi, *Animadversiones in decimum librum Diogenis Laertii, qui est De Vita, Moribus, Placitisque Epicuri*, Ludguni, 1649.

p. 29

[16] Marx never realised his plan to write a larger work on the Epicurean, Stoic and Sceptic philosophies. p. 29

[17] This refers to the following passage from the book by Karl Friedrich Köppen, *Friedrich der Grosse und seine Widersacher*, Leipzig, 1840: "Epikureismus, Stoizismus und Skepsis sind die Nervenmuskel und Eingeweidesysteme des antiken Organismus, deren unmittelbare, natürliche Einheit die Schönheit und Sittlichkeit des Altertums bedingte, und die beim Absterben desselben auseinanderfielen" (S. 39) ("Epicureanism, Stoicism and Scepticism are the nerve muscles and intestinal system of the antique organism whose immediate, natural unity conditioned the beauty and morality of antiquity, and which disintegrated with the decay of the latter"). Köppen dedicated his book to Karl Marx. p. 30

[18] Marx quotes David Hume's *A Treatise of Human Nature* from the German translation: *David Hume über die menschliche Natur aus Englischen nebst kritischen Versuchen zur Beurtheilung dieses Werks von Ludwig Heinrich Jakob*, 1. Bd., Ueber den menschlichen Verstand, Halle, 1790, S. 485. p. 30

[19] Marx quotes from a letter by Epicurus to Menoeceus; see *Diogenes Laertii de clarorum philosophorum vitis, dogmatibus et apophthegmatibus libri decem* (X, 123).

p. 30

[20] *Gymnosophists*—Greek name for Indian sages.   p. 41

[21] *Ataraxy*—in ancient Greek ethics—tranquillity. In Epicurean ethics—the ideal of life; state of the sage who has attained inner freedom through knowledge of nature and deliverance from fear of death.   p. 45

[22] The manuscripts of "General Difference in Principle Between the Democritean and Epicurean Philosophy of Nature" and "Result" have not been found.

p. 45

[23] Characterising here the gods of Epicurus, Marx, obviously, had in mind the remark by Johann Joachim Winckelmann in his book *Geschichte der Kunst des Altertums*, 2 Teile, Dresden, 1767: "Die Schönheit der Gottheiten im männlichen Alter besteht in einem Inbegriff der Stärke gesetzter Jahre und der Fröhlichkeit der Jugend, und diese besteht hier in dem Mangel an Nerven und Sehnen, die sich in der Blüte der Jahre wenig äußern. Hierin aber liegt zugleich ein Ausdruck der göttlichen Genügsamkeit, welche die zur Nahrung unseres Körpers bestimmten Teile nicht vonnöten hat; und dieses erläutert des Epicurus Meinung von der Gestalt der Götter, denen er einen Körper, aber gleichsam einen Körper, und Blut, aber gleichsam Blut, gibt, welches Cicero dunkel und unbegreiflich findet" ("The beauty of the deities in their virile age consists in the combination of the strength of mature years and the joyfulness of youth, and this consists here in the lack of nerves and sinews, which are less apparent in the flowering of the years. But in this lies also an expression of divine self-containment which is not in need of the parts of our body which serve for its nourishment; and this illuminates Epicurus' opinion concerning the shape of the gods to which he gives a body, which looks like a body, and blood, but which looks like blood, something which Cicero considers obscure and inconceivable").   p. 51

[24] *Hyrcanian Sea*—ancient name of the Caspian Sea.   p. 51

[25] The reference is probably to the commentaries by Johann Baptist Carl Nürnberger and Johann Gottlob Schneider on the following editions: *Diogenes Laertius. De vitis, dogmatibus et apophthegmatibus liber decimus graece et latine separatim editus* ... a Carolo Nürnbergero, Norimbergae, 1791 (the second edition appeared in 1808) and *Epicuri physica et meteorologica duabus epistolis eiusdem comprehensa*. Graeca ad fidem librorum scriptorum et editorum emandavit atque interpretatus est. Jo. Gottl. Schneider, Lipsiae, 1813.   p. 54

[26] This is not Metrodorus of Lampsacus, the disciple of Epicurus, but Metrodorus of Chios, the disciple of Democritus, named incorrectly by Stobaeus (in the author's note) as the teacher of Epicurus. The same lines may be found in the fifth notebook on Epicurean philosophy (see this volume, pp. 96 and 486).   p. 61

[27] Two fragments from the Appendix have been preserved: the beginning of the first paragraph of Section Two and the author's notes to Section One. The general title of the Appendix, which is missing in the first fragment, is reproduced here according to the contents (see this volume, p. 33). The text of this fragment corresponds almost word for word to the text of the third notebook on Epicurean philosophy (see this volume, pp. 452-54) and was written in an unknown hand on paper of the same kind as the text of the notebook. On this ground some scholars assume that this fragment does not belong to the Doctoral dissertation, but is part of a non-extant work on ancient philosophy. The content of the fragment, however, and the quotations from Plutarch in it are closely connected with the

author's notes to the Appendix (see this volume, pp. 102-05). As the available data do not yet permit a final decision as to where this fragment belongs, in this edition it is included in the Doctoral dissertation.   p. 74

[28] The reference is to Plutarch's mystic conception of three eternally existing categories of men.   p. 74

[29] In the manuscript of the author's notes all quotations are given in the original — Greek or Latin. While Marx, in the *Notebooks on Epicurean Philosophy*, quotes Diogenes Laertius according to Pierre Gassendi's edition (Lyons, 1649), in his notes to the dissertation he quotes from the Tauchnitz edition of Diogenes Laertius, *De vitis philosophorum libri*..., X, T. 1-2, Lipsiae, 1833.

Editorial explanatory insertions are given in square brackets when necessary.
                                                                                   p. 77

[30] *Massilians* were the citizens of the city of Massilia, now Marseilles, founded circa 600 B. C. as a Greek colony by Ionic Phocaeans.

The battle of Marius with the German Cimbri tribes who invaded Gaul and Northern Italy took place in 101 B. C. near Vercelli.   p. 84

[31] Marx refers here to the struggle between different trends in the German philosophy of the late thirties and early forties of the nineteenth century.

By the *"liberal party"* Marx means here the Young Hegelians. The most advanced of the Young Hegelians (Ludwig Feuerbach, Bruno Bauer, Arnold Ruge) took the stand of atheism and political radicalism. In answer to this evolution of the Left wing of the Hegelian school, the conservative German philosophers united under the banner of the so-called positive philosophy — a religious-mystical trend (Christian Hermann Weisse, Immanuel Hermann Fichte Junior, Franz Xaver von Baader, Anton Günther and others), which criticised Hegel's philosophy from the right. The "positive philosophers" tried to make philosophy subservient to religion by proclaiming divine revelation the only source of "positive" knowledge. They called negative every philosophy which recognised rational cognition as its source.   p. 86

[32] Marx cites (in the manuscript in French) from the book *Système de la nature, ou des Loix du monde physique et du monde moral*. Par. M. Mirabaud, Secrétaire Perpétuel et l'un des Quarante de l'Académie Française, Londres, 1770. The real author of the book was the French philosopher Paul Holbach, who for the sake of secrecy put the name of J. Mirabaud, the secretary of the French Academy, on his book (J. Mirabaud died in 1760).   p. 102

[33] Both Friedrich Schelling's works quoted by Marx (*Philosophische Briefe über Dogmatismus und Kriticismus* and *Vom Ich als Princip der Philosophie, oder über das Unbedingte im menschlichen Wissen*) appeared in 1795. Later Schelling renounced his progressive views and turned to religious mysticism. In 1841 Schelling was invited by the Prussian authorities to the University of Berlin to oppose the influence of the representatives of the Hegelian school, the Young Hegelians in particular.
                                                                                   p. 103

[34] Marx probably refers to the 13th lecture on the history of religion delivered by Hegel at the University of Berlin during the summer term of 1829.   p. 103

[35] The reference is to Kant's critique of different ways of proving God's existence in his *Kritik der reinen Vernunft* (Critique of Pure Reason).   p. 104

[36] Marx refers to the following remark made by Kant in his *Critique of Pure Reason* in

connection with the speculation on the logical meaning of the elements of reasoning (subject, predicate and the copula "is"): "... A hundred real talers do not contain the least coin more than a hundred possible talers. For as the latter signify the concept, and the former the object and the positing of the object, should the former contain more than the latter, my concept would not, in that case, express the whole object, and would not therefore be an adequate concept of it. My financial position is, however, affected very differently by a hundred real talers than it is by the mere concept of them (that is, of their possibility). For the object, as it actually exists, is not analytically contained in my concept, but is added to my concept (which is a determination of my state) synthetically; and yet the conceived hundred talers are not themselves in the least increased through thus acquiring existence outside my concept."

p. 104

[37] *Wends*—old name of West Slavic tribes.

p. 104

[38] At the end of 1841 and beginning of 1842 Marx made a new attempt to publish his dissertation. He drafted the beginning of a new preface in which many passages were altered or crossed out. It was probably at the same period that he wrote the note against Schelling (see this volume, p. 103) which was inserted in Marx's handwriting in the copy of the manuscript.

p. 106

[39] *Comments on the Latest Prussian Censorship Instruction* was the first work written by Marx as a revolutionary journalist. It was occasioned by the censorship instruction of the Prussian Government of December 24, 1841. Though formulated in moderate liberal terms, the instruction actually not only retained but intensified the censorship of the press. Written between January 15 and February 10, 1842, just after the publication of the instruction in the press (it was published in the *Allgemeine Preussische Staats-Zeitung* No. 14, January 14, 1842; Marx cites from this publication), the article was originally intended for the *Deutsche Jahrbücher* under the editorship of Arnold Ruge (see this volume, p. 381) but because of the censorship restrictions it was published only in 1843 in Switzerland in *Anekdota* which contained works by oppositional authors, mostly Young Hegelians.

Excerpts from the article were reprinted in the *Mannheimer Abendzeitung* Nos. 71 and 72, March 26 and 28, 1843.

In 1851 Hermann Becker, a member of the Communist League, made an attempt to publish Marx's collected works in Cologne. On the author's initiative the first issue began with this article (see *Gesammelte Aufsätze von Karl Marx*, herausgegeben von Hermann Becker, 1. Heft, Köln, 1851). However, the publication was ceased because of the government repressions.

The first English translation of the article appeared in *Writings of the Young Marx on Philosophy and Society*, New York, 1967, pp. 67-92, and an excerpt from it in *Karl Marx. Early Texts*, Oxford, 1971, pp. 26-30.

p. 109

[40] The reference is to the *Bundesakte* adopted by the Congress of Vienna on June 8, 1815. The Act proclaimed the formation of a German Confederation consisting initially of 34 independent states and four free cities. The Act virtually sanctioned the political dismemberment of Germany and the maintaining of the monarchical-estate system in the German states.

Article 18 of the Act vaguely mentioned a forthcoming drafting of uniform instructions providing for "freedom of the press" in the states of the German Confederation. However, this article remained on paper. The Provisional Federal Act on the Press of September 20, 1819 (it remained provisional for ever), introduced preliminary censorship for all publications of not more than 20 signatures (actually all periodicals) throughout Germany as well as a series of other restrictions. p. 115

[41] *Lettre de cachet*—a secret royal order for the imprisonment or exile of any person without judge or jury. This method of reprisals against oppositional elements and undesirable persons was widely used in France in the period of absolutism, especially under Louis XIV and Louis XV. p. 116

[42] An allusion to the negotiations of Prussian diplomats with the Pope concerning the disagreements between the Prussian Government and the Catholic Church known as the "Cologne" or "church conflict". The conflict concerning the religious denomination of children of mixed marriages between Catholics and Protestants arose in 1837 with the arrest of C. A. Droste-Vischering, Archbishop of Cologne, who was accused of high treason for refusing to obey the orders of Frederick William III, the King of Prussia. It ended in 1841 under Frederick William IV with the Prussian Government yielding to the Catholic Church (see Marx's letter to Ruge of July 9, 1842, pp. 389-90 of this volume). p. 118

[43] The article *Proceedings of the Sixth Rhine Province Assembly. First Article. Debates on Freedom of the Press and Publication of the Proceedings of the Assembly of the Estates* was Marx's first contribution to the *Rheinische Zeitung für Politik, Handel und Gewerbe.* Marx began his work as a contributor and in October 1842 became one of the editors of the newspaper. By its content and approach to vital political problems, the article helped the newspaper, founded by the oppositional Rhenish bourgeoisie as a liberal organ, to begin a transition to the revolutionary-democratic positions.

The appearance of Marx's article in the press raised a favourable response in progressive circles. Georg Jung, manager of the *Rheinische Zeitung,* wrote to Marx: "Your articles on freedom of the press are extremely good.... Meyen wrote that the *Rheinische Zeitung* had eclipsed the *Deutsche Jahrbücher* ... that in Berlin everybody was overjoyed with it" (MEGA, Abt. 1, Bd. 1, Hb. 2, S. 275). In his comments on the article published in the *Rheinische Zeitung* Arnold Ruge wrote: "Nothing more profound and more substantial has been said or could have been said on freedom of the press and in defence of it" (*Deutsche Jahrbücher,* 1842, S. 535-36).

In the early 1850s Marx included this article in his collected works then being prepared for publication by Hermann Becker (see Note 39). However only the beginning of the article was included in the first issue. The major part of the text which had been published in the *Rheinische Zeitung* No. 139 was left unprinted. The end of the article was intended for the following issue, which was never published.

A copy of the *Rheinische Zeitung* which Marx sent from London to Becker in Cologne in February 1851 with the author's notes on the text of the articles (mostly in the form of abbreviations) intended for the edition Becker was preparing has recently been found in the archives of Cologne University library. This copy of the newspaper proves that Marx thought of publishing—partly in an abridged form—many of his articles written for the *Rheinische Zeitung.* However, his plan was not realised. Marginal notes show that the articles "Communal Reform and the *Kölnische Zeitung*" and "A Correspondent of the *Kölnische Zeitung* vs. the *Rheinische Zeitung*" belong to Marx. These articles have never been published in any collection of Marx's works.

In English an excerpt from the *Proceedings* was published in *Karl Marx. Early Texts,* Oxford, 1971, pp. 35-36. p. 132

[44] Marx devoted three articles to the debates of the Sixth Rhine Province Assembly, only two of which, the first and the third, were published. In the first article Marx

proceeded with his criticism of the Prussian censorship which he had begun in his as yet unpublished article "Comments on the Latest Prussian Censorship Instruction". The second article, devoted to the conflict between the Prussian Government and the Catholic Church, was banned by the censors. The manuscript of this article has not survived, but the general outline of it is given by Marx in his letter to Ruge of July 9, 1842 (see this volume, pp. 389-90). The third article is devoted to the debates of the Rhine Province Assembly on the law on wood thefts.   p. 132

45 *Assemblies of the estates* were introduced in Prussia in 1823. They embraced the heads of princely families, representatives of the knightly estate, i.e., the nobility, of towns and rural communities. The election system based on the principle of landownership provided for a majority of the nobility in the assemblies. The competency of the assemblies was restricted to questions of local economy and administration. They also had the right to express their desires on government bills submitted for discussion.

The Sixth Rhine Province Assembly was in session from May 23 to July 25, 1841, in Düsseldorf. The debates dealt with in the article took place during the discussion on publication of the proceedings of the assemblies (this right had been granted by the Royal edict of April 30, 1841) and in connection with petitions of a number of towns on freedom of the press.

Citations in the text are given according to the *Sitzungs-Protokolle des sechsten Rheinischen Provinzial-Landtags*, Koblenz, 1841.   p. 132

46 The reference is to the article "Die inlandische Presse u. die inlandische Statistik", published in the *Allgemeine Preussische Staats-Zeitung* No. 86, March 26, 1842. Marx cited mainly from this article, and also from two other articles, "Die Wirkung der Zensur-Verfügung vom 24. Dezember 1841" and "Die Besprechung inlandscher Angelegenheiten," published in the same newspaper in Nos. 75 and 78, March 16 and 19, 1842, respectively.   p. 132

47 *Vossische Zeitung*—the name given after its owner to the daily *Königlich privilegirte Berlinische Zeitung von Staats- und gelehrten Sachen*.   p. 132

48 *Spenersche Zeitung*—the name given after its publisher to the *Berlinische Nachrichten von Staats- und gelehrten Sachen* which was a semi-official government organ at the beginning of the 1840s.   p. 132

49 Marx ironically compares Prussian officialdom's enthusiasm for statistics with the ancient philosophical systems which assigned a special importance to signs and numbers. He hints in particular at the ancient Chinese "I Ching" writings, of which Confucius was considered in the nineteenth century to be one of the first commentators. According to the philosophical conception laid down in them, *ku* signs, which were formed from various combinations of three continuous or broken lines, symbolised things and natural phenomena.

When calling Pythagoras the "universal statistician" Marx had in mind the ancient Greek philosophers' conceptions of number as the essence of all things.
p. 134

50 The reference is to positive philosophy. See Note 31.   p. 134

51 By this Marx meant Heraclitus' maxim: The dry soul is the wisest and the best.
p. 135

52 The reference is to the Provisional Federal Act on the Press for the German states adopted on September 20, 1819 (see Note 40).   p. 138

[53] The reference is to the *historical school of law*—a trend in history and jurisprudence which originated in Germany at the end of the eighteenth century. Its representatives (Gustav Hugo and Friedrich Carl von Savigny) tried to justify the privileges enjoyed by the nobility and the existence of feudal institutions by eternal historical traditions. An assessment of this school is given by Marx in the article "The Philosophical Manifesto of the Historical School of Law" (see this volume, pp. 203-10).   p. 138

[54] By the decision of the Vienna Congress of 1815, Belgium and Holland were incorporated in the single kingdom of the Netherlands, Belgium being actually subordinated to Holland. Belgium became an independent constitutional monarchy after the bourgeois revolution of 1830.   p. 143

[55] *Ku*—see Note 49.   p. 155

[56] Marx cites these and the following lines of Hariri's poem from Friedrich Rückert's *Die Verwandlungen des Abu Seid von Serug, oder die Makamen des Hariri*, Stuttgart, 1826.   p. 170

[57] This work is the beginning of a critical article which Marx planned to write against the abstract, nihilist treatment of the problem of state centralisation in the article by Moses Hess, "Deutschland und Frankreich in bezug auf die Zentralisationsfrage," which was published in the Supplement to the *Rheinische Zeitung* No. 137 of May 17, 1842.

Marx's article was evidently not finished. The part which was written has survived in manuscript form.

It was first published in English in *Writings of the Young Marx on Philosophy and Society*, New York, 1967, pp. 106-08.   p. 182

[58] This article was occasioned by attacks on the trend of the *Rheinische Zeitung* on the part of the influential *Kölnische Zeitung*, which defended the Catholic Church in the 1840s. In 1842 the *Kölnische Zeitung*, under the editorship of Karl Hermes, a secret agent of the Prussian Government, took an active part in the campaign against the progressive press and progressive philosophical trends, the Young Hegelians in particular.

The article was published in English in the collections: K. Marx and F. Engels, *On Religion*, Moscow, 1957, pp. 16-40, and *Writings of the Young Marx on Philosophy and Society*, New York, 1967, pp. 109-30.   p. 184

[59] Marx cites Lucian from *Griechische Prosaiker in neuen Übersetzungen*. Fünftes Bändchen, Stuttgart, 1827, S. 176.   p. 185

[60] *Vedas*—ancient Hindu religious and literary works in verse and prose written over several centuries, not later than the sixth century B. C.   p. 191

[61] This wording is given in Article 3 of *la Charte octroyée*—the fundamental law of the Bourbon monarchy proclaimed in 1814, and in *la Charte bâclée* proclaimed on August 14, 1830, after the July bourgeois revolution in France. While introducing some changes into the constitution of the French monarchy (certain restrictions of royal power, lowering of age and property qualifications, the practice of open debates in the Chambers, etc.), the second charter retained essentially the main principles laid down in the charter of 1814 granted by the Bourbons after the restoration.   p. 192

[62] Here and further Marx cites from *Allgemeines Landrecht für die Preussischen Staaten*, second edition, Berlin, 1794.   p. 192

[63] *Code Napoléon*—a civil code published in 1804; it was introduced also in West and South-West Germany conquered by Napoleon and continued in force in the Rhine Province after its union with Prussia in 1815. It was a classical code of bourgeois society.   p. 192

[64] An allusion to the participation of the editor of the *Kölnische Zeitung* Hermes in the oppositional movement of the German students in his youth.   p. 194

[65] *Corybantes*—priestesses of the goddess Cybele; *Cabiri* were priests of the ancient Greek divinities. The Corybantes and Cabiri were identified in Asia Minor with the Curetes, priests of Rhea, the mother of Zeus. According to mythology the Curetes clashed their weapons to drown the cries of the infant Zeus and thus saved him from his father, Cronus, who devoured his own children.   p. 196

[66] By this Marx means the attacks of the German press against the philosophical critique of religion which began with Strauss' book *Das Leben Jesu*, the first volume of which appeared in 1835.   p. 196

[67] *Deutsche Jahrbücher*—abbreviated title of the Left Hegelian literary-philosophical journal *Deutsche Jahrbücher für Wissenschaft und Kunst*. The journal was published in Leipzig from July 1841 and edited by Arnold Ruge. Earlier (1838-41) it came out under the title *Hallische Jahrbücher für deutsche Wissenschaft und Kunst*. Its name was changed and publication transferred from the Prussian town of Halle to Saxony because of the threat of suppression in the Prussian state. However, it did not last long under its new name. In January 1843 it was closed by the Government of Saxony and its further publication was prohibited throughout Germany by the Federal Diet (Bundestag).   p. 196

[68] When this article was published in the *Rheinische Zeitung*, one of the sections, "The Chapter on Marriage", was banned by the censors. It appeared in full only in 1927. In the present edition the article is reproduced, as in all previous complete publications, according to the manuscript, which is extant.

The article was published in English in *Writings of the Young Marx on Philosophy and Society*, New York, 1967, pp. 96-105.   p. 203

[69] *Papageno*—a character in Mozart's opera *Die Zauberflöte*, a bird-catcher who clad himself in feathers.   p. 203

[70] The reference is to a pamphlet written by the German jurist Friedrich Carl von Savigny in 1838 on the occasion of Gustav Hugo's jubilee—the fiftieth anniversary of his being awarded a doctor's degree: *Der Zehente Mai 1788. Beytrag zur Geschichte der Rechtswissenschaft* (Berlin, 1838).   p. 207

[71] Marx cites the first volume of Benjamin Constant's *De la religion* (Book 2, Ch. 2, pp. 172-73, Paris edition, 1826). A detailed synopsis of this work written by Marx in Bonn in 1842 has survived.   p. 207

[72] Marx refers here to the preaching of "free love" in the works of some of the Young Germany writers.

Young Germany—a group of writers which emerged in the 1830s in Germany and was influenced by Heinrich Heine and Ludwig Börne. The Young Germany writers (Karl Gutzkow, Ludolf Wienbarg, Theodor Mundt and others) came out in defence of freedom of conscience and the press, their writings, fiction and journalistic, reflecting opposition sentiments of the petty-bourgeoisie and intellectuals. The views of the Young Germans were politically vague. Soon the majority of them turned into mere liberals.   p. 208

[73] An allusion to Savigny's book *Vom Beruf unsrer Zeit für Gesetzgebung und Rechtswissenschaft,* Heidelberg, 1814, and to Savigny's appointment as Minister of Justice for the revision of the law in 1842.   p. 209

[74] This article was written in connection with the attacks made by the German philosopher Otto Friedrich Gruppe on Bruno Bauer's book *Kritik der evangelischen Geschichte der Synoptiker.* Attacking the leader of the Young Hegelians in his pamphlet *Bruno Bauer und die akademische Lehrfreiheit,* Gruppe tried under the guise of non-partisanship and neutrality in philosophy to discredit Bauer as a critic of the gospel sources. In his article Marx cites and slightly paraphrases Gruppe's statement: "The writer of these lines has never served any party and has not been influenced by anybody." The Young Hegelian journal *Deutsche Jahrbücher* replied with a series of articles in defence of Bruno Bauer.   p. 211

[75] Marx expounds the statement made by the Protestant theologian Joachim Neander in his book *Das Leben Jesu Christi in seinem geschichtlichen Zusammenhange und seiner geschichtlichen Entwickelung dargestellt,* Hamburg, 1837, S. 265, and quoted by Bruno Bauer in his *Kritik der evangelischen Geschichte der Synoptiker* (Bd. 2, S. 296).   p. 212

[76] Citation from Bruno Bauer's *Kritik der evangelischen Geschichte der Synoptiker.* Citations from the New Testament are given according to this work (Bd. 2, S. 297, 299 and 296).   p. 213

[77] This article is the first written by Marx for the *Rheinische Zeitung* after he became its editor. The article in No. 284 of the Augsburg *Allgemeine Zeitung* against which Marx polemises was published on October 11, 1842, under the title "Die Kommunistenlehren".

In English the article was published in *Writings of the Young Marx on Philosophy and Society,* New York, 1967, pp. 136-42, and in Vol. 1 of *On Revolution,* New York, 1971, pp. 3-6.   p. 215

[78] The reference is to a report from Berlin on August 21, 1842, reprinted in the *Rheinische Zeitung* No. 273, September 30, 1842, from Weitling's journal *Die junge Generation* under the title "Die Berliner Familienhäuser".   p. 215

[79] Marx means the critical article "Die Augsburger *Allgemeine Zeitung* in ihrer tiefsten Erniedrigung" published in the journal *Mefistofeles. Revue der deutschen Gegenwart in Skizzen und Umrissen,* issues 1 and 2, 1842.   p. 215

[80] The reference is to the tenth congress of scientists of France which took place in Strasbourg from September 28 to October 9, 1842. It was attended by scientists from Germany, Switzerland, Great Britain, Belgium, Russia and other countries. One of its sections discussed proposals made by the followers of Fourier for improving the social position of the non-propertied classes. The report cites Edouard de Pompery's speech in which he compared the proletariat's struggle against private property with the struggle of the bourgeoisie against feudalism.

This report, an excerpt from which Marx quotes below, was published in the *Rheinische Zeitung* No. 280, October 7, 1842, with a note: "Strassburg, 30. Sept."   p. 216

[81] This refers to the following proposition from Emmanuel Sieyès' *Qu'est-ce que le tiers état?* published in 1789 on the eve of the French revolution: "What is the third estate? Everything.—What was it until now in the political respect? Nothing.—What is it striving for? To be something."   p. 216

[82] An allusion to the revolutionary. actions of the proletariat in England and France. In August 1842 Manchester was one of the centres of Chartist agitation and a massive strike movement; in May 1839 a revolt organised by the secret revolutionary Society of the Seasons took place in Paris; the Lyons weavers rose in 1831 and 1834.
p. 216

[83] The reference is to an article datelined: "Karlsruhe, 8. Oktober", published in the Augsburg *Allgemeine Zeitung* No. 284. Excerpts from this article are printed below.
p. 219

[84] This refers to an article datelined: "London, 5. Oktober 1842", published in the Augsburg *Allgemeine Zeitung* No. 284.
p. 219

[85] *Autonomists*—the name given to the members of former landowning families of princes and counts who, on the basis of the Federal Act of 1815, retained the right to dispose of their hereditary estates at their discretion irrespective of the general legislation on inheritance, trusteeship, etc.
p. 220

[86] This apparently refers to the book by Wilhelm Kosegarten, *Betrachtungen über die Veräusserlichkeit und Theilbarkeit des Landbesitzes mit besonderer Rücksicht auf einige Provinzen der Preussischen Monarchie,* in which the author criticised the parcelling out of the landed estates and upheld the restoration of feudal landownership.
p. 220

[87] This refers to the article "Die Kommunistenlehren" published in the *Allgemeine Zeitung* of October 11, 1842, and criticised by Marx in his article "Communism and the Augsburg *Allgemeine Zeitung*".
p. 223

[88] *Proceedings of the Sixth Rhine Province Assembly. Third Article. Debates on the Law on Thefts of Wood* is one of the series of articles by Marx on the proceedings of the Rhine Province Assembly from May 23 to July 25, 1841. Marx touched on the theme of the material interests of the popular masses for the first time, coming out in their defence. Work on this and subsequent articles inspired Marx to study political economy. He wrote about this in the preface to his *A Contribution to the Critique of Political Economy* (1859): "In the year 1842-43, as editor of the *Rheinische Zeitung,* I first found myself in the embarrassing position of having to discuss what is known as material interests. Debates of the Rhine Province Assembly on the theft of wood and the division of landed property; the official polemic started by Herr von Schaper, then Oberpräsident of the Rhine Province, against the *Rheinische Zeitung* about the condition of the Mosel peasantry, and finally the debates on free trade and protective tariffs caused me in the first instance to turn my attention to economic questions."

Excerpts from the speeches by the deputies to the Assembly are cited from *Sitzungs-Protokolle des sechsten Rheinischen Provinzial-Landtags,* Koblenz, 1841.
p. 224

[89] The second article written by Marx on the proceedings of the Rhine Province Assembly, banned by the censors, was devoted to the conflict between the Prussian Government and the Catholic Church or the so-called church conflict (see Note 42).
p. 224

[90] Marx refers to the Criminal Code of Karl V (*Die peinliche Halsgerichtsordnung Kaiser Karls V. Constitutio criminalis Carolina*), approved by the Reichstag in Regensburg in 1532; it was distinguished by its extremely cruel penalties.
p. 226

[91] The reference is to the so-called barbaric laws (*leges barbarorum*) compiled in the fifth-ninth centuries which were records of the common law of various Germanic

tribes (Franks, Frisians, Burgundians, Langobards [Lombards], Anglo-Saxons and others).   p. 232

[92] *Dodona*—a town in Epirus, seat of a temple of Zeus. An ancient oak grew near the main entrance to the temple with a spring at its foot; oracles interpreted the will of the gods from the rustling of its leaves.   p. 244

[93] The fact mentioned took place during the siege of Antwerp in 1584-85 by the troops of King Philip II of Spain, who were suppressing the Netherland's revolt against absolutist Spain.   p. 257

[94] The reference is to the Barebone's, nominated, or Little Parliament summoned by Cromwell in July and dissolved in December 1653. It was composed mainly of representatives of the Congregational Churches who couched their criticism in religious mystic terms.   p. 258

[95] *Tidong*—a region in Kalimantan (Borneo).   p. 260

[96] An allusion to the debate of the Sixth Rhine Province Assembly on a bill against violations of game regulations, which deprived the peasants of the right to hunt even hares.   p. 263

[97] This note was a footnote to an article marked "Vom Rhein" printed in the same issue. The article in its turn was a reply to a previous article printed in the Supplement to the *Rheinische Zeitung* Nos. 265, 268, 275 and 277, September 22 and 25 and October 2 and 4, 1842, under the title "Fehlgriffe der liberalen Opposition in Hannover".   p. 264

[98] The reference is to *la Charte bâclée*, proclaimed on August 14, 1830 (see Note 61).   p. 264

[99] In 1837 King Ernst Augustus and his supporters made a coup d'état in Hanover. They abolished the 1833 Constitution which was moderately liberal (according to it ministers were appointed by the king but were responsible to the provincial assembly) and revived the fundamental state law of 1819 which retained representation on the estate principle and drastically restricted the rights of the provincial assembly. Liberal circles in Hanover attempted to restore the 1833 law. Their demand was formulated in a protest by seven professors of the University of Göttingen (Dahlmann, Gervinus, the brothers Wilhelm and Jacob Grimm, Ewald, Albrecht and Weber) who were subsequently deprived of their chairs and some of them banished. The controversy on the constitutional questions in Hanover was transferred to the Bundestag, which by a decision of 1839 sanctioned restoration of the law of 1819. The new constitutional Act of the King of Hanover in 1840 re-asserted the principal clauses of the law.   p. 264

[100] This article and the article "A Correspondent of the *Kölnische Zeitung* vs. the *Rheinische Zeitung*" which is closely linked with it (see this volume, pp. 277-79) were written on the occasion of a sharp polemic launched in the press on the proposed reform of local administration in towns and villages of the Prussian provinces. For the Rhine Province this reform meant the abolition of progressive elements in local government which had survived from the time of the French revolution and Napoleon I. The struggle for their preservation and development assumed the form of defending these principles against Prussian absolutism and monarchically orientated nobility.

The *Rheinische Zeitung* played a leading part in this struggle. Already in August 1842 its editorial board publicly stated its views on this matter. From November 3 to December 1 the paper published in its Supplement a series of articles entitled "The Reform of the Rhenish Administration", written by Claessen, a member of the paper's Board of Directors. These articles contained demands for unification and equality of urban and rural local administration, publicity of local administration sessions, extension of their rights and reduction of bureaucratic control over them. Reflecting the Prussophilism and anti-democratic sentiments of a certain section of the Rhenish bourgeoisie the *Kölnische Zeitung* attacked the *Rheinische Zeitung* in its "Summing Up" published on November 1, 1842. On November 11 and 16 the *Kölnische Zeitung* continued the polemic by publishing short items containing attacks on Claessen's articles and insinuations against the *Rheinische Zeitung*. The two articles mentioned here were in answer to these attacks (see Note 43).   p. 266

[101] In this note Marx laid down the principal lines for the criticism of the Divorce Bill which he later developed in the *Rheinische Zeitung* in a special article (see this volume, pp. 307-10). Preparation and discussion in government quarters of the Divorce Bill making the dissolution of marriage much more difficult was kept in great secrecy. However, on October 20, 1842, the *Rheinische Zeitung* published the Bill and thus initiated broad discussion on this subject in the progressive press. Prior to this article by Marx, the *Rheinische Zeitung* had published a brief article on the new Bill under the title "Bemerkungen über den Entwurf einer Verordnung über Ehescheidung, vorgelegt von dem Ministerium für Revision der Gesetze im Juli 1842" (*Rheinische Zeitung* No. 310, November 6, 1842, Supplement). Marx mentions the article in this item which was written in the form of an editorial note to another article devoted to the same subject, "Der Entwurf zu dem neuen Ehegesetz".

Owing to the general dissatisfaction with the government Bill, Frederick William IV was compelled to abandon his intention of carrying it through.

The publication of the Bill and the resolute refusal of the *Rheinische Zeitung* editorial board to name the person who had sent the text of it to the paper was one of the reasons for the banning of the *Rheinische Zeitung*.

In English this note was published in *Writings of the Young Marx on Philosophy and Society*, New York, 1967, pp. 136-38.   p. 274

[102] This refers to the law of the Kingdom of Prussia codified in 1794; it reflected backwardness of feudal Prussia in the sphere of law and justice.   p. 275

[103] This note reflects Marx's desire as the editor of the *Rheinische Zeitung* to use the liberal wording of the Cabinet Order on the press, to which Frederick William IV frequently resorted with demagogic aims, so as to provide juridical barriers against the persecution of the paper being prepared by the censorship and to repulse the harassing action on the part of governmental officials and the reactionary press. Marx resorted to similar tactics also on other occasions when forced to do so by the situation.   p. 280

[104] The trend pursued by the *Rheinische Zeitung* after Marx became its editor was a source of apprehension for the Prussian authorities. Oberpräsident of the Rhine Province von Schaper wrote to Berlin stressing that the tone of the paper was "becoming more and more impudent and harsh". By his order Regierungspräsident of Cologne von Gerlach demanded on November 12, 1842, the dismissal from the editorial board of Rutenberg (whom the authorities considered to be the initiator of the radical trend) and conveyed the instructions of the censorship ministries on changes in the paper's trend. The editorial board replied with a letter by the publisher Engelbert Renard who was the official manager of the paper. As can be seen from the rough copy, the actual author of the letter was Marx.

The arguments put forward by Marx deprived the government representatives of grounds for banning the paper, although it is obvious from von Schaper's report to the censorship ministers on December 17, 1842, that they did not abandon the intention of bringing a suit against the editors of the *Rheinische Zeitung*, in particular the author of the article "Debates on the Law on Thefts of Wood", for "impudent and disrespectful criticism of the existing government institutions". However, having no formal grounds for prosecution, the authorities had temporarily to confine themselves to intensifying censorship measures (change of censors, etc.).   p. 282

105 This refers to articles published in the Supplement to the *Rheinische Zeitung*: "Auch eine Stimme über 'eine Hegemonie in Deutschland'" (author, Friedrich Wilhelm Carové; signed 'Vom Main'), No. 135, May 15, 1842; "Hegemonie in Deutschland", No. 146, May 26, 1842; and "Weitere Verhandlungen über die Hegemonie Preussens", No. 172, June 21, 1842, when Marx was not yet editor of the newspaper.   p. 283

106 This note was published in the *Rheinische Zeitung* as a footnote to the article "Die hannoverschen Industriellen und der Schutzzol". It has not yet been proved who the author of this item was. Some scholars doubt whether it was written by Marx.
                                                                    p. 286

107 *"The Free"* (*Die Freien*)—a Berlin group of Young Hegelians, which was formed early in 1842. Among its prominent members were Edgar Bauer, Eduard Meyen, Ludwig Buhl and Max Stirner (pseudonym of Kaspar Schmidt). Their criticism of the prevailing conditions was abstract and devoid of real revolutionary content and ultra-radical in form; it frequently discredited the democratic movement. Subsequently many representatives of "The Free" renounced radicalism.

When Marx had become editor of the *Rheinische Zeitung*, he took steps to prevent "The Free" from using the newspaper as a mouthpiece for their pseudo-revolutionary statements. On his conflict with "The Free" see his letter to Arnold Ruge, November 30, 1842 (this volume, pp. 393-95). The article quotes almost word for word from Herwegh's letter of November 22, 1842 to the *Rheinische Zeitung*.   p. 287

108 This is an editor's note quoted from the *Rheinische Zeitung* No. 322, November 18, 1842. The report referred to was published in issue No. 317 of the paper on November 13, 1842.   p. 290

109 Here and elsewhere is quoted the article mentioned below, "Leipzig (Julius Mosen u. die *Rhein. Zeitung*)," which was published in the *Allgemeine Zeitung* No. 329, November 25, 1842.   p. 290

110 Marx wrote this work in reply to an article in the *Allgemeine Zeitung* which tried to justify the Prussian Government's attempts to substitute the establishment of the all-German Assembly of the Estates for the introduction of the constitution. The article criticised by Marx, "Berlin, im November. Über die Zusammensetzung der ständischen Ausschüsse in Preussen", was published in the Supplement to the *Allgemeine Zeitung* Nos. 335 and 336, December 1 and 2, 1842 (below are quoted passages from this article). For reasons of tactics Marx made the reservation that the polemics were directed against the opinion of the conservative press on the Prussian state institutions and not against these institutions themselves. This enabled him to criticise them severely and expose their spurious constitutionalism.

Commissions of the estates of the provincial assemblies were set up in Prussia in June 1842. They were elected by the provincial assemblies out of their membership (on the estate principle) and formed a single advisory body—the United Commissions. With the help of this body which was but a sham representative assembly, Frederick William IV planned to introduce new taxes and obtain a loan.

An excerpt from this article was published in English in *Karl Marx. Early Texts*, Oxford, 1971, pp. 55-57.   p. 292

[111] This is an excerpt from the law of March 27, 1824, introducing an assembly of the estates in the Rhine Province and adopted on the basis of the law on the provincial assemblies of the estates promulgated in Prussia on June 5, 1823.   p. 294

[112] *Mediatised lands* were former imperial fiefs which were previously held directly from the Emperor but afterwards became dependent on princes, on the King of Prussia in the given case; their holders retained some of their privileges, including personal membership of the Assembly of the Estates.   p. 303

[113] *Virilstimme* was an individual vote enjoyed in the assemblies of the estates by persons of knightly (noble) descent and individual German cities by virtue of privileges granted them in the Middle Ages.   p. 303

[114] On the Divorce Bill and the stand of the *Rheinische Zeitung* on this question see Note 101. The article was published in English in *Writings of the Young Marx on Philosophy and Society*, New York, 1967, pp. 138-42.   p. 307

[115] Late in 1842 the German governments intensified persecutions of the opposition press. The Cabinet Order of December 28, 1842, prohibited distribution of the *Leipziger Allgemeine Zeitung* in Prussia for the publication, in its issue of December 24, of a letter by Georg Herwegh, a democratic poet, to King Frederick William IV, accusing him of breaking the promise to introduce freedom of the press. The *Rheinische Zeitung* editor's defence of the persecuted press required particular courage because the paper was increasingly threatened with government repressions.

Each section of the article was published in the *Rheinische Zeitung* under its own title, the general title was given by the Institute of Marxism-Leninism of the CC CPSU.   p. 311

[116] This refers to the report marked "Köln, 4. Jan.", published in the *Kölnische Zeitung* No. 5, January 5, 1843.   p. 315

[117] This refers to the report marked "Vom Rhein, den 4. Jan.", published in the *Rhein- und Mosel-Zeitung* No. 6, January 6, 1843.   p. 315

[118] The reference is to the events connected with the abolition of the Constitution by the King of Hanover in 1837 and the protest against this arbitrary act by seven liberal professors of Göttingen University who were subjected to repressions (see Note 99). The Hanover events evoked a wide response all over Germany. The *Leipziger Allgemeine Zeitung* came out in defence of the Göttingen professors.
                                                                             p. 316

[119] The allusion is to the Augsburg *Allgemeine Zeitung*. At the end of 1842 and beginning of 1843 the newspaper again made a number of attacks against the *Rheinische Zeitung* (in particular, in No. 4, January 4, 1843), stating its intention to polemise on principles with the latter but failing to supply any weighty arguments. In reply, the *Rheinische Zeitung* of January 12, 1843, carried a polemical article by

Marx against the *Allgemeine Zeitung*, which is published in this volume together with the reply to the paper's attacks which he made on January 3, 1843 (see this volume, pp. 359-60). p. 318

[120] See Note 115. p. 319

[121] This refers to the report marked "vom Niederrhein", which was published in the *Kölnische Zeitung* No. 9, January 9, 1843. p. 319

[122] This refers to the article "Die preussische Presse" published in the *Rheinische Zeitung* No. 6, January 6, 1843. p. 320

[123] See Note 110. p. 321

[124] Here and below Marx quotes the report marked "Köln, 10. Jan.", published in the *Kölnische Zeitung* No. 11, January 11, 1843. p. 322

[125] This refers to two reports published in the *Rhein- und Mosel-Zeitung* No. 11, January 11, 1843, the first of which is marked "Koblenz, den 10. Jan." and the second "Vom Rhein, den 9. Jan." p. 324

[126] This refers to the report marked "Koblenz, den 13. Jan.", published in the Supplement to the *Rhein- und Mosel-Zeitung* No. 15, January 15, 1843. p. 328

[127] The *Rheinische Zeitung* No. 348, December 14, 1842, carried, on Marx's initiative, an unsigned article marked "Von der Mosel", written by the democratic lawyer P. I. Coblenz. The situation in the Mosel was also dealt with in another article marked "Bernkastel, 10. Dez.", published in issue No. 346. They were printed for the purpose of drawing public attention to the distress of the Mosel peasants and censuring the prejudiced and inattentive attitude of the government circles towards their complaints. The publication of these articles led to two rescripts from von Schaper, Oberpräsident of the Rhine Province, to the newspaper, accusing the Mosel correspondent of distorting the facts and slandering the government. Von Schaper demanded answers to a number of questions, in the hope of securing in effect a disavowal of the accusations levelled at the government. On December 18, issue No. 352 of the *Rheinische Zeitung* published the rescripts and asked the author to write a reply to them. However, as Coblenz was unable to produce sufficient grounds for his theses and disprove the accusations made against him, Marx took the task upon himself in order to use the polemics against von Schaper to expose the Prussian socio-political system. At the time the present announcement of the forthcoming reply to the Oberpräsident was published Marx was gathering material for his article "Justification of the. Correspondent from the Mosel". p. 331

[128] This article was written by Marx instead of P. I. Coblenz, the author of the report "Von der Mosel", in reply to the charges levelled against the latter in the rescripts of von Schaper, Oberpräsident of the Rhine Province (see Note 127). Marx was unable to carry out his programme for a reply in full—out of five questions he managed to answer only two. Further publication was banned by the censor. The manuscript is not extant. Subsequently a report datelined "Von der Mosel in Januar 1843" entitled "Die Krebsschäden der Moselgegend", which coincided with the formulation of the third point of a reply Marx had planned to give, appeared in the book by K. Heinzen, a contributor to the *Rheinische Zeitung*, *Die Preussische Bureaukratie* (Darmstadt, 1845, S. 220-25). However, the content was strictly factual, and the style of this item differed from those parts of Marx's article which had been published. At present it is still difficult to tell for certain

who the author of this report was, but it may be assumed that what Heinzen published under this heading was one of the previously unpublished articles by Coblenz, whom Marx defended, rather than the continuation of Marx's article.

The publication of the article in defence of the Mosel correspondent provided the immediate pretext for the government, at the insistence of the king, to pass a decision on January 19, 1843, banning the *Rheinische Zeitung* as from April 1, 1843, and imposing a rigorous censorship for the remaining period. The decree was promulgated on January 21.

The article was published in part in English in *Writings of the Young Marx on Philosophy and Society*, New York, 1967, pp. 143-48.   p. 332

[129] This refers to the Prussian Government's new censorship instruction (see Note 39).   p. 332

[130] See Note 39.   p. 350

[131] The two items published here under a title supplied by the Institute of Marxism-Leninism were printed in the *Rheinische Zeitung* in reply to the attacks of the Augsburg *Allgemeine Zeitung* (see Note 119).   p. 359

[132] These notes are the draft reply written by Marx to disprove the accusations contained in the ministerial rescript of January 21, 1843, which ordered suppression of the *Rheinische Zeitung* as from April 1, 1843, and imposed a rigorous censorship for the remaining period. The manner in which Marx replied was determined by his purpose of shielding the *Rheinische Zeitung* against government repressions and securing a repeal of the ban, but not at the cost of a change in its political line. Hence the Aesopean language which he uses in elucidating the paper's stand on questions of principle in the social life of Germany.   p. 361

[133] Marx apparently refers to *Das Neue eleganteste Conversations-Lexicon für Gebildete aus allen Ständen*, published in Leipzig in 1835. On p. 255 of this book it was stated that Hegel came to Berlin in 1818 so that "his doctrine might be turned into a state philosophy".   p. 362

[134] This refers to the article "Eingesandt aus Preussen" published in the *Allgemeine Königsberger Zeitung* No. 30, February 4, 1843.   p. 362

[135] This charge was provoked by the article "Die russische Note über die preussische Presse" published in the *Rheinische Zeitung* No. 4, January 4, 1843. The article criticised Russian tsarism and the interference of its representatives in German affairs for the purpose of suppressing the opposition press. The publication of this article called forth a Note of protest from the tsarist government.   p. 364

[136] Marx reproduces almost word for word the Prussian censorship instruction of October 18, 1819.   p. 364

[137] *Ultramontanes*—supporters of ultramontanism, a trend in the Roman Catholic Church advocating greater papal authority. In the Rhine Province Catholics were in opposition to the Prussian Government, which supported the Protestants.
                                                                            p. 364

[138] This refers to the separatist ideas advocated by Johannes Joseph von Görres in 1838 in the *Historisch-politische Blätter für das Katholische Deutschland* published in Munich.   p. 364

[139] This refers to Karl Marx's article "The Supplement to Nos. 335 and 336 of the Augsburg *Allgemeine Zeitung* on the Commissions of the Estates in Prussia" (see this volume, pp. 292-306).   p. 365

[140] This refers to the negotiations between Prussia and Russia which were held in the summer of 1842 on the questions of concluding a trade agreement and cancelling, under the pressure of German public opinion, the 1830 Convention with Russia concerning extradition of deserters, prisoners of war and criminals.   p. 365

[141] The Cabinet Order of October 14, 1842, obliging the editorial boards of newspapers to publish government officials' refutations of incorrect data given in these newspapers, was published in the *Rheinische Zeitung* No. 320, November 16, 1842.

The editorial note on this Order ironically remarks that whatever the author's intentions it constituted "a perfect guarantee of the independence" of the press and recognition of its social significance.   p. 365

[142] The quotations which follow are from the article marked "Vom Rhein, den 6. März", published in the *Rhein- und Mosel-Zeitung* No. 67, March 8, 1843.

p. 366

[143] The *Rhein- und Mosel-Zeitung* was published in Koblenz. Further on in the text Marx refers to it as the "Koblenz newspaper".   p. 367

[144] Marx further quotes from the article "Friedrich v. Sallet ist tot!" published in the *Trier'sche Zeitung* No. 63, March 6, 1843. This obituary to the German anti-clerical poet was attacked by the pro-Catholic editors of the *Rhein- und Mosel-Zeitung*, which carried in issue No. 70, March 11, 1843, an article entitled "Friedrich v. Sallets *Laien-Evangelium*". Marx severely criticises both this article (excerpts from which are also quoted) and attempts of the *Trier'sche Zeitung* article to describe Sallet as an author with religious beliefs.   p. 370

[145] *Sanbenito*—a yellow robe worn by heretics sentenced by the Inquisition when they were led to the place of execution.   p. 372

[146] This refers to the article marked "Vom Rhein, den 11. März", published in the *Rhein- und Mosel-Zeitung* No. 72, March 13, 1843. Marx quotes from this article below.   p. 373

[147] After the publication of the rescript of January 21, 1843, which suppressed the *Rheinische Zeitung* as from April 1, 1843, Marx directed his efforts to secure its repeal. Neither the refutation of the charges against the newspaper (see this volume, pp. 361-65), nor the petitions of the inhabitants of Cologne and other cities of the Rhine Province in defence of the paper succeeded in shaking the government's decision. At the end of January 1843 Marx was already thinking of resigning the editorship (see letter to Ruge of January 25, 1843, p. 397 of this volume), but he did not consider it possible to carry out his intention at the height of the campaign for the repeal of the ban. In March, however, he believed that changes in the editorial board could provide a chance of saving the newspaper, and made up his mind to resign officially from his post. He handed over his duties to Dagobert Oppenheim. Marx was probably prompted to do so also by his unwillingness to take upon himself the responsibility for a possible change of line of the newspaper by which the liberal shareholders wished to prolong its existence.

Notwithstanding Marx's resignation, the royal rescript was not repealed. The last issue of the newspaper appeared on March 31, 1843.   p. 376

[148] Marx's thesis, together with his applications in German and Latin, was recorded under No. 26 on April 13, 1841, in the Jena University Register. On the same day Bachmann, the Dean of the Faculty of Philosophy, and a group of professors signed a highly commendatory review on it (see this volume, pp. 705-06). On

April 15 Marx was awarded the degree of Doctor of Philosophy and received his
diploma (see illustration).   p. 379

149 In mid-April 1841, after he had been awarded the degree of Doctor of
Philosophy, Marx moved to Trier and in July of the same year to Bonn, because
he had intended to enlist as Privat-Docent at Bonn University. In view of the
government persecutions of progressive scientists (in the autumn of 1841 Bruno
Bauer, a Young Hegelian, was banned from lecturing at Bonn University), Marx
had to give up his plans for an academic career and become a publicist.

From January till March 1842 Marx stayed in Trier in the family of his fiancée,
Jenny von Westphalen.

Marx's correspondence with Arnold Ruge was occasioned by his intention to
contribute to the opposition periodicals of the time including the *Deutsche
Jahrbücher,* edited by Ruge.   p. 381

150 This refers to Ludwig Feuerbach's review of Karl Bayer's book *Betrachtungen über
den Begriff des sittlichen Geistes und über das Wesen der Tugend* published in the
Hallische Jahrbücher for 1840.   p. 381

151 The full title is *Anekdota zur neuesten deutschen Philosophie und Publicistik* which Ruge
planned to publish in Switzerland. The first issue of the almanac (1843) carried
Marx's article "Comments on the Latest Prussian Censorship Instruction" and
also articles by Ludwig Feuerbach, Karl Friedrich Köppen, Arnold Ruge and
others.   p. 382

152 The reference is to Bruno Bauer's book *Die Posaune des jungsten Gerichts über Hegel
den Atheisten und Antichristen. Ein Ultimatum,* which was published anonymously in
early November 1841. Bauer wrote it in August and September 1841 with some
assistance from Marx. Bauer and Marx intended to publish the second part of the
book as their joint work. However, their co-operation soon came to an end, chiefly
because Marx, who wanted to link advanced philosophy more closely with politics, was dissatisfied with Bauer's tendency to confine himself to radical criticism of
theology. After Marx had left Bonn for Trier in January 1842 to see the father of
his fiancée, Ludwig von Westphalen, who was dying, Bauer published the second part of *Die Posaune* as a separate book entitled *Hegels Lehre von der Religion
und der Kunst von dem Standpunkte des Glaubens aus beurteilt* (Leipzig, 1842) without
the section which was to be written by Marx — a treatise on Christian art.   p. 382

153 The article did not appear in the publication for which it was written. The
manuscript is not extant. Later on Marx set forth his criticism of the
constitutional monarchy in his *Critique of Hegel's Philosophy of Law* written in the
summer of 1843 (see present edition, Vol. 3).   p. 383

154 In the autumn of 1841 Bruno Bauer was banned from lecturing by Eichhorn,
Minister of Religious Worship, Education and Medicine, and in March 1842 he
was suspended from the post of Privat-Docent of Theology at Bonn University for
his atheistic views and opposition statements. Bruno Bauer's letter mentioned by
Marx has not been found.

Lit de justice — sitting of the old French Parliament which was held in the
presence of the king, whose directions in that case acquired the force of law.
                                                                        p. 383

155 This refers to the Cabinet Order of February 18, 1842, concerning revision of the
earlier decrees of the Prussian Government (the Cabinet orders of March 6, 1821,
and of August 2, 1834) according to which, in respect of certain judicial proceedings, the French Penal Code and trial by jury, which had been applied so far

in the Rhine Province, were replaced by Prussian law and secret hearing. Under pressure from the discontented Rhenish bourgeoisie the Prussian Government revised these decrees. However the Cabinet Order of February 18, 1842, contained a number of reservations which in fact retained the Prussian law for cases of high treason, malfeasance, etc. **p. 384**

156 This is how Marx ironically calls the official newspapers published in Germany at the time. **p. 384**

157 Marx was unable to realise his intention to move to Cologne at the time (see this volume, p. 389). About April 10, 1842, he was to go to back to Bonn where he stayed with interruptions due to visits to Trier for family reasons till early October of the same year. **p. 385**

158 *Spandau*—a fortress in Brandenburg, later included in Great Berlin. It was used for a long time as a prison for state criminals. **p. 386**

159 Of the list of articles given by Marx only one was published, namely, "The Philosophical Manifesto of the Historical School of Law", in the *Rheinische Zeitung* (see this volume, pp. 203-10). **p. 387**

160 Friedrich Rudolf Hasse's *Anseln von Canterbury*, Part I, was published in 1843, Part II appeared in 1852. **p. 388**

161 Marx had to leave for Trier at the end of May 1842 because his younger brother Hermann had died. During his stay in Trier (till mid-July 1842, when he returned to Bonn) his conflict with his mother, which had begun earlier, grew more acute. Henriette Marx was displeased with her son's refusal to embrace an advantageous government or academic career. She stopped paying him allowance and prevented him from receiving his share of his father's estate. On account of this Marx had to postpone his marriage with Jenny von Westphalen and, moreover, found himself in very straitened circumstances. **p. 389**

162 See Note 89. **p. 389**

163 On "The Free" see Note 107.
    Marx refers to the article in the *Königsberger Zeitung* No. 138, June 17, 1842, which announced the aims and tasks of "The Free". The article was reprinted in the *Rheinische Zeitung* No. 176, June 25, 1842, and marked "Aus Berlin". **p. 390**

164 Ruge's article was published in the Supplement to the *Rheinische Zeitung* No. 268, September 25, 1842, under the title "Sächsische Zustände". **p. 391**

165 This refers to an unsigned article published in the Supplement to the *Rheinische Zeitung* No. 226, August 14, 1842, under the title "Ein Wort als Einleitung zur Frage: entspricht die Rheinische Kommunal-Verfassung den Anforderungen der Gegenwart?".
    The above-mentioned articles by Karl Heinrich Hermes against Jewry were published in the *Kölnische Zeitung* (Nos. 187 and 211, and in the Supplement to No. 235, July 6 and 30, and August 23, 1842). **p. 391**

166 Apparently, Marx had in mind the unsigned article "Aus dem Hannoverschen" published in the *Rheinische Zeitung* No. 241, August 29, 1842. **p. 392**

167 The unsigned article "Das Juste-Milieu" was published in the Supplement to the *Rheinische Zeitung* Nos. 156, 228, 230, 233 and 235 of June 5 and August 16, 18, 21

and 23, 1842. The author of this article was the Young Hegelian Edgar Bauer, a
leader of "The Free". It was directed against the half-hearted attitude of the
liberals. It criticised them from the positions characteristic of "The Free", that is,
from the positions of complete rejection of any progressive role of the liberal
opposition to the absolutist feudal system. The clamorous tone of the article served
as a pretext for persecutions of the progressive press.   p. 392

[168] Marx moved to Cologne in the first half of October 1842, and on October 15 he
became editor of the *Rheinische Zeitung*.

The first English translation of this letter appeared in *Karl Marx. Early
Texts*, Oxford, 1971, pp. 52-54.   p. 393

[169] Concerning the conflict between the Prussian authorities and the editorial board
of the *Rheinische Zeitung*, which began in November 1842, see Note 104.

p. 395

[170] This refers to the rescript of January 21, 1842. For a criticism of this rescript
see Marx's article "Marginal Notes to the Accusations of the Ministerial Rescript"
(pp. 361-65 of this volume).   p. 396

[171] Marx refers to the 1842 Divorce Bill. See Note 101.   p. 396

[172] See Note 39.   p. 397

[173] Marx published the announcement of his resignation from editorship of the
Rheinische Zeitung on March 17, 1843. See Note 147.   p. 397

[174] This refers to the radical monthly *Der Deutsche Bote aus der Schweiz*, which
Herwegh was planning to publish in Zurich in 1842 and to which Marx was invited
to contribute. The plan of the publication did not materialise. Articles by various
authors written for it were published in the summer of 1843 in a collection entitled
Einundzwanzig Bogen aus der Schweiz.   p. 397

[175] Marx intended to enlist progressive German and French intellectuals to
contribute to the prospective journal *Deutsch-Französische Jahrbücher*.

The publication of the journal was started by Marx and Ruge only at the
beginning of 1844, after Marx had moved to Paris in the autumn of 1843. Only
one double issue appeared. Its publication was discontinued mainly due to
disagreements between its editors.

The first English translation of Marx's letter appeared in *Karl Marx. Early
Texts*, Oxford, 1971, pp. 58-60.   p. 398

[176] Robert Eduard Prutz's article entitled "Die Jahrbücher der Gegenwart und die
deutschen Jahrbücher" was published in the Supplement to the *Rheinische Zeitung*
No. 43, February 12, 1843. The author's intention was to prove that the journal
Jahrbücher der Gegenwart (editor Albert Schwegler, published in Stuttgart and
Tübingen), the publication of which had been announced in the press, could not
be regarded, judging by its ideological tendency, as a continuation of the *Deutsche
Jahrbücher*, which had been suppressed by the Government of Saxony.   p. 399

[177] Marx refers to the pamphlet by Arnold Ruge and Otto Wigand entitled *An die
Hohe Zweite Kammer der Sächsischen Ständversammlung. Beschwerde über die durch ein
Hohes Ministerium des Innern angeordnete und 3. Januar 1843 ausgeführte Unterdrückung der Zeitschrift "Deutsche Jahrbücher für Wissenschaft und Kunst"*, published in
early 1843 in Brunswick.

The review of this pamphlet by Pfützner was published in the Supplement to the *Rheinische Zeitung* Nos. 71 and 73, March 12 and 14, 1843. p. 399

[178] Ruge's correspondence with the German censors was published in the first volume of *Anekdota zur neuesten deutschen Philosophie und Publicistik* under the title "Aktenmässige Darlegung der Cenzurverhältnisse der Hallischen und Deutschen Jahrbücher in den Jahren 1839, 1841, 1842". p. 400

[179] The *Notebooks* written by Marx in 1839 served as preparatory material for his future work on ancient philosophy and were widely used in his doctor's thesis (see this volume, pp. 25-106). The *Notebooks* sum up the results of Marx's research into ancient philosophy and, besides his own views, contain lengthy excerpts in Latin and Greek from the works of ancient authors, chiefly of the Epicurean school of philosophy. The extant manuscript consists of seven notebooks of which five (notebooks 1-4 and 7) carry the heading "Epicurean Philosophy" on the cover. The covers of notebooks 2-4 bear the inscription "Winter Term, 1839." The covers of notebooks 5 and 6 are not extant. The fifth notebook has several pages missing. The last five pages of the sixth notebook contain excerpts from Hegel's *Encyclopaedia*, under the heading "Plan of Hegel's Philosophy of Nature"; as these are not connected with the main content of the *Notebooks* they are published separately (see this volume, pp. 510-14).

The *Notebooks* were first published in 1927 in Marx/Engels, *Gesamtausgabe*, Bd. I. That edition included mainly the text written by Marx himself without the excerpts or his commentaries on them. The full text was first published in Russian in the collection: Marx and Engels, *From Early Writings*, Moscow, 1956. In the language of the original (with parallel translations into German of the Latin and Greek quotations) the work was first published in Marx/Engels, *Werke*, Ergänzungsband, Erster Teil, Berlin, 1968.

An excerpt from the sixth notebook was published in English in *Writings of the Young Marx on Philosophy and Society*, New York, 1967, pp. 51-60.

The present edition gives the quotations from Greek and Latin authors in English. Greek and Latin terms and expressions have been left untranslated only when they were used in the German text in the author's digressions and commentaries. Vertical lines made by Marx in the manuscript for emphasis are reproduced here in the margins. In quotations from the works of Diogenes Laertius (Book X), Sextus Empiricus and Plutarch, the editors give, in square brackets, Roman figures to denote chapters and Arabic figures to denote paragraphs in accordance with the division of the text accepted in publications of the works of these authors. In some cases there are editorial interpolations within quotations (also in square brackets) made on the basis of the sources used by Marx to reconstruct the meaning. The general title corresponds to the author's headings of individual notebooks and to his definition of the subject of the investigation (see foreword to the dissertation, this volume, p. 29). p. 403

[180] This treatise of Aristotle is not extant. The passage referred to is to be found in Aristotle, *De partibus animalium* (I, 5). p. 424

[181] In his translation Marx quotes Epicurus according to Petri Gassendi, *Animadversiones in decimum librum Diogenis Laertii, qui est De Vita, Moribus, Placitisque Epicuri*, Ludguni, 1649. p. 424

[182] The followers of Epicurus received this name because the school of Epicurus in Athens founded in 307-06 B. C. was situated in a garden. The Garden became the main centre of materialism and atheism of Ancient Greece. p. 427

[183] Marx apparently quotes Jakob Böhme from Ludwig Feuerbach's book *Geschichte der neuern Philosophie von Bacon von Verulam bis Benedict Spinoza*, Ansbach, 1833, S. 161.   p. 455

[184] The fifth notebook is not extant in full. The beginning, including the cover, has been lost and the extant part has some pages missing. Still extant are also some separate sheets containing the continuation of the excerpts from the works of Seneca and Stobaeus, the beginning of which is in the extant part of the notebook, and the relevant excerpts from the works of Clement of Alexandria. In the collection *From Early Writings* (Russ. ed., 1956), these sheets were included in the sixth notebook, which is extant also without its cover or the usual author's list of works quoted. There are good grounds, however, for including them in the fifth notebook as was done in Marx/Engels, *Werke*, Ergänzungsband, Erster Teil, Berlin, 1968. The arrangement of the material of notebooks 5 and 6 in this edition corresponds to that in the *Werke*.   p. 479

[185] There are no excerpts from Book VI of Lucretius' poem *On the Nature of Things* in the extant manuscript of the *Notebooks*.   p. 490

[186] See Note 180.   p. 496

[187] Apparently Marx refers to Chapter IX of Book One of the *Metaphysics* in which Aristotle criticises Plato's teaching.   p. 497

[188] The reference is to the *Enneads*, a work by Plotinus.   p. 498

[189] There are no excerpts from Cicero's *Tusculanae quaestiones* in the extant manuscript though it is mentioned by Marx on the cover of the seventh notebook. But the seventh notebook contains excerpts from Cicero's work *De finibus bonorum et malorum*, which is not listed on the cover.   p. 501

[190] The *Plan of Hegel's Philosophy of Nature* consists of brief notes on the content of those paragraphs of Hegel's work *Encyclopädie der philosophischen Wissenschaften in Grundrisse*, 3 Aufl., Heidelberg, 1830, which deal with the philosophy of nature. These notes were made by Marx in 1839 in three versions on five pages of the sixth notebook. The first version covers §§ 252-334 of Hegel's book and most closely reproduces the order in which Hegel sets forth his material. Marx departs from Hegel's terminology here only in separate cases. The second version covers fewer paragraphs dealing with the philosophy of nature but it is marked by greater independence in systematising the material and in terminology. Most original in this respect is the third version, which, though brief, expounds the contents of Hegel's philosophy of nature more fully than the previous ones.   p. 510

[191] This section contains several poems from Marx's three albums of poems written in the late autumn of 1836 and in the winter of 1836-37. According to his daughter Laura Lafargue and his biographer Franz Mehring, who had access to his manuscripts after his death, two of these albums bore the title *Book of Love*, Part I and Part II, and the third, *Book of Songs*. Each had the following dedication: "To my dear, ever beloved Jenny von Westphalen." The covers of the albums with the titles and dedications are not extant. Some poems from these albums were later included by Marx in his book of verse dedicated to his father (published below in full). Recently a copybook and a notebook belonging to Karl Marx's eldest sister Sophie were discovered among the documents of Heinrich Marx's heirs in Trier. Alongside verses by different people they contain some by the young Marx. Most of them were taken from other copybooks, but some were new.

Marx was very critical of the literary qualities of his early poems but he believed that they conveyed his warm and sincere feelings (see this volume, p. 11). Later on, his view of them grew even more critical. Laura Lafargue, for example, wrote, "My father treated his verses very disrespectfully; whenever my parents mentioned them, they would laugh to their hearts' content." (*Aus dem literarischen Nachlass von Karl Marx, Friedrich Engels und Ferdinand Lassalle*, Stuttgart, 1902, S. 25-26.) In 1954 the Institute of Marxism-Leninism of the CC CPSU came into possession of the two albums of Marx's early verse from the inheritance of his grandson Edgar Longuet, and in 1960 Marcel Charles Longuet, Marx's great-grandson, presented the Institute with the third album. A number of poems from these albums drew the attention of Marx's biographers and translators and were published at various times, chiefly abridged, in different publications, in particular, in the books: *Aus dem literarischen Nachlass von Karl Marx, Friedrich Engels und Ferdinand Lassalle*, Stuttgart, 1902; J. Spargo, *Karl Marx*, New York,) 1910; M. Ollivier, *Marx et Engels poetes*, Paris, 1933; Marx/Engels, *Werke*, Ergänzungsband, Erster Teil, Berlin, 1968; and the magazines *Yunost* (Youth) No. 11, Moscow,1958, and *Inostrannaya Literatura* (Foreign Literature) No. 1, Moscow, 1968. p. 517

[192] This album contains 12 poems of which the ballads *Lucinda, Distraught* and *The Pale Maiden*, and the poem *Human Pride* were later included by Marx in the book of verse dedicated to his father (see this volume, pp. 565-71, 581-83, 612-15, 584-86). p. 517

[193] This album is the bulkiest of the three dedicated to Jenny von Westphalen. It contains 53 poems of which *Yearning, Siren Song, Two Singers Accompanying Themselves on the Harp* and *Harmony* were included by Marx in the book of verse dedicated to his father (see this volume, pp. 538-39, 542-45, 574-75, 580-81). p. 521

[194] This album contains 22 poems of which *Song to the Stars* and *The Song of a Sailor at Sea* were included by Marx in the book of verse dedicated to his father (see this volume, pp. 608-09, 610-11). Passages from the poems *My World, Feelings* and *Transformation* published in this volume appeared in English in the translation by Meta L. Stern in the book: J. Spargo, *Karl Marx*, New York, 1910, pp. 42, 43 and 44. p. 523

[195] In this book the young Marx collected samples of his early poetical writings, including ballads, sonnets, romances, songs, translations of Ovid's elegies, scenes from *Oulanem*, a tragedy in verse, epigrams and jokes. It had as a supplement chapters from his satirical novel *Scorpion and Felix*. Marx mentioned this book in his letter of November 10-11, 1837 (see this volume, p. 17). Two poems, *The Fiddler* and *Nocturnal Love* (published in the first section of this volume), were published by Marx in 1841 in the journal *Athenäum*. The order of the poems in the book differs slightly from the order in the contents drawn up by Marx.

The book was first published in full in German in 1929. Subsequently separate poems were reprinted in biographies and other publications.

The poem *To the Medical Students* and excerpts from *Epigrams* were published in English in R. Payne's book *Marx*, New York, 1968, *Oulanem* in *The Unknown Karl Marx* by the same author, New York, 1971, pp. 55-94. p. 531

[196] The reference is to Christoph Gluck's opera *Armide*. p. 540

[197] The age of Marx's father is stated in this document inaccurately. According to latest investigations, Heinrich Marx was born in 1777, not in 1782 (see H. Monz,

Karl Marx und Trier, Verhältnisse-Beziehungen-Einflusse, Trier, 1964, S. 130).
                                                                              p. 635

[198] Concerning Marx's gymnasium examination papers see Note 1.

On August 17, 1835, his teacher Küpper wrote the following comment on the present composition: "It is profound in thought, brilliantly and forcefully written, deserving of praise, although the topic—the essence of union—is not elucidated, its cause is dealt with only one-sidedly, its necessity is not proved adequately."

This essay was first published in English in R. Payne's book, *The Unknown Karl Marx*, New York, 1971, pp. 39-43.   p. 636

[199] The manuscript of Marx's essay in Latin was underscored in many places by the examiner Johann Hugo Wyttenbach, headmaster of the gymnasium. In the margins there are a number of remarks in Latin, some of which deal with the content of the work. Thus, there is the following remark at the end of the first paragraph, "See what a broad, almost limitless task you set yourself when you intend to examine the question in this way." The words at the beginning of the seventh paragraph, "That the Augustan age was unlike this no one can deny", were commented as follows: "You should have avoided altogether any comparison of this kind and description of the period preceding the Carthaginian Wars as well as the epoch of Nero." There is a correction to the following words in one of the last paragraphs, "Tacitus also speaks of Augustus and his age with the utmost respect": "Not at all! See *Annali*, I, 1-10. But you could have refrained from such disquisitions".

The general remarks at the end of the manuscript signed by Wyttenbach and Loers, teacher of Latin and Greek, say, "With the exception of some passages, which called forth the above remark, and a few mistakes, particularly at the end, the composition reveals a profound knowledge of history and of Latin. But what atrocious handwriting!"

This essay was first published in English in R. Payne's book, *The Unknown Karl Marx*, New York, 1971, pp. 44-48.   p. 639

[200] In addition to the certificate of maturity issued to Karl Marx by the Trier gymnasium there are extant rough copies of the certificate, an excerpt from the record of the graduation examinations at the Trier gymnasium, an extract from the report, and a list of the pupils who took the examinations.

The first rough copy of the certificate, which is kept in the archives of the Trier gymnasium, gives a more detailed account of the graduate's knowledge of Greek: "His knowledge and ability in regard to understanding the classics are almost as good as in Latin, but his skill in translating the classics read at the gymnasium is less owing to lack of solid knowledge of grammar and because he is less sure than in Latin, although he often succeeds in explaining correctly even the more difficult passages; on the whole, he translates quite satisfactorily."   p. 643

[201] Some letters of Heinrich Marx to his son have reached us in a very bad condition. Undecipherable words or phrases are marked by dots in square brackets. Square brackets are also used to indicate tentative interpretation of illegible words or phrases.

Not a single one of Karl Marx's replies to his father's letters during his stay at Bonn University (October 1835-July 1836) has been preserved. Of his correspondence with his father during his subsequent stay in Berlin (he moved there late in October 1836 from Trier where he had spent his summer vacation and become engaged to Jenny von Westphalen) only one letter dated November 10-11, 1837, remains (see this volume, pp. 10-21).   p. 645

202 Apparently Heinrich Marx refers to §§ 7 and 60 of Immanuel Kant's *Anthropologie in pragmatischer Hinsicht*, Königsberg, 1798.   p. 648

203 The letter bears mainly illegible markings and separate words apparently added later by Karl Marx.   p. 653

204 The certificate of release is extant in the form of a copy written by an unknown person and submitted to Jena University together with the other documents sent there by Marx when he applied for a doctor's degree for his treatise on the history of ancient philosophy (see Note 148).   p. 657

205 The letter has not been found.   p. 662

206 The letter was addressed to his wife and son. Apparently, it was first sent to Henriette Marx in Trier, and from there to Karl in Berlin.   p. 674

207 These lines are Heinrich Marx's last letter to his son. Heinrich died on May 10, 1838.   p. 694

208 Passages from this letter were published for the first time in Russian in the book: P. Vinogradskaya, *Jenny Marx*, Moscow, 1964, pp. 20, 55-57.
The end of the letter is missing.   p. 695

209 The original has a note written by Marx in the right-hand corner: "Permission to issue the leaving certificate to Herr Marx, student of [the Faculty of] Law, [...] 18.3.41."

Before the text filled in by the student the form has the following notification: "In accordance with the Ministry directives of September 26, 1829, every student must occupy at lectures during the whole term only that seat the number of which is stated by the respective tutor in the record sheet. If any student is prevented from attending lectures for several days or longer due to any circumstances, no one is allowed to take his seat under any pretext."   p. 699

210 The certificate bears the remark "To No. 26" made in April 1841 at Jena University on registration of the application and other documents submitted by Marx for the award of a doctor's degree (see Note 148).   p. 703

211 See Note 148.   p. 705

212 Jenny von Westphalen uses ironically the expression "Hegeling gentlemen", a derogatory name given to the followers of Hegel by their rabid opponent Heinrich Leo, historian and publicist. Leo wrote against the Young Hegelians the pamphlet *Die Hegelingen. Actenstücke und Belege zu der s. g. Denunciation der ewigen Wahrheit*, Halle, 1838.   p. 707

213 The announcement of the publication of Bruno Bauer's book *Kritik der evangelischen Geschichte der Synoptiker* and his three small articles were carried in the Supplement to the *Allgemeine Zeitung* of August 1, 1841.   p. 708

214 This petition was compiled on January 30, 1843, and illegally circulated among the inhabitants of Cologne. By February 18 it had been signed by 911 citizens. The petition was rejected on March 31, 1843.

Similar petitions requesting the lifting of the ban on the *Rheinische Zeitung* were addressed to the King of Prussia from Aachen, Barmen, Wesel, Düsseldorf and a number of other towns. However, all steps taken in defence of the newspaper were fruitless.   p. 710

215 The joint meeting of the shareholders of the *Rheinische Zeitung* and the editorial board was held in the Cologne casino and lasted for six hours—from 10 a. m. till 1 p. m. and from 5 p. m. till 8 p. m. The debates were so long because of a sharp struggle between the moderate-liberal majority of the meeting who were prepared to denounce the radical-democratic views expounded by the newspaper and to have the petition couched in a tone of loyalty, and those who stood for firm defence of the right of the opposition press to exist. The latter were headed by Marx and upheld his policy as editor. The record of Marx's statements was very brief. Marx and his followers, however, succeeded in persuading the meeting to refrain from officially denouncing the trend of the newspaper (the petition denounced only the sharp tone of its statements), and this gave the radicals grounds for signing it despite its extremely moderate form.

Brief reports of the meeting were carried in the *Aachener Zeitung* No. 46, February 15, and in the *Frankfurter Journal* No. 52, February 21, 1843.

The minutes of the general meeting of the shareholders were later published with insignificant changes in the book *Rheinische Briefe und Akten zur Geschichte der politischen Bewegung 1830-1850*, Essen, 1919, Bd. 1, S, 436-47. The present volume reproduces the minutes according to the book of minutes.   p. 712

216 For details concerning the conflict, see Note 104. This was followed by von Schaper's reply to Renard on November 19, 1842 (see *Rheinische Briefe und Akten zur Geschichte der politischen Bewegung 1830-1850*, Essen, 1919, Bd. 1, S. 380-82).
                                                                                    p. 714

217 The newspaper was suppressed within the borders of Prussia by the Cabinet Order of December 28, 1842 (see this volume, pp. 311-30 and Note 115).
                                                                                    p. 717

218 Part of this petition was published as a footnote in the book *Rheinische Briefe und Akten zur Geschichte der politischen Bewegung 1830-1850*, Essen, 1919, Bd. 1, S. 448.
                                                                                    p. 725

219 See Note 175.   p. 728

220 This apparently refers to the book: Marie Lafargue (Laffarge), *Memoires de Marie Cappelle, veuve Lafarge, écrits par elle-même*. In 1841 another book on the same subject was published in Leipzig: *Marie Lafarge, verurtheilt als Giftmischerin und angeklagt als Diamantendiebin. Criminalgeschichte der neuesten Zeit.*   p. 729

NAME INDEX

A

Adelung, Johann Christoph (1732-1806)
— German philologist, author of
a number of works on German
etymology and grammar.— 628

Aeschylus (525-456 B.C.) — Greek
tragic poet.— 30, 31, 68, 444

Aesop (6th century B.C.) — semi-
legendary Greek author of fables.— 374

Agrippa, Marcus Vipsanius (c. 63-12
B.C.) — Roman general and statesman.— 641

Alexander of Macedon (*Alexander the
Great*) (356-323 B.C.) — general
and statesman of antiquity.— 34,
189, 432

d'Alton, Eduard (1772-1840) —
professor, lectured on the history
of art at Bonn University.— 657

Ammon, Christoph Friedrich von (1766-
1850) — German Protestant theologian.— 205, 400

Amyclas (4th century B.C.) — Greek
philosopher.— 88.

Anaxagoras of Clazomenae (Asia Minor)
(c. 500-428 B.C.) — Greek philosopher.— 66, 405, 417, 435-36, 467,
469, 470, 490

Anaximander of Miletus (c. 610-546
B.C.) — Greek philosopher.— 486

Anselm, archbishop of Canterbury
(1033-1109) — born in Italy,
medieval theologian, representative of early scholasticism.— 388

Antisthenes of Rhodes (2nd century
B.C.) — Greek historian and
philosopher.— 40, 80, 501, 504

Apelles — Greek philosopher, contemporary and disciple of Epicurus.—
447

Apollodorus of Athens (2nd century
B.C.) — Greek writer, compiled
Chronology of historical events.— 81

Apollodorus of Athens (late 2nd century
B.C.) — Epicurean philosopher,
wrote a biography of Epicurus.—
81

Arcesilaus (c. 315-c. 240 B.C.) — Greek
sceptic philosopher, founder of
the New Academy.— 465

Archelaus (5th century B.C.) — Greek
philosopher, disciple of Anaxagoras.— 428

Archestratus (4th century B.C.) —
Greek poet, author of a satirical poem on gastrology.— 72, 101

Archimedes (c. 287-212 B.C.) — Greek
mathematician famous for his discoveries in mechanics.— 87

Aristippus (c. 435-c. 360 B.C.) — Greek philosopher, founder of the Cyrenaic school.— 37, 77, 404, 504

Aristotle (384-322 B.C.) — Greek philosopher.— 19, 34, 35, 38, 42, 48, 50, 51, 53, 54, 55, 56, 58, 59, 63, 66, 67, 69, 78, 79, 81, 87, 88, 90, 91, 92, 93, 96, 98, 101, 189, 201, 220, 410, 420, 424, 426, 427, 435, 439, 440, 441, 446, 459, 462, 490, 492, 496-500, 504

Aristoxenus of Tarentum (born c. 354 B.C.) — Greek philosopher, disciple of Aristotle, author of *Historical Notes*; famous primarily for his works on the theory of music.— 88

Arnim-Boytzenburg, Adolf Heinrich von, Count (1803-1868) — Prussian statesman, Junker, Minister of the Interior (1842-45) and Prime Minister (March 19-29, 1848).— 362, 710

Athenaeus (late 2nd-early 3rd century) — Greek rhetorician and grammarian.— 101

Augustine, Saint (Sanctus Aurelius Augustinus) (354-430) — Christian theologian and philosopher.— 50, 90, 198, 205

Augustus (Gaius Julius Caesar Octavianus) (63 B.C.-14 A.D.) — Roman Emperor (27 B.C.-14 A.D.).— 639-42

B

Bachmann, Carl Friedrich (1785-1855) — German philosopher, professor at Jena University.— 379, 705

Bacon, Francis, Baron Verulam, Viscount St. Albans (1561-1626) — English philosopher, naturalist and historian.— 19, 201

Balbus (Lucius Cornelius Balbus) — Roman consul (40 B.C.).— 502

Baumdahl, C.— 713

Bauer, Bruno (1809-1882) — German philosopher, Young Hegelian.— 20, 196, 211-14, 370, 381, 383, 386, 390, 395, 399, 400, 708

Bauer, Edgar (1820-1886) — German publicist, philosopher, Young Hegelian; Bruno Bauer's brother.— 392, 399

Bauer, H. L.— lecturer at Berlin University.— 700, 704

Baur, Ferdinand Christian (1792-1860) — German theologian, leader of the Tübingen school, professor.— 493-95

Bayer, Karl (1806-1883) — German philosopher.— 381

Bayle, Pierre (1647-1706) — French sceptic philosopher.— 47, 48, 50, 89, 90, 505

Bendermacher— notary in Cologne, a shareholder of the *Rheinische Zeitung.*— 713

Béranger, Pierre Jean de (1780-1857) — French song-writer.— 174

Bernadotte, Jean Baptiste Jules (1763-1844) — French marshal; later King Charles XIV (John) of Sweden and Norway (1818-44).— 398

Bernard of Clairvaux (Bernard, Saint) (c. 1091-1153) — French Catholic theologian.— 175

Berncastel— Trier physician.— 654

Bloemer, F.— Cologne lawyer, a shareholder of the *Rheinische Zeitung.*— 713

Böcking, Eduard (1802-1870) — German lawyer, lecturer at Bonn University.— 657

Böhme, Jakob (Bohemus, Jacobus) (1575-1624) — German artisan, pantheist philosopher.— 176, 190, 455

Boileau-Despréaux, Nicolas (1636-1711) — French poet of Classicism.— 627

Boismard— a shareholder of the *Rheinische Zeitung.*— 713

Boisserée, J.— a shareholder of the *Rheinische Zeitung.*— 713

Boisserée, Wilhelm— a shareholder of the *Rheinische Zeitung.*— 713, 724

Brandis, Christian August (1790-1867) — German historian of philosophy, participated in publishing the works of Aristotle.— 79, 87

Brockhaus, Johne Friedrich (1800-1865) — German publisher.— 723

Brucker, Johann Jakob (1696-1770) — German historian of philosophy.— 57, 94

Brüggemann, Theodor (1796-1866) — Prussian Royal Commissioner, member of the examination commission at the Trier gymnasium.— 644, 647

Bruno, Giordano (1548-1600) — Italian thinker, materialist and atheist, developed Copernicus' teaching on the structure of the universe. — 492

Buhl, Ludwig Heinrich Franz (1814-c. 1882) — German publicist, Young Hegelian, author of pamphlets in the *Patriot* series.— 303

Bulis (5th century B.C.) — Spartan.— 181

Bülow-Cummerow, Ernst Gottfried Georg von (1775-1851) — German publicist and politician, expressed the views of the Prussian Junkers.— 216, 321, 365, 384

Bürgers, Ignaz (c. 1815-1882) — Cologne assessor, a shareholder of the *Rheinische Zeitung*.— 712, 716, 719, 723, 724

C

Cabet, Étienne (1788-1856) — French publicist, utopian communist, author of *Voyage en Icarie*.— 360

Caesar, Gaius Julius (c. 100-44 B.C.) — Roman general and statesman. — 132, 553, 628

Campanella, Tommaso (1568-1639) — Italian philosopher, one of the early utopian communists.— 201

Campe, Johann Julius Wilhelm (1792-1867) — German publisher and bookseller, from 1823 onwards an owner of the Hoffmann & Campe Publishing House in Hamburg; in 1830s published works by authors of the Young Germany group.— 391

Camphausen, Ludolf (1803-1890) — German banker, a leader of the Rhine liberal bourgeoisie; Prime Minister of Prussia from March to June 1848.— 366-68, 374, 713, 719, 722

Carneades of Cyrene (c. 214-c. 129 B.C.) — Greek sceptic philosopher, founder of the New Academy.— 483

Cato, Marcus Porcius (234-149 B.C.) — politician and writer in ancient Rome.— 271

Cervantes Saavedra, Miguel de (1547-1616) — Spanish writer.— 124

Cetto — Trier merchant.— 726

Chamisso, Adelbert von (1781-1838) — German romantic poet.— 19

Charinus — Athenian archon in 308-307 B.C.— 480

Charles I (1600-1649) — King of Great Britain and Ireland (1625-49), beheaded during the revolution.— 156

Charles Martel (c. 688-741) — actual ruler of the Frankish state (from 715) under the last Merovingians, mayor of the palace of the Carolingian dynasty.— 618

Christiansen, Johannes (1809-1853) — German lawyer, historian of Roman law, professor at Kiel University.— 386

Chrysippus (c. 280-c. 205 B.C.) — Greek stoic philosopher.— 72, 101, 485, 501

Cicero, Marcus Tullius (106-43 B.C.) — Roman orator, statesman and philosopher.— 29, 37, 38, 40, 41, 43, 46-49, 51, 60, 77, 79-82, 89, 90, 95, 189, 472, 501, 504, 507

Claessen, Heinrich Joseph (1813-1883) — German physician and politician; member of the Board of Directors of the *Rheinische Zeitung.*—270, 277, 712, 714, 715-18, 719, 721, 722, 723, 729

Clarke, Samuel (1675-1729)—English theologian and philosopher.—190

Cleanthes (331-232 B.C.)—Greek stoic philosopher.—18

Clemens, Heinrich (c. 1818-1852)—student at Bonn University, later lawyer.—647

Clement of Alexandria (*Titus Flavius Clemens Alexandrinus*) (c. 150-c.215)—Christian theologian, philosopher.—37, 77, 80, 90, 487, 488

Clentgen—Trier landowner.—726

Clinias (4th century B.C.)—Greek philosopher, Plato's friend.—88

Clovis I (c. 465-511)—Frankish king of the Merovingian dynasty (481-510).—627

Cohen, S. B.—a shareholder of the *Rheinische Zeitung.*—713

Colotes of Lampsacus—Greek philosopher, contemporary and disciple of Epicurus.—79, 457-63, 464

Columbus, Christopher (1451-1506)—Italian navigator, discoverer of America.—444

Condorcet, Marie Jean Antoine Nicolas Caritat, Marquis de (1743-1794)—French sociologist, Enlightener, was active in the French Revolution, Girondist.—202

Considérant, Victor Prosper (1808-1893)—French publicist, utopian socialist, disciple and follower of Fourier.—220

Constant de Rebecque, Henri Benjamin (1767-1830)—French liberal politician, publicist and writer.—207

Copernicus, Nicolaus (*Mikolaj Kopernik*) (1473-1543)—Polish astronomer, founder of the heliocentric theory.—175, 201, 361

Cotta, Gaius Aurelius (c. 120-c. 73 B.C.)—Roman orator, politician, consul in 74 B.C.—37, 503

Cramer, Andreas Wilhelm (1760-1833)—German lawyer and philol-ogist, professor of Roman law at Kiel University.—19

Cromwell, Oliver (1599-1658)—one of the leaders of the English revolution, Lord Protector of England, Scotland and Ireland from 1653 onwards.—142

D

De Jonge, J.—a shareholder of the *Rheinische Zeitung.*—713

Demetrius of Magnesia (lst century B.C.)—Greek writer, compiler of works on ancient thinkers and philosophers.—40, 80

Democritus (c. 460-c. 370 B.C.)—Greek philosopher, a founder of the atomistic theory.—25, 32, 34, 35, 37-46, 50, 52-59, 61-66, 70, 73, 77-84, 87-89, 91-93, 96, 405, 427, 457, 459, 473, 486, 487, 498, 499, 503, 504, 507

Descartes, René (1596-1650)—French dualist philosopher, mathematician and natural scientist.—423

Des Maizeaux, Pierre (1666-1745)—French critic and historian, published the works of Leibniz, Bayle and other philosophers.—78

D'Ester, Karl Ludwig Johann. (1811-1859)—German democrat and socialist, a physician by profession; a shareholder of the *Rheinische Zeitung,* later member of the Cologne community of the Communist League.—712

Dézamy, Théodore (1803-1850)—French publicist, utopian communist.—360

Dietz, Johann Wilhelm—printer and publisher, a shareholder of the *Rheinische Zeitung.*—713

Diogenes Laertius (3rd century A.D.)—Greek historian of philosophy, compiler of a vast work on the ancient philosophers.—39, 40, 42, 53, 56,

58, 59, 77, 79-83, 87, 88, 90-100, 405, 410, 417, 423, 427, 486, 488

Diogenes of Babylon (c. 240-c. 150 B.C.) — Greek stoic philosopher.— 501

Diogenes of Sinope (c. 404-c. 323 B.C.) — Greek philosopher, one of the founders of the Cynic school.— 140

Dionysius (c. 200-c. 265) — bishop of Alexandria, author of a work against the atomistic philosophers. — 43, 56

Döbereiner, Johann Wolfgang (1780-1849) — lectured on chemistry at Jena University.— 706

Donner.— 662

Duns Scotus, John (c. 1265-c. 1308) — Scottish philosopher, scholastic, nominalist.— 134

E

Eichhorn — Chief Privy Councillor of Justice and Attorney General of the Rhine Court of Appeal in Berlin.— 666, 669

Eichhorn, Johann Albrecht Friedrich (1779-1856) — Prussian statesman, Minister of Religious Worship, Education and Medicine (1840-48).— 362, 383

Elizabeth I (1533-1603) — Queen of England (1558-1603) — 141

Empedocles (c. 483-c. 423 B.C.) — Greek philosopher.— 37, 78, 428, 459-61, 469

Enfantin, Barthélemy Prosper (1796-1864) — French utopian socialist, one of the closest disciples of Saint-Simon.— 220

Engels, Karl — a shareholder of the *Rheinische Zeitung.*— 713

Engels, Ph. — a shareholder of the *Rheinische Zeitung.*— 712

Epicharmus (c. 540-c. 450 B.C.) — Greek dramatist.— 37, 78, 428

Epicurus (c. 341-c. 270 B.C.) — Greek materialist philosopher, atheist.—

25, 29, 30, 32-34, 36-73, 77-83, 88, 89-97, 99-101, 189, 405, 406, 408, 409, 410, 412, 415-34, 444, 454-63, 464-65, 469, 478-88, 492, 500-05, 507-09

Esch, A. W. — a shareholder of the *Rheinische Zeitung.*— 712

Esser — Chief Privy Councillor of the Rhine Court of Appeal in Berlin.— 661, 667, 669, 682

Euripides (c. 480-c. 406 B.C.) — Greek dramatist.— 444

Eurydicus (correctly *Eurylochos*) (late 4th-3rd century B.C.) — Greek philosopher, disciple of Pyrrho the Sceptic.— 81

Eusebius of Caesarea (c. 264-c. 340) — Christian theologian, author of works on church history.— 42, 43, 54, 56, 80-83, 92-95

Evers.— 690

F

Fay, Gerhard (1809-1889) — German barrister, Councillor of Justice in Cologne, Chairman of the Board of Directors of the *Rheinische Zeitung.*— 712, 714, 722, 723, 724

Fénelon, François de Salignac de La Mothe (1651-1715) — French prelate and writer; became archbishop of Cambrai in 1695.— 208

Feuerbach, Ludwig Andreas von (1804-1872) — German materialist philosopher.— 94, 196, 197, 370, 381, 386, 399, 400, 728

Feuerbach, Paul Johann Anselm, Ritter von (1775-1833) — German lawyer, specialised in criminal law; Ludwig Feuerbach's father.— 19

Fichte, Immanuel Hermann von (1796-1879) — German philosopher and theologian; son of Johann Gottlieb Fichte.— 388

Fichte, Johann Gottlieb (1762-1814) — German philosopher, representative of classical German philosophy.— 119, 175, 201, 208, 494, 577, 624

Fleischer, Karl Moritz (1809-1876) — German publicist, contributor to the Rheinische Zeitung.— 400

Fould, Achille (1800-1867) — French banker and politician, Orleanist, later Bonapartist.— 302

Fourier, François Marie Charles (1772-1837) — French utopian socialist.— 220

Franklin, Benjamin (1706-1790) — American politician, diplomat, took part in the War for Independence, scientist, physicist and economist.— 618

Frederick the Great (1712-1786) — King of Prussia (1740-86).— 284

Frederick William III (1770-1840) — King of Prussia (1797-1840).— 355, 672

Frederick William IV (1795-1861) — King of Prussia (1840-61).— 216, 271, 280, 283, 356, 357, 397, 710, 711, 714, 725

Freytag, Georg Wilhelm (1788-1861) — Orientalist, rector of Bonn University.— 658

Friedrich Karl Alexander (1801-1883) — Prussian prince.— 677

Fries, Jakob Friedrich (1773-1843) — German philosopher, lecturer at Jena University.— 706

G

Gabler, Georg Andreas (1786-1853) — German Hegelian philosopher, professor at Berlin University.— 700, 704

Galileo Galilei (1564-1642) — Italian physicist and astronomer, founder of mechanics.— 138

Ganganelli, Giovanni Vincenzo Antonio (1705-1774) — Roman Pope Clement XIV (1769-74).— 371

Gans, Eduard (c. 1798-1839) — German philosopher of law, Hegelian.— 699, 700, 703, 704

Gärtner, Gustav Friedrich (died 1841) — German lawyer, professor at Bonn University.— 20

Gassendi, Pierre (1592-1655) — French philosopher, adherent and advocate of Epicurus' atomistic theory; physicist and mathematician.— 29, 57, 94, 405, 417, 418, 423

Geppert, Karl Eduard (1811-1881) — classical philologist, Privat-Docent in Berlin from 1836 onwards.— 700, 704

Gerlach, Karl Heinrich Eduard Friedrich von — Prussian official, Regierungspräsident in Cologne (1839-44).— 282, 285, 396, 714, 720

Gluck, Christoph Willibald (1714-1787) — German composer.— 540

Göbbels, T.— a shareholder of the Rheinische Zeitung.— 713

Goethe, Johann Wolfgang von (1749-1832) — German poet.— 112, 137, 155, 246, 385, 436, 578, 579, 580

Goettling, Karl Wilhelm (1793-1869) — German philologist, lecturer at Jena University.— 706

Goeze, Johann Melchior (1717-1786) — German theologian, Lutheran pastor.— 328

Görgen.— 655

Gorgias of Leontini (c. 483-c. 375 B.C.) — Greek sophist philosopher.— 498

Görres, Johannes Joseph von (1776-1848) — German writer, philologist and historian, exponent cf Catholicism.— 199, 364

Gottsched, Johann Christoph (1700-1766) — German writer and critic, early Enlightener.— 178

Grach, E.— 635

Gratianus, Franciscus (approx. 12th century) — Italian monk, author of a treatise on canon law.— 19

Gratz, Peter Alois (1769-1849) — professor at the Faculty of Catholic Theology, Bonn University (1819-25); inspector of schools in Trier (1825-39).— 650

Grolmann, Karl Ludwig Wilhelm von (1775-1829) — German lawyer, author of works on criminal and civil law.— 19

Grotius, Hugo (Huig de Groot) (1583-1645) — Dutch scientist, jurist, a founder of the natural law theory.— 201

Gruppe, Otto Friedrich (1804-1876) — German publicist and philosopher; in 1842 and 1843 wrote two pamphlets against Bruno Bauer. — 211-14

Guizot, François Pierre Guillaume (1787-1874) — French historian and statesman; virtually determined home and foreign policy of France from 1840 to the February 1848 revolution.— 238, 316

Günster.— Trier lawyer.— 649

H

Haan, Johann Heinrich (1804-1871) — Cologne businessman, member of the Board of Directors of the Rheinische Zeitung.— 712, 719, 724

Haass—a shareholder of the Rheinische Zeitung.— 712, 714, 719, 721, 724

Haizinger, Amalie (1800-1884) — German actress.— 709

Haller, Albrecht von (1708-1777) — Swiss naturalist, poet and publicist. — 144

Haller, Karl Ludwig von (1768-1854) — Swiss lawyer and historian, supported restoration of feudal monarchist institutions.— 144, 209

Hamacher, Wilhelm (1808-1875) — German teacher; from 1835 taught German at the Trier gymnasium. — 644

Hand, Ferdinand Gotthelf (1786-1851) — German philologist, lecturer at Jena University.— 706

Hansemann, David Justus (1790-1864) — German capitalist, a leader of the Rhine liberal bourgeoisie; Prussian Minister of Finance from March to September 1848.— 349, 351

Hardenberg, Karl August von, Prince (1750-1822) — Prussian statesman, Foreign Minister (1804-06 and 1807), Chancellor (1810-22).— 362

Hariri, Abu-Mahommed (1054-1122) — Arab scholar and poet.— 170

Hasse, Friedrich Rudolf (1808-1862) — German theologian, professor at Bonn University.— 387

Heffter, August Wilhelm (1796-1880) — German lawyer.— 699, 703

Hegel, Georg Wilhelm Friedrich (1770-1831) — classical German philosopher.— 18-20, 29, 84, 85, 87, 103, 196, 201, 309, 325, 362, 400, 439, 491-97, 500, 533, 576, 577, 707

Heim— preacher.— 678

Heine, Heinrich (1797-1856) — German revolutionary poet.— 18, 394

Heineccius, Johann Gottlieb (1681-1741) — German lawyer, author of works on the history of Roman law.— 12

Heinzen, Karl (1809-1880) — German publicist, radical, a shareholder of the Rheinische Zeitung.— 713, 720, 722, 724

Hellwitz, H.—a shareholder of the Rheinische Zeitung.— 713

Hennequin, Victor Antoine (1816-1854) — French lawyer and publicist, follower of Fourier.— 219

Henry VIII (1491-1547) — King of England (1509-47)— 141

Heraclitus (c. 540-c. 480 B.C.) — Greek philosopher, one of the founders of dialectics.— 34, 35, 135, 201, 494

Herder, Johann Gottfried von (1744-1803) — German writer and literary theorist.— 203

Hermann— 729

Hermes, Karl Heinrich (1800-1856) — German publicist; in 1842 one of the editors of the *Kölnische Zeitung.*—185-94, 390, 391

Hermippus of Smyrna (c. 200 B.C.)—Greek writer, biographer of ancient philosophers.—81

Herodotus (c. 484-c. 425 B.C.)—Greek philosopher.—53, 58, 59, 64, 68, 181, 410, 417, 486

Herrmanns, J.—a shareholder of the *Rheinische Zeitung.*—713

Herstatt, J.—a shareholder of the *Rheinische Zeitung.*—713

Herwegh, Georg (1817-1875)—German democratic poet.—287, 291, 319, 322, 323, 394, 395, 397

Herz, L.—713

Hesiod (approx. 8th century B.C.)—Greek poet.—501

Heuser, F. G.—a shareholder of the *Rheinische Zeitung.*—712

Heuser, Georg—a shareholder of the *Rheinische Zeitung.*—713

Hippocrates (c. 460-c. 377 B.C.)—Greek physician, father of medicine.—444

Hobbes, Thomas (1588-1679)—English philosopher.—201

Hoffmann, Ernst Theodor Amadeus (1776-1822)—German writer.—629

Hofmann—Trier acquaintance of Marx's father.—653

Holbach, Paul Henri, Baron d' (1723-1789)—French philosopher, Enlightener.—102

Homer—semi-legendary ancient Greek epic poet.—37, 78, 205, 388, 428, 447, 475, 487, 501

Hommer, Joseph Ludwig Aloys von (1760-1836)—bishop of Trier.—654

Hontheim, F. M. von—a shareholder of the *Rheinische Zeitung.*—713, 715, 716, 719, 722, 723, 724

Horace (*Quintus Horatius Flaccus*) (65-8 B.C.)—Roman poet.—642

Horst, J.—a shareholder of the *Rheinische Zeitung.*—713

Hugo, Gustav (1764-1844)—German lawyer, professor of law at Göttingen, founder of the historical school of law.—203-09

Hume, David (1711-1776)—British philosopher, historian and economist.—30, 208, 628

Hutten, Ulrich von (1488-1523)—German poet, supporter of the Reformation, participant in and ideologist of the knights' uprising of 1522-23.—328, 330

Hydarnes (5th century B.C.)—Persian satrap.—181

I

Idomeneus of Lampsacus (c. 325-270 B.C.)—Greek philosopher, disciple of Epicurus.—481, 482

Irenaeus (c. 130-c. 202)—Christian theologian; in 177 became bishop of Lyons, criticised the tenets of various heretical sects and vindicated the doctrines of Christianity.—497

Irnerius (c. 1050-1130)—founder of the Bologna school of glossators (Italy).—626

J

Jaehnigen—German lawyer.—661, 666, 667, 669, 676, 682

James I (1566-1625)—King of Great Britain and Ireland (1603-25).—141

Jenny—see *Westphalen, Jenny von.*

Julian, Flavius Claudius Julianus, the Apostate (c. 331-363)—Roman Emperor (361-363)—190

Jung, Georg Gottlob (1814-1886)—German publicist, Young Hegelian, one of the managers of the *Rheinische Zeitung.*—386, 712, 715, 717, 721, 723, 724

Juvenal, Decimus Junius Juvenalis (born in the 60s-died after 127)—Roman satirical poet.—146

K

Kamp, Johann Heinrich—a shareholder of the Rheinische Zeitung, deputy of the Sixth Rhine Province
Assembly.— 712, 716, 720, 721,
723

Kant, Immanuel (1724-1804)—classical
German philosopher.— 17, 18, 104,
119, 175, 204, 206, 207, 208, 388,
577, 624, 628, 648

Karr, Alphonse (1808-1890)—French
publicist and writer, author and
publisher of Les Guêpes, a satirical
monthly.— 316

Kaufmann—lottery organiser in
Bonn.— 653

Kaufmann, M.—a shareholder of the
Rheinische Zeitung.— 713, 720, 724

Kaufmann, Peter (1804-1872)—German economist.— 357

Klein, Ernst Ferdinand (c. 1744-
1810)—German lawyer, author ot
works on criminal and civil
law.— 17

Kleinerz—acquaintance of Karl
Marx.— 655, 669

Köppen, Karl Friedrich (1808-1863)—
German publicist and historian,
Young Hegelian.— 30, 386

Kosegarten, Wilhelm (1792-1868)—
German publicist.— 216, 220

Krämer—Bonn engineer.— 387

Krause—judge at Berlin University.—
704

Kropp, Mathias—office employee in
Trier.— 635

Krug, Wilhelm Graugott (1770-1842)—
German philosopher.— 628

Kühn—a shareholder of the
Rheinische Zeitung.— 713

Kühn, W.—a shareholder of the
Rheinische Zeitung.— 713

Küpper (died 1850)—teacher of religion at the Trier gymnasium.— 644

L

Laffarge, Marie (née Capelle)
(d. 1853)—was accused of poison-
ing her husband and sentenced to
hard labour for life; released by
Louis Napoleon Bonaparte;
proved her not being guilty in
Memoires (1841) and Heures de prison (1853).— 729

Lais (5th-4th century B.C.)—name of
several Athenian hetaerae or courte-
sans.— 29

Lancelotti, Giovanni Paolo (1511-
1591)—Italian lawyer, professor
of canon law.— 19

Lancizolle, Karl Wilhelm von Deleuze de
(1796-1871)—German lawyer,
author of works on the history of
the German states.— 704

Lange, Joachim (1670-1744)—German
theologian, professor at Halle.—
201

Lauterbach, Wolfgang Adam (1618-
1678)—German lawyer, author of
works on Roman law.— 19

Law, John (1671-1729)—Scottish
economist and financier, Minister
of Finance of France (1719-
20).— 142

Leibniz, Gottfried Wilhelm (1646-
1716)—German philosopher and
mathematician.— 37, 57, 78, 190,
477, 628, 647

Leist—Councillor of the Court of
Appeal, a shareholder of the
Rheinische Zeitung.— 712, 716, 718,
721

Leo, Heinrich (1799-1878)—German
historian and publicist, opponent
of the Hegelian school.— 209

Leonteus of Lampsacus (approx. 3rd
century B.C.)—Greek philosopher,
disciple of Epicurus.— 37, 77, 457

Leroux, Pierre (1797-1871)—French
publicist, utopian socialist.— 220

Lessing, Gotthold Ephraim (1729-
1781)—German writer, dramatist,

critic and philosopher, early Enlightener.— 17, 178, 328, 680

Leucippus (5th century B.C.)—Greek
philosopher, father of the atomistic theory.— 53, 55, 59, 79, 82, 87,
91-93, 486, 498, 503

Lichtenstein, Martin Heinrich Karl
(1780-1857)—Deputy Royal Governmental Plenipotentiary at Berlin University.— 704

Locke, John (1632-1704)—English
dualist philosopher and economist.— 624, 647

Loebell, Johann Wilhelm (1786-
1863)—German historian, Dean
of the Faculty of Philosophy at
Bonn University.— 658

Loers, Vitus (died 1862)—German
philologist, taught ancient languages at the Trier gymnasium,
assistant director from 1835.— 644,
647, 648

Louis XIV (1638-1715)—King of
France (1643-1715).— 142

Louis XVIII (1755-1824)—King of
France (1814-15 and 1815-24).— 398

Louis Philippe I (1773-1850)—duke of
Orleans, King of the French
(1830-48).— 398, 628

Louise (*Auguste Wilhelmine Amalie
Luise*) (1776-1810)—Queen of
Prussia, wife of Frederick William
III.— 672

Lucian (c. 120-c. 180)—Greek sati-
rist.— 185, 190

Lucretius (*Titus Lucretius Carus*) (c. 99-
c. 55 B.C.)—Roman philosopher
and poet.— 48, 49, 51, 53, 57, 59,
62, 65, 73, 89-91, 93-94, 96-98, 101,
190, 416, 440, 464, 466, 469-71,
474, 475, 489

Luden, Heinrich (1780-1847)—German historian, professor at Jena.—
17, 706

Luther, Martin (1483-1546)—German
theologian, writer, prominent figure in the Reformation, founder
of Protestantism (Lutheranism) in
Germany.— 175, 194, 284, 328, 330,
371, 579

M

Machiavelli, Niccolò (1469-1527)—Italian politician, historian and writer.
— 161, 201

Maecenas, Gaius (*Cilnius*) (b. between
74 and 64-d. 8 B.C.)—Roman
politician, associate of Emperor
Augustus, patron of letters. His
character as patron of literature
and science has made his name a
household word.— 641

Malebranche, Nicolas de (1638-1715)—
French philosopher.— 190

Mallinckrodt, G.—a shareholder of the
Rheinische Zeitung.— 712, 724

Marheineke, Philipp Konrad (1780-1846)
—German Protestant theologian,
historian of Christianity.— 391

Marius, Gaius (c. 156-86 B.C.)—Roman general and statesman, consul (107, 104-100, 86 B.C.).— 84

Martin, St. (c. 316-400).— 619

Marx, Eduard (1826-1837)—brother
of Karl Marx.— 20, 648, 663, 674,
682, 689

Marx, Emilie (1822-1888)—sister of
Karl Marx.— 694

Marx, Heinrich (1777-1838)—father
of Karl Marx; lawyer, Councillor
of Justice in Trier.— 10, 11, 19-21,
531, 533, 534, 635, 643, 646-82,
683-94, 701

Marx, Henriette (née *Pressburg* or
Presborck) (1787-1863)—mother
of Karl Marx.— 20, 635, 645, 648-
49, 652, 654, 655, 661, 664, 665,
671, 674, 676, 677, 682, 683, 685,
686, 689, 693, 694

Marx, Henriette (1820-c. 1856)—sister
of Karl Marx.— 694

Marx, Hermann (1819-1842)—brother
of Karl Marx.— 662, 683.

Marx, Karl (1818-1883).— 10-15, 17-
21, 27, 28, 29, 635, 643-709, 712,
715, 723, 727-30

Marx, Karoline (1824-1847)—sister of
Karl Marx.— 694

Marx, Louise (1821-1865) — sister of Karl Marx.— 694

Marx, Sophie (1816-1883) — sister of Karl Marx.— 666, 671, 674, 677, 685, 691, 693

Mary I (1516-1558) — Queen of England (1553-58).— 141

Mayer, Eduard — Cologne lawyer member of the Board of Directors of the Rheinische Zeitung.— 391, 712, 719

M'Douall, Peter Murray (1814-1854) — Chartist leader.— 219

Medem — secretary of Berlin University.— 704

Memmius, Gaius (1st century B.C.) — Roman tribune, orator and poet.— 94

Menoeceus — contemporary and disciple of Epicurus.— 406, 488

Merkens, Heinrich (1778-1854) — German merchant, Chairman of the Board of Trade in Cologne, liberal, deputy of the Sixth Rhine Province Assembly.— 366-68, 374

Metrodorus of Chios (approx. 4th century B.C.) — Greek philosopher, disciple of Democritus.— 81, 95, 427, 479-80, 487

Metrodorus of Lampsacus (c. 331-c. 277 B.C.) — Greek philosopher, disciple of Epicurus.— 447

Meurin — court councillor, senior Finance Department official.— 662, 666, 669, 673, 682

Mevissen, Gustav von — a shareholder of the Rheinische Zeitung; in 1848 member of the Frankfurt National Assembly.— 724

Meyen, Eduard (1812-1870) — German publicist, Young Hegelian, one of the leaders of the Berlin circle "The Free".— 390, 393, 394, 395

Mirabeau, Honoré Gabriel Victor Riqueti, Comte de (1749-1791) — prominent figure in the French Revolution.— 139, 202

Mittweg — Trier lawyer.— 726

Molière (pseudonym of Jean Baptiste Poquelin) (1622-1673) — French author of comedies.— 322

Montaigne, Michel Eyquem de (1533-1592) — French sceptic philosopher.— 205

Montesquieu, Charles Louis de Secondat, Baron de La Brède et de (1689-1755) — French philosopher and sociologist, Enlightener.— 161, 202, 227

Morel, M.— a shareholder of the Rheinische Zeitung.— 713

Mosen, Julius (1803-1867) — German romantic writer.— 289-91

Mühlenbruch, Christian Friedrich (1785-1843) — German jurist, specialist in Roman law.— 19

Mülhens, J.— a shareholder of the Rheinische Zeitung.— 712, 718

Müller — Trier notary.— 653

Müller, J.— a shareholder of the Rheinische Zeitung.— 713

Müller, Johannes (1801-1858) — German anatomist and physiologist, Dean of the Medical Faculty at Berlin University.— 654, 655

N

Napier, Sir Charles (1786-1860) — British admiral.— 708

Napoleon I Bonaparte (1769-1821) — Emperor of the French (1804-14 and 1815).— 142, 192, 201, 244, 398, 628, 673

Nausiphanes (4th century B.C.) — Greek philosopher, follower of Democritus.— 81

Nell, Georg Friedrich von — owner of a timber business in Trier.— 662

Neocles (4th century B.C.) — Epicurus' father.— 77

Nero (Nero Claudius Caesar Augustus Germanicus) (37-68) — Roman Emperor (54-68).— 640, 641

Newton, Sir Isaac (1642-1727) — English physicist, astronomer and mathematician.— 190, 647

Nicolai, Christoph Friedrich (1733-1811) — German writer, supporter of enlightened absolutism; opposed Kant and Fichte.— 494

Nicolaus of Damascenus (born c. 64 B.C.) — Greek historian and philosopher, follower of Aristotle.— 37, 77, 405

Notz, von — major of an infantry regiment in Trier, father of Heinrich von Notz, Karl Marx's schoolmate.— 669

Nürnberger, Johann Baptist Carl (1762-1807) — professor of philosophy and mathematics at Dortmund.— 54

O

Ochse-Stern, A.— a shareholder of the Rheinische Zeitung.— 713

Octavianus, Gaius Julius Caesar — see Augustus.

Oken, Lorenz (1779-1851) — German naturalist and natural philosopher. — 134

Oppenheim, A.— a shareholder of the Rheinische Zeitung.— 712, 718

Oppenheim, Dagobert (1809-1889) — German publicist, Young Hegelian, one of the managers of the Rheinische Zeitung.— 391-93, 712, 714, 715, 716, 718, 721, 729

Oppenhofen — secretary of Bonn University.— 658

Origen of Alexandria (c. 185-c. 254) — Christian theologian, one of the Fathers of the Church.— 495

Orleans, Philip II, Duke of (1674-1723) — regent of France (1715-23).— 142, 205

Overath, Christians von — a shareholder of the Rheinische Zeitung.— 713

Ovid (Publius Ovidius Naso) (43 B.C.-c. 17 A.D.) — Roman poet.— 17, 533, 548, 621

P

Pacius, Giulio (1550-c. 1635) — lawyer, specialist in canon law.— 626

Parmenides of Elea (c. 540-480 B.C.) — Greek philosopher.— 37, 81, 461

Pericles (c. 490-429 B.C.) — Athenian statesman, leader of the democratic party.— 181, 189

Peter I (The Great) (1672-1725) — Tsar of Russia from 1682, Emperor from 1721.— 120

Petrasch, Carl — Trier official.— 635

Pfützner — German advocate, Dresden correspondent of the Rheinische Zeitung.— 399

Phalaris (c. 571-555 B.C.) — tyrant of Acragos (Agrigentum) in Sicily. He is said to have burnt prisoners alive in the brazen figure of a bull.— 479

Philip II (1527-1598) — King of Spain (1556-98).— 257

Philoponus, Joannes (John the Grammarian) (late 5th-early 6th century) — Greek philosopher and theologian.— 54, 92, 94

Plassmann — a shareholder of the Rheinische Zeitung.— 712

Plato (c. 427-c. 347 B.C.) — Greek philosopher.— 35, 37, 66, 88, 219, 427, 439, 440, 459, 462-63, 483, 492, 493-98, 636

Pliny, the Younger (c. 62-114) — Roman statesman and writer.— 621

Plotinus (c. 204-270) — Neoplatonic philosopher.— 498

Plutarch (c. 46-c. 120) — Greek moralist writer, philosopher.— 29, 30, 33, 37, 50, 51, 53, 59, 60, 74-84, 89-95, 102, 431, 432, 442-58, 462-63, 464, 465, 466-69, 505

Polyaenus of Lampsacus — Greek mathematician and philosopher, contemporary and disciple of Epicurus.— 480

Pompey (Gnaeus Pompeius Magnus) (106-48 B.C.) — Roman general and statesman.— 126, 135

Posidonius of Apameia (c. 135-c. 51 B.C.) — Greek stoic philosopher. — 37, 77, 405

Praxiphanes (4th century B.C.) — Greek philosopher, follower of Aristotle. — 81

Propertius (c. 49-15 B.C.) — Roman poet. — 658

Protagoras of Abdera (c. 480-c. 411 B.C.) — Greek sophist philosopher. — 498, 503

Proudhon, Pierre Joseph (1809-1865) — French publicist, economist and sociologist, a founder of anarchism. — 220

Prutz, Robert Eduard (1816-1872) — German poet, publicist and literary historian, connected with the Young Hegelians. — 399

Ptolemy (*Claudius Ptolemaeus*) (2nd century A.D.) — Greek mathematician, astronomer and geographer, founder of the geocentric conception of the universe. — 175

Puggé, Eduard (1802-1836) — German jurist, professor of law in Bonn, disciple of Savigny. — 658

Pustkuchen-Glanzow, Johann Friedrich Wilhelm (1793-1835) — German pastor; author of parodies against Goethe. — 533, 578

Pyrrho (c. 365-c. 275 B.C.) — Greek philosopher, founder of ancient scepticism. — 81, 428, 429

Pythagoras (c. 571-c. 497 B.C.) — Greek mathematician and philosopher. — 66, 134, 427

Pythocles — Greek philosopher, contemporary and disciple of Epicurus. — 44, 58, 68, 99, 418, 481

Q

Quednow, F. — 541

R

Rabe — an acquaintance of Karl Marx's father. — 655

Rath, J. J. von — a shareholder of the *Rheinische Zeitung*. — 712, 723

Rath, J. P. von — a shareholder of the *Rheinische Zeitung*. — 713

Raupach, Ernst Benjamin Salomo (1784-1852) — Prussian playwright. — 628

Rehfues, Philipp Joseph von (1779-1843) — extraordinary governmental plenipotentiary and curator at Bonn University. — 658

Reichard, B. — a shareholder of the *Rheinische Zeitung*. — 713

Reichstadt, Napoleon François-Joseph Charles, Duke of (1811-1832) — son of Napoleon I and Marie Louise, a claimant to the French throne. — 398

Reimarus, Hermann Samuel (1694-1768) — German philosopher and philologist, Enlightener. — 19

Reimbold, C. — a shareholder of the *Rheinische Zeitung*. — 713

Reinhard — privy councillor of justice, advocate. — 661, 682

Reinhold, Ernst Christian Gottlieb (1793-1855) — German philosopher, lecturer at Jena University. — 706

Rembrandt van Rijn (1606-1669) — Dutch painter. — 171

Renard, Joseph Engelbert (1802-1863) — Cologne bookseller officially known as responsible editor of the *Rheinische Zeitung*. — 712, 714

Richardson, Samuel (1689-1761) — English novelist, representative of sentimentalism. — 205

Rick, J. B. — a shareholder of the *Rheinische Zeitung*. — 713

Ritter, Heinrich (1791-1869) — German historian of philosophy. — 55, 79, 92, 435, 498, 499

Ritter, J. — a shareholder of the *Rheinische Zeitung*. — 713

Ritter, Karl (1799-1859) — German geographer, professor at Berlin University. — 700, 704

Robespierre, Maximilien François Marie Isidore de (1758-1794) — French revolutionary of the end of the eighteenth century, leader of the Jacobins, head of the revolutionary government (1793-94)— 119

Rochow, Gustav Adolf Rochus von (1792-1847)— Prussian Minister of the Interior (1834-42).— 362

Rogge, A.— a shareholder of the Rheinische Zeitung.— 713

Rosinius, Carlo Maria (1748-1836)— Italian historian and archaeologist, commentator and publisher of Epicurus.— 56, 93

Rousseau, Jean Jacques (1712-1778)— French philosopher and writer, Enlightener.— 201, 202, 205

Rüb— a shareholder of the Rheinische Zeitung.— 713

Rudorff, Adolf Friedrich (1803-1873)— German professor of law, lecturer at Berlin University.— 700, 704

Ruge, Arnold (1802-1880)— German radical publicist and philosopher; Young Hegelian.— 277, 381, 382, 383, 387, 389, 391, 393-400, 728

Rutenberg, Adolf (1808-1869)— German publicist, Young Hegelian; in 1842 member of the Rheinische Zeitung editorial board.— 285, 391, 393, 394

S

Sack, Karl Heinrich (1789-1875)— German Protestant theologian, professor in Bonn.— 388

Sallet, Friedrich von (1812-1843)— German poet.— 370-72

Salomon, von— judge at Bonn University.— 658

Sandt— advocate in Berlin, councillor of justice.— 662

Sandt, Gottfried Alexander Maria Robert (1786-1839)— advocate in Cologne, brother of the former.— 662

Saturninus (Lucius Herennius Saturninus)— Roman politician.— 457

Savigny, Friedrich Carl von (1779-1861)— German jurist, head of the historical school of law; Minister of Justice for the revision of the law in 1842-48.— 15, 19, 699, 703

Schäfer.— 634

Schaper, von— Prussian official, Oberpräsident of the Rhine Province (1842-45).— 282, 331, 332-36, 358, 714

Schaubach, Johann Konrad (1764-1849)— German astronomer, author of researches on the history of ancient astronomy.— 47, 58-60, 89, 95, 486

Schelling, Friedrich Wilhelm Joseph von (1775-1854)— representative of classical German philosophy, opposed the Hegelian school.— 18, 103, 105, 196

Scherer.— 713

Schiller, Johann Christoph Friedrich von (1759-1805)— German poet and dramatist.— 112, 136, 291, 578, 628

Schlegel, Friedrich von (1772-1829)— German literary critic, philologist and poet, a theoretician of romanticism.— 494, 657

Schleicher, Robert— Trier physician.— 726

Schlick, Alois— music master at the Trier gymnasium (1827-38).— 647

Schmidt, Karl— agent of the Julius Wunder bookselling firm in Leipzig.— 19

Schmidthänner— assessor in Berlin, acquaintance of Karl Marx.— 20

Schneemann, Johann Gerhard (1794-1864)— historian, teacher at the Trier gymnasium.— 644

Schneider, Johann Gottlob (1750-1822)— German philologist, author of researches on ancient natural science.— 53

Schön, Heinrich Theodor von (1773-1856)— Prussian statesman.— 362

Schriever.— 669

Schriever, M-lle.— 669

Schulze, Friedrich Gottlob (1795-1860) — lecturer at the Faculty of Philosophy at Jena University.— 706

Schwegler, Albert (1819-1857) — German theologian, philosopher, philologist and historian.— 399

Schwendler, Heinrich (1792-1847) — priest, French teacher at the Trier gymnasium.— 644

Sehrmeyer, J. F.—a shareholder of the *Rheinische Zeitung.*— 713

Seligmann, A. L.—lawyer, a shareholder of the *Rheinische Zeitung.*— 713, 717, 720, 721

Seneca, Lucius Annaeus (c. 4 B.C.-65 A.D.) — Roman stoic philosopher.— 41, 44, 80-83, 90, 479, 484

Sextus Empiricus (2nd century A.D.) — Greek sceptic philosopher.— 37, 39, 59, 65, 78, 80, 92, 95, 96, 417, 427, 429, 431, 447, 492, 499

Shakespeare, William (1564-1616) — English dramatist and poet.— 139, 194, 236, 250, 256, 268, 288, 289, 290, 291, 323, 359, 617

Sieyès, Emmanuel Joseph (1748-1836) — French abbot, participated in the French Revolution.— 170, 216

Simplicius (6th century A.D.) — Greek Neoplatonic philosopher, commentator of Aristotle.—42, 43, 55, 63, 79, 82, 83, 88, 90, 92, 94-96, 417

Socrates (c. 469-399 B.C.) — Greek philosopher.— 35, 37, 66, 189, 427, 432, 436-39, 457, 461, 464, 483, 490, 492-94, 498

Solger, Karl Wilhelm Ferdinand (1780-1819) — German philosopher, art theoretician.— 17

Solon (c. 638-c. 558 B.C.) — Athenian statesman and legislator.— 177

Sotion of Alexandria (2nd century B.C.) — Greek philosopher.— 37, 77, 405

Sperthias (5th century B.C.) — Spartan.— 181

Spinoza (Baruch or Benedict) (1632-1677) — Dutch philosopher.— 54, 112, 118, 201, 496

Stahl, Friedrich Julius (1802-1861) — German jurist and politician.— 209

Steffens, Henrich (Henrick) (1773-1845) — German naturalist, writer and philosopher, Norwegian by birth.— 699, 703

Stein, Heinrich Friedrich Karl, Reichsfreiherr vom und zum (1757-1831) — Prussian statesman and reformer; held high posts in 1804-08.— 362

Stein, Karl—a shareholder of the *Rheinische Zeitung.*— 712

Steininger, Johann (1794-1874) — teacher of mathematics and physics at the Trier gymnasium, geologist.— 644

Sterne, Laurence (1713-1768) — British novelist, a founder of sentimentalism.— 113

Stilpo of Megara (4th century B.C.) — Greek philosopher, follower of Socrates.— 37, 464, 479, 480

Stobaeus, Joannes (c. 5th century A.D.) — Greek writer, compiled works of ancient authors.— 42, 44, 55, 56, 60, 65, 81, 83, 88, 89, 93, 95, 96, 481, 484, 486

Strauss, David Friedrich (1808-1874) — German philosopher and publicist, Young Hegelian.— 197, 370

Stucke, Karl Friedrich (1800-1871) — German physician, member of the Board of Directors of the *Rheinische Zeitung.*— 398, 713, 724

Swedenborg (Swedberg), Emanuel (1688-1772) — Swedish philosopher.— 87

T

Tacitus, Cornelius (c. 55-c. 120) — Roman historian.— 17, 131, 642

Talleyrand-Périgord, Charles Maurice de (1754-1838) — French diplomat, Minister of Foreign Affairs (1797-99, 1799-1807, 1814-15), represented France at the Vienna Congress (1814-15).— 398

Talma, François Joseph (1763-1826) — French tragedian.— 539

Terence, Publius Terentius Afer (c. 190-159 B.C.) — Roman author of comedies.— 316

Tertullian (Quintus Septimius Florens Tertullianus) (c. 150-c. 222) — Latin church father.— 190

Thales of Miletus (c. 640-c. 547 B.C.) — Greek philosopher, founder of the Miletus school.— 192, 432, 494

Themistius (4th century A.D.) — Greek philosopher, commentator of Aristotle.— 87

Themistocles (c. 525-c. 460 B.C.) — Athenian general and statesman, held important state and military posts.— 492

Thibaut, Anton Friedrich Justus (1772-1840) — German jurist, specialist in civil law, historian and critic of Roman law.— 12

Thiers, Louis Adolphe (1797-1877) — French statesman and historian, Prime Minister (1836, 1840); in 1871 head of the Versailles government, organised the suppression of the Paris Commune.— 316

Thomé, Wilhelm (1810-1846) — Cologne physician, member of the Board of Directors of the *Rheinische Zeitung*.— 712

Thucydides (c. 460-c. 395 B.C.) — Greek historian, author of *The History of the Peloponnesian War*.— 181

Trendelenburg, Friedrich Adolf (1802-1872) — German philosopher, author of a commentary to Aristotle's works.— 38, 78

U

Uhland, Johann Ludwig (1787-1862) — German romantic poet.— 154

V

Vahrenkamp, E. — a shareholder of the *Rheinische Zeitung*.— 713

Vanini, Lucilio (1585-1619) — Italian philosopher.— 323

Vatke, Johann Karl Wilhelm (1806-1882) — German Protestant theologian, Hegelian, professor at Berlin University.— 381, 388

Vauban — Bonn acquaintance of Karl Marx and Jenny von Westphalen.— 708

Velleius (Gaius Velleius) — Roman senator.— 43, 501

Vencelius — Trier physician.— 726

Vidocq, François Eugène (1775-1857) — French secret police agent, supposed author of *Memoirs*; his name is used to mean a clever agent and swindler.— 202

Vill, V. — a shareholder of the *Rheinische Zeitung*.— 713

Virgil (Publius Vergilius Maro) (70-19 B.C.) — Roman poet.— 109, 709

Voltaire, François Marie Arouet de (1694-1778) — French philosopher, historian, satirical writer, Enlightener.— 114, 144, 178, 202, 205, 323, 385

W

Walter, Ferdinand (1794-1879) — German jurist, Dean of the Faculty of Law at Bonn University.— 650, 657, 658

Welcker, Friedrich Gottlieb (1784-1868) — German philologist, lecturer at Bonn University.— 657

Welker, Ch. — a shareholder of the *Rheinische Zeitung*.— 713

Wenning-Ingenheim, Johann Nepomuk von (1790-1831) — German jurist, professor of civil law at Landshut and Munich universities.— 19

Westphalen, Caroline von (died 1856) — mother of Jenny von Westphalen.— 399, 674, 683, 685, 709, 729

Westphalen, Edgar von (1819-c. 1890) — brother of Jenny von Westphalen, and Karl Marx's schoolmate.— 683, 695

Westphalen, Ferdinand Otto Wilhelm Henning von (1799-1876) — Prussian statesman, Minister of the Interior (1850-58), stepbrother of Jenny von Westphalen.— 386

Westphalen, Jenny von (1814-1881) — childhood friend, fiancée and from 1843 wife of Karl Marx.— 11, 397, 399, 517, 523, 524, 557, 559, 586, 664, 666, 668, 670, 671, 673, 674, 676, 681, 683, 685, 688, 690, 691, 693, 695-98, 707-09, 727-30

Westphalen, Johann Ludwig von (1770-1842) — father of Jenny von Westphalen, privy councillor in Trier.— 27, 28, 383, 674, 681, 685, 708

Westphalen, Karl Hans Werner von (1803-1840) — stepbrother of Jenny von Westphalen, jurist.— 669

Wieland, Christoph Martin (1733-1813) — German writer.— 123

Wienenbrügge, Christian Hermann (c. 1817-1851) — student of the Faculty of Philosophy at Bonn University, later schoolmaster in Trier.— 647

Wiethaus — Prussian official; in late 1842 and early 1843, censor of the *Rheinische Zeitung*.— 396

Wigand, Otto (1795-1870) — German publisher and bookseller, owner of a firm in Leipzig which published radical writers' works.— 19, 381

Winckelmann, Johann Joachim (1717-1768) — German historian of ancient art, Enlightener.— 17

Winkler, Karl Gottlieb Theodor (pseudonym *Theodor Hell*) (1775-1856) — German writer and journalist.— 140

Wittenberg.— 699, 700

Wolf.— 628, 729

Wolff, Christian von (1679-1754) — German philosopher, physicist, mathematician, biologist, economist and jurist.— 201, 628

Wolff, Oscar Ludwig Bernhard (1799-1851) — German writer and literary historian, professor at Jena University (1830-51), friend of Heinrich Heine.— 380

Wyttenbach, Johann Hugo (1767-1848) — German historian and teacher, director of the Trier gymnasium (1815-46).— 644, 648

X

Xenocrates of Chalcedon (c. 396-c. 314 B.C.) — Greek philosopher, Plato's disciple, head of the Old Academy.— 459

Xenophanes of Colophon (c. 580-c. 470 B.C.) — Greek philosopher and poet, founder of the Eleatic school.— 66, 79, 500

Xylander (*Holtzmann*), *Guiliemus* (*Wilhelm*) (1532-1576) — German Hellenist, publisher of a number of works by Greek and Latin classics.— 431

Z

Zeno of Citium (c. 336-c. 264 B.C.) — Greek philosopher, founder of the Stoic school.— 501

Zeno of Elea (5th century B.C.) — Greek philosopher.— 79, 483, 492

Zuccalmaglio, Ferdinand Joseph Maria von (born 1790) — Prussian tax inspector, chief of the Trier Cadastre Bureau.— 337-41

Zumpt, Karl Gottlob (1792-1849) — German philologist, specialist in Roman literature, professor at Berlin University.— 704

Zuntz-Bonn, A. — a shareholder of the *Rheinische Zeitung.*— 713

INDEX OF LITERARY AND MYTHOLOGICAL NAMES

Abraham (Bib.) — 728

Achilles — the greatest of the Greek heroes in Homer's *Iliad.* — 555

Adam (Bib.) — 123, 169, 178

Aeolus (Gr. Myth.) — the god of the winds. — 491

Aether (Gr. Myth.) — upper regions of space, seat of Zeus. — 554

Ahasuerus — Wandering Jew, a character of many German legends and poems. — 630

Ajax (the Greater) (Gr. Myth.) — son of Telamon, king of Salamis, distinguished for his great strength and bravery; fought in the Trojan War. — 617

Amenthes (Myth.) — 85

Apollo — Greek god of the arts. — 104, 172, 436, 440, 581, 625

Argus (Gr. Myth.) — a hundred-eyed monster set to watch Io. — 625

Atlas — a titan of Greek mythology often represented as bearing the heavens on his shoulders. — 99

Balaam (Bib.) — 540

Banquo — a character in Shakespeare's *Macbeth.* — 627

Cerberus (Class. Myth.) — a sleepless dog guarding the entrance of Hades. — 75, 453, 484

Christ, Jesus (Bib.) — 78, 208, 212, 213, 370, 371, 488, 493, 494, 636-39

Cornwall — a character in Shakespeare's *King Lear.* — 194

Christopher, St. — patron saint of travellers, said to have been a man of exceptional strength. — 253

Cupid — the Roman god of love. — 291

Danaïdes (Gr. Myth.) — daughters of Danaüs who were condemned to pour water into a bottomless pitcher in Hades for slaying their husbands. — 75

David (Bib.) — King of Israel. — 578

Demeter (Gr. Myth.) — the goddess of the fruitful earth. — 465

Deucalion (Gr. Myth.) — son of Prometheus, renewed the human race after the deluge. — 491

Diana — a character in the play *Donna Diana* by Moreto. — 709

Doll Tearsheet — a character in Shakespeare's *King Henry IV*, Part Two. — 359

Don Carlos — a title character in Schiller's drama. — 626

Epimenides (Gr. Myth.) — a Cretan prophet said to have spent more than half a century in sleep. — 133

Eulenspiegel (Ulenspiegel), Till — a hero of German popular tales. — 212

Eve (Bib.) — 728

Falstaff — a character in several of Shakespeare's plays. — 268, 359

Faust — doctor, hero of a medieval German legend and a character in Goethe's tragedy. — 579, 580

Gabriel (Bib.) — one of the seven archangels in the Judaic and Christian religions. — 573

Gloucester — a character in Shakespeare's *King Lear.* — 291

Gratiano — a character in Shakespeare's *The Merchant of Venice.* — 256

Gretchen — the principal character in Goethe's *Faust.* — 580

Hector — one of the principal characters in the *Iliad* by Homer. — 447

Helen — according to a Greek legend, a daughter of Zeus and Leda, wife of Menelaus, King of Sparta; the most beautiful woman of her time. — 628

Hephaestus (Gr. Myth.) — a fire- and smith-god. — 431

Heracles — the most popular hero in Greek mythology. — 34, 460

Hermes (Gr. Myth.) — a messenger and herald of the gods, patron of

travellers, merchants and thieves.—
32, 185

Hulda—prophetess in Jerusalem.—318

Icarus (Gr. Myth.)—son of Daedalus, a legendary inventor and artist; he perished in a flight on artificial wings of wax and feathers.—556

Israel (Jacob) (Bib.)—144

Ixion—a king of the Lapithae; for insolence towards Hera he was banished to hell, where he was tied to a perpetually revolving wheel.—484

Jehovah (Bib.)—199

Jesus—see *Christ, Jesus.*

Joshua (Bib.)—201

Jonas (Jonah)—a prophet (Bib.)—212, 213, 214

Judas Iscariot (Judah) (Bib.)—one of the twelve apostles, betrayed Christ.—144, 370, 371

Juno—in Roman mythology, queen of the gods, sister and wife of Jupiter.—501

Jupiter (Jove)—supreme god of the Romans, identified with the Greek Zeus.—112, 481, 501, 554

Lear—the principal character of Shakespeare's *King Lear.*—291

Leda (Gr. Myth.)—the wife of Tyndarus, King of Sparta; Zeus was enamoured by her exceptional beauty.—384

Leviathan (Bib.)—a sea monster.—196

Lucretia—according to a Roman legend the wife of Tarquinius Collatinus, dishonoured by Sextus (son of Tarquin), committed suicide. This led to the fall of the king and the establishment of republican government.—628

Luke (Bib.)—one of the evangelists.—213

Mark (Bib.)—one of the evangelists.—213

Maia (Gr. Myth.)—a daughter of Atlas and Pleïone, the eldest of the Pleiades, and the mother of Hermes.—185

Marsyas (Gr. Myth.)—silenus of Anatolian origin; challenged Apollo to a contest with his lyre; Apollo, who won the contest, flayed him alive.—625

Mary Magdalene (Bib.)—616

Matthew (Bib.)—one of the evangelists.—212

Mephistopheles—a character in Goethe's *Faust,* the name of the evil spirit.—593, 622

Mignon—a character in Goethe's *Wilhelm Meisters Lehrjahre.*—618

Minerva (Rom. Myth.)—the goddess of wisdom.—34, 501

Moloch—a god of the ancient Phoenicians and Carthagenians, and also of the Hebrews in the late years of Hebrew Kingdom, to which child sacrifices were offered. The name is synonymous with a cruel force constantly requiring new victims.—104

Moses (Bib.)—205, 580, 626

Musa (Gr. Myth.)—a musician and soothsayer.—501

Oedipus (Gr. Myth.)—son of Laius and Jocasta, according to oracles, was to kill his father and marry his mother.—556

Orpheus (Gr. Myth.)—a poet and musician who was able to charm stones and tame wild beasts with his music.—501

Pallas Athena—the Greek goddess of wisdom and war.—34, 126, 172, 492, 578

Pan—the Arcadian god of forests, son of Hermes, patron of shepherds, hunters, beekeepers and fishermen.—185

Paul, the Apostle (Bib.)—37, 78, 488

Phaethon (Gr. Myth.)—the son of Helios. Driving the chariot of the sun he dropped the reins and fell into the river.— 554

Pistol— a character in Shakespeare's *The Merry Wives of Windsor, King Henry IV*, Part Two, and *King Henry V.*— 359

Pluto (Gr. Myth.) — the god of the nether world and fertility.— 185

Portia— a character in Shakespeare's *The Merchant of Venice.*— 256

Posa— marquis, a character in Schiller's *Don Carlos.*— 395

Poseidon (Gr. Myth.) — the god of the sea.— 465

Prometheus (Gr. Myth.) — a titan who stole fire from the gods and gave it to men, for which deed he was bound to a crag.— 30, 31, 68, 491

Pythia— priestess of Apollo and prophetess at Delphi.— 440

The Queen of South (*Sheba*) (Bib.) — 213

Mrs. Quickly— a character in Shakespeare's *The Merry Wives of Windsor, King Henry IV*, Part One, and *King Henry IV*, Part Two.— 359

Richard III— a character in Shakespeare's *Chronicles.*— 250

Sancho Panza— a character in Cervantes' *Don Quixote.*— 124, 211

Sassafras— a character in Wieland's *Der Neue Amadis.*— 123

Shylock— a character in Shakespeare's *The Merchant of Venice.*— 236, 256

Sibyl— one of several women in antiquity believed to possess prophetic powers; *Sibylline Books*, fabled to be sold by a Sibyl, played an important part in the religious life of Ancient Rome.— 359

Sisyphus— King of Corinth. For cheating the gods he was condemned to push a rock to the top of a hill from which it rolled down again.— 484

Solomon (Bib.) — King of Israel.— 212, 213, 629

Susannah (Bib.) — wife of Joakim, unjustly accused by the elders; was saved from death by Daniel.— 590

Telegonus— son of Odysseus and Circe, set off in search of his father and killed him not knowing who he was.— 556

Telephus— a character in Homer's *Iliad.*— 555

Thersites— a character in Greek legends, Homer's *Iliad* and Shakespeare's *Troilus and Cressida.*— 388, 617

Tristram Shandy— the principal character in Laurence Sterne's *The Life and Opinions of Tristram Shandy, Gentleman.*— 113

Venus (Rom. Myth.) — the goddess of beauty and love.— 578

Vesta (Rom. Myth.) — the goddess of the hearth and fire.— 501

Zephyr (Myth.) — the west wind, bringing warmth and rain.— 553

Zeus (Gr. Myth.) — the supreme god.— 172, 196, 465, 475, 492, 578

INDEX OF QUOTED
AND MENTIONED LITERATURE

WORKS BY KARL MARX[a]

(anon.) *The Ban on the "Leipziger Allgemeine Zeitung"*
— Das Verbot der *Leipziger Allgemeinen Zeitung.* In: *Rheinische Zeitung* Nos. 1, 4, 6, 8, 10, 13 and 16, January 1, 4, 6, 8, 10, 13 and 16, 1843.— 396

(anon.) *Comments on the Latest Prussian Censorship Instruction*
— Bemerkungen über die neueste preussische Zensurinstruktion. Von einem Rheinländer. In: *Anekdota zur neuesten deutschen Philosophie und Publicistik*, Bd. 1, Zürich und Winterthur, 1843.— 381, 383

(anon.) *The Divorce Bill. Criticism of a Criticism*
— Zum Ehescheidungsgesetzentwurf. Kritik der Kritik. In: *Rheinische Zeitung* No. 319, November 15, 1842.— 308

(anon.) *Justification of the Correspondent from the Mosel*
— Rechtfertigung des ††-Korrespondenten von der Mosel. In: *Rheinische Zeitung* Nos. 15, 17, 18, 19 and 20, January 15, 17, 18, 19 and 20, 1843.— 396

(anon.) *The Leading Article in No. 179 of the "Kölnische Zeitung"*
— Der leitende Artikel in Nr. 179 der *Kölnischen Zeitung.* In: *Rheinische Zeitung* Nos. 191, 193 and 195, Beiblätter, July 10, 12 and 14, 1842.— 390

(anon.) *The Philosophical Manifesto of the Historical School of Law*
— Das philosophische Manifest der historischen Rechtsschule. In: *Rheinische Zeitung* No. 221, Beiblatt, August 9, 1842.— 387

(anon.) *Proceedings of the Sixth Rhine Province Assembly. First Article. Debates on Freedom of the Press and Publication of the Proceedings of the Assembly of the Estates*
— Die Verhandlungen des 6. rheinischen Landtags. Von einem Rheinländer. Erster Artikel. Debatten über Pressfreiheit und Publikation der Landständischen Verhandlungen. In: *Rheinische Zeitung* Nos. 125, 128, 130, 132, 135 and 139, Beiblätter, May 5, 8, 10, 12, 15 and 19, 1842.— 387

Renard's Letter to Oberpräsident von Schaper
— An den Oberpräsidenten der Rheinprovinz von Schaper.— 714

---

[a] Editions in the language of the original are given only in cases when they were published during the author's lifetime.— *Ed.*

WORKS BY DIFFERENT AUTHORS

Aeschylus. *Prometheus vinctus.*— 30, 31, 68

Aristoteles. *De anima* libri tres, Jenae, 1833.— 38, 48, 78, 90, 505
— *De caelo.*— 51-55, 66-67, 91, 92, 93, 98, 99, 101
— *De generatione animalium.*— 42, 81, 424
— *De generatione et corruptione.*— 54, 56, 88, 92, 93, 411
— *De generatione et corruptione.* In: *Commentarii Collegii Coimbricensis Societatis Jesu, in libros de generatione et corruptione Aristotelis Stagiritae.*— 411
— *Metaphysica.*— 38, 55, 56, 58, 66, 67, 78, 79, 87, 92, 95, 98, 410, 426, 435, 439, 446
— *Physica.*— 63, 87, 96, 411
— *Physica.* In: *Commentarii Collegii Coimbricensis Societatis Jesu, in octo libros physicorum Aristotelis Stagiritae.*— 411
— *Rhetorica.*— 19

Augustinus, A. *De civitate Dei,* libri XXII, Leipzig, 1825.— 198, 205
— *Epistolae.*— 50, 90

Athenaeus, *Deipnosophistarum* libri XV.— 101

Baconi Baronis de Verulamio, F. *De dignitate et augmentis scientiarum,* Londini, 1623.— 19, 201

Bauer, B. *Die gute Sache der Freiheit und meine eigene Angelegenheit,* Zürich und Winterthur, 1842.— 400
— *Kritik der evangelischen Geschichte der Synoptiker,* Bd. 1-2, Leipzig, 1841.— 213, 214
— *Leiden und Freuden des theologischen Bewusstseins.* In: *Anekdota zur neuesten deutschen Philosophie und Publicistik,* Bd. 2, Zürich und Winterthur, 1843.— 400
— [a review:] *Die Geschichte des Lebens Jesu mit steter Rücksicht auf die vorhandenen Quellen dargestellt von Dr. von Ammon,* Bd. 1, Leipzig, 1842. In: *Anekdota zur neuesten deutschen Philosophie und Publicistik,* Bd. 2, Zürich und Winterthur, 1843.— 400
— (anon.) *Die Posaune des jüngsten Gerichts über Hegel den Atheisten und Antichristen. Ein Ultimatum,* Leipzig, 1841.— 382, 385

[Bauer, E.] *Das Juste-Milieu.* In: *Rheinische Zeitung* Nos. 156, 228, 230, 233, 235, Beiblätter, June 5, August 16, 18, 21 and 23, 1842.— 392, 399

Baur, F. C. *Das Christliche des Platonismus oder Sokrates und Christus. Eine religionsphilosophische Untersuchung,* Tübingen, 1837.— 493-97

Bayer, K. *Betrachtungen über den Begriff des sittlichen Geistes und über das Wesen der Tugend,* Erlangen, 1839.— 381

Bayle, P. *Dictionnaire historique et critique* [article: Epicure].— 47, 48, 50, 89, 90

Bible.— 144, 370, 385, 629
John.— 607, 622-25
Luke.— 213
Mark.— 213
Matthew.— 212

Brucker, J. *Institutiones historiae philosophicae usui academicae iuventutis adornatae,* Lipsiae, 1747.— 57, 94

Buhl, L. *Die Bedeutung der Provinzialstände in Preussen,* Berlin, 1842.— 303

Bülow-Cummerow [E. G. G. von]. *Preussen, seine Verfassung, seine Verwaltung, sein Verhältnis zu Deutschland*, Berlin, 1842.— 384

[Carové, F. W.] *Auch eine Stimme über "Eine Hegemonie in Deutschland".* In: *Rheinische Zeitung* No. 135, Beiblatt, May 15, 1842.— 283

Cervántes de Saavedra, M. *El Ingenioso hidalgo Don Quixote de la Mancha.*...— 124

Christiansen, J. *Die Wissenschaft der römischen Rechtsgeschichte im Grundrisse*, Bd. 1, Altona, 1838.— 386

Cicero. *De fato* liber singularis.— 43, 49, 50, 81, 89, 90
— *De finibus bonorum et malorum* libri V.— 37, 40, 41, 46, 49, 60, 77, 79, 80, 81, 89, 90, 95, 507-09
— *De natura deorum* libri III.— 37, 40, 43, 46, 51, 77, 79, 81, 82, 89, 91, 501-04
— *Tusculanarum quaestionum* libri V.— 40, 41, 80, 501

[Claessen, H.] *Die Reform der rheinischen Gemeinde-Ordnung. Zweiter Artikel. Ueber Unterschiedenheit der Gemeinde-Ordnung für Stadt und Land.* In: *Rheinische Zeitung* Nos. 312, 314, 317, Beiblätter, November 8, 10 and 13, 1842.— 270
— *Die Reform der rheinischen Gemeinde-Ordnung.* In: *Rheinische Zeitung* Nos. 307, 310, 312, 314 and 317, Beiblätter, November 3, 6, 8, 10 and 13, 1842.— 277, 278

Clemens Alexandrinus. *Stromatum* libri VIII. In: *Opera graece et latine quae exstant...*, Coloniae, 1688.— 37, 77, 80, 90, 487, 488

Coblenz, P. I. *Bernkastel, 10. Dez.* In: *Rheinische Zeitung* No. 346, December 12, 1842.— 331
— *Von der Mosel, 12. Dezember.* In: *Rheinische Zeitung* No. 348, December 14, 1842.— 331, 332

Constant de Rebecque, B. de. *De la religion considérée dans sa source ses formes et ses développements*, Deuxième édition, Paris, 1826, Tome premier.— 207

Cramer, A. W. *De verborum significatione tituli pandectarum et codicis cum variae lectionis apparatu*, Kiliae, 1811.— 19

Dézamy, T. *Calomnies et politique de M. Cabet. Réfutation par des faits et par sa biographie*, Paris [1842].— 360

Diogenes Laertius. *De clarorum philosophorum vitis, dogmatibus et apophthegmatibus libri decem.* Liber decimus. Epicurus. See: Petrus Gassendi, *Animadversiones in decimum librum Diogenis Laertii, qui est de vita, moribus, placitisque Epicuri*
— *De vitis philosophorum* libri X..., T. 1-2, Lipsiae, Tauchnitz, 1833.— 37, 38, 39, 40, 42, 44, 48, 53, 56, 58, 77, 79-83, 87, 88, 90, 91, 92, 93, 94, 95, 96, 97, 98, 99, 100, 101

Epicurus. *Fragmenta librorum II. et XI. de natura in voluminibus papyraceis ex Herculano erutis reperta ...* latine versa ... commentario illustrata a Carolo Rosinio, ex tomo II. voluminum Herculanensium emendatius edidit suasque adnotationes adscripsit Io Conradus Orellius, Lipsiae, 1818.— 56, 93, 509

Eusebius Pamphilus. *Praeparatio evangelica ...* Franciscus Vigerus ... rec., Latinè vertit, Parisiis, 1628.— 40, 42, 43, 54, 56, 60, 80-83, 92, 93, 95

Feuerbach, J. P. A. *Lehrbuch des gemeinen in Deutschland gültigen peinlichen Rechts* (4. Aufl., Giessen, 1808, 12te Originalausgabe, 1836).— 19

— *Revision der Grundsätze und Grundbegriffe des positiven peinlichen Rechts*, 2.Teile, Erfurt resp. Chemnitz, 1799-1800.— 19

Feuerbach, L. *Geschichte der neuern Philosophie von Bacon von Verulam bis Benedict Spinoza*, Ansbach, 1833.— 57, 94
— *Vorläufige Thesen zur Reformation der Philosophie.* In: *Anekdota zur neuesten deutschen Philosophie und Publicistik*, Bd. 2, Zürich und Winterthur, 1843.— 400

Fichte, J. G. *Grundlage des Naturrechts nach Prinzipien der Wissenschaftslehre*, Jena und Leipzig, 1796-97.— 12

Gaertner, G. Fr. von. *Ueber die Provinzial-Rechte. Sendschreiben an den Königl. Geheimen Justiz- und vortragenden Rath im hohen Justiz-Ministerium zu Berlin, Herrn A. W. Goetze*, Berlin, 1837.— 20

Gassendi, P. *Animadversiones in decimum librum Diogenis Laertii, qui est de vita, moribus, placitisque Epicuri*, Lugduni, 1649.— 29, 57, 94, 405-16, 417-24, 426-28, 489

Goethe, J. W. von. *Faust.*—579-80
— *Rechenschaft.*—112
— *Reineke Fuchs.*—246
— *Verschiedenes über Kunst.*— 137
— *Der Zauberlehrling.*— 155

Gratianus. *Concordia discordantium canonum* (in: *Corpus iuris canonici*).— 19

Griechische Prosaiker in neuen Übersetzungen, Bd. 15, Stuttgart, 1827
— *Lucians Göttergespräche.*—185

Grolman(n), K. von. *Grundsätze der Criminalrechts-Wissenschaft*, 4. Aufl., Giessen, 1825.— 19

Gruppe, O. F. *Bruno Bauer und die akademische Lehrfreiheit*, Berlin, 1842.—211-14

Haller, K. L. von. *Restauration der Staats-Wissenschaft oder Theorie des natürlich-geselligen Zustands; der Chimäre des künstlich-bürgerlichen entgegengesetzt*, Bd. 1-6, Winterthur, 1816-34.— 144

Hansemann, D. *Preussen und Frankreich, staatswirtschaftlich und politisch, unter vorzüglicher Berücksichtigung der Rheinprovinz*, Leipzig, 1834.— 349, 351

Hariri—see Rückert

Hegel, G. W. F. *Encyclopädie der philosophischen Wissenschaften im Grundrisse*, 3. Ausg., Heidelberg, 1830.— 495
— *Grundlinien der Philosophie des Rechts oder Naturrecht und Staatswissenschaft im Grundrisse*, Berlin, 1833. In: *Georg Wilhelm Friedrich Hegel's Werke*, Bd. 8.— 309
— *Phänomenologie des Geistes.* In: *Georg Wilhelm Friedrich Hegel's Werke*, Bd. 2, 2. Aufl., Berlin, 1841.— 400
— *Vorlesungen über die Geschichte der Philosophie.* In: *Georg Wilhelm Friedrich Hegel's Werke*, Bd. 14, Berlin, 1833.— 500

Heine, H. *Die Nordsee. 1. Zyklus: Frieden.*— 18, 394

Heineccius, J. G. *Elementa iuris civilis secundum ordinem Pandectarum, commoda auditoribus methodo adornata*, Amstelodami, 1728.— 12

[Hermes, C. H.] *Köln, 5. Juli; Köln, 29. Juli: Letztes Wort an Hrn. Philippson zu Magdeburg.* In: *Kölnische Zeitung* Nos. 187, 211, 235, Beiblätter, July 6, 30, August 23, 1842.— 391-92

Herodotus. *Historiae.*— 181

Hesiodus. *Theogonia.*— 501

[Hess, M.] *Deutschland und Frankreich in Bezug auf die Centralisationsfrage.* In: *Rheinische Zeitung* No. 137, Beilage, May 17, 1842.— 182, 183

[Holbach, P.-H.-D., baron d'.] *Système de la nature. Ou des loix du monde physique et du monde moral.* Par M. Mirabaud, Vols. 1-2, Londres, 1770.— 102

Hugo, G. *Lehrbuch des Naturrechts, als einer Philosophie des positiven Rechts, besonders des Privatrechts,* 4. Aufl., Berlin, 1819.— 203, 204, 205, 206, 207, 208, 209

[Hume, D.] *David Hume über die menschliche Natur aus dem Englischen nebst kritischen Versuchen zur Beurtheilung dieses Werks von Ludwig Heinrich Jakob,* 1. Bd.: *Ueber den menschlichen Verstand,* Halle, 1790.— 30

Juvenalis. *Satirae.*— 146

Kant, I. *Anthropologie in pragmatischer Hinsicht,* Königsberg, 1798.— 648
— *Metaphysische Anfangsgründe der Rechtslehre,* Königsberg, 1797.— 17

Klein, E. F. *Annalen der Gesetzgebung und Rechtsgelehrsamkeit in den Preussischen Staaten,* Bd. 1-26, Berlin und Stettin, 1788-1809.— 17
— *Grundsätze des gemeinen deutschen peinlichen Rechts nebst Bemerkung der preussischen Gesetze,* 2. Ausg., Halle, 1799.— 17

Köppen, C. F. *Friedrich der Grosse und seine Widersacher. Eine Jubelschrift,* Leipzig, 1840.— 30

Kosegarten, W. *Betrachtungen über die Veräusserlichkeit und Theilbarkeit des Landbesitzes mit besonderer Rücksicht auf einige Provinzen der Preussischen Monarchie,* Bohn, 1842.— 220

Lancelotti, G. P. *Institutiones iuris canonici.*— 19

Lauterbach, W. A. *Collegium theorico-practicum. Ad L. Pandectarum Libros methodo synthetica,* Vols. 1-43 und Register, Tübingen, 1690-1714.— 19

[Leibniz, G. W.] *Lettre de Mr. Leibniz à Mr. Des Maizeaux, contenant quelques éclaircissemens sur l'explication précédente, & sur d'autres endroits du système de l'harmonie préétablie etc.* Hanover ce 8 Juillet 1711. In: *Opera omnia,* T. 2, Genevae, 1768.— 37, 78

Lessing, G. E. *Laokoon, oder über die Grenzen der Mahlerey und Poesie. Mit beyläufigen Erläuterungen verschiedener Punkte der alten Kunstgeschichte,* Berlin, 1766.— 17
— *Eine Parabel. Nebst einer kleinen Bitte und einem eventualen Absageschreiben,* Braunschweig, 1778.— 328

Lucianus— see *Griechische Prosaiker in neuen Übersetzungen*

Lucretius. *De rerum natura* libri sex..., Vol. I, Lipsiae, 1801.— 416-17, 440, 464, 466-69, 470-78, 489-91
— *De rerum natura.*— 48, 49, 51, 53, 57, 59, 62, 65, 73, 90-91, 93-98, 100, 101

Luden, H. *Geschichte des teutschen Volkes,* Bd. 1-12, Gotha, 1825-37.— 17

Marheineke, Ph. K. *Einleitung in die öffentlichen Vorlesungen über die Bedeutung der Hegelschen Philosophie in der christlichen Theologie,* Berlin, 1842.— 391

Molière, J. B. Poquelin. *Les Fâcheux.*—322

Montesquieu, Ch.-L. de. *De l'esprit des lois,* T. 1, Genève, 1748.—227

Mosen, J. *Der Congress von Verona*, Berlin, 1842.—289-91
— *Herzog Bernhard.*—291
Mühlenbruch, Ch. Fr. *Doctrina pandectarum*, Vol. 1-3, Halis Saxonum, 1823-25 (3. Ausg., 1838).—19

Ovid. *Tristia.*—17, 533

[Pfützner.] *Ueber die Broschüre an die hohe zweite Kammer der sächsischen Ständever-sammlung.* In: *Rheinische Zeitung* Nos. 71 and 73, Beiblätter, March 12 and 14, 1843.—399
Philoponus. In: *Scholia in Aristotelem*
Plato. *Parmenides.*—497
— *Res publica.*—440
— *Timaeus.*—497
Plotinus. *Enneads.*—498
Plutarchus Chaeronensis. *Commentarius Ne suaviter quidem vivi posse secundum Epicuri decreta, docens.* In: *Quae extant omnia,* cum latina, interpretatione Hermanni Cruserii, Gulielmi Xylandri..., T. 2: *Continens Moralia.* Gulielmo Xylandro interprete, Francofurti, 1599.—51, 81, 90, 91, 102, 103, 431, 442, 443, 445-53, 455-56
— *Adversus Colotem.*—37, 39, 59, 61, 77-80, 95, 442, 457-58, 459-62, 463, 464, 465
— *De animae procreatione e Timaeo.* In: *Varia scripta, quae moralia vulgo vocantur...,* T. 6, Lipsiae (1815, 1820, 1829) (Tauchnitz).—50, 90
— *Caius Marius.*—84
Proudhon, P.-J. *Qu'est-ce que la propriété? Ou recherches sur le principe du droit et du gouvernement....* Premier mémoire, Paris, 1840.—220
[Prutz, R.] *Die Jahrbücher der Gegenwart und die deutschen Jahrbücher.* In: *Rheinische Zeitung* No. 43, Beiblatt, February 12, 1843.—399
[Pseudo-Plutarch.] *De placitis philosophorum libri V.* In: Plutarchus Chaeronensis, *Varia scripta, quae moralia vulgo vocantur...,* T. 5, Lipsiae (1815, 1820, 1829) (Tauchnitz).—37, 44, 54, 60, 77, 79, 81, 83, 89, 92, 93, 94, 95

Reimarus, H. S. *Allgemeine Betrachtungen über die Triebe der Thiere, hauptsächlich über ihre Kunst-Triebe, zum Erkenntniss des Zusammenhanges der Welt, des Schöpfers und unser selbst,* [Hamburg,] 1760.—19
Ritter, H. *Geschichte der Philosophie alter Zeit,* 1. Teil, Hamburg, 1829.—55, 79, 92, 435, 498-500
Rousseau, J.-J. *Du contrat social; ou principes du droit politique,* Amsterdam, 1762.—205
[Rückert, F.] *Die Verwandlungen des Abu Seid von Serug, oder die Makamen des Hariri,* Stuttgart, 1826 (Tübingen, 1837).—170
[Ruge, A.] *Aktenmässige Darlegung der Censurverhältnisse der Hallischen und Deutschen Jahrbücher in den Jahren 1839, 1841, 1842.* In: *Anekdota zur neuesten deutschen Philosophie und Publicistik,* Bd. 1, Zürich und Winterthur, 1843.—400
— *Das "christlich-germanische" Justemilieu. Die Berliner "literarische Zeitung". 1842. Januar und Februar.* In: *Anekdota zur neuesten deutschen Philosophie und Publicistik,* Bd. 2, Zürich und Winterthur, 1843.—400

— *Sächsische Zustände*. In: *Rheinische Zeitung* No. 268, Beiblatt, September 25, 1842.— 391

Ruge, A., and Wigand, O. *An die Hohe zweite Kammer der sächsischen Ständeversammlung. Beschwerde über die durch ein hohes Ministerium des Innern angeordnete und am 3. Januar 1843 ausgeführte Unterdrückung der Zeitschrift "Deutsche Jahrbücher für Wissenschaft und Kunst"*, Braunschweig, 1843.— 399

Sallet, Fr. von. *Laien-Evangelium*, Jamben, Leipzig, 1842.— 370-72

Savigny, Fr. C. von. *Das Recht des Besitzes*. Eine civilistische Abhandlung (1. Aufl., Giessen, 1803, 6. Aufl., Giessen, 1837).— 15, 19
— *Der zehente Mai 1788. Beytrag zur Geschichte der Rechtswissenschaft*, Berlin, 1838.— 204

Schaubach, J. K. *Ueber Epikur's astronomische Begriffe nebst einem Nachtrage zu Nr. 195 des A[llgemeinen] Anz[eigers] d. D. 1837*. In: *Archiv für Philologie und Paedagogik*, Bd. 5, Heft 4, Leipzig, 1839.— 47, 58, 89, 95

Schelling, F. W. J. *Philosophische Briefe über Dogmatismus und Kriticismus* (1795). In: *F. W. J. Schelling's philosophische Schriften*, Bd. 1, Landshut, 1809.— 103, 105
— *Vom Ich als Princip der Philosophie, oder über das Unbedingte im menschlichen Wissen* (1795).— 103

Schiller, F. W. von. *Über naive und sentimentalische Dichtung.*— 112
— *Die Worte des Glaubens.*— 136

Scholia in Aristotelem. Collegit Christianus Aug. Brandis. In: Aristoteles: *Opera*, ed. Acad. Reg. Borusica, Vol. 4, Berolini, 1836.— 39, 42, 43, 48, 54-55, 61, 63, 79, 81, 83, 87-88, 90, 92, 93-96

Seneca. *Opera, quae exstant, integris Justi Lipsii, J. Fred. Gronovii, et selectis variorum comm. illustrata*, T. 1 u. 2, Amstelodami, 1672.— 44-45, 83, 90, 479-84
— *De constantia sapientis, sive quod in sapientem non cadit injuria.*— 480
— *Ad Paulinum de brevitate vitae liber unus*, T. 1.— 483
— *De vita beata ad Gallionem fratrem liber unus*, T. 1.— 480, 483
— *De otio aut secessu sapientis libri pars*, T. 1.— 479, 483
— *Ad Aebucium liberalem de Beneficiis libri VII*, T. 1.— 51, 90, 482, 483
— *Ad Lucilium epistolae*, T. 2.— 41, 80-82, 479-84
— *Ad Lucilium naturalium quaestionum libri VIII*, T. 2.— 44-45, 83, 482
— *De morte Cl. Caesaris*, T. 2.— 484

Sextus Empiricus. *Opera, quae exstant. Magno ingenii acumine scripti, Pyrrhoniarum hypotyposeon libri III, ... Adversus mathematicos, hoc est, eos qui disciplinas profitentur, libri X ...*, Coloniae Allobrogum, 1621.— 37, 41, 59, 63, 65, 78, 80-81, 92, 95, 96, 427-30, 499, 500

Shakespeare, W. *Hamlet, Prince of Denmark.*— 204, 273
— *Julius Caesar.*— 366
— *King Henry IV*, Part One and Part Two.— 268, 323, 359
— *King Lear.*— 194, 289, 290, 291
— *Life and Death of King Richard III.*— 250, 617
— *The Merchant of Venice.*— 236, 256
— *A Midsummer Night's Dream.*— 139
— *Othello, the Moor of Venice.*— 288
— *Troilus and Cressida.*— 617

Simplicius. In: *Scholia in Aristotelem*

Solger, K. W. F. *Erwin. Vier Gespräche über das Schöne und die Kunst,* 2 Teile, Berlin, 1815.— 17

Spinoza, B. *Ethica ordine geometrico demonstrata et in quinque partes distincta.* In: *Opera...,* Amsterdam, 1677.— 54, 112, 469

Sterne, L. *The Life and Opinions of Tristram Shandy, Gentleman.*— 113

Stobaeus, I. *Sententiae, ex thesauris graecorum delectae... Huic editioni ac. ... Eclogarum physicarum et ethicarum libri duo...,* Aureliae Allobrogum, 1609.— 42, 44, 46, 56, 60, 61, 65, 82, 83, 88, 89, 93, 96, 481, 484-86

Tacitus. *Germania.*— 15
— *Historiae.*— 131
Terence. *Andria.*— 316
Tertullianus. *De Carne christi.*— 190
Themistius. In: *Scholia in Aristotelem*
Thibaut, A. F. J. *System des Pandekten-Rechts,* Bd. 1-2. Jena, 1803-05.— 12
Thucydides. *De Bello Peloponnesiaco libri VIII.*— 181

Ueber ständische Verfassung in Preussen, Stuttgart und Tübingen, 1842.— 303

[Uhland, L.] *Die Rache.*— 154

Vanini, L. *Amphitheatrum aeternae providentiae....*— 323
Vatke, W. *Die menschliche Freiheit in ihrem Verhältnis zur Sünde und zur göttlichen Gnade,* Berlin, 1841.— 381
Vergil. *Aeneis.*— 109
Voltaire, Fr.-M. A. de. *La Bible enfin expliquée.*— 323
— *L'enfant prodigue.* In: *Oeuvres complètes de Voltaire,* Tome septieme, Gotha, 1784.— 114

Wenning-Ingenheim, J. N. v. *Lehrbuch des Gemeinen Civilrechtes, nach Heise's Grundriss eines Systems des gemeinen Civil-Rechtes zum Behuf von Pandecten-Vorlesungen,* Bd. 1-3, München, 1822-25 (4. Aufl., München, 1831-32).— 19
Wieland. *Der Neue Amadis.*— 123
Winckelmann, J. *Geschichte der Kunst des Alterthums,* 2 Teile (Dresden, 1764, 1767).— 17

DOCUMENTS

Allgemeine Gesetz wegen Anordnung der Provinzialstände. Vom 5ten Juni 1823—see *Gesetz-Sammlung für die Königlichen Preussischen Staaten. 1823*
Allgemeines Landrecht für die Preussischen Staaten, 2. Aufl., Berlin, 1794 (Neue Ausgabe, Berlin, 1804).— 192-93
Capitularia regum Francorum. In: *Monumenta Germaniae historica. Legum* T. 1 und 2. Hrsg. von G. H. Pertz, Hannover, 1835-37.— 19

La Charte Constitutionnelle, das ist: Verfassungs-Urkunde der Franzosen, franz. und deutsch, Berlin, 1830.— 192-93

Gesetz-Sammlung für die Königlichen Preussischen Staaten. 1823, Berlin [1824].— 294

Gregorius XVI. Encyclica *Mirari vos*, August 15, 1832.— 323

[*Instruktion über die Verwaltung der Gemeinde und Institutenwaldungen in den Regierungsbezirken Koblenz und Trier.*] Koblenz, August 31, 1839.— 335

Mitteilungen des Vereins zur Förderung der Weinkultur an der Mosel und Saar zu Trier, H. IV.— 337, 338, 339, 340, 341, 342, 343

Preussischen Landrecht—see *Allgemeines Landrecht für die Preussischen Staaten*

Sitzungs-Protokolle des sechsten Rheinischen Provinzial-Landtags, Coblenz, 1841.— 137-49, 152-60, 168-74, 175, 176-80, 224-26, 228, 229, 235, 236, 237, 238-40, 242, 243-59

Zensuredikt *Erneuertes Censur-Edict für die Preussischen Staaten exclusive Schlesien*, Berlin, December 19, 1788.— 350

Zensuredikt *Verordnung, wie die Zensur der Druckschriften nach dem Beschluss des deutschen Bundes vom 20sten September d. J. auf fünf Jahre einzurichten ist. Vom 18ten Oktober 1819.* In: *Gesetzsammlung für die Königlich Preussischen Staaten,* 1819, No. 20.— 111, 114-19, 124-25, 128-29, 285, 350

Zensurinstruktion der Preussischen Regierung vom 24. Dezember 1841. In: *Allgemeine Preussische Staats-Zeitung* No. 14, January 14, 1842.— 109, 111, 114-20, 122-25, 128-30, 351, 353

ANONYMOUS ARTICLES AND REPORTS
PUBLISHED IN PERIODIC EDITIONS

Aachener Zeitung

No. 277, October 6, 1842: *Aachen, 6. Oktober. Kommunisten in Preussen.*— 222

No. 293, October 22, 1842: *Aachen, 22. Okt.*— 222, 223

Allgemeine Preussische Staats-Zeitung

No. 75, March 16, 1842: *Die Wirkung der Zensur-Verfügung vom 24. Dezember 1841;*

No. 78, March 19, 1842: *Die Besprechung inländischer Angelegenheiten, ihre Ausdehnung u. natürlichen Bedingnisse;*

No. 86, March 26, 1842: *Die inländische Presse u. die inländische Statistik.*— 132-36

Allgemeine Zeitung

No. 284, October 11, 1842: *Die Kommunistenlehren.*— 215, 219, 220, 222
Karlsruhe, 8. Oktober.— 219
London, 5. Oktober 1842.— 219

No. 329, November 25, 1842: *Leipzig (Julius Mosen u. die Rhein. Zeitung).*— 290, 291

Nos. 335 and 336,
December 1 and 2, 1842,
Beilagen: *Über die Zusammensetzung der ständischen Aus-
                                    schüsse in Preussen. Berlin, im November.*—
                                    292, 293, 294, 295, 296, 297, 298, 299,
                                    300, 303

No. 360, December 26, 1842:   *London, 20. Dez. (Atlas), Fussnote.*— 359

No. 4, January 4, 1843:   *München, 2. Jan.*— 359-60

Düsseldorfer Zeitung

No. 5, January 5, 1843:   *Berlin, vom 1. Januar.*— 315

Elberfelder Zeitung

No. 315, November 14, 1842:   *Schreiben aus Berlin, vom 10. November.*— 287

No. 5, January 5, 1843:   *Elberfeld.*— 315, 316
                                    Schreiben aus Berlin, vom 30. Dez.—315

Frankfurter Journal

No. 349, December 19, 1842,
Beilage: *Coblenz. 18. Decbr.*—342

Kölnische Zeitung

No. 179, June 28, 1842:   *Köln, 27. Juni.*— 184-95, 202-03

No. 309, November 5, 1842,
Beilage.— 266-68
No. 315, November 11, 1842:   *Köln, 10. Nov.*— 268-71

No. 319, November 15, 1842:   *Berlin, 11. Nov.*— 280

No. 320, November 16, 1842,
Beilage: *Köln, 14. November.*— 278

No. 365, December 31, 1842:   *Leipzig, 27. Dez.*—313, 319

No. 5, January 5, 1843:   *Köln, 4. Jan.*— 315

No. 9, January 9, 1843:   *Vom Niederrhein.*— 319, 320

No. 11, January 11, 1843:   *Köln, 10. Jan.*— 322, 323

Königlich Privilegirte Preussische Staats- Kriegs- und Friedens-Zeitung

No. 138, June 17, 1842.— 390

Mefistofeles. Revue der deutschen Gegenwart in Skizzen und Umrissen
Nos. 1 and 2, 1842:   *Die Augsburger "Allgemeine Zeitung" in ihrer
                                    tiefsten Erniedrigung.*—215

Rheinische Zeitung für Politik, Handel und Gewerbe

No. 146, May 26, 1842,
Beiblatt: *Hegemonie in Deutschland.*— 283

No. 172, June 21, 1842,
Beiblatt: *Weitere Verhandlungen über die Hegemonie
                                  Preussens.*— 283

No. 226, August 14, 1842,
Beilage: *Ein Wort als Einleitung zur Frage: entspricht
                                  die rheinische Kommunal-Verfassung den
                                  Anforderungen der Gegenwart?*— 334

No. 241, August 29, 1842:   *Aus dem Hannoverschen, 25. August.*— 392

Nos. 265, 268, 275 and 277,
September 22 and 25, October
2 and 4, 1842, Beiblätter: *Fehlgriffe der liberalen Opposition in Han-
                                  nover.*— 264

No. 273, September 30, 1842:   *Die Berliner Familienhäuser.*— 215

No. 280, October 7, 1842:   *Strassburg, 30. Sept.*— 216

No. 292, October 19, 1842:   *Pfalz, 12. Okt.*— 222

No. 310, November 6, 1842,
Beiblatt: *Bemerkungen über den Entwurf einer Verord-
                                  nung über Ehescheidung, vorgelegt von dem
                                  Ministerium für Revision der Gesetze im Juli
                                  1842.*— 274

No. 314, November 10, 1842:   *Köln, 9. Nov.*— 271

No. 317, November 13, 1842:   *Vom Main.*— 290, 291

No. 322, November 18, 1842:   *Redaktionelle Note.*— 290

Rhein- und Mosel-Zeitung

No. 6, January 6, 1843:   *Vom Rhein, den 4. Jan.*— 316

No. 11, January 11, 1843:   *Vom Rhein, den 9. Jan.*— 325, 326

                                  Koblenz, den 10. Jan.— 324, 327, 328

No. 15, January 15, 1843,
Beilage: *Koblenz, den 13. Jan.*— 328, 330

No. 67, March 8, 1843:   *Vom Rheine, den 6. März.*— 366, 367

No. 70, March 11, 1843,
Beilage: *Friedrich v. Sallets Laien-Evangelium.*— 370

No. 72, March 13, 1843:   *Vom Rhein, den 11. März.*— 366, 373, 376

Trier'sche Zeitung

No. 63, March 6, 1843:   *Friedrich v. Sallet ist tot!*— 370

INDEX OF PERIODICALS

Aachener Zeitung—see *Stadt Aachener Zeitung*

Abendzeitung—a literary daily published in Dresden in 1817-50 and in Leipzig in 1851-57.—140

Allgemeine Königsberger Zeitung—see *Königsberger Allgemeine Zeitung*

Allgemeine Preussische Staats-Zeitung (Berlin)—a semi-official organ of the Prussian government published under this title from 1819 to 1843; appeared six times a week.—132, 133, 134, 135, 136, 262, 313, 317, 356, 362, 387

Allgemeine Zeitung (Augsburg)—a conservative daily founded in 1798; published in Augsburg in 1810-82.—135, 196, 215-23, 283, 288, 289, 290, 291, 292, 300, 315, 318, 359, 360, 708

Anekdota zur neuesten deutschen Philosophie und Publicistik (Zurich and Winterthur)—a two-volume collection published in 1843, edited by Arnold Ruge. Among its contributors were Karl Marx, Bruno Bauer and Ludwig Feuerbach.—382, 385, 389, 391, 393

Archiv für Philologie und Pädagogik (Leipzig)—published from 1831 to 1855 as a supplement to the magazine *Neue Jahrbücher für Philologie und Pädagogik.*—89

Augsburger Zeitung—see *Allgemeine Zeitung*

Berliner politisches Wochenblatt—a conservative weekly published from 1831 to 1841 with the participation of Karl Ludwig von Haller, Heinrich Leo, Friedrich von Raumer and others; it was patronised by King Frederick William IV.—144, 196, 216

Berlinische Nachrichten von Staats- und gelehrten Sachen—published six times a week from 1740 to 1874. In the early 40s of the 19th century it was a semi-official government paper; was also known after its publisher as *Spenersche Zeitung.*—132

Correspondent—see *Staats- und Gelehrte Zeitung des Hamburgischen unpartheiischen Correspondenten*

Deutsche Jahrbücher für Wissenschaft und Kunst—a literary and philosophical journal, a continuation of the *Hallische Jahrbücher*, published from July 1841 by the Left

Hegelians in Leipzig and edited by Arnold Ruge. In January 1843 it was suppressed by the Saxon government and prohibited throughout Germany by order of the Federal Diet.— 196, 381, 382, 390, 396, 398

Deutsche Tribüne (Munich, Hamburg)—a radical newspaper published from 1831 to 1832; eventually suppressed by the government.— 392

Deutscher Musenalmanach (Leipzig)—a liberal annual published from 1829 to 1838 and edited by Adelbert von Chamisso and Gustav Schwab.— 19

Deutsch-Französische Jahrbücher—a yearly published in German in Paris, edited by Karl Marx and Arnold Ruge. Only the first issue, a double one, came out in February 1844.— 398, 728

Didaskalia. Blätter für Geist, Gemüth und Publicitat (Frankfurt am Main)—a literary supplement to the *Frankfurter Journal*, published from 1826 to 1903.— 287

Düsseldorfer Zeitung—a daily published under this title from 1826 to 1926; was liberal in the 40s of the 19th century.— 315

Elberfelder Zeitung—a daily published from 1834 to 1904; was conservative in the 30s and 40s of the 19th century.— 287, 315, 316

Frankfurter Journal (Frankfurt am Main)—a daily founded in the 17th century and published up to 1903; was liberal in the 40s of the 19th century.— 342

Gemeinnütziges Wochenblatt (Bernkastel)—a weekly published in the mid-30s of the 19th century.— 352

Les Guêpes (Paris)—a satirical monthly published by the French radical publicist Alphonse Karr from 1839.— 316

Hamburger Correspondent—see *Staats- und Gelehrte Zeitung des Hamburgischen unpartheiischen Correspondenten*

Hannoversche Zeitung—a daily, organ of the Hanover government, founded in 1832.— 390

Historisch-politische Blätter für das katholische Deutschland (Munich)—a clerical magazine published from 1838 to 1923.— 316, 324, 325, 328, 329

Jahrbücher—see *Deutsche Jahrbücher für Wissenschaft und Kunst*

Jahrbücher der Gegenwart (Stuttgart and Tübingen)—a weekly published from July 1843 to 1848, edited by the theologian Albert Schwegler.— 399

Journal des Débats politiques et littéraires—a conservative daily published in Paris from 1789; a government organ during the July monarchy.— 135

Kölnische Zeitung—a daily published under this title from 1802 to 1945; defended the Catholic Church in the 30s and early 40s of the 19th century.— 184, 185, 193, 196, 202, 266, 268-73, 277-78, 280, 313, 315, 318, 319, 320, 321, 322, 323, 370, 390

Königlich Privilegirte Preussische Staats- Kriegs- und Friedens-Zeitung (Königsberg)—a daily published under this title from 1752 to 1850; was radical in the 40s of the 19th century.— 201, 390

Königlich privilegirte Berlinische Zeitung von Staats- und gelehrten Sachen—a daily published in Berlin from 1785; also known as the *Vossische Zeitung* after its owner.— 132

Königsberger Allgemeine Zeitung—a daily published from 1843 to 1845; semi-official organ.— 362

Leipziger Allgemeine Zeitung—a daily published from 1837; was radical in the early 40s of the 19th century. At the end of December 1842 it was suppressed in Prussia; in Saxony it appeared until April 1, 1843.—311, 313-16, 317-18, 323, 324, 325, 326, 327, 329, 396, 717

Literarische Zeitung (Berlin)—a literary paper published once or twice a week at the expense of the government from 1834 to 1849.—400

Mannheimer Abendzeitung—a radical daily published from 1842 to 1849.—222, 223

Mefistofeles. Revue der deutschen Gegenwart in Skizzen und Umrissen (Leipzig and Kassel, 1842, Münster, 1843-44)—a magazine published from 1842 to 1844 by the liberal publicist Friedrich Steinmann; only five issues appeared.—215

Mittheilungen des Vereins zur Förderung der Weinkultur an der Mosel und Saar zu Trier—organ of the Trier Society for the Promotion of Viticulture in the Mosel and Saar area, published in the early 40s of the 19th century.—337, 342-43

Münchener politische Blätter—see *Historisch-politische Blätter für das katholische Deutschland*

Le National (Paris)—a daily published from 1830 to 1851; in the 40s—organ of the moderate republicans.—237

Preussische Staats-Zeitung—see *Allgemeine Preussische Staats-Zeitung*

Rheinische Zeitung für Politik, Handel und Gewerbe—a daily published in Cologne from January 1, 1842, to March 31, 1843. It was founded by representatives of the Rhenish bourgeoisie opposing Prussian absolutism. Some of the Young Hegelians contributed to it. In April 1842 Karl Marx began to contribute to it, and in October of the same year he became one of its editors and turned the paper into a mouthpiece of revolutionary-democratic ideas.—182, 194, 201, 215, 216, 217, 220, 222-24, 265, 266, 270, 271, 272, 273, 277, 278, 279, 282-85, 286, 288-91, 299, 307, 315, 318, 319, 321, 322, 324, 325, 327, 328, 330, 331, 332-35, 336, 360, 361, 362-65, 366, 367, 373, 374, 376, 387, 389, 397, 400, 710, 711, 712, 714-19, 721, 723, 725-26

Rhein- und Mozel-Zeitung (Koblenz)—a daily Catholic paper published from 1831 to 1850.—315, 316, 322, 323-29, 357, 366, 367, 368, 369, 370, 371, 372, 373, 374, 375

Spenersche Zeitung—see *Berlinische Nachrichten von Staats- und gelehrten Sachen*

Staats- und Gelehrte Zeitung des Hamburgischen unpartheiischen Correspondenten—a paper published under this title from 1814 to 1869; conservative in the 40s of the 19th century.—196, 283, 316

Staats-Zeitung—see *Allgemeine Preussische Staats-Zeitung*

Stadt Aachener Zeitung—a daily published under this title from 1815 to 1868; in the 40s of the 19th century, organ of the anti-clericals.—222, 223

Tribüne—see *Deutsche Tribüne*

Trier'sche Zeitung—a daily founded in 1757; published under this title from 1815. It became a radical organ in the early 40s of the 19th century.—370, 371

Vossische Zeitung—see *Königlich privilegirte Berlinische Zeitung von Staats- und gelehrten Sachen*

SUBJECT INDEX

A

Absolute idea— 10, 85, 491-92
Abstraction— 8, 44, 48, 50-52, 56, 62-63, 65, 71, 73-76, 104, 392, 413, 419, 424-25, 426, 435, 437, 439, 441, 452, 453-55, 457, 464, 471, 475-76, 490-93, 505
Accidens— see *Substance*
Activity, practical— 439
Administration— 344-48
   — communal system— 267, 270, 271, 277
Agnosticism— 428
Aim— 438, 439, 636
   — and means— 3, 7
Alexandrian school of philosophy— 34-35, 189-90, 491
Alienation (Entfremdung)— 61, 62, 64, 509
America, North— 162, 167
Analogy— 65, 69, 119, 413, 493, 494
Ancient philosophy— 420, 423, 428, 432, 436
   See also *Greek philosophy, Roman philosophy*
Animal— 3, 75, 189, 230-31, 446, 452-53
Anthropomorphism— 66-67
Antinomy— 39, 59, 70
Antiquity, the— 190, 419-20, 423
   See also *Ancient philosophy, Classics, Greece, ancient, Rome, ancient*

Appearance— see *Essence and appearance*
Arbitrariness— 130, 441, 473
Art— 11, 19, 52, 189, 371, 431, 492, 636, 640, 642
   — Dutch— 171
   See also *Sculpture*
Assembly of the estates— 136-37, 145-51, 293, 297-301, 303, 304, 321, 322
Assembly, political— 151
Astrology— 66-70
Astronomy— 66-70, 170
   —Copernicus' discovery— 201, 361
Ataraxy— 51, 68-70, 72, 419, 432, 443, 449-50
Atheism— 68-70, 190-91, 323, 393, 395
   — and existence of God— 103, 104-05, 425
   — in antiquity— 29-31, 69-71
   — in the Middle Ages— 323
Athens, ancient— 137, 492
Atomistics— 32, 38-39, 42, 46-65, 70-71, 73, 412-16, 419, 424, 426, 430, 432, 441, 454-56, 470-78, 498-99, 505
   — concept and qualities of the atom— 48-49, 51-58, 60-64, 414, 475, 486
   — and teaching on essence— 58-62, 476-77, 478
   — and chance and necessity— 52, 412-13, 415
   — and teaching on motion— 47-49, 416

— repulsion of atoms—46, 47, 52, 53, 70, 416
— declination of atoms from the straight line—46, 47-51, 53, 416, 472-75
Authority—310, 506

B

Babylon, ancient—432
St. Bartholomew's night—197
Becoming—463
Being—38, 42, 45, 50, 51, 62, 63, 415, 416, 454, 455-56, 458, 462, 463, 471, 473, 505
Belgian revolution of 1830-31—143
Belgium—143
Berlin—303, 386, 390
Bible—144
See also Gospels
Bliss—451
Body, bodies—58-59, 424, 432, 444
— celestial body—70-72, 418-20
Books, book publishing—164, 175, 398
Bourgeoisie—169, 216
Brain—195
Bureaucracy—126, 131, 343-45, 347-48, 349, 363, 365
— and state—131, 321, 344-45
— and people—321
Byzantium—200, 318

C

Castes—230
Categories, philosophical—71, 155, 426
— Categorical imperative (Kant)—439
Catholicism—117, 197, 199, 316, 324-25, 329, 389-90
See also St. Bartholomew's night
Cause—43, 44, 50, 430
Censorship—109, 122-31, 165
— and freedom of the press—132, 133, 139-41, 153-55, 158, 159, 161, 162-64, 177, 181, 351, 353, 356-57, 393, 396
— censor—165, 166
— and police—161-62, 164, 166-67
See also Press
Centralisation—298, 299
Chance—see Necessity and chance
Chartism—216
China—126

Christianity—29, 116-17, 190-92, 197-201, 370-71, 400
— and its ties with philosophy—495-96
— its world outlook—371-72, 431, 432
— redemption, the—478
— and Christ as religion personified—494
See also Catholicism, Church, Protestantism
Church
— and state—117-18, 198-200, 274-75
— Christian—495
— and ancient philosophy—29
— Fathers of the Church—29, 37, 495
See also Clergy
Classes—121, 123, 234, 235
— and state—126, 129
Classics, the—202, 468-69, 475
See also Mythology
Class struggle—216
Clergy—302, 325
Commissions of the estates in Prussia—292, 297-306
Communism (communist ideas, communist movement)—215-21, 393, 394
Community—246, 335
Concept—12, 15, 48, 49, 52-54, 60-64, 66, 104, 309, 410, 413, 416, 426, 437, 455, 505
Concrete, the—424, 490
Consciousness—42, 61, 72-73, 74, 84-85, 131, 413-15, 419, 420, 422, 424-25, 454, 505, 506, 509
— ordinary, common—415, 448, 457, 494
— philosophical—416, 441, 448, 457, 506
— philosophising—419, 425, 440
— sensuous—74, 425
— individual—421, 491, 492
Contradiction—12, 38, 41, 45, 47-49, 53-58, 61, 62, 64, 71, 72, 73, 85, 86, 212, 414, 419, 429, 440, 491, 504
Court and legal procedure—166, 254-55, 259, 260-61, 384
See also Prussia
Crime—228, 229, 235, 236, 251, 252-53

Critique— 85, 86, 104
Cuba— 262
Cult— 66, 172, 199
— worship of animals— 230, 263
Culture— 165, 167, 195, 292, 636
Custom— 230-33
Customs Union— 219, 365
Cynics— 34, 35, 491
Cyrenaics— 34, 35, 431, 504

D

Death— see *Life and death*
Definition, determination— 12, 60-61, 413, 415, 425, 429-30, 438, 443, 448, 498
Deity, divinity, god, gods— 3, 4, 18, 30-31, 121, 144-45, 147, 168, 169, 199, 230, 425, 430-31, 437, 495, 506
— pagan— 104, 172
— of antiquity— 51, 68, 84, 104, 172, 430, 432, 435, 436, 475
— Christian— 104, 636-39
— ontological proof of the existence of god— 103-04
— concept of god in Epicurean philosophy— 30-31, 51, 66, 418, 432, 450-51, 473, 505. 639
— as seen by Aristotle— 189
— as seen by Lucretius— 474-75
— as seen by Plato— 636
— as seen by Plotinus— 498
— as seen by Plutarch— 84, 449-51
Despotism— 130, 160, 177
Determinism— 43, 48, 49, 415, 418, 473-74
Development— 12, 60
— philosophical— 462
— political— 178, 202
Dialectics— 18, 264, 412, 443, 451-52, 457-58, 491-92, 493-94, 498, 504
District president— 355, 357
Divorce— 274, 275, 307-10
See also *Family, Marriage*
Doctors' club— 19
See also *Young Hegelianism*
Dogmas, religious— 191-92, 197, 200
Dogmatism— 12, 45
Dualism (of Anaxagoras)— 435
Duty— 3

E

Eclecticism— 34-35
Education— 154, 193, 208, 289, 292, 438
Egypt, ancient— 176
Eleatics (*Eleatic school of philosophy*)— 436, 504
Elements (*in ancient philosophy*)— 469-70, 486
Empirical, the— 448-49
Empiricism— 41, 45, 58, 65, 73, 76, 413, 432, 438-39, 448-49, 453-54, 456-57, 494-96, 499
Energy— 436
England— 178, 219, 286, 302
— history— 156
— constitution— 302
— industry— 286
— labour movement— 216
— the press— 141, 142, 311-12, 317
— and problems of communism— 215-16, 219
See also *Chartism*
English revolution of 1640-60— 142
Enjoyment, pleasure— 447, 449-51, 473
Enlightenment, the— 144, 161, 202, 203, 205
Epicurean philosophy— 29, 30, 34-36, 46, 50, 71-72, 101, 404-509
— its principle— 71-73, 412, 415, 445-46, 505-06
Epoch— 182, 491-92, 500-01
Epos, epic poetry— 475
Equality (social)— 230, 347
See also *Inequality* (social)
Essence and appearance— 39-40, 45, 61-65, 68-69, 71, 471
Estates— 145, 169, 170, 175-76, 177-80, 231, 232, 241, 262, 292-306
— princely— 138, 141, 143, 145, 152, 169, 240
— knightly— 138, 145, 146, 148, 151, 156, 169, 239
— urban— 138, 169, 170, 239
— in Plato's Republic— 440, 495
See also *Peasantry, Workers*
Ethics— 35, 68, 504
See also *Morality*
Evil—see *Morality*
Existence— 469-70, 505-06
— and essence— 61, 71, 309-10

— empirical—76, 454
— and appearance—64
Experiment—167
Externalisation (Entäusserung)—54, 57

F

Family—308-09
See also *Divorce, Marriage*
Fear—74, 75, 448, 452-53, 455
Fetishism—189
Feudalism—230
Feuerbachianism—386, 400
Fichte's philosophy—12, 18, 494, 577
Forests and forest-owners—237-38, 239-40, 246-47, 250-53. 260, 262
Form and content—15, 35, 36, 43, 70-72, 129, 264, 282, 360, 420, 430, 454-55, 456, 469-70, 509
Fourierism—216, 220
France—239-40
— and the press—143, 167, 311-12, 318
— history—142, 398
— constitution—302, 303
— landed property—302-03
— workers' movement—216
— and problems of communism—216, 219
See also *Enlightenment, French philosophy, French revolution of 1789-94, French revolution of 1830 (July), Huguenots*
"The Free"—390, 393-95
Freedom—42, 47, 62, 72, 85, 131, 132-33, 144-45, 151, 157, 171-74, 199, 200, 230, 256, 260, 264, 286, 301, 359, 365, 385, 392, 394, 397, 418, 421, 443, 444, 640-62
— abstract—419
— from premises—432, 473, 474, 478
— inner—209, 414, 415, 421, 444, 448, 449, 468, 491-92, 496
— and individual—161-62, 169, 208, 301, 306, 334
— of speech—355, 357-58, 432
— of the press—114-15, 132-81, 224, 337, 349, 353
— and law—162

— and constitution—392
— and arbitrariness—162, 165
— and censorship—154, 155, 158, 163-64, 166-67, 397
French philosophy—423
French revolution of 1789-94—139, 143
See also *Jacobin dictatorship*
French revolution of 1830 (July)—264
Friendship—see *Morality*

G

German literature—140-41, 178, 290-91, 382
German philosophy—140, 195
See also *Feuerbachianism, Fichte's philosophy, Hegelianism, Kantianism, Schelling's philosophy*
Germany—114-15, 138, 219, 283
— national character—172-73
— literature—140-41
— and philosophy—140-41
— and the press—139-40, 168, 284, 312-13, 315-17, 318-19, 326-37
— censorship in—139-40
See also *Berlin, German literature, German philosophy, Prussia, Saxony*
Good, the—see *Morality*
Gospels—199, 212, 370-72
Government—121, 143, 155
Greece, Ancient—34, 35, 51, 189, 202, 430, 432, 436-37, 500
See also *Athens, ancient, Sparta, ancient*
Greek philosophy—29-30, 34-37, 66, 69-70, 419-20, 423-30, 432-441, 490-500, 504, 505
— character of—413, 494
— contradictions of—71, 425, 439
— and astronomy—65, 66, 68-70, 72-73
— and religion—497
— philosophy of Aristotle—34, 35, 69-70, 424, 504
— philosophy of Democritus—35, 39, 40, 44, 46, 52, 62, 65, 473
— philosophy of Socrates—35, 436-39, 492
See also *Alexandrian school of philosophy, Eleatics, Epicurean philosophy, Ionian philosophy, Plato's doctrine,*

Pythagoreans, Scepticism, Sophists, Stoicism
Guilds— 257

H

Hansa— 369
Health— 444-45
Hegelianism— 18-20, 29-30, 84-86, 103, 385, 391, 439, 491-93, 510-14
    See also *Young Hegelianism*
Heretics, heresies— 139, 323
Hero— 35
Historical school of law— 203-10, 387
History— 8, 10, 19, 168, 179, 182, 195, 230, 317-18, 636
Holland— 142, 143
Holy Alliance— 199
Homoeomeria (of Anaxagoras)— 470, 485
Huguenots— 197, 199
Hypothesis— 73

I

Ideal— 8
Idealism— 11-12, 17-18, 28
Ideality— 76, 412, 414, 435-36, 439, 440, 454
Ideas— 4, 8, 18, 21, 28, 65, 85, 122, 154, 172, 196, 220-21, 423, 439, 462, 478, 494-96
    See also *Absolute idea*
Identity— 419, 451, 464
Ignorance— 202
Illness— 163, 444
    See also *Health, Life and death*
Immanent— 85, 86, 414, 448-49, 471, 474-77, 493, 494, 497-98
Immortality— 455, 478
Individual— 76, 164, 168, 182, 251-52, 348-49, 432, 438, 439, 444, 448-51, 453-55, 457, 462, 468, 473, 475, 497
    See also *Hero, Man, Personality*
Individual, particular and general, the— 35, 36, 50, 52, 56-57, 62, 71-73, 165, 431, 444, 454-55, 457, 493
Industry— 286
Inequality (social)— 230
Infinity, infinite, the— 60-61, 499

Inquisition— 197, 372
Instinct— 505
Institutions— 130-31
Intellect— 30, 44, 63, 305
Intelligence— 293, 300-05
Interests— 302
    — general— 243, 305, 345
    — estate— 299, 300-01, 302-03, 304, 305
    — private— 228, 236, 239-42, 246-50, 254, 256-62, 301, 302, 343-44, 345, 347-48
    — and state— 241, 302, 304, 344, 347-49
    — people's interests— 312
Investigation, research— 111-14, 188, 468-69
    See also *Experiment, Method*
Ionian philosophy— 424, 435
Ireland— 199
Irony (as a form of philosophy)— 493-94

J

Jacobin dictatorship— 119
Jews, Jewish question— 391-92, 400
    See also *Judaism*
Journalism— 125, 333
    See also *Literature, Press*
Judaism— 199, 400
    See also *Jews*
Judgment— 135, 437, 438, 451
July revolution— see *French revolution of 1830*
Jurisprudence— 20, 165, 274, 275

K

Kantianism— 18, 104, 119, 206, 428, 440, 577
Knowledge— 38, 60, 62, 84, 428, 429, 432, 458, 498, 506

L

Landed property, landownership— 220, 224, 235, 246, 293-95, 300-03, 305, 306

Law, laws— 12, 15, 17, 19, 109-12, 114, 115, 119, 120, 121, 122, 161-66, 168, 183, 198, 200, 202, 204-10, 227, 230-33, 235, 257, 260-62, 273, 275, 308, 309, 335, 355, 438, 445, 640-41
— civil — 209, 232, 233
— constitutional — 198, 209
— private — 15, 17
— public — 12, 252
— patrimonial — 237
— and personality — 243
— and equality — 347
— and freedom of opinion — 119-22, 145, 161, 162
— and censorship — 130, 165
— and private interest — 236-37, 257, 345
— Roman law — 12, 233
— medieval criminal law — 260
— Prussian — 201, 275, 307
— Chinese — 260
Leap— 75, 454
Legislation— 232, 243, 308, 309, 364, 365, 384
Liberalism— 137, 180, 264, 304, 365
— French — 283
— German — 172, 283
— pseudo-liberalism — 110
Life and death— 11, 35, 153, 163, 164, 309, 454-55, 456, 479, 492
See also *Health, Illness*
Literature— 164, 167, 398, 642
— its history — 176
See also *Books, Classics, German literature, Journalism, Poetry, Press, Writer*
Logic— 18, 34, 44-45, 104, 292, 293 298, 445, 473, 504
Love— see *Morality*

M

Man— 3, 4, 7-9, 33, 52, 65, 74, 75, 104-05, 158-59, 191-92, 300-01, 310, 428, 432-35, 436-37, 438, 450-54, 455-57, 505, 636-37
— and state — 199-200, 306
See also *Individual, Personality*
Marriage— 192, 193, 204, 207, 274, 275, 307-10
See also *Divorce, Family*

Materialism (abject) — 262
Mathematics— 12, 40, 201
Matter— 15, 61-64, 70-72, 441
Measure— 491
Metaphysics as part of idealistic philosophy— 12, 17, 35-36
Method— 60, 61, 69, 70, 71, 182, 204, 413, 419, 424, 426
Middle Ages— 29, 134, 146, 197, 234, 260, 286, 369
Mind— 73, 85, 110, 468-69
Monad— 48, 492
Monarchy
— absolute — 119
— constitutional — 382
Morality— 84, 118-19, 120, 164, 209, 274, 307-10, 312, 319, 372, 435, 468, 624, 636-37
— good, the — 51, 158-59, 439, 446, 448-49, 451, 456
— evil — 51, 158-59, 445-46, 448-49, 451-52
— friendship — 53, 309-10
— love — 75-76, 453, 498
See also *Duty*
Motion— 48, 49, 51, 412, 415, 437, 439, 440, 473-74, 490
Mysticism— 73, 140, 152
Mythology— 30, 42, 66-70, 85, 104, 172, 185, 196, 431, 454, 475, 491, 492, 497-98
See also *Classics, Deity*

N

Napoleonic Code— 192-93, 201-02
Natural science— 18, 167
Nature— 3, 12, 18, 45, 52, 71, 72, 112, 234, 295, 309, 431, 468, 508, 637
— sensuous — 18, 65
— spiritual — 18
Necessity and chance— 42-45, 52-53, 337, 412, 415, 419, 441, 443, 445-46, 473, 478, 492
Negation— 426, 441, 493
Netherland revolution of 1566-1609— 257
Notion— 415, 421, 426
Number— 133, 435

O

Official, officialdom— 130, 343-45
See also Bureaucracy
Opposites— 38, 41-42, 61, 429, 504
Opposition— 137, 364
Outlook (world)— 499
Ownership— 303, 317

P

Pantheism— 423-24
Parcellation— 220, 347
Part and whole— 348
Particularism— 144
Parties, political— 120, 202, 312
Patriotism— 129
Peasantry— 177, 179, 180, 294, 299
See also Poor
Penal code in Germany— 226
People— 137, 141, 144-45, 164, 167,
  168, 176, 227, 251, 265, 292, 296,
  306, 309, 312, 320-21, 333, 347,
  351, 353, 506, 636
Personality— 10, 122, 229, 243, 266,
  334, 354, 436, 494, 499, 504-06
See also Hero, Individual, Man
Philistinism— 390, 456, 458, 545
Philosophy— 15, 17-19, 29-31, 35, 36,
  62, 84-87, 183, 191, 195-96, 201,
  202, 395, 429, 431, 488, 494, 497-
  98, 500, 507
  — and external world— 491
  — and practice— 85, 197, 491
  — and science— 429, 496
  — and religion— 196, 198, 487,
    493, 495-96
  — philosophy of law— 12, 274
  — history of— 29, 101, 423, 431,
    490-93, 506
  — objective universality of— 491
  — philosopher— 84-85, 200, 201,
    432-40, 450, 452, 457, 462-63
See also Ancient philosophy, French
philosophy, German philosophy,
Spinoza's teaching
Philosophy of nature— 504
  — ancient— 25-73, 84-87, 431-35,
    440-41, 468-71, 500, 504
  — of Hegel— 510-14
Pietists— 478

Plato's doctrine— 35, 439, 440, 462-63,
  490, 497, 636
Poetry— 11, 17, 174-75, 371-72
Police— 161, 166, 191
Politics— 117, 118, 284-85, 351
Poor, the— 230, 232, 234-35
Positive philosophy— 86
See also Schelling's philosophy
Possibility and reality— 43, 44, 72, 415,
  443, 444
Poverty— 332, 343, 347
Predicate— see Subject
Prejudice— 70
Premises— 420, 423, 431, 441, 473, 478
Press— 155, 157-58, 164, 167-68, 176,
  177, 198, 292, 314-15, 316-17, 333,
  334, 336, 348-49
  — and revolution— 143
  — and people— 137, 167-68, 176,
    336, 348-49, 351, 352-55
  — popular— 159, 313, 314, 315-17
  — conservative— 292, 363
  — censorship— 109, 131, 140, 158-
    59, 163-64, 167-68, 176-77, 316
  — press legislation— 161-62, 164
  — in Belgium— 143
  — in England— 141, 142, 311
  — in France— 143, 167, 311
  — in Germany— 140, 167, 196,
    197, 288-92, 311-30, 359, 363
  — in Holland— 142
  — in Prussia— 110, 124, 132-37,
    140, 184, 196, 197, 266-73,
    277-79, 280-82, 311, 336, 337,
    349-51, 353-56, 361-65, 373
  — in Switzerland— 144
  — in the U.S.A.— 167
See also Censorship, Freedom, Journalism, Literature
Principle— 413, 414, 418-19, 426, 427,
  436, 487
Profession— 3-9
Progress— 202, 364, 397
Proof— 506
Property— 199, 204, 229, 232-34, 252,
  257, 303, 305, 306
  — private— 220, 232, 234, 240-
    41, 251, 252-53, 255
  — of monasteries— 232
See also Landed property
Protective tariffs— 286
Protestantism— 197, 199, 212

Provincial assemblies and assemblies of the estates in Prussia — 137, 138, 145-46, 147, 148-51, 179-81, 224, 226, 229, 235, 237, 239-40, 241, 246, 248, 254, 258, 259, 260-61, 262, 299-302, 303-05, 364, 396

Prussia — 135-36, 282-83, 302, 303, 318, 365, 384, 389-90, 396-97
— state system — 296-98, 302, 321, 353-64, 362, 363, 384, 394, 396-97
— legal procedure — 130, 236-37, 238, 240, 307, 355, 384
— press laws — 109-11, 114-19, 121-31, 132, 133, 139, 264, 280-83, 285, 332, 335, 349-50, 357, 365, 397
— laws on marriage — 274-75, 307-10, 365
— and Russia — 365
See also *Berlin, Commissions of the estates in Prussia, Press, Provincial assemblies and assemblies of the estates in Prussia, Rhine Province*

Psychology — 85, 130
Publicity — 334, 350, 351, 353, 355, 384
Public opinion — 164, 269-71, 349, 353-54
Punishment — 162, 228-29, 235, 251-52
Pythagoreans — 48, 66, 426, 435, 436

Q

Quality and quantity — 54-58, 76, 454-55

R

Rationalism in religion — 116, 200
Reality — 39, 44, 60, 72, 84-85, 435-36, 437, 439, 444
See also *Possibility ana reality*
Reason — 4, 105, 113, 151-52, 168, 197, 200, 202, 204, 295, 419, 508-09, 639
— νοῦς (in Anaxagoras) — 435, 490
Redemption — see *Christianity*
Reflection — 42, 64-65, 84, 419, 439, 441
Reform, legal — 364
Regularity — 69, 422

Relation(ship) — 38. 52, 438-39, 452, 457, 493-94
Relativity — 443
Religion — 8, 18, 30, 116-18, 144, 152, 173, 189, 190, 191, 197, 198, 230, 274, 285, 323, 371-72, 384, 386, 394-95, 438, 493, 494
— general principle — 121
— as philosophy of transcendence — 497
— and philosophy — 196, 493
— and science — 190-91
— and state — 199-201
— and secular authority — 118
See also *Atheism, Christianity, Church, Deity, Judaism, Mysticism, Mythology, Pietists*

Republic — 200
Revolution — 113
See also *Belgian revolution of 1830-31, English revolution of 1640-60, French revolution of 1789-94, French revolution of 1830 (July), Netherland revolution of 1566-1609*

Rhine Province — 140, 179, 180, 258, 261-62, 283, 284, 310, 330, 335, 355, 364, 365, 389-90
— Mosel region — 332-58
See also *Provincial assemblies and assemblies of the estates in Prussia*

Right — 164, 199, 228-32, 235, 240, 248, 252, 256, 347, 384
— customary — 230-32, 234, 235
— private — 233, 252, 253, 255
— public — 233, 255
— of the state — 253, 256
— right to property — 234, 252
— and private interest — 248, 257, 259, 262
— patrimonial — 252
— as a privilege — 145-46
— legal position — 316, 327
See also *Court and legal procedure, Crime, Custom, Jurisprudence, Law, Legislation, Punishment*

Roman philosophy — 189-90
— philosophy of Lucretius — 48, 51, 62, 65, 72-73, 416, 468-71, 475
Rome, ancient — 35, 119, 189, 318, 431, 640-42
See also *Classics*
Russia — 120, 365

S

Saxony— 391

Scepticism— 29, 30, 34-36, 38-39, 45, 106, 189, 410-11, 415, 423, 427, 429-30, 432, 436, 464, 492, 504

Schelling's philosophy— 103, 105

Science— 8, 11-12, 18-20, 29-30, 40-41, 84, 111-14, 133, 429, 636-37
  — and religion— 190
  See also *Astronomy, History, Investigation, Method, Philosophy*

Sculpture— 51, 431, 437

Self-consciousness— 30, 35, 39, 45, 52, 63, 65, 66, 70, 71-73, 85-86, 104, 165, 418, 493, 506

Semblance— 10, 39-40, 45, 64, 309, 421, 430, 444

Sensation, sensuousness— 39, 40, 45, 64-66, 69, 74-75, 135, 295, 413, 418-20, 425, 435, 448, 451, 454, 458-59, 462-63, 465, 469-71, 473-74

Serfdom— 139

Slavery— 162

Social relations— 4, 337

Society— 3-8, 120, 130, 137-38, 166, 234
  See also *Classes, Family, Public opinion, Social relations, State*

Sophists— 436-38, 504

Soul— 50, 413-15, 449, 452-53, 454, 496, 504-05

Space— 12, 48, 62, 64, 70, 71, 134

Sparta, ancient— 34, 181

Speculation (speculative philosophy)— 29-30, 35-36

Spinoza's teaching— 119, 201, 496

Spirit— 424, 428, 430-32, 436-41, 443, 444, 448, 491

State, the— 12, 120-22, 126, 129, 166, 183, 200, 249-255, 295, 302-06, 309, 317-18, 347-49, 384
  — its origin— 200
  — and civil society— 234-35, 347-48
  — and private interest— 235-36, 240-41, 245, 250, 251, 256-57, 303
  — system of organisation— 296, 321, 344, 346, 382, 392
  — and government— 155, 176, 182

  — and law— 256-57, 384
  — and religion— 189, 198-200
  — and church— 198-99
  — and philosophy— 195, 201-02
  — as seen by ancient philosophers— 409-10, 435, 440, 494, 495
  — in antiquity— 435
  — estate representation— 302, 303
  — Christian— 117, 199-201, 400
  — theocratic— 199
  — despotic— 130, 177
  See also *Bureaucracy, Classes, Government, Law, Monarchy, Parties, political, Police, Politics, Republic, Right*

Stoicism, stoics— 29-30, 34-36, 43, 59, 70, 72-73, 101, 189, 432, 493, 501, 504, 638-39

Subject— 437-39, 506
  — and object— 113
  — and predicate— 438, 458

Subjectivity— 72, 437, 439, 444

Substance— 426, 430-31, 432-41, 452-53, 455-56, 469-71, 474, 475
  — and accidens— 63-65

Supernaturalists— 478

Switzerland— 142, 144

System, philosophical— 35, 84-85, 505, 506

T

Tautology— 104, 425

Teleology— 422

Terrorism— 119, 372

Theology— 30, 74-76, 197, 447

Theory and practice— 40-42, 84-85, 220-21, 432, 436, 441, 451

Thinking— 38, 42, 45, 113, 425, 439, 458, 471

Time— 33, 48, 63-65, 70, 441, 443

Trade— 286, 368

Tragic fate— 202

Truth— 8, 39-40, 111-14, 191-92, 457-58, 494, 497, 636

U

Unity and difference— 74, 295-97, 413, 453-54, 458, 476, 491

V

Vedas, the — 191
Void — 48, 58, 441, 471, 474, 478

W

Weight — 55-57, 60, 70
Whole and part — see *Part and whole*
Will — 137, 244, 308
 — *of the people* — 309, 321

Workers (working class) — 195, 216
World — 61-62, 63, 64, 413, 419, 424-
 26, 439, 440, 472, 475, 478, 491,
 497
Writer — 119, 174-75

Y

Young Germany — 208
Young Hegelianism — 192, 194
 See also *Doctors' club, Hegelianism*